# BRAZIL
## UP CLOSE

# The Sensuous & Adventurous Guide

## Pamela Bloom

D1069316

HUNTER
PUBLISHING

HUNTER PUBLISHING, INC.
130 Campus Drive
Edison NJ 08818, USA
Tel (732) 225 1900; Fax (732) 417 0482

1220 Nicholson Road
Newmarket, Ontario L3Y 7V1
Tel (800) 399 6858; Fax (800) 363 2665

ISBN 1-55650-755-0
© 1997 Pamela Bloom
© 1998 Revised Edition

For complete information about the hundreds of other travel guides offered by Hunter, visit us online at:

**www.hunterpublishing.com**

Maps by Kim André

Cover photo by W. Hille (Leo de Wys); all others by author.

2 3 4 5

## About The Author

Pamela Bloom is a music and arts critic, travel, and fiction writer, whose work has appeared in *The New York Times*, *The Chicago Tribune*, and *The Los Angeles Times*, as well as *High Fidelity*, *Musician*, *Downbeat*, *Seven Days*, *Connoisseur*, and *Elle* magazines, among others. She received a B.A. in comparative literature from Trinity College (Hartford, CT), attended Dartmouth College, and also studied opera at Indiana University and the

Juilliard School of Music. She taught the history of Brazilian jazz at the New School for Social Research in New York, and has presented multimedia lectures on Brazilian music and culture at the Ballroom Club in Manhattan, for their annual Brazilian jazz series.

A world traveler, Pamela Bloom has pursued writing assignments in China, Spain, Greece, and the Caribbean, as well as throughout the U.S.A. As a dedicated Brazilophile, she has danced in Rio's Carnaval with the Portela Samba School, interviewed the country's top musicians and traveled extensively within Brazil. A native of Houston, Texas, she presently resides in New York City.

## To My Readers

One day late in the summer of 1985, I was walking down West 65th Street in Manhattan, wondering why the Brazilian at my side was not as madly in love with me as I was with him, when suddenly he handed me his headphones and purred, "Pamela, you must *leesen* to *deese*."

From that moment on, when I first heard the voice of the great Elis Regina singing the songs of Milton Nascimento, my life irrevocably changed. Like many before and after me, it was the wings of song that carried me into the heart and soul of Brazilian culture, one that at first seemed so exotic, but has since come to feel like second skin. As a music critic, I've had the rare opportunity of sitting down to talk with the country's greatest musicians, visiting their homes in Brazil, watching them record, and listening like a child at their feet as they discussed their dreams and visions and the ineffable power of their music. In 1986, I even had the wondrous joy of dancing with the Portela Samba School in Rio's Carnaval.

Still, nothing can match the privilege of writing this *Up Close Guide* (and its previous incarnations, the first three editions of *Fielding's Brazil, 1993, 1994 and 1995* ). Being able to travel to over 60 cities and villages – meeting the locals, tasting their food, surfing their waves, tramping their forests, and yes, even getting bitten by their bugs – has allowed me to begin to understand what makes up Brazil, and, more importantly, what makes a Brazilian. The very size and diversity of this tropical country defies simple stereotype, but there is one thing that is certain: anyone who travels to Brazil with an open heart is sure to return home with an incurable case of *saudade* – an indefinable Portuguese word that is translated most often as "unrequited longing." The late Brazilian composer Antônio Carlos Jobim immortalized that feeling in the music of bossa nova, but for travelers it can mean only one thing: book a return passage as fast as you can.

Frankly, I wrote this guidebook for the kind of tourist who wants to engage himself body and soul in Brazil and Brazilian culture. In fact, I have always written the kind of guidebooks I wanted to read – one that not only inspires adventure, but also demystifies any obstacles to travel. As such, in *Brazil Up Close*, you'll find not only straight-from-the-hip tips about hotels, restaurants, and tours, but also first-person narratives and interviews that bring the color of Brazil to life. In fact, there's enough information and background here that non-Portuguese speaking tourists may never have to hire a private guide to explain what they're looking at. In this new edition, I have included not only the major tourist destinations, but some really out-of-the-way excursions for those who want a few extra thrills.

And especially new for this edition are contributions by some really gonzo travelers who shared with me their private and very confessional over-the-top adventures in Brazil (see the section *Up Close Deep Throats*, below).

The best thing advice anyone ever gave to me about traveling in Brazil was from Adam Carter of Brazil Nuts, who said (with no tongue in cheek), "Hope for the best and expect everything to go wrong." And he's right: like anywhere else in the world, in Brazil you get the room you pay for (and sometimes less), but no travel writer or agency can foresee quirks in personal service, change of administration, and just the plain bad luck of getting that one room where the air-conditioning is busted and the sewage has backed up. And no one can make anyone show up on time in Brazil! Truth is, Brazil is a country of continuous movement and unpredictability, and a guidebook at its best can only point to the way, not carve it in stone.

A most important section of this book is dedicated to ecotravel in Brazil. In an era when clean air, pure water and rich soil are at a premium, Brazil remains one of the leading destinations in the world for those who want to scale mountains, traverse rainforests, veg out on beaches, or trek through the backcountry on horseback. As you'll be able to tell from my first-person accounts, I managed to happily survive all these adventures, proving you don't have to be in Olympic shape to enjoy yourself in Brazil. But even before you turn a page, make a promise to me that you will become the most eco-conscious traveler ever. This means traveling light, disposing of garbage properly, not throwing cigarette butts on the forest or beach, and not unduly disturbing fauna or flora above or under the sea. In other words, as they say in Brazil, *preserve a natureza* (preserve nature) and by doing so we'll preserve the planet.

Most importantly, I have taken the issue of my readers' personal safety deeply to heart. More than anything, I want to see you return home from Brazil happy, healthy, and with your valuables intact. As with all large cities throughout the world, the major cities of Brazil do have their share of crime, but there is absolutely no reason why anyone should be deterred from visiting the country because of that. Safety is largely a matter of common sense and caution, and throughout this book I have given numerous safety tips which, if followed precisely, can go a long way to ensuring your well-being. While incidents do occur, I have not experienced any threatening situations in the many years I have traveled through Brazil – although I did return from the Amazon with a few nasty ticks. For eco-travelers, included in the back of the book is an extensive health kit, one which you should study months prior to a trip to the backlands. In any case, I would love to hear from you about your trip, your likes and dislikes, and any suggestions for future editions of this guide. After all, it was thousands of 18th-century *bandeirantes* (pioneers), not just one that opened up the interior of Brazil to the rest of the world. If only we in the 20th century could be half as adventurous.

So get out the suntan lotion, pack your sexiest swimsuit, and head out with me to one of the most glorious spots on this Earth. As they say in Brazil, *Vai com Deus* (Go with God) and, as I like to add, *May you return with a song in your heart.*

PAMELA BLOOM

## New To This Edition: Up Close "Deep Throats"

Having written over 700 pages of this guide myself, I finally decided I simply couldn't continue to check out every single zone of pleasure in Brazil all by myself (kinda selfish, huh?). So I invited some fellow Brazilophiles to share their tips, opinions, and exotic adventures so that you can know that *other* people besides myself actually survived going to Brazil. With the courage of *bandeirantes*, they have bared their souls on everything from the best *pousadas* in Parati to dancing in Olinda's Carnaval to riding over the pampas of Rio Grando do Sul to partying till after dawn on the remote beaches of Morro de São Paulo in Bahia. This year's Deep Throats are:

**Mike Salvo** is young, handsome, musical, short, and, except for his Long Island Portuguese, could pass for a Brazilian. A freelance photographer, he's traveled up and down the backroads of North and South America, but somehow got stuck on Northeastern beach towns due to what he calls a "strange, inexplicable twist of fate" (UFOs, Mike?). A die-hard blues fan, Mike takes his harmonica wherever he goes, which probably explains why there's always a crowd attached to him. I love his tips because you *know* he has "suffered" for them.

**Theodore Maclean Folke** must have had a few past lives in Brazil. Addicted to traveling through the country, he's currently finishing up a comic novel set in the Northeast called *The Gringo and the Piranha* (get back, P.J. O'Rourke). He's also the Travel Editor of the *U.N. Secretariat News*, which gets him free trips to wild places on a minute's notice. I love Ted because he's lost his heart more times than I have in Brazil.

**Bonnie Kassel**, an internationally recognized corporate artist, tells me she has traveled and cooked all her life. She's lived in Belgium, Mexico, Kenya, and Turkey, explored the jungles of Central America, Indonesia, Egypt, and the Sahara, and loves to get lost in big exotic markets (this I believe!). The founder of *Adventurous Appetite*, she now takes people around the world – just to eat weird new things. She's also a passionate lover of museums and has given me lots of tips on new ones. Bonnie isn't afraid to tell me when she's found a better (and cheaper) *pousada*.

**Mitchell Torton** first visited Brazil in 1984 as a freelance journalist covering Brazilian politics and cinema. For 10 years he represented VARIG Airlines in Washington, DC. Recently, he joined as General Manager the Brazil Nuts Consulting Group, an independent travel-marketing company. Mitch supports the growth in eco-tourism, but believes that sustainable development should also extend to Brazil's social and cultural heritage. But give him some flippers and a snorkel and he's outta here.

**Christine Chauvin**, part Brit, part French, left a cushy job at Sotheby's to roam the globe, write about it, and entice others to follow her. Today she heads her own travel consultancy, which allows her to take horsebackriding groups to the most exotic locales in the world. She writes a great newsletter called *Travel Log*, in which she details her equestrian treks through Rio Grande Do Sul, the Pantanal, and many other places. I've never seen her in the flesh, but I imagine she is in frightfully good shape.

All Deep Throat contributions are carefully accredited, so do note that every other opinion in this book is mine! If you would like to be considered as an *Up Close* Deep Throat for my next edition and have tips, adventures, suggestions, or complaints, please contact me through Hunter Publishing (130 Campus Drive, Edison, NJ 08818), or by e-mail: BrazilSoul@aol.com.

## Acknowledgements

A book of this magnitude could never have been written without the support of literally hundreds of people, both in Brazil and back home. Without a doubt, initial thanks must go to Michael Hunter of Hunter Publishing, who saw the value of supporting travel to Brazil, not to mention my particular passion and perspective.

Anyone who has traveled throughout Brazil knows the road is strewn with visible and invisible helpers along the way. First and foremost, my deepest thanks goes to the offices of the Brazilian Tourist Office in New York and Funtur and Embratur in Rio de Janeiro for having helped me plan my initial sojourns throughout Brazil.

Tourist professionals, both governmental and private, bent over backwards to make my research seem more like fun. A kiss and hug (*um beijo um embraço*) go to Trajano Ribeiro, former president of Rio Tur, Sylvia Mangabeira of the São Paulo Convention Bureau, the tourist boards of the states of Santa Catarina, Paraná, Pará, Rio Grande do Sul, Amazonas and Bahia, as well as the cities of Recife, Máceio, Natal, João Pessoa, Brasília and Belém. Gracious thanks to André Von Thuranyi, who inspired my derring-do in the Amazon and the Pantanal.

A special *biejo* goes to three Secretaries of Tourism who kept me awake and entertained beyond the call of duty: José Luiz Nogueira of Cáxambu, Ivan Canzioni of Farroupilha, and, especially, Fernando César Mesquita of the state of Maranhão, who introduced me to the unforgettable dunes of Parque dos Lençois. Beatrice Imbiriba, now Secretary of Tourism of Santarém, continues to the very model of an ecological warrior.

For memories that will last a lifetime, an eternal *abraço* goes to: Massimo Ferrari of São Paulo for several nights of unsurpassable dining; Túlio Marques Lopez Filho of Belo Horizonte for a superlative weekend on horseback; Humberto Morim of TV Amazonas in Manaus for making me feel like a star; and Luis Claudio Ferreira and Celso Losado of Arraial d'Ajuda for simply being themselves.

Brazil is one of those countries where mystical help is just around the corner. Deep gratitude goes to Fernando do Oxalá, *pai de santo* in Belo

Horizonte, for his words of wisdom and encouragement, União Vegetal's Mestre Felipe Belmonte in Brasília and Mestre Alberto in Salvador for several nights of illumination; Marilena Simões in Belo Horizonte for her accurate psychic readings, and Vida Vidmar at Transamérica Hotel for her enlightening lunch.

A nod of deep gratitude to Georgia Christgau of *High Fidelity* magazine, Don Shewey of *Seven Days* magazine, Jon Pareles of the *New York Times*, and Cathy Cook of *Taxi* magazine, who welcomed my articles on Brazilian music, and especially to Mark Rowland of *Musician* magazine, who sent me off on a wild, unforgettable roadtrip with Milton Nascimento.

Particularly regarding the first edition of *Brazil Up Close*:

Extra-special gratitude – for years of friendship and service – must be extended to Neiva Duarte of BeloTur, whose knowledge and love of the state of Minas Gerais has been her greatest gift to me. She is the best representative of Mineiro soul that I know.

My political understanding of Brazil has been deeply transformed by hours spent over churrasco, pizza and cold *chopp* with Eduardo Sanovicz, Chief of the Tourism Department in Santos, in the state of São Paulo. His love of, and dedication to, social reform continues to inspire my life. Many thanks to his staff, who made me feel like family.

Special gratitude for their indefatigable support goes to Claudio Heckmann and Robert Falkenburg of F&H Consulting, who continue to support the finest in Brazil and have never let me down.

In New York, thanks for deep friendship goes to Faye Levey, whose early morning chats, and Karen Modell, whose late-night chats kept me going. In Houston, deep thanks to Dr. Kim Bloom and family, Dr. Kerry Bloom and family, and to my parents, Mitzie Muntz Bloom and the late Dr. Manuel G. Bloom, for their love, support and patience beyond all common sense.

And always, to my lifelong *bem-amigo* Carlos Alberto Saldanha Leite in Rio, without whose *jeitinhos* and packing genius I would never have been able to return home. But most of all, I would like to thank the Igreja Messianica Mundial (called Johrei Fellowship in the United States) and particularly Rev. Tetsuo Watanabe, for the opportunity of sharing their vision of paradise on earth and for having implemented it so beautifully in Brazil. *May the model of your Sacred Grounds spread far beyond Brazil.*

## Money Alert!

The state of the Brazilian economy is infamous for its unpredictability and sudden change. As such, exchange rates have had a long history of instability, and even periods of relative stability (as the last one starting in 1994) should be considered suspect and liable to change. As such, rates in this book are only estimated, and the reader should use them as a guideline only, checking with specific establishments on an individual basis.

## Dedication

To Maneco Bueno, whose record collection recharted the course of my life; And to my mother, who continues to survive beautifully my trips to Brazil.

BRAZILIAN EMBASSY
WASHINGTON, D.C.

The Ambassador

July 5, 1996

Ms. Pamela Bloom

*Dear Ms Bloom,*

My wife and I would like to thank you very much for thoughtfully giving us your newly published guide to adventure in Brazil. Congratulations on a job well done. Your book will certainly entice the curiosity of many prospective visitors to Brazil. As I think your book attempts to show, Brazil is such a large, complex many-countries-in-one-country that there can always be found reasons for visiting us. We Brazilians welcome all and each visitor with whom we are pleased to share the wonders, the riches, the life, and the soul of a great nation.

PAULO-TARSO FLECHA DE LIMA
Ambassador of Brazil

# Contents

# Maps

# INTRODUCTION

Brazil is a land of exotic collision. Cows lumber across multilaned highways, battery-powered TVs blare away in the jungle, and some of the world's most sophisticated music wafts from its sorriest ghettoes. In Brazil's modern metropolises, skyscrapers surge like icons toward heaven, while only blocks away languish beaches of such incredible beauty they can only be called paradise. Hot spices, hot rhythms, and hot climes all jangle together, producing a cultural mélange that favors mystics and marketplaces. And yet, just a few kilometers away are cold winters, *sauerkraut* and European-style beerfests. Simply, Brazil is a third-world country with a sometime first-world face, a persona that often tricks not only its own people, but even the savviest of travelers.

Long called a sleeping giant, Brazil is just now wiggling its gargantuan toes and waking from a hibernation that has, with a few notable exceptions, kept it politically and economically dazed for most of the 20th century. To some keen observers, Brazil has been likened to an adolescent struggling to find itself in the face of an enormous but chaotic inheritance. From its birth as a Portuguese colony with unlimited promise, it has steadily passed from being an unwieldy empire, an ambitious republic, and a repressive dictatorship into the still-struggling democracy it is today, supported firmly, if cautiously, by the world's major powers. As the biggest country in South America, Brazil boasts both some of the greatest wealth and the greatest inequality in the world – at times, even the sunshine seems unfairly distributed. Yet what makes Brazil so attractive as a travel destination is its diversity. Just as there is no one topography that represents the richness of the nation's resources, there is no one color of Brazilian, though the stunning coffee-colored *mulata* has come to represent, for better or worse, a definite standard of natural beauty. But to the surprise of most tourists, there are also German blue-eyed blondes in the south, Indian-angled cheekbones in the Northeast, Japanese almond eyes in São Paulo, and dark Italian features in the extreme south, not to mention the black-faced descendants of African tribes, whose religious beliefs, music, dance, culture, and cuisine support the very core of Brazilian culture itself.

Travelwise, Brazil has lain buried under a burden of misconceptions. Ask the average American to name the first thing that comes to mind at the mention of Brazil, and the answer will probably be: monkeys, Spanish, elephants, naked pretty girls, and Carnaval – though not necessarily in that order. In truth, there are monkeys in Brazil (in the rainforest, not roaming the streets); Spanish is spoken by a few, but Portuguese is the national language; elephants, to my knowledge, have *never* been sighted in the jungle; but there *are* definitely lots of pretty girls, though not naked, except during Carnaval, when flinging off one's brassiere becomes nearly an act of national pride. As for other easily puncturable myths, the Brazilian bombshell Carmen Miranda probably did more than any other "goodwill ambassador" to perpetuate the idea that all Brazilians walk around with fruit on their heads. Sure, in the interior, particularly in Bahia, women gracefully carry piles of laundry, luggage and even crates of fruit on their heads without missing a beat, but visit a disco in a big city like Rio or São Paulo and you'll find Brazilians dress more stylishly than most North Americans.

Today, Brazil is a country where you can travel between centuries in a matter of hours. There's the Amazon jungle, where Indians live in the Stone Age; 18th-century villages, where you'll find horses hitched to posts; 19th-century *fazendas*, or ranches where cowboys still ride the range; fashionable 20th-century cities, where international trends set the style; and even one arresting city called Brasília, whose avant-garde buildings proudly face toward the 21st century. There are even tiny villages, like São Tomé das Letras in Minas Gerais, that seem totally out synch with real time – dare I say *otherwordly*. It's not for nothing that Brazil has gained the reputation for hosting some of the most famous UFO sightings in the world.

The continuous clash between first- and third-world values is something that no tourist can escape. Even within one city, upper-class grande dames take afternoon tea in plush beachside hotels, while only blocks away, high up on the hillside, families of 10 crowd into huts that disappear regularly under mudslides. It's impossible to travel through the country without taking both realities into account, and yet most tourists, unless they travel far into the backlands, will not be assaulted with a continual display of wretched poverty. Somehow the tropical beauty, especially along the seashore, soothes some of the harsher social realities – even for Brazilians, who appear able to delight in the simple pleasures of sun, surf, and sand. This is not to discount the very real problems faced by a majority of the population, particularly in the Northeast: high infant mortality rate, drought, homelessness, malnutrition, and disease. But even in the worst possible circumstances, there is an indefinable Brazilian spirit that manages to transcend human misery, or at least absorb and transmute it into song, dance, and religious fervor. Frankly, I have never seen such shining, luminescent eyes than on the faces of some hearty souls who struggle to survive in the Amazon jungle.

# Where To Go

Brazilian explorer José de Paula Machado wrote that "Brazil is a country in which space is its most important heritage, the ecosystem its language, and the natural resources still its greatest secret." Space, indeed, is Brazil's middle name. The fifth largest land-rich country in the world, Brazil is also the most populous country in Latin America, with over 150 million people. With the exception of Chile and Ecuador, Brazil's borders touch every country in South America – a fact that requires continual diplomacy. Although the country boasts a land mass larger than the continental United States, its people are crammed into a very small area. Forty-five percent of the population crowd in the southern region, which represents only 14% of

the territory. The Amazon rainforest occupies 42% of the total mass, although it is home to fewer people than live in New York City. Despite the construction of the ultra-modern capital of Brasília, the central plateau remains relatively uninhabited.

Brazil thrives on its colorful regionalism. There are six distinct regions, each with its own geography, climate, racial makeup, and cultural traditions. To meet the political and social needs of each, however, is an ongoing challenge for the federal government.

The area most known to tourists is the **Southeast**, dominated by the beachside city of Rio de Janeiro and the industrial capital of São Paulo. Also here is the mining state of **Minas Gerais**, its fashionable capital Belo Horizonte, and the small legion of historical towns that continue to preserve the flavor of 18th-century Brazil. Geographically, the region is divided between a slender coastal zone and an elevated plateau banked by a narrow mountainous range. With the exception of the ports in Rio and Santos, most of the area, sculpted by rolling hills, enjoys a temperate climate with a clear winter and summer.

The smallest of Brazil's regions, the **South**, makes up 7% of the national territory and has experienced a boom since the 1950s. Located below the Tropic of Cancer, it boasts a subtropical climate with all four seasons, including frosts and occasional snowfall. In the states of Paraná, Santa Catarina, and Rio Grande do Sul, there is a distinctive mix of Italian, German, Polish and Russian immigrants, many of whom speak their native languages and perpetuate their homeland's cuisine. Home to the Brazilian cowboy, called the *gaúcho*, the extreme south is blessed with magnificent rolling hills, picturesque valleys, and fertile wine country; but the region's greatest natural wonder is the **Iguaçu Falls**, which plunge through a gorge of the Iguaçu River along the Argentina-Paraguay border.

The **Central West** is an elevated plateau that reaches 3,300 feet above sea level and is called the Planalto Central. It is divided into areas of forest (mostly in the north) and woodland savannas known as *cerrado*. This scrubland, when cleared, has actually proven quite fertile, inspiring southern farmers to develop large soybean and cattle-grazing plantations. In the middle of this plateau stands the nation's futuristic capital, **Brasília**, a mirage of modernism in an otherwise sparse region.

The **Northeast** is the third largest region, covering 18% of the country. Once the center of the sugar industry during colonial times, it has remained underdeveloped due to life-threatening droughts, but is not underpopulated. Some of the country's best beaches are here, its coastline rewarded with sunshine year-round. Among the best coastal resort cities are Arajú in the state Sergipe, Maceió in Alagoas, Recife in Pernambuco, João Pessoa in Paraíba, Natal in Rio Grande do Norte, Fortaleza in Ceará, and São Luis in Maranhão (all capitals of their respective states). Located here is also the state of **Bahia** and its capital, **Salvador**, the center of Brazilian black culture and one of the most colorful and folkloric parts of Brazil.

Legend and harsh reality come together in the region known as **Amazônia**, home to the vast, mysterious Amazon jungle and the enormous river of the same name. Modern cities, quaint port villages, and isolated jungle huts all await the intrepid tourist, who may indulge in a variety of adventures over land, swamp, and river. Just south of the Amazônia is the magnificent swampland known as the **Pantanal**, a veritable paradise of exotic animals and birds, whose migrations depend on biannual flood tides.

# What To Do

Brazil is best known for its **sensuous beaches** – more than 4,600 miles of Atlantic coastline. The sophisticated beach scene in Rio is in a class by itself (the further you go from the city, the hipper it gets), but each Brazilian beach city boasts its own personality. After Rio, Salvador is the second most frequented coastal destination, enjoying a massive bay and numerous primitive coves in its outlying districts.

Beaches outside Recife are known for their wild, unspoiled locales, while some of the most exotic beaches (colored sand, windswept dunes, moonscape rocks) are situated outside Fortaleza. One of the most memorable beach diversions in the country is the *jangada* boat ride in Máceio, where you can sail to the middle of the ocean, get out of the boat, and stand up. Natal is particularly famous for its voluptuous sand dunes, traversed by wild buggy rides that will leave you breathless, if a little queasy. Some of the best scuba diving in the world can be found off the northeastern coast, on the primitive island of Fernando de Noronha. Encroaching upon the edge of the Amazon, the city of São Luis combines picturesque beaches with rich folklore and a beautifully restored colonial center. In the extreme southern state of Rio Grande do Sul, the beaches of Torres boast craggy grottoes and wooded cliffs reminiscent of Druid country.

Perhaps Brazil's biggest draw, and least publicized asset, is the amazing array of ecologically oriented **adventure** vacations, many of which are included in this book. If the Amazon forest is your thing, you can stay overnight in a treehouse lodge, float down a tributary in a canoe, fish for man-eating piranhas during the day, or hunt for alligators at night. If exotic birds are your fancy, you can trek through the Pantanal on horseback, in canoe, or by jeep, depending on the time of year. If you're keen on mountains, you can scale rugged peaks in the state of Rio de Janeiro or Minas Gerais, where you might also take an overnight horseback trek around the mountains (my favorite eco-trip).

**Culture** hounds will find plenty to do in Brazil. Just an hour north of Rio in the German-influenced town of Petrópolis is the restored imperial palace of the Portuguese royal family, a must-see for monarchy buffs. A few hours south of Rio is the historical town of Parati. One could spend two weeks just walking the cobblestone streets of Minas Gerais' colonial towns – Ouro Preto, Mariana, São João del Rei, and Tiradentes – soaking up the remnants of the Brazilian baroque era as seen in magnificient ecclesiastical art and architecture and heard in musical recitals played on rare instruments.

A novel idea is to design a **culinary** trip through Brazil. First on the agenda should be the wine country in the state of Rio Grande do Sul, where you can visit wineries, indulge in tasting, and dine on home-made breads, cheeses and salamis prepared by Italian-descended families. With every cuisine represented, São Paulo is truly the culinary capital of South America, not to mention the home of some of the greatest five-star chefs in the world. Rio is renowned for its seafood, and the spicy Afro-Brazilian cuisine of Bahia is an art unto itself. Minas Gerais is characterized by the hearty fare miners ate in centuries past, today best eaten at a traditional country farm with drunken cowboys singing over your shoulder. The German beer, *weinerschitzel*, and chocolates make a trip to the German-influenced state of Santa Catarina well worth while. And you simply haven't met the challenge of the Amazon jungle until you find yourself eye-to-eye with a grilled *tucunaré* or other regional fish that is so big its head rolls off the plate. (For more suggested itineraries, see *Best of Brazil, Itineraries*, on page 33.)

# How To Go

The most important thing to decide before you go to Brazil is what kind of traveler you are. Do you want an adventure, and how much? Would you rather have an agency make all your reservations, or do you want to wing it alone? How self-reliant are you, or do you prefer to be coddled? Is your idea of a vacation a deserted beach where you can snooze all afternoon, or do you prefer to be revved up by physical challenges? Are you traveling with children or valuable equipment that can't be replaced? Do you like to mingle with the upper crust, or would you rather meet locals who live a simpler life? Every single option can be found in Brazil, and you must gauge your accommodations and activities accordingly. If you communicate clearly to your travel agent or tour operator, even trips through the jungle can be arranged to suit your state of fitness, age and ecological desire. Believe it or not, even senior citizens over 70 have been glimpsed hooting up a storm in the rainforest.

# Is Brazil Expensive?

Can I afford Brazil? This question is asked by many tourists and, while the answer depends on your personal tastes and budget, the answer is a resounding yes. Prices in Brazil are not as dirt-cheap as they were 15 years ago, but they remain cheaper than the Caribbean or Europe. The airfare from the United States will be one of your biggest financial setbacks, but there are ways to scope out reduced fares through package deals, air passes, advance purchases, and courier services. Once in Brazil, you can go the luxury route at fabulous resorts or stay in relatively low-priced *pousadas* or inns, even bargaining for a hammock on the porch of a local. A good meal practically anywhere in the country can be had for under $7, an excellent one for $15-20, and world-class haute cuisine for no more than $35 per person. If you start off the day with a big breakfast (a substantial buffet is included in the rate of most hotels) you could probably get by on just one more meal a day (fueled, perhaps, by a few inexpensive snacks). Depending on the exchange rate (as variable as a bad love affair), you may often discover that your dollar is worth much more by the time you leave Brazil than when you arrived – a quirk of international travel that can inspire glee or regret.

# Why Go?

If you're still looking for one overriding reason to go to Brazil, here it is: Brazil is just plain fun – as are Brazilians, who are among the warmest and most hospitable people in the world. It's been said that you could put any Brazilian on a stage anywhere in the world and he or she would instantly become a star. Simply, in Brazil emotionality is an art form, the ability to dance second nature, and even young boys from *favelas* can beat out complicated sambas on the side of a beer can. All that pent-up passion to sing and dance explodes come Carnaval every Feb., when Brazilians in every part of the country take to the streets to celebrate the coming of *Quaresma* (Lent) with parades, masquerades, and an explosive effusion of rhythms. Known worldwide is the gargantuan parade in Rio's Sambódromo – a highly organized yet exuberant parade involving over 70,000 dancers, singers and models. The party, countrywide, is open to tourists, who need do nothing but hang loose in a flow of merrymaking that ranges from the merely joyous to the outrageously sexy.

# How To Use This Guide

The best way to get acquainted with Brazil through this book is to read the first chapters up to Rio, followed by the introduction to each region. Then, according to your interest, move on to the introduction to each city, also perusing the descriptions of the beaches, as well as the sections on *Excursions*. Hotels and restaurants have been listed in such a way as to facilitate clarity and to give you a quick idea of what's available in all price ranges. Because the "culture" of Brazil differs from region to region, I have included this kind of information within each particular area to preserve their distinctive flavors.

# SURVIVING BRAZIL IN STYLE

## Before You Go

---

### Accommodations

---

Accommodations in Brazil run from the Fantasy Island resort hotel to the jungle lodge adorned with mosquito nets. In between are excellent five-star city hotels, four- and three-star establishments that are clean, sometimes stylish and often reasonably priced, quaint *pousadas* (or inns) in historical houses, and – for the truly budget minded – two-star hotels, youth hostels, and simple pensions with ceiling fan. Most hotels are rated according to a five-star scale by EMBRATUR, the official tourist board. Be aware, however, that the board's values are not always equivalent in different regions of the country (or comparable to international standards). The quality of five-star properties in Rio and São Paulo is variable, but more often competitive with international expectations. Such hotels usually offer an array of facilities, including excellent pools, gourmet restaurants, fashionable decor, exercise equipment and/or sauna, boutiques and fine service. As you move up the northeast coast and into the Amazon region, three-star hotels will sometimes challenge American standards of cleanliness, and those rated with two stars, unless otherwise stated, can only be recommended for backpackers.

A recent tourist trend, particularly in Rio, São Paulo and Belo Horizonte, are apart-hotels, which are usually exquisitely decorated apartments costing much less than five- and sometimes four-star hotels. They are excellent choices for families, large groups, or even singles wishing to escape the tourist hubbub of larger hotels. Youth hostels are generally upbeat and clean, do not discriminate by age, and provide an extremely valuable social network.

Room rates fluctuate greatly throughout the year, not only because of inflation, but in response to the various seasons. During low season (Mar.-June and Aug.-Nov.), a 20% discount is not uncommon, but you or your agent must ask for it. The highest rates are charged between Dec. and Feb. (end of Carnaval), the month of July, and especially the weeks around Carnaval. Reservations should be made up to six months in advance during Carnaval and other regional folkloric events, such as Oktoberfest in Blumenau.

Excellent package deals can be obtained through various private tour companies that you will find listed under *Package Deals* below and the

*Specialty Tours* chapter in the back of the book. If you fly on Varig Airlines, you can receive up to a 10% discount on Varig hotels, which often includes a transfer from the airport. (Varig properties include the Tropical Hotels in Santarém, Manaus and Iguaçu Falls.)

> **UP CLOSE TIP**: *Members of the Brazilian Concierge Association told me that concierges at all four- and five-star hotels severely screen the guests of clients (particularly those who are heading for their rooms). Unless guests are dressed in "attire appropriate to the style and class of the hotel," they are not permitted upstairs (i.e., they had better not look like prostitutes). Clients who return to their hotel with obvious prostitutes (male or female) in tow are politely asked to take them elsewhere, "for the sake of the client's own security." (Some irate clients have checked out immediately in such circumstances, but the concierges remain firm in this matter.) The best bet is to go to a motel, which is actually cheaper and rented by the hour, specifically for this purpose. Barra has many motels; the good ones are located on the highway to the Sheraton.*

## Youth Hostels

For a list of youth hostels in Brazil, write **Youth Hostels Contej**, Estácio de Sá/Rua Vinicius de Moraes,120, Rio de Janeiro, Brazil.

# Air Travel To Brazil

International flights from the US to Brazil run between five and 12 hours, depending on city of departure and destination. Prices and conditions change frequently. Those listed here should be used as a guideline only. When speaking with your agent or the airline directly, inquire if any new nonstop Brazilian destinations – Recife, Salvador or Manaus – have been added since the writing of this book.

**VARIG AIRLINES**, ☎ *800-468-2744*, Brazil's national carrier, is one of the best ways to start off your Brazilian vacation. (I love Varig Airlines and am proud that they represent Brazil!) While other airlines may be cheaper, Varig is known throughout the travel industry as one of the best carriers in the world, consistently providing punctual arrivals, excellent food, and cheerful, efficient service. I have never had an uncomfortable or distressing flight on Varig. Today its copartnership with Delta has improved service beyond accolade. Executive-class seats are considerably more comfortable than tourist class, and their meals (along with those of first class) are unexpected delights with extensive hors d'oeuvres and desserts, well-heated entrées, fine cheese and breads – one might even complain that there is too much food! Films (generally two) shown throughout long flights are usually the latest releases. Best of all, charming Brazilian flight attendants give you the opportunity to try out your Portuguese and will answer your questions.

From North America, Varig offers wide-body services to Brazil through four gateways: New York, Atlanta, Miami, and Los Angeles. There are nonstop flights from New York and Miami to both São Paulo and Rio.

Atlanta flies nonstop to São Paulo, and then on to Rio. On Mon., Miami has nonstop flights to São Paulo, and then on to Rio.

*Fare Guideline:* The nonstop New York-Rio flight (coach, Jan. 8-June 20, three-day stay, seven-day advance purchase, ticketed three days within reservation) cost $921 in 1996. Penalty to change return flight: $100.

Varig passengers traveling to Rio de Janeiro, Brasília, Porto Alegro and Curitiba may now reserve a cellular phone to use during their stay, with more cities being added. Fees for daily rental, minimum usage, and security are all waived; renters receive a 10% discount on all calls. Reservations for the service must be made 72 hours in advance through a travel agent or Varig.

**American Airlines,** ☎ *800-433-7300*, provides the following routes: Miami-Belo Horizonte direct, Miami-Rio nonstop, Miami-São Paulo nonstop, JKF-Miami-Rio and JFK-São Paulo nonstop. Flights from other American cities, including Los Angeles, fly through Miami.

*Fare Guideline:* The flight from New York's JFK-Rio (through Miami) in low season (Jan. 11-June 30, coach, five- to 30-day stay, seven-day advance purchase) cost $921 in 1996 season. Under the same conditions, the New York's JFK-São Paulo is the same price.

**United,** ☎ *800-538-2929*. United flies to three Brazilian destinations: Rio, São Paulo and Belo Horizonte. Stateside ports of departure include New York (JKF, La Guardia and Newark), Miami, Chicago and Los Angeles. Any combination of connecting flights from other American cities can be arranged.

*Fare Guideline:* The direct flight from New York's JFK to Rio (Jan. 11-June 20, coach, five- to 30-day stay, seven-day advance purchase) cost $921 in 1996. Under the same conditions, the LA-Rio flight costs $849.

**Aerolinas Argentinas,** ☎ *800-333-0276*, flies from New York, Miami and Los Angeles to Rio and São Paulo, making a stopover in Buenos Aires.

*Fare Guideline:* For the New York-Rio flight (stopping in Buenos Aires, Jan. 18-June 20, coach, 14-day to three-month stay, 14 days in advance) the 1996 season price was $1,326. If you plan to stay in Buenos Aires before going on to Brazil, the price rose to $1,752.

**VASP,** ☎ *800-732-8277*, a Brazilian airline, flies to São Paulo nonstop from New York, Miami and Los Angeles (ongoing connection to Rio). A direct flight Miami-Recife is on Mon., Fri. and Sat., but differs from month to month.

*Fare Guideline:* For the New York-Rio flight, (Jan. 8-June 30, coach, seven- to 21-day stay, seven-day advance purchase), cost $859 in 1996. During Carnaval, there is a $60 surcharge. Connections to most other Brazilian cities can be made.

For information about packaged vacations and discount flights, see *Package Deals* below.

## Jet Lag

International flights from New York and Miami usually leave at night and arrive in Rio between 7 a.m. and 9 a.m. Although there are no remarkable differences in time zones from most US destinations (see *Time Zone*, below), you may be exhausted from fidgeting in your seat all night long. For tips to combat travel stress, see the *Health Kit for the Tropics* at the back of the book.

## Package Deals

The cheapest way to reach Brazil is to buy your transcontinental ticket through a wholesaler. These independent operators and travel agents buy tickets in bulk and sell them at discounted rates and/or arrange package tours that include ground transportation, hotels, transfers from airports, and stops in several cities. Many agencies work on an FIT system, which allows them to contour a package vacation according to your specific needs. Carnaval packages often include tickets to the Sambódromo Parade. Prices from year to year can change drastically depending on inflation in Brazil (and worldwide!). Your best bet is to call around to many operators and find the lowest price for your particular itinerary. Three reliable wholesalers:

The **Brazilian American Cultural Center**, 20 West 46th Street, New York, NY 10036 (☎ *212-730-1010*, or toll-free *800-222-2746*) is not only a wholesaler but a membership club that requires a $20 fee. The BACC membership allows you to take advantage of round-trip fares that are sometimes $400 below fares listed by the airlines. Included in the membership fee is a subscription to *The Brasilians*, the organization's newspaper, which gives up-to-date news from Brazil. For a $15 fee, BACC will also secure a visa for you. You must first request an application, then mail them the completed form with one 2" x 2" photo and a check or money order payable to BACC. The company will then process your papers through the Brazilian Consulate. This service is especially good for travelers who don't live near a consulate.

**Ladatco**, 2220 Coral Way, Miami, FL 33145; (☎ *800-327-6162*). A specialist in Latin American travel, Ladatco has been in business for 26 years. President Michelle Shelburne offers numerous packages (one 14-day itinerary includes Salvador, Rio, Brasília, Manaus, and a stay in the jungle). She can also arrange discounts on air travel and tailor-make any agenda.

**Ipanema Tours**, 8844 West Olympic Blvd., Suite C, Beverly Hills, CA 90211 (☎ *800-421-4200*), offers a 5% discount to clients (10% to travel agents) on all international flights. The agency handles all of South America and can tailor itineraries to suit. Carnaval packages are also available.

For more package tours, charters and cruises, see *Specialty Tours* at the back of the book.

## Airport Tax

You will be charged US $18 for international flights (if you stay in Brazil over 24 hours) and US $1-$3 on local flights, payable when you check in. To facilitate matters within Brazil, have small change in Brazilian currency ready.

# The Best Time To Visit

Anyone interested in Brazil must experience Carnaval *ao vivo* (live) at least once in his life – whether it's in Rio, Salvador, Recife, or a folkloric city like São Luis (for dates, see the end of the chapter on Carnaval). Do avoid July, a school vacation month, when hotels are packed and rates excessive. Regional folkloric festivals are great fun, such as the beer-swilling Oktoberfest in Blumenau (Oct.), Círio de Nazaré in Belém (second Sun. of Oct.), and *bumba-meu-boi* in São Luis (June). New Year's Eve in Rio and Salvador offers huge processions of white-clad celebrants who perform ceremonies on the beach. Wine-tasting in the state of Rio Grande do Sul is best done Jan.-Mar. while the grapes are still fresh on the vine. The best time to visit the Amazon and the Pantanal is in Aug. (For more information on climatic conditions and when to visit, see the *Hands-On* section of each city.)

# Consulates

The **Brazilian Consulate General** in the US is located at 630 Fifth Avenue, New York, NY 10020; (☎ *212-757-3080*). Brazilian Consulates are also located in Chicago, Houston, Los Angeles, San Francisco, Washington, D.C. and Puerto Rico. Visas and general information may be obtained from these offices.

   In England, the **Embassy of Brazil** is at 32 Green St., London WTY 4AT.

   For American consulates in Brazilian cities, see the *Hands-On* section at the end of the city chapter.

# Customs

Upon arrival from any international flight, foreign visitors pass through customs – usually a quick and painless process. Follow the crowd to the inspection site and have your passport, visa, and card of embarkation ready. (On the plane, the flight attendant will have handed you the embarkation card – a declaration card – to fill out.) Guard this card with your life; it must be shown on departure. Your best bet is to attach it securely to your passport immediately.

   Besides clothing and personal belongings, visitors may carry a radio, a tape deck/cd player, a computer, a typewriter, and cameras for their personal use only. Though luggage is usually not inspected, it will be difficult, for example, to explain why you need 10 radios for your personal use. Your legal allowance is $500 in gifts (an additional $1,000 in taxable gifts) and $300 of duty-free goods – liquor, cigarettes, etc. – bought at the airport.

## Documents

A **valid passport** and **visa** are required before entering Brazil. Visas may be obtained in person at the Brazilian Consulate, or you may write the head consulate in New York (for addresses in the US, see above). You'll need 2" X 2" photo (black-and-white or color), your passport, and your airline ticket (or itinerary confirmed by your travel agent) as well as a completed signed application. Tourist visas obtained in person are free; those transacted by a messenger service cost $10. You may also use local visa service agencies. Tourist visas now last up to five years.

**Business visas** may be obtained by presenting a passport, photo, completed application and a letter from your company detailing the purpose of your trip. If possible, avoid having to fly on a business visa; they are more complicated and hassle-inducing than normal tourist visas.

You should also carry with your passport the official record of your vaccinations, particularly if you're going into the jungle. If you become sick or if an epidemic breaks out, a physician can determine your susceptibility. If you pass into bordering countries, you may be required to show proof of vaccinations.

Brazilians love letters of introduction. If you are doing special research, collect as many signed references as you can. Business cards are also impressive and prove you are a serious professional.

## Language

Brazilians will deeply appreciate even the slightest effort you make to speak Portuguese, even if it's a garbled mess. In general, Spanish is a help, but it will only get you so far. Brazilians have the uncanny ability to understand Spanish, although if you speak only Spanish, you will be floored when you first hear Portuguese – the rhythm, accent, and sensibility are totally different, although more than a few words may be similar. (Written Portuguese, on the other hand, is much easier for Spanish-speaking travelers to decipher.)

Even if you speak Portuguese, you will find that regional accents vary profoundly. Southerners actually speak with a kind of cowboy twang, and Northeasterners speak extremely fast and clipped. Sometimes even Brazilians don't understand each other, and actors from the interior have been known to undergo diction classes before they're allowed on stage and screen.

Still, it's very possible to travel throughout Brazil without any facility in Portuguese or Spanish. Just make sure all your travel arrangements are made in advance and join group tours rather than wander around alone in the backcountry. In fact, Brazil without Portuguese (or even "Porto-Spanglish") can be a great international adventure. In southern cities, such as Blumenau, Nova Petrópolis, and Gramado/Canela, German is spoken as a second language, and throughout the wine country in Rio

Grande do Sul, many Italian-born families are well versed in their mother tongue. There is also a large Japanese-speaking community in São Paulo.

> **UP CLOSE TIP from Mike Salvo:** *Take photographs of your family, pets, even that last snowstorm from home when you travel through Brazil. I discovered it was a great way to bridge the cultural gap and make friends, especially as I couldn't speak the language well.*

Receptionists at four- and five-star resorts usually speak English, along with some travel agencies in Rio, Salvador, São Paulo, and Manaus. Usually, at least one person at a city or state tourist information center speaks English. Fluent English, however, is another matter. Although many can understand English, because of the huge influx of foreign music and film, Brazilians have little opportunity to practice speaking and hence, are extremely shy. If you are speaking English to anybody (no matter how fluent they may seem), speak slowly (but do not shout), use simple words and grammar, and be on the lookout for misunderstandings. Brazilians tend to mix up the words "he" and "she," and often confuse negative constructions. They also speak more through body language than through words. (See *Language* at the end of this book for a brief introduction to some of the more common phrases that might come in handy.)

---

# Money

---

Traveling to Brazil with a large amount of cash is as risky as it is elsewhere (because once it's stolen, it's gone). However, when the dollar is strong against the Brazilian currency, it's your best bet for value, particularly if you exchange small amounts at a time. My personal choice is to carry a mixture of cash, credit cards and traveler's checks, stashed in different places. If recent trends are to be believed (though they never are in Brazil), the re-evaluation and establishment of the *real* has brought a tentative stability to the exchange situation. Credit cards (MasterCard, Diner's Club, Visa and American Express) are accepted at most four- and five-star hotels, and many restaurants in the larger cities. Clothing stores and boutiques often give discounts if you pay in Brazilian currency.

If you are traveling into the interior and away from large cities, make sure you have exchanged enough money to pay for everything in Brazilian currency because you will be hard pressed to find anyone who will accept traveler's checks or dollars.

If you run out of money while traveling, the easiest way to receive extra funds is through cash advances on your credit card, but note that you can only receive the money in Brazilian currency. Remember to bring personal checks with you to facilitate this negotiation. American Express will cash up to US$1,000 on green cards and $5,000 on gold once a week, exchanged at the official tourist rate (offices can be found in Rio, São Paulo, Manaus and Salvador). Banco do Brasil also handles money forwarded on Visa. In New York the **Brazilian American Cultural Center** (☎ *212-730-1010*) will make transfers in dollars to Brazil.

It's best to have already exchanged some Brazilian currency (small bills) before you arrive to pay for airport tips and taxis. There is usually an exchange house or bank in the airports of major cities.

(For more information on exchanging money in Brazil, see *Currency Exchange* below, under *While You're There*.)

# Photography

Film and developing often cost twice as much in Brazil as it does in the States, so stock up before you go. Carry all film in a protective lead-lined bag to protect it from damaging x-rays at airport security stations and take it out of your hand luggage before you pass through any metal detectors in airports. Do not pack expensive equipment in checked baggage; it could get damaged or stolen. In the rainforest, keep film well protected from moisture and humidity.

# Safety

Brazil has received an undeserved reputation for being totally and irrevocably dangerous. True, in the big cities – Rio, São Paulo, Salvador, and Recife – you must exercise extreme caution and not walk around like a neon sign for robbers. This means carrying as little money on your person as possible, not wearing jewelry (leave gold watches at home), and not brandishing expensive-looking cameras. Don't leave valuables strewn about your hotel room; use the safe inside your apartment or at the front desk. Take taxis, especially at night, and don't exchange money with people you meet on the street. Use common sense.

As you move away from the big cities, you'll happily discover laid-back, crime-free areas. In some cities, like Nova Petrópolis in Rio Grande do Sul, the residents don't even bother to lock their car doors. Frankly, the trick is to look like you have nothing to steal.

You can do a lot for your own safety by becoming an expert traveler. This means double-checking your airline schedules, always knowing where your passport and travel documents are, and carrying your cash, credit cards, traveler's checks, and ID in separate places. Never carry your wallet in a back pocket. Carry backpacks in front of your body. Invest in a money bag that straps inside your clothes, around your stomach, chest or ankle.

And don't think crime only happens in Brazil. There's been a rash of airport thefts reported in the US; the most targeted ones are Kennedy, La Guardia, Newark, Boston, Miami, and Los Angeles. Entire bags have been stolen or relieved of packed cameras, laptops, credit cards, portable phones, jewelry, scuba equipment, and even golf clubs. For protection, don't carry expensive-looking luggage or attach American Express platinum card tags. Buy adequate locks and use them. Pack only clothes and carry anything valuable with you on board. If you don't want to lose it, don't check it.

## Vaccinations

Yellow fever vaccination is highly recommended if you are visiting rural areas or the Amazon jungle. It's always a good idea to update your tetanus vaccination. Immunizations for hepatitis and typhoid are suggested for rural and jungle travel. For more in-depth information, see *Health Kit for the Tropics* at the end of the book.

## What To Pack

Before going to Brazil, it's important to check the climate of the areas you will visit (see each region) and also consider whether you will be spending most of your time in metropolises, small back-road towns, or the jungle. In very hot weather, tropical clothing (light cottons or silks) is essential. Businesspersons in Brasília and São Paulo wear suits and dresses but, in general, jeans and t-shirts are the fashion. All seem to be worn with a sexy, stylish flair.

Most Brazilian fashion feeds on extreme seduction – skirts are very short, pants are tight (or very baggy) and tops for women are skimpy. Think anti-dowdy. Although you may not want to do as Brazilians do, it is a good idea (for safety's sake) not to look like a tourist. Don't even think about wearing a loud, garish tropical shirt, any t-shirt with BRAZIL or I LOVE RIO blazoned across it, or any large handbag that looks as though you're carrying a microwave oven. Instead, invest in a waist-pouch to carry your small necessities (cheap ones can be bought from street vendors in Ipanema and Copacabana in Rio) and/or consider carrying your money in a body pouch underneath your clothing.

For most Americans, what to wear on a Brazilian beach is a dilemma. If you want to look like a Brazilian, probably no bathing suit you can buy in the States will be small enough. Simply, most Americans on the beach look like they are either a) dressed for winter or b) wearing a diaper (I was personally accused of the latter during my first visit). On the other hand, if you are anything but petite, most Brazilian bathing suits will not fit you, or at least certainly not cover what you are used to covering. One option for women is to buy a large scarf and tie it native-style around the waist; you can also buy adjustable bathing suit tops that can regulate the amount of flesh you expose. Fair-skinned travelers should give real consideration to coverups for skin protection; the tropical sun is more intense than it seems.

What you wear on your feet is a prime factor in determining your trip's pleasure quotient. Most of Rio's streets are cobblestone or uneven pavement, and you won't be happy in anything that has a high heel. Flat, lightweight tennies or well-grounded walking shoes are best, though Brazilian women do wear high heels at night (okay if you take cabs). A pair of sturdy sandals is also important, as well a cheap pair of beach sling-ons. Cowboy boots tend to be too hot (not to mention bulky to pack), but fashionable Brazilians have taken to the miniboot, the kind that just grazes the bottom of your jeans. Runners will want to throw in their jogging shoes to join the throngs that turn out at dusk and dawn in nearly every seaside city.

Brazilians live to dress up at night. They take hours after work getting ready to go out for dinner, even though they may end up looking nonchalantly casual in an open shirt and nice slacks, or a short sexy dress. Only in the very elite restaurants are men required to wear ties; a jacket is sufficient in most cases. If you are going out with Brazilians, they will, upon meeting you, check out just how fashionable and coordinated you look, even in the smallest city. If you're going high society, matching shoes and a bag are expected, and fashionable (if fake) jewelry is a must. No matter what one's social class, in Brazil taking care for one's physical appearance is a sign of self-respect.

I'll discuss jungle attire at more length in the chapters on the Amazon regions, but do note that at some point you will have to come out of the jungle, and Brazilians don't take kindly to muddy, smelly, wild-looking barbarians, no matter how great their jungle stories are. Make sure you bring an extra pair of pants or a skirt, a clean pair of shoes, and a nice shirt if you want to partake of anything in the city that's civilized.

# While You're There

## Bringing Home Brazil

Varig Airlines is entirely accommodating when it comes to traveling home with a *berimbau* – a large, one-stringed instrument attached to a round gourd. Wrap the bow separately in heavy packing paper and send it through with your luggage. Carry the gourd with you as hand luggage.

US Customs allows returning residents of the US to bring home duty-free articles totaling up to $400. This includes up to 100 cigars, 200 cigarettes (from one carton), and one liter (33.8 fluid ounces) of alcoholic beverages. When shipped, gifts up to $50 in fair retail value may be received by friends and relations to the US free of duty and tax.

Among prohibited articles considered injurious to the public welfare are: absinthe, liquor-filled candies (where prohibited by law), narcotics, obscene articles and publications, and switch blades (unless you are a one-armed person who uses a switchblade knife for personal use). Most fruits and vegetables are either prohibited or require an import permit. Meat, livestock, poultry, and their byproducts (sausage, pâté) are either prohibited or restricted from entry, depending on the animal disease condition in Brazil.

If you are traveling with medicines containing habit-forming drugs or narcotics (i.e., cough medicine, diuretics, heart drugs, tranquilizers, sleeping pills, depressants, stimulants, etc.), you must properly identify all drugs, carry only the quantity you will normally need, and have ready a prescription or written statement from your personal physician confirming you are under a doctor's care and in need of these drugs for your personal health while traveling. See *Health Kit*, at the end of the book.

Plants, cuttings, seeds, and certain endangered species either require an import permit or are prohibited. Wildlife and fish are subject to certain import and export restrictions, prohibitions, and quarantine requirements. All ivory and ivory products, except antiques, made from elephant ivory are prohibited. If you are contemplating purchasing articles made from materials such as tortoise shell, leather, whalebone, ivory, skin, or fur, contact the **US Fish and Wildlife Service, Department of the Interior**, Washington, D.C. 20240, *before you go.*

## Business Hours & Holidays

Most businesses and stores open at 9 a.m., break for lunch between noon and 2 p.m., and re-open between 2 and 5 p.m. Mon.-Fri. Shops in Ipanema and Copacabana in Rio tend to open 9 a.m.-1 p.m. on Sat. Banks open 10 a.m. to 4:30 p.m. Mon.-Fri. Many businesses close up shop for the five days of Carnaval leading up to Ash Wednesday. Museums throughout the country are generally closed on Mon.

Businesses, with the exception of restaurants, shut down completely for the following Brazilian holidays. As in the States, some offices may shut down not on the official date, but on the Monday closest to it, for a long weekend.

| | |
|---|---|
| January 1 | New Year's |
| Carnaval | Five days prior to Ash Wednesday |
| March/April | Good Friday and Easter Sunday |
| April 21 | Tiradentes' Day |
| May 1 | Dia do Trabalho |
| June 10 | Corpus Christi |
| September 7 | Independence Day |
| October 12 | Nossa Senhora da Aparecida (Our Lady of the Apparition) |
| November 2 | Dia dos Finados (All Souls Day) |
| November 15 | Proclamation of the Republic |
| December 25 | Christmas (most restaurants closed) |

## Climate

Brazil's climate varies according to latitude and elevation. Seasons are opposite to the Northern Hemisphere; winter runs June-Sept. and summer Nov.-Mar. Average temperatures during the summer range from 25-40°C (75-100°F). Warm tropical weather extends north from Rio de Janeiro throughout most of the year. South of Rio – in the states of São Paulo, Santa Catarina, Paraná and Rio Grande do Sul – the climate is temperate, with warm summers, cold winters, and the occasional snowfall in the far south.

# Communications

## Mail

On a good day, it takes about five days to a week for a letter from Rio to reach New York. On a bad day, it might take a few years. Anyone sending packages to Brazil should note that all packages are opened by post office officials and that restrictions apply.

The easiest way to mail an envelope is to hand it to your concierge, who will mail it for you or sell you stamps at a small markup. There are usually post offices in major airports. Express post, registered mail, and parcel service operate both domestically and internationally.

## Newspapers

Most major cities have at least one newspaper and sometimes two that offer listings of local events in music, theater, film, and dance. *O Jornal do Brasil* is Rio's version of *The New York Times*, as is *A Folha de São Paulo* in São Paulo. In Rio, Brasília and São Paulo, it is relatively easy to locate *The International Herald Tribune, The Miami Herald,* and *The Wall Street Journal,* as well as international version of *Newsweek* and *Time* magazines. A daily English-language newspaper, *The Latin America Daily Post*, circulates in Rio and São Paulo. I've even glimpsed copies of *Musician* and *Downbeat* magazines in Rio – albeit for more than twice the price. At larger newsstands and airport bookshops you can find other foreign newspapers and magazines, along with some paperback novels in English.

## Telephones

The phone line in Brazil has a mind of its own. Many numbers seem perpetually busy, and you can be suddenly disconnected for no apparent reason. Be patient. Local calls can usually be made free of charge from your hotel (check ahead of time). You can also call locally from streetside phone booths that require tokens, called *fichas*, which you can pick up quite cheaply at the newsstand. Buy at least two packs of five at one time, since each *ficha* lasts for only three minutes. When you first pick up to dial, put two or three tokens in at once, since disconnections come fast and without warning. You can also buy phonecards, which serve the same purpose, although not all phones can take them.

## Calling Brazil/Calling Home

Some of the better hotels offer direct dialing; when the hotel operator becomes involved, calls can often take up to a half-hour or more to place. Hotels often charge up to a 25% service fee or more for international calls; to save money, patronize the city phone company called EMBRATEL, where you will be directed to a private booth and given a key that opens the phone. You pay the receptionist after you make the call. Phone companies operate at most airports as well.

### International Calls to Brazil

From the States, dial 011-55, followed by the area code (without the preceding 0) and number.

### International Calls from Brazil

For direct dial to the US, dial: 00-1, area code, number; to Great Britain 00-44, area code (without the preceding 0), number; to Ireland 00-353, area code (without the 0), number; to Australia 00-61, area code, number.

For collect calls, dial the International operator: 000-111.

### National Calls within Brazil

For direct-dial: 0 plus the area code; collect calls (not in a hotel): dial 107.

# Electricity

Electric voltage is not standardized in Brazil. What we consider "house current" in the States can be found generally only in the city of Manaus in the Amazon and in some five-star hotels. The current is commonly 127 volts, while the city of Brasília uses 200 volts. Plugs have two round holes, so if you want to use hairdryers, shavers or other appliances from home, you will need a converter kit that has an adapter. Check your appliances before leaving: some have a switch that can be turned to 110 or 220-volt current (110-volt appliances work normally on 127-volt current). Computers should always be used with a surge protector because they draw more power.

Most four- and five-star hotels supply hairdryers in the bathroom, or you can ask for one. Just check the voltage before plugging anything in. One warning: even with a converter, my electric steamer pooped out after a few weeks.

# Emergencies

In the case of any emergency, do not hesitate to contact the consulate of your own country in the nearest Brazilian city. US embassies are the official diplomatic arm of the federal government abroad. Embassies are usually located in capital cities, and US consulates are the local offices of embassies. Consulates represent American interests, including commercial concerns. US consulates can replace a lost or stolen passport, help find medical assistance, assist in an evacuation, or contact family members at home. You have the right to request a consular officer to visit you in jail if you are arrested overseas. Consulates are informed by the foreign government when Americans are arrested, but don't expect these offices to help you with travel plans. The State Department recommends that Americans who visit a country for longer than one month register with the nearest available post. If you are a concerned family member of someone traveling abroad, contact the Office of Overseas Citizens Services at ☎ *202-647-5225* (a 24-hour hot line).

**Brasília** (US Embassy)
Avenida das Nacoes, Quadra 801, Lote 3
☎ 011-55-61 321-7272

**Rio de Janeiro** (US Consulate General)
147 Avenida Presidente Wilson
☎ 011-55-21 292-7117

**São Paulo** (US Consulate General)
933 Rua Padre Joao Manoel
☎ 011-55-11 881-6511

## Hair Salons

Excellent hair salons and barbershops can be found in most five-star hotels. I would not, however, suggest getting your hair permed or colored anywhere in Brazil. Products sold in Brazil tend to be harsher than their American counterparts, and my own hair actually started to fall out from a combination of bad products and overbleaching from the tropical sun. Manicures are not expensive, but do bring your own tools for health's sake. And don't be startled – Brazilian manicurists have a way of globbing polish all over your fingers, then cleaning up the residue later. But the final result is usually excellent.

## Health

For information regarding jungle diseases, see the *Health Kit for the Tropics* in the back of the book.

## Cholera

Cholera was declared epidemic in Brazil in 1992, but it need not scare away informed tourists. Long called the poor peoples' disease, it largely attacks populations with untreated sewage and no access to clean drinking water. Unless you are traveling in rural areas and/or drinking tap or river water, you stand almost no risk of getting sick. The US Centers for Disease Control also recommend that all visitors to Latin America avoid consuming ice, salads, tap water, foods sold by street vendors, raw fish, and cooked food served cold. For more information, see *Health Kit for the Tropics*.

## Safe Sex

Brazil now has the third largest number of recorded HIV infections in the world (about one million people infected, 20% of them women). Among the factors contributing to its proliferation is the large amount of bisexual activity, heterosexual anal sex, an active gay population, a lack of efficient blood testing practices, and the sharing of needles, particularly in the upper class, where drugs were deemed fashionable in the late 1970s and 1980s. Young prostitutes who come down from the *favelas* (shanties) often believe in magical potions made by the Indians or think using a bidet is sufficient for cleansing germs. Despite a television blitz campaign warning about the danger of unsafe sex and the proliferation of Benetton billboards featuring enormous multicolored condoms, few couples take preventive measures. Brazilian men often refuse to use condoms out of ignorance or stubbornness, and women are loathe to press the issue. Furthermore, the Brazilian condom is vastly inferior to ones you may be familiar with, and is prone to breakage.

A foreign traveler's best bet is to pack a sufficient supply of American condoms, use them *unstintingly*, giving the leftovers to Brazilian friends, who will be delighted to receive them. If you must buy condoms in Brazil, they can be found in most pharmacies, under the name *camisinha* or *camiseta de Venus* (note the word *camiseta* alone means T-shirt).

## Doctors & Pharmacies

If you have a medical emergency, ask your concierge to recommend a doctor (some five-star hotels have doctors and nurses on call). If the problem is extremely serious, contact your country's nearest consulate (see under *Consulates*, above) and ask for help in returning home as quickly as possible. Simply, Brazilian hospitals tend to be overcrowded and not up to American standards. If you find a competent doctor (usually referred by a friend or your concierge – and they do exist!), he or she will probably give you more time than the American counterpart, exhibit more gracious behavior, and even call you at home to follow up on your condition. Frankly, all private health care I received in Brazil, from traditional Western medicine to more oriental/holistic practices, turned out to be excellent.

If you travel with prescription drugs, carry a copy of the prescription with you (for customs and emergency refills). Do note, however, that many drugs needing prescriptions in the States are purchasable over the counter in Brazil, though their quality can't be vouched for. Strangely, other non-prescription products in the States, such as homeopathic remedies (Bach Flower Remedies, in particular) and some antihistamines, require a prescription from a certified practitioner.

Receiving prescription drugs (or even vitamins) from home while in Brazil is tricky. All overseas packages are opened, and you will be required to pick up the box at a government agency, as well as show three copies of the prescription and a letter from the doctor stating why these products cannot be bought in Brazil. To Brazil's credit, however, a care package of vitamins I never picked up in Rio was actually returned to my mother, the sender – totally intact! – a mere 12 months later.

Shiatzu and acupressure practitioners are well trained in Brazil and provide excellent service. Make sure, however, that any needles have been disinfected before they are used on you, or bring your own set.

## Water

For health reasons, drink only bottled water wherever you go in Brazil. In small towns you can order it at bars or in restaurants and even Amazon jungle lodges serve bottled water. If you are camping, you must carry your own. You're asking for cholera and any number of other diseases if you drink river water or some tap water, purified or not. Most hotel rooms are supplied with bottled water in the mini-bar. Avoid brushing your teeth with tap water. For more tips, see *Health Kit for the Tropics* at the back of the book.

# Money/Currency Exchange

In the past, one of Brazil's ways to handle inflation has been to knock off zeroes from its present currency, then change the name. At press time, the currency is the *real* (pronounced ray-OW); the plural is *reais*, (pronounced ray-ICE), though it may have changed by the time you read this (but *dat's Brazil!*). Contrary to popular belief, there is really no longer a black market for exchanging currency here. There are, however, three levels of exchange: the *oficial*, or official rate, which Brazilians pay to buy air tickets and foreign currency; the slightly higher tourist rate called *dólar turismo*, generally offered to tourists at official exchange houses called *câmbios*, and the even higher parallel rate, called *dólar paralelo*, which is so rarely made available to tourists that it's not worth thinking about. Despite attempts by the federal government to stabilize the *real* in relationship to the dollar, rates still vary slightly from day to day. You can always check the morning newspapers before exchanging money.

During periods when the US dollar is considerably stronger than the Brazilian currency in use, everybody on the streets will want to exchange money with you. This is really asking for trouble, because you may find yourself in the middle of a set-up and never see your money again (and that's the least of it!). *Câmbios* are the safest place to exchange money and traveler's checks; often you are escorted to a private back room where the exchange takes place. Make sure you receive a receipt. Avoid exchanging money at your hotel because the rate is usually lower than the official one.

## Cutting Costs

Because severe inflation and the fluctuating fees of air travel may make determining costs difficult, prices quoted by travel agents can change weekly. Traveling during off-season is the best way to save money and most hotels offer discounts if you ask. Other strategies include joining a prepackaged tour; taking full advantage of your hotel's large "American" breakfast and skipping lunch; foregoing a hotel with a pool in a seaside city; renting a room without a view; buying an Airpass for travel within Brazil (see page 9); and carrying a map so you won't get cheated by taxi drivers. Soda, bottled water, and candy bars in your mini-bar can run up to $2 each; so make a stop at the neighborhood store or bar and stock up. If you prefer to travel with your own bottle of scotch or rum, buy some at the duty-free shop before you leave the States. Don't use credit cards, to avoid the surcharge. Make overseas telephone calls direct or (most preferably) at the public phone company. Take advantage of the large breakfast buffets that are included in most hotel rates. Lunching at a *rodízio* (an all-you-can-eat steakhouse) could last you all day. Regularly verify all meal checks and hotel bills for accuracy; "mistakes" are often made. Finally, become well-acquainted with the currency before using it so you won't confuse the bills.

## Pricing

From my vantage point (six-month lead time before publishing), and given the unpredictable flow of the Brazilian economy, it is almost impossible to suggest prices for the 1997-98 seasons. Hotels and restaurants in this book are listed by category, since inflation can play havoc with prices overnight. As a loose guideline, the figures below show average expenses for a visitor to Rio de Janeiro (São Paulo, Salvador and Recife) in the spring of 1996. (Smaller cities came in slightly lower for comparable quality.)

### Average Tourist Expenses (US$)

| | |
|---|---|
| HOTEL* room for one with tax | 167.00 |
| DINNER* with tax and tip, but no drinks | 32.45 |
| Beer | 2.36 |
| Big Mac hamburger | 2.16 |
| TAXI | |
| Base charge | 1.26 |
| Each additional km. | .45 |
| From the airport | 25.00 |
| CAR RENTAL PER DAY | |
| Midsized car with unlimited free mileage | 81.00 |
| Gas per gallon | 1.89 |
| AVERAGE DAILY EXPENSES | 284.00 |

* Note that prices for hotels are higher during Carnaval and in high season (Dec.-Feb., July).

* Good news! Individual portions are most often so large in Brazilian restaurants that two can share one plate (except in nouvelle cuisine restaurants, where the portions are miniscule).

## Price Charts

HOTELS (standard double)
Very expensive .............................. Over $150
Expensive................................. $80-150
Moderate ................................. $40-80
Inexpensive ............................... Under $40
RESTAURANTS (per person)
Expensive................................. Above $25
Moderate ................................. $10-25
Inexpensive ............................... Under $10
"All cards" means that all major credit cards are accepted.
MC - MasterCard; V- VISA; DC -Diners; AE American Express

## Tipping

There are no service taxes charged in Brazil, but most hotels and restaurants add a 10% service charge unless otherwise specified. Look for the sign *não taxa de serviço* ("no service tax") or *serviço não incluso* ("service not included"), suggesting you should leave a tip. If a service charge is added, or if you want to leave more, feel free to do so – remember you're in a third-world country where maids, waiters, manicurists, porters, and other service people can barely subsist on minimum wages.

On a good tour, tip a guide between $5 and $10 for a half-day trip. They usually make very low wages, despite being multilingual and well educated. Do note that they probably receive commissions from any stores they steer you to.

In Rio and Salvador, in particular – and most anywhere, actually – especially if you are sitting at a sidewalk café, street children or beggars may ask you for money or food. Follow your conscience, but be aware that the request is sometimes a ploy to get attention while a third party lifts your belongings.

## Police

Contrary to popular belief, the police in Brazil can be helpful to tourists, especially in Rio, where special forces maintain watch over the beaches. If you're in trouble, don't hesitate to approach one even if he/she doesn't speak English; he will find someone who does. (I was saved during Carnaval by one charming officer who made sure I got to my proper samba school.) However, if you are the victim of petty theft, the best thing to do is notify the concierge and manager of your hotel. Filing a complaint with the federal police may be a waste of time unless you want to file an insurance claim.

Don't get nervous if you see armed policemen stopping cars on the street or highways near *favelas* (slums). They are most probably making routine searches for drugs.

## Restrooms

Memorize this phrase: *"Onde fica o toalete?"* ("ON-gee FEE-cah oh twah-LETCH-ee?"). That will get you a finger pointed to the nearest restroom. Women's restrooms (also called *banheiros*) are usually marked M for *mulher* (woman), and S is for *senhor* (man). Adequate facilities can be found at most restaurants, and if you are not trailing sand, the more casual ones will probably let you use them without dining. Toilet paper is not uniformly present in public restrooms, so I'd suggest carrying your own supplies (such as Handiwipes) or snitching a few sheets of tissue from your hotel room. Bus stations usually have clean facilities, with an elderly woman handing out a stiff, torturous paper for a few cents. Most hotel rooms come with regular toilets, as well as European-style bidets. If you're camping out, you'd better come prepared.

## Shopping

Fine clothes, though stylish, have become extremely expensive in Brazil, often costing more than comparable items in the States. Centers of fashion are Rio and São Paulo, which boast extremely modern shopping malls, as well as chic neighborhood boutiques. Best buys are leather shoes and bags, particularly if you take advantage of end-of-season sales (look for the words *promocão* or *liquidação*.)

Most native crafts can be bought in Rio, but they will usually cost twice as much as they do in their states of origin. Unabashed bargaining is expected at open-air markets and bazaars, but use discretion in finer stores and boutiques, where you might still be able to wrangle discounts on large jewelry purchases if you speak to the owner or manager.

## Time Zones

Brazil has three time zones, though most of the country is three hours behind Greenwich Mean Time. This region occupies eastern Brazil, and parts of central (including Rio de Janeiro, Salvador, São Paulo, Brasília, Recife, and Belém.) That means when it's noon in New York, it's 2 p.m. in Rio de Janeiro. The second zone, which is four hours behind GMT, encompasses the states of Mato Grosso and Mato Grosso do Sul and most of Brazil's north (such as Manaus, Corumbá, Rio Branco, Porto Velho, Cuiabá, and Campo Grande). Far western Brazil (Acre and the western edge of Amazonas) is five hours behind GMT. For Daylight Savings Time, clocks go forward an hour on the second Sun. in Nov. and are set back on the second Sun. in Mar. The city of Belém is not in the habit of following this schedule, so double-check your flight schedules.

# Transportation

## Air

Brazil is a big country (as the musician Caetano Veloso once said, "kinda too big"), and the distances between major cities are enormous. If you are planning to visit more than one city here, consider buying Varig's **Brazil Airpass.** For a basic cost of $440, you receive one to five flight coupons (six, if Santarém is included), which allow you to make that many flights within a 21-day period. (You may also make two connections via any of the following cities: Brasília, Fortaleza, Manaus, Recife, Rio, Salvador, and São Paulo.) Additional coupons can be purchased for $100 each. Note that you must plan your itinerary carefully, as some cities, especially in the Northeast, will require several connections. Also, the Airpass must be purchased outside Brazil (though you need not be flying internationally on Varig), and it may be used only on domestic Varig flights. It is not valid on the Rio/São Paulo shuttle between Congonhas and Santos Dumont airports. Depending on your itinerary, this Airpass can save you hundreds of dollars, since domestic travel within Brazil is extremely expensive.

Other airlines within Brazil are **Transbrasil, TAP, Taba,** and **VASP.** Transbrasil flights are usually at night and connections aren't always convenient.

For travel by bus, car, and tram within Brazil, see below.

### Computers & X-rays

Laptop computers should be carried with you in your hand luggage. DO NOT EVER send them through a Brazilian x-ray machine. Otherwise, you may find your entire software program and files wiped out, as I did. Travelers headed for the rainforest should protect their computer and diskettes from humidity and moisture by wrapping the case in an extra plastic bag.

### Airport Transfer

Taxis are always available at airports. Airport buses into the city are much cheaper, and usually drop you off in front of five-star hotels. City buses are also usually available heading to the city's center or main terminal. Special taxis can often be obtained at a central post near the exit of the airport, where you pay in advance, then give your receipt to the driver. These taxis generally cost about 10% more than the regular fares, but are considered safer and are guaranteed to get you to your destination. Have the name and address of your hotel on hand. Some hotels, especially those booked through package deals, will provide transfers to and from the airport, so check in advance.

## Flight Confirmation

Confirm all flights at least 24 hours in advance (international flights, 48 hours); otherwise, you risk losing your reservation. And keep a check on the weather at your destination. Some of the planes flying between Northeastern destinations and in the Pantanal are small.

## Luggage Damage

Luggage can get damaged on the best airlines. Reports should be made to an airline official at the airport, but unless the bag is totally dysfunctional, you are better off biting the bullet, especially if you aren't staying too long in the city. In general, suitcases are taken to be repaired, not replaced, a delay that could cause you even greater grief.

Do make sure that all luggage (hand and checked) is well identified with your name and home address.

# Bus

Bus travel can be an invigorating way to see the countryside, if a little demanding. Most buses are not air conditioned, but the breeze is refreshing, and the tickets are cheap. Chickens and other small animals traveling with their owners may be sharing the bus with you. In most cases, seats are reserved by numbers, which are taken seriously. Ask for a seat next to the window (*janela*), which is generally cooler. Buses stop frequently (about every three or four hours), and bus terminals with snack bars, casual restaurants, newsstands, and bathrooms can provide colorful glimpses of native life. A viable trip by bus is down the southern coast from Rio to the seaside cities of Ubatuba, Santos, and Guarujá. Reservations for buses should be made as far as possible in advance, especially on weekends and during high season.

Custom-designed, air-conditioned buses called *leitos* are more expensive but luxurious, sporting reclining chairs for overnighters and sandwiches and cookies in cardboard boxes. The Salvador-Ilhéus route in the state of Bahia is an excellent overnight trip.

In seaside cities, such as Salvador, Maceió, Natal, and Recife in the Northeast, special tourist buses take bathers down the main beach drag.

City buses are boarded from the back and payment in exact change should be given to the cashier, who sits in the rear. You exit from the front. City buses, however, are usually not the best option for a first-time tourist. They are almost always packed, and crime is prevalent. In fact, you couldn't pay me to ride one anymore. There are many, many reports of buses being held up by bandits who demand everybody's money and jewelry (one thief sent back the silver since he was only interested in gold!).

# Driving

Brazilian drivers are maniacs. (Is there a better reason why the Formula One races are held in Rio?) They ride on each other's bumpers, make turns from opposite lanes, run stop signs and red lights and, most of all, love to swoop down and park on the sidewalk next to your foot. If you have the mind of a madman it might suit you fine, but I couldn't suggest driving a great deal in Brazil unless you are settling down there and have no choice. Outside the large cities, which usually have paved and/or cobblestone streets, roads run from passable in the south to awesomely hazardous in the Pantanal, where four-wheel-drive is an absolute necessity.

If you insist on hiring a car, you will find rental agencies in most airports and in all major cities. Officially, you are required to have an international driver's license, but a few extra bucks might curtail that requirement. Gas in Brazil is more than twice the cost in the US, while the state-subsidized alcohol is slightly less.

Pedestrians should note that the police in Rio advise drivers *not* to stop at red lights at night to avoid being held up. As a pedestrian, look both ways several times when crossing the street and keep an eye out for speeding cars. Pedestrians in Brazil do not have the right of way.

## Taxis

Taxi drivers, particularly in Rio and Salvador, have long been notorious, but are slowly being educated that their honest service deeply affects tourism, and thus the country's economy. Here are some tips to avoid being carried miles out of your way and stiffed for an outrageous fee.

- ☐ Know where you're going and have your destination written in Portuguese on a piece of paper, as well as the best route there, recommended by your concierge.
- ☐ Because of inflation, rates are constantly changing, but up-to-date prices must be displayed on a chart pasted on the back window. See that the taxi meter, located in the front seat next to the wheel, starts when you do, and check the chart yourself at the end of the ride. A surcharge is collected on Sun. and after 10 p.m., so check the second table of prices.
- ☐ If you are returning to your hotel, call out to the porter to verify the charge, or hail a policeman if you see one.
- ☐ Special air-conditioned taxis, which are safer, are usually found lined up in front of fine hotels, but they invariably run almost twice as much as the normal fee. Rates are determined in advance, so ask.
- ☐ Hire a car and guide for the day or by the hour.
- ☐ Attend night-time shows with tour groups, which provide transfers by private coach.
- ☐ To hail a cab in Brazil, stand up on the curb and point your finger to the ground, not up! Otherwise, taxi drivers think you are waving at them.
- ☐ Always carry the name, address and telephone numbers of your hotel tucked inside your shoe in case your wallet or purse gets stolen.

## Train

There are few trains in Brazil and you are generally better off taking the bus. A few daily trains run between Rio and São Paulo, and two trains weekly between Rio and Belo Horizonte.

## Traveling With Kids

Brazil is an extremely family-oriented country. Highchairs are available in numerous restaurants, and many hotels do not charge for children under five. Baby-sitters are often available at resort-style hotels, whose private grounds and excellent security make them ideal for families. The best examples of this are the Rio Sheraton in Rio de Janeiro, Nas Rocas Resort in Búzios (near Rio), the Transamérica Hotel and Praia do Forte in Bahia, and the Pratagy-Eco Hotel in Maceió in the Northeast. Kids love the jungle lodges in the Amazon and would do well taking a lazy boat trek through the Pantanal. However, a child who goes on an adventure tour must be accompanied by an adult, and should be old enough to take directions without misinterpreting or balking.

# The Best Of Brazil

### Best Hotels

Sheraton Rio (Rio), Caesar Park (Rio, São Paulo and Fortaleza), Maksoud Plaza (São Paulo), Hotel Tropical (Manaus), Laje de Pedra (Canela), Solar de Nossa Senhora do Rosário (Ouro Preto)

### Best Restaurants

Massimo (São Paulo), Satyricon (Rio), Claude Troisgros (Rio), Mariu's (Rio), The Place (São Paulo), Saint Honoré (Rio), Café Colonial Bela Vista (Gramado), Lá Em Casa (Belém), Dona Lucinha (Belo Horizonte), Chez Dadette (Belo Horizonte)

### Best Resorts

Transamérica Hotel (Comandatuba Island), Praia do Forte (Bahia), Pratagy Eco Hotel (Maceió), Floresta Amazônica Hotel (Alta Floresta, Mato Grosso), Genipabú (Natal), Hotel Casa Grande & Senzala (Recife)

### Best Eco-trips

Horseback riding outside Belo Horizonte, *jangada* (raft) rides in Maceió, dune surfing in Natal, dawn cruise to Parrot Island near Belém (Amazon), Expeditour's Pantanal Triangle Cruise, camping and trekking in Chapada dos Guimarães, hiking through Serra da Bocaina, scaling the mountains of Petrópolis, traversing the Pantanal's Transpantaneira Highway

## Best Beaches

Grumari Beach (Rio), Piatã (Salvador), Praia do Forte (Bahia), Praia de Ponta Negra (Natal), Praia de Francês (Maceió), Jericoacoara and Taiba (Fortaleza), Caeheta and Porto de Galinhas (Recife).

## Best Ranches & Jungle Lodges

Ariau Jungle Tower (Manaus), Fazenda Xaraes and Pousada Caiman (Pantanal)

## Best Pousada

Pousada do Vale dos Veados (Bocaina National Park)

## Best Historical Sites

Parati (Rio de Janeiro), Ouro Preto and Mariana (Minas Gerais), São Luis and Alcântara (Maranhão), Olinda (Pernambuco)

## Most Spiritual Sites

Rio and Salvador on New Year's, Ouro Preto, São Lourenço and Caxambú, (Minas Gerais), Iguaçu Falls, Chapada dos Guimarães, Solo Sagrada (Guarapirangá, São Paulo)

## Most Artistic City

Congonhas (Minas Gerais)

## Best Scuba

Island of Fernando de Noronha

## Best Outdoor Market

Belém (Para)

## Best Party Towns

Porto Seguro and Arraial d'Ajuda (Bahia)

## Safest Locations

Transamérica Hotel (Bahia), Fernando de Noronha (island) Praia do Forte (Bahia), Chapada dos Guimarrães (Mato Grosso), historical towns and spa towns of Minas Gerais, Santarém (Pará), Blumenau and Joinville (Santa Catarina), Nova Petrópolis and Torres (Rio Grande do Sul)

## Best Sites for UFOs

Sugarloaf (Rio), São Tomé das Letras and São Lourenço (Minas Gerais), Chapada dos Guimaráes (Mato Grosso), Alta Floresta (Mato Grosso), Amazon jungle

---

### Vp Close Awarò For Social Action

The city of Santos (in the state of São Paulo), which has overcome enormous social obstacles (the highest AIDs rate, polluted beaches, and horrendous slums) through vigorous leftist-supported programs devoted to the welfare of the common people, today sports beautiful, usable beaches, an attractive, flower-strewn main drag, and has become a model for the country in AIDS prevention. *Felicidades!*

---

# Itineraries

Brazil offers so many diverse destinations that the most difficult task of your trip may be selecting an itinerary. Mixing and matching experiences – cultural, adventure and relaxation – can be fun, or you can focus on one region or one particular interest. Do note that jumping from north to south may require multiple flight connections, and could mean a full day of travel. A novel idea is to cruise from the States to Brazil on an oceanliner, dock in the Northeast or the Amazon, then fly on to other parts of the country. People with little time, like businesspersons, should particularly take a look at the sections in each chapter marked *Excursions* because they usually entail only a few hours' travel time (by car, bus, or boat) from the main city. In the following itineraries, remember to add two more days for international travel to and from Brazil.

### Brazil Sampler

Fly to Rio, 3 days in Rio; 4 days in Minas Gerais; 3 days in Salvador; 1 day in Brasília; 2 days in Iguaçu Falls; 4 days in Manaus (Amazon jungle)

### Best Beaches Tour

Fly to Rio; 2 days in Grumari Beach in Rio; 3 days in Angra dos Reis, including Parati; 3 days at Transmérica Resort on Comandatuba Island in Bahia; 2 days in Natal (dunesurfing); 3-5 days in Fortaleza and surrounding beaches

### Northeast Beaches

Fly to Salvador; 3 days in Salvador; 3 days at Praia do Forte in Bahia; 2 days in Maceió; 3 days in Recife and Olinda; 2 days in Natal; 3 days in São Luis

### Ecological (Multiple Ecosystems)

Fly to Rio; 1 day in Rio to experience the urban Atlantic rainforest (Tijuca Forest); 3-4 days in Serra da Bocaina (state of Rio de Janeiro); 3 days in Belo Horizonte horseback riding around the mountains; 2 days in Foz do Iguaçu (waterfalls); 3 days in São Luis, including Lençois National Park (dune park); 4 days in a lodge or cruise in the jungle outside Manaus (Amazon rainforest); 4 days in the Pantanal

## Amazon Forest

Four days in Belém (including cruising the river); 2 days in Santarém; 2-3 day boat ride down Amazon River in Manaus; 3 days in a jungle lodge; 4 days in Alta Floresta in Mato Grosso

## Spiritual

Four days in Ouro Preto, Mariana, São João del Rei and Tiradentes (colonial Catholic Brazil); 3 days in Salvador, including Cachoeira (heart of Afro-Brazilian religion); 2 days in Brasília (New Age); 4 days in Chapada dos Guimaráes and the Pantanal (natural and extraterrestrial)

## Natural History

Fly to Natal; 4 days in Fernando de Noronha (island scuba diving); 4 days at Praia do Forte (Sea Turtles Conservation Project); 2 days at Iguaçu Falls (one of world's greatest wonders); 4 days in Pantanal (Caiman Ecological Lodge)

## Trekking & Camping

Fly to Rio or São Paulo; 4 days in Serra da Bocaina; 4 days in the Pantanal and Chapada dos Guimarães tableland; 3 days Iguaçu National Park; 4 days in the Amazon jungle from Belém, Santarém or Manaus

## Cultural & Folklore

Arrive in Rio; 1-2 days in Parati; 4 days in Ouro Preto (Mariana, Rio, São João del Rei and Tiradentes); 3 days in Salvador; 3 days in Recife and Olinda; 3 days in São Luis, Maranhdo

## Musical

Three days in Rio (samba shows, pagode on the beach and jazz clubs); 2 days in São Paulo (discos and jazz clubs); 2-3 days in Belo Horizonte (Minas Gerais school of musicians in local jazz clubs); 3 days in Salvador (Afro-Brazilian drumming and *axé*, Bahian regional pop music); 2-3 days in São Luis (samba, reggae and regional music)

## Culinary

Three days in Rio (seafood and international gourmet); 2 days in São Paulo (international 5-star cuisine); 2 days in Santa Catarina (German delicacies); 4 days in the wine country of Rio Grande do Sul; 2 days in Minas Gerais (Mineiro regional fare); 3 days in Salvador (Bahian specialties); 2 days in Belém (Amazonian cuisine)

For agencies that focus on special-interest tours, see the back of the book.

# ROOTS

**P**ristine beaches, crystalline waters, luxurious vegetation – the Brazil the first European explorers saw was nothing less than a terrestrial paradise: "one so well favored that if it were rightly cultivated it would yield everything," said one enthusiastic chronicler. Today, after 500 years, that sentiment of perpetual promise is still being bantered about by supporters and critics alike, and exactly how to cultivate that wealth has remained a continuous challenge. If Brazil has had one major obstacle through its tumultuous history, it has been its gargantuan size – a girth so preposterous as to make near impossible any attempt to maneuver a reasonable distribution of wealth. Ever since the first explorers ventured onto Brazilian shores in 1500, their primary approach has been the Manifest Destiny creed of "explore and conquer"; today, that philosophy cuts at the heart of the world's ecological debates regarding the importance of Brazilian rainforests to the planet's survival.

## The First Europeans

The **Portuguese** were the first Europeans to set foot in Brazil, and in the late 15th and 16th centuries, there was already a mingling of many cultures – Iberians, Celts, Phoenicians, Greeks, Carthaginians, Romans, Visigoths and Muslims. In a society dominated by the Church, religious motives for expansion played at least a supporting role – the hope was to defeat the enemies of the Christian faith in Africa and carry the word of God to the continent. The Crown's more pressing goal, however, was to create a direct all-water trade route with the Orient that would break Italian domination and bring a cascade of riches to Portugal. Not surprising, then, that crass materialism and the most sublime spiritual intent mingled in the Portuguese sailor with almost fanatical fatalism. Those who risked passage across the vast unknown seas to the New World had to be not only adventuresome and fearless, but also unquestionably loyal to the Crown.

Under the appointment of Manuel I, the explorer **Pedro Alvares Cabral** set forth with 13 ships and 1,200 men to follow up Vasco da Gama's claims, departing from Lisbon on Mar. 8, 1500. The voyage to India began routinely enough, but on Apr. 20, after a whirlwind storm, the fleet unexpectedly sighted weeds and reeds in the ocean. Two days later, at approximately 17° south latitude, land appeared, which Cabral christened **Ilha da Cruz** (Island of the Cross). Some say his fortuitous discovery was a nautical mistake; others believe he intentionally veered off course, either on a hunch or on instructions from the throne. In any case, the Court paid little attention to this discovery until **French and British pirates** began to raid the spice ships. Later merchants, attracted to the plentiful stands of brazilwood, a source of excellent red dye, would rename the new territory **Terra do Brasil** (Land of Brazil).

The **native people** who shyly met those first expeditioners at what is now Porto Seguro in Bahia were friendly, even generous in their innocence. According to conservative historians, there were around 2.5 million native Indians living in Brazil at the start of the 16th century. They had lived there undisturbed for hundreds of thousands of years (possibly having migrated from Asia over 430,000 years before). Fragmented into small tribes, the majority were **Tupí-Guaraní**, who tended to be short and bronze-colored, with long straight black hair. Though the Tupis tended toward cannibalism when provoked (they ate the first bishop to arrive in Bahia), they had become masters of tropical survival, cleaning and pruning just enough land for their own crops, wearing no clothes, and indulging in intricate body designs. Although they were not equal in culture to the sophisticated Aztecs of central Mexico, the Mayas of Yucatan and Guatemala, or the Incas of Peru, they had developed a strong tradition of **spirituality**, in which the *pajé*, or **shaman**, communed with nature spirits and prescribed herbal medicines culled from the forest. As visionary as they were, however, what these tribal shamans tragically did not foresee was the future decimation of their race.

# The First Progenitors

To be fair, the first white men the Indians encountered were not exactly the cream of humanity, but they had their strong points. As was the case with most New World colonies, among the first to inhabit Brazil were *degredados*, **exiled criminals** ordered to live among the Indians and learn their language. While they may have been rough and uncouth, these lowlifes were at least equipped with the one thing upon which the future of the Portuguese colony depended. According to Brazilian sociologist Gilberto Freyre, the blending of the Lusitanian and Amerindian cultures was facilitated primarily by one major factor: a favorable attitude toward miscegenation – in other words, lust. Since Portuguese women were excluded from the first colonies, the conquerors, who were already accustomed to the dark-skinned beauty of the Moorish, African, and Asian females, soon discovered a veritable paradise. Some men, like Diogo Alvares (renamed Caramuru) in Bahia, actually sired an entire village of miscegenated offspring. As a result, a new race quickly appeared – the *mameluco* or *caboclo* – a blend of European and Indian blood well adapted to the physical demands of the land. In return, the Indian taught the white man the best methods for farming and hunting, introduced him to new crops like manioc, and showed him the best way to pass the night in the tropics – in a hammock.

# Missionaries

As ship captains bartered with the Indians, exchanging trinkets for brazilwood, a temporary truce was enjoyed. But soon enough, **Jesuit missionaries** set out to convert "the heathens," supervising their education and encouraging them to dress like Europeans. At the same time, the arriving colonists, supported by daring explorers, were rounding up conquered Indians as candidates for **enforced labor**. In time, the Jesuits would severely antagonize the Court with their viewpoint that the enslavement of Indians was contrary to Christian doctrine, but the fathers themselves managed to violate their subjects' basic human dignity by systematically stripping them of their animistic beliefs and instinctual lifestyle. Though some Indians became acculturized, most either rebelled, ran away or, more frequently, succumbed to death when their immune systems proved too weak to fight even the slightest Western germ.

By the end of the 16th century, about 100 ships were sailing annually from Lisbon to Brazil. To discourage the French privateers scoping the coast, King João III in 1532 sent **Martim Afonso de Sousa**, along with colonists, plants, seeds, and animals, to found the first settlement at São Vicente (somewhere near Santos). Established at this time was the pattern of **land distribution** that would influence Brazilian history for centuries – 15 captaincies of about 60 leagues in length, divided among 12 donnees and extending all the way to the Tordesillias Line. The owners could tax, impose justice, divide the land into sesmarias, and be expected to rent their land in the name of the king. Only two of the captaincies survived – **Pernambuco**, where sugar plantations flourished, and **São Vicente**.

Disappointed by the lack of progress, João III appointed **Tomé de Sousa**, a loyal soldier who had served in Africa and India, as the first governor in charge of all military and civil administration. Beyond the French, Portugal's biggest headache was the **Dutch**. (Owing to a legitimate right of succession, the Portuguese Crown in 1580 had passed to the heir of the Spanish throne – making both Portugal and Brazil dominions of Spain for 60 years.) Although the Dutch, in the guise of the **Dutch West Indies Company**, occupied the Northeast for 30 years, they were eventually defeated in a near-massacre campaign that pitted Catholics against Protestants. In 1555, the French occupied what is now the city of Rio de Janeiro, but few colonists were seduced away from Europe, and they were finally driven out by the Portuguese in 1565. In 1624, a Dutch fleet off the coast of Salvador took the governor by surprise, burned the Jesuit College, and massacred priests until they were expelled nine months later by a hastily assembled Spanish and Portuguese fleet. The occupation of Recife by the Dutch lasted a brutal 24 years, replete with ambushes, outrageous taxes, and mounting hostilities, until the colonists themselves sent them packing.

# Motley Crews

The conquest of the vast, mysterious Brazilian interior was due mostly to the *bandeirantes*, a rugged breed of men propelled as much by their own personal dreams of glory as by loyalty to the throne. Ever in search of gold, diamonds, and Indians, these Brazilian explorers set out mostly from São Paulo – on mules, on foot, and in canoes – forging waterways and paths that would eventually appear on the maps of the coming empire. The motley crews that banded together under their own flag almost always included a priest (sometimes craftier than his colleagues), a few fierce Indian fighters and, later, botanists, who dared to explore the Amazon, Uruguay and Paraguay rivers. It was the *bandeirantes* who led the first expeditions to Minas Gerais when gold was discovered in Sabará in 1695, and later in Ouro Preto, Mariana, and elsewhere. In 1719, the gold rush opened the path to Cuiabá in Mato Grosso – a 2,175-mile obstacle course from São Paulo that led through hostile tribes, voracious mosquitoes, sweltering heat, and dangerously flooded rivers. The herculean efforts of the *bandeirantes* finally paid off, and by the middle of the 18th century it was Brazilian gold that was keeping the Portuguese throne afloat.

Brazilians are fond of saying that they have never had a bloody revolution. In truth, Brazil does enjoy the reputation of being the only South American colony to have achieved independence through peaceful means, but that doesn't include the many who died trying to amass power before and after. The most famous of the aborted rebellions was the *Inconfidência Mineira*, hatched by 12 prominent citizens in Ouro Preto, who were inspired by the success of the 13 former British colonies up north. The conspirators betrayed each other before they even began, except for the self-avowed leader, **Tiradentes**, whose gruesome execution would make him a national hero after Brazil gained its independence. In 1807, Napoleon's invasion of Portugal forced the royal family to take refuge in Rio, declaring it the temporary capital of the Portuguese Empire. On the suggestion of French minister Talleyrand, the portly, good-natured prince named João III made his tropical home into an official kingdom and actually grew genuinely fond of it, despite the constant complaining of his wife, the Spanish princess Carlota Joaquina. In 1816, following the death of his demented mother, Maria I, he ascended to the Portuguese throne in his own right as **King João VI** and did not return to Lisbon until liberal revolts demanded his presence back home five years later. When he finally bid farewell to Brazil, he felt quite nostalgic about leaving the cosmopolitan city he had transformed from a small, unimposing village.

# Constitutional Emperor & Perpetual Defender of Brazil

As João VI sailed home, he left behind as regent his 23-year-old son **Pedro**, with the advice that he should take up the crown of Brazil if it should part from Portugal, lest it fall into the "hands of an adventurer." Although Pedro was a talented and complex young man, his education had been sorely neglected and his undisciplined childhood eventually gave way to a lusty adulthood. A dashing horseman, composer, and friend to the Italian composer Rossini, he lived openly with his mistress, the beautiful Domitila de Castro, in a relationship considered one of the great love stories of the Americas. Together, they had five children. Unfortunately, as a ruler, Pedro alternated between autocratic and democratic behavior, eventually battling the **Côrtes**, the parliamentary body, which demanded his return to Portugal. On Sept. 7, 1822, the short step to **independence** was taken on a dusty road between Santos and São Paulo when Pedro received a slew of messages: one from the **Côrtes** reducing his power, others from friends pushing for independence, and the most powerful one from his wife, who urged him to fight with the words: "Pedro, this is the most important moment of your life." With the fire of a *bandeirante*, Pedro unsheathed his sword right on the banks of the Ipiranga River and gave the infamous cry "Independence or Death." On Dec. 1, 1822, in typical royal splendor, he was crowned "**Constitutional Emperor and Perpetual Defender of Brazil**."

The US became the first country to recognize the newly independent empire on May of 1824, when President James Monroe officially received José Silvestre Rebelo as chargé d'affaires. By the end of 1825, Portugal acknowledged the independence of its former colony in return for two million pounds sterling, though the "bill" and Pedro's allowance to use the honorary title of Emperor of Brazil infuriated Brazilians, further enflaming anti-Lusitanian sentiment. A disastrous war with Argentina, domestic disorganization, and a rampant money crisis aggravated by promises to free the slaves eventually forced Pedro to abdicate with the following announcement: "I prefer to descend from the throne with honor rather than to go on reigning as a sovereign who has been dishonored and degraded. Those born in Brazil no longer want me for the reason that I am Portuguese. My son has the advantage over me that he is Brazilian in birth. He will have no difficulty in governing." The son he was talking about – the one he would leave behind as he sailed for Lisbon – was a five-year-old child.

Although **Pedro II** was a mere pawn of his courtiers when he mounted the throne at the age of 14, he achieved full maturity in only a few years. By 1847, he was ruling firmly, free of all political influences, emerging as a symbol of order and prosperity for various regional groups. At the time, Brazil was overwhelmingly rural, and Pedro II reasoned that he needed the support of those who dominated the fields – namely the plantation owners (sugar, coffee and cacão). In retrospect, most historians praise Pedro for his honesty, integrity, and moderation, though a few have complained that his tolerance dampened any progressive vision.

# National Unity

The presence of the royal Braganças in Rio for 30 years forged a most needed sense of unity in the new empire. In fact, they became the only European monarchs to ever set foot on their American domains. During their reign, Brazilians acquired the habit of looking to Rio as the center of power, and they saw in the monarchy a guarantee of national unity and security. At the urging of the emperor himself, a **constitution** was written advocating some of the major tenets of early 19th-century liberalism – free trade, sanctity of private property, and capitalistic incentives. Unfortunately, these directives proved disastrous and had the effect of further subordinating the Brazilian economy to the needs of the capitalistic markets of the North Atlantic.

The relative sense of **national unity**, however, gave emotional space for long-repressed tensions in the interior to arise. Black slaves rebelled against masters; Indians rose up against whites; old scores with Portuguese noblemen were settled. The **Cabanagem Rebellion**, a bloody 10-year uprising of the dispossessed, exploded in the Amazon when mixed-breed rebels invaded Belém and killed the governor of Pará. Uprisings in Maranhão, Pernambuco, Bahia, and Rio Grande do Sul further threatened the stability of Pedro's administrative powers. Although he was ostensibly an intelligent ruler, Pedro's foreign policy led Brazil directly into the bloodiest war in South American history – the **War of Triple Alliance**, from 1864 to 1870. Although Paraguay initially started the hostilities by invading Uruguay and parts of Mato Grosso, Brazil had antagonized its neighbor by blocking access to the sea. Though Paraguay was deeply humiliated, losing over 75% of its male population, it did fight gallantly and caused great damage to Brazil.

# Slavery

Due to the rise of the **plantation culture** in the interior, the color of the average Brazilian began to change drastically. As **sugar** and **tobacco industries** dominated the economy, the need for extensive labor ballooned, and when Indians proved unsuitable, millions of Africans were stripped from their tribal communities and shipped to Brazilian ports beginning in the 17th century. For 300 years, the ignominious **slave trade** continued, and some historians claim that Brazil imported a half-million more slaves than did all of Spanish America. Most labored under a hot sun on the sugar plantations of Bahia and Pernambuco; in Minas Gerais, slaves toiled under even less humane conditions in the underground **gold mines**. While many tried to preserve their African culture through religious practice, food, dance, and music, others fled to refugee enclaves called *quilombos*. As the winds of abolition wafted through Brazil on a British current, the backlash to preserve slavery incited even more racism and bloodshed. The slave trade was finally abolished in 1854, but slavery itself remained legal, requiring the impassioned oratory of lawyer Joaquim Nabuco to turn the final tides of sentiment. On May 13, 1888, Brazil achieved the notorious distinction of being the last country in the Americas to abolish slavery.

# The End Of The Monarchy

The political fallout from such a humanitarian gesture did not ultimately serve Pedro's administrative position. Threatened by the loss of labor, enraged landowners turned on him, as did the liberal intellectuals clamoring for a republic; even the military had not forgiven the debacle of the Paraguayan War. Without a shred of resistance, military forces led by **Marechal Deodoro da Fonseca** marched into Rio on Nov. 15, 1869, effectively announcing the end of the monarchy. Though invited to remain, Pedro II insisted on exile, dying impoverished in a humble Parisian hotel.

The end of the monarchy ushered in an era of **military involvement** that would color Brazilian politics up to the present day. Twenty years after marching into Rio, Fonseca declared himself a dictator. Unsupported by his own troops, he was forced to resign two weeks later. His successor, **Marechal Floriano Peixoto**, took command, proving himself even more incompetent, until finally stepping down in favor of the first elected civilian president, Prudente de Morais.

# The Good, the Bad & the Ugly

For the first 30 years of the 20th century, Brazilian leaders oscillated between the good, the bad, and the ugly. The surge of the coffee industry shifted the base of power away from the sugar fields of Bahia to the coffee fields of São Paulo and the dairy farms of Minas – a political trend that came to be known as *café com leite* (coffee with milk). Between 1890 and 1930, large-scale immigration further spiked the ethnic mix, as the Japanese headed to São Paulo, Italians to the wine-producing lands of the extreme south, and Germans to the cool, fresh climes of Santa Catarina. **Rubber** joined the boom-bust economy as millions of *Nordestinos* (Northeasterners) moved into the Amazon to tap rubber – that is, until a sly British conspiracy to smuggle seedlings out of the jungle eventually exploded Brazil's world monopoly.

# The Second World War

As regional interests began to dominate the federal scene, political graft slowly set in. During World War II, Brazil passively sided against Germany; on the homefront, the economy was weakened by the disastrous collapse of the coffee market as two million sacks of beans lingered unwanted in storage – a million more than the world consumed in one year. The year 1929 marked the beginning of an 18-year domination of government by one man – **Getúlio Vargas**. Though he lost the 1929 presidency in a legitimate election, a military junta immediately seized power from the elected opposition and passed Vargas the sash of office four days later. In one dramatic act, the old republic ended just as it had begun – with military intervention.

For nearly a generation, Vargas managed to rule the country from every possible political position: as chief of a provisional government (1930-1934), as constitutional President elected by the Congress (1934-1937), as dictator (1937-1945), and finally as constitutional President elected by the people (1951-1954). Born to a rich ranching family in Rio Grande do Sul, Vargas proved to be gifted with unusual political acumen, though he never quite demonstrated the megalomaniacal tendencies of Latin dictators like Juan Perón of Argentina (to whom he was often compared). Urged on by a group of young, idealistic supporters, he managed to nationalize the oil, steel, and electricity industries and standardized a health and social welfare program that brought him working-class kudos long after his death. But to effect such drastic changes, Vargas had to create his own power, which he did by declaring himself dictator and renaming his regime **O Estado Novo** (The New State). World War II found Vargas siding with the Allies, only after the US offered massive aid in return for naval bases, but it was his own army that forced him to resign upon their return from fighting troops in Italy. From 1945 to 1950, **Marechal Eurico Gaspar Dutra** ran an insipid regime, opening the door to Vargas' defiantly triumphant return in 1950. This time, however, military enemies and crushing inflation undermined his popularity, particularly when he raised taxes for the middle class. Events turned tragic when **Carlos Lacerda**, a famous journalist who had publicly called Vargas a communist, barely survived an assassination attempt; a shot meant for him killed one of his bodyguards instead. Evidence pointed to one of Vargas' own bodyguards, though the president was never directly implicated. Nevertheless, when the High Command eventually demanded Vargas' resignation, the politician countered with a swift response that left the country in shock. After writing a dramatic farewell note, he retired to his bedroom in the Palácio do Catete in Rio and shot himself through the heart.

# Brasília

An interim government ruled until a most industrious, truly visionary physician from Minas Gerais turned the country on its head. **Juscelino Kubitschek** (known to his supporters as JK), marched into Brazilian politics with faith in the interior and a commitment to modernism, all symbolized in the construction of a new, decidedly futuristic capital called Brasília. Suddenly, with new highways, avant-garde architecture, and a thriving automotive industry, Brazil shot into international prominence as a modern country to contend with. Although JK can be credited with bringing Brazil out of the horse-and-cart era, his successor, **Jânio Quadros**, inherited a financial nightmare, riven with by debts incurred in the construction of Brasília, and worsened by Quadros's own autocratic temper and his friendliness to Cuba (the latter shocking the military). When Quadros suddenly resigned seven months after taking office (citing "terrible forces" against him), the military stepped in, severely reducing the power of his succeeding vice president, **João Goulart**, and instituting a parliamentary system. A plebescite in 1963 returned full power of the presidency to Goulart, whose land reforms and social programs veered him dangerously to the left. As the cost of living soared and middle class opposition swelled, the military accused Goulart and his government of being communists and again usurped power in a bloodless coup on Mar. 31, 1964. Within four hours of taking power, before Goulart fled to Uruguay, the leaders of the coup received a telegram from President Lyndon B. Johnson congratulating them on their maneuver. Generous American aid and loans would soon follow.

# Trials & Tribulations

For the next two decades, Brazil was at the mercy of a **military dictatorship**, where presidents were chosen in secret by the army and where individual human rights were severely abused. The regime never hesitated to use violence in pursuing its agenda. The most repressive era was the Médici years, between 1969 and 1974, when "subversives" were tortured and killed and even the lyrics of popular songs were censored. Nevertheless, aided by harsh measures, the economy surged between 1974 and 1979, giving rise to the "Brazilian Miracle," as it was called – boom years of unprecedented prosperity, though its riches barely touched the legions of the impoverished majority. The 1980s reverted to hard times as the Latin American debt crisis exploded and foreign loans dried up; the interest alone on Brazil's foreign debt outstripped the nation's ability to pay. The last military president, **João Baptista Figueiredo** intentionally paved the way for the end of the regime – rescinding press censorship, calling for an amnesty for political prisoners, and even allowing Congressional elections – but he could not surmount growing public hostility over the failing economy.

# Democratic Elections

It seemed as if the sun would finally rise on Brazil in 1985 when 75-year-old elder statesman **Tancredo Neves** was chosen by an electoral college comprised of Congressional and state delegates to be Brazil's first civilian president in 21 years. Aided by humanitarian insight, Neves, considered the most competent moderate to oppose the military, was able to unite rival factions – until he was rushed to the hospital with a bleeding tumor the night before he was to take office. Thirty-eight days and seven operations later, he died of septicemia, though a few suspected foul play. (His surgeons were brought to trial for incompetency.) His vice-president, **José Sarney**, a staunch conservative from the northeast state of Maranhão, attempted to gain the support of liberals through populist land reforms, but his indecisive nature, not to mention institutionalized government corruption, helped to fuel the foreign debt that reached a devastating $120 billion.

By the time he left office, Sarney was so out of favor that crowds regularly greeted him with showers of bricks. Still, nationalistic fever had gained prominence, leading the government to declare a moratorium on the foreign debt and instigate strict measures against foreign investment. By 1988, inflation had become so outrageous (700%) that a new, powerful president was needed to avoid another military takeover. In 1989, **Fernando Collor de Mello** became the first president elected by popular vote in 30 years. He was the scion of a wealthy Alagoas family who, as governor of his home state, had become famous for hunting down *marajás* – retired generals and former public servants who were living illegally on multiple pensions. Beating out the Worker's Party, Collor brought a new sophistication to Brazil's international image with his movie-star good looks, beautiful wife, and personal derring-do. (He once took over the controls of a 727 jet on his way to the White House to meet President Bush.) Only hours after taking office, however, he totally shook up the country when he froze the banks – an anti-inflationary plan that pleased those without money (their buying power remained stable), but infuriated those who had any assets. (No one could withdraw from their accounts for at least a period of six months.) Eventually, most of the money was returned – with interest – but not before many in the middle class had to drastically change their lifestyles.

# Scandal

The **Collor Plan**, a complicated financial agenda geared toward salvaging the failing economy (including the privatization of government-owned industry), was generally been hailed as a positive step, but its workability was obscured by one scandal after another throughout Collor's administration. To the delight of the press, the first brouhaha began with his minister of economy, **Zélia Cardoso de Mello** (no relation to Collor), an extremely intelligent but somewhat graceless woman who eventually resigned under political pressure after her illicit affair with a married Cabinet member was uncovered. (She later went on to marry the country's most beloved comedian.) Collor's own wife, **Rosane Collor**, in a series of scenes straight out of a Brazilian soap opera, was accused of illicit spending and deposed from an honorary position (her public tears upstaged only by her husband's dramatic disposal of his wedding ring into a lake before they were subsequently reconciled). Finally, on the eve of Rio '92, the finance manager of Collor's election campaign was accused of embezzlement by the president's own brother, who also publicly accused the President of using cocaine. Complicating the scenario was the fact that the finance manager was trying to compete with the Collor family's newspaper and radio conglomerate in Alagoas, "coincidentally" run by the brother.

In June 1992, Collor addressed the public in an impassioned 6½-minute speech denouncing the scandal, effectively clearing the way a few days later for a monumental repackaging of the foreign debt with the International Monetary Fund. Yet, as Congressional investigations provided more evidence of fund-milking by Collor, his wife, and key administrators, public and legislative pressure swelled, demanding the President's swift resignation.

# Recovery & Renewal

**Itamar Franco**, Collor's low-profile Vice President, succeeded to the presidency in the fall of 1992, but he quickly lost popularity through indecisiveness, lack of humor and a penchant for changing his cabinet ministers on a whim. In the meantime, Collor, along with his wife, prepared to face criminal charges. In spring 1993, a bid for the return to a monarchy was overruled by popular vote, though many supported it, not as a joke but as a desperate attempt to change the dire economic crisis.

With the Presidential elections of 1994, Brazil began to mark a new political trajectory that now has observers predicting the country just might claim back its right to a reasonable financial future. As a result of policies instigated by **President Fernando Henrique Cardoso** (a sociologist and former professor in American universities who beat out the Worker's Party), Brazil is now, for the first time in decades, enjoying both solid economic growth and price stability. Latin America's biggest economy by far at $650 billion, it is expected to grow by 4% in 1996, repeating 1995's rise. Inflation, which soared more than 40% per month in early 1994, fell to 20% around Feb. 1996.

All these changes are inspiring foreign investors to jump aboard. In the first 40 days of 1996, $4.5 billion of portfolio investment entered the country, with much more projected. President Cardoso continues to impress upon foreign skeptics that what happened in Mexico – as he described it, "where people didn't know the real state of the economy" – will never happen in Brazil, due to its active press, strong business groups, and an observant, if divisive, Congress. According to an interview with *Business Week* in 1996, Cardoso claimed that the **Real Plan**, which his administration instigated, has brought about the greatest income redistribution in Brazil's history to date, not exactly lessening the gap between rich and poor but at least increasing consumption and private-sector investment. Given the enormous task facing any new government in Brazil, the Cardoso administration has at least achieved a minor miracle – lassoing that gargantuan monster and putting it back on track.

# INTRODUCING BRAZIL

## Inside Brazilians

**A**nything is possible in Brazil. That's the attitude to adapt if you're planning to do any traveling or business. Given that special Brazilian temperament, however, nothing is ever accomplished by a push and a shove. The currency in this country is not money so much as **charm** (though a few discreetly placed bucks never hurt anyone). Even though most of Brazil remains a third-world country, the sophistication of the upper class has filtered into every level of society, mostly through the extravagant soap operas that dominate the air waves. Simply, Brazilians are worldly and should be treated as such; some remote farmers I met in the Amazon jungle had just watched the entire coverage of the Gulf War on their battery-powered TVs.

There's no question that Brazil labors under a seemingly perpetual economic crisis – a fact of life that can profoundly influence all **financial relationships**. Most prices can be bargained down, but it depends on your attitude and technique – even with a street vendor, you should negotiate with grace, humor, and dignity. It is totally tasteless to bargain shamelessly in restaurants or commercial stores, though if you are Brazilian it's perfectly fine (nearly expected) to complain about the high prices. Asking politely for a *desconto* (or **discount**) is another matter. Hotels in low season tend to respond favorably to the idea – if you have the gumption to ask, preferably in advance (see *Accommodations* on page 9). The same holds true for a fashionable boutique or jewelry store, particularly if you are buying a substantial amount. (Be savvy enough, however, to distinguish between a true discount and one that is based on already wildly inflated prices.) Sometimes paying in cash (usually Brazilian currency) can inspire a discount; what also helps is to smile, look beseeching, then offer to pay in cash.

Brazilians often misinterpret American straightforwardness as brusqueness, and if you learn to soothe your Western impatience, you will find many more social doors opening. Unfortunately, numerous Brazilian women have complained to me that American men tend to treat them all as (please pardon the language) whores. To be politic, I think the misunderstanding mostly has to do with sexy standards of tropical dress, which should be reinterpreted by Americans as merely national style. True, in the big cities, particularly around touristic hotels, there are lots of prostitutes, but you will rarely find them among the legions of professional guides and shopgirls, many of whom are quite conservative, no matter how short their skirts are. If you want to date a Brazilian, ask with the same grace you accord women at home.

**Social kissing** is one national habit that causes undue consternation among North Americans. Even when meeting professionally, most women kiss each other hello and good-bye on both cheeks (really, two pecks in the air), though two men (or a man and woman) in a corporate situation usually just shake hands. Industries such as tourism and arts & entertainment usually find everybody kissing everybody, no matter how well they know each other. If a Brazilian acquaintance introduces you to his or her mother, especially if you've been invited to dinner, get ready to kiss. When in doubt, you can always shake hands. The thing to remember is that this kind of double-cheek kissing has really nothing to do with deep-seated affection, though it is a sign of how important even superficial displays of warmth are to Brazilians. If you feel awkward or mess up, those acquainted with American mores will probably forgive you.

In terms of **personal address,** Brazilians can be both respectfully formal and charmingly casual. When introduced socially, a Brazilian might give only his or her first name (indeed, at times in Brazil it seems that nobody has a last name). The truth is, most people have four or five names, the combination of which – if told to you – you would no doubt forget. While first names are commonly used, titles of respect – *senhor* for men and *dona* for women – are used as a sign of politeness with strangers and also to show respect to an elder or someone from a different social class. As such, guides or hoteliers often addressed me as Miss Pamela, and I always addressed my elderly landlady in Rio as Dona Vitória. Children always address their parents as *o senhor* or *a senhora* in place of the equivalent "you," a form also expected in matters of business. A pleasant way to address a government official or older colleague is to call him *Doutor*, followed by his or her first name (i.e., Doutor Fernando, or Doctor Fernando). The trick is to keep the sarcasm out of your voice.

**Family life** is important to most Brazilians. Due to the financial crisis, adult children often live at home long after their American counterparts would, a condition now identified by Brazilian psychologists as severely extended adolescence. Until 1985, divorce was illegal in this Catholic country, giving rise to a subculture of adultery (the poet and lyricist Vinícius de Moraes was famous for his numerous wives/lovers/companions). Today, you will find many men over 40 already on their second wife – usually young, pretty women in their 20s – while the legion of divorced upper- and middle-class women continues to swell. Both married men and women tend to take lovers, but given the machismo still rampant, women must remain more discreet. In fact, men accused of murdering their wives for adultery often go unconvicted, as do the majority of rapists. A feminist movement is only now beginning to have a voice in Brazilian politics, but most women will admit that they are still judged on the basis of their looks, not their capabilities.

What truly separates Americans from Brazilians is **punctuality.** Basically, never expect a Brazilian to be on time or to apologize for being late (yes, even up to two hours). Tardiness is simply not considered a problem in

Brazil, and if you ever comment on it adversely, you will only be met with a quizzical look. On the other hand, every time I was late for a business meeting, it always seemed to matter to somebody. The rule in Brazil, I guess, is expect to wait, but never keep anyone else waiting.

**Smoking** seems to be a universal activity among Brazilians, even those who live in the Amazon jungle and particularly guides, who tend to blow their smoke in your face as you trek through the rainforest. An estimated 50 million Brazilians smoke, or about a third of the population – a higher proportion than the US, where about a quarter of adults smoke. And the average Brazilian smokes more than his American counterpart: over 3,100 cigarettes each year, compared to 2,500 a year in the US. In Sept., 1996, the mayor of São Paulo, Paulo Maluf (a former smoker married to a smoker) signed an executive order banning smoking in all places where food is served, including bars – to the disgruntlement of a lot of citizens. It's one of the toughest bans in all of Latin America, where smoking is not only tolerated but widely accepted. As of 1996, smoking in São Paulo was also prohibited in shopping malls and supermarkets.

While the rest of the country is hardly as stringent, I was nevertheless surprised at how many times I was politely asked if someone's smoking would bother me. (I had the distinct impression I was expected to say no; most Brazilians are too socially accommodating to ever admit to offense.) If you really can't stand the smoke, the best way to curtail it is to plead severe allergies.

Brazilians, in general, have impeccable **table manners,** and are often shocked by more casual American mores. They eat nearly everything (including pizza) with knife and fork (held in the right and left hand respectively, European-style, without changing), and the habit runs deep. It was not until I brought a Brazilian friend to New York that he saw for the first time "sophisticated" people eating barbecue ribs with their fingers.

Among habits that will shock you is the Brazilian manner of getting a person's attention, particularly in stores or restaurants. It's common to snap one's fingers, hiss, and make a sound like sssssh (as if telling one to be quiet). Waiters are accustomed to these signals, though you may feel a bit uncomfortable using them. Also, Brazilians use toothpicks found on the dining table to clean their teeth after meals, though they always shield their mouth with one hand. (This is more true of the men, but women are not excluded.) Brazilians love to color their conversations with dramatic **hand gestures,** much like Italians. The first time I saw a native frantically shaking his hand from his wrist and snapping his finger I thought he was having an epileptic fit. The gesture, common among all classes, actually means "you are gonna get it." A "thumbs up" gesture is commonly used by all sexes to mean "great." One gesture you should totally avoid is the common American gesture for okay (thumb and forefinger touching with the last three fingers raised). In Brazil, it's equivalent to a four-letter word.

Most **business** in Brazil is done in social situations: over drinks, during two- or three-hour lunches, and at evening receptions and cocktail parties. While laws exist to be broken in Brazil (a favorite national saying), bureaucratic **red tape** has felled many a foreigner, particularly those trying to acquire permission from federal agencies in Brasília. What you need most are personal contacts: that is, friends (or, at least, friends of friends) in high places. Most important, however, is your own behavior, especially if you can acquire the reputation of being *simpatico*. The word variously means you are a joy to be with, you are not an American boor, you can be trusted in delicate situations and, just possibly, you might make a good lover. The next best thing to be called is *esperto*, or clever. Maybe it's a sign of the financial times, but these days *esperto* is most often applied to somebody smart enough to have made a million dollars, no matter how.

And cleverness in Brazil always comes with a touch of humor – that pinch of sugar that helps the medicine go down, particularly in the midst of chaos. For example, a recent Brazilian AIDS-awareness campaign was inspired to tap an unusual spokesman – a talking penis named Braulio – that is, until people with the same name as Braulio protested vehemently. "Buddy" was next suggested as a possible alternative.

The **Amazon jungle** is at the heart of heated political controversy these days, so for those heading to the wilds, here's a word of advice: Don't go with the self-righteous attitude that Brazil is destroying the rainforest while the rest of the world is innocently suffering the consequences. Keep your mind open, talk to as many people as possible, and don't come to hasty conclusions. Brazilians complain that tourists blame every Brazilian they meet for the ecological destruction of the planet. It's not a fair assumption and, worse, you will lose out on developing a lot of great friendships.

As for **romance,** Brazilians are just plain sexy, and there's no getting around it. Even those lacking in traditional physical charms have a certain *je ne sais quoi*, a way of expressing their life force that can have devastating effect. In normal conversation, Brazilians like to look their partner straight in the eye, and in true Latin fashion they love to touch (though a light finger on your arm doesn't necessarily signal sexual interest). On the other hand, many Brazilians might say, "What doesn't signal sexual interest?" Simply, Brazilians are big flirts, big heartbreakers and totally irresistible.

### UP CLOSE TIP: For Women Only

*After more than a decade of experience in this topic, I have yet to nail the exact quality of machismo in Brazil. It is more charming, more subtle, yet at times more brutal than in other Latin American countries. More and more, women are working outside the home, but it seems that a woman's first responsibility is still to her family and she is rarely allowed the freedom to come and go like a man. Consequently a foreign woman traveling alone in Brazil is still a point of enormous intrigue. Blondes, in particular, seem to evoke the same kind of fantasies that darker-hued women inspire in Northerners. Pinching is rare (more common are intense stares and light-hearted flirtation). How you dress and carry yourself have some influence over how you are received. If you don't want to encourage attention, you might consider wearing a fake wedding ring, although this will only slow down action, not stop it. Frankly, it's my observation that Brazilian men seem to be perpetually within a hair's breadth of an erotic thought. Consequently, in no circumstances should you go off into dark places with a man you do not know, or traipse off alone into the jungle with only a male guide. On the plus side, women traveling alone are often treated with great deference; old ladies will be glad to watch your luggage at bus stations while you use the bathroom.*

*Just use your head about whom to trust. If you are traveling to São Paulo or Rio, the Caesar Park Hotel is especially attractive for single women, and the southern states of Brazil are particularly hospitable.*

# Cuisine

Brazilian food is hearty, colorful, and delicious. You will not go hungry. Brazilians are big meat eaters – and for good reason: southern beef from Rio Grande do Sul and cuts imported from Argentina are among the tastiest in the world. If a small town has only two restaurants, at least one of them is sure to be a **steakhouse**: a *churrascaria*, where you can order grilled beef à la carte, or a *rodízio*, an all-you-can-eat buffet where formally dressed waiters serve up to 18 cuts of meat until you yell quits. For a single moderate price, you start off with chicken hearts, ham, sausage and gizzards, then work up to chicken, filet mignon and prime rib. Most often included in the price are side dishes or an extensive salad bar. If you pace yourself properly, one meal at a *rodízio* could hold you for a couple of days.

A beautiful Bahian woman in traditional dress selling *acarajé*, fried bean cake, in Salvador. Photo by Stephen Geller Katz.

**UP CLOSE TIP:** *Ask for the "prato feito," or "sortido," the prepared dish of the day – usually a great bargain, particularly in smaller cities.*

The **national dish** of Brazil is *feijoada*. Throughout the country most restaurants serve it on Sat., though it can often be found on Weds. (especially in the finer hotels of Rio). The original version was invented by black slaves during the colonial period, who creatively employed the leftovers from their master's table. Today, making a good *feijoada* is a fine art (it takes all day to prepare), and you're expected to eat it at a leisurely pace, among good friends or family. The basic element is a black bean stew, to which is added an intriguing lineup of dried, salted and smoked meats, including pork, tongue, pork loin, ribs, sausage and bacon. (Chefs at more sophisticated restaurants tend to leave out some of the more traditional ingredients such as pig's ears, tail, feet, and snout.) Uninitiated foreigners are sometimes put off by the dark, "witchy" look of the simmering pots, but steel yourself and dig in: the dish is truly delicious, if a bit heavy.

Nearly every region boasts its own delicacies. Rio's cuisine is as international as they come, but local specialties focus on excellent grilled fish, lobster, fine **fish stews** called *caldeiradas*, and some of the best pizza in Brazil. Cuisine in Minas Gerais tends toward short ribs, heavy bean dishes and to-die-for *torresmos* – fried pork rinds. Bahian cuisine is spicy, most often orange in color (from the dendê palm oil), and based around seafood. The most exotic **fish dishes** can be found in the Amazon, where anything from piranha to pirarucu is fried, stewed, broiled, and poached. In the more German-inspired cities – such as Blumenau and Joinville in the state of Santa Catarina – superb wienerschnitzel, spätzle, and sauerkraut can be washed down with a dark, frothy beer. Some of the best **pastas** can be found in the wine country of the extreme south.

And new trends pop all the time. Becoming a preferred Sun. habit these days, especially in Rio de Janeiro, is a dish called *cozido*. Born of Portuguese-Spanish heritage, the dish consists of various meats – beef (dried and fresh), chicken and sausage – cooked with vegetables like squash, okra, kohl potatoes, and sweet potatoes. *Pirão*, a thick meal made of manioc flour combined with broth and peppery sauces, is served on the side.

Young boys in the Amazon eking out a living selling produce.

**Vegetarians** need not worry in Brazil. While you should avoid eating raw vegetables or unpeeled fruits, rice and beans are universally served in every restaurant, omelettes are easy to find, and *legumes cozidos* (cooked vegetables) can be prepared by any chef. In some of the larger cities, like Rio, São Paulo, and Brasília, there are good macrobiotic restaurants, as well as a variety of health-conscious vegetarian counters. Delicious **tropical fruits** are among Brazil's natural wonders, in shapes, sizes, and colors you have probably never seen before. They are made into ice creams, smoothies, and compotes, among other things. More familiar fruits are apples, melons, strawberries and bananas, as well as mangoes, pineapples, guavas, passion fruits, persimmons and tamarinds, not to mention the more exotic specimens like bacuri and cupuaçu.

Considering the time Brazilians spend in **sidewalk cafés**, noshing has become a national art. In the south, afternoon teas called **café colonials** nearly reach full-meal status, with plate after plate of sweets (*doces*) and small, savoury pastries (*salgadinhos*, a triangular or oblong concoction of deep-fried manioc filled with meat, fish, or cheese). Another snack not to miss is *pão de queijo*, small hot cheese-filled rolls served piping hot by many stand-up coffee bars throughout the cities. It's wonderful for breakfast, washed down with *café com leite* (coffee with milk).

Drinking spirits takes on new meaning in Brazil. *Cerveja* or **beer** seems to be a national battle cry, and Brazilian natives have an uncanny ability to drink all night and not get unduly drunk. Even children sip *cerveja*. The best brands are **Brahma** and **Antarctica**. *Chopp* is **draft beer** and goes best with *hors d'oeuvres*. Made from sugarcane, the local firewater, *aguardente* (also known as *cachaça* or *pinga*) is cheap and powerful. *Caipirinha* is a lethal concoction made with *cachaça* and lime slices crushed inside a glass full of sugar and ice. Competing with the ubiquitous Coke is the native-made *guaraná*, a tangy carbonated soft drink distilled from the berry of the same name. (Diet soda, once only found in the larger cities, has recently been spotted in the smallest towns of the interior – a sure sign of modernism.) Good before or after meals, *batidas* are rum-based liqueurs made with various flavors such as coconut or chocolate.

**Wines** produced in the south of Brazil are quite fine. Among the best names are **Casa Valduga** (available in five-star hotels and restaurants), **Maison Forestier** and **Peterlongo** (champagne). When in doubt, ask the maitre d' for suggestions. *Tinto* is red, *branco* is white, and *rosé* is rosé; dry wines are referred to as *seco*, sweet wines as *suave*. As for spirits, there are few good Brazilian whiskeys, and imports are usually expensive.

Brazil takes great pride in one of its most important exports – **coffee.** *Cafezinho* (sugar-laced espresso served in tiny cups) is nearly a ritual. It is taken frequently throughout the day and you are sure to be offered one at a business meeting. (It's a little impolite to refuse, though it's probably nicer to refuse than to choke over it, which I usually do – it tastes like gasoline to me.) In general, most Americans find Brazilian coffee too strong, but *café com leite* (coffee with hot milk), served at breakfast, helps to cut some of the tang. Finding fresh milk for coffee at any time other than breakfast, however, is like looking for the Grail, though fine restaurants may have delicious whipped cream called chantilly. (Ask for it – it's a life-saver in *cafezinho*.)

The best place to buy packaged Brazilian coffee is at the airport's duty-free shop on your way back home. I heard the prices are cheaper on the second floor.

Bottled **mineral water,** *água mineral* (a must for all travelers; see *Health Kit* at the back of the book) can be found in nearly all restaurants and counters and is delicious. You can order it carbonated (*com gás*) or not (*semi gás*). The best brand is **Caxambú.**

(For more information regarding regional cuisine, see under the individual regions.)

### UP CLOSE TIP: Salt
*Food in Brazil comes heavily salted, and if you are used to cutting back, you will find your first bite a veritable shock. Don't be shy when ordering to ask for "sem sal" (without salt). You can always add more yourself.*

More and more restaurants are serving food by the kilo; you serve yourself from a buffet and pay for the weight of the food on your plate. Seafood buffets are especially fun. Also, look for ice cream buffets, where you can make your own wild sundaes (this is to die for!).

# Traveler's Guide To Brazilian Spirits

Although 70% of Brazilians are Catholic, 100%, it's been said, believe in something else. That "something else" ranges from African spirits, Indian fetishes and gypsy love potions to trance channelers, psychic healers and extraterrestrials. No matter where you go in Brazil, you are sure to run into something or somebody that smells otherworldy. "I'm not a real believer, but you can never tell..." is not an uncommon phrase here. I've met government officials who are self-proclaimed *bruxos* (witches), and even respected businessmen who regularly consult psychics. Prior to her son's election in 1989, the mother of ex-President Fernando Collor secretly met with an American trance medium to scope out her son's political chances. It's public knowledge that the federal government annually consults the *Umbanda* roll, which predicts events for the coming year. These practices so exasperate the Pope that rumors of excommunicating the entire country regularly abound.

**Catholic worship** can reach fanatic proportions in Brazil, though each year the number of devotees is dwindling. On Oct. 12 of each year, hundreds of thousands flock to the Basilica of Aparecida on the highway between Rio and São Paulo to celebrate the founding patron saint of Brazil, **Our Lady of Conception.** The city of Congonhas, which displays the sculpted prophets of the artist Aleijadinho, has long been the site of spontaneous healings. In Belém, religious tensions reach such a fervor during the Cirio de Nazaré parade that fights regularly break out among penitents pushing each other to catch hold of the rope shielding the sacred

Madonna. In cathedrals throughout the country, there are special rooms full of letters, photographs and plastic heads and body parts symbolizing prayers that have been answered. At a famous grotto outside Torres in Rio Grande do Sul, you'll find staunch believers climbing up the torturous stone staircase on their knees. In small villages, devotees carry ponderously heavy crosses for hundreds of miles in payment for healings.

The syncretism of Catholicism and the African Yoruban religion finds expression in the Afro-Brazilian cult worship called *candomblé*. During colonial times, slaves were not allowed to practice their native trance religions, so they clothed the African divinities in the guise of Catholic saints – a double-faced identity that's been preserved to this day. *Candomblé's* basic principle is that the body of the believer through possession becomes the instrument of communication between divine forces and mortals. Worshippers who receive signs by the spirits of their potential mediumship undergo extensive training, including months of seclusion, ritual baths, and initiations that involve smearing animal blood and chicken feathers on their foreheads. The religious ceremonies themselves are great, with shows of African drumming and frenetic dancing, all designed to provoke the initiate to fall into a trance. Although white upper-class devotees are rare in *candomblé*, the maternal heads of these *terreiros*, or churches, are often powerful spiritual figures in the community. Among the most famous of these was **Mãe Menininha,** the supreme priestess of Gantois (one of the oldest *terreiros* in Brazil) and a favored spiritual mother among artists such as novelist Jorge Amado and composer Dorival Caymmi. Although Mãe Menininha was a staunch traditionalist, she was also a true daughter of

Trance worship finds many forms in Brazil. Above, Fernando de Oxalá, a *pai de santo* in Belo Horizonte, is possessed by a female divinity during a *candomblé* session.

syncretism; her office, where she received visitors, was decorated with pictures of Jesus, Omulu (an African divinity) and John F. Kennedy.

An underlying theme of Brazilian spirituality is the **cult of the feminine**. It's no wonder that in this beachfront country the "Goddess of the Ocean" would exert a powerful grip on the collective psyche. Considered the syncretistic equivalent of the Virgin Mary, the Afro-Brazilian goddess **Iemanjá** inspires reverence on a national scale: witness the celebrations held on New Year's throughout the country. On Dec. 13 in Praia Grande near São Paulo, Dec. 31 in Rio, and Feb. 2 in Salvador, her worshippers offer flowers, perfume, and lipstick at the edge of the sea. In the south of Brazil along the seashore of Torres, the mesmeritic power of Iemanjá has been transformed into **legends of mermaids**, who seduce unsuspecting sailors with their siren-like song and beauty.

Among the most democratic of the visionary cults is *Umbanda,* which arose in 1908 when a 17-year-old boy during a spiritualist session questioned why the spirits of *caboclos* (mixed breeds), blacks, and Indians were never channeled. Subsequently, he began to channel the spirit of an enlightened Indian named Seven Crossroads, as well as a Preto Velho (old black man), who cured sick people. Today, *Umbanda* sessions, which are free of charge, are performed only for the sake of healing and, in contrast to *candomblé*, use no drums or chanting. Many of Brazil's artists and musicians have participated, however fleetingly, in *Umbanda*. During the 1980s, Gilberto Gil entitled one of his tunes *Um Banda Um*, a play on words between the name of the cult and the phrase "One (Music) Band."

Along the beach of Copacabana, as well as in forest grottoes and near waterfalls, you'll no doubt stumble upon the remains of a *Macumba* ritual. Erroneously equated with *Umbanda*, *Macumba* is actually a form of black magic that arose out of Quimbanda Bantu fetishes and witch doctor rituals. Public sessions are held after midnight in dark forests; the spirits are supposedly of the lowest level, and *trabalhos*, or magical work, is performed ostensibly to undo evil. Dishes of food and candy are often left out as appeasement to the gods, and under no circumstances should these offerings be disturbed – even dogs have the good sense to sniff and walk away. Cigars, popcorn, bowls of manioc flour, black candles, and ribbons are sure signs of *Macumba*.

Although the Portuguese colonialists were raised on the mystical stories of their black nurses, the enlightened whites of Rio longed to find a seemingly more civilized way of believing in spirits. The **court of the Emperor Dom Pedro II** was well peopled with shamans, including a doctor who did laying-on-of-hands and another who communicated with spirits. In 1858, the work of French spiritualist **Allan Kardec** was brought back from Europe by a nobleman who had it translated into Portuguese, immediately inspiring a subculture of white spiritualists who began experimenting with automatic writing, table rapping, and healing. Today, numerous adherents of Kardec-inspired philosophies practice healing, laying-on-of-hands, and exorcisms without the benefit of drumming, drugs, or the incentive of money.

Today in Brazil the influence of *candomblé* and other spiritualistic practices reaches throughout all strata of society. Upper-class Brazilian families sometimes sneak patients out of mental hospitals to be healed by a *mãe de santo* with spirit medicine. Anyone visiting the dressing room of singer Maria Bethânia after a show will be greeted in a darkened room thick with incense and cluttered with dripping candles, with pictures of her favorite spirit guides placed before her mirror. In the darker cults, however, spirit possession is used to manipulate clients and to provoke fear. Even within *candomblé* one *mãe de santo* has publicly admitted that not all examples of trance possession are real. Fights have been known to break out in *terreiros* when two members claim to be receiving the same spirit simultaneously – a sticky situation that must be resolved by the *mãe* or *pai de santo* with Solomonlike diplomacy.

Long before black slaves arrived in Brazil, however, native **Indians** were practicing **shamanistic rituals** that required the services of a *pajé*, or medicine man. He understood the therapeutic power of plants and allowed himself to be possessed by nature spirits to cure disease. Throughout the Amazon, legends arose that are still believed today, mostly regarding the *matinta pereira* and the *pai do mato*, sylvanlike spirits who love to befuddle humans. Today, *candomblé do caboclo* and a cult called *batuque* call upon such legendary Indian spirits as Iracema and Peri during ritual trance work. Travelers to the Amazon may actually inquire about meeting a *pajé* – a request still so rare that you are bound to meet the real thing.

In the last few decades, the discovery of certain hallucinogenic jungle plants has given rise to two popular cults that use an organic mixture (known in the States as ayahuasca) to invoke spiritual visions. Branches of the independent organizations **Santo Daime** and **União Vegetal** can be found throughout the country (though mostly in Rio, Salvador, and the Amazon), having attracted adherents from all walks of life, including celebrities and artists who gleefully retell their psychedelic experiences on talk shows. Although the drug (actually, a ritually prepared concoction of two Amazonian plants) was illegal for many years, recent government research has proved the thick, bitter liquid (ironically called *chá* or tea) is neither addictive nor harmful, despite its side effects of extreme gastrointestinal distress (most first-timers succumb to intense vomiting or diarrhea). Men, women (sometimes even during childbirth), and children are known to partake of this drug, though advisories are given to forgo meat, alcohol and, in some cases, sex prior to the ritual. *Santo Daime*, the more orthodox of the two cults, often makes participants stand or dance in one place for hours, while the more liberal *União Vegetal* plays classical and Brazilian jazz to accompany the seated group ritual. American travelers should note that it is illegal to transport ayahuasca back to the States, and that there have been numerous cases of confiscation at customs. If you are interested in participating in any of these groups, it is best to do so through personal contacts.

Psychics and psychic healers have many adherents in Brazil. One of the most famous and respected is **Francisco Candido Xavier** (nicknamed Chico). Born in 1910 of humble origins, this craggy-faced mulatto barely managed to finish primary school, but one day, while working as a day laborer, he began channeling poetry from 56 dead writers. The poems were so good that Brazil's finest literary critics were unable to dispute their authenticity. The book, published under the title *Parnassus Beyond the Grave*, became the first of hundreds Xavier would write regarding spirituality and health. For years, Xavier has given psychic medical consultations to thousands who stream to his home in Uberaba, Minas Gerais. The latest visitors have found the medium himself extremely ill.

Another famous psychic healer was **José Arigó,** who, with the supposed help of the spirit of a dead German physician known as **Dr. Fritz,** was seemingly able to perform psychic surgery using only a rusty paring knife. Despite persecution by the government, Arigó was, over a number of years, able to heal thousands of people; it was rumored he even received a silver box inscribed with thanks from Pope Pius XII. Following Arigó's death, at least 13 other Brazilian psychics have surfaced, claiming to channel the same Dr. Fritz and performing operations (though, apparently, none have yet gotten Dr. Fritz's German accent quite right). That the establishment now accepts such activities as more or less believable was made apparent in a recent report by *Veja* magazine (the *Newsweek* of Brazil), which only half-jokingly asked, "Will the real Dr. Fritz please stand up?"

Given the above interest, it's not surprising that one of the most popular American writers in Brazil has been Shirley MacLaine, whose esoteric-oriented book *Dancing in the Light* describes two other astounding Brazilian psychics. Among the middle-class, New Age interest is intense, and yearly conventions featuring crystals, psychics, and astrologers are often held at five-star hotels like the Bahia Othon in Salvador. Although Brazil is home to enormous pockets of **natural crystals,** they were not considered much more than pretty rocks until about 10 years ago, when the demand from the States made Brazilians reconsider their esoteric (and, hence, commercial) value. Now you can find traditional jewelers setting stones for "healing purposes," and you can also purchase excellent raw crystals and rocks. The best place to buy them is in the state of Minas Gerais.

There is also a thriving **holistic health** community found not only in the big cities, but in such remote areas as Cuiabá in Mato Grosso. There you'll be able to find shiatzu practitioners, acupuncturists, masseurs, and homeopaths. The city of Brasília, in particular, is populated with numerous healers who use color, sound, and aroma. Brazilians adore natural health cures; spa towns featuring mineral waters and baths attract millions of health seekers south of Minas. And ever since the singing superstar Xuxa began taking dips in waterfalls on the advice of her personal psychic, Marilena Simões of Belo Horizonte, thousands have been flocking to *cachoeiras* around the country. Herbs of all kinds, cultivated throughout the Amazon, are generally accepted as medicine. Sold at homeopathic stores and herb markets, they are said to cure anything from impotence to heart and blood diseases.

As for **extraterrestrials,** it is difficult to travel through Brazil without meeting numerous people who have sighted UFOs. Among the most famous locations are the **Amazon jungle, Brasília, Rio de Janeiro, Chapada dos Guimarães,** and **São Tomé das Letras** in Minas Gerais – the latter an entirely eccentric village made of stone where some residents claim to have conversed with extraterrestrials for the last 30 years. A half-hour from São Tomé is a highly respected community of contemplatives founded by

**Trigueirinho,** a former film director turned guru and author who claims to have continuing contact with beings from outer space.

A deep strain of **millennarianism** has run for centuries throughout Brazilian history; today, religious groups like the **Euboise Temple** in São Lourenço, Minas Gerais, fervently hold to the conviction that the birthplace of the Third Millennium will take place in that area. Groups in Brasília feel the same way about their own city, as do individuals in the town of **Chapada dos Guimarães** in Mato Grosso, the geocentric point of South America. A community already gearing for the end of the world is **Abra di Garça,** an alternative village in the interior of Mato Grosso where only the international language Esperanto is spoken.

One of the most unusual communities, which incorporates spirits from all races and planetary systems, is **Vale do Amanhecer,** or Valley of the Dawn, a dusty village outside Brasília. Founded by a feisty ex-trucker known as Tia Neiva (Aunt Neiva), the community is based on her channeled visions and has trained over 3,000 mediums. Brazilians from all over descend on the village to be healed inside a brashly colored temple full of icons of Indian, black and extraterrestrial spirits. As per the group's philosophy, no money is charged and no religious dogma other than a form of spiritualism is promoted. According to local police, the village is a model of harmony. While the outer visuals of the community look silly – residents dress in tacky Renaissance outfits (according to channeled injunctions from Tia Neiva) – its inhabitants all seem to be "normal" people and are gracious to visitors. One young psychotherapist I met there was developing her psychic skills to deal more skillfully with her own patients. Despite the community's eccentricities, the national press is always petitioning it for spiritual advice during such phenomena as eclipses, harmonic convergences and ecological disasters.

An old woman in São Tomé das Letras in Minas Gerais awaits extraterrestrials as she cleans up.

Brazilians have a high threshold for shock, but a recent scene on the national TV station startled even the most jaded. In an act of unprecedented fury, Sergio von Helder, a bishop in Brazil's extremist Universal Church of the Kingdom of God, actually beat up a nearly life-size statue of the Virgin Mary (Brazil's national saint in the form of Our Lady of Aparecida). Referring to her cultlike status in his speech, he said:

"We want to show one thing to Brazil, that (saints) don't work," he said. "This is not a saint at all," he said with a kick. "This is not God."

But von Helder represents one of the fastest-growing movements in Brazil – Protestant evangelicals, who in the last decade have won nearly 15 million converts (13% of the population) in this still predominantly Catholic nation of 155 million, and millions more across Latin America.With their emphasis on personal spiritual experience, strict morality, and upward mobility, they offer Brazil's poor an unbeatable message: a chance at a better life, not just a better afterlife.

Its radical appeal for change overshadows the 70's liberation theology, which called for social reform and redistribution of wealth, but had little success. Today even the Catholic Church has since largely abandoned its leadership in social reform movements.

Few of Brazil's booming evangelical churches, however, have been as quick to seize on these Brazilian quirks as the **Universal Church**, known for its aggressive recruitment and extreme attacks on other religions. Founded in 1977 by Edir Macedo, a charismatic televangelist and savvy businessmen in the mold of Jim Bakker and Jimmy Swaggart, the church now has 2,100 temples in Brazil and an annual budget of $735 million, making it the country's 34th-largest business.

Its astounding growth is based in part on the reach of its media empire, including a nationwide television station, 30 radio stations, a daily newspaper, a recording company and a magazine.

Once-poor, now savvy businessman Macedo, who lives in Long Island, NY, tracks his holdings via laptop computer in 34 countries on five continents. His followers consist mostly of poor devotees who put their stock in the message of a world filled with battling devils, including the saints of other religions and evil spirits who lure believers with drink, cigarettes, and other vices.

Triumphing over those devils involves in part clean living and church exorcisms, but mostly on making large donations to the church.

# Carnaval

*Samba: Capacity for sustained episodes of intense unambivalent joy.*
from *Samba* by Alma Guillermoprieto

Brazilians didn't invent Carnaval but, probably more than any other country in the world, they sustain it. A festival of unbridled emotion, Carnaval in Brazil has many faces – from the televised grand parade in the Sambódromo and the fashionable upper-crust balls in private clubs to the streetside frenzies that anyone can join. For four days businesses close, drinks flow freely, inhibitions of body and mind are shed without caution. To an outsider, it looks like so much indulgence, but for those who live in the *favelas* (slums), where the so-called samba schools were first born, Carnaval invokes a fierce sense of tradition, a unifying force that provides political, emotional, and even spiritual nourishment to those who feel deeply disenfranchised from the (mostly white) center of power.

No matter what one's social status, sexual preference, or style, Carnaval is a time to be whatever one isn't during the rest of the year – to inhabit for a brief moment the cloak of a prince, the skirt of a vamp – to have a stage big enough and brash enough to express one's deepest desires. Yet

Mind, body, and soul melt into one communal frenzy during Rio's Carnaval.

Carnaval is also about the sheer joy of music – the color, rhythm, and soul of samba. If you've never had the urge to sing and dance in the greatest Broadway musical in history, you cannot begin to understand the frenzy Carnaval enflames in its most willing victims.

## Beginnings

The Bacchanalian urge dates back to Greco-Roman times, when during late fall, hierarchy was happily dissembled and princes, politicians, philosophers and paupers all mingled with lower-class ladies in orgiastic assembly. As the Catholic Church slowly usurped control, the festivities were severely condemned, but nevertheless allowed to flourish in a tamer version restricted to the days preceding Ash Wednesday. With a nod to their own appetites, food-loving Italians adopted the phrase *Carne Vale*, "farewell to meat," a salute that soon included all kinds of flesh.

In Brazil, the origins of Carnaval were more impish than erotic. The festival entered the country on the wings of the Portuguese *entrudo*, a term used to describe the naughty if somewhat childish acts of mischief performed by the Portuguese in the name of religiously sanctioned **fun.** By the middle of the 19th century, *cariocas* were taking to the streets on the Sun. before Ash Wednesday to lance water bombs and rotten lemons; a painting by the French artist Debret shows a young Rio man giddily dousing the face of a black slave girl with flour. After a parade of upper-class young men managed to secure a proper brass band, a Portuguese shoemaker, considered "an athlete at beating soles," invented a unique bass drum beat that immediately took root – later becoming the *Zé Pereira*, or percussive fanfare that still begins every Carnaval samba. While waltzes and polkas were played at Parisian-inspired masquerades, a musical class war was being waged on the street, as police tried to quell the raucous African *candomblé* drums by ordering drunken revelers back home. But the upper classes could not control themselves either; at one memorable São Cristavão ball, even the Emperor Dom Pedro II, a self-avowed party boy, got himself pushed into a fountain.

## The First Samba

It was not until samba was born as a musical form that Brazilian Carnaval began to find its true dancing legs. Historians claim the infectious rhythm slipped into Rio from Bahia around the turn of the century, conceived in the backyard of Tia Ciata, a well-to-do black woman who opened her home to the aspiring musicians of the neighboring hills. Out of those fiery jam sessions in 1916 sprang the first samba, *Pelo Telefone* (On the Telephone) – a jovial if saucy tune, with insinuating comments about the chief of police. Inspired by their own creativity, the *favelados* didn't take long to complain that only middle-class whites and blacks seemed to have the privilege of parading down the main avenues of Rio. Since the *favelados* used to rehearse near an old teacher's college, they called their makeshift organization an *escola de samba* (samba school) and dubbed themselves *Deixa Falar* (Let Them Talk), an obvious snub to the upper crust. Their debut was dazzling, and by the next year five more black communities were following in their footsteps.

Out of this early creative explosion was forged the irrepressible personality of the *sambista* – one who not only plays samba, but eats it, loves it, and dreams it morning till night. As one observer wrote, "A *sambista* happens to be a human being in whom the soul is more apparent than the flesh, his spirit more recognizable than substance." Uninhibited but generous, and bohemian to the core, a *sambista* can invent great poetry despite being illiterate and compose great tunes with no knowledge of music. Invariably, even the greatest *sambistas* never made money, but their friendships and contacts crossed cultural bounds. At the funeral of **Sinhô**, one of Rio's most famous *sambistas*, hundreds of prostitutes, malandros, and underworld characters crowded in next to hard-core intellectuals, after which everyone headed out together to grieve at the neighborhood bar.

The building boom in Rio after World War II profoundly affected Carnaval. As numerous dwellings were razed in Botafogo and Copacabana to make way for middle-class housing, thousands fled to the squalid shantytowns, taking with them their passion for music, dance, and most of all, *desfile* (the parade). By 1935, rules fixed by the city Carnaval commission banned any other musical instruments except mandolin and percussion to accompany the parade singer. During the early 1960s, before the coup that would submerge Brazil into its two-year dictatorship, white journalists, artists, and musicians slipped into the blackest *favelas* to soak up "roots" – a collaboration that would soon birth samba's cooler child – sweet bossa nova. (For more information, see *Sounds of Brazil*, page 72.) Though middle-class whites were still a rarity in the late 1960s, by the 1970s they were a welcome minority, and by the late 1980s some schools, like Mangueira, were not only boasting white *alas* (battalions, literally "wings"), but black chiefs in charge of the most expensive white wings.

## The Sambódromo

In 1983, architect Oscar Niemeyer, who had designed the city of Brasília, changed the face of Carnaval in Rio when he built its new home, called the Sambódromo (or Sambadrome) – actually, nothing more than a wide cement pavement hugged on both sides by bleachers and boxes. At first glance, the overwhelmingly bland features of the structure shocked many a devotee, but as soon as the extravagant color and panache of the parade filled its empty spaces, the stadium's very insipidity showed itself to be a virtue. Today, the Sambódromo parade is broadcast two weekends in a row on national TV – a phenomenon that nearly obscures any other form of national or international news. As happens in a class-biased economy, the tickets for the Sambódromo parade are outrageously expensive, but there is nothing like being so close to the dancers that you can swim in their passion and get wet from the sweat. As such, Brazilians who can afford it spend thousands of dollars to rent boxes for their families and friends, who immediately proceed to get sloshed on a 24-hour rotation. (For information about tickets, see page 71.)

Better than watching the Sambódromo parade, however, is to dance in it. Tourists are welcome, but if you don't have the time (or courage) to participate, do read *Samba*, Alma Guillermoprieto's stunning account of what it takes to pull off a parade – from the inside of the *favela*. Amid drug trafficking, murders, poverty, and despair, Verdi-sized productions are designed, carpentered, sewed, sequined, and rehearsed to reasonable perfection, and most often at the price of great personal sacrifice. Individual costumes have become so pricey lately (sometimes two or three times the monthly minimum wage), that *sambistas* sometimes go for days without eating just to save up. For, within the universe of Carnaval, to *sair* (go out) at Carnaval is not only a matter of pride; for many it's a condition of soul. For those devotees who can afford it, parading with two or three schools per Carnaval is not uncommon; a friend of mine in New York with unearthly endurance manages five!

In the midst of such blatant commercialism, many people have begun to wonder whether the real spirit of Carnaval is dying. Truth is, that death knell has been rung ever since the 1800s, when Carnaval first began to lose its folkloric elements. And yet, year after year, certain parts of the festival remain resistant to diffusion, and that is the natural creative fervor of the people themselves – a fierce lot who, despite all odds, seem to perpetually rise to the occasion. Today, the real thief of Carnaval is the economic crisis and its uncontrollable inflation, which has given rise to the desperate need for international tourists. Although exhibitionism is at the heart of the Brazilian personality, even hard-core *sambistas* today complain that the blatant nudity and lascivious role-playing is eating away at the true spirit of Rio's Carnaval – all done, they say, merely for the sake of the camera. In actuality, the truly "uncivilized" behavior takes place these days in the upper-class balls, where outlandish sexual displays are photographed in every detail on late-night TV. It's no exaggeration to say that the sex channels on American cable TV have nothing over these televised Roman orgies, among whose guests are numbered famous politicians, celebrities, and girls from "good families." Tourists who venture forth to such parties should at least go forewarned; though some, like the Gay Balls, are outrageously funny, anyone burdened with an extreme sense of prudishness would be happier staying home and watching the events tubeside.

## The Parade

At first glance, the Sambódromo's parade can seem as mystifying and chaotic as the trees of the rainforest, but once you know what to look for, you'll become as discerning as the panel of judges. Since the parade is actually a fierce competition between 14 schools, a certain regulated structure is adhered to, around which the creativity of each school is allowed to flourish. Annually required of each school is an overriding theme, which unveils itself like an operatic plot through costume, decor, song, and dance. Since *sambistas* have a great passion for "roots," historical themes are often favored; the best are those that tap the dreams of the masses, like "The Brazilian Utopia," which Portela boasted in 1985 when I danced with them. (Political barbs in Carnaval can get sticky, however. In 1960, Império Serrano was actually petitioned by the Paraguayan embassy to change its theme – The Paraguayan War – to avoid re-humiliating Brazil's now friendly neighbor. In 1996 the same school included a float carrying nearly 100 landless Brazilian peasants, part of a tribute to sociologist Herbert de Souza, who has led a campaign in Brazil against hunger, misery, and violence. Following the demise of some shantytowns hard-hit by recent floodings, one school from the Cidade de Deus slum paid tribute to its dead by silently walking the Sambadrome route accompanied only by the beat of single drum. Carnaval 1996 also marked another innovation for Brazil: the condom machine. Brazilian AIDS activists, preaching "self-service safe sex," installed the machines on Rio's beachfronts, and handed out millions of free condoms to revelers.

Designing the productions for each school is the *carnavalesco*, most often a white stage designer (and, more recently, art school graduates), who must invent original designs, while remaining true to each school's personality. Portela, for example, is known for its muscular verve, Beija-Flor for its extravagant lushness, and Mangueira for its populace appeal.

## The Lineup

Each school's parade usually opens with the **abre-alas**, which may consist of a very simple painted sign or an elaborate float recounting the major theme. Directly afterwards is the **Comissão de Frente** – consisting of the directorate of the school, usually attired in silk hats, gloves, and spats. After pausing before the judge's box for a quick inspection, they execute a well-drilled maneuver and step aside as the school passes in front of them. Behind them are the **children's wings**, followed by the **Bahianas** – usually older women of enormous girth, or at least of enough personal stature to carry off wearing the traditional hoop skirts that are so heavy they must be suspended from one's shoulders by straps. (In olden days, men used to dress as *Bahianas*, because the costume's skirts provided an ideal hiding place for knives and other weapons.) Today, the heart-felt spirit of the *Bahiana* wing carries the soul of the school; Mangueira's is the most famous and most traditional. Other schools have taken to dressing their "mothers" in newspaper clippings or, as in one year, Statues of Liberty – an artistic license that caused wild controversy.

In between elaborate floats full of half-naked women dances the most important member of the school – the **mestre-sala**. The majordomo of the parade, the *mestre-sala* is the pivot around which all the choreography revolves, best performed by a tall, slim fellow who is both graceful and agile. Usually dressed like a Dumas musketeer or a Louis XV courtier, he accompanies the *porta-bandeira*, or flagbearer, often the prettiest girl in the school. As he pirouettes around her, she gracefully twirls about holding the school's flag – not such an easy task since many a girl has gotten tangled up in the folds. Appearing singly or in pairs among the many *alas* are the *destaques*, fabulously dressed women and men of great beauty whose sequined and pearled costumes are usually heavier than they are.

## The Musicians

The guts of the parade, however, is the **bateria**, a percussion ensemble of 300 men (and women of late!) who march forward looking as though they're on their way to slay Goliath. Although the uninitiated observer may hear only a Mack truck wall of sound, the beauty of the percussion section is its intricate interplay of rhythm and color, created by a wily assortment of native instruments that are played with so much force that blood often runs. The **surdo**, or bass drum, sets the two-four beat of the school's original samba, a dull thud achieved by dampening the skin of the drum with one's hand. The gypsy-style **pandeiro** is rather like a tambourine, its metal disks jingling as the performer, usually a great ham, twirls it up over his head, between his legs, and around pretty women. The *tamborim*, a small round shallow drum, is played with two long thin sticks, effecting a velvety ratta-ta-tat. In contrast, the *agogô*, a short iron bar with two or three hollow cups, adds a shrill piercing tang, like the beating of an anvil. Chit-chit chit-chit is the sound made by the *chocalho* (or *ganza*), a rattle from the Northeast made of sheet metal and filled with pebbles. Add to the mélange a couple of frying pans and the *cuica*, the Carnaval clown – a small steel barrel open at one end and skinned on the other, into which a stick is attached to the center of the membrane. Great *cuica* players can cajole sighs, screams, and laughs from their instrument. To coordinate all these sounds is a steely-eyed conductor of enormous discipline, whose troops are expected to receive his stop-and-start whistles as commands from God.

Holding this opera together is the school's song, written anew each year and sung by dancers and audience alike. Usually, the songs have been played on the radio for weeks, and lyrics can be found in the program. Even if you don't speak a word of Portuguese, or don't understand anything about the themes, you will recognize a good samba. The best ones are infectious, irresistible. They grab your heart, pull you to your feet and, along with the screaming crowd, carry you off. Believe me, it won't pass you by.

## Carnaval On The Street

For those who don't make it to the Sambódromo or the balls, there's always "street Carnaval" – in Rio, led by *blocos*, neighborhood groups who carry out their parades all throughout Ipanema and Copacabana, as well as the colonial sections downtown. Founded in 1965, **Banda de Ipanema** is probably the most popular Carnaval street band in Rio. The usual point of concentration is Praça General Osario around 4 p.m.

The first day of street festivities is Saturday, two weeks before Carnaval begins. Other days to join in are Carnaval Saturday and Tuesday, before Ash Wednesday. **Simpatia E Quase Amor** (Sympathy is Almost Love) is the name of a 10-year-old *bloco* which, in 1994 at least, held its spectacular throughout Ipanema. **Suvaco do Risto** paraded through Jardim Botânico in 1994. **Clube do Samba**, perhaps the most well known, is led by the singer João Nogueira; rehearsals, often held in Recreio Beach at the bar Rio Orla, have been described as "supertropical." **Bloco de Segunda** paraded last year through Botafogo, a mixture of irreverence and disorganized fun. (For more information, see names and addresses on pages 71 and 72.)

### UP CLOSE ADVENTURE from the author

"Don't look at her, don't touch her, don't even think about her!"

It's midnight, three weeks before Carnaval, and Russo, the *mestre sala* (main dancer) of Portela, one of the Rio's greatest samba schools, has just introduced me to his colleagues. On the pockhole streets in this lower-class district, where my very white skin speaks volumes of my origins, Russo is simply trying to protect me from flirtatious mishap, having assumed the role of my "Carnaval Papá" after hours of privately teaching me samba's hip-swinging steps. Though Russo is mostly a gigolo in real life, his goal with me is to get me prepared to *desfile* (or parade). When I finally master the Carmen Miranda wrist twists (I am the only one in the school who is doing them!), I think he must feel exactly like Henry Higgins.

Truth is, practicing for Carnaval in the district of Portela without Russo would have been like going to Harlem after dark – alone. Yet, as his privileged guest, we trail giddily down the blocks, trying to stay in line, follow the beat, and sing the words of our school song all at the same time. Locals who can't afford to parade this year sit on their roofs, beer cups in hand, and cheer us to victory. Even in our civilian fatigues, there is already a fierce devotion starting to form.

Come Carnaval night, all 5,000 Portela dancers and musicians find themselves backstage at the Sambadrome, on a wide avenue awaiting our turn to parade. Dressed, half-dressed, wings, feathers and sequins dragging behind us, we look like escapees from a Fellini movie. At 3 a.m. we start to inch forward toward the blaring stadium awash with floodlights. With the 50 other dancers in my small group, I am dressed like a very sexy *morego* (vampire bat!), which I only later discover represents the IMF, or the "blood-sucking" International Monetary Fund (draining the Brazilian economy). Some of us practice our steps; others drink; a gorgeous mulatta model in a voluminous beaded historical gown lies down on her back and drags on a cigarette. Then it's two minutes to go, and some of our unisex bats suddenly file out and face the wall – it takes a few seconds to realize they are relieving themselves of superfluous beer. And then the cannon booms and we're off. I am swept up in a tornado of arms and legs, chiffon in my throat, shoes falling off, brasierre slipping downwards (I am one of the few still wearing one!), my heart bursting with orgiastic joy as I catch smiles, cheers, that one handsome face I will never forget who looks me straight in the eyes and gives me his thumbs-up. I can't see Russo, but I know he is in the front of the school dancing his soul off, and in that moment everything he has ever taught me about samba comes reeling back: Love it, be it, survive it. And suddenly, a mere 15 minutes later, it's over, we've reached the end of the runway, but because it's the end of the night's schedule – we all turn around like lemmings and dance our way back, while the audience piles out from the bleachers above and the drums goes wild and everyone becomes one delirious mess.

By the time I finally find Russo, as exhausted and pent-up as I am, there are no words I can find – in any language – to express my now samba-ized heart. In any case, I don't have to... we just look at each other and cry.

---

(For more information on how to attend Carnaval festivities in Rio, see *Hands-On Carnaval* at the end of this chapter.)

## Bahia

The author "undercover" in Carnaval.

Salvador's Carnaval couldn't be more different than Rio's – some connoisseurs claim that it's better. In Salvador, the entire festival is a massive, hot, sweaty street affair, the linchpin of which are *trio elétricos*, amped-up flatbed trucks that hark back to a hillbilly duo in the 1950s who toured the city during Carnaval in a beat-up Chevy playing pop and folk tunes. Today, the *trio elétricos* in Salvador have three musicians, flashing lights, and thousands of people trailing after them through the city streets. At some point during Carnaval, the various bands meet in Praça Castro Alves, playing anything from samba to *frevo* to a new rock-influenced samba called *deboche*. During the 1980s, even reggae infiltrated the menu, creating a new hybrid by the 1990s and new superstars, such as the dynamite performer Daniela Mercury. Some of the best music comes from organized cultural groups like the Grupo Cultural Olodum, on the Pelourinho and the Ata Ketu, which situates itself at the Praça da Sé. In the weeks preceding Carnaval, their *blocos* hold fabulous rehearsals near the clubhouse.

Also, don't miss the *afoxés*, or spiritual processions of the Filhos de Ghandi, on Rua Gregorio de Matos, near the Pelourinho. You'll recognize them by their white papier-maché elephants or by their mascot, who looks uncannily like the original Gandhi. For other outdoor parties, check the northern beaches near the Hotel Rio Vermelho and Ondina. The city's official tourist office, **Bahiatursa,** Rua Francisco Muniz Barreto, 12 (☎ 321-2463), can provide you with schedules, parade routes and tickets, where necessary. Also check the special supplements in the newspapers on Thurs. and Sat.

# Pernambuco

The stars of the Northeastern Carnaval, **Recife** and its colonial sidekick, **Olinda**, explode with *frevo*, a feverish, fast-stepping rhythm that sounds as though it's stuck on a perpetual upper. Instead of grooving on hip-swinging samba, *frevo*-ites seem to spend most of their time jumping up and down in a vertical fashion, twirling huge parasols that hark back to the ones carried by slaves to shade their masters. The costumes of *frevo* dancers tend toward knee-britch stockings and floppy shirts, but anything is allowed. Some even indulge in Indian headdresses and lots of body paints.

Although Recife does have street celebrations, you'd be a fool to miss Olinda and its city-wide party that fills the historical cobblestone streets with a panache all its own. Strewn with streamers and gas lanterns, the colonial city takes on the look of a Christmas tree, the sidewalks becoming cement beds for the thousands of drunken revelers unable to make it home. (Many local residents escape to the nearby Jesuit seminary in search of peace and quiet.) The festivities start the Sun. before the official opening of Carnaval, when the Virgem do Bairro Novo, a traditional *bloco*, parades down the seafront road followed by huge crowds. On Fri. night and during the day, huge *bonecos* – papier-maché stuffed puppets representing folk heroes or savage caricatures of local personalities – are also paraded over the cobblestones. Homemade *pinga* (sugarcane liquor) flows like water; revelers take baths in the public fountains; and at some point the major *blocos* all meet at the junction of four corners with a rousing hurrah.

Accommodations must be made months in advance: all or part of a house may be rented out for the four days ($150-$800), or you can knock on doors and bargain.

> **UP CLOSE TIP:** *Hotel reservations in Rio (and any major city like Salvador and Recife/Olinda) should be made as far in advance as possible. For the best rooms, call at least six months prior to the event.*

## UP CLOSE ADVENTURE from Mike Salvo

I was not prepared for Carnaval in Olinda.

I couldn't imagine a more perfect setting. The cobblestone streets winding past baroque fountains, the colonial buildings, the ancient churches fringed by gardens and palm tress – Olinda is a page out of time, and so was my first Carnaval...

I took a public bus from Boa Viagem to the outskirts of Olinda and just followed all the other people who, like me, were following the sounds of the drums at the top of the hill. It was morning, but the streets were already crowded and people were eating, talking, and gathering themselves for another day of madness. By midday the fiesta was in full swing, music was everywhere, and dancing was bliss. Troops of drummers 50-150 strong marched the streets, beating and singing in an Olodum chant style. Cars loaded with speakers crept down side streets cranking out *frevo* and Daniela Mercury. Musica Bahiano drifted out of bars. It was an orgy of rhythms orchestrated by chance and the wonderful *blocos* of Olinda. At times different processions would converge – *frevo* dancers with their umbellas, people with elaborate costumes, the beautiful, the drunk, and the dirty all dancing together.

Grandmothers were drinking on their front porch selling homemade bottles of *Pao do Indio*, literally translated (so I was told) as "Indian Dick." I was warned to go easy on this stuff – a homemade brew of cachaça, honey, guarana, and 22 mysterious Amazonian herbs – but the sun was so hot and the dancing so furious that I drank my share and then some. By nighttime I was buzzing, and as the magic of Carnaval kicked in, I realized the buses had stopped running and I was drunk, lost, and basically homeless (since I had lost my address).

Somehow I found my way back to town when I literally bumped into a woman I had met in Boa Viagem. We looked at each other and then she grabbed my hand and pulled me into a nearby apartment. Sula was from Olinda and we joined a party at her friends' house. There was great food and she made me a super *vitamin suco* (juice smoothie) with guarana that fixed everything. I had just become my old self again when Sula called me into another part of the house where her friend, a well-known local artist, painted our faces like psychedelic cats. Outside the drums were gaining intensity and you could feel the rush of energy beginnning a new cycle – this one until sunrise and the end of Carnaval.

But while the masses were sleeping I had to get back to Recife and catch my night flight to Miami. My travel friends who had opted for a quieter Carnaval at a beach house were a bit worried when I arrived at their place with a weird smile and bits of paint on my face. While I slept they packed for me. Somewhere in mid-flight I woke up and wondered what was real and what was a dream. I started going through my backpack when I discovered a note written on a bar napkin.

The words swam into view and I slowly deciphered the Portuguese: "You are like a cloud that passes slowly by, unable to stop or even touch the ground. You are pushed by the wind and soon you will be gone. I will miss you. Kisses, Sula." Alas, I never knew her last name or her address, but perhaps one day I will meet her again and thank her for saving me – and Carnaval.

# Hands-On Carnaval (Rio)

## Tickets

If you want to visit Rio during Carnaval, it's best to buy a package tour that includes airfare, accommodation, and tickets at the Sambódromo – you'll save money and possible grief. You can also buy tickets for the Sambódromo parade starting in Dec. at the **Meridional Bank**, or call **A1ô Rio Tur,** ☎ *242-8000*. After Jan. 16, Rio Tur will sell tickets for tourists in Setor 9; ☎ *297-7117*. The concierge of your hotel may be able to obtain tickets for you at the last minute, but rest assured he will charge a hefty commission. A better bet is to ask at almost any travel agency in Rio – they receive just a 10% commission. In 1996, prices ranged from $70-$220. For $540, **Blumar,** Rua Visconde de Pirajá, 550, sala 108 (☎ *21 511-3636*), arranged for viewing, marching, and a tour of a costume maker.

## Balls

All you need to attend a Carnaval ball is a large dose of courage, a desire to wear few clothes, and a ticket, which may be bought directly through the individual clubs (call in advance). Your concierge may be able to advise you which ball would suit your particular life-style.

**Copacabana Hotel**: 1702 Avenida Atlântica; ☎ *255-7070*. One of the most elite parties in the city, requiring usually formal attire or Carnaval costume.

**Roda Viva**: Avenida Pasteur, 520; ☎ *295-4045*. Mostly tourists.

**Yacht Club**: Avenida Pasteur, 333; ☎ *295-4482*. Mostly high society.

**Clube Sirio Libanês**: Rua Marquês de Olinda, 38 (Botafogo); ☎ *551-9942*. Mostly artists and tourists attend this ball, which goes under various names: Atlantic Ball, Tourists' Ball or Artists' Ball.

**Scala**: Avenida Afrânio de Melo Franco, 296 (leblon); ☎ *239-4448*. Famous for its flamboyantly outrageous "Gala Gay" ball, attended by people of all sexual persuasions, including tourists.

**Hippopotamus Prive Discotheque**: Rua Barão da Torre, 354; ☎ *247-0351*. High society with *feijoada* on the Sat. of Carnaval week starting at 8 p.m. You must buy a T-shirt in advance to wear on the date.

**Clube Monte Libano**: Avenida Borges de Medeiors, 701; ☎ *239-0032*. Artists and high-class prostitutes usually frequent the "Night in Bagdad" ball on the Tues. of Carnaval week.

## Samba School Rehearsals

Even though you might not be in Rio during the actual Carnaval events, you can still visit the samba schools during their practice sessions. In fact, some of the best times to visit are the weeks before Carnaval. All rehearsals start at 10 p.m. on Sat. night unless otherwise indicated. Call first to verify the day. The most popular performance is the **Beija Flor samba school** on Morro da Urca, every Mon. night at 10:30 p.m., where you can see snippets of one of Rio's best extravaganzas against a beautiful natural backdrop. For reservations, ☎ *541-3737*. During high season, they also perform Thurs. and

Sat. nights at other locations in the South Zone. Check the newspaper. Also entertaining, if touristy, is the floor show at **Sugarloaf,** where you can take good photos. Other school locations are: **Portela,** Rua Clara Nunes, 81 (Madureira); ☎ *390-0471;* **Bella-Flor,** Rua Pracinha Wallace, Paes Leme, 1562 (Nilópolis); ☎ *791-2866;* **Acadêmicos do Saigueiro,** Rua Silves Teles, 104 (Vila Isabel); ☎ *238-5564.* Sat. at 11 p.m.; **Estação Primeira de Mangueira,** Rua Visconde de Niterói, 1072 (Mangucira); ☎ *234-4192.*

### Blocos

**Bloco de Segunda/Gatio,** Rua Humberto de Campos, 699-C (Leblon); ☎ *294-5535.* **Clube do Samba,** Rio Oria, Avenida Sernametiba, 16696 (Recreio). **Simpatia E Quase Amor/Clube do Condominio,** Rua Albreu Fialho, corner of Rua Pacheco Leão, 780.

During the Carnaval period of 1996 until Mar., the city of Rio sponsored free concerts of Brazilian music on the beach at Ipanema on weekend evenings. Call to see if they are offering this again.

> **UP CLOSE TIP:** *During Carnaval, most hotels raise prices or require minimum stays of four to five nights – or both. To save money, inquire about apart-hotels (like apartments, but with maid service and kitchens – especially if you are traveling with a group or with children).*

### Breakfast During Carnaval

Five-star hotels offer the best breakfast spreads during Carnaval. Try the **Copa Cabana Palace, Caesar Park, Rio Palace,** or the **Sheraton,** where the buffets are massive, exotic and as fresh as the dawn.

# The Sounds Of Brazil

The majority of Brazilians may be poor, but they boast one of the richest musical cultures in the world – a sensuous mélange of African, Indian, and European influences. In any major city you'll find jazz artists of international renown, fine local musicians specializing in regional rhythms, and even world-class dancers executing the sexy moves of samba, *lambada,* reggae and *forró.* Some of the best music can be found at impromptu jam sessions on the beach or in tiny bohemian bars where guitar-strumming singers croon out cool bossa nova. And no world-music fan should ever miss the big arena concerts given by riveting performers such as Milton Nascimento, Gilberto Gil and Caetano Veloso – proponents of a highly sophisticated strain of pop music called **MPB,** or *música popular brasileira.*

## Roots

The rhythmic vitality of Brazilian music stems from the native Indians, who accompanied their pantheistic rituals with an exotic blend of rattlers, shakers, and panpipes. Starting in the 17th century, black slaves imported from Africa brought along the hot, impassioned drumming of their *candomblé* rituals. Slow, heartbreaking ballads were added by the first Portuguese colonists, who accompanied themselves with *cavaquinhos* (similar to the ukulele), the *bandolim* (mandolin), bagpipes, and the Portuguese guitar.

From the very beginning, sensual body movement accompanied Brazilian music. From the lundu of the Portuguese court to the hip-grinding *lambada* of the last decade, Brazilians have consistently demonstrated their knack for inventing undulating dances. Many were inspired by the erotic dances of African slaves, the undulating gestures traveling with only a little refinement to the salons of the ruling class. Samba itself is said to have been derived from the slave dance called *umbigada*, in which a sharp pelvic thrust signifies the entrance of each successive soloist. Even European-imported dance rhythms like the polka and the mazurka were eventually tropicalized into the *maxixe*, a flamboyant tango that became the rage during the 1920s.

Slowly, a passion for gorgeous melody began to surface in Brazil. During the 1930s and 40s, the songs of **Dorival Caymmi,** one of the country's classic songwriters, romantically evoked the seaside sensuality of Bahia. Ary Barroso's beloved ballad *Aquarela do Brazil* (known to most of the world as "Brazil") signaled to North America that something languid and subtle was happening down south. In 1958, a brand-new sound called bossa nova would rock the Brazilian music scene and eventually the world's.

## Bossa Nova

Musically, the times were ripe for revolution. Optimism was high; Juscelino Kubitschek was pushing Brasilia; film, theater, and painting were thriving. Bohemian musicians gathered in the cafés of Ipanema and Copacabana to jam and write songs. The singer Johnny Alf and the composer Luis Bonfá were already shaping the loud, brassy strains of samba with a soft jazz, but it was the strange harmonies and cooled-down beat of the song *Chega de Saudade* that truly shocked the public and marked the beginning of MPB. The composer was the yet-unknown **Antônio Carlos Jobim** and the performer was **João Gilberto,** an eccentric musician who managed to simultaneously recreate all the rhythms of a samba band on his solo guitar. His awesome instrumental technique would influence generations of musicians, but in truth it was his sad-teddybear voice that perfectly embodied the tender wistfulness of bossa nova. Even today, Gilberto still plays so softly that audiences must sit on the edge of their seats to hear him.

Though he died in 1994, **Antônio Carlos Jobim** (who was often called Tom) remains the undisputed master of bossa nova – a classically trained musician who infused his sleepy, sensuous tunes with Ravel-inspired harmonies and unexpected blues notes. Over the next 35 years, Jobim's songs, often written with Vinícius de Moraes, one of Brazil's greatest poets, would be recorded by literally thousands of musicians worldwide – the most prominent among them being Frank Sinatra and the American saxophonist Stan Getz. Though Jobim continued to mine the genre until his death, many consider the peak of his bossa nova expression to have been the 1960 movie version of *Orfeo Negro* (Black Orpheus), Jobim's and Moraes' musical play that retold the Orpheus myth through the eyes of two poor lovers during Carnaval. In fact, it was that movie that did more to promote the exotic romanticism of Brazil (and thus international tourism) than other commercial propaganda. Brazilophiles should run to rent the Academy Award-winning movie, now available on video. That Jobim's unexpected death was mourned as a national loss indicates just how deeply bossa nova had defined the soul of Brazil.

Though many singers, including Astrud Gilberto, Flora Purim, and Gal Costa, became famous for singing bossa nova, there was one special voice that gave it its soul. Born in Porto Alegre, **Elis Regina** was called *furacão*, or "hurricane" by her admiring public. Though neither pretty nor particularly glamorous, she was enfused with a naturalness of voice and spirit that seemed to render anything she sang a hit. Those who loved her singing style were swept away by her prodigious emotionality that could swing from intense joy to profound sorrow in seconds. A favored muse of Jobim's, she also recorded renditions of Milton Nascimento's greatest hits that nearly eclipsed his own. In 1982, Elis died from an accidental overdose at the peak of her career – a tragedy deeply felt by the entire country.

## Tropicália

By the late 60s, bossa nova's sweet strains weren't sufficient to quell the public's growing despair over the military regime. A cult of the absurd suddenly emerged from the state of Bahia, calculated to shock the middle class from their complacency. Spearheaded by singer/songwriter **Gilberto Gil** and his best friend **Caetano Veloso,** the movement called *Tropicália* pitted electric guitars against berimbaus (a native one-stringed instrument), freely borrowing from international influences in what was dubbed "neo-cultural cannibalism." At a time when all Brazilian singers wore dark suits and ties, Gil and Veloso bounded on stage with long hair and bellbottoms, spouting Dada-esque lyrics that few understood. Their eccentricity got them arrested and eventually exiled from Brazil, but when they returned two years later they reactivated careers that have since become the most enduring in the country.

If any one Brazilian musician represents the successful synthesis of disparate parts, it is Gilberto Gil. Raised the son of a doctor in a country village near Salvador, Gil absorbed a musical environments that included not only the nasal cries of street singers, *trios elétricos*, and the folk accordion of Luiz Gonzaga, but also the Beatles, the Rolling Stones and Bob Dylan. The passion to make sense of this international collusion has underscored Gil's entire 30-year career, and since his return to Brazil in 1972, his albums have shown an ever-increasing knack for being primal, contemporary and futuristic all at the same time. A consummate lyricist, Gil writes about a wide range of concerns, from the profoundly spiritual to the hotly political. A song lambasting the Pope was banned from Brazilian TV in 1985, but it didn't diminish Gil's popularity; in the early 90s he was elected to the city council in Salvador and remains a leading force in the Brazilian Green Movement, which supports ecological activism.

**Caetano Veloso** is considered one of Brazil's greatest poet-composers. He was born in Santo Amaro, a small coastal town near Cachoeira in Bahia. Although few of his 20-odd albums have gone gold, he has emerged at the age of 50-plus as a world-class performer, still mesmerizing audiences with his doe-like good looks, sweetly seductive presence, and a searing intelligence partial to irony. Caetano's styles run the gamut from bossa nova and rock to avant-garde and samba, but his lyrics are the true standouts: full of Joycean-invented words, internal rhymes, and cryptic allusions. In 1986, his American debut on Elektra/Nonesuch was heralded by many American critics as one of the top 10 albums of the year.

The ultimate muse of the Tropicália movement, and Brazil's biggest singing star today, is **Gal Costa**. A fellow Bahian, she met Caetano as a young girl and recorded her first song (his *Domingo*) in 1967. While Gil and Veloso were living in exile in London she continued to interpret their songs with a raw, earthy voice that has since grown into a reedlike instrument of astonishing flexibility. Part hippie, part torcher, part elegant lady, she is painfully shy in person, but her self-consciousness becomes transformed onstage into shining vulnerability. Her repertoire ranges from samba and rock to folkloric rhythms like *frevo* and *baião*, but she truly excels in bossa nova.

The sister of Caetano Veloso, singer/songwriter **Maria Bethânia** has carved her own niche in MPB, despite her brother's fame and her own anti-diva personality. In 1978, she became an overnight sensation when she replaced the ailing singer Nara Leão in a highly controversial stage show, but it was her 1979 album, *Alibi*, that shot her to national prominence – a lush collection of ballads sung in her inimitable husky croon. In recent years, Bethânia (as she is called) has added socially conscious songs to her repertoire, a gesture that has lent her the persona of a mystical Joan Baez.

## Minas & Milton

Arguably the most important Brazilian songwriter in terms of international influence is **Milton Nascimento,** one of a constellation of musicians from Minas Gerais, a state known for its introspective people and deep religiosity. Blessed with one of the greatest voices in jazz history, Milton can soar effortlessly from a heartfelt baritone to an angelic falsetto, but he is also equally revered for his profound melodies and rhythmic ingenuity that derives from an exotic cache of influences, including the Portuguese *fado*, the Mineiro folk ballad called *toada,* the Beatles, Gregorian chants, and *nueva canción*. Among Milton's best early albums, the 1971 *Clube da Esquina* featured such other local artists as Lô and Marcio Borges, Beto Guedes, Ronaldo Bastos, Fernando Brant, and Toninho, all of whom would later establish their own impressive careers. Although Milton ascribes to no one religion in particular, his albums are infused with a profound spirituality and almost prophet-like affinity with the human condition. In 1973, when the military dictatorship censored his lyrics, the wordless cry of his falsetto on the album *Milagre dos Peixes* expressed more political protest than words ever could. In one his latest album *Txai,* he incorporates chants and percussion from Amazonian tribes to riveting effect.

The most ingenious ensemble from Minas is **Uakti,** a quartet of classically trained musicians who make their own instruments. Other notable Mineiros, whose records you might find only in Minas, are the singer/songwriter **Flavio Venturini,** keyboardist **Tuilio Mourio,** and singer **Tadeu Franco,** a heartthrob who often performs in local clubs.

## More MPB

MPB has been pushed forward by the creativity of numerous musicians who continue to transcend genres while carving out their own unique identities. **Chico Buarque,** the son of one of Brazil's greatest intellectuals, has written not only an impressive array of songs but novels, plays, and literary analyses. Another songwriter with an instantaneously recognizable sound is **Ivan Lins.** A former chemical engineer, Lins was brought to the public eye by Elis Regina, who propelled his song "Madalena" into posterity. Although many of Lins' songs have been recorded by such American artists as Patti Austin, Ella Fitzgerald, and Dave Grusin, Lins is often his own best interpreter. His concerts are always joyous explosions of romantic sentiment.

A born rhythmist, **Jorge Ben** developed his own guitar style simply because he couldn't imitate João Gilberto's. *Mas Que Nada,* his biggest hit, shot to international fame in 1966 in the hands of Brazilian bandleader Sergio Mendes. Still thriving 25 years later, Ben is known for shows that turn into tribal parties pumped by a transcontinental black groove.

**João Bosco** is one of Brazil's most daring songwriters, a post-modern troubadour who wildly flips between boleros, flamenco, jazz, and classical styles. With his lyricist, the ex-psychiatrist **Aldir Blanco,** he has written songs that range from the surreal to the socially conscious, in languages as diverse as Tupi, French, Yoruban, and his own invented phonemes.

Singer/songwriter **Djavan** was born in the northeastern state of Alagoas, but has long transcended his folkloric roots to create a pan-American sound hailed internationally for its radiant melodies and jazzy, undulating rhythms. Steering clear of political controversy, Djavan focuses more on love songs and highly danceable tunes; *Luz,* one of his best albums, features Stevie Wonder.

## Northeast

During the late 70s and 80s, singers and songwriters from the Northeast and Amazônia have catapulted to national attention as regional beats like *forró* and *maracatú* proved themselves disco-friendly. Part court jester, part serious balladeer, **Alceu Valença** is a perennial presence in Olinda's Carnaval and the king of *forrock* – an explosive mix of *forró* amplified by electric guitars and rock drums. His songs, written with partner **Geraldo**

**Azevedo,** are much like *cordels* – the pulp-story narratives that document the misery and miracles of Northeastern existence.

Entering her fourth decade as sexy as ever, singing sensation **Elba Ramalho** continues to magnetize fans worldwide with her irrepressible energy and infectious repertoire that marries Northeastern rhythms with Caribbean dance mixes. Other prominent names in the Northeast are **Dominguinhos,** one of Brazil's greatest accordionists, **Zé Ramalho,** a *sertanejo*-styled guitarist, and **Fagner,** a romantic pop balladeer. From Amazônia has sprung the popular singer **Fafa de Belém,** and *lambada* singer **Beto Barbosa.**

## The South

The musical traditions in the south are just now enjoying a surge of popularity, especially among youths looking to revitalize their *gaúcho* roots. Among their role models is the hippie-looking **Renato Borghetti,** a young accordionist who plays folkloric tunes with a modernistic flair. More mainstream, **Kleiton and Kledir,** two brothers from Rio Grande do Sul achieved national fame with their "country rock" sound during the late 70s and 80s; in more recent years, Kledir has been pursuing a fine solo career.

## Tropical Rock

For the last three decades, Brazilian rock has been brewing underground, slowly working its way up in the last 10 years to guitar-slashing anger. The father of the movement was singer **Roberto Carlos** who, with his partner **Erasmo Carlos,** promoted a good-time rock that counterbalanced the social concerns infiltrating bossa nova. Today, Roberto remains Brazil's best-selling artist, having savvily maneuvered his Lothario-like image into that of a slick, middle-aged balladeer. Also an early proponent of Brazilian rock, **Rita Lee** began her career with the Dali-influenced **Os Mutantes** (The Mutants), but later evolved into a light, sassy pop singer trading on native rhythms and sly humor.

As the democracy of the 80s took hold, a new generation of rockers, freed from censorship, conquered the air waves. The wildly theatrical **Blitz** opened the door for other hard rockers like **Barão Vermelho** and **Kid Abelha,** who took the 1985 Rock in Rio concert by storm. The most ingenious rock group of the last two decades has been **Os Paralamos do Successo,** a bass, drum and guitar trio (filled out with brass) who have incorporated *lambada, afoxé,* and *coco* in a wild Caribbean party mix. Nearly as ebullient is the work of **Lulu Santos,** who describes his own style as "Brazilianized, tropicalized, Latinized rock."

Irreverence reaches state-of-the-art with rocker **Ney Matogrosso,** whose outlandish stage attire situates him somewhere between Elton John and Carmen Miranda. Despite his feminine voice (higher than most females) and his flagrant strutting, Matogrosso continues to draw crowds that defy sexual definitions or age categories. His contributions to the rock genre have included a spirited fusion with *virá*, a syncopated Portuguese folk style played with great verve on the accordion.

It's not surprising that Brazilian punk emerged from the sons of the military in Brasília, a city where the monotony of the architecture alone is enough to make a kid go crazy. One of the most enduring has been **Legão Urbana,** who in 1983 stumbled on stage in disheveled jeans and torn T-shirt (unheard of in Brazil) and reveled in a frenetic, Cure-influenced protest rock. The city of São Paulo has also spawned hundreds of rock groups; among the biggest sellers has been **RPM** and **Titãs,** a group of young men who sing everything from *brega* (old-fashioned) ballads to two-chord punk, reggae and funk.

The rock star who most deeply affected Brazilian society in the last two decades was **Cazuza,** an electrifying performer whose venom-filled lyrics attacked social hypocrisy and political deception. An open bisexual, Cazuza discovered he had AIDS in 1987, but continued to perform in public, sharing the reality of the epidemic with his fans. By the time he died in 1990, his last two albums had reached multiplatinum success.

## Avant-Garde

Full-dimensional musicianship reaches its pinnacle in two Brazilian composers revered worldwide by jazz fans for their inventiveness, prodigious output and sheer genius.

**Hermeto Pascoal**, an albino who looks uncannily like Santa Claus, can coax a musical sound out of anything that dares to cross his path – from a blade of grass to teapots, sewing machines, kitchen utensils and even bleating piglets. Despite his stubby fingers, Hermeto is a piano virtuoso, master accordionist, percussionist and wind player, capable of improvising profoundly moving melodies as well as the most intricate of rhythms. Accompanied by his tightly rehearsed band, his shows are always exhilarating. Many musicians (foreign and Brazilian) make pilgrimages to his commune outside Rio just to audit his all-day rehearsals. As iconoclastic as Hermeto is the composer **Egberto Gismonti,** a conservatory-trained guitarist and pianist whose works are fascinating abstractions of Brazilian folklore, world-beat music and free-form jazz. Since 1978 he has been influenced by an ongoing relationship with Amazonian Indians, whose percussion sounds are often heard in his work.

## Percussionists

It's not surprising that some of the best percussionists in the world have sprung from Brazil. Among them is **Airto Moreira** who, along with his Brazilian-born wife, singer **Flora Purim,** has profoundly influenced American jazz, bebop, funk and pop. The provocative stage presence of **Naná Vasconcelos,** a virtuoso on the cuica and berimbau, often resembles that of a jungle shaman. The most famous of samba percussionists is **Marçal,** the former director of the Portela Samba School. **Olodum** is the

Bahia-based pop group, propelled by *afoxé*, percussion and vocals, that was brought to international prominence on Paul Simon's *Rhythm of the Saints* album.

## Other Instrumentalists

The list of Brazilian jazz artists who thrill fans around the world is endless. Among guitar masters is **Baden Powell**, an early bossa nova advocate who has made extensive research into Afro-Brazilian traditions. **Oscar Castro-Neves,** an early colleague of Jobim's now based in the States, is one of the most enduring bossa nova composers spinning out tenderly evocative albums. **Ricardo Silveira**, a former lead-guitarist for Milton Nascimento, has established himself as a formidable soloist with his fusion-driven albums. In a more classical vein is the **Duo Assad**, two guitar-playing brothers whose superb repertoire ranges from baroque airs to free-form jazz. On the horizon is the brilliant guitarist **André Geraissati**, whose superlative technique and profound lyricism pushes the edges of jazz, fusion and the avant-garde.

The most talented jazz pianist to come out of Brazil today is **Eliane Elias** (now based in New York), acclaimed for her impressive piano technique, deep lyrical affinity and rhythmic inventiveness. Running in close competition is the effervescent **Tânia Maria**, who has maintained a successful transcontinental career as a jazz singer, pianist and composer for several decades. Young keyboardist **Rique Pantoja** also has recorded several fusion albums in the States, the latest with trumpeter Chet Baker.

Other fine instrumentalists include trumpeters **Claudio Roditi** and **Márcio Montarroyos**, both of whom have carved solid reputations in the jazz field; fusion sax player **Leo Gandelman**, (sometimes called the "Brazilian Kenny G") and the avant-garde saxophonist **Perelman**. Among the best ensembles is the long-running **Azymuth**, whose numerous albums have been well-received in the States. **Banda Savana,** formed in 1988, is a 19-piece jazz band whose lush, sophisticated arrangements of Jobim tunes and others are dedicated to preserving the roots of Brazilian music.

Among singers not already mentioned, the best are **Zizi Possi**, an impeccable stylist whose voice approaches Barbra Streisand's in terms of purity and control; **Simone**, a female ex-basketball player known worldwide for her husky, near-baritone voice; **Marisa Monte**, an instant success in her 20s and the most likely heir apparent to Gal Costa; and **Adriana Calcanhoto**, whose punklike irreverence is matched only by her masterful jazz chops and superb writing skills. Popular samba singers include **Beth Carvalho, Alcione, Martinho da Vila,** and **Paulinho da Viola**. (See the selective *Discography*, at the back of the book.)

> **UP CLOSE TIP:** *The most exciting singer on the Brazilian scene these days is* **Daniela Mercury**, *a samba-reggae singer/dancer who began attracting thousands in her home state of Bahia and is now conquering fans worldwide. Her powerful good looks and magnetic presence inspired a New York Times critic in 1993 to aptly describe her as "sex on two wheels." Don't ever miss her shows!*

## UP CLOSE ADVENTURE from Mike Salvo

"Traveling in backcountry Brazil, I found that my musical instruments were a doorway to meet people, make friends, and discover new things. On one trip through the state of Ceará, my guitar and I became both student and teacher on beaches and around the bonfire. When I traveled through Bahia, I put smiles on many unsuspecting faces when I took out my blues harp and played. One time I ended up surrounded by a spontaneous *capoeira* circle in the middle of nowhere. I was playing near the road and the local little kids began dancing around. Soon, a young guy with a berimbau walked by and we began to play together – a strange mix of instruments and styles that somehow managed to blend. (Both the berimbau and the blues have their roots in Africa and then evolved separately in North and South America.) A circle formed and two people would enter and perform the acrobatic martial arts dance with our strange music weaving around them. This spontaneous and joyous expression on a dusty street in the middle of nowhere remains one of the purest experiences of music I've ever had."

# Literature & The Arts

## Literature

The beginnings of Brazilian literature in the 18th century were marked by the emergence of the French Revolution, the great Encyclopedists, and the war for independence in North America. Though Portuguese influence remained strong, Brazilians in the 19th century began to create their own literary expressions. All the multicultural and multiracial issues of the burgeoning country are deeply reflected in Brazilian literature.

Considered one of Brazil's greatest novelists, **Joacquim Maria Machado de Assis** (1839-1908) became the first president of the Brazilian Academy of Letters in 1897. *The Epitaph of a Small Winner* (published as *Memórias Pósthumous de Bras Cubas* in 1881) became a true Brazilian classic, providing a realistic, if unflinching look at the foibles of Brazilian society in the late 19th century.

**Euclides da Cunha** (1866-1909) authored one of the most important novels in Brazilian literature: *Os Sertões* (translated as *Rebellion in the Backlands*), an uncompromising description of the impoverished existence of Northeasterners and their fight for survival and integrity. The novel tells the true story of Antônio Conselheiro, the chief of a poor village in Bahia who managed to repulse several police invasions until his entire community was massacred.

Jose Pereira de Graça (1868-1931), a diplomat in Europe, combined the age's latest aesthetic and philosophical ideas with his own investigation into the problems of modern Brazilian life. In his 1902 novel *Canaan*, he explored the life of German Pomeranian colonists in the state of Espirito Santo and the conflicts arising from the multicultural mélange.

Among cultural historians, the most outstanding is **Gilberto Freyre** (1900-1988). His three-volume study of Brazilian social history (*Order and Progress, The Mansions and the Shanty*, and *The Masters and the Slaves*) are so richly detailed they read like novels, offering an unprecedented peek behind the closed doors of all strata of Brazilian society throughout its history.

Born in 1912, **Jorge Amado** is certainly the best known and most popular of all Brazilian novelists. His novels, such as *Terras do sem fim* (*The Violent Land*) and *Gabriela, cravo e canela* (*Gabriela, Clove & Cinnamon*) have been published in over 40 foreign editions. Some, such as *Gabriela*, have been made into well-received films. Amado, born in Salvador, steeps his books in Afro-Brazilian folklore; as such, they are must-reads for anyone traveling to Bahia.

**Carlos Drummond de Andrade** (1902-1987) was the first Brazilian poet to gain wide recognition in the post-modern period. Stylistically, he takes a critical though realistic attitude toward himself, his fellowman and society, and his works have attained great critical acclaim as masterpieces in the Portuguese language.

## Painting

The first painters of the 16th century were **Jesuit** and **Benedictine missionaries**. On the heels of the Dutch expeditions in the mid-17th century came **Flemish artists**, who painted flora and tropical scenes. Eighteenth-century **Brazilian baroque** art reaches its zenith during the gold cycle in the cities of Ouro Preto, Salvador, Recife, and Olinda. In the 19th century, artists were influenced by successive European trends – **late Neo-classicism**, **Romanticism**, and **Impressionism** – while artists of the 20th century were inspired by **Academicism** and **Modernism**.

**Cândido Portinari** (1903-1962) is Brazil's best-known painter, and the most outstanding artist of this century. Before leaving art school in Paris, he committed himself only to Brazilian themes for the rest of his life. Upon his return to Brazil, he developed into a social commentator through his art, defining the genre so deeply that critics now divide the history of Brazilian painting into two periods – before and after Portinari.

Portinari's best loved painting was done in tempera and entitled **Tiradentes**. The depiction of this immortal hero of Brazilian independence was actually fashioned after his friend, Luis Carlos Prestes, a Brazilian communist leader.

Portinari's larger murals clearly show the influence of the 14th- and 15th-century Italian painters, such as Giotto and Piero della Francesca, as well as the Mexican muralist Diego Rivera. The United Nations headquarters in New York City displays two of Portinari's finest murals,

**War** and **Peace**. In his later works, the artist abandoned dramatic social themes for historical subjects, beginning with the discovery of Brazil.

## Sculpture

The finest sculptor and one of the greatest Brazilian baroque architects was **Antônio Francisco Lisboa**, the son of a Portuguese architect and an African slave. A more detailed account of his work and life can be found in the chapter on Minas Gerais, a state where most of his greatest sculptures and paintings are located.

# RIO DE JANEIRO

**N**early all visitors catch their breath when they first glimpse Rio from the window of a plane. That fabulous white shoreline curving crescent-like around the azure-blue ocean, the mysterious jungle-like mountains towering above the city's sinuous streets, and the hundreds of tiny tropical islands that dot the natural southern bay all combine to make Rio a city of startling beauty, if not perpetual promise. For the 10 million people who live here, Rio is like a tempestuous lover one can never imagine leaving. Some other cities may have more money or more culture, but none have the beach, the sun, and the *joie de vivre* of Rio de Janeiro.

Sugarloaf Mountain rises like a totem over Rio de Janeiro
(as seen from Corcovado Mountain).

An intricate weaving of man and nature, Rio is unique among the cities of the world in that most of its important landmarks are natural rather than man-made: **Corcovado Mountain**, with its imposing statue of Christ the Redeemer; **Pão de Açucar** (Sugarloaf Mountain) standing guard at Guanabara Bay, and **Copacabana Beach**, that irrepressible stretch of sand as alive in legend as it is in fact. Against this sensual backdrop, and behind the facade of first-world glamour, however, lies a more bitter reality that engulfs at least 40% of the city's population – pit-level poverty. Crowded into slum dwellings, called *favelas*, that hang precariously from the mountainsides, these rural poor, many of whom fled to Rio from the droughts in northeastern Brazil, only now have begun to receive a voice in a culture that has traditionally separated them from the upper-class neighborhoods lining the shore. Rio may have fine restaurants, ultra-chic shopping, and exotic nightlife, but for many, the very heart of the city lies in these downtrodden neighborhoods, for it's from here that Carnaval, Rio's greatest theatrical production, is constantly being reborn, a free-for-all celebration fueled as much by creative passion as it is by living life on the edge.

But pleasure in Rio doesn't end with Carnaval – in fact, the city's sensuous delights last year-round. And they can be exceedingly simple: an early-morning jog down a fabulous beach, an afternoon hike through a tropical rainforest, an exquisite sunset-splashed vista overlooking the city, or just the cool taste of a delicious *água de coco*, ice-cold coconut water, straight from the shell. For the shopper, there are bustling open-air markets, boutiques with tight sexy clothes, and some of the best jewelry stores in the world. For the gourmet, Rio de Janeiro offers up some of the finest chefs in South America. For the adventuresome, there's scuba and skydiving and treks up the mountains. And for the soulful, there is music and art, dance and magic, and black voodoo cults.

To be in Rio is to be in tune with the ever-changing play of the sunlight, with the eternal movement of the rushing waves, with the incessant beating of *candomblé* drums, and with the ubiquitous rhythm of samba tapped out on the side of a matchbox.

*Carioca* is the Indian word given to the first settlements of Rio, but the word has also come to refer to the stereotypical personality of Rio's inhabitants – sensual, indolent, uninhibited, and irrepressibly hedonistic. A *carioca* is an improviser, a jester, a creature whom the sea has somehow made asystematic. For a *carioca*, nothing is certain and anything is possible – especially if one has mastered the art of *jeitinhos*, clever little maneuvers that are always helped by a handful of *reais*. In contrast to the hardworking *Paulistanos* (from the city of São Paulo), *cariocas* know how to party and they have, it's been claimed repeatedly, *no* inhibitions. But there's a sadness that also underlies their spirit. "The same satirist who can joke about Rio can sit down and cry in the street," says the writer José Augusto Ribeiro, who's talking not only about the nature of the *carioca's* personality but about *carioca* street life itself.

Day and night Rio's sidewalks and plazas are crowded with shoppers and vendors, lovers and loners, a cacophony of bargaining, negotiating, and flirting filling the air. On a perfect Fri. afternoon, with a hot sun and a clear sky, you won't find many people left in the office.

## Dream Assignment

I'll never forget the first time I met the *carioca* spirit face to face. Several years ago, I was sent by a magazine on a dream assignment – to join a samba school in Rio and dance in Carnaval. Since I would be staying on for several

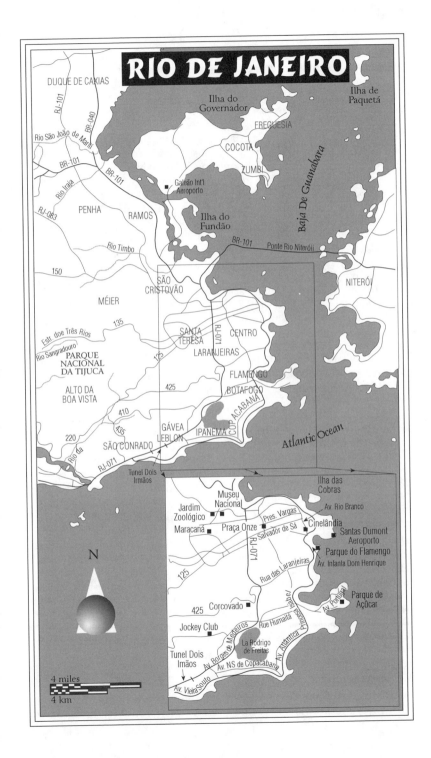

months, I rented a small room in Copacabana from Dona Vitória, an elderly widow who rose at dawn every day to bake cookies for high-society parties. One night, when we were discussing whether she should leave the door unlocked for me, I muttered something about having found a new boyfriend, and was perhaps – well – not coming home. For a moment she looked confused, then suddenly she threw out her arms and hugged me. "Ah, *querida*, go! Have fun, eat, dance, laugh, make love! Life is so short!" In that brief moment, the joy of her *carioca* spirit blazed through me, and as I shut the door behind me, I felt somehow I'd been blessed.

Sometimes (no, more often than not), the *carioca* spirit gets out of hand. A few years back, on a Sat. night, when the clocks were supposed to go forward one hour to mark the end of summertime, the mayor felt it was a little unreasonable to deprive the people of an extra hour of sunshine on the beach. So, aided by TV and radio announcements, he actually defied federal law, and for 48 hours, nobody knew exactly what time it was. The mania, which had driven airport controllers crazy, swiftly ended on Mon. morning when a stern presidential dictum told the mayor to stop messing with Mother Nature and get back into Greenwich Mean Time. *Cariocas* simply thought the whole show hilarious.

These days there is still great joy in Rio, but there's also much that reminds me of the Wild Wild West – hot, gritty, chaotic, more than a little dangerous, yet always exciting, a fount of nonstop stimulation. Indeed, after a recent visit to Rio, it seemed to me that New York in comparison was moving in slow motion. All that speed and excitement, however, can often add up to mayhem and mishap. And the question that's probably on your mind right now is: *Is Rio safe?*

To be frank, the answer is complicated and not so easily reduced to a simple yes or no. I suppose the really truthful answer is: *No, it's not safe, but that shouldn't stop you from going.*

Contrary to popular opinion, Rio is not the world's most violent city – it actually ranks eighth, behind such crime meccas as Johannesburg and Medellin. However, the audacity of its criminals, the corruption of the police, and the city's seemingly unsolvable poverty problem have left even Rio's long-time residents uneasy about venturing out alone at night. Kidnapping of private citizens, especially wealthy executives or their children (in broad daylight), has reached such proportions in Rio that businessmen reportedly spent over $1.2 billion in 1995 on bodyguards, alarms, armored guards, and other private security. In recent years, there have also been tales of tourists who were assaulted on Copacabana Beach by gangs of street boys. Stories also abound about Carnaval disasters, especially stolen wallets from drunken tourists. Gays, both tourists and natives, have been subjected to extremely violent crimes; straight men, too, have been misled and assaulted by knife-wielding transvestites.

However, when all is said and read, I would like to add (for whatever it's worth) that NOTHING HAS EVER HAPPENED TO ME (thank God!) in all my visits to Rio (or Brazil, for that matter) and I hope it never will. And what's my secret? Besides probably having an overworked guardian angel, I stay very much aware at all times, use my New York City street savvy constantly, and I *never* walk around wearing expensive accessories or clothes. More than anything, I try to blend in with the crowd.

I have been encouraged by recent developments in Rio indicating that *cariocas* aren't about to lie down (at least, on this point). In late Nov. 1995, tens of thousands turned out for a city-wide march to protest the rising crime rate and to show their support for **Viva Rio**, the citizens' anti-crime coalition which hopes to raise $500 million to improve the police force and living conditions in the city's 500 crime-plagued slums. Since 1994, the state government of Rio de Janeiro has pursued a security program in the city called **SPAT** (Special Police Force for the Protection of Tourists), which provides police assistance at 25 tourist sites around the city, including the two airports, bus station, Botanical Garden, Praça Mauá, Sugarloaf and Corcovado Mountain. (On my last trip, I was comforted to see groups of strong, handsome policemen walking down the beach in Copacabana.) In addition, a special beach police force known as **DEAT** is located at Avenida Afrânio de Mello Franco in Leblon, ☎ *511-5112.*

## Exotic Adventures

No tourist should view Rio as merely one city. It is the center of a larger environ that holds a myriad of eco-travel possibilities and you should never get stuck for your whole trip in Copacabana, no matter how much you may love it. Within hours of Rio proper are so many fascinating day trips and overnight excursions that you can have the most exotic adventures without ever flying to another city. Years ago, travelers would spend a week or 10 days in Rio glued to one beach; today, using the information in the chapter *Excursions from Rio*, you can use the same time exploring the beach resorts of the **Costa do Sol**, the deserted islands of **Angra dos Reis**, the historical city of **Parati**, or the magnificent forests of **Serra da Bocaina** with a minimum of effort and a maximum of pleasure. This new expanded Rio is simply a multifaceted treasure that's still being developed and awaiting explorers. For anyone in search of the ultimate in fantasy as well as adventure, Rio – city and state – remains, as it has for centuries, the superlative paradise.

# History

As with the discovery of Brazil just two years earlier, the **Portuguese** stumbled on the future city of Rio de Janeiro by nautical mistake. On the **Jan. 1, 1502**, a fleet sent by the King of Portugal to survey the newly found territories sailed merrily into Guanabara Bay, thinking it was a river. Even after the confusion was cleared up, the name stuck – hence, Rio de Janeiro, or River of Janeiro. In 1555, desperate for their own stake in the New World, the French, under the command of the Vice-Admiral Durand de Villegaignon, reconnoitered an area around the bay and dubbed it France Antartique. The Portuguese governor **Mem de Sá** valiantly attacked the invaders on several occasions, even establishing a fort on the **Morro do**

**Castelo** (where the Santos Dumont Airport stands today), but it was not until a prolonged siege in 1567 that he was able to expel them. Once relieved from French hands, the city grew rapidly, supported by the excellent harbor and the fertile soil, which proved perfect for sugarcane.

In the 15th and 16th centuries, to be Portuguese was to be Roman Catholic, and one of the earliest records of Rio contains an account of a Portuguese bishop who warded off shipwreck in 1647 by praying to Our Lady of Copacabana and, in gratitude, rebuilt the chapel. The bishopric of Rio was established in 1676, but it wasn't until 1763 that Rio was made the capital of the colony, not only because it was closer to the military threat but also because it could serve as a lookout for the flow of wealth from the mines of Minas Gerais. As gold was discovered in the hinterlands, Rio quickly became home to a small affluent class. Despite the filth, the stench and the overwhelming heat, a mid-18th-century visitor could still describe a certain elegance prevailing in the streets – ladies wore black veils over one eye and men were carried in chairs or hammocks, trailed by at least one or two barefoot servants dressed up in finery. Meanwhile, the port, an important leg in the South American-European-African trade and a magnet for contraband, throbbed with activity. Most of what remains from that time can be found close to the harbor, notably the beautiful **São Bento Monastery**, the **Convento de Santo Antônio**, and the **Praça XV**, full of colonial administrative palaces.

## Dom João's Reign

With the arrival in Rio of the Portuguese court of **Dom João VI**, the city suddenly gained a caché of glamour. The city Dom João and his 1,500 nobles discovered on arrival was a sleeping beauty; of its 60,000 inhabitants, 24,000 were Portuguese, 12,000 were slaves, and the rest a contingent of English and French desperate for something to do. Immediately the ruler threw open the port to free trade, but by 1808 the harbor was so full of foreign ships that nary a Portuguese one could be seen.

Still, the presence of the royal family helped focus Rio as the center of power. In the first decades of Dom João's reign, universities, medical schools, and naval academies were established, while the new printing press churned out the first issues of *Gazeta do Rio de Janeiro*. Curious visitors from the remote provinces even made the long trek to the tropical city, invariably surprised to find such a European mode of life.

Rapid urbanization began to alter Rio. By the end of the 1850s, Rio had become the largest city in South America, with a population exceeding a quarter of a million. Large numbers of aristocratic planters were now indulging in the pleasures of the city, dividing their time between the noisy, friendly streets and the more sedate salons. Women went mad over French fashions, an obsession that has remained to this day. The crown even honored that obsession by inviting a French cultural mission to Rio and years later founding the French-staffed **Academy of Fine Arts**. Most notable in this group of talented French instructors was the artist **Jean Baptiste Debret**, whose brush depicted memorable scenes of that epoch.

By the last half of the 19th century, Rio had become a bustling metropolis. The English traveler William Hadfield, returning after a 16-year absence, marveled at how the population had burgeoned to 600,000. All the principal streets had been paved and an efficient drainage system installed. The new streets were wide and lined with buildings whose beautiful architectural style Hadfield commended. New public markets and shops provided a variety of wares, and coaches, carriages and omnibuses pulled by mule teams crowded the main streets illuminated by gaslight. Even then, the infamous *carioca* personality was already beginning to form. In a French memoir of the 19th century, the author observed that young ladies from the best families of Rio were flirting outrageously with lads right inside the Imperial Chapel – exactly as they would 100 years later in the cafés along the city's most beautiful beaches.

Throughout the last half of the 19th century, hundreds of mule trains headed for Rio, discarding their cargo of precious coffee at the train station to await shipment to foreign ports. By 1890, the capital had more than a million inhabitants and boasted many characteristics of a first-class American city, with one exception – no good hotel. Students and other visitors were forced to find lodging in monasteries that were no longer functioning. Still, the American traveler Maturin M. Ballou reveled in the hospitality of the city, with its beautiful fruit trees and gardens enlivened by monkeys and caged parrots, as well as its wonderful French meals. Ice cream, a miracle food in a tropical country, was first spotted at the Hotel do Norte during the early days of Pedro II, and the novelty spread throughout the century. Francioni's, the first ice cream parlor to boast tropical flavors, became a popular meeting place, with its enormous shade trees and exotic fruit drinks.

Of course, many travelers complained about the heat and the beginning of the slums that would later climb up the mountainsides as blatant proof of the inequality of wealth. But by the end of the century, colonial mercantilism had given way to the modern pulse. Trams and trains were installed, and the first tunnel through the mountains of Alaôr Prata was built in 1892. Additional access was provided with the **Leme Tunnel** in 1904, all providing impetus for the transformation of Copacabana into single family houses.

In the early 20th century, Copacabana and Ipanema were nothing more than sleepy fishing villages, but accelerated growth during World War II saw the first high-rises dot the strand. During the 30s, the international jet set swarmed down on Rio, stimulated by a handful of Hollywood movies, like Fred Astaire's *Flying Down to Rio*, with its chorus line of beautiful girls doing the samba on the wings of a jet.

The late composer Antônio Carlos Jobim used to harbor nostalgia for that Ipanema of the pre-bossa nova wave, "when the streets were empty and the fish were so big we were afraid to go in the water! (as he once told me in an interview)." Yet it was Jobim himself, with poet Vinícius de Moraes, who put Rio on the map during the 60s with *The Girl from Ipanema* and other beautiful songs, such as *Corcovado*, that later became international jazz standards.

Even as Rio surrendered its status as the country's capital to Brasília in 1960, a new building boom began to transform the shoreline. Luxury hotels such as the Caesar Park, the Rio Palace, the Meridien and the Sheraton Rio were added to a lineup that had traditionally centered around the elite Copacabana Palace Hotel. At the same time, the *favelas*, or slums, were burgeoning with the influx of immigrants from the arid Northeast, forging a subculture of despair and poverty beneath the glamorous sheen of *carioca* life.

With the commercialization of Carnaval in the late 60s and the building of the Sambódromo (an open-air theater for the Carnaval parade) in 1975, what had once been a folkloric festival of the masses was now being transmitted worldwide through satellite TV, popularizing the culture and drawing new fans from the States, Europe, and even Japan.

In the 90s, the advent of AIDS, as well as the severe economic crisis, somewhat dampened the sense of outrageous licentiousness that had characterized the Carnavals of years past, but what has started growing in its place is a new sense of responsibility, foresightedness, and cooperation, particularly in light of the United Nations Conference on the Environment that was held in Rio in 1992.

For the first time in years, roads have been improved, taxi drivers reeducated, and the general public enlisted to renew the sense of hospitality that has made Rio such a *cidade maravilhosa* (marvelous city) for hundreds of years.

# A Bird's Eye View

The city of Rio de Janeiro is two longitude lines east of New York City, putting it two hours later on the Greenwich Mean Time scale. Smack on the Tropic of Capricorn, it shares the same longitude (and the same hot, humid climate) as much of the Kalahari Desert in Botswana, Africa.

Rio is the capital of the state of Rio de Janeiro (one of the smallest states in Brazil), which is flanked to the south by the state of São Paulo, in the west by Minas Gerais, and in the north by Espirito Santo. With an area of 728 square miles, the city of Rio is only second in size to São Paulo, and is the third largest port in the country.

The modern city of Rio is divided into two zones: **Zona Sul** (south) and **Zona Norte** (north). Downtown, the commercial center of the city, lies in between and is the site of a number of historical blocks (see *Rio By Foot*, page 106). In general, most tourists avoid the more industrial North Zone and spend their time on the beaches, all of which are located in the South. But you will certainly make the pilgrimage north if you visit Rio's great temple to soccer, the world-class **Maracanã Stadium.**

Neighborhoods in Rio are called *bairros*. In the South Zone, the name of the *bairro* is synonymous with the name of its beach. The most famous, of course, are **Copacabana** (with its extension, **Leme**) and **Ipanema** (with its extension, **Leblon**). A few miles west along the southern shore lie **São Conrado** and **Vidigal**, home of Rio's most luxurious resort hotels.

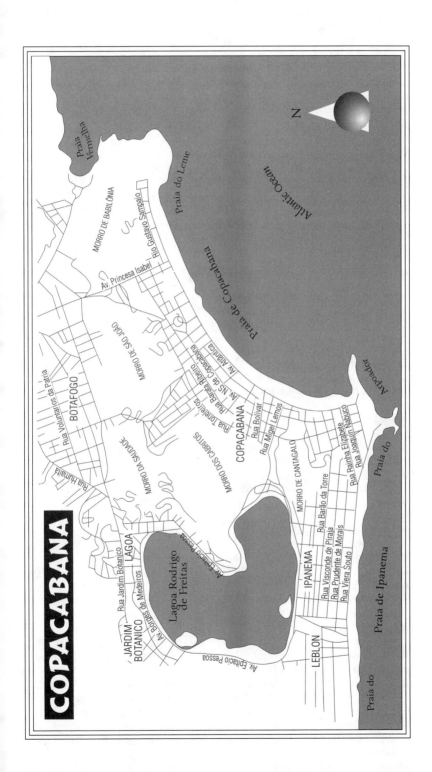

Even farther to the west is **Barra da Tijuca**, a nine-mile beach that's considered to be the Mercedes Benz of beaches and the most promising development area in the city. Following the southern shoreline of the Atlantic Ocean, you will eventually reach the most remote beaches of **Recreio dos Bandeirantes, Grumari**, and **Guaratiba**. In 10 years' time, these outlying primitive beaches will probably be as developed as Ipanema – so go now.

Less touristic neighborhoods with their own beaches also include **Botafogo** and **Flamengo**, northeast of Copacabana. Both are fashionable middle-class neighborhoods that enjoyed their heyday a few decades ago, although Botafogo still boasts some of the best restaurants in the city. **Urca**, situated at the base of Sugarloaf Mountain, is a quiet, elite neighborhood that offers a spectacular view of the city from its coastline.

# Sights

## Corcovado

The greatest symbol of Rio de Janeiro's soul is the enormous statue of **Christ the Redeemer** that towers over the city on the 2,400-foot-high mountain called Corcovado. Clearly seen from numerous points throughout the city, the 120-foot-high figure of Christ, with his arms outstretched to an expanse of 75 feet, seems to be welcoming, if not embracing the multitudes that throng to the city seeking work, pleasure, and a pocketful of dreams. At night, illuminated in lush, golden light, the statue takes on a preternatural glow, appearing almost to rise mystically from the dark sky. No matter what your religion, it takes only a few days in Rio to orient yourself to the statue's omnipotent presence.

The massive mountain of **Corcovado** was a focal point for *cariocas* long before the soapstone-and-concrete statue was completed in 1931 to commemorate (albeit 10 years late) the centennial of Brazilian independence. **Dom Pedro I**, in particular, loved to trek up and down the trail to escape his more princely duties – but no doubt he was also greatly influenced by the stunning panoramic view of his kingdom. In 1885, in an effort to entice less athletic visitors, Dom Pedro's son (later Pedro II), commanded the construction of a passenger train that would rise to the peak through lushly forested landscapes. Thankfully, that forest is still intact, and today one of the best ways to reach the monument is to follow this same path on a much modernized tram.

Visit Corcovado early in your stay; the view will convince you that Rio is still one of the most beautiful cities in the world. Locating your hotel may be difficult from the south side of the platform, but you can follow the voluptuous curves of Copacabana and Ipanema Beach all the way to Leblon, as well as to the crystal blue waters of the Lagoa Rodrigo de Freitas. Closer in, you'll be able to glimpse the leafy backstreets of residential neighborhoods like Botafogo, Cosme Velho, and Laranjeiras, and there are excellent views of Sugarloaf, Guanabara Bay, and Flamengo Park. From the northern platform, you can see the most industrial parts of the North Zone, along with glimpses of the encroaching vegetation that represents some of the last untouched Atlantic rainforest on the east coast (and the home of some very poor *cariocas*). Don't forget to look up into the eyes of the Christ. To catch the entire figure on film, you'll have to find a way to lie down on the ground and shoot upwards.

The best time to visit Corcovado is on a clear day around three or four in the afternoon when dusk begins to settle over the city. And don't write-off cloudy days – one of the most exciting moments is when the sun finally breaks behind the statue, magically backlighting it. The tram ride lasts about 20 minutes, after which you must climb 220 semi-challenging steps to the base of the statue. (Although there are various levels for rest, refreshment and observation, anyone with a heart condition should think twice about this climb.)

The statue of Christ called Corcovado reigns over the city of Rio de Janeiro.

**UP CLOSE TIP:** *The wind is strong: hats and sunglasses may take flight. Unfortunately, during high season, the numerous crowds can turn your visit into a push-and-shove affair, particularly at peak hours. Don't be surprised if you're accosted on the way down by a salesman with a ceramic plate embossed with your face – your photo was secretly snapped on your way up. You should not feel obligated to buy. Postcards, film, and souvenirs are often much more expensive here than down below in the city.*

---

### Vital Stats

- ☐ The Christ weighs over 1,000 tons.
- ☐ Its hands and face were sculpted by French artist Paul Landowski, aided by Brazilian engineers.
- ☐ The lighting was designed by Marconi.

---

❖ **GETTING HERE:** *The easiest way is to sign up for an organized tour (see the list of travel agencies in "Hands-On Rio"), which either takes you to the Cosme Velho train station or to the base of the statue. You can also take city bus #583, which leaves from Copacabana and goes to the train station. Private car or cab can also take you to the base of the statue (or train) and wait for you while you tour the site. The train, winding around a tropical paradise, leaves every 20-30 minutes from 8:30 a.m.-6:30 p.m. and costs about $2.50 round trip. Agency tours usually cost $20-25 and include both Corcovado and Sugarloaf in a half-day itinerary.*

---

## Pão de Açucar

If Corcovado is the soul, Pão de Açucar must be the rock-solid heart of Rio. This huge granite and quartz mountain sits on the edge of the shoreline of the Urca Peninsula, staunch and immovable, like a sentinel protecting its charges from a threatening ocean. Thousands of years ago, the 1,500-foot-high mountain must have made an excellent lookout for the Tupi Indians who populated the area and were rumored to have cannibalized colonists. Though no one really knows the origin of the mountain's name, it does sound remarkably like the Indian phrase *pau-hn-açugua*, meaning a high and pointy hill. Other scholars believe the name originated from the Portuguese, who thought the shape of the hill resembled a loaf of sugarcane, or *pão de açucar*.

That Pão de Açucar is a classic tourist attraction should not daunt the more esoteric traveler. From its peak of 1,300 feet is a view as stunning as Corcovado's and the best view of Corcovado itself. To the west is the entire scope of Copacabana and Ipanema beaches, to the north the district of Botafogo with Corcovado behind, to the east the neighborhoods of Laranjeiras, Flamengo, Santa Teresa, and Guanabara Bay, and to the south the Atlantic Ocean. In 1912, a rickety cable of wooden carriages probably frightened more visitors than it thrilled as it rumbled up the mountainside, but today you can ride to the top in a modernized cable car that holds up to 75 passengers.

The most romantic time to visit Sugarloaf is at sunset, when the mountain is bathed in ever-deepening hues of pink. Even the twinkling lights of the slums fiercely clinging to the hillsides seem picturesque in the glow of twilight. The cable-car trip has two stages. It first stops at the **Morro da Urca**, where there is a large restaurant and entertainment complex. The second stop takes you to the peak, which can become quite windy on overcast days. At night, the temperature turns decidedly nippy, so take a sweater and hold on to your hat and sunglasses so that they don't go sailing off toward Copacabana. A camera is a must.

> **UP CLOSE TIP:** *Film, batteries, and souvenirs bought at Sugarloaf will actually cost about two to three times the normal rate, so stock up before you go.*

With some inventiveness, you could actually spend the entire day here. There is a great tropical bird collection with screaming toucans and macaws, as well as a small playground (but, seriously, was that an alligator I saw slithering about, or just a big lizard?). Every Mon. evening at 10 p.m., the Beija-Flor Samba School presents a well-received show featuring authentic Carnaval costumes and near-naked *sambistas*. Rock concerts are often held in the amphitheater, and during the afternoon you may overhear some young bloods or even famous artists practicing for their shows.

The latest eco-trend at Sugarloaf is to forego the sissy cable car and actually climb the damn thing. (The first recorded scaling was made by an Englishwoman in 1817.) Though I personally cannot attest to the glories of this trek, it's rumored to take about two days and you don't need a special permit. You must, however, hire a guide. Call **Rio Tur** (☎ *242-8000*).

> ❖ **GETTING HERE:** *Many travel agencies offer half- and full-day tours that include Sugarloaf. It's very easy to go by yourself, however. Every taxi driver knows it – just make sure he/she takes the direct route. From Copacabana you can take the #511 bus. Cars run from 8 a.m.-10 p.m. at 30-minute intervals, or continuously if the demand is heavy. A tourist information booth manned by Rio Tur can answer any questions you may have about Rio in general. For more information, ☎ 541-3737.*

## Santa Teresa

If old Rio exists anywhere, it is in the winding cobblestone streets and Victorian mansions perched precariously on the hillside in the district of Santa Teresa. During the 19th century, prosperous landowners and businessmen constructed high-walled gardens and fabulous homes here to take advantage of the cooling winds and remote privacy, and even today the isolated neighborhood retains much of its distinctive, if slightly bohemian charm.

For years the most colorful way to appreciate the neighborhood was to take the *bonde*, an open-air streetcar that moseys over an antiquated track from a station near the New Cathedral in Largo da Carioca. In recent years the trolley has been a target of lightning-fast assailants who jump on and off the usually jam-packed trains. These days, policemen ride shotgun on most trams, but they can't guarantee your safety. If you do decide to brave the trolley, leave all valuables at home and sit near the security guard.

> **UP CLOSE TIP:** *If you take the tram, don't take your camera, and carry only the money you need for the day, preferably inside your clothes. The better way to see the neighborhood is to hire a private car (see Hands-On Rio).*

### Chácara do Céu Museum

*Rua Almirante Alexandrino, 316, store B;* ☎ *232-6570. Tues.-Sun., noon-10 p.m.*

This is one of the major stops in Santa Teresa. The modernist mansion was formerly the home of Raymundo de Castro Maia, one of Rio's leading industrialists, whose dabblings in the art world managed to amass one of the greatest private collections in Brazil. Adorning the walls are works by Brazil's finest modernists, such as Portinari, Di Cavalcanti, and Volpi, as well as impressive originals by Picasso, Matisse, Dali, Modigliani, and Monet. Outside, the landscaped gardens invite contemplative walks, as well as offering awesome views of the bay and downtown Rio.

Afterwards, gear up for a slightly uphill jaunt to the district's most bohemian hangout – **Bar do Arnaudo** – where you'll find some of the best artists and intellectuals passionately discussing the day's latest political mess.

## Tijuca Forest

☎ *224-3242. Hours: 8 a.m.-5 p.m. daily. Free.*

Long before the first colonists arrived, 95% of Rio and much of southern Brazil was blanketed with dense tropical rainforest that cooled the heated air and provided a magnificent self-sufficient ecosystem for literally thousands of lifeforms. Sadly, only 9% of that chain, known as the **Atlantic Forest**, remains in any visible form (having endured a destruction rate decidedly more devastating than that of the Amazon forest). The good news, however, is that a sizable portion of this forest can be found right in the middle of Rio – in the **Tijuca National Park**.

By some estimates the largest city forest in the world (about 175 square km.), the area of the park was once the property of a wealthy nobleman who slashed and burned the forest to make way for coffee plantations. By the 1850s, however, the city managed to replant 100,000 trees and a second growth flourished. Today the park is an eco-paradise of stunning waterfalls, exotic jungle trails, tropical flowers, and even Tarzan-like swinging vines. Tour buses usually stop at the best views: the **Vista Chinesa**, 38 meters high (125 feet), with a homage to the Chinese immigrants who came to work on tea plantations; the **Mesa do Imperador**, where Dom Pedro I and his family loved to romp; and the **Dona Marta Mirante**, with a riveting view of Botafogo, Sugarloaf, and Guanabara Bay. The **Mesa do Imperador** is the best place to picnic, and if you follow the map, you can hike the trails alone. For the kind of eco-trekking you will remember for a long time, hire a private guide, who will provide expert leadership, security, and even specialized birdwatching and botany tours. Don't forget to wear your swimsuit under your hiking shorts: taking a dip in one of the many waterfalls is a sensuous experience you will never forget. Near the **Cascatinha de Taunay** is one of the most delightful waterfalls, the rustic **Mayrink Chapel**, most notable for the altar painting by the great Brazilian

20th-century master, Cândido Portinari. Two restaurants within the park offer dining options from rustic to more-than-rustic. The better one, called **Os Esquilos** (The Squirrels), serves only adequate food, but is surrounded by enormous trees and the chirping of birds.

❖ **GETTING HERE:** *Many travel agencies offer bus tours through Tijuca Forest, but in most cases you'll just see the trees from the window. A great guided trek (offering a superb way to experience the wet, moist, and cool crunchiness of the Atlantic chain) is supplied by **Rubéms Topelem** (☎ 256-8297, 236-6400), the owner of Bicho Solto, a two-person eco-agency, and a former physicist with poetry still in his veins – he knows enough about tropical botany to make tangled roots and slimy fungus a joy. Tours last about 2½ hours ($35) and you can extend it by visiting a favela. During winter, the forest can get cool, so take a jacket; it's a great option for a gray Rio day since sun rarely penetrates the forest anyway.*
*If you want to take public transportation (not recommended), catch bus #221 from Praça XV de Novembro, or #223 or 234 from the main bus terminal.*

## Jardim Botânico

*Rua Jardim Botânico, 10008; ☎ 274-4897. 8:30 a.m.-6 p.m. Mon.-Fri. Fee: $2.*

This luxurious ecological paradise was the creation of Dom Jõao VI, who designed a living laboratory to test the many exotic spices and plants his farmers imported from the East Indies. The 34-acre **Botanical Garden** boasts over 8,000 different kinds of trees and plants, as well as 268 enormous royal palms majestically lining the main promenade like courtiers. The grounds, part cultivated, part jungle, are a relaxing place to stroll, picnic, and birdwatch among the many ponds, shady leafed clearings, and stunning 18th-century bronze fountains. There is also a museum, a botanic library, and an exotic plants collection, including the famous Victoria Régis water lilies from the Amazon that look like Mad Hatter saucers.

**UP CLOSE TIP:** *For an extra-special experience of the Atlantic rainforest, consider a two-day/night excursion to the city of Acadia (about a 90-minute drive from Rio). Jeeps will transfer you to the small village of Lagoa das Lontras, where you commence an easy 3½-hour trek through the rainforest. After a refreshing swim in the São Pedro River, another trek (medium-hard) lasts about 1½ hours. A campsite is made in a natural granite cave that accommodates up to 12 people. The next day a visit to the ruins of a church is followed by a feijoada lunch and eventual return to Rio. A biologist guide accompanies the tour, and rucksack, mattress, raincoat, and sleeping bag are all provided. For more information contact: **Diana Turismo**, Av. N.S. de Copacabana, 330; ☎ 255-2296.*

## Quinta Da Boa Vista

Formerly owned by the Jesuits, the sprawling grounds of this natural park were later appropriated by Dom João VI for use by his family. Today, the city-owned complex, which can be enjoyed in a full day, includes the **Jardim Zoológico** (the zoo) and the **Nacional Museu** (National Museum), as well as hundreds of acres of fine shaded park.

The zoo is a wonderful place to watch Brazilian families in action and also offers a close-up of Brazil's finest jungle creatures, even if the caged animals do appear to be a little depressed. Alligators, monkeys, snakes, and big cats abound, as do some impressive African elephants. The tropical bird collection is out of this world, but the star is Tião, a big black ape who became famous for throwing water on the mayor and still seems to be in a perpetual funk.

> **UP CLOSE TIP:** *The unshaded sidewalks of the zoo can get extremely hot, so bring a sun hat, shade, and lots of sunscreen. Most important: keep track of young boys who may be enviously eyeing your camera equipment.*

Children will adore taking the little train through the park, which ends at the national museum, a palatial estate displaying prehistoric fish skeletons, artifacts from Pompeii, crafts by American and Amazonian Indians, macumba statues, and folkloric crafts. Within the park itself, canoes can be rented for paddling around the ponds, and shows are often performed on a Grecian-columned stage in the middle of a lake. The sprawling park is a perfect place for picnics and strolls, although weekends are often crowded.

❖ **GETTING HERE:** *Take the metro to the Estação Cristóvão stop, or bus #472 or 474 from Copacabana.*

## Parque do Flamengo

*Av. Infante Dom Henrique, 85.*

Mostly frequented by residents of the neighboring *bairro* of the same name, **Flamengo Park** is the biggest city park in the world. Stretching from Botafogo Beach to the Santos Dumont Airport, it runs alongside the Marina da Gloria, as well as Flamengo Beach, and was the vision of the famous botanical professional Paisagista. He used the landscaping artistry of Roberto Burle Marx, who managed to plant over 13,000 trees representing nearly every Brazilian species. Completed in 1960, the complex boasts two restaurants, excellent jogging and biking trails, basketball, soccer and tennis courts, playgrounds and a sports arena. On Sun., northbound traffic is closed so that visitors can stroll, play and flirt in the street. The park also houses the **Museum of Modern Art** and the **Carmen Miranda Museum**, as well as the **World War II Soldier's Memorial**. The park is wonderful for children, and is best visited in the accompaniment of a private guide.

# Museums

## Fine Arts

### Museu de Arte Moderna

*Av. Infante D. Henrique, 85 (Parque Brigadeiro Eduardo Gomes, Flamengo);*
☎ *210-2188. Tues.-Sun., noon-6 p.m.*

In 1952, the architect and urbanist Afonso Eduardo Reidy received 40,000 square meters (10 square acres) on the landfill of Flamengo to construct Rio's Museum of Modern Art. Inaugurated in 1958, the hangar-type construction is considered to be the acme of modernist style (others think it looks merely like an airport hangar). MAM (as it is affectionately called) has become a space for innovation and the ever-changing showcase of local culture, hosting the main artistic movements of Rio, such as the "Neoconcretism" of the 50s and the "Nova Figuração" (New Design) of the 60s, among others.

A fire in 1978 destroyed 90% of its collection, but in recent years about 4,000 important works have been donated by Gilberto Chateaubriand, one of Brazil's most renowned collectors. These include works by Anita Malfatti, Do Cavalcanti, Portinari, Panceti, and Djanira. Besides a library that specializes in the arts, you'll also find a fine movie collection, a research center, art workshop and arena for fairs. The restaurant makes this a nice stop for lunch, particularly if you are visiting Flamengo Park and beach.

### Museu Nacional de Belas Artes
### (National Fine Arts Museum)

*Av. Rio Branco, 199 (downtown);* ☎ *240-0068. Tues.-Thurs., noon-4:30 p.m., Sat. & Sun. 3-6 p.m. Free.*

This is one of the most beautiful buildings in downtown Rio. It was constructed in 1908 in French Renaissance style to imitate the Louvre, but was first used to house the National Academy of Fine Arts. Since 1937, when the museum was installed, the collection has grown to over 20,000 pieces, including paintings and sculptures of both native and international artists. The permanent exhibition offers an interesting overview of Brazilian culture as it developed over the centuries. Photography is prohibited. If you'd like a specialized guide who speaks fluent English, call for an appointment.

❖ **GETTING HERE:** *Take the metro to Carioca station or a city-bound bus to Av. Rio Branco.*

# Historical

## Museu Histórico Nacional

*Praça Marechal Ancora;* ☎ *220-5829 or 240-2092. Tues.-Fri. 10 a.m.-5:30 p.m., weekends and holidays 2:30-5:30 p.m.*

An architectonic treasure, the building that houses Rio's National Historical Museum boasts its own colorful history. Once the site of the 17th-century Santiago fortress at the base of Castelo Hill built to defend Guanabara Bay, it later became a military prison where slaves were detained and tortured. Since 1922, when the building was used for exhibitions during Brazil's Centennial celebrations, it has served as a museum. The collection of over 130,000 objects, from furniture and weapons to painting and sculpture. Sections tell the story of Brazilian history from the moment Cabral discovered its shores up to the time of the Republic in 1889. There is also a research library and an archive of manuscripts.

## Museu Da República

*Tues.-Sun. from noon-5 p.m. Free.*

From 1887 to 1960, when the capital of Brazil was transferred to Brasília, the Catete Palace was the private residence and headquarters of the country's presidents. Today it's a historical museum starting where the national historical museum leaves off – at the beginning of the republic. It features presidential memorabilia, including the bedroom where President Getúlio Vargas committed suicide. In 1985 the museum was restored; in evidence still are exquisite stained-glass windows and an impressive skylight. The Folklore Museum (see below) is nearby.

> ❖ **GETTING HERE:** *Take the subway to the Catete stop. Rua do Catete, 153;* ☎ *225-4873 and 225-4875.*

## Museu da Imagem e do Som

*Praça Rui Barbosa, 1, Praça XV (downtown);* ☎ *262-0309. Mon.-Fri. 1-6 p.m.*

The development of Brazil's social history as told through books, film, photos, records, and tapes. Fascinating photos of Rio from the first 40 years of this century. Call to verify hours.

# Music & Theater

## Museu Villa-Lobos

*Rua Sorocaba, 200 (Botafogo);* ☎ *266-3845.*

Established in 1960, in honor of Brazil's most famous classical composer, Heitor Villa-Lobos. If you don't know his works already, look up his **Bacchianas Brasileiras No. 5** for high soprano, one of the most beautiful pieces of classical music. The museum has a display of personal possessions and original scores. Tapes and records are on sale.

## Museu Carmen Miranda

*Parque Brigadeiro Eduardo Gomes, in front of #560 of Av. Rui Barbosa (Flamengo); ☎ 551-2597. Tues.-Fri. 11 a.m.-5 p.m., weekends and hols 1-5 p.m.*

Revel in the fruit-basket headdresses and tight ruffled dresses of the Brazilian songbird whose memory still lingers on in the drag queens of Miami. Stock up on T-shirts, postcards, and records. Located in Flamengo Park, near the Hotel Glória.

# Native Culture

## Museu do Indio (Indian Museum)

*Rua das Palmeiras, 56 (Botafogo); ☎ 286-8899. Mon.-Fri. 10 a.m.-5 p.m.*

A must if you're headed for the Amazon, this small but discriminating collection of Indian artifacts tells the story of native life in Brazil. Exhibitions range from dress, jewelry, weapons, and daily utensils to a fascinating selection of native music and language. Researchers will also find the stock of documentary films on contemporary aboriginal issues provocative.

## Museu do Folclore

*Rua do Catete, 179; ☎ 285-0441. Fri. 11 a.m.-6 p.m.; weekends and holidays 3-6 p.m.*

A wealth of art, artisanry, costumes, and utensils by popular Brazilian artists working with folk traditions. A good introduction.

## Casa do Pontal

*3295 Estrada Pontal*

> **UP CLOSE TIP from Bonnie Kassel:** *"Just outside of Rio in Recreio dos Bandeirantes, near the beaches of Grumari and Prainha is* **Casa do Ponyal**, *THE best folk art museum I have seen anywhere in Brazil. Frenchman Jacques Van de Beuque, now in his 70s, has spent the last 40 years collecting and has built a small museum with his own money. Pressing buttons activates hundreds of carved and painted wooden figures – some life-sized. Any lover of art must come here. Since it's near the beach, there are a couple of typical thatched roof restaurants for a simple grilled fish lunch."*

# Rocks, Gems & Jewelry

## Museu H. Stern

*Rua Visconde de Pirajá, 490.*

Among Brazil's greatest natural resources are the scores of semi-precious crystals and gemstones discovered mostly in the state of Minas Gerais since the 18th century. The art of creating fine jewelry from these stones is a well-developed Brazilian craft – a process that can be seen in the lapidary workshops of one of the country's leading jewelers, H. Stern. A free 15-minute tour conducted in a multitude of languages (through earphones) will guide you through the cutting and polishing of the stone to the design and construction of the finished piece. In the small museum on the same site you'll view some of the world's largest uncut gemstones, both polished and raw. For big purchases, helpful salesmen who speak excellent English will assist you in private. Most clients at four-star and five-star hotels receive invitations that include free transportation, but you can also call one of the company's many outlets and arrange an appointment.

Also try: **Museum Amsterdam Sauer**, Rua Garcia D'Avila, 105 (Ipanema); ☎ 512-4746.

## Astronomy

### Planetário da Cidade do Rio de Janeiro

*Praça Padre Leonel França;* ☎ *274-0096.*

A bit disappointing if you've visited Epcot Center, but Rio's only planetarium still attracts those interested in the constellations of the southern hemisphere. The 45-min. shows are held on Sun.: 4:30 p.m. for children, 6 p.m. for teenagers, and 7:30 p.m. for adults, with all explanations in Portuguese. The classical music soundtrack is both relaxing and inspiring. On Wed. when the sky is clear, an astronomer allows visitors to peruse the night skies through a telescope around 6:30 p.m.

# Galleries

The thriving art community in Rio has numerous galleries, the finest of which are listed below. Check the newspapers for announcements of openings, or ask the concierge if you're staying in a five- or four-star hotel. Personal tours of galleries and museums may be guided by Paulo César, ☎ *(21) 208-8369*, who himself is an up-and-coming abstract and naif artist.

### Naif Art (African & Folkloric Tendencies)

**Galeria de Arte Jean Jacques**, Rua Ramon Franco, 49; ☎ *542-1443.*

### Contemporary Art

**Galeria Saramenha,** Shopping da Gávea, Rua Marques de São Vicente, 52, loja 165; ☎ *274-9445.* **Galeria Bonino,** Rua Barata Ribeiro, 578 (Copacabana); ☎ *235-7831.*

### Traditional Art (Brazilian Artists in European Styles)

**Galeria Europa**, Av. Atlântica, 3056 B; ☎ *256-4574.* **Galeria de Arte Borghese**, Shopping da Gávea, Rua Marquês de São Vicente, 52; ☎ *259-6793.*

# Artist Studios

Buying work at the artist's studio rather than a gallery can save you up to 50%. You also get the opportunity to meet the artist in person and discuss his work (not to mention, snoop around his studio). The following artists open their studios to interested clients. Call to make appointments in advance.

### Contemporary Abstract & Naif

**Barão de Morallis**, Rua Torres Homem 440, casa 14 (101), Vila Isabel; ☎ 208-8369.

### Conceptual Colorist

**Anisio Carvão**, Rua Souza Lima, 138, apt. 1301; ☎ 287-6800.

### Academic & Abstract Painting

**Rubens Monteiro**, Rua Evaristo da Veiga, 35, apt. 1513; ☎ 240-2751.

### Northeast Regionalist & Abstract

**Wanderley Santana**, Rua Mem de Sá, 72, apt. 502; ☎ 222-4772.

# Especially For Children

You may find it a horrifying thought, but children will love Rio. There are plenty of things to do that will keep them entertained, happy, and safe. Rio-friendly children should either be so young they won't remember the trip or old enough to follow directions immediately. (Children should never be left alone.) Hotels like the Inter-Continental and Rio Sheraton, which are more isolated from the hubbub of the city, are safer for small children. Here are some suggested activities for kids of all ages, even the ones over 40.

### Fazenda Alegria ("Happy Farm")

*Estrada da Boca do Mato, (Vargem Pequena);* ☎ *342-9066.*
*Sat., Sun. and holidays 10 a.m.-5 p.m.*

A popular ecology farm for kids with waterfalls and pettable animals, including lambs and mini-ponies. Lunch is available.

### Jardim Zoológico (Zoo)

*Quinta da Boa Vista;* ☎ *254-2024. Daily 9 a.m.-4:30 p.m. $2.*

Besides 2,500 animals, there are snack bars, clean toilets, and acres of adjoining grounds for picnics. (See above.)

## Mini-Rio Barra Shopping

*Av. das Américas, 4666;* ☎ *325-5611. Daily, 10 a.m.-10 p.m. About $6.*

While the adults shop, kids will enjoy the playground on the first level, which almost rates as a small circus. Bumper cars, airplane rides and boat rides for the wee-sized.

## Tivoli Parque

*Av. Borges de Medeiros (Lagoa);* ☎ *274-1846. Thurs. and Fri. 2 p.m.-8 p.m., Sat. 2-10 p.m., and Sun. 10 a.m.-10 p.m.*

An amusement park open every day during the afternoons in Lagoa, with a special Mini-Tivoli for children 2 to 10. *Cariocas* usually spend two-three hours there; you can go anytime and find it full.

## Flamengo Park

The largest landscape project in Rio, with jogging and bicycle tracks, tennis courts, places for picnics, museums and restaurants. (See above.)

## Planetário (Planetarium)

*Rua Padre Leonel Franca, 240 (Gávea);* ☎ *274-0096.*

Special shows for adults and kids.

## Lokau

*Av Sernambtiba, 5800 (Barra da Tijuca),* ☎ *433-2429.*

If you're bathing at the beaches in Barra with children, don't miss a trek to Lokau (The Spot). Built on a small estate, it hosts a menagerie of animals, including ducks, toucans, monkeys, and peacocks, as well as an expensive open-air restaurant. Children can be let loose to roam around on their own. Eat on the outdoor deck facing the Lagoa of Marapindi, full of tiny protected alligators. (See *Culinary Rio*.)

## Babysitters

The concierge of your hotel will most likely be able to find you a reliable babysitter.

# Rainy Days In Rio

There may come a day in your stay in Rio when you've either overstayed your time in the sun (and you're so red you can't sit down) or, God forbid, it's raining. Rio is a sad city on a rainy day; the sea turns mopey gray, the sky hangs ominously over the mountaintops, and even Corcovado disappears in the fog. To keep you from moping in your hotel room and complaining about how much money you're wasting, here are some suggestions to take up the slack.

- ☐ Visit the **Museum of Fine Arts** and take a long lunch next door at the elegant **Café do Teatro.**
- ☐ Browse the chic stores at **Barra Shopping Ctr**, take lunch at Guimas, a movie, then a few rides at the amusement park.
- ☐ Visit a great health club like **AKXE**, where there's a fantastic Olympic-sized pool, great-looking members, and state-of-the-art equipment.
- ☐ **Souvenir shop** for the perfect crystal-carved bird or chess set down Rua N.S. de Copacabana.
- ☐ Visit the **Carmen Miranda Museum** and learn to sing *Down South American Way* with the right accent.
- ☐ Visit the **H. Stern Museum** and workshop (they'll pick you up), design your own jewelry, then pay for it on credit.
- ☐ Visit the **studios of up-and-coming artists**, followed by **afternoon tea** at the Caesar Park Hotel or the Meridien Hotel.
- ☐ Check **neighborhood cinemas** in Copacabana and Ipanema – they usually offer new American films with Portuguese subtitles (an interesting way to learn bad words in Portuguese).
- ☐ Sleep in, take brunch at the **Confeitaria Colombo**, take another nap, then indulge in an all-night orgy of Rio by dark.
- ☐ Get drunk at the **Garota de Ipanema Bar** and try to whistle all the bossa nova classics you know.
- ☐ Check out the music stores and listen to the latest releases.

## A Must On Sundays

### São Bento Church

*Rua Dom Gerardo, 68 (downtown);* ☎ *291-7122. 8 a.m.-5:30 p.m. Sun. mass at 10 a.m.*

Built in the neighborhood of Saúde on one of the original four hills that once marked colonial Rio, São Bento ranks as one of the most beautiful and richly adorned churches in the country. Construction was begun in 1617 on land bequeathed to Benedictine monks who had sailed from Portugal via Bahia; the architect, sculptor, and painter were all priests who lived on the site during construction. The entire facade remained simple in contrast to the deeply baroque interior – an intentional device to shock the parishioners into awe as they entered through the portals. When the French invaded Rio in the 18th century, a cannon was placed in the temple to protect it. In 1938, the church, monastery, and hill became a national patrimony.

The dark and humid atmosphere inside the church is steeped in mysticism. Large silver censors handmade in the 18th century hang from the ceiling, and the seven-tiered, gold-inlaid altar is strewn with gold-leafed curlicues, saints, and candelabras in every possible nook. Particularly exquisite is the rendering of the Madonna breast-feeding the baby Jesus surrounded by cherubs. On Sun., a marvelous **choir of monks** singing Gregorian chants accompanies the high Benedictine mass replete with incense and carillons, making it one of the most transcendent musical experiences in Rio. The officiating priest may go on interminably about such favorite Latin topics as infidelity, but feel free to leave early or take photos, as long as you don't disturb the other worshippers. Also, leave time to stroll around the lovely landscaped gardens that look down on Guanabara Bay and Praça Mauá, once a seedy port that's now being renovated.

The church is on a slight incline reached by an elevator at Rua Dom Gerardo, 40, or you may walk or drive up the hill. After services, walk to Av. Rio Branco and catch a taxi.

## Villa Rio

*Estrada da Gavea, #728;* ☎ *322-1444.*

**From Bonnie Kassel:** "Located in the lush hills of São Conrado, this is one of the last great plantation houses with beautiful gardens, and open to the public on Sun. for *feijoada*. Often there is music as well. Polished mahogany floors, and colonial paintings of saints take you back centuries. Owner Cesarina is an incredible cook and opening her house to the public is how she's managing to keep the house and land intact."

# Rio By Foot

This is an energetic walking tour of downtown, which focuses on what's left of historical Rio. On this route, however, are also shopping diversions and enjoyable pit stops, so you can make the excursion a full-day outing. Of course, many travelers will not want to give up their day at the beach to see churches and old palaces, but for architecture buffs and art connoisseurs, this walk can give an exciting glimpse of what it was like to live in Rio from the 17th century on.

> **UP CLOSE TIP:** *Best time to take this tour is on Thurs. and Fri. to catch the outdoor markets. Weekends will give you more breathing space, but always watch out for your purse or wallet.*

### Praça XV

The best place to enter the heart of historical Rio is here, where Dom João VI did. It was at the waterfront in 1808 that the King of Portugal, fleeing Napoleon's conquering armies, first arrived in southern Brazil, and where, 81 years later, his grandson, Pedro II, would be forced by the newly declared republic to return to Portugal in exile.

### Palácio Imperial

A few steps from the docks, on the square originally known as **Largo do Paço** looms the formidable white palace with green shutters and grilled balconies that was originally built in 1743 for the local governor of what are now the states of Rio de Janeiro and Minas Gerais. Later, it was where Dom João and his family both lived and worked. It was also here, on the palace steps, in 1888, that Princesa Isabel proclaimed all of Brazil's slaves free – an act that was accompanied, at least for the moment, by cheering crowds and dazzling fireworks. In recent years, the magnificent architecture of the palace has been restored to reflect its former glory in the 1850s and is primarily used for concerts and exhibitions.

## Cândido Mendes Escola Técnica de Comércio

Walking down Rua Premiero de Março, you'll come to what is now a law school but was formerly a monastery where the colorful Queen Maria I of Portugal (the mother of João VI) often resided while in Brazil. Known as Dona Maria, she was officially declared a madwoman by the powers that be (epilepsy – the true cause of her raving fits – was not medically recognized until 200 years later), and she spent the rest of her years here, until her death in 1816, under house arrest.

## "Antigo Cais do Periodo Canal"

Walking towards the overpass, turn left at the sign and soon you'll come upon an 18th-century fountain, where servants had to arrive by canoe to fill their jugs with water (the ocean at that time flowed up this far!). Notice that the stonemaker showed himself to be a nationalist by incorporating gray Brazilian granite with Portuguese white marble. To the side of the imperial palace is the statue of General Osário – hero of the Paraguayan War in 1894; his mummified body is actually buried underneath.

## Arco de Telles

On the northern side of the square is this colonial arch dating back to the 18th century. It was built by a rich traditional family named Telles and the same architect who built the imperial palace.

## Travessa do Comércio

Behind the arch runs a narrow cobblestone alleyway with authentic, centuries-old architecture, one of the most charming streets in Rio. In the 18th century, this street, definitely the boulevard of power, linked the palace to Rua Ouvidor, where the common folk lived.

## Bolsa de Valores

The first building to the right of the arch is the home of Rio's stock exchange. During the 19th century, the grilled verandas, tall roofs and neoclassic columns of the upper-class homes above street level contrasted starkly with the Mack-the-Knife set of beggars, prostitutes and thieves who populated the seedy taverns below. Dom Pedro I, a libidinous fellow, loved to frequent the *travessa*'s bars in disguise. Stories are numerous; it's been said that one night, as a group of hooligans unwittingly harassed him, a young man who suddenly recognized the ruler jumped up and yelled, "At your service, Your Majesty!" The audacious act inspired the drunken Pedro to dub him his personal secretary on the spot.

On Thurs. and Fri., the square bursts with energy as vendors cram into the cobblestone plaza hawking every item imaginable – from clothes to handicrafts to food and antique coins.

## Travessa do Comércio

On this street is the house where **Carmen Miranda,** the Brazilian bombshell, lived with her family during the 20s and 30s (#13, second floor). Her mother owned a cheap restaurant down below on street level. Note how the street becomes so narrow that an antique lamp connects to both sides of it.

## Rua do Ouvidor

Turn right here and you'll eventually come across some good restaurants (lunchtime only). On the cross street, Rua Mercado, one of the most noted restaurants, **Cabeça Grande,** is over 70 years old. Turning left on Rua Rosário to Rua dos Mercadores (a street so narrow it makes a pretty frame for the church at its end), you'll discover Galeria Paulo Fernandes.

## Galeria Paulo Fernandes

*Rua do Rosário, 38, 2nd floor (corner at Rua dos Mercadores);* ☎ *253-8582. Tues.-Fri., 10 a.m.-8 p.m.; weekends, 2 p.m.-6 p.m.*

The exhibition is sure to be among the most avant-garde in Brazil at this brand new art gallery; even the skylight is impressive, leftover from colonial times, and the balcony gives a connoisseur's view of the street below. Beside the gallery building, you'll find a superb outdoor brass sculpture by artist **Nelson Felix**, nicknamed "La Donna é Mobile," because of its identifiably female shape that blows in the wind.

At this point you may return the way you came (back to the Imperial Palace) and cross Av. Primeiro de Março to the Nossa Senhora do Carmo da Antiga Sé (see below). Alternatively, continue to walk down the street beside the gallery to Rua Visconde Itaboraí to what was formerly Banco do Brasil, and which is now an impressive cultural center.

## Espaço Cultural dos Correios (Cultural Corridor)

*Open 10 a.m.-10 p.m., Tues.-Sun.*

One hundred and ten years old, the bank was founded by a Portuguese family in 1808 and now houses the pride of Rio – an impressive array of cultural events throughout its six floors, including art exhibits, videos, historical archives and free musical performances. Ride the stylish green Greek Revivalist elevator to the charming teahouse on the second floor, where you may enjoy lunch and afternoon tea. There are several computerized information centers with what-to-do-in-the-city listings in English.

## Casa Franca-Brasil

On the right of the bank is this white-and-orange Customs House, the most important Classic Revival building in Brazil. Inside, an enormous hall suggests the facade of a Greek temple (though the columns are wood). Interesting temporary exhibitions are often held here. Outside, take a look at the **palmito decorativo**, a most unusual tree whose branches seem to stream down like a cascade of dreadlocks.

If you have returned to the Imperial Palace and Praça XV, cross Av. Primeiro de Março.

## Nossa Senhora do Carmo da Antiga Sé

This church, built in the 1750s, is where Dom Pedro I was crowned as the first Constitutional Emperor and Perpetual Defender of Brazil in 1822. Since 1808 it was used as the city's cathedral until the 1970s, when the New Cathedral was built. It's a fine example of Portuguese architecture in Rio, with its pure-gold adornments and original blue tiles. Visit the cathedral store and check out the eerie plastic heads brought by parishioners who have prayed for their loved one's healing. When the person is healed, the heads are placed on one of the side altars in the cathedral as tokens of gratitude. Mass is held on Wed. at 9 a.m. and Fri. at 12:20 p.m.

## Igreja da Ordem Terceiro de Nossa Senhora do Monte do Carmo

This beautiful church was founded in 1761. The magnificent rococo facade is matched only by the chapel's stunning silver altar, decked with arabesque flowers, candelabras and a multi-tiered throne featuring statues of the Divine Mother and Jesus. The stalls housed rich families, who most often came to church just to be seen. The seven altars represent images of Christ in his various worshipped forms. Today it's considered very fashionable to be married here. Mass is held daily on the hour from 8 a.m. to 1 p.m.

## Igreja de Nossa Senhora da Candelária

At the end of Rua Primeiro de Março you'll emerge onto Praça Pio X, where an 18th-century church stands. Constructed between 1775 and 1898, this neoclassical structure, with a stunning painted cupola, ranks as the largest and richest church of Imperial Brazil. Its origin harks back to the 17th century, when a Portuguese couple, about to be shipwrecked, prayed to Saint Candelária and promised to build a chapel in her name if their boat did not sink. Miraculously, they were saved and, in gratitude, they built a small chapel at the first harbor they met. The present structure, a marvelous marriage of baroque and renaissance revival styles, took over a century to complete and was fashioned after the Basilica of Estrela in Lisbon.

Walk back to Nossa Senhora do Carmo and turn left at Beco dos Barbeiros to watch the street vendors sell tickets for the lottery called Jogo do Bicho.

## Jogo do Bicho (The Animal's Game)

The illegal (but usually tolerated) game, which runs daily at 2 p.m., with results by 3 p.m., was invented by the baron who owned the old zoo to advertise its treasures to the public. Today, I'm told, the game is so honest that nobody would dare not pay you, although the bankers of the game, who are shunned by high society, are forced to find their social status as presidents of samba schools. (In 1993, a scandal ensued when I was in Brazil as a group of so-called "bankers" were arrested for gambling, an event which threw the samba schools into temporary disarray.) Usually, the areas where the tickets are sold are among the safest in the city, since hidden Mafia-like security is always on patrol.

## Café Sublime

While you're deciding whether to play Jogo do Bicho, stop on the corner for a *cafezinho*, or maybe a *suco de maracajú* (fresh juice). This kind of juice bar, called a *botequim*, is where *cariocas* come after work to relax, schmooze, and show off their new girlfriends.

## Livraria São José

Turn down the cobblestoned Rua do Carmo to this fascinating antique bookstore, where you may find old maps of Rio, as well as used books on anything from music and poetry to physics.

## Rua do Ouvidor

The street of fashion during the 19th century, Rua do Ouvidor was filled with French corsets and gowns, as well as fashionable cafés and restaurants. Walking toward Av. Rio Branco down the cobblestone street, look right and left down the pedestrian streets that cross Rua do Ouvidor, full of *camêlos*, street vendors who peddle everything from cheap cosmetics to dubious cassette tapes and batteries. Take the time to browse and use your best bargaining tricks. Lining Rua do Ouvidor are several banks where you may exchange money and traveler's checks.

## Avenida Rio Branco

Eventually you will arrive at the city's center of commercial power ever since it was inaugurated on Nov. 15, 1905, under the name Avenida Central. In 1912, it was renamed Rio Branco to commemorate the Baron of Rio Branco, José Maria da Silva Paranhos Júnior, whose brilliant legal defenses of Brazil's borders added over 342,000 square miles of land (approximately the size of France) to its territory. Conceived originally as the Champs Elysées of Rio, during the early 1900s the avenue was dotted on both sides by fashionable cafés and boutiques and frequented by upper-class ladies who leisurely strolled down it, followed by their colorful retinues of well-dressed, but barefoot servants.

Crossing Av. Rio Branco, walk toward Rua Gonçalves Dias, where you will see the remains of a group of old Rio buildings. Once fashionable homes, these three-story buildings, with their pink, white, orange and light-blue facades, are now restaurants and shops. From Av. Rio Branco, turn left on Rua Gonçalves Dias, heading for the Confeitaria Colombo.

## Confeitaria Colombo

*Rua Gonçalves Dias 32/36;* ☎ *232-2300; open 8:30 a.m.-6:30 p.m.*

This is a traditional *fin-de-siècle* teahouse and a masterpiece of art nouveau. Originally a meeting place for the intellectuals and artists of Rio, it has retained its magnificent tile floors, stained glass ceiling and humongous Belgian mirrors framed in jacaranda wood. Order a complete tea (*chá completo*) to feast on a parade of dishes that include sweets, breads, and salty hors d'oeuvres, or indulge in some luscious Viennese-style pastries while the piano player bangs out old-fashioned waltzes.

## Praça Floriano

If you're interested in more involved dining, head back toward Av. Rio Branco to this area of Rio that looks like Paris revisited. Since the elite *cariocas* of the late 19th century aped everything Gallic (French was their second language), it was only natural that the city's finest buildings should also emulate Louis XVI style.

## The Teatro Municipal

A small-scale replica of the Paris Opera, the theater has hosted international artists of ballet, opera, and theater ever since its opening in 1909. (To take a tour of the theater, you must make an appointment in advance; English-speaking guides will probably be available.)

## Café do Teatro

If you didn't fill up at Confeitaria Colombo, stop for lunch at the theater's adjacent restaurant, considered one of the best in Rio, as well as being one of the most flamboyantly appointed. Affecting the atmosphere of a chic underground cave, the restaurant boasts huge ceramic tableaus of Assyrian-influenced Persian themes, marked by marble columns and elegant piano music. Even the outside foyer is magnificently arrayed with a tiled tableau of Moliere's *Le Bourgeois Gentilhomme*, among others. Head across the street to the Museum of Fine Arts.

## Museu Nacional de Belas Artes (Museum of Fine Arts)

*Av. Rio Branco, 1991; ☎ 240-0068. Tues.-Fri. noon-4:30 p.m.,*
*Sat., Sun., and holidays 3 p.m.-6 p.m. Free.*

In 1816, the French Artistic Mission arrived in Brazil to arrange the official teaching of art. Ten years later it founded the Imperial Academy of Fine Arts, which exhibited works of both students and teachers as well as those donated by the Imperial family. When the school went public, its name was changed to the National Fine Arts School, which was housed in this building beginning in 1908. In 1937, the museum was officially installed to house the school's collection, which includes over 20,000 pieces. As such, it is the best place to view 19th-century academic Brazilian painting. (One sidelight: when construction started at the turn of the century, builders found the remains of boats, suggesting the waters of the bay had once flowed this far north.)

## National Library

*Av. Rio Branco, 2191; ☎ 240-9229. Mon.-Fri., 9 a.m.-8 p.m.; Sat., 9 a.m.-3 p.m.*

Next door to the museum is one of the most important libraries in South America – The National. It is the sixth largest in the world, with over four million books, including documents brought by the royal family as well as important treaties. If it looks like the Military Academy of Paris, that's because it was patterned after it, evoking Louis XVI style. Situated on the steps around the buildings are numerous vendors selling used records and books; you might pick up some old bossa nova classics. All these buildings are part of the district called **Cinelândia**, so named for the many old-fashioned cinemas that dot the area. These days the neighborhood has been all but usurped by the gay community, which uses the area as a hangout, although singles of all orientations tend to congregate during the day at the numerous cafés and bars.

## Largo Da Carioca

From the Museum of Fine Arts, find the street on the right of the Opera House – Março de 13 – and walk directly to this colorful public square where street vendors hawk their goods, and where artists and like-minded bohemians traditionally congregate.

## Church & Convent of Santo Antônio

Santo Antônio was built between 1608 and 1620 on a low hill overlooking the square. The exquisitely adorned Church of Saint Francis dates from the 18th century. The hill on which the two churches stand is the remains of landfill that was excavated to become Flamengo Park. Santo Antônio (Saint Anthony) is the patron saint of marriages, and young *carioca* girls still come here to light candles in the eternal hope of landing a mate (a perpetual ritual for some, since eligible men in Rio are scarce, so I'm told). June 13 gets practically every single girl and her mother out of hiding when a huge celebration for the saint's birthday is held. If you're in a marrying mood, here's how to make a *pedido* (prayer-request). At the vendor stalls in the church's courtyard, buy a little silver-colored statue of Saint Anthony holding the baby Jesus (called *Santo Antônio com o menino Jesus solto para arranjar um namorado*), then remove the baby Jesus and tell Saint Anthony you will only return the infant when your lover appears. (I actually tried this ploy, but eventually gave up in frustration and returned the baby to Santo Antônio out of pity.) If this strikes you as too religious, another fine remembrance is the key chain made in the shape of a tiny *cachaça* bottle with the image of Saint Anthony inside! As you wander through the church, note the turquoise cherubs sitting on the organ pipes, the Portuguese-crafted image of Christ adorned with a crown of thorns, and the authentic yellow and blue-and-white Portuguese tiles. Before leaving, you can even place a written wish in the crack of the picture frame of Saint Anthony with the Madonna and Child.

## Igreja Da Ordem Terceira Da São Francisco Da Penitência

*Largo da Carioca, 5 (Centro);* ☎ *262-0197. Mon.-Fri., 1 p.m.-5 p.m.*

Next door to Santo Antônio, this church was initiated in the mid-18th century (although the order was constituted as early as 1610). It is the second richest church in Rio, a true example of baroque style (remember that the baroque era arrived late in Brazil, dependent on the discovery of gold in Minas Gerais). The church will probably be closed for repair, but you may call ahead and request special permission to enter. The visit will be worth it, as the images inside are of great beauty and artistic value, in particular the tableau of Saint Francis and the Crucified Jesus at the altar.

## Catedral Metropolitana (Metropolitan Cathedral)

*Rua dos Arcos, 54 (Lapa);* ☎ *240-2669. Mon.-Sat., 7 a.m.-6 p.m.; Sun. 9 a.m.-6 p.m.*

Take the underpass walkway (more or less safe) in front of the convent. You'll be passing under the 36 arches of the Aqueduct da Carioca, one of Rio's best landmarks, designed to carry fresh water from the Santa Teresa neighborhood to the public fountain in the Largo da Carioca. Inaugurated in 1976 after 12 years of work and still unfinished today, the cathedral's stark modernistic construction has been the center of controversy among *cariocas* – one that seems to be falling on the side of those who can't stand it. Actually, the huge cone-shaped construction (83 meters/125 feet high) resembles one of the great Mayan pyramids, and I personally find its airy, New Age spaciousness appealing, though perhaps not exactly appropriate for a baroque Catholic mass. The main door, sculptured with 48 bronze reliefs, is considered the Portal of Faith, and each of the colors used in the imposing stained-glass windows variously symbolize the doctrine of faith (blue), the one gospel for all races (red), and the victory of the Crucifixion (yellow). Beside the main altar stand the protector saints Sebastian and Anna.

*Note:* bathing suits and shorts are not permitted, but culottes are acceptable.

## Capela das Almas

This 17th-century book recording the baptism of slaves can be seen in the basement of the cathedral. Walk through the parking lot to visit the Ossário, a bathhouse-type crypt where the bones of former parishioners are kept. (The sign reading "Don't leave your ashes on the floor" refers to cigarette smokers!)

If you're aching by this time to return to your hotel (probably in Zona Sul), walk up Av. Rio Branco to the bus terminal on Rua São José, where you can take an air-conditioned bus. Your best bet, however, especially if it's hot, is to grab a taxi.

## Praça Tiradentes

Walk back under the aqueduct to Largo da Carioca, then left along Rua Carioca, arriving soon at Praça Tiradentes. This is named after the leader of the so-called Minas Conspiracy of 1789, a complicated political plot that attempted to overthrow the Portuguese rule. (For more information, see the chapter on Minas Gerais.)

## Praça da República

Three blocks west along Rua Visconde do Rio Branco is the Praça da República in the Campo Santana. Spurred on by the arrival of the Portuguese royal family to Rio, the Count of Rezende started to urbanize this area in 1808, and the park was inaugurated in 1880, becoming the site of the court's most popular parties. In 1889 the square was the site for the proclamation of the republic by the Marechal de Deodoro da Fonseca, at which point it got its official name. Today the beautiful landscaped park, suggesting an English style, is an oasis from the agitation of downtown. Unfortunately, it's not considered a safe place to kick back.

# Where To Stay

Whether you stay three days or three weeks in Rio, choosing the accommodation appropriate to your needs can go a long way toward assuring a happy, even safe vacation. As a city geared for pleasure, Rio offers hotel rooms for every budget – from the most princely suites with wraparound verandas to modest digs for under $30-40 a night. If you've come to Rio to tan, you'll be glad to know that the best hotels are located right in the Zona Sul (or South Zone), along the beaches of Copacabana, Ipanema and Leblon. In fact, if your hotel boasts an address on Avenida Atlântica or Avenida Delfim Moreira, all you'll have to do is cross the street and throw yourself into the waves.

EMBRATUR, the official tourist board of Brazil, uses a star rating system, but the results are not really comparable to North American standards, though they do suggest the availability of certain facilities, as well as prices. In general, all five-star hotels have a pool, nightclub, at least two excellent restaurants, a bar, gym, sauna and hair salon. Four-stars generally boast a good restaurant, bar and sauna. Three-stars usually differ from four-stars only in a slight downgrading of decor, while two-stars, with no extra amenities, offer only breakfast. Every hotel room has air conditioning. Where you'll really feel the crunch is in the quality of the "American" breakfast included free of charge in all rates. Five-star hotels outdo each other with fabulous spreads of breads, cheeses, meats, fruits, and often freshly made omelets, while a two-star hotel won't serve more than a roll and coffee.

**Location** is important. Copacabana, while one of my favorite areas, is not the safest or quietest place to stay these days; however, it is at the heart of the city's pulse, and many of the best restaurants, as well as nightly hangouts, are within walking distance. The beaches of Ipanema and Leblon attract more "beautiful people," while Barra these days is considered the hippest beach, with the most preserved shoreline and the highest quotient of celebrity sightings.

If you're concerned about **safety**, the Caesar Park and the Meridien Hotel both provide excellent beach security, with hidden patrols surveilling the strand in front of the hotels at all times. The safest beachside hotel is probably the Sheraton Rio, on an isolated strip of sand that is closely patrolled by its staff. Unfortunately, it's 30 minutes from the South Zone. The best hotels have safes in the rooms, as well as professionally secured drawers behind the reception desk. If you stay at a three- or two-star hotel without room safes, don't bring *any* valuables, and think twice before you rent a security box.

No question about it – staying in a luxurious hotel like the Caesar Park or Rio Palace can be a memorable experience, but if you can't swing it, here's how to save substantial bucks without feeling the pinch. Hotels located a few blocks from the main beach drags are generally cheaper, and the walk isn't bad – *cariocas* are used to seeing bathers stroll through the streets wearing only a coverup. And who needs a pool in Rio, anyhow? Restaurants, hair salons, bars and nightclubs at fine hotels are always open to the public. As for exercise equipment, you might have more fun buying a tourist pass at a neighborhood gym, where you're bound to meet more natives.

For some, a good option is one of the newly trendy **apart-hotels** – residences that are run like hotels but are actually private, completely stocked apartments that may be rented daily. They usually run half the price of hotels and often are better decorated. Those in Barra have all been built in the last five to seven years. Breakfast and maid service is usually included, although the kitchen is fully equipped for cooking. These accommodations are especially good for families or large groups wanting to budget, although the quality of some apart-hotels is so superb you often can't believe the price.

Anyone arriving in Rio without a reservation in high season is living damgerously. The best rooms are sure to be taken, and you will be lucky to find anything suitable. Reservations for Carnaval and during New Year's must be made six months in advance.

If you want to stay at a five-star hotel and don't have time to research them, the American-based, Brazilian-owned **F & H Travel Consulting** can steer you to excellent selections and make all arrangements. Contact: 2441 Janin Way, Solvang, CA 93463; ☎ *800-544-5503*; fax *(805) 688-1021*.

## Rates

Room rates given in this guide usually refer to high season, but note that rates around Carnaval and other prime holidays may be double. Discounts during low-season sometimes run as high as 20%.

### Price Chart (standard double)

| | |
|---|---|
| Very expensive............................ | Over $150 |
| Expensive ................................ | $80-150 |
| Moderate................................. | $40-80 |
| Inexpensive............................... | Under $40 |

# Five-Star Hotels

## Caesar Park

*Av. Vieira Souto, 460 (Ipanema); ☎ (21) 525-2525; fax 521-6000.*

Perhaps the most elegant hotel in Brazil, the Caesar Park in chic Ipanema winningly combines first-class professional service with the kind of luxuries international tourists demand. And for good reason – the Japanese management is part of the Leading Hotels of the World. Which is not to say that Brazilian charm does not abide everywhere; from the mints on your pillow at night to the excellent *feijoada* buffet on Sat., the hotel does everything to make its guests feel the high rates are worth it. The lobby, with its oriental rugs, tropical flowers, and huge grand piano, is immediately inviting, though not exactly the place for screaming kids. The private rooms are just as lavish. The standard, superior, and deluxe suites differ primarily in the view and floor level. Becoming a preferred choice for singles is the *solteiro*, a nook of a studio with single bed, special furnishings, and a magnificent mahogany desk. The white-and-wicker breakfast room resembles a charming teahouse; breakfast is an impeccably arrayed buffet with a chef who prepares fresh omelettes.

The Petronius has been long considered one of the finest restaurants in Rio, serving classical European cuisine; Mariko is also the best Japanese restaurant, although its sushi is outrageously expensive. An English-style pub, the prettiest around, offers the kind of soft bossa nova you rarely hear on the radio. A small pool is easily usurped by the beach across the street, but it does offer private tanning space. The hotel's special security force takes the sting out of beachcombing: two lifeguards (one stationed rooftop) constantly keep sight of clients, who may be identified by the yellow beach tag supplied to each room. A special Carnaval kit includes a ball for guests and visitors, as well as samba shows during meals. In 1993, the hotel began sponsoring music and arts programs throughout the city; if you attend these performances, you can receive a 20% discount at their most prestigious restaurant, Petronius, overlooking the shoreline of Ipanema. *221 apts. Very expensive. All cards.*

## Copacabana Palace

*Av. Atlântica, 1702 (Copacabana);* ☎ *(21) 255-7070; fax 235-7330.*

Certainly one of the oldest landmarks along the southern coast, the Copacabana Palace has never lost its reputation as the town's most elegant address; in fact, its palatial facade always reminds me of a great white wedding cake. Inside, old money talks loud; unfortunately so does old furniture. In recent years the English group Orient Express purchased the hotel and made extensive renovations; in 1995 it was named Hotel of the Year by *Quatro Rodas*, the Brazilian travel Bible. Photos from 1923 show the newly built hotel surrounded by untamed space; now it's wedged in by high-rises, elegant jewelry stores, an exotic flower shop, and dozens of apartment buildings. The Palace's enormous pool has been compared to that of the Beverly Hills Hilton, not only for its size but for its social-climbing activity. Guests might be lucky enough to stumble over a society wedding in the chandelier-filled Salão Nobre, with its massive wraparound veranda. The main building has 10 floors, the annex has six, filled with 75 suites. Deluxe rooms hold double beds, a desk, and art deco lamps; standards are somewhat smaller. Any room with a veranda overlooking the beach is the place to be on New Year's Eve. Newly decorated rooms are cheerful, light and soundproofed.

The breakfast room is one of the most pleasant in Rio, with freshly made pancakes and omelettes, and the highly formal Bife de Ouro restaurant serves international cuisine with an Italian buffet every Thurs. Teatime, a tradition among Brazilian women with stiffly teased hair, is a cultural event not to be missed; make reservations a week in advance. For high season, rooms must be booked six months ahead. *223 apts. Very expensive. All cards.*

## Everest Rio Hotel

*Rua Prudente de Moraes, 1117 (Ipanema);* ☎ *(21) 287-8282; fax 521-3198.*

Tucked into a side street of Ipanema a few easy blocks to the beach, the 17-year-old Everest Rio is a five-minute walk from Chaika's, one of my favorite stops for pizza and ice cream sundaes. The lobby is elegant with burnt-orange leather couches warming the speckled marbled floors. On weekdays the hotel is filled with executives; weekends attract pleasure-seeking tourists. Promotions are available year-round. Standards have only a slice of ocean view squeezed between high-rises; deluxe rooms look out to the Lagoa and Corcovado. The pool on the top floor lies under an open sky, and a separate playground will keep children occupied. Sauna is available for men only. An elegant restaurant with live music is open to the public, and the coffee shop off the lobby is especially attractive, with flowered banquettes and a fast-food counter. Three convention salons cater to large groups. A hair salon and small boutique are also on premises. *166 apts. Expensive. All cards.*

## Glória

*Rua do Russel, 632 (Glória);* ☎ *(21) 205-7272; fax 245-1660.*

One of the most beautiful white facades in the city, the recently refurbished Glória is actually two hotels in one – the first, a five-star page out of *Art and Antiques* magazine, and the second, a budget alternative for large and small groups. The owners, who live on the 10th floor, are antiques fiends who shop the world to furnish the Glória's rooms with an individuality unsurpassed in Brazil. The classical lobby brings back memories of *Dangerous Liaisons*, with sculptured ceilings, love seats, crystal chandeliers, and antique phones that really work. The suites are just as lavish; incredibly enough, there's never been one theft. Suites with two rooms are individually designed and boast some kind of objet d'art in every corner. The best buy is the Imperial Suite, draped in satin and brocade, with Oriental carpets, an antique French receptionist desk, and sculptured arches over the bed. Only the standard rooms remain nearly featureless, though they are large enough to fit three single beds with room to spare. Ask for a reformed standard, which usually includes Oriental rugs and antique sofas. Singles may love Room 802, which, despite a strangely skinny bed, boasts an exquisite mahogany desk and colored chandelier. A few suites and superiors on the 4th floor have sit-on verandas. With its full view of downtown and the Marina da Glória, the panoramic pool is a lovely place to relax at sunset. The gourmet restaurant **La Grita** offers a different cuisine daily. The dark, sexy, cavern-like bar is open till 1 a.m. During Carnaval, the Glória hosts the Concurso de Desfile – a costume competition famous in the city. *700 rooms. Moderate-expensive. All cards.*

## Inter-Continental Rio

*Av. Pref. Mendes de Moraes, 222 (São Conrado);* ☎ *(21) 322-2200; fax 322-5500.*

The Inter-Continental is a large, sprawling hotel situated in one of the recently developed condo areas outside Rio proper. Despite its size, however, the hotel is so intelligently designed that it is virtually impossible to get lost; presently it's reminiscent of a dated Club Med. An elegant arcade of shops and restaurants winds around to a sensuous pool complex, offering a children's pool and several waterfalls. Breakfast is served poolside in an open-air restaurant, which doubles as a breezy lunch buffet. The 20 cabanas facing the pool are perfect for families. Appointed in lime green, beige, and mauve, the spacious standards differ from the deluxes only in their view; in fact, many prefer the standards for their eclectic vistas of ocean, mountain, and Corcovado. All rooms have direct-dial telephones and safes; most bathrooms have tubs and hairdryers. A business center includes a stunning meeting room with free drinks and canapés, international access TV, videos, and journals, and a multilingual secretary. There is a charge for use of the tennis courts. Guests may use the Gávea Golf Club for a hefty fee. Dining options are richly varied, including "the best hamburgers south of Miami" at a '50s-style luncheonette. Improbably hungry guests can also walk a block to São Conrado Fashion Mall, the chic-est in Rio, which is packed with other eateries. Special activities in July will keep children out of your hair, so you can spend the day drinking *cachaça* at the bar inside the pool, or sunbathing at the beautiful beach across the street. The hotel is also a perfect spot for viewing the hang gliders diving off Lookout Rock. *463 apts. Expensive. All cards.*

## Rio Internacional

*Rio Av. Atlântica, 1500 (Copacabana);* ☎ *(21) 295-2323; fax 542-5443.*

The two-year-old Internacional Rio is a well-coordinated, well-organized hotel that serves executives, as well as international tourists. A sleek modern sheen characterizes the decor of both the corridors and the apartments. Deluxe rooms are extremely spacious, in black, white, and gray, with muted lighting and verandas that make them an excellent choice for New Year's. The attractive marble bathrooms come with tub/showers. In the suites, a Japanese sliding door separates the bedroom from the sitting room. A gastronomic festival featuring the cuisine and music of different cultures is held every two months. Breakfast is taken in a sleek and modern wraparound restaurant with a fabulous view of the beach. The sixth-floor business center is stocked with computers, telex, fax, typewriters, and multilingual secretaries. Compact and sleek, the lobby bar is known for its special *caipirinhas* – honey, *cachaça*, and a few drops of Cointreau. *117 apts. Expensive. All cards.*

## Marina Palace

*Rua Delfim Moreira, 630 (Leblon);* ☎ *(21) 259-5212; fax 294-1644.*

Located along the beach in the high-class neighborhood of Leblon, so expect to find rich people sunning next to you. An elegant hush seems to pervade this hotel; corridors are wood-paneled with muted lighting. Bedrooms, individually decorated, all have brightly colored spreads with enamel and wood headboards; wicker chairs and glass-topped tables make a stylishly upbeat effect. Standard rooms offer a view of the beach, but also a peek at the rooftops of the neighboring apartment building – terrific, considering all the nude suntanning. Suites face the ocean. Clients include lots of Americans, Japanese, French, and Germans, who appreciate the fine service. The pool on the open rooftop is minuscule, but it does offer a 360° view of the city. There are two restaurants and a hair salon. *160 apts. Expensive. All cards.*

## Le Meridien

*Av. Atlântica, 1020 (Leme);* ☎ *(21) 275-9922; fax 541-6447.*

The French-owned Meridien is one of Rio's most lavish hotels and knocks itself out to provide the best possible service for its international clientele. One of its biggest advantages is its location in the family-filled neighborhood of Leme – five minutes from Rio Sul shopping center, around the block from excellent restaurants and fast-food joints, and across the street from some of the most exotic shows in Rio. Entrance into the hotel is dramatic: escalators quickly shoot you up to the second-floor reception, where elegant red-suited clerks greet you in a lobby lush with huge crystals and overstuffed banquettes. Even the young elevator boys, their chin-strap caps perched jauntily on their heads, look as if they just stepped out of an MGM movie. Standards – spacious, with an added entrance hall – are done in shades of blue, with plush carpets and a partial view of the sea. Superior rooms boast a full view of the sea, though windows are not uniformly clean. Most impressive are the enormous luxe suites, with raised living area, pillow couches, queen-sized bed, two bathrooms, and trellised shutters opening onto the sea. All bathrooms have tubs, make-up mirrors, 110 volts and Hermès toiletries. The hotel's special festivities are legendary: the New Year's Eve Ball, the Carnaval Costume Parade and Competition, and Oct. international backgammon tournaments. A strong conciergerie takes care of all tickets for excursions and entertainment. The troop restaurants are all first-class. Café de la Paix is a Toulouse-Lautrec-style salon where society ladies gather each afternoon for extravagant teas; Le St. Trop Café, overlooking the beach, is the place to sample French pastries and Brazilian delicacies; around the pool, a daily barbecue buffet serves four kinds of meat and numerous salads; and Le Saint Honoré, on the top floor, offers the best nighttime view of the beach. For late-night music, Le Rond Point Bar, on the first floor, is a chrome-and-glass wonder, with real Magrittes, a stunning wraparound bar, backgammon tables, and sexy maroon couches. *496 apts. Expensive. All cards.*

## Rio Atlântica Suite Hotel

*Av. Atlântica, 2964 (Copacabana);* ☎ *(21) 255-6332; fax 255-6410.*

Built in the last couple of years, the Rio Atlântica has been carefully designed to remain beautiful for years to come. Despite its slick, modern facade, many have observed that the hotel's interior "looks just like Rio," perhaps because of its natural lighting, raw brick walls, and sand-colored decor. The marble lobby comes complete with waterfall, and you must pass an irresistible deli counter before reaching the reception. Half-Swiss, half-Brazilian owned (50% belongs to TV Globo), the hotel brings a Swiss sense of organization to its 228 rooms (120 of which may be booked as two-room suites). The bedrooms, a delightful mix of mauves and gray-greens, are filled with fine furniture; showers hanging from the ceiling are perfect for tall people. Unlike other five-star hotels, here all apartment floors are tiled, not carpeted, to avoid the mustiness that pervades many seaside accommodations. There are also three handicapped suites, as well as some nonsmoking rooms. The outdoor pool has been designed to make swimmers feel they are on a boat in the middle of the ocean. Health-minded guests will adore the gorgeous weight room stocked with Nautilus, imagine pedaling away on a bike in full view of the sea. Dry and wet saunas are also available for a fee, as is massage. A real plus is the 70-seat mini-theater, which hosts premieres in simultaneous translations. A 24-hour takeout service offers some of the best Swiss pastries and pastrami in Rio; even if you're not a guest, stop by for some beach snacks. The Café ao Ponto coffee shop, with its pink luminescent lighting and art nouveau ceiling, looks transplanted from New York. A more formal Swiss-style restaurant serves top-class cuisine. A drugstore, Timberland shoe shop, and H. Stern jewelry store complete the picture. *228 rooms. Expensive. All cards.*

## Rio Othon Palace

*Av. Atlântica, 3264 (Copacabana);* ☎ *(21) 521-5522; fax 521-6697.*

The flagship property of the Othon chain, which has nine hotels in Rio alone, the Rio Othon is geared more toward families than the Meridien or Copacabana Palace. The lobby is dark, cool, and intimate, with numerous couches; the only blemishes are the jewelry store employees, ready to pounce on you as you walk by. Standard rooms with partial ocean views offer adequate space, attractive quilted spreads and plush carpets. The bathrooms in marble and tile are smallish, though each contains a scale, hair dryer and makeup mirror. Executive suites with two bathrooms are bright and sunny, with terrific views that nearly extend out over the beach; the master bedroom is separated from a sitting room by sliding doors. Deluxe rooms can hold an extra bed and sport tiny verandas. The pool is located on the top floor, and the skylight bar gives a wraparound view of the Forte de Copacabana and the west end of the beach, including the Vidigal *favela.* The VIP floor has a 24-hour butler, an executive breakfast room with open bar at night, and a small living room with international newspapers. The coffee shop is a tropical wonder, with waterfalls gracing the back walls. A fancier restaurant, Estância, overlooks the ocean. The gym, with weight machines and sauna, alternates days between the sexes, and the house masseur will even come to your room. Hair styling for women is also available. The lobby bar, a nice place to crash, features a Brazilian singer nightly. *581 apts. Expensive. All cards.*

## Rio Palace

*Av. Atlântica, 4240 (Copacabana);* ☎ *(21) 521-3232; fax 247-3582.*

Enough said that Frank Sinatra and Paul McCartney stay here. Big, posh, and splashy, the Rio Palace fulfills a tropical dream some tourists still pine for – like having brunch on your balcony overlooking the beach. That's why the twin-tower hotel is usually sold out for New Year's Eve – its verandas offer a perfect view of the macumba rituals down below. Moreover, the hotel is extremely user-friendly; clerks are fluent in English, and a special guest-relations director will even do your personal shopping. The pool complex can only be called gloriously self-indulgent; two large pools front and back are so situated as to catch the rays of the sun all day long. Medium-sized rooms are brightly decorated with brocade spreads and dark maroon rugs; all bathrooms come with hairdryers, toiletries, and phone, as well as tub/showers. A glass-enclosed restaurant serves one of the largest breakfasts in the city, with health-food options and a dazzling array of breads, croissants and tropical fruit juices; you can also eat outside on a terrace overlooking the beach. The 8th-floor Imperial Club, for executives, offers a butler, open bar and full secretarial services, as well as elegant meeting rooms. A salon with wicker chairs and a great view of the beach makes afternoon tea a special event. A panoramic elevator takes you to a five-star French restaurant, Le Pré Catalan, and to the Horse's Neck Bar, a dark English pub with live jazz nightly. Replete with antiques from the era of Dom Pedro II, the lobby itself makes an elegant statement, even if the adjacent bar seems to attract certain high-class "ladies" looking for business. The hotel is also connected to the Casino Atlântico, a shopping mall open from 10 a.m.-8 p.m. One warning: Be careful when entering and leaving the hotel as it's a prime spot for thieves. Security, however, is always on hand. *415 apts. Expensive. All cards.*

## Sheraton Rio Hotel & Towers

*Av. Niemeyer, 121 (Vidigal);* ☎ *(21) 274-1122; fax 239-5643.*

A 40-minute drive out from Copacabana is one of the most complete beach resorts in Brazil. With a circular driveway opening onto its Hollywood-style lobby, the Sheraton offers a five-star ambience compatible with any top-class hotel in the world. In fact, guests may completely miss the sense of being in chaotic Rio. With the hotel situated on a lone cliff overlooking an isolated beach, security is excellent; the only access is by a single staircase constantly patrolled by the staff. The 45 special suites are the stuff honeymoon dreams are made of: gauze-canopied beds, bamboo and brocaded walls, thick shag rugs, potted plants and white-shuttered windows opening onto dramatic crashing waves. Even the pastel-colored standards are highly stylish, with verandas, carpeted floors and sliding glass doors. All rooms have safes and bathtubs; most have hairdryers – the only difference in rooms is the amount of ocean view. VIP services are available for the first four floors, known as the Towers, including a business center, private breakfast room and courtesy tea and bar. A nonsmoking floor is offered. The Sheraton has the best hotel gym in Rio, with a full line of exercise equipment, all-day classes, massage, and sauna. Five restaurants include a top-class Italian eatery, a sushi and teriyaki bar, an outdoor barbecue, a Casa da Cachaça, where you can sample native spirits, and an à la carte restaurant with different cuisine nightly. An outdoor amphitheater holds concerts during high season, and special children's activities are offered during the summer. There's no shuttle bus to the city, but a 24-hour car service is available, and public transportation runs close to the hotel. Completing the sense of a self-sufficient city is a bevy of outrageously priced souvenir and clothes shops. *617 apts. Expensive. All cards.*

# Four-Star Hotels

### Califórnia Othon

*Av. Atlântica, 2616 (Copacabana); ☎ and fax (21) 257-1900.*

Computer-organized efficiency vies with the old-world charm here. The building is narrow, sandwiched between other apartment buildings on Copacabana's main beach drag. Standards are large, but lack any view worth opening the drapes for; superiors have a small view. Furniture is somewhat dated, but bathrooms were attractively remodeled in 1988. Antique light fixtures add a smidgen of style. All rooms have safes. The colonial restaurant has established a good rep for quality, comfort and large plates of pasta. There is no pool, but next door is a typical pizzeria and a sidewalk café. *110 apts. Moderate. All cards.*

### Copa D'Or

*Rua Figueiredo Magalhães, 875 (Copacabana); ☎ and fax (21) 235-6610.*

Management at this three-year-old hotel claims the Copa D'Or is a four-star hotel with five-star service, and I saw nothing to dispute this claim. The hotel's only drawback is that it's located five blocks from the beach, but a free shuttle service will transport you to the beach and shops. A medium-sized pool provides a 360° view of the city. Special handicap showers are available in the top-class executive suites, which also have two TVs, two bathrooms, shower/tubs, safes and Spanish TV. Deluxe rooms can hold three single beds tightly; there are no standard rooms. Windows are double-glazed to mute the sound of the city street. A special culinary floor holds a sushi bar, an elegant French restaurant, and a salmon-colored breakfast room with woodpaneled floors and floor-to-ceiling mirrors. Excellent lunch buffets are served, with one hot dish, lavish desserts, and plenty of salads for vegetarians. Guests may indulge in sauna and massage; the minimal gym contains a mechanical bike and one weight machine. *198 apts. Moderate-expensive. All cards.*

### Leme Othon Palace

*Av. Atlântica, 656 (Leme); ☎ (21) 275-8080; fax 275-8080.*

The philosophy of the Othon hotels is fast evolving from large groups to more personalized attention, but structural changes at the Leme Othon have taken more time to develop. A friendly doorman in formal attire greets you, but a strange sculptured wood wall in the lobby dampens the charm. And the lobby lounge seems impossibly small for such a big hotel. In general, however, rooms are large; deluxe rooms are enclosed by a glassed-in veranda, but furniture is often no more than utilitarian. Standards have the same veranda, but sadly show only a slice of ocean view. All rooms have safes and baths with separate showers. The hotel seems unusually popular with Italian tourists, which perhaps explains the frequent appearance of polenta and carpaccio on the menus. La Forchette restaurant serves local and international cuisine, as well as *feijoada* on Sat. The coffee shop is good for fast food, drinks, and omelettes until midnight. The Leme Pub, with a small dance area and intimate leather banquettes, has a citywide reputation for ambience and good live music on Thurs., Fri., and Sat. nights. *193 apts. Moderate-expensive. All cards.*

## Luxor Copacabana

*Av. Atlântica, 2554 (Copacabana);* ☎ *235-2245; fax 255-1858.*

The Luxor chain in Rio (three hotels) continues to uphold its reputation for fine service and efficiency. Standards of upkeep are impeccable at the Luxor Copacabana, whose furnishings and architecture suggest the feel of a cottage inn. Renovated in 1991, the hotel, which is ideally located on the beach drag, is usually full. Standard rooms are cheerful and attractive, though not particularly spacious, and lack any worthy view. Superior rooms offer a partial view of the ocean with a veranda on which you must stand in order to see the waves. The best bet is the super-deluxe suite, with queen-sized bed and a veranda with a garden. The lobby lounge is situated away from the street in the back of the hotel. Breakfast is taken in a charming tea room facing Av. Atlântica. There is no pool. *120 apts. Moderate-expensive. All cards.*

## Luxor Regente

*Av. Atlântica, 3716 (Copacabana);* ☎ *(21) 287-4212; fax 267-7693.*

The relatively substantial size of Luxor's largest hotel belies the intimate feel that characterizes this elite four-star. Rooms are situated among towers and annexes in a maze-like fashion, and can accommodate beachgoers who want a beautiful (if noisy) view of Copacabana, as well as tourists looking for calmer hideaways in the hotel's interior. The friendly and efficient service is among the best in Rio. The noted restaurant Forno e Fogão offers hearty cuisine at moderate prices – a good bet even if you aren't staying at the hotel. *250 apts. Expensive. All cards.*

## Luxor Continental

*Rua Gustavo Sampaio, 320 (Leme);* ☎ *(21) 275-5252; fax 541-1946.*

Tucked away on a leafy back street of Leme, this Luxor is situated a tiny block away from the hubbub of the beach drag. As such, its prime location can take full advantage of the hominess of Leme, with a pizzeria on every block, as well as drugstores, ice cream parlors, stationery stores, and travel agencies in abundance. Having spent 10 days here once, I grew to feel at home in this smallish hotel, whose staff is excellent and whose restaurant serves a great chicken soup. Corner rooms offer the best view of the beach; otherwise, you will be looking out onto the picturesque side streets and hills of Leme. All rooms come with color TV and mini-bar. The bar serves drinks until the wee hours. *282 apts. Expensive. All cards.*

## Marina Rio Hotel

*Av. Delfim Moreira, 696 (Leblon);* ☎ *(21) 239-8844; fax 259-0941.*

Next door to the Marina Palace, the Marina Rio is the former's kid sister – a pint-sized version with 69 rooms and one of the prettiest restaurants in the city. The large bedrooms are elegantly appointed, with fine wood headboards and lush brocaded spreads. Unfortunately, all rooms are perfumed to disguise smoke smells and, although I was assured Johnson & Johnson anti-allergic spray is used, the effect is intense. There are no nonsmoking floors. Room service is available 24 hours a day, and guests may use the pool, hairdresser, and sauna at the Marina Palace. *69 apts. Moderate-expensive. All cards.*

## Olinda Othon

*Av. Atlântica, 2230 (Copacabana);* ☎ *and fax (21) 257-1890.*

Sculptured beams and antique chandeliers give the lobby of this Othon its Belle Époque beauty. Despite its age (nearly half a century), the Olinda has managed to stay both current and traditional; even the well-kept corridors exude an old-world charm. Standards are comfortably sized, with an extended area for dressing; however, the views are so nonexistent it's best to keep the drapes closed. Deluxe rooms with attractive tapestry bedspreads have excellent views of the ocean, though no verandas. Unfortunately, rooms with views tend to absorb the traffic noise down below. Suites, excellent for New Year's Eve, include an extra sitting room with a veranda overlooking the beach. Electronic keys provide extra security, and all rooms are supplied with safes. The one restaurant offers an Italian menu, and a pianist can be heard nightly in the lobby and bar. A hairdresser is available. *96 apts. Moderate–expensive. All cards.*

## Ouro Verde

*Av. Atlântica, 1456 (Copacabana);* ☎ *(21) 542-1887; fax 542-4597.*

The Swiss-owned Ouro Verde has long been known as an elite exec hotel, but tourists will find it one of the most charming traditional establishments in Rio. Built in 1951, the Ouro Verde sports the kind of spacious architecture that was possible only in years past, with much of the original sculptured moldings still intact. From the moment you're welcomed through the large brass gates by the formal doorman, you feel as though you've checked in at an elegant Swiss inn. The huge bedrooms are beautifully furnished, with deep blue carpets, floral spreads, antique desks, and colonial-style couches. The deluxes face the ocean with a huge veranda; an extra sitting room can also be connected. Standards face Corcovado and the rooftops of Rio. Bathrooms are light and bright, with tub/showers. Intriguing are the massive walk-in closets, originally built to accommodate immigrant families who arrived with their sailor trunks. Execs will like the secretarial services, including fax, telex, and multilingual typewriters. A wood-and-leather bar illuminated with antique street lamps opens onto a plant-strewn terrace. A lovely reading room with fresh flowers looks out onto a flowering atrium. The Ouro Verde Restaurant overlooking Copacabana Beach serves top-class French cuisine. *66 apts. Moderate-expensive. All cards.*

### Savoy Othon

*Av. N.S. de Copacabana, 995 (Copacabana);* ☎ *and fax (21) 521-8282.*

This choice Othon hotel is perfectly situated for sugar addicts: On one side is Babuska, the best ice cream parlor in Rio; on the other is Kopenhagen, the city's finest chocolate store. Perhaps to assuage the guilty, the lobby is steeped with antique religious paintings and pious folkloric art. The hotel's ambience, however, is all smiles; many employees have worked here over 20 years, so a family feeling abounds. Because it's two blocks from the beach, no ocean views are available, but rooms are attractive, with a Scottish plaid theme. The deluxe rooms have a couch bed and two singles, giving a grand feeling of space; standards are a bit tighter. Don't be surprised if a neighbor's bathroom noises resound through the thin walls. All rooms have safes and tub/showers. The Savoy Grill, now open to the public, serves typical Brazilian food for lunch and dinner. Room service is available 24 hours a day, and the bar is open from 4 p.m. to midnight. One disadvantage: the hotel is situated on a busy commercial street where homeless families sometimes camp out. A bevy of souvenir shops, movie theaters, and restaurants are also right around the corner. *15 apts. Moderate-expensive. All cards.*

# Three-Star Hotels

### Bandeirantes Othon

*Rua Barata Ribeiro, 548 (Copacabana);* ☎ *and fax (21) 255-6252.*

Located on a busy street two blocks from the shoreline, the Bandeirantes is serviceable, though not dripping in charm. Although the lobby is minuscule, rooms are not particularly cramped, but they are rather featureless. Standards, although the same size as deluxes, are quieter and overlook the rooftops of Rio. Some apartments have a tiny but very clear view of Corcovado. One restaurant doubles as a coffee shop, which is good for omelettes, sandwiches, and desserts. Room service lasts till midnight. There is no pool, but a pizzeria is right next door, and there's a nightclub across the street. *90 apts. Moderate. All cards.*

### Castro Alves Othon

*Av. N.S. de Copacabana, 552 (Copacabana);* ☎ *and fax (21) 255-8815.*

Built in the boom following the end of World War II, the Castro Alves is situated on a very busy commercial street a few blocks back from the beach. As such, you may have to stumble over small dogs and frantic shoppers just to get to the front door. Fortunately, the lounge, with a minuscule bar, has been placed in the back of the hotel for a more relaxed ambience. All rooms were renovated in 1989. Today, antique furniture and mauve motifs add a little oomph. Standards boast huge salmon drapes that open onto a small veranda with an excellent, though distant, view of Corcovado. Deluxe rooms with sitting verandas look onto a leafy park called the Praça Serzeldo Correia. All rooms have safes and extremely old color TVs. Breakfast is served in **La Mole**, a connecting restaurant under separate ownership that has proved a popular medium-priced lunch and dinner spot. A beauty salon is located in the adjacent building. *72 apts. Moderate. All cards.*

## Excelsior Copacabana

*Av. Atlântica, 1800 (Copacabana);* ☎ *(21) 257-1950; fax 256-2037.*

This charming off-white, colonial-style edifice, part of the Horsa chain, is superbly situated right in the middle of Copacabana's beach drag, surrounded by popular restaurants and souvenir shops. Next door is an apartment building filled with the country's top actors and socialites. Friendly receptionists speak good English and a special concierge will arrange all excursions and entertainment reservations. Halls and doorways are paneled in maple, lending a whiff of old-world sophistication. Claustrophobia-prone guests should opt for the superior and deluxe rooms. The super-deluxes come with a balcony facing the sea, as do suites. Safes are available only at the reception. There is no pool. A lounge area doubles as an art gallery, and the American bar is open until midnight. The restaurant serves international and typical Brazilian food, with a *feijoada* buffet on Sat. *220 apts. Moderate. All cards.*

## Ipanema Tower

*Rua Prudente de Morais, 1008 (Ipanema);* ☎ *and fax (21) 521-3011.*

Nineteen of these 90 modern two-bedroom apartments are reserved for rental to tourists and are delightful for the price. Terraces allow you to revel in the atmosphere of Ipanema. Its restaurant, the Four Seasons offers a delectable array of appetizers. Good rates for a four-day stay during Carnaval. *Moderate. All cards.*

## Lancaster Othon

*Av. Atlântica, 1470 (Copacabana);* ☎ *(21) 541-1887.*

A doorman waits under the canopied facade of this Othon built with the generosity of space characteristic of the 1950s. A voluptuous marble staircase winding upwards from the lobby recalls another era, although elevators are available for the faint of heart. Deluxe rooms are actually suite-size, with a veranda facing the ocean and sliding glass-and-wood doors that open to a second room. Standards are equally spacious, though minus the ocean view. Some guests may be put off by some carpet stains and scratched furniture. All three meals are served in a restaurant that is a strange mixture of quiet elegance and screeching TV. In warm weather, you may sit on the front patio overlooking Copacabana Beach and drink fabulous tropical cocktails. Just watch out for the cars that pull up on the sidewalk. *67 apts. Moderate. All cards.*

## Mar Ipanema

*Rua Visconde de Pirajá, 539 (Ipanema);* ☎ *(21) 274-9922; fax 511-4038.*

The five-year-old Mar Ipanema boasts a privileged location down the street from Giorgio Armani on Ipanema's main shopping drag. For a three-star hotel it is remarkably well kept. Argentines, who seem to have the knack of discovering good budget hotels, make up the majority of the clientele, but Americans are welcome. All rooms are carpeted, with modern furniture and color TV with VCR and CNN. The only difference between the standard and superior is the floor level, but the view of downtown Ipanema is not worth the extra bucks. The restaurant – small but spunky – serves three meals, and the lobby bar remains open till midnight. *81 apts. Moderate. All cards.*

## Praia Ipanema

*Rua 706 Vieira Souto;* ☎ *(21) 521-3011, fax 239-6889.*

Ideally located on the oceanfront of Ipanema Beach, this medium-sized hotel is simply furnished, but a favorite among foreign budget-watchers who take advantage of the small verandas or the full or side ocean views. Four-night stays during Carnaval are some of the best deals in the city. *Moderate. All cards.*

## Rio Copa Hotel

*Av. Princesa Isabel, 370 (Leme);* ☎ *(21) 275-6644; fax 275-5545.*

Located down the street from the Meridien Hotel on a busy avenue leading to Rio Sul Shopping Center, the Rio Copa is a comfortable, attractive hotel only two blocks from the beach. Attention to details, such as the cool gray tones of the elevator, has helped make the hotel an oasis of calm in contrast to the city street outside. Those looking for excellent living space will be rewarded here. Standards are a lovely mix of cool grays and blues and comfortable furniture. Deluxes come with an extra room that holds a sofa bed. Double-glass windows and heavy drapes keep street noise to an absolute minimum. A pool and sauna should be installed soon. One restaurant serves all three meals. Room service and the small bar is open till midnight. Check-out time quickly fills the tiny lobby with fast-talking Venezuelans and Paraguayans, but consider that part of the local color. *110 apts. Moderate. All cards.*

## Trocadero Othon

*Av. Atlântica, 2064 (Copacabana);* ☎ *and fax (21) 257-1834.*

Brazilians, Argentines, Chileans, and Italians seem to favor this Othon much more than North Americans. The windows are a bit greasy and the lobby has retained a slight mustiness. Deluxes and suites have full ocean views; the standards, somewhat tight for space, look out onto the side and back of the hotel. If you insist on the budget route, however, make sure you ask for a lateral standard. Only a few deluxe rooms have tubs. All rooms have safes. A hair salon is available to guests. There is no pool. The Trocadero's trump card is the Moenda Restaurant, known throughout the city for its Bahian cuisine. Whether you are a guest or not, don't miss the opportunity to try this unforgettable cuisine. *116 apts. Moderate. All cards.*

# Two-Star Hotels

## Hotel Carlton

*Rua João Lira, 68 (Leblon);* ☎ *(21) 259-1932; fax 259-3147.*

For a two-star hotel, the Carlton gives seedy a good name. So the couches are a little tattered and the bedroom lights hang strangely from the ceiling, but the bathrooms are clean and cheerfully tiled, and the suites are an excellent budget idea for four people. Standards have no view; superiors look out onto a leafy back street of Leblon. Rooms usually come with two single beds; double beds must be requested. All rooms have safes, mini-bars, and air conditioning. *45 apts. Inexpensive. All cards.*

## Ipanema Inn

*Rua Maria Quitéria, 27 (Ipanema);* ☎ *(21) 287-6092, fax 511-5094.*

Pleasant carpeted rooms with colorful drapes and marble-topped tables make this small hotel seem like a neighborhood home. Clean and upbeat, the hotel attracts many Argentines and Americans. Bathrooms are attractively tiled and there is ample closet space. TVs are optional for a small fee. Beach service includes umbrellas and towels. The restaurant serves only breakfast and snacks. *56 apts. Inexpensive. All cards.*

## Predia/Leme

*Av. Princesa Isabel, 7, loja 14/15;* ☎ *(21) 275-5449.*

Unsuspecting tourists without a reservation are often brought here by crafty taxi drivers, who profess they know a great deal. And surprisingly, they're right. One of the best-kept secrets in Rio, the Predia/Leme is neither luxurious nor elite, but it is cheap. Double rooms have air conditioning, TV, and mini-bar. Clients who stay a week might receive a 10% discount. Some rooms even have full views of the sea, and the money you save on accommodations can go toward fancy dinners at the Meridien Hotel next door. *Inexpensive. No cards.*

## Hotel Praia Leme

*Av. Atlântica, 866 (Leme);* ☎ *(21) 275-3322.*

With only two floors, the Praia Leme looks as though it's about to be delicately squashed between towering buildings on Copacabana's main beach drag. Guests will almost feel as though they are staying at a private residence. Internal rooms face side streets; splurge the extra couple of dollars for a room that faces the sea. The fully carpeted rooms include a sleeper-sofa. Bathrooms are tiled, though only showers are available. There are no elevators, but the friendly staff will carry your luggage. The restaurant serves only breakfast, which you may take in your room. The lobby is comfortable, but faintly musty. You can contemplate the sea at night from the tiny bar. Children under six stay free. *22 apts. Inexpensive. No cards.*

### Hotel San Marco

*Rua Visconde de Pirajá, 524 (Ipanema);* ☎ *(21) 239-5032.*

A two-star hotel in chic Ipanema seems an anomaly, and the San Marco is. Standard rooms are similar to those at the Carlton – simple, with two single beds, formica table, safe, TV and air-cooling units. Light bulbs here hang strangely from the ceiling. Some of the wood paneling has been scratched, and I found water standing inexplicably in a pool in one bathroom. Deluxe rooms are the size of standards, but furniture appears to be new. Snack bar and room service available only between 7 a.m. and 4:20 p.m., at which time the kitchen staff apparently leaves in a hurry. The staff is friendly, but the ambience is claustrophobic. *49 apts. Inexpensive. All cards.*

### Toledo

*Rua Domingos Ferreira, 71 (Copacabana);* ☎ *(21) 257-1990.*

Anyone looking for the best cheap hotel in Rio should stop right here. Don't expect many amenities: There is no restaurant, only minimal room service, and few TVs. But the Toledo, located behind the Luxor Copacabana, is impeccably clean and even has a certain *je ne sais quoi*. The small hallways are tiled, suggesting the ambience of a guesthouse. The mini-*solteiro* is a Tom Thumb-sized single, with a tiny desk, a small wardrobe, and an extremely space-efficient bathroom. Standards, a surprise with dark blue carpeting and colorful wallpaper, can easily fit three single beds. Not all rooms have windows, but they do have air conditioning. The forgettable breakfast room is a two-flight walk-up, although breakfast may be served in your room. There's no pool, but the beach is only a block away. The receptionist speaks English (more or less), and even the brick-floor lobby isn't the least bit depressing. There is no service charge. *95 apts. Inexpensive. All cards.*

## Apart-Hotels

Apart-hotels are residences that are run like hotels, but are actually private, completely stocked apartments that may be rented daily. They usually run half the price of hotels and often are more fashionably decorated. Breakfast and maid service are included, although the kitchen is fully equipped. These accommodations are especially good for families or large groups on a budget; the quality of some is so superb that sometimes you can't believe the price.

### Rio Flat Service

*Rua Almirante Guilherme, 332 (Leblon);* ☎ *(21) 274-7222; fax 239-8792.*

This network of apartments with privileged sites in Rio, Copacabana, Leblon, and Lagoa/Humaitá offers one- and two-bedroom places with fully equipped kitchens, air conditioning, and color TV. Sauna, pool, playground, and maid service are also available, as well as a video center and a laundry room. Breakfast is included in the daily rate; children under five stay free.

### Ipanema Sweet

*Rua Visconde de Pirajá, 161;* ☎ *(21) 267-7015; fax 227-4389.*

These air-conditioned apartments are just a block from the beach. Each has a bedroom, living room, kitchen, and veranda. All rooms have color TV and duplexes with two bedrooms are available. There's also a garage, a sauna, and a swimming pool.

## Youth Hostels

For information regarding youth hostels in Rio, write or call: **Associação de Albuergues da Juventude do Estado do Rio de Janeiro** (Association of Youth Hostels for the State of Rio de Janeiro), Rua da Assembléia, 10, room 1616 (downtown), Rio de Janeiro; ☎ *(21) 222-0301.*

## Barra da Tijuca

The in place to hunker down for a spell is in Barra, one of the best beaches in Rio. In the last seven years, apart-hotels have sprung up like wildfire, many of excellent quality. The spaciousness of these facilities, as well as the safety and cleanliness of the beaches, make them ideal for families.

### Barrabella Hotel

*Av. Sernambetiba, 4700 (Barra da Tijuca);* ☎ *(21) 385-2000.*

This is the largest apart-hotel complex in Rio, located in Barra da Tijuca. It has a fine swimming pool, good food, and a hot nightclub. Apartments – one-, two-, and three-bedroom – are popular among singles and the newly divorced.

You might also try **Barra Beach Rio**, Av. Sernambetiba, 1120; ☎ *(21) 389-6333.*

# Where To Eat

Rio is a city of indulgence, and food is no exception. *Cariocas* adore eating and, thanks to the syncretic mix of cultures that has richly characterized Brazilian culture since its inception, Rio's culinary scene offers a huge array of international delights that should satisfy even the most discerning gourmet. From romantic Italian grottoes to elegant French salons, from casual seaside bars to rip-roaring barbecue houses, Rio has a restaurant for every mood, every flavor, and every pocketbook. You can spend under US $5 on open-grilled chicken or up to $100 per person for fine haute cuisine. You can nibble a "natural" sandwich walking down the beach or settle into fine-crusted pizza loaded with eggplant, anchovies and tuna. But dining in Rio is much more than the eternal search for good food. For *cariocas*, it's a time to meet friends, make new ones, show off new clothes and flirt outrageously. Dress may be casual, even in the most expensive restaurants, but *cariocas* will spend hours preparing to look good for a night on the town.

*Cariocas* not only love to eat – they love to eat a lot, and the amount of food on your plate will astonish you. Even in small, unassuming restaurants a main course of beef, for example, with the accompanying platters of rice and beans, can often serve two. The couvert usually includes bread, butter, and a plate of olives, but in the finest restaurants, like **Satíricon,** the fabulous spread of hors d'oeuvres is often as good as the meal. Couverts are automatically placed on your table the minute you sit down, so if you don't want them, refuse them. It can add an extra $2-5 to your bill.

Anyone with a yen for red meat should head for a *churrascaria* – a Brazilian-style steakhouse where some of the finest cuts of beef in South America are served. You can either eat à la carte, at restaurants like **Baby Beef,** or brave the more boisterous *rodízio* scene, such as at **Mariu's**. *Rodízio* means "rotation," referring not to the style of cooking but to the quality of service. For a set price, you stay chained to your seat while a troop of waiters, rhythmically timed to your appetite, stab the middle of your plate with metal skewers, then slice off choice pieces of beef, chicken and pork with a flourish. This decidedly macho form of dining can go on for hours until you call it quits, or until you decide to move on to dessert. Vegetarians who can at least endure looking at meat shouldn't be deterred, because the salad bars (inclusive in the set price) are full of great fresh vegetables. For some reason, Brazilians talk louder at *rodízios* than anywhere else, so expect a kind of boisterous elegance. And don't be surprised if your plate is exchanged in the middle of the meal for a clean one. The first time it happened, I thought the meal was finished, but it's just one of those many gracious gestures of Brazilian service – they want you to eat off clean plates every time.

**Fish** is superbly fresh in Rio. Because of the cholera scare, however, skip the sushi and head for the imaginatively designed kitchens of **Sol e Mar, Grottamare,** and **Satíricon,** where you can indulge in enormous *peixadas* (a potpourri of seafood in a delicate broth) or succulently grilled sea bass, squid, calamari, and lobsters. Along the beach in Barra da Tijuca are dozens of simple rustic eateries that serve a hearty plate of just-caught fried fish for about five bucks. Frequenters of Copacabana Beach need only to cross Avenida Atlântica to dine at **Príncipe,** a tradition in the neighborhood for moderately priced seafood.

As for European cuisine, it's a symbol of status in Rio. The Louis XVI architecture downtown proves just how long Brazilians have mimicked French culture in an attempt to become stylish. Recent imports to the French culinary scene, such as **Claude Troisgrois,** Rio's reigning French chef, and the masterful **Paul Bocuse** at Saint Honoré, have designed imaginative menus that they reinvent daily. Yet some of the most creative kitchens, like the Italian-styled **Ettore's,** have been fashioned by third-generation immigrants using the culinary secrets learned at their grandmother's knee.

**Home-styled** Brazilian food, however, is not to be missed in Rio – though it's not exactly easy to find. Dishes like *galinha ao molho pardo* (chicken cooked in its own blood) tastes much better than it sounds, as does *feijoada*, the Brazilian national dish made from the not-so-popular parts of the pig. (See *Cuisine*.) More an event than a meal, *feijoada* is best eaten at home in the company of friends (who have spent all day to prepare it), but barring any invitations, head for the **Caesar Park Hotel** on Sat., which is considered the best spread in Rio. And don't forget the motherland: Portuguese food specializes in codfish, and one of the warmest and most authentic places to find it is at the colorful cantina called **Adega do Valentim**.

**Vegetarians**, on the other hand, do get respect and won't feel deprived. Beyond the salad bars at *churrascarias*, there are numerous health-style restaurants downtown that serve hearty plates of veggies and grains. Pasta is readily available in Italian restaurants and you can always order rice, beans, steamed vegetables, and omelettes in any moderate-priced restaurant. Eating vegetarian is one of the cheapest ways to dine in Rio, and you'll even find brown rice (*arroz integral*) at special places.

Taking **afternoon tea** in Rio is not just a luxury from colonial days; it's a reasonable way to stave off starvation until you eat dinner at 9 or 10 p.m. (the normal time for supping in Brazil). Hotels such as the **Meridien**, the **Copacabana Palace**, and the **Caesar Park** boast superb buffets of cakes, puddings, breads, and salty pastries that rate as full meals in themselves. For decor that takes you back to the *fin de siècle*, stop by the **Confeitaria Colombo** downtown, and bring back a box of sweets for your room.

Of course, noshing has to be part of a culture that loves to sit at a sidewalk café and watch the girl from Ipanema, Barra or Leblon walk by. There's no better way to cool down geared-up nerves than with a plate of *frango à passarinha* (fried chicken bits), some good company and a cold glass of beer. The restaurant/bars I've listed under *Grazing* needed only three requirements to make the grade: They had to be well situated, well attended, and serve great *chopp* (lager beer on draft, pronounced show-pee). Add a little sunshine, and that's really all you need for a fabulous time in Rio. Restaurants are listed according to the type of food and are sometimes cross-referenced. A service charge of 10% is usually added to the bill, and you may feel free to add another 5%, though it's not expected.

## Dining Rates
(per person, minus tax, tip, and drinks)

| | |
|---|---|
| Expensive | over $25 |
| Moderate | $15-$25 |
| Inexpensive | under $10 |
| Cheap under | $5 |

"All cards" means that all major credit cards are accepted.

MC - MasterCard; V - VISA; DC - Diners; AE American Express

# Brazilian

## Bar do Arnaudo

*Rua Almirante Alexandrino, 316, store B, Santa Teresa; ☎ 252-7246. Tues.-Sat., noon-10 p.m.; Sun., 11 a.m.-6 p.m.*

Set in the colonial hillside neighborhood of Santa Teresa, this is the place to go if you've braved the streetcar to visit the Chácara do Céu Museum, one of the finest modern art collections in Rio. (Better you should take a taxi.) Family run, Arnaudo's is as homespun as you get here, cooking up the salty dried meats characteristic of Northeastern cuisine (*carne-de-sol* may look like leather, but tastes fantastic). Local artwork enlivens the walls, and you might even run into a few artists who are dying to sell. *Moderate. No cards.*

## Mala e Cuia

*Rua Raimundo Corrêa, 34 (Copacabana); ☎ 235-7994. Tues.-Sat., noon-3 p.m. and 6 p.m.-midnight; Sun., noon-5 p.m.; closed Mon.*

The winning formula here, honed in Belo Horizonte, the capital of Minas Gerais, features the state's regional cuisine – a veritable buffet feast, where diners can choose among home-styled dishes, such as *galinha com quiabo* (chicken with okra) and smoked sausages with fried pork rinds. Eat like an 18th-century goldminer. *Moderate.*

## Moenda

*Av. Atlântica, 2064 (Copacabana); ☎ 257-1834. Daily, noon-midnight.*

Moenda offers the best Bahian cuisine in Rio. Waitresses in folkloric costumes sport huge smiles and exhibit the graciousness that's synonymous with Bahia. Health-savvy tourists will appreciate the light touch to a normally heavy cuisine – less oil and fewer spices. Start off with the *acarajé com dois molhos* – a type of bean roll with fried shrimps you buy on Bahia's streets – followed by a variety of fish: the *file de namorado à Moenda* with coconut milk and palm oil sauce is delectable. For dessert the *cocada baiana com quiejo* – a coconut dish with cheese – is a sugar rush. The restaurant, at the Hotel Trocadero, looks out onto the beach with a wonderful view, but don't be surprised if the windows are dirty. *Expensive. All cards.*

## Arataca

*Rua Figueiredo de Magalhães, 28 (Copacabana); ☎ 255-7448. Daily, noon-2 a.m.*

One of the very few places in Rio to get real Amazon fare, including fresh fish, such as the delicious *tambaqui, tucunaré,* and *surubim.* Don't miss various ice cream dishes and juices made from Amazonian fruits. *Moderate. All cards.*

### Siri Mole & Cia

*Rua Francisco Otaviano, 50 (Arpoador);* ☎ *267-0894. Tues.-Sun., noon-2 a.m.; Mon. only dinner, 7 p.m.-2 a.m.*

The owner of Bargaço's in Salvador inspired his friend Agda Pereira to open this excellent restaurant for Bahian specialties. With a light touch to the normally oil-laden cuisine, the menu excels in fish stews, and the *siri mole* (soft crabs) are as refined as caviar. The gentle decor enlivened by ficus trees is pretty, and the chef manages an exact balance between spice and restraint. For starters, try the *acarajé de pilar*, a helping of *vatapá* with dried baby shrimps, then indulge in the house glory, *Sinfonia de Crustaceos* – a delirious symphony of several varieties of fish doused in coconut milk and African palm oil. If you're downtown, try Dona Agda's other restaurant for lunch only, **Pier One**, Av. Rio Branco, 1; ☎ *233-1201. Moderate. All cards.*

### Yemanjá

*Rua Visconde de Pirajá, 148;* ☎ *247-7004.*

Named for the *candomblé* goddess of the sea, this restaurant in the heart of Ipanema offers some of the best Bahian food in the city, combined with the lazy, lush atmosphere, colorful decor and balooning white skirts associated with the state of Bahia. Scrumptious are the fish or shrimp *moqueca*, cooked with coconut milk and palm oil and served over rice. *Moderate. All cards.*

## Churrascaria

### Baby Beef – Paes Mendonça

*Av. das Américas, 1510 (Barra da Tijuca);* ☎ *494-2187. 11:30 a.m.-1 a.m.*

This excellent *churrascaria* is right next to a super-size supermarket, the Paes Mendonça, so big the clerks have to travel on roller skates. Shop first, then feast next door on fine beef à la carte. The *picanha* – huge, juicy, and very tender – is my favorite cut. *Moderate. All cards.*

### Barra Grill

*Av. Min. Ivan Lins, 314;* ☎ *493-4003. Daily, 11 a.m.-midnight.*

This relatively new *churrascaria* is reaping a fine reputation, particularly among couples who patronize the love motels in Barra. Perhaps that explains the added *élan*: side plates served individually by waiters (rather than thrown on your table like frisbees). Eighteen cuts of meat, 24 salads, a hot buffet including lasagna and stroganoff – all for less than $15. The salad and dessert buffet are additional. Always make reservations, especially on Sun., when the lovers head out. *Moderate. All cards.*

### Esplanada Grill

*Rua Barão da Torre, 600 (Ipanema);* ☎ *239-6028. Daily, noon-2 a.m.*

One of Rio's chichi places for à la carte beef (even the napkins come with black bow ties), Esplanada is more expensive than a good *churrascaria* and, in my mind, not fully worth it, especially if quantity is important to you. Still, *cariocas* cough up the *reais* just to be seen in this slender wraparound salon near the Lagoa, especially on weekends, when it's packed. *Expensive. V, MC.*

## Grill One

*Av. Rio Branco, 1; ☎ 18-1331. Noon-11 p.m., closed Saturday and Sunday.*

A weekday delight, especially at lunch with the riveting view of the port and top-notch barbecue meats and unusually delicious side dishes. Try the *picanha*, a sumptuous cut not available in the US. Reservations suggested. *Expensive. AE, V.*

## Mariu's

*Av. Atlântica, 290 B (Leme); ☎ 542-2393. Daily, 11 a.m.-1 a.m.*

More typical of the barbecue houses of Rio Grande do Sul – Brazil's cowboy country in the south – this is my favorite *rodízio*-style *churrascaria* for ambience, quality, and location, right in Leme overlooking the beach. The price is steep (about $75 for two), but the quality is the best in the city. Menus, in English and Portuguese, are little slips of paper you fill out – just like grade school. Best to check everything off, including the French fries, the onion rings, and dozens of salads. You can even specify rare (*mal passado*), medium (*médio*), or well done (*ao ponto*). A few years ago, a "light" menu was introduced, which even lists the number of calories you're consuming and suggests alternatives. Desserts served in huge crystal goblets are exquisite, like the chocolate mousse and the avocado ice cream drenched in liqueur, and especially the chocolate eclairs, called profiteroles. Tell somebody it's your birthday and you'll get a cake with sparklers and a chorus of singing waiters. The owner, the young scion of a rich Brazilian family, is the Armani-suited ponytail who's bussing the clients. *Expensive. All cards.*

## Porcão

*Rua Barão da Torre, 218 (Ipanema); ☎ 521-0999; Av. Armando Lombardi, 591 (Barra da Tijuca); ☎ 399-3355.*

The name means "big pig" and probably refers to the meat; unfortunately, the mascot over the door reminds me too much of Porky (or Babe!). A chichi address in Ipanema, it's *rodízio*-style service – meaning all you can eat as fast as you can eat it. *Moderate. All cards.*

# Continental

## Alho e Oleo

*Rua Barão da Torre, 348 (Ipanema);* ☎ *287-4842. Noon-last client.*

The well-liked restaurant made its debut in Flamengo, now garnering applause in Ipanema, with the same light style: salads, homemade pastas for reasonable prices. A delicious dessert is the *pêra belle helene*, (pear served with white wine and ice cream). *Moderate. No cards.*

## Café do Teatro

*Av. Rio Branco;* ☎ *262-4164. 11 a.m.-4 p.m. Closed on weekends and holidays.*

The official restaurant of the Municipal Theatre skips the *fin-de-siècle* allure and has the atmosphere of an underground cave Moses might have loved. Huge tableaux of Assyrian slaves adorn the walls, and two sculpted sphinxes stand guard at the entrance. The fine food, funky ambience and relaxing music can cure rainy-day blues. *Moderate-expensive. All cards.*

## Clube Gourmet

*Rua General Polidoro, 186 (Botafogo);* ☎ *295-3494.*

This salmon-colored, turn-of-the-century house attracts *cariocas* who love to kvetch about the taxes they pay on their Parisian chateaux. Tourists, however, will enjoy the down-home *savoir faire*, the female bartenders and waitresses (very avant in Brazil), and an excellent lunch buffet that includes 15 salads, pasta, meat, and entrée. Dinner is more gourmet: for a fixed price you choose from three starters, two fishes and one pasta, three meats, and three desserts. For the last 12 years, owner/supervisory chef José Hugo Celidônia, a former food critic for Brazilian *Vogue* and *Gourmet*, has been developing an eclectic but highly praised menu with the help of his friends – some of the best chefs in Europe, who also teach at his amateur cooking school. Fresh products, such as butter, cream, and oranges, are trucked from his farm daily, and he boasts the best wine cellar in Brazil. "My tradition was to eat and cook with my friends," he told me, and you can still taste the good vibes in his meals. *Very expensive. No cards.*

## Pax Delicia

*Rua Maria Quitéria, 99 (Ipanema);* ☎ *247-4191. Tues.-Sat., noon-2 a.m.; Mon., 6 p.m.-midnight.*

Pax is still the hot spot, tucked into a pretty corner off Ipanema's Praça da Paz. Yellow walls, pink orchids, and white-and-tan tables say Santa Monica, but the Spanish chef brings a Latin flair to fish, like the *peixe wanda* with an almondine sauce and rice with raisins. The *filet pax*, thinly sliced grilled filet mignon, comes with a fine herbed sauce. I had time to try only the desserts, but some, like the chocolate mousse, chocolate crocante, and the *maracujá* torte are, unquestionably, the best in town. Many people just come for afternoon tea. No reservations, but between 1-3 p.m. and after 9 p.m., expect to wait. *Moderate. No cards.*

## Rio's

*Pq. do Flamengo (Flamengo);* ☎ *551-1131. Daily, noon-1 a.m.; Sun., noon-5 p.m.*

The glorious views of Guanabara Bay and Sugarloaf may be lost on the businessmen and politicos who eat at this restaurant built by the city for its official guests, but at night, with the twinkling stars, it's the peak of romance, especially if you retreat to the plushy piano bar after *cafezinho.* Dinnner is formal, but the user-friendly menus are in English and the first-class waiters are personable. Start with baked crabs or excellent crab pancakes, then move on to Spanish-style octopus, grilled seabass with creamed spinach, or the memorable Chateaubriand. Dramatic tableside productions are made for flambés. *Expensive. All cards.*

# Fast Food

## Chaika's

*Rua Visconde de Pirajá, 321 (Ipanema);* ☎ *247-7974.*

Chocolate-swirled meringues and pastries a mile high greet you on your way into Chaika's, set in the middle of Ipanema's prime shopping drag. My favorite place for non-junk fast food and desserts, Chaika's makes pizzas for one, two, or more folks, and its ice cream sundaes are not to be missed – complete with tropical umbrellas and unusual toppings. Service is lively, as is the young clientele, some of whom become obsessed with the video games next door. *Inexpensive-cheap. No cards.*

## Bob's

*Av. N.S. de Copacabana, 129 (Copacabana);* ☎ *275-7045.*

So why shouldn't a burger joint boast an American name? At least the meat is thicker and less papery than at Brazilian McDonald's, and the chocolate milk shakes are definitely healing. *Cheap. No cards.*

## Salpicante

*Rua Anibal de Mendonça, 55 (Ipanema);* ☎ *274-9996.*

A clean airy place to lunch a few blocks from the beach. Make your own salad from the bar or get more complicated with grilled chicken (less than $3) or cold roast beef. *Inexpensive. No cards.*

## Tutti Torta

*Rua Visconde de Piraj, 468 A (Ipanema);* ☎ *521-3543. Mon.-Fri., 10 a.m.-8 p.m.; Sat., 10 a.m.-6 p.m.*

Sweet and salty *tortas,* or tart-like cakes – a marvelous surprise is the torta with hearts of palm and ham. Good for quick, cheap lunch snacks a few blocks from the beach. *Inexpensive. No cards.*

## Kibes & Blues

*Av. Alvorada, 3000, loja 1014, Via Parque (Barra);* ☎ *385-0314. 10 a.m.-11 p.m.*

The house style is American luncheonette, and the music – ah well, blues, not Arabian chant – but the kibes and other Mideastern fare is authentic, filling and fast. *Inexpensive. No cards.*

## Rio Hot Dog

*Avenida Ataulfo de Paiva, 1321 (Leblon);* ☎ *259-5441.*

Beyond Yankee Stadium, these are hot dogs German-Brazilian style, with three types of sausages, plus smoked pork, and an exclusive sauerkraut made in São Paulo. Get it to go. *Inexpensive. No cards.*

# Feijoadas

## Caesar Park Hotel

*Av. Vieira Souto, 460 (Ipanema);* ☎ *287-3122. Wed. and Sat.*

Nearly everyone's choice for the best *feijoada* in Rio, the Tiberius restaurant is an elegant surrounding for the country's most famous traditional dish (see under *Cuisine*.) The huge black pots containing dried meats, bacon, salted pork, sausage, and odd parts of pig are set up buffet-style, while traditional singers in folkloric costumes serenade diners. Don't eat for 24 hours beforehand and don't miss the coconut *batidas* – an intoxicating combination of creme de coco and *cachaça. Moderate. All cards.*

## Rio Othon Palace Hotel

*Av. Atlântica, 3264, 3rd floor;* ☎ *521-5522.*

Children up to age nine eat free at the Othon's *feijoada* buffet every Sat. *Moderate. All cards.*

# Fish

## Barreado

*Estrada dos Bandeirantes, 21295 (Vargem Grande);* ☎ *442-2499.*
*Fri., 6 p.m.-midnight; Sat., noon-midnight; Sun., noon-10 p.m.*

Tourists seem to love the tropical ambiance here, with tables made of tree trunks. Portions can be shared by two persons, seafood is the house specialty, but the most famous dish is the *varreadinho*, a pumpkin stuffed with shrimp and catupiry cheese. Mon. through Thurs. Barreado accepts group reservations. *Expensive. All cards.*

### Cândido's

*Rua Barros de Alarcão, 352 (Pedra de Guaratiba);* ☎ *417-1630. Mon.-Fri., noon-6 p.m.; Sun. and Sat., noon-9 p.m.*

Given the crown by visiting French chef Paul Bocuse, who dubbed it his favorite restaurant in Rio, Cândido's looks like a dump on the beach. But *cariocas* drive an hour out to this seaside suburb to sample the fresh fish caught daily. Owner Carmen Sampaio bought the building 21 years ago when the area was only a fishing village, but it wasn't until her grilled *lula* (squid) started appearing in the social columns that she took off. Now clients wait up to an hour for a table and grilled seafood while they soak up the sun and bat off mosquitoes. Paul Bocuse claims Carmen makes the best rice in the world. After dining, stop next door at Chez Janine, a popular nightclub. Reservations at the restaurant are absolutely necessary. *Expensive-very expensive. No cards.*

### Príncipe

*Av. Atlântica, 514 (Leme);* ☎ *275-3996. Daily, noon-1 a.m.*

One of the better moderate-priced fish eateries on the beach in Leme. The maitre d' hangs out at the door, sometimes looking a bit like Mafia, but don't let that deter you. *Moderate. All cards.*

### Shirley

*Rua Gustavo Sampaio,610 (Leme );* ☎ *275-1398. Hours: noon-1 a.m.*

You will have to search for this slim reed of a restaurant tucked into a backstreet of Leme, a leafy residential neighorhood next to Copacabana, but the restaurant is a long-time favorite among residents who can afford the creative cuisine. Seafood (particularly codfish) is a specialty.

### Sol e Mar

*Av. Reporter Nestor Moreira, 11 (Botafogo);* ☎ *295-1997.*

Don't be turned off by the phrase "tourist complex." Here you'll find the best view of Guanabara Bay and Sugarloaf, first-rate service, and fine fresh fish cooked Spanish-style. A good place to come after you've visited Sugarloaf, Sol e Mar definitely serves the best fruit cocktail drinks in the city. *Camarão no coco* arrives in a big pineapple boat covered with coconut cream sauce, but the best bet is the *Festival de Pescador Mariscos* – a groaning plate of fresh grilled seafood enough for two. The desserts are extravagant – from coconut pie and chocolate mousse to *tartuffe*, a chocolate ice cream ball drenched in chocolate sauce. Many *cariocas* with big wallets have their weddings and bar mitzvahs upstairs in the glass-enclosed ballroom; a plush disco features live music nightly. *Moderate-expensive. All cards.*

# French

## Allons Enfants

*Rua Visconde de Carandaí 5, Jardim Botânico;* ☎ *239-3397.*
*Noon-4 p.m., 8 p.m.-last client.*

One of the best French restaurants in Brazil. It offers reasonable prices for dining in a charming house in a lovely neighborhood. What more can you ask for?

The young chef studied with Pierre Troisgros; Brazilian-style *feijoada* is also excellent here. Fish with unusual sauces heads the menu. *Moderate. All cards.*

## Le Bec Fin

*Av. N.S. de Copacabana, 178 (Copacabana);* ☎ *542-4097. 7 p.m.-2 a.m.*

Only 42 seats, but this classic French restaurant has remained a top-class tradition in Rio for over 40 years. The menu never budges, nor do the kiss-kiss clients who never worry about prices. Romance abounds; with its fabulous marble-and-mahogany bar, flowered chairs, and red brocaded walls, the intimate room resembles a high-class madam's salon. But generosity reigns – the philosophy is to serve sumptuous portions so that nobody leaves hungry. Lots of champagne and rabbit are common.

Reservations required on Thurs. and weekends, when you might get to glimpse singing star Roberto Carlos (said to dine here weekly). *Very expensive. All cards.*

## Traiteurs de France

*Av. N.S. de Copacabana;* ☎ *235-6440. Mon.-Sat., noon-6 p.m.; Sun., noon-3 a.m.*

Chef Patrick Balncard has turned his tiny bistro into one of the most charming dining experiences in Rio – perhaps one of the reasons why *cariocas* love all things French.

Don't be swayed by the delectable display of desserts as you enter until you dig into such winning entrées as *coq au vin* and the breast of duck. *Moderate.*

## Claude Troisgros

*Rua Custódio Serrão, 62 (Jardim Botânico);* ☎ *286-1538. Mon.-Sat.,noon-3:30 p.m. and 7:30 p.m.-12:30 a.m. Closed Sun.*

Tucked into a leafy side street of Jardim Botânico, this cozy, flamingo-pink chalet is the brainchild of 38-year-old master chef Claude Troisgros, son of one of the great chefs of Roanne, France. Only a few years ago, Claude started out with a tiny six-table bistro and one waiter (his Brazilian wife was cashier), but he quickly carved a reputation for *la cuisine française pour les tropiques* (French food for the tropics) that few have ever matched in Rio. If you're a true gourmet, money will never be wasted here; in fact, only deep concentration while eating does justice to the unusual herbs, daring combinations, and artistic design of every magnificent plate. Best to go for the fixed menu (changed weekly). The kitchen, led by well-trained António Costa when Claude is absent, isn't at all stuffy. Once a client brought a *jacaré* (crocodile) he had just caught and they baked it without blinking. The climax of any meal should be the *panaché des desserts*, which gives you an opportunity to taste a little of everything, including the miraculous chocolate mousse. *Expensive. All cards.*

## Ouro Verde

*Av. Atlântica, 1456; ☎ 542-1887. Daily, noon-midnight.*

Tucked into the first floor of the Ouro Verde Hotel, this romantic, top-class restaurant does justice to its French-and-Swiss-inspired menu. Cuts of beef are excellent, and the desserts leave nothing to the imagination. A window seat looks over a fine expanse of Copacabana Beach. *Expensive. All cards.*

## Petronius

*Caesar Park Hotel, Av. Vieira Souto, 460 (Ipanema); ☎ 287-3122.*

The newly revamped French restaurant of Rio's classiest hotel is, oddly, the best place to see the Tues. night bikers as they race next to Ipanema's shore. With ivories tinkling in the background and candles illuminating the plush room, white-gloved waiters serve on silver plates with particular grace. Start with the *carpaccio de filet* – a wonder of thinly sliced raw meat, followed by an excellent grilled sole with a devastating crunchy cashew sauce (portions are immense). The *Bandeja Imperial do Pescador* is a stupendous potpourri of fish, shrimp, and lobster for two (a bit steep at $75, but you needn't eat for days prior). The *maracajú batidas* are spectacular. For dessert, a Brazilian friend urged me to try the chocolate mousse with a side dish of soft meringues – an interesting combo. *Cafezinho*, made tableside in a glass globe, is a wonder of heat and gravity. On the way out, don't miss the live fish in the foyer: one has the face of a kitten, and the other, a lion fish, looks extraterrestrial. *Very expensive. All cards.*

## Le Saint Honoré

*Av. Atlântica, 1020 (Hotel Meridien, 37th floor, Leme); ☎ 546-0880. 8 p.m.-1 a.m.; closed Sun.*

Not only has this classic French kitchen been voted number one by the city's best critics, but the wraparound view of Copacabana Beach is one of the most romantic vistas at night. Designed by Chico Gouveia, the famous Brazilian decorator, the salon is a classy study in black, yellow, and white, with a sumptuous piano bar that suggests Cole Porter's ghost might be hanging about. Chef Michel Angier masterfully improvises on the cuisine of Paul Bocuse, offering a different weekly fixed-price menu, as well as à la carte selections. As an appetizer, caviar wrapped in salmon with tartar sauce is the most popular, followed by female frog's legs and filet of beef in a fine bordelaise sauce. Hot goat cheese usually precedes a cavalcade of exquisite chocolates. Service is elegant, in fact nearly obsequious: when I asked for a doggie-bag, nobody batted an eye. Reservations a must. *Very expensive. All cards.*

# Galetos

An American girlfriend who works in Rio claimed she was too scared to walk up to these sometimes murky-looking, open-air counters, but she's missing out on some of the best grilled chicken around. And the price is unbeatable. Salads and fries are extra; other cuts of beef can be grilled. The couvert, for a few cents, will get you fresh French bread and a condiment of diced onions and tomato – practically a meal in itself. The service is fast, the ambience casual, and the natives quite friendly. A good option for takeout.

### O Crack dos Galetos

*Av. Prado Junior, 63, loja C (Copacabana). 11 a.m.-4 a.m. daily.*

A block from the beach, and a block from the Meridien Hotel, next to a self-service laundromat called Lave Lev. There's even an erotic nightclub next door. *Cheap. No cards.* Also try their branch on Rua Domingos Ferreira, 197; ☎ 236-7001.

### Quick Galetos

*Rua Duvivier, 284 (Copacabana).*

Open-air counter near the Hotel Internacional Rio. *Cheap. No cards.*

# German

### Bar Luiz

*Rua Carioca, 39; (Downtown); ☎ 262-6900. Mon.-Sat., 11 a.m.-11:30 p.m.*

The smoke is thick, the tables tight, and the noise meter rambunctious, but this lovable joint in the publishing district is the meeting place for the Woodwards and Bernsteins of Rio. More than a century old, the German-style restaurant remains packed nightly after 8:30 p.m., while guests fiercely devour the famous knockwursts, sauerkraut, smoked chicken, potato salad, and pickles. Even the waiters seem straight out of a brusque Jewish deli, but the *chopp*, ice-cold draft served in generous pitchers, is pure *Brasileiro*. Nearby is the **Cine Iris**, a 200-year-old building that shows porn flicks, but the terrain, I was told, is rough. *Inexpensive. DC only.*

# Gimmicks, Goofballs, & Games

## Torre de Babel

*Rua Visconde de Pirajá, 128 A, Ipanema;* ☎ *267-9136. Mon.-Sat. noon-4 p.m. and 8 p.m.-2 a.m.*

The name means Tower of Babel, and the hodgepodge of artists, painters, and actors who own it wanted a joint to indulge their individual whims. Consequently, the windows are filled with Brazilian kitsch; opera videos play on a huge screen at lunch; nights and weekends alternate between live concerts, video premieres, poetry readings, and fashion shows. Just come for hors d'oeuvres and the interesting people, or dig into the eclectic, health-savvy menu: grilled vegetables with curry, chicken with chutney, and stone-baked codfish. Worth babbling over is the *Negão de Bebel* (Portuguese for big, black man), a wicked slab of fudge that will adhere to the roof of your mouth. The humor-studded restaurant, hidden behind a jungle of plants on Ipanema's main shopping drag, may be hard to find, but look for the topless mannequin with a menu pasted on her chest. *Inexpensive. No cards.*

## Mostarda

*Av. Epitácio Pessoa, 990 (Lagoa);* ☎ *287-7629. Daily 7 p.m.-4 a.m.*

The restaurant started with a group of Portuguese and Spanish owners and an obsession. So successful was the menu, made almost entirely with mustard, that a gorgeous new branch was built overlooking the Lagoa, complete with a disco upstairs. Sit on the veranda outside, or ask for a window seat on the second story, then start off with an explosive cocktail that comes with sparklers. Meats are often as big as their plates. After 9:30 p.m., the tables upstairs are taken. A huge line for the disco starts around 10:45 p.m. Sun.-Thurs; if you are having dinner, you are invited to dance free. *Moderate. AE only.*

# Ice Cream

## Babuska

*Rua Anibal de Mendonça, 55 (Ipanema) and Rua Rainha Guilermina, 90 (Leblon).*

Best ice cream parlor in Rio. Banana chocolate chips and coconut are among the top flavors. *Cheap. No cards.*

## Mil Frutas

*Rua Jardim Botânico, 585.*

One of the best flavors is *chocolate com laranja* (chocolate with orange). *Cheap. No cards.*

# Italian

## Enotria

*Rua Frei Leandro, 20 (Jardim Botânico);* ☎ *246-9003. Weekdays, 12:30-3:30 p.m. and 8 p.m.-12:30 a.m.; Sat. 8 p.m.-1 a.m.; Sun. 12:30 p.m.-5 p.m.*

The *Guita 4 Rodas*, Brazil's travel bible, has in the past awarded Enotria the Best Restaurant in Brazil, and all agree the quality has not wavered at its new address. Today's portions are even more generous. An excellent wine list accompanies such delicacies as smoked surubin *carpaccio*, risotto with sausage and saffron, and *filé* with cashew nuts. Reservations a must. *Very expensive. DC, MC.*

## Arlecchino

*Rua Prudente de Morais, 1387 (Ipanema);* ☎ *259-7745. Mon.-Sat. 7 p.m.-2 a.m.; Sun. noon-2 a.m.*

The harlequin decor of this two-story, brick-and-wood house recalls the clowns from the 17th-century Commedia del'Arte, but the cuisine is post-modern Italian. A buffet of iced fish greets you in the foyer, so fresh they're still moving. The owners from northern Italy offer excellent fresh seafood salad, along with specialties such as the *pasta bucatini al cartocci* (with fish and mushrooms) and the risotto with asparagus and scampi. Service is first class, though a tad snobby, and prices are continually changing. *Very expensive. No cards.*

## Da Brambini

*Av. Atlântica, 514 (Leme);* ☎ *275-4346. Daily noon-1 a.m.*

The newest addition to the beach drag in Copacabana is an absolute delight. Superb Italian cuisine in tranquil, friendly environs; even the pasta sauces come piping hot. The *penne alla boscaiola*, with white sauce and mushrooms, was such a joy. We still dream about it. *Moderate. All cards.*

## Ettore

*Av. Armando Lombardi, 800, loja D;* ☎ *399-5611. Sun.-Thurs. noon-1 a.m., Fri.-Sat. noon-2 a.m.*

Natural rock walls and wooden pews make this famed Italian eatery seem like a peasant's grotto, but the antipastos, pizzas, and pastas are fit for a king. Owner Ettore Sinalschi learned to cook from his Italian grandmother, who inspired such creations as *tagliatelle modo mio* (pasta with thin strips of filet mignon and dry mushrooms) and the *gamberotti* (seven pillowlike pastas filled with shrimp and ricotta). Pizzas arrive with a very refined crust, and desserts, like the chocolate eclair, manage to be silky and firm simultaneously. The takeout counter is to die for. Reservations recommended. *Moderate. No cards.*

### Florentina

*Av. Atlântica, 458 (Leme);* ☎ *275-7698.*

No reservations needed for this user-friendly cantina across the street from Leme Beach. Pizza, ice cream sundaes, and pastas for reasonable prices in a boisterous setting. *Inexpensive. All cards.*

### Gattopardo

*Av. Borges de Medeiros, 1426 (Lagoa);* ☎ *274-7999. 6 p.m.-4 a.m. daily.*

A great place for elite pizza with fine, crunchy crust. Socialites and theater people adore the Amaral, with tomatoes, eggplant, green and yellow peppers, anchovies, tuna, and olives. Extremely fine pastas with lots of cheese, basil, and tomatoes. *Moderate. No cards.*

### Grottamare

*Rua Gomes Carneiro, 132 (Ipanema);* ☎ *287-1596. Daily 7 p.m.-1 a.m.*

Wood-beam structures and exotic bouquets give this noted 11-year-old restaurant its tropical *élan*. Intimate seating is found behind the magnificent bar made out of a boat or in the main dining room, where the service is formal, but exceedingly friendly. The cuisine is Adriatic, meaning from the sea, and the Italian chef/owner, Paolo Neroni, goes to great extremes to please the most subtle palates. So good was our first appetizer – *pizza branca* sprayed with butter and rosemary – that we could have eaten it all night. Specialties are fish grilled *na brasa* (barbecue style); but my favorite was the *peixada* (for two), a glorious black pot of lobster, shrimp, squid, and filets steeped in a broth light enough to preserve flavor. Desserts, like the *torrone* – Italian ice cream with crystallized fruits – are intense. *Expensive. All cards.*

### Satyricon

*Rua Barão da Torre, 192 (Ipanema);* ☎ *521-0627. Daily noon-2 a.m.*

Rock in Rio graduates like Paul Simon and Sting swear by this elite eatery, which offers the best fish in Rio, not to mention celebrity sightings on a good night. The Roman owner, Miro Leopardi, is the biggest fresh fish exporter in Brazil – hence the still wiggling fresh-water display when you enter. For starters try the *Gran piatto di mare*, a cornucopia of six types of fresh seafood in natural shells. For entrées, pick your own fish, from swordfish to seabass to *tamboril* (a very white fish), as well as the accompanying sauce, or go for the Italian-made *pasta all'aragosta*, with lobster, champagne, basil, and tomato is stylish perfection. The salmon-colored walls, avant-garde art, tropical plants, and Roman arches may seem a bit faux-Californian, but Brazilians call it classy. Some gastronomics come just for the extravagant dessert menu or to hang out at the bar. Reserve on weekends. *Expensive. All cards.*

### Le Streghe

*Rua Prudente de Moraes, 129, Ipanema;* ☎ *287-7146. 8 p.m.-2 a.m.*

This restaurant, disco, and piano bar is popular with the rich, 30-plus set, as well as tourists who want to splurge and dress up. The piano bar is brocaded in mauve and dominated by a huge grand piano; the upstairs restaurant is more tropical, with flowered tablecloths and bamboo beams. The kitchen, under the baton of Stefano Monti, the Italian owner, has a thing for fresh white truffles. And the 13 desserts are renowned, particularly the pineapple flambé. Don't forget to visit the neighboring disco **Calígola**, run by the same owner. *Very expensive. No cards.*

# Oriental

### Nova China

*Av. Epitácio Pessoa, 1164 (Lagoa);* ☎ *287-3947. Mon.-Fri. 7 p.m.-2 a.m.; Sat. and holidays, noon-1 a.m.; Sun. noon-midnight.*

Nothing surprising on the Chinese menu here, but the servings are honest and the environs unquestionably pleasant – a renovated colonial-style home overlooking the Lagoa. *Moderate. AE, MC.*

### Kioto

*Rua Ministro Tavare de Lyra, 105, 3rd floor (Flamengo);* ☎ *205-9197.*

Sequestered at the top of a snooker salon, in a street everyone passes but nobody knows by name, the Kioto casually mixes Japanese with Chinese. If you can't decide on sushi, sashimi or tempura, there's always sweet and sour pork. *Inexpensive. All cards.*

### Chinese Palace

*Av. Atlântica, 1212-A (Copacabana);* ☎ *275-0145.*
*Noon-3 p.m., 6 p.m.-midnight.*

Chinese food in Brazil usually doesn't come cheap, nor is the quality spectacular. What the Palace has going for it is location – on the beach – and a plate of unusually crispy and spicy spare ribs. And the spring rolls are at least recognizable. *Inexpensive-moderate. All cards.*

### Take D'Or

*Hotel Copa D'Or, Rua Figueiredo Magalhães, 875 (Copacabana);* ☎ *235-6610.*

A sushi bar for executives, prepared by Nobu San, a recent import from Japan. The real thing. But think twice about cholera. *Expensive. All cards.*

# Pizza

### Caravella

*Rua Domingo Ferreira at the corner of Rua Bolivar. Postal 5-1/2 (Copacabana).*
The best pizza in Rio. Period. *Moderate. No cards.*

### Fratelli Leblon

*Av. General San Martin, 983;* ☎ *259-6699. Mon.-Thurs. 7 p.m.-1 a.m.; Fri. and Sun. 1 p.m.-1 a.m.*

The Italian-born owner claims the pizzas are equal to those back home in Genoa, but even more impressive are the 32 fine-crusted varieties, with exotic Brazilian combinations. *Moderate. All cards.*

### Parmê

*Rua Furani 4 (Botafogo);* ☎ *551-5500. Weekdays 11 a.m.-midnight; 11 a.m.-2 a.m. on Fri. and Sat.*

Tues. is *rodízio*-pizza night, which means maybe up to 10 different kinds, all you can eat. Plus, two can eat for the price of one. *Moderate. No cards.*

### Antonello

*Av. Lineu de Paula Machado, 696 (Lagoa);* ☎ *274-5854. 6 p.m.-last client; closed Tues.*

Five thousand pizzas are sold every month here, in this beautiful house in Lagoa. Considered one of the top chic pizzarias.

### La Maschera di Pulcinella

*Rua Farme de Amoeda, 102 (Ipanema);* ☎ *287-3792. Weekdays, 7 p.m.-1 a.m.; Weekends, 1 p.m.-1 a.m.*

Lots of locals think the couverte (what they put on the table without asking) is the best in the city – at least, it's the most abundant with pizza, mozarella cheese, tiny cordona bird eggs, carpaccio, and four types of bread – and then you order the entrée. Try the hearty house wine, Villa Chiopris, with the *peixe no sal grosso* (fish baked in salt). *Expensive. AE, DC.*

Also see **Gattopardo** under *Italian*.

# Portuguese

### Adega do Valentim

*Rua da Passagem, 178 (Botafogo);* ☎ *541-1166. Daily, noon-1 a.m.*

With the salamis and garlic hanging from the ceiling and the Portuguese guitar trickling down from upstairs, all you need is Columbus to feel as though you've landed in Lisbon. The classiest Portuguese food in Rio, Valentim's always guarantees a great spread. The owner, Valentim, with his Telly Savalas face, is one of those rare people at peace with his lot, and every corner of his restaurant exudes his warmth. Ask him to suggest an appetizer, called *petiscos* – all of them sumptuous and filling. Codfish – a Portuguese delicacy – has a million versions here, but I prefer the *salmon na brasa*, barbecue grilled, with almond-spiked rice. Portions are huge and can often serve two. The way they make coffee at your table will make you want to buy the pot. Alvarinho, a wonderful 1948 Portuguese wine, can run you about $200. *Expensive. All cards.*

## Antiquarius

*Rua Aristides Espindola, 19 (Leblon); ☎ 294-1049. Daily noon-2 a.m.*

One of the most chichi restaurants in Rio, Antiquarius has the kind of exalted reputation that sometimes can't be lived up to. Portuguese-inspired inventions with codfish are popular, as is the grilled octopus. Desserts are spectacular but usually steeped in an egg base that might require developed taste buds. Surrounded by such beautiful antiques and people, you might as well get dressed to kill. Reservations are recommended. *Very expensive. No cards.*

# Vegetarian/Natural

## Natural

*Rua Barão da Torre, 171 (Ipanema); ☎ 267-7799. Daily 11:30 a.m.-11:30 p.m.*

A homey brick house with good vegetarian and health-oriented food. Lunch only served at the location in Botafogo: Rua 19 de Fevereiro, 118 (Botafogo). *Cheap. All cards.*

## Celeiro

*Rua Dias Ferreira, 199 (Leblon); ☎ 274-7843. 11:30 a.m.-5 p.m.; closed Sun.*

Creative salads, pastas and salty pastries, made with organically grown products.

## Sabor Saúde

*Rua Ataúlfo de Paiva, 630-A (Leblon); ☎ 239-4396. Daily 9 a.m.-10:30 p.m.*

One of Rio's best health restaurants, where the owner claims the vegetables are cultivated in tiny groups without toxins. For those addicted to brown rice, green vegetables, and fresh fruit, enjoy. *Cheap. All cards.*

## Downtown

Downtown is full of vegetarian and health-oriented restaurants open for lunch – popular among working girls and guys. Among the better ones are:

## Cheio de Vida

*Av. Treze de Maio, 33, sala 403; ☎ 232-6645. Mon.-Fri. 11:30 a.m.-4 p.m. for lunch, and from 6:30 p.m.*

Difficult to locate (take the escalator up), but feast on the brown rice, green vegetables, and yam torts with soybean hamburgers. *Cheap. No cards.*

## Greeness

*Rua Sacadura Cabral, 233; ☎ 263-8016. Daily 11 a.m.-3 p.m.*

Eight salads, vegetable soups, wholewheat bread, and a hot dish with four side orders. *Cheap. No cards.*

# Teatime, Snacks, Sweet Tooths

### Biscuit

*Rua Carvalho de Mendonça at the corner of Rua Rodolfo Dantas (Copacabana);*
☎ *541-8648.*

In the heart of Copacabana, here's a good place to snatch a fast tea with luscious waffles, croissants, *pão de queijo*, and coffee with cream. Try the crêpes suzettes. *Inexpensive. No cards.*

### Casa do Pão de Queijo

*Av. N.S. de Copacabana, 336 (Copacabana);* ☎ *235-6424.*

A treasure box for the best *pão de queijo* in Rio – tiny, delicate rolls of cheese bread that melt in your mouth and are addictive. *Cheap. All cards.*

### Confeitaria Colombo

*Rua Gonçalves Dias, 32/36;* ☎ *232-2300.*

Established almost 100 years ago, this traditional pastry shop-cum-restaurant in the nervous heart of downtown evokes an old-time atmosphere, with its fabulous sculptured walls and rinky piano. So a little seediness has set in – the pastry show is still impressive and the slow service just adds to the old-world charm. Waffles are excellent, and if you ask for a plate of *salgados*, you'll be served an array of salty biscuits and *torts*. For afternoon tea, try the *chá completo* – a dazzling service of cakes, toast, biscuits, sweets, and beverage. A visual must-see for architecture buffs – even the organ music sounds like a 19th-century horror show. There's also a smaller version in Copacabana at Avenida N.S. de Copacabana, 890; ☎ *257-8960. Moderate. No cards.*

### Cervantes

*Av. Prado Junior, 335 (Copacabana);* ☎ *275-6147.*

Artists and TV stars crowd in here after midnight for snacks and sandwiches. Inexpensive and filling. *No cards.*

### Doce Delicia

*Rua Anibal de Mendonça, 55, lojas C and D (Ipanema):* ☎ *259-0239. Mon.-Fri. 11 a.m.-midnight; weekends, 11 a.m.-8 p.m.*

An extension of the Pax restaurant, this delectable teahouse two blocks from the beach is a perfect place to escape the heat. The desserts, like the *maracujá* pie, come straight from one of the best chefs in the city, and the salad bar looks clean.

### La Thé Lautrec

*Av. Atlântica, 1020 (Hotel Meridien, 3rd floor, Leme);* ☎ *275-9922. Noon-2 a.m.*

This *fin-de-siècle* café, with frosted glass and antique lamps, recalls teatime with Toulouse Lautrec. The 4 p.m.-6:30 p.m. cavalcade of sweets, breads, and salty delights is a tradition among society ladies who arrive with their just-coiffed hair and cellular phones, but the fabulous spread will delight anyone with a late-afternoon craving. The iced chocolate drinks are perfect for relieving sunstroke and the chocolate cake is superb. *Moderate. All cards.*

## Pérgula

*(Copacabana Palace Hotel) Av. Atlântica, 1702. For reservations, ☎ 255-7070, ext. 497. Mon.-Fri., 4 p.m.-7 p.m.*

Newly installed by Brit-born Annie Phillips, a former stewardess and graduate of the Cordon Bleu, afternoon tea at the Copacabana Palace is a hoot. In a cheery salon overlooking the wickedly large pool, Annie personally serves you hot chocolate or at least a dozen kinds of foreign teas from huge silver urns; then the formal waiters bring on Scottish pancakes, scones, and muffins. You are then invited to feast from a buffet of assorted finger sandwiches, hot Brazilian canapés, and a selection of sweets, cakes, and ice cream, including the most delicious fresh blackberries I've ever tasted. You'll find all sorts here: Brazilian socialites in Chanel suits, students from the American School, elite birthday parties, and just a few tourists. Sweet flute and guitar add to the luxurious calm. For a fixed price, you could eat enough for lunch and dinner combined. *Moderate. All cards.*

# Bars For Grazing & Cruising

## Academia da Cachaça

*Rua Conde Bernadote, 26, loja C.*

A sidewalk café between Leblon and Gávea, famous for every kind of *batida* under the sun. The recipe is sugarcane brandy, lemon, sugar, or honey, and a variety of flavors from chocolate to strawberry. *Inexpensive. No cards.*

## Bar Lagoa

*Av. Epitácio Pessoa, 1674.*

The waiters are a little dense at this seaside bar (the most-oft-heard phrase is "*Garcon, pelo amor de Deus,*" or "Waiter, for the love of God"). But the *chopp* is honest, and the place is always packed. *Inexpensive. No cards.*

## Restaurante Meia Pataca

*Copacabana Beach.*

Probably the most frequented street-side café bar on Av. Atlântica – famous for its *chopp* and for the prostitutes who might sidle up for some business. If you don't find the action amusing, or if you have children in tow, it's best not to linger.

## 1900

*Rua Capitão Salomão, 55 (Botafogo); ☎ 266-7497. Daily 6 p.m.-last client.*

The newest bar in Botafogo, with historic stone walls and a replica of the old street car that circles around the veranda loaded with drinks. *Carpaccio* made with *carne-de-sol* (sundried meat) gives you a taste of the Northeast.

## Caneco 70

*Av. Delfim Moreira, 1026 (Leblon);* ☎ *294-1180; 10 a.m.-4 a.m.*

On the Tues. night of the city bike run, you'll find hordes of cyclists hanging here for a *chopinho regenerador* (a little rejuvenating beer!). The majority chow down on pizza *cortadinha à francesa* and the *bolinhos de bacalhau* (codfish balls) for a quick pick-me-up. *Inexpensive. No cards.*

## Bar Garota de Ipanema

*Rua Vinícius de Moraes, 49 (Ipanema);* ☎ *267-8787.*

It was here in 1960 that Tom Jobim and Vinícius de Moraes wrote the song *The Girl from Ipanema* and never looked back. Just two crazy guys who fell for a blonde passing their barstools every day without ever saying *alô*. Of course, she sure sidled up after they got famous, but that's another story. That's about all this bar has going for it, but nostalgia runs deep. During Carnaval this corner of Ipanema, a few blocks from the beach, attracts the most flamboyant personalities, usually in drag. *Inexpensive. No cards.*

# In Barra

## Giannetto

*Av. Sernambetiba, 5800 (Barra da Tijuca);* ☎ 433-2429.

A former mechanical engineer with a gift for cooking has opened one of the most honest Italian restaurants in Rio. Unusual offerings like squid salad, vegetarian antipastos, and eggplant marinated in white wine set the menu apart from the rest. The array of rigatonis, macaronis, and etceteronis are all winners. The pesto sauce is considered perfect. *Moderate. All cards.*

## Lokau

*Av. Sernambetiba 13500 (Barra da Tijuca);* ☎ 982-0549. *Noon-midnight.*

One of plastic surgeon Ivo Pitanguy's favorite spots, Lokau is an informal but pricey eatery on its own dock facing Lagoa de Marapindi – a lake full of protected baby alligators. Families with children love to come here since free-range ducks, swans, chickens, and toucans are all part of the open-air decor, but it can also be very romantic. Grass-hut tables add to the tropical allure, and kids can spend hours on the tire swings. *Muqueca* – a Bahian fish stew with palm oil – is especially good. Despite the formidable prices, the joint is packed on weekends. *Expensive. No cards.*

## Nau Catarineta

*Av. Sernambetiba, 760 (Barra da Tijuca).*

One of the most romantic spots in Rio, this cavern-like, candlelit joint about 40 min. from Copacabana is a secret among lovers, who go for the dark lights, the hors d'oeuvres, and the sexy drinks called *batidas afrodisiacas*. (The *ostra virgem*, or virgin oyster, with vodka, cream of coconut, and pineapple juice, is particularly fine.) Fondues are also a turn-on. Go early, since the place gets packed after 8 p.m. and there are no reservations. *Moderate. All cards.*

## Peixe Frito

*Av. Fernando Matos, 371 (Barra da Tijuca);* ☎ 492-9494. *Daily noon-midnight; Sun. noon-10 p.m.*

The fish lover's version of a *churrascaria* – an all-you-can-eat buffet of grilled fish, fish-inflected salads, and shrimp-defined stews; then the waiter serves you fried shrimps, stuffed crabs, and fried squid till you drop. Families come from the beach, but the high-beamed wood ceilings keep the noise currents circulating. About $12 per person, but sometimes women receive a 20% discount. Reservations a plus. *Moderate. No cards.*

## Cervejaria Biruta

*Av. Sernambetiba, 6470 (Barra da Tijuca);* ☎ 433-2769.

The place to drink forever in Barra – a restaurant with a decor complex featuring at least nine different environs, from a Texas saloon to a Roman café to the old Rio train station. Go before dinner for excellent *cerveja* and a plate of thinly sliced cold cuts called *gamela de linguiças variedas,* or pig out on the many hors d'oeuvres. *Inexpensive. No cards.*

# Off-Barra

## Kaçua

*Rua Senadora Carneiro, 220 (Recreio);* ☎ *437-9310. Mon.-Thurs. 11 a.m.-midnight; Fri. and Sat. 11 a.m.-last client; Sun. 11 a.m.-6 p.m.*

At a beach on the outskirts of Barra, this is Northeastern cuisine for everyone's palate, including the palm-oil delicacies of Bahia and the dried salty meats called *carne-seca.* At the animated bar, order a *caipirinha* made from exotic Amazonian fruits.

# In São Conrado

All restaurants in São Conrado Fashion Mall are pricey.

## Guimas Restaurant

*São Conrado Fashion Mall.*

Frequented by celebs and musicians, this light, airy bistro makes a perfect lunch stop for shoppers at São Conrado Fashion Mall. Menus in English offer chicken breast with blue cheese and fish filet cooked with slices of papaya and covered with Gorgonzola cheese. The salad with warm mushrooms is excellent. While you wait for your food, feel free to doodle on the white paper tablecloths with crayons. *Expensive. All cards.*

## Alvaro's

*São Conrado Fashion Mall.*

Famous for its *chopp* and huge portions of excellent fish. Also dine on shrimp omelettes and filet mignon. *Expensive. All cards.*

## Lagostão

*São Conrado Fashion Mall, Estrada da Gávea, 899, loja 206-A;* ☎ *322-0269.*

Excellent seafood. *Expensive. No cards.*

## Valentino's Il Ristorante

*Av. Niemeyer, 121;* ☎ *274-1122.*

Top-class Italian cuisine located at the Sheraton Rio Hotel & Towers. Go for lunch and spend the day poolside or at the stunning secluded beach, then finish off with dinner at the hotel's outdoor barbecue grill. *Expensive. No cards.*

# Nightlife

*Cariocas* party hard and they party late. You may find yourself asking, "Don't these people ever have to get up for work in the morning?" That's when you'll realize it's not a good idea to do business before noon in Rio. Truly, *cariocas* seem to have limitless energy for late-night fun, and even during the weekdays you'll find popular restaurants packed from 10 p.m. on. For a tourist, however, there's only one way to survive the nightlife in Rio, and that's by taking a nap between 6 and 8 p.m. every night. By 9 p.m. you'll be ready to dine at a fashionable hour, and by 11 p.m. you can start cruising the scene.

There are two faces of nightlife in Rio – one touristic and the other pure *carioca*. First-time visitors will probably feel compelled to witness at least one samba extravaganza, featuring near-naked mulattas (cream-colored gals) who flick off their bras, samba to rapid-fire drum licks, and parade around like the Folies Bergère on uppers. The real musical culture, however, is better found in the small **piano bars** and **jazz clubs**, where you can settle back and groove on the sensual sounds of *música popular brasileira* (or MPB, a term that refers to the music of bossa nova, Milton Nascimento, Gilberto Gil, Caetano Veloso, and many others). The country's most famous singers can often be found performing at large venues like **Canecão** or the **Imperador**, where you can nosh and drink at small tables. Check the newspapers or ask your concierge who is playing.

**Discos** don't get hot until after midnight, when *cariocas* take to the floor to do what they've done naturally since birth – sing and dance their hearts out. You may be surprised by all the American and Brit rock that the DJs play, not to mention reggae and funk, but there's a joy that exists in Brazilian nightclubs that seems absent in the overly pretentious clubs of, say, New York. Simply, in Rio, people love to express themselves, and the enthusiasm is contagious. Some clubs have special drug-free matinee parties for teens, and some discos even hold roller-skating sessions – with instruction! Single women may go to most discos alone, though rest assured, you will be stared at and probably hit upon. And men should be careful about exactly who is picking them up. Transvestite prostitutes are rampant in Rio (and often violent), and some seduction scenes are just foreplay for wallet-snatching or more. (One way to discern gender, I've been told, is to check out the size of the feet and the wrists!)

For the more regionally minded, a stop at a *gafieira* or *forró* **hall** is essential. Here you'll find some of the best ballroom dancers in South America or, as in the case of the latter, high-spirited native dancing propelled by a Northeastern beat. Big bands often play in these clubs, and the action remains hot until 4 a.m. These dance halls are rarely situated in fashionable neighborhoods, but decent commonfolk attend them, and there are rarely outbreaks of trouble.

The samba shows may not be enough to satisfy everyone's erotica quotient. In this section, I've included an agenda of clubs that offer live sex shows and striptease, but they should be investigated with caution. One of the recent rages in Rio, however, has been the wildly successful **Os**

**Leopardos**, which features good-natured male striptease on one night for women only, and presentations for mixed couples and gays on others. The show is tasteful but not tame, and *carioca* girls have been flocking to hold their engagement parties there.

# Late Night To Dawn

One of the best ways to wind up a night of great partying is at one of the plushly romantic hotel bars, like the **Meridien** or the **Caesar Park**. Top-class hotels such as these usually feature the city's best local musicians, always gracious enough to take personal requests. And after-hours jam sessions at clubs such as **Jazzmania** and **People Down** are often better than the regular shows, with famous friends of the soloists sitting in.

And as the night prowling winds down, there's nothing better than breakfast at dawn – that is, before you hit the sheets to get back to the beach by noon. If you're not staying at a hotel with a fabulous breakfast buffet, head for the **Rio Palace Hotel**, where you can indulge in the freshest croissants, cakes, fruits, and omelettes while you watch a glorious sun rise over Copacabana.

A few words of caution for all kinds of night revelers. Don't get so intoxicated that you forget who you are, and remember to take taxis to and from your destination. Carry only the amount of money you will need to get you through the night. If you can, stay away from darkly lit areas.

# Piano Bars

### Chico's Bar

*Av. Epitácio Pessoa, 1560 (Lagoa);* ☎ *287-3514.*

Where Brazilian musicians and out-of-town colleagues come to jam until the wee hours – plush, dark, and sexy. *Moderate. All cards.*

### Rio's

*Pq. do Flamengo (Flamengo);* ☎ *551-1131. Noon-3 a.m.*

Part of the restaurant called Rio's, this made-for-romance piano bar is a dark, cushy den with mood-making music – one of the sexiest places in Rio. *Moderate. All cards.*

### Saint Honoré

*Av. Atlântica, 1020 (Hotel Meridien, 37th floor, Leme). Noon-3 p.m.; 8 p.m.-1 a.m.*

A plush piano bar adjacent to the even plusher French restaurant in the Hotel Meridien. *Moderate-expensive. All cards.*

## Vinicius Bar

*Av. N.S. de Copacabana, 1144; ☎ 267-1497. Opens at 8 p.m. Live music weekdays 9 p.m.-2 a.m.; weekends 9 p.m.-4 a.m.*

One of the best attended, 30-something bars for live music and dancing, Vinícius is right next to a good steakhouse in a prime area of Copacabana. A tradition among *cariocas*, it seats about 350 people, who come to soak up the solid bands and rip up the dance floor. Tourists will feel welcome – the tables are close and the natives friendly. The joint is named after one of the most beloved lyricists and poets in Brazil – Vinícius de Moraes – though when I was there, nary a Brazilian tune or lyric was heard. Cover charge. *Moderate. All cards.*

## Alberto's

*Av. Copacabana, 7 (Leme); ☎ 275-4099.*

Just two blocks from Leme Beach, here's that tiny musical bar that only the locals know about. So maybe the record companies aren't knocking down their door (the house guitar/singers are a bit *desafinado* and even the guest performers sometimes sound like they're braying), but everyone's soul is in the right place and you might even rub knees with an ex-soccer player. The sexy Latin owner (he loves boleros) sometimes plays keyboards, especially on Tango nights (Tues., Thurs., and Sat.) when a young Argentine duo twirls center-stage. By the time you arrive, the club may have hopped to another corner, so have your concierge check the address. Bahian specialties and typical meats are served for a moderate price; music cover is about $2. On weekends you'll need a reservation as there are only 10 tables.

# Jazz Clubs

## Au Bar

*Av. Epitácio Pessoa, 864 (Lagoa); ☎ 259-1041. Mon.-Sat. 6 p.m.-2 a.m.*

The newest success story in Rio, this compelling bar has become the place to listen to Brazilian music – romantic, dark and cave-like, with Spanish arches and a view of the twinkling Lagoa. Live Brazilian music (usually piano, bass, guitar, and voice) runs from 5-11 p.m.; starting at 11 p.m., there's a 1½-hour show with well-known national singers, like jazz great Leny Andrade. Sun. features classical music. Music cover until 12:30 a.m. Reservations for shows should be made about two days in advance. *Moderate. No cards.*

## Jazzmania

*Av. Rainha Elizabeth, 769 (Ipanema); ☎ 227-2447. Opens daily 9 p.m.; shows start at 9:30 p.m. (two shows in summer).*

This jazz club for people who love good music (especially Brazilian jazz) was opened about 10 years ago and was recently reinaugurated with a fabulous sound system. Come early to catch the wraparound vista of

Ipanema Beach, stay for dinner, then listen to such greats as Egberto Gismonti, Edu Lobo, and Leila Pinheiro. The Blues Project runs Feb.-Apr., featuring international stars such as John Hammond, Hy Rodgers, and Sugar Blues. *Moderate. No cards.*

## Le Rond-Point

*Av. Atlântica, 1020 (Copacabana);* ☎ *275-9922.*

A plush chrome-and-glass bar at the Meridien Hotel, with real Magrittes on the wall and a fiery house band that excels in MPB. *Moderate. All cards.*

## Mistura Fina

*Rua Garcia D'Avila, 15 (Ipanema);* ☎ *259-9394.*

This casual restaurant with outdoor tables attracts young upper-crust *cariocas* who dig the live band that cooks from 10 p.m.until 2 a.m. Before that, it's a great place to enjoy soft guitar and piano. *Inexpensive. No cards.*

## People Down

*Av. Bartolomeu Mitre, 370-A;* ☎ *294-0547.*

The upstairs club called People is private, but People Down (downstairs) offers some of the best sounds from Brazil and abroad in an intimate setting. Frequenters of the famous Blue Note in Manhattan will be reminded of that haunt.

## Rio Jazz Club

*Av. Atlântica, 1020;* ☎ *541-9046. Thurs.-Sat. 11 a.m.-last client.*

Top stars like rocker Lobão moonlight here, possibly because of the excellent acoustics. Check papers for current performances.

## The Queen's Legs

*Av. Epitácio Pessoa, 5030 (Lagoa);* ☎ *226-3648. Sun.-Thurs. 7 p.m.-2 a.m.*

Lovers of jazz congregate for jam sessions on Tues. nights here, where the windows look out on romantically illuminated Lagoa (lake). Thurs.-Sun., a fine singer remakes classic Brazilian popular music (MPB). Best offer on the menu is the filet mignon.

## Music Bar

*Estrada da Barra da Tijuca 1636-H (Itanhangá);* ☎ *492-5250. Daily 10 a.m.-last client, Sun. till 6 p.m.*

The spot to hear music in Barra – if you can put up with the Madonna videos, you'll get a glimpse of Caetano Veloso in between sets of live renditions of classical MPB Weds.-Sun. *Moderate. AE.*

## Night's Rio

*Parque do Flamendo, in front of Morro da Viúvav;* ☎ *55-1131.*

MPB graduates and aspiring stars perform here. Check the newspaper for current acts.

## Oriente/Ocidente

*Mercado São José Rua das Laranjeiras 90. Tues.-Sun. 5 p.m.-midnight.*

You can't phone ahead, but it's worth checking out who's playing jazz or *bossa*'n'blues at this club in a neighborhood that offers little else. *Cariocas* city-wide crowd in to hear stars like Victor Biglione. *No cards.*

## Zeppelin

*Estrada do Vidigal, 471;* ☎ *274-1549. Weds. and Sun. 8 p.m.-2 a.m.;*
*Fri. and Sat. 10 a.m.-3 a.m.*

A novel way to meet people when you're linguistically challenged – at this game club, where pros and near-pros at darts, chess, backgammon, and cards congregate. The clientele can be elegant. The view of the beach, preferred by romantics, is spectacular. Live music.

Excellent bars with live music can be also found at the **Meridien**, **Rio Sheraton**, **Rio Othon**, **Rio Palace**, and the **Caesar Park** hotels.

# Samba Shows

## Plataforma 1

*Rua Adalberto Ferreira, 31;* ☎ *274-4022.*

Featuring one of the city's best parades of Brazilian beauties, this popular variety show has a new twist these days – mulatto boys, who waggle their booties on a platform that extends far into the audience. Here, you'll get a more authentic sense of the samba parade: The costumes are better than Oba Oba and the spirit more earthy than Scala. Like a variety show in Harlem during the 20s, the show includes a sultry mulatta singer with an operatic range and a chorus of gorgeous coffee-colored girls with figures big to small. There's also a very sexy *gaúcho* dancer who does a flaming rope trick that's out of this world. Extremely dramatic, a tribute to Bahia and *candomblé* features drummers who nearly fall into trance. And the gravity-defying acrobatics of the *capoeiristas* are terrific. Seats are close together, and the maitre d' always asks each country to get up and sing. Better learn *New York, New York.*

## Scala 1/Scala 11

*Av. Afrânio de Melo Franco, 296;* ☎ *239-4448. 8 p.m.-4 a.m.*

The most sophisticated show in Rio, Scala is more like the Folies Bergère – rich and snazzy, with an international flair, although some *cariocas* prefer the more folkloric spirit of *Plataforma*. Fine international cuisine is also served in a luxurious setting, with crystal chandeliers and black marble stairs. Highly recommended is the *Tournedos à la Scala*, with mushroom sauce, sautéed potatoes, and *risotto alla Piemontese*. Shows start at 9 p.m., but you can stay and dance until 5 a.m.

## Dancing Samba

Dancing samba well is an art, so think about taking a few lively lessons. Classes are held at the **Só Arte Escola de Dança**, Rua Assunção, 207 (Botafogo); ☎ 286-6522, but check their schedule in advance. Then head for a samba rehearsal at a samba school (see *Index*), or the following "samba clubs," where simple folks dance "couples-samba" thigh to thigh. The music might get screechy, but that's the point. (Call in advance to check times.) Your best bets are: **Olímpico Clube,** Rua Pompeu Loureiro, 116 (Copacabana), ☎ 235-2909; and **Nega Fulô,** Rua Conde de Irajá, 132 (Botafogo), ☎ 266-6294.

Try the following for *forró*, that nearly manic, upbeat dance of the Northeast. These clubs are often fly-by-nights, so ask your concierge to confirm. **Forró do Leblon,** Rua Bartolomeu Mitre, 630 (Leblon); and **Forró do Copacabana**, Av. N.S. de Copacabana, 435.

# Candomblé

Any organized *macumba* or *candomblé* for tourists is sure to be less than the real thing. The trance religion, a syncretism of African and Catholic images, is an extremely private affair, replete with powerful drumming, incense, and congregants falling into unconscious trances. Hence, finding a good *terreiro* (the equivalent of a church service) in Rio is not the easiest task, nor would you want to wander there alone, as they are sometimes located in poor neighborhoods not exactly hospitable to strangers. Ask your concierge if he can arrange something for you, usually on a Sat. night. Reserve a private car to take you and pick you up, or better yet, have the car wait for you. If all else fails, **Fenician Tur**, Av. N.S. de Copacabana, 335, loja B; ☎ 235-3843, conducts a *macumba* tour on Wed. nights starting at 7 p.m. for about $45, but the authenticity cannot be vouched for. Theatrical presentations of *macumba* distilled for the general public are held at the club **Terreiro-Um**, Av. Borges Medeiros, 3192; ☎ 226-0577. Call for times.

# Musical Theaters

### Canecão

*Av. Wenceslau Bráz, 215;* ☎ *295-3044.*

The major venue for the city's largest acts, Canecão resembles the smaller clubs in Atlantic City. Check in the newspaper to see who's playing – you might get Tom Jobim, Gal Costa, or Simone. Large screens amplify the stage performance – I once saw Roberto Carlos singing with his own image 30 years younger – eerie. If you sit at a table, order some drinks and a plate of *petiscos*, but if you pay by card, it will take forever to leave. Tickets, about $25, usually go on sale a week before performances and must be bought at the box office. You can also sit in cheaper, bleacher-type seats on the sidelines, but the view isn't great.

### Metropolitan

*Av. Ayrton Senna (via Park Shopping).*

This is the best place to see big shows, six times the size of Canecão, underneath the shopping center called Park Shopping. Peter Frampton played here. Despite the size, all seats have a good view.

## Rock & Video

### Show Point

*Rua Maria Quitéria, 42 (Ipanema);* ☎ *521-5393. Tues.-Sun. 6 and 9 p.m. shows.*

A coffeehouse Americana-style with a Broadway obsession. Videos of musicals are played upstairs; downstairs you'll find the newest rock groups during the week, and more famous ones on the weekends. *Moderate. No cards.*

## Discos

### Ritmo

*Estrada do Joáo, 256 (São Conrado);* ☎ *322-1021.*

This 400-seat club with disco is considered the prime spot to find a rich boyfriend. It's also where some of the best international jazz musicians from Brazil perform. Every Sun. night a group called Terra Molhado does Beatles covers perfectly.

### The Ballroom

*Rua Humaitá 110,* ☎ *537-7600.*

Blues to funk to pagode, the shows here are usually extravaganzas, with dancing to follow.

### Hippopotamus

*Rua Barão da Torre, 354;* ☎ *247-0351.*

*Cariocas* will swoon if you say you're going to Hippopotamus, Rio's most exclusive private club. If you're staying at a five-star hotel (and some four-stars), you need only show your hotel ID card, but check first. Weekends are packed with chichi Brazilians. Minimum. *Expensive. No cards.*

### Stop Night

*Av. Atlântica, 1910;* ☎ *255-7583. Daily from 11:30 p.m.*

Located on the beach in Copacabana, this disco caters to the 25-and-under set, who can understand why there's a coffin in the middle of the dance floor. Upstairs, under a planetarium of lights, a small circular dance floor looks out on the beach. On weekends, live music starts at 11 p.m., and sometimes up to 1,000 people cram in to dance under the tropical plants and rock walls. Dress glitter.

## Hi Fi Night

*Capital du Chope, Rua Arnaldo Quintela, 43 (Botafogo);* ☎ *541-9944.*
*Sat. 10 p.m.-4 a.m.*

In late 1994, this club was put on everyone's calendar as the city's best dance option in the city, even if the music is a bit too American with its black R&B and loud percussive rock.

## Babilônia

*Av. Afrânio de Melo Franco, 296;* ☎ *239-4448.*

Thurs. and Sun. are a blast at Babilônia, with roller-skating (including instruction) starting at 9 p.m. At 10:30 p.m. the place transforms into a hot disco. Afternoon sessions from 4-8 p.m. on the weekends cater only to teens.

## Resumo da Opera

*Av. Borges Medeiros, 1426. Thurs.-Sun., from 10 p.m.; Sat. and Sun. 4-10 p.m.*
*(for 14-18-year-olds).*

Next to Gattopardo Café and Teatro Lagoa, this is the latest trend-setting club owned by Ricardo Amaral, a businessman who understands Rio's night pulse. Special matinee sessions for teens on Sat. and Sun. are drug-free.

## Help

*Av. Atlântica, 3432;* ☎ *521-1269.*

Usually only tourists stumble into this neon-blaring disco on Av. Atlântica – most *cariocas* wouldn't be caught dead there. On the other hand, it seems to be a good disco for single men on the prowl, but beware of prostitutes. You might be charged for your affections.

## Zoom

*Largo de São Conrado, 20 (São Conrado);* ☎ *322-4179.*

Hip young couples frequent this glitzy disco in São Conrado, with its razzmatazz light show and excellent sound system. Six bars keep the social interaction hot.

# Dancing/Gafieiras

Ballroom dancing Fred-and-Ginger style holds a powerful sway over *cariocas*, with special clubs called *gafieiras* allocated for exactly that style. Even if you don't dance, the sight of world-class performers, as well as experienced commoners doing the cha-cha, the samba, and the Brazilian tango will make your heart flutter. A code of behavior dominates the scene, however. A woman cannot refuse an offer to dance, and there may be no "indecent" gestures made between dancing couples. There's even a security man watching to ensure that the unwritten rules are obeyed.

## Asa Branca

*Av. Mem de Sá, 17;* ☎ *252-4428.*

A fabulous New Orleans-style mansion more than 100 years old houses the most sophisticated dance hall in Rio. Even Prince Charles passed through its ornate portals, where well-known Brazilian artists perform live. The house band is infectious. *Moderate. No cards.*

## Estudantina

*Pr. Tiradentes 79/1st floor (Centro);* ☎ *232-1149. Thurs.-Sat. 10:30 p.m.-4 a.m.*

Here's the best *gafieira* in Rio, where you'll find serious dancers who know how to have fun. You'll have to brave a rough part of town to get there, but the clientele is respectable. Be on the safe side and take a taxi to the second-story flat. Once inside, you'll be impressed by the tight band and skillful feet. The best day to go is Thurs. *Inexpensive. No cards.*

## Elite

*Rua Frei Caneca, 4/1st floor (Centro);* ☎ *232-2317. Sat. 11 p.m.-4 a.m.; Sun. 10 p.m.-3 a.m.; Fri. 5-11 p.m.*

Another version of Estudantina, where there's a variety of live bands and the women usually pay half price. *Inexpensive. No cards.*

## Sassaricando

*Estrada do Joá, 151 (São Conrado);* ☎ *322-3911. Thurs.-Sat. 10 p.m.-4 a.m.; Sun. 8 p.m.-2 a.m.*

A post-modern *gafieira* with neon ambience, colored mirrors, and full orchestra playing the hits of Frank Sinatra and Ary Barroso. Tango is the passion on Thurs. nights, and Sun. is dominated by Latin rhythms. Timid singles are helped by a card system that lets the waiters deliver your name and number to a prospective date.

# Pagode

The tropical beat blasting the ears of the new and old generations is *pagode*, a heart-stopping, energetic cousin of samba born in the Northeast and played (in its pure form) on banjo and *repique de mão* (a kind of tambourine). During Carnaval, and possibly throughout the year (do check), the group **Amizade** presents Pagode do Tatuí on Copacabana Beach in front of the Praço do Lido on Fri. nights around 11:30 p.m. Also, near Ponto 19 on Avenida Atlântica, you might find spontaneous *pagode* peformances Thurs.-Sun. in front of the kiosk. Don't hesitate to join in dancing. Indoor clubs that sponsor *pagode* performances include the following:

## Resumo da Opera

*Av. Borges de Medeiros, 1426 (Lagoa);* ☎ *274-5895 Wed.-Sat. 10 p.m.-4:30 a.m.*

On Thurs. and Sun., *pagode* reigns in this nightclub at the end of the evening following a heavy diet of dance music.

## Café de Espanha

*Rua Vitória da Costa 254 (Humaitá); ☎ 286-3141. Thurs. 10:30 p.m.-3 a.m.*

This is the *pagode* in-spot, where chart-hitting groups like **Sem Querer** and **Fundo do Quintal** preside.

## Ilha dos Pescadores

*Estrada da Barra, 793 (Barra da Tijuca); ☎ 494-3485. Wed., Thurs. and Sun. 10 p.m.-3 a.m.*

A highly successful house that plays only *pagode*, with a capacity for 3,500 persons and a bar that's always full. Average age here is 20!

## Wells Fargo

*Rua General Urquiza, 102 (Leblon); ☎ 274-7986. Sat. 10 p.m.-5 a.m.*

Usually dominated by the well-known *pagode* group **Gostoso Veneno**, with clientele (around age 16) barely out of the crib. Call before to confirm.

> **UP CLOSE TIP:** *In 1993 Roberto de Regina, a medical doctor, Renaissance scholar, and director of the Camerata Antique de Curitiba, began giving fabulous harpsichord recitals on his massive estate in Guaratiba, inside a medieval chapel he refurbished. Following the performance in full Middle Ages regalia, guests are treated to a chicken curry dinner, then transported home. A little anachronistic for Brazil (since the Middle Ages never ocurred here), but the music and the environs are reportedly charming. Only Fri.-Sun. For more information call* **Super Fly**, *Av. Epitácio Pessoa, 3624, room 20; ☎ 322-2286.*

## Romantic Evenings In Rio

☐ Take a night drive around the Lagoa with the golden-lit Christ marking your way, stopping off for Mexican food at Lagoa Charlie's or chop suey at Nova China.

☐ Settle into the cozy piano bar at Mariu's in Leme, where there's no cover and the bar opens at 5 p.m. Alcoholic tropical concoctions are delicious, as well as the virgin fruit cocktails with *creme de leite*, orange juice, and strawberries.

☐ Take a moonlit stroll around the Marina da Glória, topped off by a cocktail or dinner cruise on the Albacora Yacht. Night cruises with dinner on board are held on Thurs., Fri., and Sat. from 9 p.m. to 1 a.m. During the week, dinner only aboard the anchored ship. For reservations, ☎ 205-6496.

☐ Snuggle up in the piano bar at Rio's Parque do Flamengo; ☎ 551-1131 and groove on the soft jazz until 2 a.m.

☐ Ride a horsedrawn carriage through the colonial streets of Ilha da Paquetá (Paquetá Island). Get there by ferry, leaving from Praça Quinze daily. Stay the day and eat a twilight dinner in a typical village restaurant.

☐ Catch the sunset from any of the following places: Corcovado, Sugarloaf, Fishermen's Walk in Leme, Urca facing the Rio-

Nitéroi Bridge, São Conrado facing Gávea Mountain, and from any point around the lagoon.
- ☐ Bathe under a waterfall in Tijuca Forest, followed by a picnic lunch at the Emperor's Table.
- ☐ Dance cheek-to-cheek at Asa Branca.

# Erotic Rio

The real eroticism in Rio is free – it's in the waves, in the music, in the lilt of a walk, or the smile of a beautiful woman or man. There is, however, a subculture of porn to be had in Rio, though it doesn't come highly recommended. There's no law prohibiting live sex on stage, and erotic clubs in Rio have gained a reputation among world travelers, especially Germans, but to tell the truth, most people find these shows unartistic, animalistic, and violent. On the other hand, that may be exactly what you're looking for. Many of the clubs near the Meridien are fly-by-nights, with names and addresses changing quickly for whatever reasons your imagination can supply. A good source for information is your concierge, who may have already approached you if you are a single man traveling alone. While I can't be an arbiter of morality in this guide, I do feel obligated to pass on a few warnings: Fights break out often at these clubs, and assaults on tourists are not uncommon. Some taxi drivers won't even take you to them. If you do go, leave all your jewelry, credit cards, and passport in your hotel safe; take only enough money to last you the night, and hide a little extra cash in your shoe.

## Barbarela Boite

*Show Av. Princesa Isabel, 263 A;* ☎ *275-7348.*

Considered to have the most beautiful women performing striptease. Some explicit sex. Located near the Meridien Hotel, in front of the Hotel Plaza Copacabana. Call for show times. *MC only.*

## New Scotch Boite

*Av. Princesa Isabel, 7;* ☎ *275-5499. Daily 4 p.m.-7 a.m.*

The erotic show is amplified by the presence of a discotheque, samba show, and striptease with a bevy of mulattas with prodigious figures. Located directly across the street from the Meridien, with six shows nightly; an opportunity to party. *No cover, no minimum.*

## La Cicciolina

*Av. Princesa Isabel, at the corner of Rua Viveiro de Castro 15-A;* ☎ *275-8949.*

Named after the Italian porn star turned politician turned artist, Jeff Koons' ex-wife, this bar offers two erotic shows per night. Call for times. *Cover charge plus two-drink minimum.*

## An Exception To The Rule: Erotica For All Seasons

### Os Leopardos

*Teatro Alaska, Av. Copacabana, loja Hotel;* ☎ *247-9842. Fri. and Sat. at midnight, Thurs. and Sun. at 9:30 p.m.*

You can't blame this one on the bossa nova, but the latest trend in Brazilian big cities is male striptease – that is to say, artistic male striptease! A racier, and *more serious* version of Chippendales in the States, the original show was called "Night of the Leopards," which made its way around the club scene until it landed these days at the Teatro Alaska, once a seedy gay theater, now resurrected into funkydom. These days, lots of girls hold their engagement parties here, with the bride pouring champagne on the "leopard" of her choice. For the strip finale, which includes some of the most beautiful men in Rio, the participants must come onstage with a hard-on – an effect that looked to these rather inexperienced eyes like Birnam Wood advancing. The show is enlivened by several transvestite MC's, the best of which is Rogéria, an international star with blonde hair and a great voice that deserves kudos. Do slink down in your chair if you don't want to be dragged up onstage at the end to give baths (yes!). Obviously, you have to be in the mood for this kind of show, but the night I went, the theater was equally divided between gays, couples, straight men, and single women, all having a good-natured hoot. Women should also look for spin-offs at other clubs, sometimes called "Casa das Mulheres" (Women's House), which present ladies-only shows.

*Note:* The Teatro Alaska, in a shopping mall off of Av. Atlântica in Copacabana (near the Rio Palace Hotel), is today better illuminated and secured so that it is safe to attend. Next door, you might note the evangelical church, which always seems to hold loud services just at the time of the show!

## Sex Stores

### Complement Sex Shop

*Av. Nossa Senhora de Copacabana, 581, loja 306 (Copacabana);* ☎ *255-9348.*

Accoutrements of the sport, including lingerie, aphrodisiacs, videos and appliances. A discreet shop (third floor) on the main shopping drag of Copacabana, but I wouldn't suggest that a single woman go alone.

## Escort Services

Escort services that provide more than massage or mere company abound in Rio, and advertisements can be found in tourist brochures and newspapers – using the tag words *Massagem* or *Relax*. The concierge of your hotel will not even blink an eye if you ask for his assistance. However, do note: Although prostitution is not against the law in Brazil, there are few, if any, regulations concerning health, so consider it an extremely dangerous pastime since many prostitutes carry the HIV virus. The services of a more elite class of women are supplied by **Scort Girls**, which serves businessmen needing anything from a chic companion for a night on the town to a traveling secretary and more.

# Gay Rio

Gay life in Brazil has played a colorful if somewhat veiled role in Brazilian culture ever since colonial days. A riveting book on the subject is *Perverts in Paradise*, written by one of the founders of the gay movement in Brazil, who has made a fascinating, if controversial analysis of the gay influence on politics, religion, and the arts. Today, a number of Brazil's most beloved musicians are openly gay and/or bisexual, but it has never colored their popularity. In fact, the most flamboyantly gay performer, Ney Matogrosso, numbers among his fans a lot of older women who adore his campy clothes and outrageous behavior. Carnaval seems to bring out latent transvestism in a number of men, many of whom are not gay, yet revel in the opportunity to blur social distinctions and indulge in sexual fantasy.

All this is not to say that the gay lifestyle is readily accepted in Brazil. Gay bashing is not uncommon, and the fact that a number of transvestite prostitutes have murdered unsuspecting clients has not gone over well in the community. The AIDS epidemic has severely dampened blatant sexual license as well, especially during Carnaval, and anyone traveling to Brazil to live out sexual fantasies should think twice – if not three or four times. It cannot bear repeating enough: No sexually active person, gay or straight, should ever travel to Brazil without condoms. (For more information about safe sex, see *Health*, on page 23.)

## The Scene

Rio is the gay capital of South America. Since Argentina forbids transvestism, international devotees of the art eventually find their way here, particularly during Carnaval. **Cinelândia** downtown and other places in Lapa have long been traditional gay hangouts, but they remain unsavory, even by *carioca* standards. It's common knowledge that rich, foreign gays tend to stay at the **Copacabana Palace**; as such, a thin strip of beach in front of the hotel, called "The Bolsa," attracts a lot of *movimento*. Another gathering place is the monthly club called **Turma Okay**, Rua do Rezende, 43, located at Rua Gomes Freire downtown. Other places that attract a gay crowd are:

### Maxim's Bar/Restaurant

*Av. Atlântica, 1850-A (Copacabana);* ☎ *255-7444.*

Located in front of the Hotel Excelsior, this bar/restaurant attracts the same clientele as the Copacabana Palace. *Feijoada* is served on Sat., and the fish is considered outstanding. *Moderate. All cards.*

## Le Boy

*Poste 6, Rua Raul Pompeia, near the Stúdio. Copacabana movie house.*

Owned by a Frenchman, this disco attracts a sophisticated gay crowd.

## Basement

*Av. N.S. de Copacabana, 1241 LJ I.*

A new disco in Copacabana caters to all types, with an emphasis on gay.

## Underground

*Prado Junior, 36.*

A disco in the red-light district.

## Tamino Bar

*Rua Arnaldo Quintela, 26 (Botafogo); ☎ 295-1849.*

Transvestites hang out in the Galleria Alaska. Gays tend to congregate near the Excelsior Hotel near Rua Paulo Freitas.

## Carnaval

The main gay ball, called the **Grande Gala G**, is usually held at Scala Av. Afrânio de Melo Franco, 296 (Leblon); ☎ 239-4448. All kinds of guests and tourists may attend, though the final roll call tends to be predominantly gay. In 1991, the Sugarloaf Ball ended up all gay. Trends change with the years, so inquire when you arrive.

# Shopping

As the largest shopping center in South America, Rio is an exotic blend of first-world and third-world goods. You can browse for designer labels in modern shopping malls, bargain wildly for native crafts at street fairs, or negotiate wholesale prices in some of the finest jewelry stores in the world. Whether you're looking for a last-minute costume for Carnaval or the latest mini-bikini, you'll be able to find it in Rio.

The two main shopping streets in Rio are **Rua Visconde de Pirajá** in Ipanema and **Avenida Nossa Senhora de Copacabana** in Copacabana, both only a few blocks from the beach. They are, however, as different as day and night. Ipanema, of course, is the much more chic place to shop; it's full of tiny, expensive boutiques with merchandise of international quality, including exquisite luggage, gorgeous evening dresses, fine leather jackets, and elegant men's wear. Some of the snappiest stores, however, are tucked into the many side streets that cross Rua Visconde de Pirajá. Days could be spent just wandering up and down, perusing the small but highly selective stocks.

Experiencing the vibrancy of Copacabana's main shopping area is a must for those who want to throw themselves into the heart of Rio. Avenida Nossa Senhora de Copacabana stretches for about two miles, from Avenida

Princesa Isabel (where the Meridien is located) to Rua Francisco Otaviano, but most businesses and vendors are concentrated between Rua Sá Ferreira and Avenida Princesa Isabel, with the busiest blocks directly behind the Copacabana Palace Hotel. The name of the street means Our Lady of Mercy and it dates back to the 18th century, when some Peruvian Quechua Indians gave a statue of the saint to the city. The avenue is so popular that sometimes you have to squeeze your way through crowds, but you will no doubt also pass homeless families of young women and children camped out on the sidewalk. If you feel like giving money, follow your conscience. From the boutiques to the streetside vendors, shoppers will discover everything they need (and don't need) – from fresh fruits, shoes, and lingerie to batteries, cheap watches, and even those complimentary airline slippers resold for a buck. (In 1994, the massive proliferation of these sidewalk vendors can only be attributed to the economic crisis.) There are also cinemas and record stores and tiny malls with benches and even waterfalls. And there are dozens of luncheonettes, juice bars, and casual restaurants where you can fill up on salads, rice, and meat for under $10.

Along the sidewalk on **Avenida Atlântica** in Copacabana, especially on weekends, street vendors set up stands of bikinis, towels, leather bags, maps and various sculptured art made out of semi-precious rocks. (Other crafts fairs are listed below.) Stone-carved birds precariously perched on chunks of crystal are great buys and are usually half the price of those found in stores. If you become obsessed with these birds (as I did), you will find that the better ones evoke unique personalities. They make excellent gifts (even the tiny ones that go for around $3-5). Just make sure you repack them exceedingly well in newspaper – don't depend on store-wrapped techniques. Sadly, many birds in my crystal menagerie arrived home with their heads or wings snapped. Soapstone sculptures don't travel well either.

Fairs are a good place to pick up souvenirs and less expensive craftwork, and a number of them, like those in Copacabana and Ipanema, are directly geared toward the tourist. Here, you should bargain like crazy, but watch your purse at all times, particularly when you take your money out to pay. Wandering through the vegetable and flower markets held weekly in the South Zone is also fun, and pretty girls are usually offered free samples.

Other fine souvenirs include the *figa* (a charm or statue made in the shape of a clutched fist, a sign of good luck in Brazil, though tradition says you can't buy one for yourself); folkloric-dressed dolls; Indian artifacts; berimbaus (stringed instruments made out of a gourd); clocks, coasters, letter openers, and chess sets made out of semi-precious stones; rose-quartz crystal balls; lace handiwork from the Northeast; hammocks (though they're much cheaper in Amazônia); music tapes; and tropical bird calendars.

Choice stops for shopping are listed below. General business hours are from 9 a.m.-6 p.m. Mon.-Fri. and 9 a.m.-noon on Sat. Shopping centers are generally open Mon-Fri. 10 a.m.-10 p.m. and Sat. 10 a.m.-8 p.m. Stores usually don't close for lunchtime siestas.

# Clothes: For Women Only

## Blu 4

*Rua Visconde de Pirajá, 444, # 126/129 (Ipanema). Mon.-Fri. 9 a.m.-7 p.m., Sat. 9 a.m.-2 p.m.*

Brightly colored T-shirts and jersey dresses.

## Daboukir

*Rua Visconde de Pirajá, 225 E (Ipanema). Mon.-Fri. 9 a.m.-7 p.m., Sat. 9 a.m.-1:30 p.m.*

Classy short dresses and chiffon gowns for last-minute affairs.

## Elle et Lui

*Rua Visconde de Pirajá, 393A (Ipanema). Mon.-Fri. 9 a.m.-7 p.m., Sat. 9 a.m.-12:30 p.m.*

As boring as sophistication comes in Brazil – seriously yuppie fabrics and cuts at very high prices. If you wear clothes like this, why not just buy them in the States?

## Folic

*Rua Visconde de Pirajá, 540, loja B (Ipanema); ☎ 239-8997.*

Exquisite women's clothing with high-class sexy touches. A branch in Rio Sul Mall, Barra Shopping and downtown at Rua Gonçalves Dias, 49.

## Heckel Verk

*Rua Visconde de Pirajá, 547, loja E (Ipanema); ☎ 239-8891.*

Fine Brazilian designer with one-of-a-kind outfits. Just don't run into the glass door (everybody does).

## Krishna

*Rua Garcia D'Avila, 101 (Ipanema). Mon.-Fri. 9 a.m.-7 p.m., Sat. 9 a.m.-1 p.m.*

Exquisitely stylish silk and linen separates. Stores in Leblon and Barra Shopping, with a special children's section in São Conrado Fashion Mall.

## Optimo's by Leilah

*Rua Visconde de Pirajá, 351/loja 109 (Ipanema).*

Exquisite handmade leather and suede dresses. It's just a hunch, but if you really want something, bargaining with sophistication might bring down the high prices.

## Piccola Gente

*Rua Visconde de Pirajá, 371 (Ipanema). Mon.-Fri. 9 a.m.-7 p.m.*

Stylish baby clothes.

## Sagaró

*Rua Visconde de Pirajá, 295 (Ipanema).*

Good-quality, stylish women's shoes.

## Comercial SA

*Rua Visconde de Pirajá, 592, loja B (Ipanema).*

The shop that entranced me – where upper-class madames buy their maids, valets, and chauffeurs their near-colonial-style uniforms.

## Mariazinha

*Rua Visconde de Pirajá, 365-B (Galeria Fiamma/Ipanema).*

Chic women's shoes and handbags.

## Pucci

*Rua Visconde de Pirajá, 371 (Galeria Paranhos/Ipanema).*

Excellent-quality women's shoes.

# Bikinis

## Miss Bikini

*Rua Visconde de Pirajá, 177 (Ipanema);* ☎ *521-1574.*

Full line of one- and two-piece suits. *All cards.*

## Bum Bum

*Rua Visconde de Pirajá, 187, loja C (Ipanema);* ☎ *287-4493.*

"Bum Bum" in any language probably means the same thing. *No cards.*

## Sunkini

*Rua Visconde de Pirajá, 602, loja B. (Ipanema). Mon.-Fri. 9 a.m.-7 p.m., Sat. 9 a.m.-2 p.m.*

Snappy collection of bikinis and one-piece suits – both the kind you could wear back in the States and the kind you can't.

# Used Clothes

The rage in Rio is shopping for *seminovo* (semi-new) clothes from the upper-class elite, more than a curiosity, especially if you're in the mood for Givenchy, YSL, and other classical clothes. The philosophy is: *Reciclar é o chique ecológico* (recycling is ecologically chic). Here are some popular stores:

**Dois Tempos**
Rua Dias Ferreira, 64, room 206 (Leblon) . . . . . . . ☎ 512-4500
**Magic**
Rua Visconde de Pirajá, 169, # 602 (Ipanema) . . . ☎ 287-2010

# Clothes: For Men Only

### Eduardo Guinle

*Rua Visconde de Pirajá, 514-A (Ipanema).*

Elegant men's sports clothes, including oversized tropical shirts that won't embarrass you when you wear them in Boise.

### Giorgio Armani

*Rua Visconde de Pirajá, 559-A (Ipanema).*

The name speaks for itself.

### Pullman

*Av. N.S. de Copacabana, 897 (Copacabana).*

Fine men's wear.

### Saint Gall

*Av. N.S. de Copacabana, 420-C (Copacabana).*

Chic, understated men's wear.

### Dijon

*Rua Garcia D'Avila, 110 (Ipanema).*

Stylish men's wear.

# Costume Jewelry, Etc.

### Alana Bijoux

*Rua Visconde de Pirajá, 580/103 (Ipanema);* ☎ *259-7794.*
*Mon.-Fri. 9 a.m.-7 p.m., Sat. 9 a.m.-4 p.m.*

Small but excellent selection of knockoff watches, earrings, hair pieces, and whatnots for startling prices. *All cards (but 15% added).*

### Shok Presentes

*Rua Visconde de Pirajá, 580-A (Ipanema).*

Perfumes, cosmetics, and costume jewelry.

# Cosmetics

### Boticário

*Rua Visconde de Pirajá, 540 (Ipanema).*

One of Brazil's great success stories, Boticário has its own factories that make all-natural perfumes, anti-allergic cosmetics, shampoos, and soaps. The masculine line is also very popular. You can find these stores throughout Brazil. *All cards.*

## Fine Jewelry

Fine jewelry stores seem to be everywhere you look in Rio – from the lobby of your hotel to the airport and in every main shopping street and mall. As one of the world's largest suppliers of gold and semi-precious stones, Rio can offer anything from diamonds and emeralds to aquamarines, blue and gold topaz, tourmalines, and rubellites.

Unless you're a pro, stick to the top stores, which can guarantee the quality of your purchase and will treat you with deference. **H. Stern**, perhaps the biggest name in Brazil, makes it easy for tourists at five-star and four-star hotels by inviting them to a free tour of their workshop and main headquarters, located at Rua Visconde de Pirajá, 490; transportation is provided. The other big names in Brazil are **Amsterdam Saur**, as well as **Moreno, Natan, Masson,** and **M. Rosenmann.**

## Music

One of the best ways to remember Brazil is to go home with its music. In Rio, you can find not only the best albums of Brazilian popular music, but also a smattering of various regional artists as well. And don't forget the great masters of Brazilian classical music, such as Heitor Villa-Lobos. What's terrific is that you can usually listen to recordings on the store's equipment before you buy them (this habit began a few years back when customers kept bringing back records they didn't like and demanding refunds). Salespersons will usually be helpful, and checking out the newest hits is a great way to while away a rainy day in Rio. It's also not a bad idea to check whatever you do buy before you leave the store; the sealed cassette I bought of sexy Bahiana Daniela Mercury turned out to be Roberto Carlos singing out-of-date love songs.

Sad to say, recorded music is much more expensive here than in the States. Some of the best buys are videos – of Carnaval, bossa nova, and even erotica.

### Gabriela Discos

*Av. N.S. de Copacabana, 683 (Copacabana); Rua Visconde de Pirajá, 422 (Ipanema) and Rio Sul Shopping Center.*

One of the best record stores for new releases.

### Cocoon

*Av. N.S. de Copacabana, 98-A (Copacabana);* ☎ *295-2596 and Rua Gustavo Sampaio, 676 (Leme);* ☎ *541-2596.*

A full line of jazz, pop, and videos. The store in Leme is the best.

### Copadisco

*Av. N.S. de Copacabana, 340 (Copacabana);* ☎ *235-2977.*

A full line of MPB, rock, jazz, *lambada,* and video tapes of Carnaval and erotica. *V, DC.*

## Souvenirs, Crystals & Semi-precious Gems

### Ely's Gem, Jewelry & Souvenirs

*Av. N.S. de Copacabana, 249, loja D–E (Copacabana).*
*Mon.-Fri. 9 a.m.-7:30 p.m., Sat. 9 a.m.-6 p.m.*

Some of the best selections of crystal-carved birds, as well as jewelry, coasters, clocks, and chess boards made out of semi-precious stones. The huge raw amethysts are gorgeous. *All cards (dollars and traveler's checks).*

### Rio Souvenirs Ltd.

*Rua Fernando Mendes, 28-D, at the corner of Av. N.S. de Copacabana (Copacabana).*
*Mon.-Fri. 9 a.m.-7 p.m., Sat. 9 a.m.-3 p.m.*

Largest collection of mulatta samba dolls dressed à la Carmen Miranda and in a variety of Carnaval costumes – excellent for little girls. *No cards.*

### Rising

*Rua Santa Clara, 50, room 301-302 (Copacabana);* ☎ *256-3287.*
*Mon.-Fri. 9 a.m.-10 p.m., Sat. 9 a.m.-4 p.m.*

A small, soothing gem and crystal store for those who are seriously into healing. Owner Miumar Mothé, who comes from a traditional family rooted in the mining business, can speak only a little English, but she is one of the foremost esoteric experts on crystals in Brazil. There's a good selection of raw crystals and semi-precious stones, but most charming are the amazingly lifelike wood carvings of gnomes. Courses (in Portuguese) are also given on UFO-ology, tarot, runes, Bach Flowers, and numerology. Open house is held on Fri. night at 8 p.m. for those who want to meet like-minded souls.

## Pharmacies

Pharmacists give shots and also dispense advice freely. You can also buy some toiletries, and there's usually a big scale in kilos. The following pharmacies are open 24 hours and some English is spoken:

**Farmácia Piauí**
Av. Ataúlfo de Paiva, 1283A (Leblon) . . . . . . . . .  ☎ 274-8448
**Farmácia Piauí**
Rua Barata Ribeiro, 646 B (Copacabana) . . . . . . . .  ☎ 255-7445
**Farmácia do Leme**
Av. Prado Júnior, 237 (Copacabana) . . . . . . . . . .  ☎ 275-3847

**Leme Pharmacia**
Corner of Rua Prado Junior and Viveiros de Castro.
A 24-hour pharmacy in Leme.

# Books & Magazines

## Alpharrabio

*Rua Visconde de Pirajá, 365-B/loja B (Ipanema).*

Duck around the bend in this shopping center to find a funky antique bookstore full of 30-year-old Brazilian magazines and even older books. Sifting through dust piles, I even found a pre-*Manchete* magazine with pictures of the 1956 Carnaval.

## Astral e Magicos

*Rua Visconde de Pirajá, 595, loja 108 (Ipanema);* ☎ *512-3365.*
*Mon.-Sat. 9:30 a.m.-7 p.m.*

A small book and crystal store with New Age paraphernalia, including tarot cards, runes, incense, and trance music.

## Nova Galeria de Arte

*Av. N.S. de Copacabana, 241, loja D. (Copacabana);* ☎ *255-4055.*
*Mon.-Fri. 9 a.m.-7 p.m., Sat. 9 a.m.-5 p.m.*

A fine bookstore in Copacabana where you can buy such classics as *Brazilian Cookery, Traditional and Modern* by Margarette de Andrade, and the beautiful picture book, *Botanical Gardens of Rio de Janeiro* by Tom Jobim (the composer) and Zeka Araújo. *All cards.*

## Livrarias Sicilianas

*Av. N.S. de Copacabana, 591 (Copacabana).*

One of the biggest and best chains in Brazil, with an impressive selection of American and foreign magazines, including the *Harvard Business Review* and lots of rock magazines. Also, a lot of esoterica, including the works of French psychic Alan Kardec, who profoundly influenced the spiritualist movement in Brazil.

### Unilivros

*Av. N.S. de Copacabana, 445/A (Copacabana);* ☎ *235-1594.*

Full of interesting books on esoterica and spirituality in Portuguese. Also unearthed were several copies of *Birds of Brazil* in English and Jacques Cousteau's *Amazônia*, a classic adventure-photo album.

# Luggage & Handbags

### Victor Hugo

*Rua Visconde de Pirajá, 507 (Ipanema). Mon.-Fri. 9 a.m.-7 p.m., Sat. 9 a.m.-4 p.m.*

Best name for leather in Brazil, with finely crafted women's purses, wallets, and exquisite luggage. Luscious leather backpacks run about $125. A branch can also be found in Rio Sul Shopping Center.

### A Mala do Rio

*Rua Dias da Rocha, 9-A (Copacabana);* ☎ *237-7021.*

Good luggage for last-minute overweights. Just one note: if you buy luggage in Brazil, be careful when picking it up at the airport in the States; there'll be many Brazilians with similar luggage on your flight.

# Foods

### Kopenhagen Chocolates

*Av. N.S. de Copacabana, 583A (Copacabana). Mon.-Sat. 9 a.m.-9 p.m., Sun. 10 a.m.-6 p.m.*

Simply, the best chocolates in Brazil. A gift from here would be most appreciated by any Brazilian. Get some for yourself. *All cards.*

### Paes Mendonça Hipermercado

*Av. das Américas (Barra da Tijuca). Mon. 2 p.m.-10 p.m., Tues.-Sat. 8:30 a.m.-10 p.m.*

"Hiper" is even bigger than super in Portuguese – here is the country's most famous oversized supermarket, and probably the only one in the world that doesn't allow you to take photos. Which is unfortunate, because pretty young clerks zoom through the aisles on roller skates wearing very short skirts. Anything that's available in Brazil is here at a good price, including gourmet cheeses, Argentine butter, and all sorts of dietetic products. More important, this is the place to see Brazilian culture in action, but notice that you will rarely see a single woman shopping alone. Expect crowds, watch your wallet, and whatever you do, don't stand on the orange lines in front of the checkouts, or the roller skaters will zoom you down.

---

## Natural Food Stores

### Amigos do Trigo

*Rua das Laranjeiras, 462, loja 7; ☎ 255-5590. Mon.-Sat. 7 a.m.-5 p.m.*

A bakery and natural foods stand since 1984, Amigos offers freshly baked, 100% wholewheat loaves of bread, cookies, cakes, oatmeal, and other products. Another larger health food store is right around the corner in the same shopping center.

Among others you might try are: **Cereal Panificação Integral**, Rua Siqueira Campos, 143, loja 87, ☎ 237-2999; **Vida Integral Produtos Naturais**, Rua Figueira Magalhães, 741, loja H, ☎ 237-0748; and **Macro Nature Produtos Macrobióticas e Naturais**, Rua Miguel Lemos, 51, loja F, ☎ 247-3941.

---

# Photo Development

### Klub Foto

*Rua Visconde de Pirajá, 318 (Ipanema).*

Two nice Jewish brothers who do excellent development, fast.

### Kronokoma Foto

*Rua do Russel, 344-loja E (Glória); ☎ 285-1993.*

The most professional photo lab in Rio. Slides developed in two hours, contact sheets in six. Prints take a week. Near the Hotel Glória.

### Revelação

*Rua Visconde de Pirajá, 511 (Ipanema). Mon.-Sat. 8 a.m.-7 p.m.*

One-hour express development. (Other one-hour stands can also be found at Rio Sul and Barra shopping centers.)

---

# Shopping Centers

I have a deep passion for the shopping malls of Rio. The top three, **Rio Sul**, **São Conrado Fashion Mall** and **Barra Shopping Center**, are all modern, with-it malls, where you can pick up anything from toothpaste and fine shoes to evening clothes and sexy beachclothes. Not to mention jeans, jeans, jeans – a Brazilian obsession. If you get overwhelmed by the third-world buzz, these air-conditioned oases make for a few cool hours of diversion or even a full day's distraction, such as at Barra, with its myriad forms of entertainment.

### Rio Sul

*Rua Lauro Muller, 16 (Botafogo). Mon.-Sat. 10 a.m.-10 p.m.*

Closest shopping center to Copacabana, Rio Sul is a modern multilevel mall of 400 shops with a great ice cream and yogurt stand on the first floor and a culinary floor of intriguing fast foods on the top. The shopping center is about a $2 ride from the Meridien Hotel, but don't walk as you have to go through a tunnel. Many hotels have complimentary bus service. The best bets include **Bee Infantil** for children's wear, **Sapasso** for shoes, **Canteen** for women's wear, **Ocean Pacific** for surfwear, **Bijoux Access** for costume jewelry and accessories, and **1 Hora Revelações** for photo development.

## São Conrado Fashion Mall

*Estrada da Gávea, 899 (São Conrado). Mon.-Sat. 10 a.m.-10 p.m.*

This sophisticated two-level mall near the InterContinental Hotel has the classiest stores in Rio. It offers highly fashionable children's clothes at **Joanna João**, knitwear at **Asparagus**, Carmen Miranda T-shirts at **Boy's House**, leather bags, shoes, and belts at **Carmen**, teen sportswear at **Philippe Martin and Company**, traditional Northeastern lace at **Borogodó**, fine linen dresses at **Chocolate**, expensive Brazilian shoes at **Mezzo Punto** (they give a tiny gold shoe as a present that allows discounts on future purchases), women's clothes at **Champagne**, Banana Republic styles at **Bill Bros.**, and books at **Livrarias Siciliana**. Hair stylist Alan Duran at **Parruchiere** is one of the best in Rio.

## Barra Shopping

*Av. das Américas, 4666 (Barra da Tijuca). Mon.-Sat. 10 a.m.-10 p.m.*

Some consider Barra to be the best mall in Rio. Located in Barra da Tijuca, it boasts three cinemas, an amusement park for children, an ice-skating rink, Rio's only bowling alley, video games, and restaurants from fine foods to McDonald's. Air-conditioned buses run from most hotels to the mall. Best bets include **Bee** for unisex wear, **Gabriela Discos** for music, **Temper Roupas** for men's wear, **Formosinho** for sportswear, **Love Rio** for souvenirs, and **Le Postiche** for leather goods and accessories.

## Rio Design Center

*Av. Ataúlfo de Paiva, 270 (Leblon).*

A mecca for interior designers, with numerous showrooms featuring the finest in home furnishings. There are also several art galleries, as well as antiques stores.

## Shopping Center Casino Atlântico

*Av. Atlântica, 4240 (Copacabana).*

Attached to the Rio Palace Hotel, this small mall features souvenir shops, jewelry stores, and antiques shops with inflated prices. There's also a tea room and a dark, relaxing atrium.

# Fairs

## Hippie Fair (Copacabana)

*Praça do Lido. Sat. and Sun. 8 a.m.-10 p.m.*

About 300 artisans exhibit and sell paintings, sculptures, ceramics, leather goods, jewelry, clothing, and dolls. A fine place to bargain for the perfect gift. Remember, the knickknacks that look like nothing always seem to look 10 times better when you get them home.

## Hippie Fair (Ipanema)

*Praça General Osório between Ruas Jangadeiros and Teixeira de Mello. Sun. 9 a.m.-6 p.m.*

A large, crowded open-air market that has rarely lived up to its reputation. The stop is obligatory, though, for first-time tourists, who may find the leather bags, lace embroidery, and hippie-style jewelry enticing. Don't carry snatchable bags and keep your wits about you. Bargain like crazy.

## Daily Fair (Copacabana)

*In front of Rio Othon Hotel, Av. Atlântica, 3264. Daily 6 p.m.-midnight.*

Various handicrafts, paintings, and sculptures.

## Northeast Fair

*Sun. from 6 a.m.-1 p.m. in the Campo de São Cristavão, close to the Quinta da Boa Vista.*

Vendors in traditional Northeast clothes sell a variety of crafts, typical foods, and clothing accompanied by the strains of the *zabumba* (bass drums) and *sanfonas* (accordions). Good buys are colorful hammocks, leather sandals, and straw items. Take the bus marked São Cristavão #461 from Ipanema or #463 from Copacabana.

## Praça XV Square

*Near the Arco dos Telles. Thurs. and Fri.*

One of Rio's oldest fairs peddles everything from local foods to handicrafts and coins.

## Antiques Fair

*Praça Antero de Quental (Leblon). Sun. from 10 a.m.-6 p.m.*

Held by the Rio de Janeiro Antique Dealers Association.

## Antiques Fair

*Praça Marechal Ancora (downtown). Sat. from 8 a.m.-5 p.m.*

You can bargain for pricey European antiques from the 18th century.

# Hands-On Rio

## Beauty Salons

Most five-star hotels have good beauty salons, with manicurists on hand. The best hair salons in the city are listed below:

**Jambert Haute Coiffeur** (Av. Gal San Martin, 1010; ☎ *259-7198*) has French and high-class cuts for women of all ages.

**Nonato** (Rua Visconde de Pirajá, 414; Leblon. ☎ *287-6297/521-3938*). This is Rio's most famous stylist for both men and women. Nonato cuts the hair of actors and musicians.

**Pauletti** (Copacabana Palace Hotel, Av. Atlântica 1702; ☎ *255-7070*) offers reliable, inexpensive cuts for men only.

**Lynda Hartley**, Rua Siqueira Campos, 85C (Copacabana); ☎ *236-0595/257-5192*. A full-service unisex salon with manicures, facials, electrolysis, and ultra-extraordinary beauty treatments.

## Climate

Depending on the season (remember, they are reversed below the Equator), I have at times wilted from Rio's heat or shivered from its ocean wind. Generally, though, Rio's weather is beach-perfect – warm and humid, with averages between 75 and 96°F. During the Brazilian summer (Dec.–Mar.), temperatures can rise as high as 104°F, but frequent downpours tend to cool the air. May usually is rainy. Temperatures from July to Sept. can plummet to 62°F, but usually average around 72°. The best month to go in off-season is Sept. – before it gets too hot for comfort. Nearly all hotels and good restaurants have air conditioning.

## Communications

### Mail

The easiest way to send a letter is to hand it to your concierge, who will mail it for you or sell you stamps at a small increase in price. Postcards normally run about $1, as do letters up to 20 grams. Post offices are generally open weekdays 8 a.m.-5 p.m., and Sat. 8 a.m.-noon. (The post office in Praça Serzedelo Correia in Copacabana is open Mon.-Fri. 8 a.m.-7 p.m., Sat. 8 a.m.-5 p.m., and Sun. and holidays from 8 a.m.-noon.)

Most offices will deliver express post, registered mail, and parcel service both domestically and internationally.

The **Main Post Office** is at Rua Primeiro de Março, 64 (corner of Rua Rosário in downtown); other offices are Av. N.S. de Copacabana, 540 in Copacabana; Av. Princesa Isabel, 323A in Leme; Rua Visconde de Pirajá, 452 in Ipanema; and Av. Ataúlfo de Paiva, 822 in Leblon.

### Newspapers & Magazines

Rio has two daily papers. *O Jornal do Brasil* is the serious one; *O Globo* is the fun one with the color photos. Both have excellent listings of music, film, and theater events, as well as special exhibitions and children's events. *Veja* is the *Newsweek* of Brazil, with a special "This Week in Rio" insert. Available at international newsstands (such as the one near the Meridien Hotel on Rua Princesa Isabel) are current issues of the *International Herald Tribune, Wall Street Journal, Miami Herald*, and *USA Today*, which are flown in daily and distributed by noon.

Before you leave, write for a free copy of *Rio Life*, a British-edited newsletter catering to the English-speaking community in Rio. You'll probably want to skip fraternizing with compatriots, but you may discover tips on lifestyle, events, and private housing opportunities. You might even think about advertising for an apartment switch. Contact **Rio Life**, Caixa Postal 38025 (Gávea) CEP 22452, Rio de Janeiro; ☎ *(21) 252-0741;* fax *(21) 222-7904.*

## Telephones

See also *Communications* under *While You're There*, page 20.

Most hotel operators can place long-distance calls for you, but it will be enormously cheaper to dial direct or to go to the public telephone company at various offices throughout the city: Av. N.S. de Copacabana, 462 in Copacabana (open 24 hours); Rua Visconde de Pirajá, 111 in Ipanema (open 6:30 a.m.-midnight); downtown at Praça Tiradentes 41 (open 24 hours); Galeão International Airport (open 24 hours); Santos Dumont Airport (open 5:30 a.m.-11 p.m.); the main bus terminal, Rodoviária Novo Rio (24 hours), and the Menezes Cortes Bus Station, Rua São José (open weekdays 6:30 a.m.-10 p.m.).

Local pay phones on the street are bright orange. You must buy tokens called *fichas*, available at any newsstand. To make long-distance calls on the street, look for the blue-colored DDD phones, which require special tokens.

### Emergency Numbers

| | |
|---|---|
| Operator | ☎ 100 |
| Police | ☎ 190 |
| Ambulance | ☎ 192 |
| Fire station | ☎ 193 |

### Consulates

The consulate of your own country is your friend away from home. For any emergencies regarding diplomatic issues, including theft, personal assault, lost passports, or life-threatening illness, contact them immediately.

If you are planning to travel to neighboring countries, contact that country's consulate to obtain a visa, as well as travel and health advisories.

**U.S.**

| | |
|---|---|
| Av. Pres. Wilson (downtown) | ☎ 292-7117 |
| | ☎ 541-3898 |

**Canada**
Rua Lauro Müller, 116 (Botafogo) . . . . . . . . . . . . . ☎ 275-2137
. . . . . . . . . . . . . . . . . . . . . . . . . . . . . . . . . . . . . . ☎ 541-3898

**Argentina**
Praia de Botafogo, 228/rm 201 (Botafogo) . . . . . . ☎ 551-5498

**Chile**
Praia de Botafogo, 344
7th floor/rm 401 (Flamengo). . . . . . . . . . . . . . . . . ☎ 552-5349

**Costa Rica**
Rua Joana Angélica, 60, apt. 302 (Ipanema) . . . . . ☎ 267-5646

**Germany**
Rua Pres. Carlos de Campos (Laranjeiras) . . . . . . ☎ 553-6777

**Great Britain**
Praia do Flamengo, 284, 2nd floor (Flamengo). . . ☎ 552-1422

**Ireland**
Av. Princesa Isabel, 323, loja 1208:
(Copacabana) . . . . . . . . . . . . . . . . . . . . . . . . . . . . . ☎ 275-0196

**Paraguay**
Av. N.S. Copacabana, 583, loja 404;
(Copacabana) . . . . . . . . . . . . . . . . . . . . . . . . . . . . . ☎ 255-7572

**Peru**
Av. Rui Barbosa, 314, 2nd floor (Flamengo) . . . . . ☎ 551-6296

**Uruguay**
Praia de Botafogo, 242, 5th floor (Botafogo) . . . . . ☎ 533-6030

## Maps

Maps of the city (and the country) can be found in most bookstores, as well as at newspaper kiosks, where you may find a wandering vendor willing to part with good Brazil maps for about $3 (bargain!).

Also check at the hippie fairs along Avenida Atlântica in Copacabana.

## Money

### Credit Cards

Due to catastrophic inflation, businesses in Brazil are constantly changing their policies toward credit cards, but lately most credit cards are accepted at well-heeled restaurants and stores. In past years American Express was not unilaterally accepted but, as of 1996, policy seems to have changed. Depending on the swing of currency, some businesses may suddenly decide to accept no cards overnight. Consequently, always check before you eat or buy anything.

The **American Express** offices are at Praia de Botafogo, 228 Suite 514; ☎ *(21) 522-3854* and at Kontik Franstur Avenida Presidente Vargas, 309/4th floor, ☎ *(21) 296-3131*. For card carriers, here's a veritable oasis: services include emergency check cashing, card replacement, and foreign currency exchange. You can even have your mail sent care of the office and they will hold it for you – a good idea if you're going to be on the road a lot. There's also a 24-hour telephone service for any kind of assistance: ☎ 800-5050. The office will, at no extra charge, also confirm airline tickets, reroute tickets, and arrange hotel and car reservations, as well as all sightseeing excursions.

## Currency Exchange

See also *Money* under *While You're There*.

Most five- and four-star hotels in Rio will exchange money, but the rates are usually lower than in travel agencies or official exchange offices. Banks usually give lower rates than *câmbios* (hours: 10 a.m.-4:30 p.m.), but higher rates than hotels. Most travel agencies will exchange money, but check the newspaper in advance for the official daily tourist rate. Whatever you do, don't exchange money on the street unless it is with friends you know and trust well. I've heard lots of stories about a "newfound friend" who was never heard from again.

---

## Reliable Exchanges

IN COPACABANA
**Câmbio**. . . . . . . . . . . . . . . . . . . . . . . . . . . . . . ☎ 235-3843
Rua Santa Clara, 50 Fenician Tur Av. N.S. de
Copacabana, 335. loja B
**Banco do Brasil**. . . . . . . . . . . . . . . . . . . . . . . . ☎ 235-8992
Av. N.S. de Copacabana 335, loja B;
IN IPANEMA
**Casa Piano** . . . . . . . . . . . . . . . . . . . . . . . . . . . . ☎ 267-4615
Rua Visconde de Pirajá, 365
DOWNTOWN
**Banco do Brasil**
Av. Presidente Vargas, 328 . . . . . . . . . . . . . . . . . ☎ 271-7413
**Casa Piano**
Av. Rio Branco, 88
**Citibank**. . . . . . . . . . . . . . . . . . . . . . . . . . . . . . . ☎ 276-3636
Rua da Assembléia, 100
AT THE INTERNATIONAL AIRPORT: On departure level.

---

## Medical Emergencies

It's not a wise idea to get sick in Rio. Many doctors don't speak English, and health care, to put it politely, is generally not as advanced in Brazil as in the States. Your best bet is to contact your concierge, who can recommend you to the hotel's doctor or another physician who speaks English. For serious illnesses or death, do not hesitate to call your consulate immediately (see *Consulates*, above).

For names of doctors and dentists who speak English, call **Rio Health Collective** (Av. das Américas 4430, room 303; ☎ 325-9300, ext. 44. Hours: 9

a.m.-2 p.m.). For sunburns, low-grade fevers, colds, and tourist trots, pharmacists excel in suggesting appropriate reliefs. (For 24-hour pharmacies, see *Pharmacies* under *Shopping*.)

The following hospitals have 24-hour emergency service and doctors who speak English. Anything you can do to avoid going there, however, would be beneficial to your health.

**Miguel Couto**. . . . . . . . . . . . . . . . . . . . . . . . . . . . . ☎ 274-2121
Rua Mario Ribeiro, 117 (Gávea)
**Souza Aguiar** . . . . . . . . . . . . . . . . . . . . . . . . . . . . . ☎ 296-4114
Praça da República, 111 (downtown). . . . . . . . . . ☎ 242-4539
**Clinica Galdino Campos**. . . . . . . . . . . . . . . . . . . . ☎ 255-9966
Av. N.S. de Copacabana, 492. . . . fax . . . . . . . . . . ☎ 257-5791
General clinic with lab. Tourists welcome, English spoken.
**Dr. Sergio Kahn** . . . . . . . . . . . . . . . . . . . . . . . . . . ☎ 521-8941
Rua Visconde de Pirajá, 351, no. 811, (Fórum Ipanema)
Home . . . . . . . . . . . . . . . . . . . . . . . . . . . . . . . . . . . . . . ☎ 259-0325
Highly recommended dentist available to tourists day or night.

## Points Beyond Rio

### By Bus

Buses to all state capitals of Brazil leave 24 hours a day from:

**Rodoviária Novo Rio**, Av. Francisco Bicalho, 1; ☎ *291-5151*. Tickets may be purchased at the station (in advance) or at various travel agencies.

**Guanatur Turismo**, Rua Dias da Rocha, 16A; ☎ *286-5563*. Located in Copacabana – handles all bus reservations, but don't expect much English or excessive friendliness.

**Menezes Cortes**, Rua São José, 35 (downtown); ☎ *224-7577*. Serves all buses to the outskirts of Rio, as well as to the cities of Petrópolis and Teresópolis. You can also find air-conditioned buses to the Zona Sul from here.

### By Ferry

From the docks at **Praça Quinze de Novembro**, ferry boats and launches cross the bay every 10 minutes to Niterói (a 20- to 30-minute trip) for under a dollar. Boats also leave for Paquetá Island every 10 minutes.

### By Rail

Trains for São Paulo and Belo Horizonte leave from **Dom Pedro II station** in Praça Cristiano Otoni, downtown; ☎ *233-4090* or *233-3390*.

## Religious Services

When you're far away from home, you may want to attend church services of your own denomination, or even visit others out of curiosity. One Sun.

mass not to be missed is at the **São Bento Church**, where a group of monks chant Gregorian tunes.

CATHOLIC MASSES
**Capela de N.S. das Mercês**
Rua Visconde de Caravelas, 48 (Botafogo); ☎ *246-5664*
Sat. 6 p.m., Sun. 9:30 a.m. (both in English).

JEWISH
**Sinagoga Beit Aron**
Rua das Laranjeiras, 346; ☎ *245-8044*. Fri. 7:30 p.m., Sat. 9:15 a.m.
**Associação Religiosa Israelita**
Rua General Severiano, 170 (Botafogo); ☎ *295-6444*.
Fri. 6:30 p.m., Sat. at 8:30 a.m.

PRESBYTERIAN
**Catedral Presbiteriana do Rio de Janeiro**
Rua Silva Jardim, 23; ☎ *262-2330*. Sun. 10 a.m. and 7 p.m.

UMBANDISTA
**Tenda Espírita Mirim**
Av. Marechal Rondon, 595 (São Francisco Xavier); ☎ *261-3160*.

CANDOMBLÉ
**Palácio de Iansã**
Estrada Santa Efigênia, 152 (Taquara); ☎ *342-2176*. Sat. 10 p.m.

SPIRITUALISM
**Centro Espírita João Evangelista**
Rua Mena Barreto, after Rua Conde de Irajá. Fri.-night sessions are open to the public.

YOGA & MEDITATION
**Academia Brasileira de Yoga**
Rua Visconde de Pirajá, 318, sobreloja 204; ☎ *287-7048*.
**Centro do Tibet**
Rua Ribeiro de Almeida, 50 (Laranjeiras); ☎ *205-0583*.
**Lotus Center for Yoga**
Rua Voluntários da Patria, 375, casa 2; ☎ *246-2573*.

## Street Traffic

Here are some tips for staying safe as a pedestrian. *Carioca* drivers have been known to run red lights, cut the curbs, and even pull up on the sidewalk and park, so don't stand close to curbs, even if you're getting ready to cross. Also, look both ways before crossing because you never know when the traffic has been officially redirected. Note that even the police advise nighttime motorists not to stop at red lights to avoid theft.

## Tourist Offices

The main office of **Rio Tur**, the tourist board of the city of Rio, is at Rua da Assembléia, 10 (8th and 9th floors; ☎ 242-8000). There is a large tourist lounge where the receptionist speaks French, Spanish, and English and can ply you with brochures, maps, posters, and other information. It's open Mon.-Fri. 9 a.m.-6 p.m. Other information booths may be found at the international airport, at Sugarloaf Mountain, Av. Pasteur, 520, Urca (open 8 a.m.-8 p.m.); Marinha da Glória Aterro do Flamengo, Glória, ☎ 205-6447 (open 8 a.m.-5 p.m.); and the Rodoviária Novo Rio, Av. Francisco Bicalho 1 (São Cristóvão), ☎ 291-5151, ext. 143 (open 6 a.m.-midnight). **Turis Rio**, Rua Assembléia, 10 (7th and 8th floors) is the official tourist organ of the state of Rio de Janeiro. For information and travel assistance, ☎ 252-4512, weekdays 9 a.m.-6 p.m. A second information booth can be found at the international airport.

## Transportation

### Air

See also *Transportation* under *Surviving Brazil In Style* and *While You're There*.

**Varig Airlines** offers direct flights to Rio leaving from New York, Los Angeles, Chicago, and Miami. ☎ 800-468-2744.

**United Airlines** flies Miami-Rio and New York-Rio daily. ☎ 800-241-6522.

**American Airlines** flies New York-Miami-Rio daily. ☎ 800-433-7300.

**Japan Airlines** flies Tokyo-Rio (with a stop in L.A.) once on Sat. ☎ 800-525-3663. Varig and British Airways are the only airlines that fly to Rio from London.

Discounts on flights to Rio are available to members of the **Brazilian American Cultural Center**, 20 W. 46th St., New York, NY 10036; ☎ 212-242-7838 or 800-222-2746. For more information see *Package Deals* under *While You're There*.

**Bas-Brazil Travel Agency** offers an excellent five-night package in Rio, including airfare out of Miami, hotel, transfers from airport, and a half-day city tour for about $986 ($250 more than a budget-class airfare). For more information contact **Brazil Bas-Brazil**, 551 Fifth Ave. New York, NY 10017; ☎ 212-682-5310.

**Arrival:** All international flights and some domestic ones use the **Galeão International Airport** (pronounced Gah-ley-ow), Praça Salgado Filho (Ponte Aérea; ☎ 21 220-7728, or 21 210-2457). New facilities allow for international passengers who are flying on to other parts of Brazil to check in on the same level, so you won't have to schlep your luggage all over the terminal. In general, however, Setor A is for domestic flights, Setor B for international. Upon arrival, follow the crowds to customs, where you must present your passport, visa, and the card of embarkation you filled out on the airplane. (Remember to keep this card of embarkation because you must present it on departure.) Then follow the signs to pick up your luggage. Located about 45 minutes from Copacabana, Galeão is a modern multi-tiered structure with a post office, bank, exchange houses, restaurants, bars, and boutiques selling crystals, bikinis, T-shirts, and souvenirs. On your way home, arrive early and browse for any last-minute shopping, although rest assured, prices may be double what you'll find in the city.

For tourist information, ask for directions to the **Rio Tur** information booth, ☎ *398-4073*, where English-speaking guides will provide you with brochures, maps, and general assistance.

**Aeroporto Santos Dumont,** Praça Salgado Filho Ponte Aérea; ☎ *220-7728* or *210-2457*, is a 20-minute drive from the South Zone, just on the edge of downtown. A few air-taxi firms and the Rio-São Paulo shuttle are serviced here.

**From The Airport:** A new road from the international airport was built for Eco '92, cutting travel time to the South Zone down to about 30 minutes. The easiest way to reach your hotel from the airport is to pre-arrange a transfer with your hotel. Five-and four-star hotels and resorts sometimes provide a tourist bus free of charge; others will add a fee. But, considering you will be stumbling off the all-night flight weary-eyed and loaded down with luggage, there is nothing like being met in a foreign country by a friendly face holding a sign with your name.

Whatever you do, don't be bamboozled by young boys offering to carry your luggage or yellow-cab drivers who will try to charm you with a smattering of English. They're notorious for taking tourists way out of the way – your final bill could reach into the hundreds of dollars.

The safest bets are the special air-conditioned airport taxis operated by two firms: **Transcoopass** (☎ *270-4888*) and **Cootramo** (☎ *270-1442*), both of which have booths in the foyer outside the baggage pickup area. Fares to various parts of the city are posted at the booths. A ride to the South Zone, where most of the hotels are located, runs about $30, paid in advance (20% discount for a roundtrip). Keep the receipt, because if you leave something behind, it will be easy to retrieve.

**White radio taxis**, if you can find them, are generally reliable and charge about 20% less than the special cabs.

The cheapest way to the city is by air-conditioned **airport buses** that stop along the beach drags and at all major hotels. The fee is $5, and buses leave every half-hour from 5:20 a.m.-11 p.m. The bus takes about an hour one way, and is often the easiest way to return to the airport; ask your concierge what time it will arrive at your hotel. Remember, you must be at the airport for international flights two hours in advance, so leave at least three hours early.

Whatever you do, do not take a normal city bus loaded with luggage. You will probably be relieved of it in a hurry.

### Airline Ticket Offices In Rio

All tickets must be confirmed 24 hours in advance for domestic flights and 48 hours before international ones; otherwise, your ticket may be sold to someone else. Confirmations can be handled over the phone, but any flight changes must be made in person.

**Varig.** Offices are located throughout the city. The most central are at Rua Rodolfo Dantas 16, near the Copacabana Palace Hotel in Copacabana, and

Rua Visconde de Pirajá, 351; ☎ *(21) 287-0440*, on the main shopping street in Ipanema. The downtown office is at Av. Rio Branco 227; ☎ *(21) 220-3821.*

## International Airlines Serving Rio

**American Airlines,**
Av. Pres. Wilson, 165, 5th floor (downtown) . . . . ☎ 210-3126
**British Airways**
Av. Rio Branco, 108, 21st floor (downtown) . . . . . ☎ 242-6020
. . . . . . . . . . . . . . . . . . . . . . . . . . . . . . . . . . . . . . . ☎ 221-0922
**Canadian Airlines International**
Rua da Ajuda, 35, 29th floor . . . . . . . . . . . . . . . . . ☎ 220-5343
**United Airlines**
Av. Pres. Antônio Carlos, 51, 5th fl. (downtown) ☎ 532-1212
. . . . . . . . . . . . . . . . . . . . . . . . . . . . . . . . . . . . . . . . . ☎ 240-5060

## Popular Airlines Serving The Interior

All numbers carry a (21) prefix

**VASP**
Rua Santa Luzia, 735 (downtown) . . . . . . . . . . . . ☎ 292-2112
**TAP Air Portugal**
Av. Rio Branco, 311-D (downtown) . . . . . . . . . . . ☎ 210-1277
. . . . . . . . . . . . . . . . . . . . . . . . . . . . . . . . . . . . . . . ☎ 210-1278
**Transbrasil**
Av. Calógeras, 30 (downtown) . . . . . . . . . . . . . . . ☎ 262-6061

## Taxis

See also *Private Cars/Private Guides,* below.

The easiest way to get around Rio is by taxi. *Carioca* taxi drivers, however, are infamous throughout Brazil for both their crazy driving and their wily ways, though in the face of such outlandish inflation, who can blame them? To get the best deal for your money, consult the *Taxis* section under *While You're There.* In Rio, the common house variety – **yellow cabs** – can be hailed throughout the South Zone on main avenues, and they often line up outside tourist attractions and nightclubs. The concierges of upper-class hotels, however, tend to steer guests into the special air-conditioned taxis in their front driveway; these cabs are definitely safer and are controlled by the hotel, but they cost twice as much. You can also ask the concierge to call a **radio taxi** for you, which will be reliable and cost only 20% more than yellow cabs.

**Cootramo** and **Transcoopass**, ☎ *270-1442* and ☎ *270-4888* (respectively). These special taxis can be hired to tour the city. The advantage is that the driver will wait while you shop and dine, and follow you as you stroll.

## Buses

Hot, crowded and bumpy, city buses in Rio are only for the experienced native or the die-hard adventurer who can look Jonah's whale in the eye and not flinch. During high season, the chance of getting your pocket picked or purse snatched is more than probable, particularly if you wear loud tropical shirts or lug lots of shopping bags. Sad to say, there are numerous stories about buses being held up in Rio – though not without humor. One time a bus bandit requested only *ouro* (gold) from his passengers, then politely returned a silver watch to a rider who had coughed up everything, just in case. Avoid carrying any valuables on you, wear a money belt inside your shirt, hug your purse and backpack to your chest, don't even think about flashing your camera, and try not to look like a tourist. Have your change ready as you board the back of the bus, pay the cashier, then push through the turnstile to your seat.

If you want to travel along the beach drags, flag down a special air-conditioned bus called a *frescão*, which is specifically designed for tourists and stops at the hotels, the two airports, and downtown.

**Rodoviária Novo Rio**, Av. Francisco Bicalho, 1 in São Christovão; ☎ *291-5151*. This is the main bus station for city and state if you are traveling to the neighboring tourist cities of Petrópolis and Teresópolis.

**Menezes Cortes Rodoviária**, Rua São José; ☎ *224-7577*, is a more centrally located terminal.

## Metro

The subway in Rio is nothing like the one in New York. That is to say, it's clean, bright and one of the cheeriest places in town. Unfortunately, it's very short. Started in 1979, it's still not finished and has only two lines: **Line 1** goes from Botafogo Station to the Saens Pena Station in Tijuca; **Line 2** from Estacio Station to the Engenho da Painha Station. Combination subway-bus tickets allow you to ride special buses called *integração* to and from Botafogo Station. The **M-21** goes to Leblon via Jardim Botânico and Jóquei, while line **M-22** goes via Copacabana as far as Leblon.

During Carnaval, the subway is the best way to reach the Sambadrome, as the streets are choked with revelers and traffic jams. During most of the year, the subway operates Mon.-Sat. 6 a.m.-11 p.m., except Sun. All tickets can be bought inside the stations; the ticket is inserted into the slot at the turnstile.

For bus and subway routes, check the *Official Guide* handed out by **Rio Tur**, available at the airport and at the main office, Rua da Assembléia, 10 (8th and 9th floors) in downtown; ☎ *242-8000* (weekdays 9 a.m.-6 p.m.).

## Car Rentals

Unless you're a Formula One driver, I wouldn't suggest renting a car in Rio. (See *Driving* under *While You're There*.) Streets are hard to find, and the names are hard to spell and even harder to pronounce; *carioca* drivers are fanatics. If you must, however, the following companies offer good rates:

**Avis**
Av. Princesa Isabel, 150 (Copacabana). . . . . . . . . ☎ 542-4249
**Hertz**
Av. Princesa Isabel, 334 (Copacabana). . . . . . . . . ☎ 275-3245
**Nobre**
Av. Princesa Isabel 150 . . . . . . . . . . . . . . . . . . . . . . ☎ 541-4646

Cars may also be rented at the international airport as you exit from customs.

## Travel Agencies & Tours

There are numerous travel agencies in Rio offering half- and full-day tours of various touristic sites. The most popular tours are the Sugarloaf-Corcovado combo, Tijuca Forest, Rio by Night, and schooner trips around the islands in Angra. The following agencies work with highly personable guides who speak excellent English and are exceedingly reliable.

### Turistur

*Rua Araujo Porto Alegre, 36; ☎ (21) 240-0173/240-0560; fax (21) 240-0560.*

One of the finest travel/tourist agencies in the country, Turistur works with a large European clientele who appreciate the personalized service. However, feel free to walk in off the street and arrange a guide for the day, or make arrangements for travel throughout Brazil.

### Diana Turismo

*Av. N.S. de Copacabana 330/Co. 01; ☎ 255-2296.*

A well-run travel agency set up to serve European and American clientele with class, Diana Turismo will make all your hotel and transportation reservations, including picking you up at the airport. They also offer excellent package tours, including a special Carnaval deal as well as wonderful excursions outside Rio, such as horsebackriding in the Serra da Bocaina. In Rio, half-day tours (4½ hours) run about $26 and include a guide, pickup at hotel, city tour, and a stop at Corcovado or Sugarloaf. All rates are given in dollars, with special discounts for families of four. Package tours of the Amazon and the Pantanal are also available. Write for their itineraries.

## Private Cars & Guides

If you want something different from the run-of-the-herd tours from big agencies, hire a private guide and driver to spin you around town. Good English-speaking guides and drivers are hard to come by, but I can highly recommend the following for their reliability, expertise, and charm.

### Professor Carlos Roquette

☎ 322-4872

A relic from another century, this highly personable, if slightly eccentric 40-something art historian brings old Rio to life like no one I've ever met. For groups of any size, he offers walking tours of the old city, art museums, opera house, and "interiors" of buildings, blending philosophy, sociology and architectural trends into a seamless whole. He's also the source for any hard-to-find object or fact concerning Rio.

### Paulo Cézar

*Rua Souza Franco, 783 (Vila Isabel), casa 3, apt. 201;* ☎ *268-8499.*

Cézar is a hip, up-and-coming painter who excels in art and historical tours and can introduce you to the best galleries in the city. You may also ask to see his private studio; many people walk away with purchases.

### Rubéms Topelem

☎ *256-8297, 236-6400*

Topelem gives individual and group tours only in jeeps; his main destinations are anything ecological, including the rainforest (see under *Tijuca Forest* and *Favela Tours*). His company is called **Bicho Solto,** which means a "free animal, one that's difficult to catch."

### Maurício Basseres

*Av. Epitácio Pessoa, 3624/201;* ☎ *226-5207/286-0666.*

Charismatic with big groups and probably stimulating alone, Maurício will take you nearly anywhere for about $100 per eight hours, including Petrópolis, Búzios, Angra dos Reis, and Rio by Night. Three people will fit in his own car, or he can arrange for larger buses.

## José Wanderley

*Rua Camarista Meier, 636, B1, apt. 306 (Meier);* ☎ *594-3336, 593-7519.*

This older Brazilian gentleman must be the most honest and decent driver in Rio. For about $50 for eight hours (it may be higher by now), you can go anywhere, accompanied by his humorous commentary; excursions outside the city usually run more. He can be found in front of the Hotel Glória, but he may also be reached at his home number, above. José speaks Japanese, Italian, Spanish, and English with gusto. He will also take you to Itacuruça for a wonderful day trip that includes a schooner excursion and buffet in the islands of Angra dos Reis.

### Vaccinations

See also *Surviving Brazil In Style.*

Considering the possibility of dirty syringes and dubious vaccines, I would heartily recommend getting all vaccinations before you arrive in Brazil. Gamma globulin shots, purchased over the counter, can be administered in the hip by pharmacists behind closed curtains.

If you are desperate for other vaccinations before you go into the jungle, try the following government center:

**Posto de Vacinacāo do Ministerio da Saúde**
Praça Marechal Ancora, Praça XV de Novembro   ☎ 240-8628

### What To Wear

Rio is the most casual city in the world. No one bats an eye if you walk to the beaches in the South Zone dressed only in your bathing suit, but it's best to wear a coverup and sandals. Most restaurants (except sidewalk cafés) will expect you to wear a shirt, but ties are declassé, except in the fanciest restaurants, such as St. Honoré. Shorts, light summer dresses, cotton and linen slacks, jeans, and T-shirts will get you through the day. At night, *cariocas* dress to kill in tight, sexy dresses and fashionable slacks. Anyone planning to walk around the city should wear walking shoes or tennies because the pavements are uneven and full of holes.

# EXCURSIONS FROM RIO

**N**o one should ever get stuck in Rio for their entire Brazilian vacation. Only miles away from the hustle and bustle of the city is what I call "Greener Rio"– an eco-traveler's paradise of challenging mountain peaks, furious river rapids, fabulous deserted islands, and 19th-century historical villages right out of a movie set. These destinations, such as the **Costa do Sol** (north of Rio), the **Costa Verde** (south of Rio), and the **Serras** (the mountain chain above Rio) have long been familiar to Brazilians from Rio and São Paulo, who escape here to their second homes during summer and holidays. Today there are travel packages that are easy to arrange and even easier to follow, allowing us foreign tourists the benefit of these offbeat pleasures with minimum effort.

One of the easiest trips to make from Rio is to the historical city of **Petrópolis**, where the imperial government had its summer home during

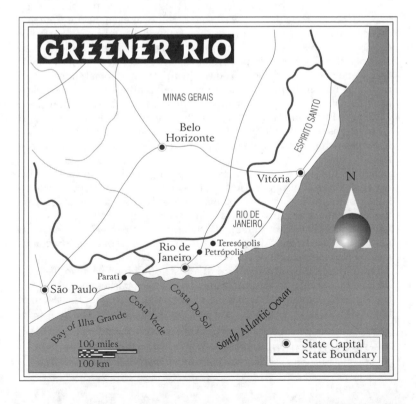

the 19th century. And just 50 miles west of Rio is the village of **Itacuruçá**, a departure point for some of the best schooner excursions in the area. Less than two hours from Rio is the elite resort of **Nas Rocas** on its own island, just a bird's fly from the internationally hip village of **Búzios**. The historically preserved village of **Parati** is a national patrimony, and probably everyone's favorite excursion outside Rio, where you can relive the early days of Brazil. For forest adventurers, one of my greatest memories was curling up into the warm quilts at the **Pousada Vale dos Veados**, tucked into the hills of the **National Forest of Serra da Bocaina** (three hours from Rio by jeep or car). The unusual local color of these environs, the added security of being away from an urban area, and the full range of sports activities available make them perfect for both families and honeymooners.

# NORTH OF RIO

## Petrópolis

Dom Pedro had a good idea when he bought a farm in this cool, mountainous area 41 miles from Rio. In 1843, his son also fell in love with the greenery and fresh air and designated the area the summer home of the imperial government. From 1889-99, Petrópolis was even the full-time seat of the government. As German immigrants found the stunning scenery not only reminiscent of home but a welcome refuge from the heat and disease of Rio, a thriving community developed, with a decidedly Gothic flavor and a nobleman's attitude. Today, many large colonial homes and mansions remain from the empire period (all pink – a curiosity scholars can't explain), as well as romantic cobblestone streets and extravagant gardens. Most tourists come to visit the **Imperial Museum** and **royal churches**, as well as to indulge in wholesale shopping along **Rua Teresa**. Eco-treks across the mountainous plains are also attracting some hardy adventurers.

A new four-lane highway wraps around a spectacular roller coaster vista between Rio and Petrópolis. The trip takes only an hour as you pass through hills, tropical forests, and banana plantations. Take the time to investigate the waterfalls along the highway and revel in the increasingly cooler temperatures. However, don't make the trip on foggy days or if the roads are slick – it's extremely dangerous, although the view of the misty clouds settling into the mountains can be truly mystical.

During the entire month of June, the **Festa do Colono Alemão** (Festival of German Immigrants) erupts into wild street parties, beer-drinking contests, and oompah bands. For more information, write the official tourist board **SECTUR**, Pr. Mariano Procópio, Petrópolis, RJ CEP 25286; ☎ *(242) 42-0316.*

> **UP CLOSE TIP:** *The entire city can be seen in a couple of hours, but the museum, churches, and some restaurants and stores are closed Mon.*

# Sights

## Terraço

Twenty minutes from Petrópolis on the highway from Rio is Terraço – a wonderful *mirante* (view) marked by a large stone cross.

## Museu Imperial

*Rua da Imperatriz, 220 (Centro);* ☎ *(242) 427-1023. Small fee.*
*Tues.-Sun. noon-5:30 p.m.*

Why are they playing *Rhapsody in Blue*? you might ask as you wander through Dom Pedro's 44-room summer palace, but somehow Gershwin's music does manage to throw into dramatic relief the extraordinary paintings, costumes, and furniture of Brazil's imperial era. With luck, by the time you arrive the royal crown, with 639 diamonds and 77 pearls, will have been put back on display, but just as remarkable are the 19th-century paintings of Rio, as well as the various musical instruments used in the era. The museum is arranged to make you feel as though you are visiting the owners of the palace, with its many rooms and salons. You'll love schussing along highly polished wooden floors on felt slippers, but all coats, cameras, packs, and umbrellas must be left at the door.

> **UP CLOSE TIP:** *The horse-drawn carriages in front of the museum will take you to the cathedral, the Santos Dumont house, and past the Imperial Museum.*

## Cathedral de São Pedro de Alcântara

*Av. Tiradentes. Open for visits Mon.-Fri. 8 a.m.-noon; Sun. 8 a.m.-6 p.m. Free.*

This imposing Gothic cathedral is where Dom Pedro II, his wife, Empress Dona Teresa Cristina, and his daughter, Princesa Isabel (now immortalized in a famous street in Rio), are entombed in sepulchres sculpted with their life-size figures in imperial regalia. Note the large painting of Pedro and his family being led unhappily to exile in Portugal in 1889. Mass on Sun. is offered at 8:30, 10, and 11:30 a.m., and 6 p.m. (weekdays 8 p.m.).

## Palácio de Cristal (Crystal Palace)

*Pra. da Confluência, Rua Alfredo Pacha. Free. Tues.-Sun. 9 a.m.-5 p.m.*

This cast-iron and stained-glass construction with stunning French chandeliers was a wedding present to Princesa Isabel, whose own pink-and-white house was a two-minute walk away. As the first prefabricated house in France, the pavilion was shipped and then re-assembled here in 1884, a wonder for the time. How easy it is to imagine magnificent balls held inside the glass walls while guests strolled in the garden outside. In fact, it was here that Princesa Isabel danced the night away in celebration of the slaves' emancipation on April 1, 1888.

## Casa de Santos Dumont

*Rua do Encanto, 124. Tues.-Sun. 9 a.m.-5 p.m.*

Brazilians cherish the idea that it was their compatriot, Santos Dumont (not the Wright brothers), who flew the first airplane in the world. A famous inventor, Dumont started in a balloon around the Eiffel Tower, then graduated to a paper plane. A debonair-looking chap of slight stature, he built a house to his own measurements, which stands today as an eccentric homage to his life.

## Florália

*Rua Octávio Maui, 1700 (Samambaia); ☎ (252) 420-4340. Daily 9 a.m.-6p.m.*

Twenty minutes from Petrópolis proper is this exquisite greenhouse with more than 100 green plants and flowers. Of course, you won't get any through customs, but at least revel in the fresh air and the beautiful specimens of rare orchids. Next door, a German-style restaurant replete with the smell of country baking offers a *chá completo* (something between breakfast, tea, and a pig-out dessert) with a buffet of breads, jellies, brownies, pâté, and chocolates for about $6. Buses from downtown stop at its doorstep.

# Sports

Hang-gliding takes off from the **Rampa da Simieriain** in the district of Simeria and the **Rampa do Parque São Vicente** in Quitandinha.

# Where To Stay & Eat

## Pousada de Alcobaça

*Rua Agostinho Goulão, 298 (Correa, RJ 225730-050); ☎ 21-1240.*

Located in Correas, a town north of Petrópolis in the Valley of the Gourmets (so-named for its fine restaurants), this once summer estate has been transformed into a charming 10-room bed-and-breakfast. The treasure is the excellent cooking of Dona Laura, whose fine pasta sauces are spiked with herbs from her own garden. No leisure program here, but do stop for a meal or tea overlooking the gardens, an exquisite blend of Italian villa, English countryside and Brazilian forest with wildflower beds, trellises, and statuary (breakfast only). *Moderate. All cards.*

## Bauernstube

*Dr. Nelson de Sá Earp. 297; ☎ 42-1097. 11 a.m.-midnight, except Mon.*

Three minutes by car from the museum, this typical German restaurant with log-cabin walls offers a roaring fire throughout winter. Antique gas lamps lend romance to the already comforting lentil soup with sausage. Hungarian goulash, bratwurst, smoked tongue, and kassler with sauerkraut are also authentic and delicious, but do try the *pato Baden Baden* – sliced duck roasted with cabbage. Apfelstrudel with schnapps for dessert is a must. *Moderate. All cards.*

## Locanda delle Mimosa

*Al. das Mimosas, 30 (Vale Florido), accessed from km. 71.5 on BR-040 to Rio de Janeiro), 15 km.;* ☎ *42-5405. Noon-4 p.m., 8 p.m.-midnight, closed Mon.-Weds. and the month of Aug.*

This delightful restaurant, ensconced in a small, but sophisticated *pousada* (six rooms), is the creation of Dânio Braga, considered Brazil's chef of the year in 1996. Top-notch modern Italian cuisine is influenced by his ancestors (pasta with real Genovese pesto), but the wine cellar is also superb. Menu changes every week, but includes delicious pizzas on Sun. *Expensive. All cards.*

---

# Shopping

---

## Rua Teresa

*Cariocas* (from Rio) descend on this meandering street to snatch up the incredibly cheap buys on shirts, jeans, knitwear, and sportswear. Prices are cheaper here than in Rio, but the style and quality might strike you as old-fashioned.

## Sandiges

*Estrada da Cascatinha, 46-Galpão 1;* ☎ *42-5868. 9 a.m.-6 p.m.*

Expect all souvenirs to be overpriced in this city; at least this store, next door to the house of Santos Dumont, has interesting stock. Crystal birds, sandstone sculptures, and a large collection of sculptured saints, including *candomblé* divinities, are available. Check out the tiny replicas of the imperial crown. *All cards.*

## In Tempore

*Rua Barão de Amazonas, 35;* ☎ *43-6100.*

Nice for a look-see, this antique store features 19th-century Brazilian colonial furniture and English stoneware, silver, and jewelry.

## Patrones

*Rua Coronel Veiga, 1321. 9 a.m.-6 p.m., closed Mon.*

A must-do on the way home is this aromatic chocolate store, where all goods are made on premises. No public demonstrations. *All cards.*

---

# Hands-On Petrópolis

---

**Private guides** are the easiest way to reach and get around Petrópolis. **Buses** also leave daily from Rio's Menezes Cortes terminal, Rua São José, 35 (downtown); ☎ *(21) 224-7577,* on the Fácil and Unica lines every 15 minutes, but the buses fill up fast. Numerous Rio-based agencies, such as **Diana Turismo,** ☎ *(21) 255-2296,* and **Turistur,** ☎ *(21) 240-0173,* offer day-trips to Petrópolis.

# Teresópolis

Fifty-six miles from Rio, within proximity of Teresópolis, lies the **Parque Nacional Serra dos Orgãos** – a national park filled with rugged, mountainous climbs, unusual rock formations, and unforgettable vistas. Visitors can roam the 27,170 acres of wild forest, waterfalls, and streams while admiring the abundant tropical flora and fauna. Located inside the park is the **Museu von Matius**, specializing in natural history.

From the top of Mirante do Soberno, Guanabara Bay in Rio can be seen in full, along with the city of Cabo Frio. Legends have come to be associated with the unusual rock formations, poetically called *Dedo de Nossa Senhora* (Finger of Our Lady), *Dedo de Deus* (Finger of God), and the *Agulha do Diablo* (Devil's Needle). It takes about four hours to climb the park's highest peak, *Pedra do Sino* (Rock of the Bell), towering at 7,422 feet.

## Where To Stay

See page 26 for price chart.

### Hotel Fazenda Rosa dos Ventos

*Estrada Teresópolis, Friburgo (RJ-130), C.P. 92967 (Teresópolis, RJ);*
☎ *(21) 742-8833, fax 742-8174.*

The only Brazilian hotel in the French Relais et Châteaux chain is so adult-oriented it won't accept children under 16 (not even the owner's grandchildren). As such, exquisite peace and calm prevail over these three chalet-style buildings set in the midst of a mountainous 250-acre private park. Spend hours on horseback following forest trails replete with bamboo or pine, swim in two hotel pools or a fresh-water lake, indulge in dry and wet saunas, or play tennis on a lakeside court surrounded by flowering bougainvillea. The food is committed Brazilian, with free cheeses, fruits, and vegetables from the farm next door. Rate includes breakfast, lunch, and occasional dinner. Reserve horses on arrival. *41 apts. Expensive. All cards.*

## Le Canton

*Estrada Teresópolis-Friburgo, 12.5 km. (Vargem Grande, near Teresópolis)*
☎ *and fax (21) 742-6202.*

The activities feel like Club Med, but the architecture is all Swiss in this fantasy maze of turrets, towers, market buildings, and town hall that comprise Le Canton. The resort handles children by making them disappear (the kiddie recreation programs last from mid-morning right through until dinner at 8 p.m.). Spend the day hiking to a waterfall, skiing on grass, or playing group volleyball. Three pools (one heated) offer good swimming. The package includes breakfast and lunch. The horse club offers four extensive tours through the mountains. *Moderate. All cards.*

# Where To Eat

See page 26 for price chart.

## Taberna Alpina

*Rua Duque de Caxias, 131;* ☎ *742-0123. Noon to 5 p.m.*

The alternative to a picnic basket in the mountains, this German beer hall proffers excellent sausage, sauerkraut, and potato salad, a tribute to the ancestors of many immigrants who settled here. *Moderate. All cards.*

## Dona Irene

*Rua Yeda, 730, Tijuca (Teresópolis);* ☎ *742-2901.*

You may need a reservation, particularly during Carnaval, to enjoy the extraordinary banquet of Russian food, homemade vodka, and great desserts. *Expensive. All cards.*

> **UP CLOSE TIP:** *Best time to stay overnight in Petrópolis or Teresópolis is during the week to avoid the weekend carioca crush, when reservations are hard to come by and rates usually higher. Also, remember to dress for cool climes (sweater, light jacket, and hiking boots).*

# Costa do Sol

This stretch of coastline north of Rio belongs to the glitter-and-be-gay set of Rio – an international hot spot that draws celebs and tourists alike. Despite the overload of pleasure-seekers, the area, which is dominated by the city of Búzios, has not yet lost its primitive edge, so go now. It is easily reached by bus or taxi (112 miles) from Rio (two hours, 10 minutes by car). The Costa do Sol requires a car to access its more remote beaches. Without wheels, foreign travelers would be best suited to the glorious resort of Nas Rocas, especially those in search of that castaway island.

# Búzios

Ever since Brigitte Bardot did her "I vant to be alone" number here in 1964 (thus magnetizing thousands of paparazzi), the seaside village of Búzios has steadily grown to become the hippest watering hole of the Brazilian elite. On any day of the week, particularly in summer, it's possible to glimpse famous actors, musicians, and artists strolling the quaint cobblestone streets and possibly bathing in the nude at one of the 23 beaches. Although some call the area Brazil's French Riviera, the village of Amaração Búzios (as it's technically known) has nevertheless retained its paradisiacal ambiance. But it is no longer a sleepy village; during summer weekends (Dec.-Mar.) the 12,000-strong population swells to more than four times that amount. These days chic, expensive stores line the main avenue, charming *pousadas* dot the shoreline, and some of the best restaurants in Rio sport branches here.

The magical weather in Búzios perhaps accounts for some of its attraction. It's called *Sol e Chuva* because it can rain at the same time the sun is clearly shining. Often dramatic, the showers are brief, and they happily cool the air.

Some say that the ghosts of 19th-century slaves still roam the peninsula where Búzios is located, about 105 miles north of Rio. In the early 1880s, the largest banana plantation in the state of Rio de Janeiro was situated here, although it was tragically destroyed by fire following a mutinous quarrel between workers and owner.

Today, mystically minded Brazilians still consider the area is haunted and claim that they can feel the souls of these slaves moaning to the wind, particularly on Rasa Island, which was a refuge for runaway slaves. Such mysticism, however, doesn't seem to dampen any of the active nightlife for which Búzios is known. Clubs stay open till 5 or 6 a.m., with a number of discos overlooking the shimmering sea.

## Sights

The philosophy of Búzios is beach, more beach, and boogie all night. The residents are extremely laid-back and infamous for their unshakable calm. Whatever you do, don't go to the center of Búzios in the morning, because nothing is open. Everyone, including the shopkeepers, is nursing a hangover, having stayed out to party on **Rua das Pedras**, until the wee hours. Instead, come around midday, when folks are just beginning to rub the sleep from their eyes. During the summer, Rua das Pedras (also known as Rua José Bento Ribeiro Dantas) is transformed into a colorful street fair. A popular meeting place day and night is **Chez Micou**, with a huge open bar and enormous TV screens.

Nightlife centers around **Estralagem**, a small charming pub with live jazz filling the outdoor courtyard and **St. Trop**, an outdoor reggae-based disco overlooking the sea. At night, "dress to kill" is the attire.

# Beaches

Búzios has 23 beaches of all shapes and sizes. **Jõao Fernandes** is perfect for swimming; **João Fernandinho** is excellent for diving; **Ferradura** is known for jetskiing; and **Praia Brava** is the nude beach. **Azedo Beach**, an easy walk from center, is where Brigitte Bardot's house was located.

# Sports

You can rent Yamaha **jetskis** on Ferradura Beach from the company **My Car**. **Kayak, scuba, surfing**, and **schooner excursions** can also be arranged.

# Where To Stay

See page 26 for price chart.

### Nas Rocas (Island Resort)

*Ilha Rasa, 10 km; reservations, ☎ (247) 29-1303, fax 29-1289.*

One of the most popular resorts in Brazil, Nasa Rocas occupies its own Robinson Crusoe island off the peninsula of Búzios. The late owner, Umberto Modiano, was a Jewish immigrant during the 40's who started exporting coffee and was offered the land on this island (then called Rasa) for dirt-cheap prices. Eight years ago, his son, an architect, designed 70 chalets to blend gracefully with the luxurious natural landscape. Exotic flowers and cactus bloom year-round, and huge boulders dot the shore; at night you can sit on the rock and watch the moon turn the sea silver. Toucans and parrots roam the grounds at will. The latter have mastered the art of stealing cherries off tropical drinks. Schooners leave daily to transport guests to the beaches of Búzios free of charge – you can even cruise all day, with a lunch stop for barbecued shrimp on Tartaruga Island. Kayaking and windsurfing are also free, and joggers will love the one-mile perimeter path around the island. Life is more laid-back here than at Club Med, with families and children enjoying the security. Suites are perfect for honeymooners; in low season singles might find the pickings slim unless they go to Búzios for nightlife. To reach Búzios you can either take a 15-minute boat ride from the hotel's marina, or hire a taxi or jeep.

Rustically appointed standards come with air conditioning and mini-bar, but no TV. On Thurs. and Sun. clients may be picked up at the airport for a set fee (about $30 per person, round trip) or the hotel can arrange a bus pickup at your hotel in Rio. Breakfast is included but lunch and dinner are extremely overpriced. *70 apts. Reservations can be made through F & H Consulting, 4545 Baseline Ave., Santa Ynez, CA 93463; ☎ (800) 544-5503. Very Expensive. All cards.*

### Pousada do Martim Pescador

*Estrada da Ponta da Sapata, lote 13-A (Praia da Manguinhos), 2.5 km.;*
☎ *(247) 23-1449, fax 23-2547.*

Leather, glass, and wood furniture transform this 13-room *pousada* into a home away from home. Your best bet is the two-room suite, which looks out on the fabulous beach of Maguinhos. Squash courts are available, as are pool, sauna, and swings. *Moderate-expensive. All cards.*

### Barracuda Pousada

*Pousada da Sapata;* ☎ *(247) 1314. Reservations,* ☎ *(21) 262-2013.*

Purple bougainvillea contrasting against the orange dirt road and vibrant green shrubs turn this modest *pousada* into a luscious tropical estate. A bit isolated, the *pousada* is about seven minutes from Centro down a scenic winding road; you must have a car. Unfortunately, the 23 individual apartments are less impressive than the grounds, but they are functional. Amenities include a pool with a bar, an indoor restaurant, and a game room with a gorgeous wood-boat bar. The beach is a five-minute walk away. *Moderate-expensive. All cards.*

### Lagostim Pousada

*Estrada de Geribá, 70;* ☎ *(247) 23-2082.*

Located 1,000 feet from Ferradurinha Beach (considered one of the most beautiful in Brazil), this colonial-style *pousada* has charm, intimacy, and comfort. Two regal suites have awesome panoramic views; the more rustic apartments and two other suites are fully air conditioned, with color TV and phone. A homey living room, pool room, dry sauna, and restaurant complete the services. Sports equipment can be rented nearby. *12 apts. Moderate-expensive. All cards.*

### Pousada Portal da Búzios

*Estrada José Bento Ribeiro Dantas (Porral da Ferradura);* ☎ *(21) 231-11, for reservations. Phone in Búzios,* ☎ *(247) 23-2283.*

The cheap option in Búzios, where "rustic" takes on new dimensions. These simple rooms, with no air conditioning, are five minutes from downtown. You'll be surprised to find a pool, but you can actually see the coast with a good pair of binoculars. Rates have been a steal in this city. Next door, the simple eatery, Fernando's Point, offers some of the best seafood in the village. *Inexpensive. No cards.*

---

# Where To Eat

---

Most of Búzios' restaurants are on **Rua das Pedras** in Centro. There are also *barracas* (counters) on the beach for snacks and drinks. Off-season from May-Dec., and especially in Aug., you may find some restaurants closed, particularly at lunchtime during the week. See page 26 for price chart.

### Satyricon

*Rua das Pedras, 500; ☎ 23-1595. 1 p.m.-2 a.m., closed Wed. (Apr.-Nov.).*

This is the original Satyricon, opened by an Italian who now manages its sister in Rio, considered one of the finest restaurants in Brazil. The couvert appetizer is a meal in itself – an extraordinary helping of two salads, marinated eggplant, mussels, and assorted fish that defines the term "generous."

### Adamastor

*Av. José Bento Ribeiro Dantas, 712 (Armação); ☎ 23-1162. 6 p.m.-midnight, noon-midnight, Nov.-Mar. Closed Mon.*

One of the most expensive eateries in Búzios. Specialties are grilled lobster. *Expensive. All cards.*

### Le Streghe

*Av. José Bento Ribeiro Dantas, 201 (Praia do Centro); ☎ 23-1311. 7 p.m.-2 a.m., Sat., Sun., and holidays 1-5 p.m., closed Mon.*

This high-class Italian kitchen is ruled by homemade pasta and a light touch on the oil. The ocean view adds a tropical élan. Reserve. *Expensive. AE.*

### Parvati

*Tr. José Luiz, 262. 1 p.m.-2 a.m.*

Good pizzas. *Inexpensive. No cards.*

# Shopping

Shopping in Búzios is for browsers, not shoppers, since everything can be bought cheaper in Rio. There are some unusual finds, however, such as the elegant batik clothes at **Patrick Juvenelle** (in a small mall called Shopping de Búzios, off Rua das Pedras). Also try the second-hand clothing at **Bisa Bizar**, Rua 223 das Pedras, 71, where you can have tea in the back room overlooking the sea.

Look for crafts on **Praia dos Ossos** and **Rua das Pedras**.

# Hands-On Búzios

## Arrival

### Bus

From Rio's Novo Rio bus station, Av. Francisco Bicalho, ☎ *(21) 291-5151*, take a bus to Cabo Frio, then take another (or a taxi) to Búzios. The bus stops at the City Square in the town center, where there is a food market on Sat.

### Air

**Costair Taxi** offers 40-minute flights from the Santos Dumont Airport to Rasa Airfield in Búzios. The benefits are magnificent views of Rio on take-off and an exciting landing in the middle of a marsh. In Rio, ☎ *(21) 220-9052*; in Búzios, ☎ *(246) 623-1303*.

## Taxi

Your hotel may be able to provide you with a private car and driver, or you can hire a radio cab. Fine private drivers are recommended in *Hands-On Rio*. This mode of transport will run up bucks, since you will have to pay for the car's return.

## Boat

You can sail to Búzios from the Marina da Glória in Rio. Rentals of schooners, sailboats and large motorboats for fishing are handled by **Escolade Vela,** ☎ *(246) 205-8646*.

## Travel Agency

**Tours Ekoda,** Av. José Bento Ribeiro Dantas, 222; ☎ *(246) 23-1490*. This company can handle tours of the village, as well as hotel accommodations and car rentals. In Rio, ☎ *(21) 240-7067*.

## Tourist Information

Brochures and suggestions can be found at the state tourist office **Turis Rio Advanced Information Office,** Rua José Bento Ribeiro, ☎ *(246) 23-6628*.

## City Transportation

If you want to do more than stick to your beachside *pousada*, you will most likely need some sort of wheels. The "in" choice and your best bet, considering the uneven roads and sandy paths, is a dune buggy, which may be rented for a whole day with a full tank of gas. For rentals contact:

**Buggies**
Rua Rui Barbosa, 51, casa 3 . . . . . . . . . . . . . . . . . .  ☎ (246) 23-1285
**Locarauto Sun Side Rent a Car**
Rua Celeste A. Costa, 30 (Manguinhos) . . . . . . . .  ☎ (246) 23-2193

# SOUTH OF RIO

## Costa Verde

The famous Brazilian essayist Rubem Braga said this about the Costa Verde (Green Coast): "Nowhere in Brazil is there such intimacy between land and sea."

Indeed, this coastal stretch south of Rio, containing more than 100 islands, is one of the most remarkable natural resources of Brazil. A stay at one of the major resorts in **Angra dos Reis**, or even a day trip to the historical city of **Parati**, is considered a special vacation by *cariocas*, who themselves long to escape the city and be pampered by well-organized facilities here. Fabulous trips to these islands, including a three-hour schooner cruise and lunch at a nearby resort, can be easily arranged through many travel agencies or through private guides (see *Hands-On Rio*), who will gladly drive you up and down the coast at your own pace. Do include on this itinerary a stop at Parati, or settle into a full-service resort such as **Portobello** in Angra dos Reis, take a cruise in the morning and visit Parati in the afternoon.

# Sights

If you ever needed to be reassured of the fertility of God's earth, take a drive along the Costa Verde. Located **south of Rio on BR 101**, the highways are so overgrown with exotic plantlife that you'll feel as though you're traversing a jungle. Five minutes from Club Med, a nearly overgrown path winds through tangled roots and rocks, leading you to a waterfall of uncommon beauty (usually a small boy along the highway will escort you there). Few will be able to forget the spicy smell of this forest, or the dozens of pink, gold, and purple flowers in ecstatic bloom. Tucked into the rocky coves are bottles and flowers, representing *macumba* shrines, and an armadillo might even cross your path. From the excellent two-way highway that curves around the Bay of Ilha Grande, you'll see barefoot boys pushing wheelbarrows along the road and old women strolling home, their heads piled high with packages. From this perspective, Angra looks like a storybook cluster of white houses and orange-tiled roofs creeping up the hillside and surrounded by a sensuously snaking sea. Unfortunately, the only things that mar the paradisiacal view are the large orange cranes of a nuclear power plant, which continues to be a point of controversy.

## Fazenda Nova Graiaú

Near the Hotel Frade stands this antiquated farm of storybook proportion. A former coconut plantation, it boasts an awesome windmill, wild ducks and geese, and superbly landscaped grounds. It can be seen from the highway and is sometimes open to the public.

## Mambucaba

This tiny beachside village halfway between Angra dos Reis and Parati is a lovely place to do nothing. Once the center of a thriving coffee trade, Mambucaba used to be the favorite of whales, who came to eat the numerous small fish swimming out of the river's mouth. Due to the agricultural crises at the end of Empire, the city fell into an era of decadence from which it never recovered, but that is exactly why it has retained its antiquated charm. An impressively adorned church, **Igreja de Nossa Senhora do Rosário**, contrasts starkly with the more modest squat houses.

The black bees (or *mambucas*), from which the city gets its name, still buzz around the area, particularly next to the bikini-clad girls, who make sugarcane drinks from raw stalks. Seaside cafés offer refuge from the sun, and if you linger long enough, you just may be asked to join in on some sambas.

## Excursions

A day's **schooner cruise** around the tropical island in the Costa Verde is an excellent idea for anyone on a tight schedule. Clients are picked up in their hotels in Rio and delivered back at the end of the day. A lunch and swim is usually included. Reservations can be made through your hotel or through full-service agencies in Rio, such as **Diana Turismo,** ☎ *(21) 255-2296*, or **Turistur,** ☎ *(21) 240-0560*. The agencies below specialize in these tours:

**Saveiros Tour,** Pr. Macilio Dias, 2; ☎ *(21) 780-1003*, is one of the most experienced operators offering day trips, including lunch, with stops at Itacuruça Island and Jaguanum.

**Tropical Angra Tur,** Cais de Santa Luiz, 231; ☎ *(24) 365-0402*, offers tours of Angra dos Reis and the Bay of Ilha Grande. Included is a buffet lunch on one of the islands.

> **UP CLOSE TIP:** *Snorkeling is often fantastic on these cruises, so ask about equipment in advance. There will be occasions when you'll have to wade to shore through knee-high water, so dress appropriately. You can get very sunburnt on these open-sea cruises, even on overcast days, so don't forget sunscreen, sun hat, coverup, and shades. And do be careful about swallowing bay water.*

## Where To Stay

See page 26 for price chart.

### Portabello

*BR-101, km. 47 (highway to Angra dos Reis), 9 km.;* ☎ *789-1495.*
*To reserve in Rio,* ☎ *(21) 267-7375.*

This five-star resort, part of the Frade chain (which has three other hotels in the area), is perfect for children. Situated on a hill overlooking the bay, the hotel transports its guests on a ski-lift from the pool area to the beach below. Jetski, kayak, and surfing are all available, as are schooner trips to **Guaiba Island**. The hotel will also transport you free of charge to the neighboring village of **Mangaratiba**, the docking-off point for hundreds of island-hopping possibilities. You may also rent a car (and/or private driver) and make the fabulous drive along the coast to the historical town of **Parati**. Across the street from Portobello is a buffalo farm, which you can visit either by tractor, by horse-and-carriage, or on horseback – a truly enjoyable sojourn. Once a month, Ligia Azevedo, the famous Braziian cosmetician, conducts a spa for guests.

Rooms have tile floors and are beach-oriented. Breakfast is included and lunch and dinner, as well as all watersports, are payable on the bead system. Sauna and tennis are included in the rate. Motorboats can be rented, and 2½-hour schooner excursions can be arranged. Reservations can be made through **F & H Consulting**; ☎ *(800) 544-5503. Expensive. All cards.*

### Portogalo

*BR 101 Norte, km.71 (Itapinhoacanaga); ☎ and fax 65-1022.*

Also part of the Frade chain, the Portogalo resort is smaller, but livelier. Hibiscus adorn the tropical bar; the white leather furniture lends a light elegance to the lobby; and the rooms are appointed in tropical chic. The water is cleaner than at Portobello because there is no river running into the sea here. All watersports are available, as are schooner excursions. Air-conditioned buses from the hotel offer transfers from all the hotels in Rio. Reservations can be made in the US through **F & H Consulting**, ☎ *(800) 544-5503. Expensive. All cards.*

### Hotel do Frade

*BR 101 Sul, highway to Ubatuba, km. 123, ☎ and fax 65-2244.*

Just 2½ hours from Rio, this enormous resort enjoys a prime location right on the beach and within walking distance of the Pico do Frade Mountain. Of the three Frade hotels along the southern coast, only this one features all watersports, as well as horseback riding, cycling and schooner cruises to the neighboring islands. An air-conditioned bus picks up all guests at hotels in Rio. Reservations can be made through **F & H Consulting**, ☎ *(800) 544-5503*; in Rio, ☎ *(21) 262-0832. Expensive. All cards.*

### Club Mediterranée.

*Villa das Pedras (beach) BR-101, km. 55 (Highway to Angra dos Reis), 16 km.; ☎ 789-1635.*

A fantastically landscaped resort using the Club Med theme. This new colonial-style village enjoys its own crescent-shaped beach between the mountains and the bay. Sports facilities include nine tennis courts, squash courts, fitness center, soccer, pool, waterskiing, windsurfing, sailing, and more. Children under four years old are not accepted, but singles may find more families here than they're looking for. A Mini-Club program keeps kids from ages six to 10 entertained. Meals and drinks are conducted on the bead system. In the States, ☎ *(800) CLUB MED* for reservations. *324 apts. Expensive. All cards.*

# Ilha Grande

It's incredible to think you can still find near-virgin beaches in the coastal stretch between Rio and São Paulo, but on Ilha Grande they're commonplace. This 122-square-mile island of mountainous jungle, with more than 100 beaches, is a perfect place to take long, picturesque hikes, particularly to the far side of the island, where the beaches are extremely primitive. On the western shores is an **ecological reserve**, where you can enjoy the island's rich variety of exotic birds, butterflies, and primates.

Ilha Grande was discovered in the early 16th century when explorer Amerigo Vespucci first roamed the coast, but it was long inhabited by Indians, who fought fiercely to defend their territory. Later, the island became known as a pirate's cove. Legend has it that one wily *pirata* named José Grego was on his way to the Straits of Magellan when he and his two daughters were shipwrecked on the isle. After he became a successful trader, one of his slaves (who, by soap-operatic coincidence, happened to be his fellow ex-pirate) fell in love with one of his daughters. Infuriated, the jealous father killed the slave and took his own daughter as his lover. Afterwards, a curse passed over the island, sweeping away all its inhabitants in a tidal wave, except for José, who managed to bury his lifelong treasures before he died a crazed man.

Looking for José's treasure will no doubt unearth some spectacular natural resources. The tiny hamlet of Abraão, where the ferry from Mangaratiba lands, boasts good skindiving about 15 minutes from shore. Beautiful unspoiled beaches, such as Canto and Crena, are about an hour away by foot. Nearby is **Freguesia Island**, a fishermen's village with an 18th-century cemetery, a colonial green-and-white church, and four separate beaches around the island's perimeter. There's also one restaurant on the far shore. Paradise on earth would be to rent the one beach home here – a four-bedroom affair with hardwood floors, white canvas furniture, and a glassed-in living room facing the ocean.

## Where To Stay

Good deals can be found on weekdays when rates are reduced in this weekend party island. Weekends are considered to run from Sat. morning to Sun. afternoon. Few rooms, if any, have air conditioning, and most are more primitive than rustic. Better accommodations can be found 90 minutes away in Parati, or across the bay at the Portobello Hotel. See page 26 for price chart.

### Pousada Mar da Tranquilidade

☎ *(243) 780-1861.*

A two-minute walk from where the ferry docks in Abraão, this stone and wood-beam inn is rustic hominess. The rooms are fan-cooled, with no TV or phone; some have mini-bars. The newer rooms are more congenial. Rates include breakfast and lunch Sat. and Sun. Check with the reception about their various island-hopping options for one- or two-day trips, including hiking and skindiving. *Moderate. No cards.*

## Camping Renato

*Av. Getúlio Vargas, 17.*

Tents may be rented at this campground, a few minutes' walk from the ferry. Outdoor showers with no curtains (you shower in your swimsuit) are available, and the $4-a-night rate includes breakfast. *Cheap. No cards.*

## Hotel Alpino

*Rua Getúlio Vargas (Abrãao; ☎ 780-1861).*

Large groups on a budget will enjoy these fan-cooled chalets with clean, modern baths and breakfast served on an open patio. Reserve in São Paulo. *☎ (11) 220-7633. 10 apts, 4 chalets. Inexpensive. No cards.*

# Where To Eat

Dining on Ilha Grande is mostly enjoyed in Abrãao. The majority of restaurants are simple and open to the fresh air. See page 26 for price chart.

## Flor da Ilha Restaurante

*Av. Beira Mar, 20.*

This is considered the choice place to eat, complete with a nightclub and a menu of steaks and pizza. Most likely you'll want to plop down beachside at one of Casarão da Ilha's stone tables and eat a plate of fried squid (*lula frita*) with a squeeze of lime. *Moderate.*

# Nightlife

Post-sunset parties are as spontaneous as the waves, but do catch the *forró* parties, featuring regional dancing from the Northeast, at Nilzo (end of the beach) on Fri., Sat., and Sun.

# Hands-On Ilha Grande

## Arrival

Daily **ferries** to Abrãao, the main hamlet of Ilha Grande, leave from the village of Mangaratiba 8:30 a.m.-4:30 p.m. (expanded schedules during summer). The trip takes 1½ hours. The dock is about 10 minutes from the Hotel Portobello and **buses** run daily from Rio.

## City Transportation

Lots of small **boats** docked in the harbor of Abrãao are willing and able to take passengers around the islands. If you're alone, you'll probably need substantial Portuguese to negotiate a price. Ask around for the boatman named Fifi, who can take up to 10 people in his flat-bottomed wood fishing boat. Bargain for a good price. A professional certified diver, Fifi also has a boat that seats 50 people and is especially equipped for divers. He can be reached c/o Pousada Mar da Tranquilidade, ☎ *(243) 288-416.*

## When To Go

Nov. through Mar. is best. Expect it to rain a little every night, but days are hot and bright. Winters are cooler and cloudier and often too cold for swimming.

# Parati

With its cobblestone streets, antique lamps, and 19th-century homes so beautifully preserved, Parati might easily be a scene out of a Jorge Amado novel – indeed, the classic film *Gabriela*, based on his novel, was masterfully filmed here. Since it was confirmed as a village in 1667, Parati and its port have witnessed incredible growth, owed in great part to the rich deposits of gold discovered in Minas Gerais. By the 18th century, as it became the major port for gold destined for Portugal, the very name Parati rang with a certain magic throughout the colony. Deserting soldiers, runaway slaves, gypsies, convicts, noblemen and gold diggers all converged on the town, creating a freewheeling population that made its day-to-day doings a veritable soap opera. Even as the gold rush diminished during the 19th century, sugar mills smoked day and night, while countless coffee plantations and cattle farms sprang up in the countryside. Unfortunately, when the Rio-São Paulo road was constructed, Parati fell victim to rerouted traffic and was only later rediscovered as an authentic, nearly untouched historical gem in the 20th century. After a new road to Angra was completed in the 1950s, artists and bohemians flooded the area and instituted new traditions of craftsware. Today, UNESCO has cited the city's six square blocks as part of the World Heritage List, and Brazil itself has named the city a national monument.

Located 149 miles from Rio (and 60 miles from Angra), Parati remains one of the country's major tourist attractions. At the same time its 26,000 residents continue to thrive on fishing and farming. Bicycles fill the streets, small shirtless boys play in the sand; everywhere there are the kinds of small-town businesses that all but get lost in larger metropolises. Walk to the waterfront and look back on a magnificent scene – the time-warped vista of colonial Brazil.

# Sights

The sweetest route to take in Parati is without objective. One of my finest memories is walking along the city's cobblestones, listening to a flutist play *Greensleeves* while I nibbled on coconut candy bought from a street vendor.

Four churches dominate the six-block historical center, perfectly exemplifying how even the Church in colonial Brazil catered to a powerful segregation according to class.

## Churches

### Igreja Matriz Nossa Senhora dos Remedios

Located on the Travessa do Gargoata, this church (1789-1873) was built for the middle class – its leafy courtyard, turquoise-and-white altar, and enormously high arches affecting a certain bourgeois élan. Climb the stairs and see the little gallery of paintings and photos in both modern and antique styles by local artists. The antique bells, which are enclosed in colonial arches, are rung every day at 6 p.m.

### Igreja das Dores

Following the river to the bay, you will reach this 19th-century church used by the noble class.

### Igreja do Rosário

Head three blocks down Rua Fresca and turn right on Rua Doutor Samuel Costa, where you will find this 18th-century church built for the city's slaves.

### Sobrado dos Bonecos

Turn left on Rua Tenente Francisco Antônio and walk two blocks to Rua Maria Jacome de Melo, to reach one of Parati's finest examples of colonial architecture.

### Santa Rita

On the same street is the city's oldest church built in 1722 for the city's mulattos.

## Museu de Arte Sacre

*Tues.-Sun. 9 a.m.-5 p.m.*

Located on Rua Santa Rita, the museum holds the city's depository of sacred art. The outdoor vegetable market is just down the street. From here, you may be lucky enough to glimpse the city's fishermen lugging in the catch of the day.

# Excursions

**UP CLOSE TIP from Bonnie Kassel:** *Go to the waterfront and bargain for a boat. You'd be crazy to come here and not spend a day sailing and swimming among the pristine islands for a day. Buses run six times a day to and from Rio.*

## Fazenda Bananal

*(Also known as Engenho da Murycana)*
*Estrada para Cunha;* ☎ *(243) 71-1153. Daily 11 a.m.-6 p.m.*

Children will adore this 17th-century colonial farm set off a dirt road about 15 minutes from Parati. During centuries past, it was used by the muleteers and pioneers as a trading post for the precious stones unearthed in Minas Gerais and São Paulo; at times, the royal family visited to fiscalize the imperial taxes imposed on the traders. Included in the grounds today is a zoo featuring animals from the Amazon, Pantanal, and Serrado Goiano, with wonderful specimens of lions, pumas, leopards, tigers, monkeys, pacas, and rare toucans and parrots. There are two swimming pools and you can even rent horses to follow the miners' trails through the forest to refreshing waterfalls.

Using many products cultivated on the farm, the restaurant **Murycana** serves typical farm foods from that era, such as *galinha ao molho pardo* (chicken in its own blood), *frango à passarinho* (fried chicken bits), and *bisteca de porco* (pork steak). On Sat. and Sun. *feijoada* is served. Delicious desserts, made from colonial recipes, may also be bought as takeout. The 48-hectare farm produces some of the best sugarcane in the area – an accomplishment, since Parati has long been known as the *cachaça* capital of Brazil. In the small marketplace, be sure to taste the various samples before you buy – flavors include tangerine, cinnamon, cherry, and exotic fruits you've probably never heard of. There's also a museum displaying various objects used in the past century, including guns and furniture.

# Where To Stay

See page 26 for price chart.

## Pousada Frade Parati

*Rua do Comércio;* ☎ *(243) 71-1114.*

Located on the historical square of the Rua do Comércio, this *pousada* rates as one of the most charming. Built as a tropical home, the fully air-conditioned rooms are cozily appointed in woods, and all have color TV and video, safe, mini-bar, and phone. An attractive swimming pool is shaded by a tropical garden. A fine restaurant serves all three meals, and breakfast is included in the rate. Transfer in an air-conditioned bus from hotels in Rio is provided for about $66 per person, round-trip. For reservations, contact **F & H Consulting** in the States, ☎ *(800) 544-5503. Moderate-expensive. All cards.*

## Pousada Pardieiro

*Rua Tenente Francisco Antôni, 74;* ☎ *(243) 71-1370.*

In Bonnie Kassel's opinion: "Elegant and sublime, this is the finest *pousada* accommodation in Parati." Totally private at the end of a cobblestone street, it boasts a colonial-style architecture, with all amenities. Several different room rates range from $90-130 for a suite. The $100 is a lovely double. *Expensive. All cards.*

## Pousada Arte Urquijo

*79 Rua Dona Geralda;* ☎ *(243) 711-362.*

This 300-year-old inn takes you back to Parati's more colorful days, with a thriving indoor garden walled in by driftwood furniture. The paintings of the owner, Malou Urquijo, an Argentinean artist, adorn the walls. Rooms look out onto the bay, the Bocaina Mountains and the city's charming whitewashed houses. Ask Malou to take you to the mineral mud baths at the far end of Jabaquara Beach, and the post-requisite rinse in the nearby waterfall. *7 apts. Moderate. No cards.*

## Pousada do Príncipe

*Av. Roberto Silveira, 289;* ☎ *(243) 71-2266.*

My Deep Throat, Bonnie, claims this *pousada* has "the best rooms for the best value in town." It's located just before you enter the old town, which is why it's cheaper. But as Bonnie says, "when you enter, the pool and gardens are so lovely that you won't care." It's also near the bus station – good if you have heavy bags. Owned by a real prince (grandson of Princess Isabel), the *pousada* is managed by Antonie Grenier, a woman who speaks perfect English and is "charming beyond description." *Inexpensive-moderate. All cards.*

## Pousada das Canoas

*Av. Roberto Silveira, 279;* ☎ *(243) 71-1133; fax 71-2005.*

Two-story, colonial-style house with color TV, mini-bar and air conditioning. The pool is surrounded by a landscaped courtyard, with rooms appointed in a blend of modern comfort and wood. *Moderate. All cards.*

## Pousada do Forte

*Alameda Princesa Isabel, 33 (Centro);* ☎ *(243) 71-1462.*

The motto here is history and leisure. This is the only *pousada* in town where all the apartments face the sea. Nearby is the Ecological Reserve do Forte. The attractive pool area is served by a grass-hut bar. *18 apts. Moderate. All cards.*

# Where To Eat

Most of the restaurants in Parati are colonial-style or open-air houses. Go for the fish in this town, most likely just pulled off the docks. See page 26 for price chart.

## Ancoradouro

*Rua da Geralda, 345; ☎ 71-2055. 11 a.m.-11 p.m., closed Tues. from Apr. to Dec.*

Typical Brazilian food. *Moderate. All cards.*

## Punto Divino

*Rua Marechal Deodoro, 129. Praça da Matriz-Centro.*

Brazilian-Italian food reflecting the roots of the owner/chef. Bonnie Kassel writes: "Superb food (and pizza), the kind one would expect in a large city. The owner, one of those gentle types, speaks English and couldn't be more helpful." *Moderate. All cards.*

## Restaurant Dona Ondina

*Rua do Comércio, 2 (Centro); ☎ 71-1473. Daily 10 a.m.-11 p.m.*

International cuisine in a colonial house complete with sunny veranda. *Moderate. All cards.*

## Fazenda Bananal

*Highway to Cunha; ☎ 71-1153.*

(See listing under *Excursions*).

## Restaurante Galeria do Engenho

*Rua de Lapa, 18; ☎ 71-2115. Daily 11 a.m.-11 p.m.*

This cool restaurant with two strong ceiling fans is situated on a side street and features fine seafood. There are 15 kinds of shrimp dishes, including grilled shrimp with such big head and eyes that you'll need a lot of courage to eat them. Excellent is the *camarão Ivan Lins*, Milanese-style shrimp fried with cheese. The calamari stuffed with cheese and shrimp were also delicious, but they may have caused a few days of bellyaches.

## Restaurante do Hiltinho

*Rua Marechal Deodoro, 233 (Centro); ☎ 71-1432. 11 a.m.-midnight.*

Creative blends of fish and seafood can be had at this well-received eatery, especially the *caldeirada* – a simmering seafood stew. Schooner trips can also be arranged. *Moderate. No cards.*

## Merlin, O Mago

*Rua Comércio, 376 (historical center); ☎ (0243) 71-2157. 7 p.m.-last client.*

Good Brazilian fare, and a restaurant particularly festive during Carnaval.

## Shopping

**UP CLOSE TIP from Bonnie Kassel: Luis Moreno Arte & Antiguidades.** *"This is an upscale art and antique shop (contemporary hand-painted bowls and platters are to die for), the quality of which one would expect in Paris or New York. Expensive, but worth every penny."*

## Nightlife

If you have a chance, catch **Mansamente**, the famous Brazilian puppet company that's been acclaimed by *The New York Times* for its avant-garde creativity with foot-high puppets and antique doll furniture.

## Hands-On Parati

### Arrival

**Buses** from the main bus terminal in Rio (Rodoviária Novo Rio) leave every three hours for Parati on the Eval line and make the trip in 3½ hours. The bus station is at Praça N.S. de Guia, ☎ *789-1495*, where you can also catch buses to Angra dos Reis, Itacuruçá, Itaguai, Muriqui, and Rio de Janeiro. **Private cars** may also be hired in Rio (see *Hands-On Rio*). As you approach Parati, tune into FM Parati 88.9 to hear advertisements for all kinds of hotels, restaurants, etc. (alas, in Portuguese).

### City Transportation

Parati can be seen on foot in a matter of hours, as all the historically appointed streets are cut off to traffic. Roam at will or pick up a map at City Hall. During the day, the town gleams like a treasure box, but at night the antique lamps lend an air of romance unsurpassed in Brazil. A fabulous night vision is the illuminated belfry and white cross of the Santa Rita church against the dark, star-specked sky. Stores are usually open till late at night.

If you haven't chartered a **boat** around the islands of Angra, here's your chance for a spectacular schooner cruise. Contact **Soberano da Costa,** in Rio ☎ *(21) 267-7794*; in Parati *(243) 71-1114*. Schooner trips are also available through **Turbo I** from noon to 5 p.m. Inquire at the store called Papelaria Disque, across from Café Parati on Rua do Comércio.

### Tourist Information

More tourist info can be obtained at City Hall, ☎ *(243) 71-1266, ext. 50.*

# Serra da Bocaina

The national park of Serra da Bocaina is simply one of the most beautiful landscapes in all of Brazil. Situated between the states of São Paulo and Rio, the park contains what little remains of the Atlantic rainforest chain. But more than an eco-reserve, it's also a receptacle for the history of colonial Brazil – it holds the old 18th-century gold route from Minas to Parati, as well as the last vestiges of the 19th-century coffee plantations. The park is a welcome vacation spot for adventuresome *Paulistas* (the city of São Paulo is only 167 miles away), and for *cariocas*, who may easily stop in Parati on their way home. Getting to the park takes guts. The only way to reach it is through SP-221, an extremely precarious rock 'n roll road that requires expert four-wheel-drive control. The only vehicles authorized to drive inside the park are on their way to Pousada do Vale dos Veados (see below).

The natural wonders of the park are seemingly endless, though signs of a burning forest are sadly in evidence. The **Mambucaba River** makes dramatic dips and tucks over rocks, creating a spectacular 2,600-foot waterfal, **Cachoeira São Isidro**. Bromeliads and rare orchids dot the landscape, as do profusions of Brazilian pines, cedars, sumaumeira (kapok), and others. The nearly extinct black monkeys roam at will, along with mountain lions, capybaras, deer, anteaters, sloths, and wild pigs. Even birdwatching is excellent, with more than 90 rare species, including toucans and parrots. A little before the entrance of the park is one of the most popular **hang-gliding** points in the country (veterans claim you can stay in the air for 10 hours). The area called **Sertão da Bocaina** is brimming with fishable trout. And hardy trekkers will adore scaling the **Pico do Gavião**, the top of which offers a superlative vista of the Bay of Parati.

A surprise to those who have been bearing the tropical heat, the park boasts low temperatures the whole year. Winter clothes are essential, as are trekking and horseback-riding gear. Also, don't forget some light clothes for skindiving and for bathing in waterfalls and natural lakes.

## Along The Way

The Rio-São Paulo road to Bocaina can be read as a documentary of what has happened to the Brazilian Atlantic rainforest. European nationalists who came in the last century spoke of the tallest trees they had ever seen; today, the land is sadly flattened, with only the mountainous regions having escaped the slashing and burning that prepared the land for sugarcane, coffee and, finally, cattle. Today, the Rio-São Paulo Highway is one of the most dangerous in Brazil (along with the São Paulo-Curitiba Highway), thanks to maniacal truck drivers. Nevertheless, signs of country life still abound. Dozens of stands sell papayas, coconuts, and enormous clusters of bright yellow bananas. Eighteenth-century towns, such as São José do Barreiro, with their grilled verandas and traditional roofs, still languish in another era, especially during the festival of St. Peter at the end of June, when the cobblestone streets overflow with people dancing *forró*.

# Where To Stay

See page 26 for price chart.

### Pousada do Vale dos Veados

*Km. 42 da Estrada da Bocaina;* ☎ *(21) 322-4849. In Rio,* ☎ *(11) 253-0660.*

In the heart of the national park, this must be the coziest, homiest *pousada* in all Brazil. Because nothing can be built in the park that does not conform to the pre-1971 style, the 50-year-old original construction has been preserved, though it's more reminiscent of frontier life. The main building, with dining rooms, living rooms, and four bedrooms, is made of wood logs and rock walls, with a traditional Brazilian tile roof. The inn is 10½ miles from the park's entrance on a wildly bumpy road; upon arrival you will immediately want to collapse in front of the roaring fire or sink into the soft colonial beds, with the deepest quilts imaginable. No electricity is used and the candle-lit rooms and wood-burning stoves turn back the centuries. Superb country-style food, grown on the farm, is served buffet-style and warmed under gas heaters.

Although it's possible to lie in a hammock all day (the view of the lake from the porch is gorgeous), you can make outstanding climbs up Gavião Peak, follow the 18th-century Mambucaba Gold trek on foot, horseback ride to a glorious waterfall, or canoe up and down rivers. Honeymooners can set their beds together overlooking fabulous trees and be woken to the call of roosters. No one speaks English here, but the small staff is so friendly you may never want to leave. Doubles are actually chalet-type apartments. All rates include full board, transfer from the city of São José do Barreiro, and all activities. Don't leave without taking home a huge loaf of homemade cheese. *Expensive. All cards.*

# Hands-On Serra da Bocaina

## Arrival

If you drive yourself (not recommended), you'll have to request permission from IBAMA (Brazilian Institute of Environmental Preservation) to trek or camp in the park.

## Getting Out

The trip out of the park is a bucking bronco ride around a mountainous valley so bumpy you'll have to hold on to the top of the jeep. I was wrecked for days after this trip (make sure your driver is sober!), but the charm and beauty of the *pousada* was worth every bruise. The environs are unforgettable, and the country folk in the area are so *simpático*, they even let me use their bathroom at midnight.

# MINAS GERAIS
## The Heart of Historical Brazil

For many people, the true soul of Brazil is found in the state of Minas Gerais. Sequestered from the coast, embraced on all sides by five different states, Minas has developed a profound culture all its own. Throughout its tumultuous history, the state has given rise to near-genius painters, sculptors, musicians, politicians, and psychics, who have not only enriched the national personality, but have found international fame far beyond their small hometowns and dusty villages. Since the late 1600s, the land itself has delivered some of the world's greatest supplies of gold, silver, iron, and other precious and semiprecious stones and metals. Yet, despite its richness, there is something ineffable about Minas, something in the color of the rust-orange soil and the voluptuous mountains, something in the air that can never be exploited or explained. If you want to understand Minas, listen to the early albums of the great Milton Nascimento – a music that is at once sensual yet spiritual. As musician Glberto Gil once told me, explaining the difference between Salvador and Minas, "In Bahia, everything is sun and celebration and joy, but in Minas everything is hidden – the mountains, the people, even the next curve on the highway is hidden away."

In the final years of the 17th century, the name Minas Gerais (or General Mines) became synonymous with El Dorado as rumors of emerald highways and diamond-studded bushes filtered through the Empire. Men, women, rich, poor, bandits, nobelmen, even monks and priests descended upon the mines from every direction, fast giving rise to a feverish society of boom towns and lawless disorder. Although 18th-century Brazil, with the help of Minas, would produce nearly 80% of the world's gold supply, most of it slipped through the fingers of the Brazilians and Portuguese into the hands of northern Europeans. A few, however, struck it rich, settling in towns such as Mariana and Ouro Preto, where they constructed cathedrals of such decorative wealth that no one dared contest their spiritual devotion. Others found more secular ways to indulge their fancies: one young diamond contractor was so entranced with his *mulata* mistress (an ex-slave) that he first built her a lake large enough to navigate a full-sized sailing ship, then he built her the ship.

Today, *Mineiros* (people from Minas) are deeply tied to their past. You will find more people here who can retell their own state's history than anywhere else in the country and, indeed, many feel a direct living lineage to it. Some of the most beloved heroes in Brazilian history hail from Minas: the rebel Tiradentes, the artist Aleijadinho, the politician Juscelino Kubitsckek (who built Brasília), and Tancredo Neves, the first president of the new democracy, who died shortly before taking office. Deeply sensitive to matters of justice, *Mineiros* have often evinced great force as a group – though sometimes to paradoxical effect. It was troops from Minas who eventually quelled the São Paulo revolt against Getúlio Vargas's regime in

1932's brief civil war, but it was also *Mineiro* divisions that moved against Rio in 1964 to ensure the success of the military coup.

Today, the tourist possibilities in Minas are so diverse you could spend an entire three-week vacation just exploring the state. If you have any sense of adventure, you absolutely must retrace the steps of the original *bandeirantes* on horseback around the rugged mountain plains – a trip I have rated as the best eco-trek in Brazil. After that, leisurely browse through the town of Ouro Preto, Mariana, São João del Rei, Tiradentes, and Congonhas, five beautifully preserved historical towns considered World Heritage treasures.

In this edition I have added several more historical cities: Diamantina and Serro, along with their neighboring villages, which boast some of the most beautiful waterfalls and trekking sights in the state. In the southern area, you can replenish body and soul at the spa towns of São Lourenço, Caxambu, and Poços de Caldas, where you can "take the waters" in elegant 19th-century style. And anyone with a yen for UFO sightings and eerie environs should immediately head for São Tomé das Letras, where it's difficult to tell the humans from the otherworldly creatures who walk the dusty, rock-strewn streets.

In a country of gracious service, Minas Gerais is famous for its hospitality. In fact, a term for the *Mineiro* personality has even been coined *Mineiradade*, a behavior forged on self-sufficiency and tempered by a profoundly sensitive nature. Stereotyped as slightly suspicious, *Mineiros* take a long time to make a friend but, once they open up, they stay your friend for life. *Mineiros* prefer to listen than talk; it's an easy bet that at a table of raucous Brazilians, the one quietly observing the others is probably from Minas. Even *Mineiro* composers sing about love in a different way. As local composer Tadu Franco explained to me, "A love song from Minas isn't just about romance; it's really universal."

# Belo Horizonte

Despite being the third largest city in Brazil, Belo Horizonte preserves the sentiment of an intimate town. The capital of Minas Gerais, it's considered by the media to be one of the best cities of South America in which to live. It's nicknamed the **Garden City** for good reason – no other metropolis in Brazil boasts streets so strewn with greenery. The unique *Mineiro* personality can be felt everywhere here: taxi drivers are more than occasionally honest, citizens are concerned and even helpful, and the cultural life, particularly the music scene, is more profound than flamboyant. The most famous dance group in Brazil, Grupo Corpo, is based in Belo Horizonte, and musicians like singer Tadeu Franco, song writer Beto Guedes, and guitarist Toninho Horta lend a sophisticated lining to the contemporary pop scene. Don't forget that Milton Nascimento's famous Clube da Esquina, the "corner" where his childhood friends hung out to make music, was right here in Belo Horizonte.

While there are a few sites in Belo Horizonte, most people use the city as a trampoline to visit the historical towns and do the spa circuit. But given the availability of some fabulous, moderately priced apart-hotels, a stay in Belo Horizonte for more than a few days could be exceedingly enjoyable. Some of the best restaurants for regional food are here, as well as an active nightlife that features both solid jazz and *sertaneja* (country music). Shopping, particularly in the chic Savassi neighborhood, is superb, and fashionable clothes are often less expensive than in Rio. New Age adherents and healers who are interested in buying large amounts of crystals (as well as jewelry) should head directly for one of the best shops in the country – IRFFI – where bulk buys are often rewarded with large discounts. As for romance: those fond of statistics may appreciate knowing there are 10 women to each man in Belo Horizonte (as opposed to São Paulo, where there are 10 men per woman).

## History

Belo Horizonte is a new city, a mere 100 years old. At the beginning of the 18th century, it was initially settled by the São Paulo explorer **João Leite da Silva Ortiz**, whose farm, Curral del Rey, became the core of the first hamlet.

On December 17, 1893, the fertile undulating landscape was chosen among five potential areas as the site for a new town. Finally, after numerous political crises in Ouro Preto, the governor of Minas, Augusto de Lima, initiated a project to build the political, cultural, and economic center of the state. With architects and engineers arriving from Rio, it took four years for the country's first planned city to be constructed. Based on Washington, D.C. and La Plata in Argentina, Belo Horizonte looks like a huge chessboard of criss-crossing streets, broken up diagonally by wide avenues. Though it was built for 200,000 people, it now holds over 2.5 million.

# Sights

## Pope's Square

In 1980, Pope John celebrated mass in what is now known as the Pope's Square. The **Monumento à Paz**, dominating the plaza, represents a testimony to world peace. Of the two triangles forming the monument, one symbolizes the energy sent to heaven through man's faith; the other represents the energy mankind receives from God. Together they form a square representing the synergistic balance that peace brings to the world. The sculptor is Ricardo Carvão Levy. Unfortunately, graffiti has defiled much of the monument. Behind the mountains surrounding the city is the deepest gold mine in Brazil, now producing over 600 kilos of gold and 300 kilos of silver per month.

## Pampulha

Anyone wanting to understand the construction of Brasília should first look at Belo Horizonte, particularly in the northern district of Pampulha, where all the principal characters in the architectural drama were situated 20 years earlier. In 1940, **Mayor Juscelino Kubitschek** (who, as President, would later oversee Brasília) asked architect **Oscar Niemeyer** and landscape designer **Roberto Burle Marx** to design the Pampulha neighborhood to attract the elite of the city. Following his signature modernist style, Niemeyer created an artificial lake, casino, restaurant, museum and church. While the museum no longer holds permanent exhibitions due to lack of funds, it is notable for its onyx ramp in the entranceway, a rich reminder of Minas' natural wealth. The restaurant, **Casa do Baile**, is still open for business, with a wonderful view overlooking the lake. From this side of the lake, Niemeyer's church, known today as the **Igreja de São Francisco de Assis**, looks like an unfortunate mistake. Up close, it is more intriguing than ugly, but like everything else Niemeyer constructed in Belo Horizonte (including the downtown public library and the Bemge Bank), the church was done in a disturbing series of curves that didn't sit well with the conservatives of the 1940s. In fact, the Archbishop refused to consecrate the church because Niemeyer, a member of the Communist party, had seemingly constructed a symbol of the sickle and hammer (the curved church and the unattached tower, respectively), though the architect vigorously denied it. Not until 10 years later would a new Archbishop finally open the church's doors. The azulejo tiles and murals, by Cândido Portinari, one of the most famous of Brazilian artists, are stunning and lend warmth to an otherwise cool, avant-garde facade. Mass is held at 10:30 a.m. and 6 p.m. on Sun. Visiting hours: Tues.-Sat. 8:30 a.m.-noon and 1:30-5 p.m.

## Nossa Senhora da Boa Viagem

*Rua Sergipe, 175*

The main cathedral of the city is characteristic of the city's temperament: homey, engulfed in greenery, with a touch of art nouveau in the colorful stained-glass windows. At any time of the day or night, you'll find *Mineiros* quietly praying on their knees as candles twinkle on the altar. The rotunda is impressively high, but it is the grounds that are most memorable. Surrounded by flamboyant and ficus trees, you'll feel as though you are sitting in the middle of a forest.

## Rua Amendoim

*Peanut Street*

It's better to show than tell ahead of time, but Rua Amendoim, in the district of Funcionários, perhaps the most famous street in Belo Horizonte, will astound you. As the street inclines upward, your car will strangely roll forward (instead of backwards). No joke. Today some people try to explain the phenomenon away by saying it's just an optical illusion (not true) or that the soil is so rich it pushes the car forward (also not true). Why the street was named Amendoim is also a mystery. (Some claim that *amendoims*, or peanuts, are great aphrodisiacs.)

## Parque Florestal das Mangabeiras

*Av. Anel da Serra and Av. Bandeirantes;* ☎ *277-0199.*
*Tues.-Sun. 8 a.m.-6 p.m.*

To get a glimpse of the Atlantic forest, as well as a magnificent view of the city from its highest peak, head for the 1,500-acre natural reserve designed by Roberto Burle Marx. For an initial orientation of the massive acreage, hop on one of the park's internal buses available every half-hour at the entrance. As you descend into the forest you will instantly feel the humidity rise and the air cool; the profusion of plant and tree life will delight any horticulturalist. Eco-trails are well marked, but you can also engage in roller-skating, watersports, and canoeing on two artificial lakes. The park's highest point, **Mirante da Mata**, a 20-minute walk from the entrance, is the place to contemplate the sprawl of the city. Free eco-oriented painting programs for children take place on Sat. Take a look at an entire flock of wild geese that arrived one day and hasn't budged since. For a spectacular nighttime view, stop by Mirante das Mangabeiras, outside the park.

❖ **GETTING HERE:** *Take a taxi or the blue #2001-C buses marked "Aparecida" from Avenida Afonso Pena.*

# Museums

## Museu Histórico Abílio Barreto

*Rua Bernardo Mascarenhas (Cidade Jardim). Hours: 10 a.m.-5 p.m., closed Tues.*

This is the best historical museum in the city. It's situated in a preserved *fazenda* (farmhouse) in Cidade Jardim, now fast burgeoning into a fashionable district. A photographic gallery reveals the mules, mud huts, and oxcarts of Belo's early days, as well as the Art Deco buildings from the 1930s and 1940s. Much more gruesome is the display of slave shackles, called "Little Angels," so-named because the masters felt the restrainers made their slaves act like "angels." In the last century, travelers from the west on their way to the coast would stop in Belo Horizonte to pray at the chapel of Nossa Senhora da Boa Viagem (Lady of the Good Trip); you can see the remains of the original altar here.

## Museu de Arte

*Av. Itacilio Negrão de Lima, 16.585 (Pampulha);* ☎ *443-4533. Daily 8 a.m.-6 p.m.*

# Excursions

## UP CLOSE ADVENTURE from the author "In The Saddle Of The Bandeirantaes"

The sky from the window of our hotel room in Belo Horizonte had looked threatening all morning, but bad weather has never daunted Túlio Marques Lopes, who offers the best eco-trek in Brazil. At noon Túlio picks us up in a jeep and roars off to his hitching post a half-hour away. By the time the 16 of us are saddled, the mist has turned to gentle rain and we bundle up in huge yellow ponchos that graze the legs of our horses. Riding a stunning Argentine horse, Túlio leads us through a cobblestone village to the mountains ahead.

Suddenly a magnificent rainbow breaks in the sky, setting a new mood. Soon, civilization is forgotten as we wind around the granite mountains and grassy valleys, the sky so dramatic in color it nearly sings. The going at times is rough as our horses step gingerly around fallen boulders and mudslides, but Túlio remains an undaunted master, keeping us in line and shouting *"coragem"* (courage) at the top of his lungs. Visions of gold rushes and wagon trains fill our minds as we teeter up the rocky embankments and even the most uncoordinated among us start to feel macho as our faithful horses sludge onward. Even after the moon rises we keep marching forward, cocooned in darkness, able to see only the faint image of a swishing tail in front of us.

Somewhere between exhausted and starving, we find our way to an isolated ranch house in the middle of nowhere, where an elderly backwoods couple prepares a hearty meal for us over a wood-stove fire (a chicken dish so traditional that the claws are still on the feet!) We pick and chew like prisoners just let out of the penitentiary, and as we polish off our last beers, scrawny farmhands serenade us with drunken country tunes. But it's another two hours back on the road until we finally collapse in the most rustic of *pousadas*. In the morning we blearily discover that we've landed our sore rumps in the quaint village of São Sebastian das Aguas Claras, a dusty, one-road town where we greet the country folk, kick up more dust, and peer into old churches and houses.

After an ice-cold dip in a nearby waterfall, we head to Dona Dica's for lunch – a treasure of the region who has been serving up traditional *Mineiro* fare with home-grown products for almost five decades. (The vegetables we eat are grown right outside her backdoor and tomorrow's chicken dinner is still squawking out back. ) A few extra beers fortify us for the long trek home; this time we traverse fast-running streams, race over flat plains, and generally feel the soul of the moon. By the time we arrive back home – muddy, scraped, and nearly paraplegic – most of us have come to feel at one with our own souls... and with the soul of *Mineiros*.

---

What makes this trip so spectacular is truly the charm of Túlio Marques Lopes, the owner, whose friends were so entranced with his weekend escapades that they forced him to go public. A former film director, lawyer and bon vivant, Túlio has developed a deep feel for the terrain of Minas, capable of convincing you that you're retracing the steps of the early *bandeirantes* (pioneers). By the time you read this, probably all of his horses will be Manga-Larga Marchadors, an Argentine breed whose *lambada*-like trots make long journeys no less than a sensual experience. And due to the difficult terrain, the pace is so slow that anybody who can stay upright on a saddle can do it; rainy days provide a little extra thrill.  Full-day and overnight trips with hotel (three meals included) are offered. More daring adventurers may arrange a special four-day trek from Belo Horizonte to Ouro Preto, which should prove to be unforgettable. In general, children under nine are not allowed, but senior citizens in good shape are welcome.

For more information, contact **Tropa Serrana**, c/o Túlio Marques Lopes, Rua Gentios 50/1041 (Belo Horizonte); fax 344-8986.

## Where To Stay

The best accommodations in Belo Horizonte are apart-hotels, some so fashionably decorated you may want to move in forever. Since the city is a business center, weekend discounts are often phenomenal. Any hotel in Savassi will situate you within walking distance of the city's best shopping; you'll also be able to stay close to excellent neighborhood restaurants and bars. Downtown hotels tend to be noisy and slightly rambunctious. See page 26 for price chart.

### Merit Plaza Hotel

*Rua Tamóios, 341;* ☎ *(31) 201-9000, fax 271-5700.*

My newest rave in Belo Horizonte is small (seemingly), chic, has huge beds, a cozy lobby bar, and a cheerful breakfast room. The French restaurant appears casual, overhanging the mezzanine, but the food, designed by Laurent, one of São Paulo's finest French chefs, will be one of your most memorable meals in Brazil. Service at the five-star restaurant is impeccable, as it is throughout the hotel itself. *Expensive. All cards.*

### Le Flamboyant

*Rua Rio Grande do Norte, 1007 (Savassi);* ☎ *(31) 261-5233, fax 261-7370.*

A perfect hotel, this 13-floor high-rise in chic Savassi offers rooms that are more like apartments with a kitchen, living room, and bedroom, complete with color TV and video, hydromassage, and central air and heat. An exquisitely decorated bar is lined with fine art and the lobby must have the world's most comfortable leather couches. Breakfast is poolside, and the chic restaurant serves lunch and dinner. The same management intends to open a similar property, Metropolitan Flat, some five blocks with futuristic gold furnishings, gym, sauna, pool, and two executive salons, plus auditorium. Businessmen at both properties receive a 10% discount; 30% on weekends. Reserve at least 10 days in advance. *30 apts. Expensive. All cards.*

### Del Rey Hotel

*Praça Afonso Arinos, 60 (Centro);* ☎ *(31) 272-2211, fax 273-1804.*

Elegant simplicity in this four-star high-rise downtown is marred only by the inevitable sounds of traffic. The location is central, across the street from the Mineral Museum and close to the park, handicraft fair, and the Palácio das Artes. Standards, all air conditioned, come with minibar and TV. The restaurant is buffet. No pool. *213 apts. Expensive. All cards.*

### Belo Horizonte Othon Palace

*Avenida Afonso Pena, 1050 (Centro);* ☎ *(31) 273-3844, fax 212-2318.*

Shaped like a huge curve, this 25-floor high-rise is a friendly, inviting hotel near the beginning of the handicraft fair downtown. All five-star service here: sauna, hair salon, boutiques, jewelry stores, and 24-hour room service. VIP services are available. Standards and deluxes are nearly identical, except the latter are higher up. Tastefully appointed, all rooms include two separate spaces delineated by a divider; all come with color TV, safe, minibar, tub, and central air. The outdoor pool boasts a spectacular view of the city, and the restaurant – Venezia – is known for its pasta. Live music on the bar nightly. In front of the hotel is a popcorn man who sells fried pieces of coconut – the most delicious junk food I have ever tasted. *302 apts. Expensive-moderate. All cards.*

### Max Savassi Suite Hotel

*Rua Antônio de Albuquerque, 335 (Savassi);* ☎ *(31) 225-6466, fax 223-0747.*

One of the city's best deals, this elite apart-hotel tucked into a leafy street of Savassi is chic, luxurious, and comfortable. Each apartment has a bedroom, living room, and kitchen, and is decorated in the style of a plush private residence. Room service is not available, but a restaurant down the street will deliver. There is a pool, sauna, luncheonette, restaurant, and high-class bar. Good discount for travel agents. *109 apts. Moderate. AE, DC.*

### Boulevard Plaza

*Avenida Getúlio Vargas, 1640 (Savassi);* ☎ *(31) 223-9000, fax 225-8438.*

Well situated, this property is more like an apart-hotel, with spacious apartments overlooking the shopping district, including a small second room in front of the bedroom. All apartments come with air conditioning, color TV, and phone. A casual restaurant is open 24 hours and a bar features live music. *44 apts. Moderate. All cards.*

### Wembley Place Hotel

*Rua Espirito Santo, 201;* ☎ *(31) 201-6966, fax 224-9946.*

Near the train and bus stations and 15 minutes from the airport, this impressive three-star budget hotel has compact but attractive apartments equipped with fully stocked mini-bars, bathroom phones and color TVs. Safes are at the reception. An intimate bar opens daily at 6 p.m. *105 apts, 2 suites. Moderate. All cards.*

### San Francisco Flat

*Rua Alvares Cabral, 967 (Lourdes);* ☎ *291-4522, fax 275-1965.*

This flat hotel resembles a mini-Maksoud Plaza (the elite hotel of São Paulo), with its inner courtyard of greenery hanging from each floor. The rooms are small, but spectacular, with a sitting room, complete kitchen, and generous beds. The price is unbelievably low. The dining room serves breakfast; nearby is a good pizza parlor. *Inexpensive. All cards.*

### Albergue da Juventude Pousadinha Mineira

*Rua Arazá, 514 (Floriota);* ☎ *44-82-05 and 446-2911, fax 442-4448.*

A youth hostel that is clean, friendly, and cheap. *Inexpensive. No cards.*

# Where To Eat

Atmosphere – from romantic to homey – is as important as the quality of cuisine. Locals leave home around 10 p.m. for dinner; any earlier and you will probably find the dining rooms empty. Some of the best regional food in the state can be enjoyed here; also listed below are hangouts where you may run into the city's most famous musicians and poets. For dessert, try *quiejo mineiro*, a local sour cheese served with a sweet slice of *goiabada* (guava jam) to cut the taste. *Doce de leite*, a caramel-like pudding sometimes topped with shreds of coconut, is also scrumptious. See page 26 for price chart.

## Churrascaria

### Mr. Beef

*Rua Gonçalves Dias, 2600;* ☎ *276-1966. 6 p.m.-last client.*

Maybe you didn't come this far to hear Simon & Garfunkel, but this Western saloon also offers some of the best steaks in town. Live music Tues.-Sat. *Moderate. All cards.*

## Eclectic Funk

### Era Vm Vez Em Chalezinho

*Rod. MG 30, km. 10/1364 (Vale do Sereno-Nova Lima);* ☎ *286-3136. Mon.-Fri. noon -3 p.m., 7 p.m.-last client. Sat. 7 p.m.-last client. Closed Christmas & New Year's.*

A Swiss chalet with a pyramid roof (for energy) may seem a bit anachronistic in Brazil, but this is one of the city's most romantic eateries. Come for drink and hors d'oeuvres, or indulge in six kinds of fondues. The coffee drinks are unbelievably good; try the *Era Um Vez* (Once Upon a Time), with coffee, coffee liqueur, banana, chocolate, sugar, ice cream, whipped cream, and cherries. For dessert try the exquisite *Pavé da Vovó*, with layers of biscuits, cream, peanuts, and whipped cream drowned in chocolate. Choose dining outdoors on a porch, or downstairs with a rinky-dink piano, upstairs with jazz or in a tiny attic. A small music cover is charged. Another branch in Santa Teresa near the old cinema features a pasta buffet with live band. *Moderate. All cards.*

## French

### Chez Dadette

*Rua Coelho de Souza, 70;* ☎ *275-1400. Noon-3 p.m., 7 p.m.-last client, closed Sun.*

One of the most respected chef/owners in Brazil. Bernadette (Dadette) Bahia Mascarenhas studied with Pierre Troisgros and trained at Lutece in New York. But the menu she's created in this upscale yet homey French bistro is the result of her worldwide travels, crossing everything from Japanese to Indian to French. Heads of state and prime ministers dine here; the filet mignon arrives with caviar, and the breast of duck with caramel sauce is her own invention. Desserts are highly creative, such as the crêpes with passion fruit mousse (the seeds of passion fruit are toasted for a crunchy topping). Dadette loves to schmooze tableside when she's not supervising the kitchen; in her spare time she restores Persian rugs for export. She's still crying about the time architect Oscar Niemeyer painted the entire map of Brasília on her wall and the cleaning lady washed it off by mistake. *Very expensive. DC, AE.*

## Regional

### Dona Lucinha

*Rua Pe. Odorico, 38 (Savassi);* ☎ *227-0562. Noon-3 p.m., 8 p.m.-midnight. (Also, Rua Sergipe, 811;* ☎ *261-5930.)*

One of the best regional kitchens. Owner Dona Lucinha offers the kind of traditional food they used to serve up on grand plantations. Eighteenth-century prints on the walls take you back in time, but it's the huge self-service buffet that will delight gourmands as well as gourmets. Feast on *feijão tropeiro*, sinfully juicy short ribs, and the best *doce de leite* (a kind of caramel pudding) that I've ever tasted. *Moderate. All cards.*

### Mala e Cuia

*Avenida Raja Gabaglia, 1617 (São Bento);* ☎ *342-1421. Tues.-Sat. 11 a.m.-midnight. Live music 9 p.m., Fri., Sat., and Sun. at 1 p.m.*

The panoramic view of the city's green hills and skyline seen from the open windows of this pink farmhouse is wonderful. The typically *Mineiro* cuisine is made the old-fashioned way (peek inside the kitchen and see the roaring fire). Onions hang from the ceiling; the sweet jam, cheeses, and marinated peppers hugging the wall are for sale. The specialty is *ao molho pardo* (chicken cooked in its own blood). Some of the vegetables are fresh from the garden. A minimal charge on the weekend covers live country-style music. *Moderate. No cards.*

### Pier 32

*Avenida Afonso Pena, 3328;* ☎ *225-0782. Mon.-Sat. 11:30 a.m.-3 p.m., 6 p.m.-last client. Sun. 11:30 a.m.-5 p.m.*

The kitchen is in the middle of this casual, nautically inspired restaurant alive with talk. At lunch, it's more business, but at night the 25-30 set settles in for a typical *Mineiro* buffet of *feijão tropeiro*, fried manioc, sausage, *farofa*, and stews. Fish and pastas are available, and a chef in top hat cooks nicely grilled *picanha* (steak). Menu changes daily, sometimes there's even rabbit. *Moderate. No cards.*

## Spanish

### Taberna Flamenco

*Rua Cristina, 1163 (Santo Antônio);* ☎ *344-8494.*

Excellent Spanish food and live flamenco music and dance. *Moderate. No cards.*

## Varied

### Cervejaria Brazil

*Rua Almorés, 78 (Funcion, ários);* ☎ *225-1099. 11 a.m.-1 a.m., weekends at 2 a.m.*

As tropical as you get this far inland, this open-air eatery with grass-hut roof is a magnet for artists and intellectuals of the city. Argentine *picanha*, a juicy chuck of beef, comes simmering on a grill with a sleeve of fat. You can also choose among 18 other kinds of meat. The smoked fish is delicious. Noshers should try the *tábua de frios* – a wooden tray laden with cheese and meats. *Moderate. MC, DC, V.*

## Taste Vin

*Rua Curitiba, 2105;* ☎ *292-5423. 7:30 p.m.-midnight, closed Sun.*

If you're dragged out late by a local, or find yourself lost after the theater, head here for the best soufflés in town; the *quiejo gruyere* (gruyere cheese) is superlative. Top it off with a profiterole cream puff filled with ice cream and sizzled with chocolate sauce. Weekends are packed. *Moderate. V, AE.*

## Restaurante Dona Dica

*Rua São Sebastião, 315 , access from BR 040 Sul (São Sebastiãn das Aguas Claras);* ☎ *547-7122. 11 a.m.-8 p.m.*

The motorbikers who race around the mountain edges discovered this simple abode 20 years ago. Today, superstars like Milton Nascimento and Elba Ramalho make the half-hour drive from Belo Horizonte for the home-cooked food of Dona Dica, owner, chef, and mother superior of this mud-floor eatery for almost five decades. Horses can be hitched right next to your table. Ask to see the kitchen, where a clay furnace bakes delicious breads and biscuits. Since 1986, Dona Dica has received a top rating in *Quatro Rodas*, the Brazilian travel Bible, and her weather-beaten face proves just how hard she's worked. On holidays and weekends, the food is always ready; other times she whips up something on the spot. (For more information, see under *Excursions.) Moderate. All cards.*

# Nightlife

## Bars with Music

After Belo-ites leave work, they head straight for neighborhood bars to relax, flirt, and negotiate their dinner dates. The best bars are in Savassi – casual, often open-air, surrounded by lush trees and vegetation. You'll find the top local musicians performing here.

## Bar Brazil

*Rua Aimorés, 108;* ☎ *225-1099. Mon.-Fri. 6 p.m.-midnight,*
*Sat. and Sun. 11 a.m.-midnight.*

This bar, the little sister to Cevejaria Brazil restaurant next door, is one of the hottest joints in town. Singer Tadeu Franco and composer Beto Guedes can usually be found here, wrapped around the stone tables, as well as anyone who's smart and sexy under 30. Those that can't fit inside the small wooden structure sit on the sidewalk. *Inexpensive. MC, DC, V.*

## A Canga & Candela

*Avenida Contorno, 6342 (Savassi);* ☎ *223-9512.*

A comfortable, well-attended club with a dance floor. Shows of *música serteneja* (country music) start at 9:30 p.m. Tues.-Sat. *Moderate. No cards.*

# Theater

Belo Horizonte attracts top Brazilian and international stars in opera, music, and dance.

## Palácio das Artes

*Avenida Afonso Pena, 1537 (centro);* ☎ *237-7333.*

Check the newspaper for listing of performances at this grand theater – opera, choral, concerts, ballet, and others.

# Nightclubs

## New Sagitarius Night Club

*Rua Alfenas, 27 (Mangabeira);* ☎ *221-9304. Mon.-Sat. 9pm. on.*

For men (executive style) only. This is considered to be the best in Brazilian striptease. *Moderate. All cards.*

# Gay Belo Horizonte

Best bars/discos for gays are **Ragã**, Rua Padre Idoreco, 95 (Savassi), ☎ 227-8403. Ragã is open Fri., Sat., Sun., starting at 10 p.m. Also try **Sam's Club**, Rua Pernambuco, 223 (Savassi), ☎ *267-5703.* It's open Fri. and Sat. starting at 11 p.m.

# Shopping

The district of **Savassi** is home to most of the best restaurants, apart-hotels, cinemas and shopping malls in the city. Located south of the Municipal Park and the Palácio das Artes, the fashionable neighborhood is bounded on the east by Avenida Contorno, on the south by Rua Congonhas, and by Rua Rio de Janeiro on the west. One of the finest mini-malls in the area is **BHZ Fashion Mall**, Rua Paraiba, 1132, offering some of the most elegant fashions for men and women in Brazil.

# Fairs

## Hippie Fair

*Avenida Afonso Pena. Sun. 8 a.m.-2 p.m.*

Artists show and sell works of ceramic, wood, weaving, metal glass-cutting, painting, graphics, and drawings.

## Flower Market

*Municipal Marker. Fri.*

Here you'll find 110 stalls offering a huge variety of plants and flowers. Many vendors grow their own plants and give good advice.

## Mercado Central

*Downtown.*

This farmer's market is in the style of a Turkish bazaar, where you must master saying the word *desconto* (discount) with an irresistible smile. Espadrilles made from buffalo hide are a swell deal. Medicinal herbs in their raw state are also for sale. If you're in the market for live animals, you won't be disappointed, though the stench is awesome (many families, or rather, their maids, buy fresh turkeys and chickens here). Remember to wash and peel any fruits.

# Crystals

## IRFF International

*Avenida Barbacena, 600 and 700 (Barro Preto);* ☎ 335-7211.

This huge store has some of the best crystals in the city, and maybe the state. Leave plenty of time to browse through hundreds of rings, necklaces, pendants, crystals (raw and polished), semi-precious stones, crystal pyramids, soapstone sculptures, and chess sets. You'll also see rocks you didn't know existed, with their healing properties marked. Groups can finagle discounts.

## Gem Center

*Rua Paraiba, 330, 5th floor (centro) Central Shopping;* ☎ 226-3900.
*Mon.-Sat. 9 a.m.-7 p.m., Sat. 9 a.m.-1 p.m.*

Extensive collection of gems, jewelry, and precious stones from Minas. Not the place to buy crystal, but good for jewelry. With 15-20 stores, you should browse, compare prices and bargain.

# Native Crafts

## Centro de Artesanato Mineiro

*Av. Afonso Pena, 1537 (centro);* ☎ 222-2544. *Tues.-Fri. 9 a.m.-9 p.m., Sat. 9 a.m.-1:30 p.m., Sun. 9 a.m.-2 p.m.*

Crafts markets representing the artists of the state.

## Serjö

*Rua Antônio de Albuquerque, 749 (Savassi);* ☎ 227-5251.
*Mon.-Sat. 9 a.m.-10 p.m.*

A chic crafts store with the best native handiwork from all over Brazil, including miniature clay nativity scenes, lacework, tapestries, and paintings. Prices are steep, but the store is worth visiting just to see the inventive stock.

# Sports

**Soccer** is played Mar.-July and Aug.-Nov. on Weds., Sat. and Sun. at the Estádio Governador Magalhães Pinto, nicknamed "Mineirão." Outside, there's a monument to Pelé, Brazil's greatest soccer player, who just may end up president of the country one day (though retired, he's still that popular). A bronze model of the sports hero's feet allows you to step into his arches. Next door is Mineirinho, the biggest sports gym in South America.

# Hands-On Belo Horizonte

## Arrival

Most flights into Belo Horizonte arrive at the modern international airport known as **Confins,** ☎ *689-2700,* about 18 miles from the center of the city. Another airport is **Pampulha,** which usually only receives shuttle flights. (Always double-check your ticket.) Avoid taking the red taxis (they cost more). The white taxis are just as good, and will take you to the center of town for about $20-$25 (be prepared for a long drive). Frequent buses will take you to the *rodoviária* (bus station) or the Terminal Turistico JK. Buses to the airport leave from both the Terminal Turistico JK and the *rodoviária* – you'll need a full hour for the trip. An air-conditioned *executivo* is your best bet; it leaves from the Terminal Turistico and takes only about 20 minutes.

## Airlines Serving Belo Horizonte

**Varig**
Rua Espirito Santo, 643 (centro) . . . . . . . . . . . . . . . ☎ 273-6060
**Vasp**
Av. Olegário Maciel, 2221 (Lourdes) . . . . . . . . . . ☎ 330-5588
(Confins) . . . . . . . . . . . . . . . . . . . . . . . . . . . . . . . . . . . ☎ 689-2411
(Lourdes) . . . . . . . . . . . . . . . . . . . . . . . . . . . . . . . . . . ☎ 330-5588
**Transbrasil**
Rua Tamois, 86 (centro) . . . . . . . . . . . . . . . . . . . . . ☎ 274-3533
**American Airlines**
Rua dos Guajajaras, 557 (centro) . . . . . . . . . . . . . . ☎ 213-1288
**United Airlines**
Rua São Paulo, 1106, sala 305 (centro) . . . . . . . . . . ☎ 261-7777

## Car Rental

**Localiza**
Avenida Bernardo Monteiro, 1567 . . . . . . . . . . . . . ☎ 800-2121

## City Transportation

### City Buses

City buses are excellent, color-coded for destination; yellow buses have cirular routes, red buses serve the center, and blue buses run diagonally. The easiest place to catch one is on Avenida Alfonso Pena from downtown.

### Taxis

Taxis are generally cheap, and much more reliable than in other big cities.

Rádio Táxi . . . . . . . . . . . . . . . . . . . . . . . . . . . . . .   ☎ 281-1700
Coomotáxi . . . . . . . . . . . . . . . . . . . . . . . . . . . . .   ☎ 418-2020
B.H. Táxi . . . . . . . . . . . . . . . . . . . . . . . . . . . . .   ☎ 215-8081

## Consulates

**U.S.A.**
Rua Fernandes Lourinho, 147, 14th floor . . . . . . .   ☎ 335-3555
**Great Britain**
Av. Afonso Pena, 852 (centro). . . . . . . . . . . . . . . .   ☎ 521-5000

## Money Exchange

**Banco do Brasil**
Rua Rio de Janeiro, 750
**American Express Master Turismo**
Rua Afonso Pena, 1867. . . . . . . . . . . . . . . . . . . . . .   ☎ 330-3600

## Points Beyond

**Daily buses,** ☎ *201-8111,* run to Brasília, Rio, Salvador, São Paulo, Caxambu, Congonhas, Diamantina, Lapinha, Mariana, Ouro Preto, Poços de Caldas, Sabará, São João del Rei, and São Lourenço. Tickets should be bought early, including the return trip (especially on weekends and hols).

## Tourist Information

Special tourist information in English can be found by calling **Alô Belo**, ☎ *220-1310.* There are centers in the bus station, and at Confins airport. The official tourist board is at **BELOTUR,** Rua Tupis, 149, 10th floor (centro).

## Travel Agency

### Vnitour

*Rua Tupis, 171 (entro);* ☎ *(31) 201-7144.*

An excellent travel agency with a helpful English-speaking staff offers tours of the historical towns. Half-day tours of Congonhas run about $78, one-day tours of Ouro Preto and Mariana about $140 (rates for two are considerably cheaper). A tour of Congonhas, São João del Rei, and Tiradentes runs $200. Airport transfers can also be arranged.

### Ouro Preto Turismo

*Shopping 5 Avenida Rua Alagoas, 1314 (Savassi);* ☎ *281-0333, fax 281-0322.*
Good service and the best prices for excursions.

## What To Wear

Businessmen tend to wear suits, but general tourists will feel comfortable wearing jeans and a neat t-shirt during the day. Dress at night is casual chic.

# HISTORICAL CITIES
## Ouro Preto, Mariana, São João del Rei, Tiradentes, Diamantina, Serro, & Caraça

There is no other place where a visitor can so steep himself in the richness of Brazil's historical past than in the *cidades históricas* (historical cities) near Belo Horizonte. Originally colonized in the late 17th century by the *bandeirantes* (those rough and rugged pioneers who heeded the cries of gold emanating from the Mineiro hills), these satellite villages quickly developed from rambunctious mining camps into gracefully constructed towns with beautiful two-story mansions, cobblestone roads and, most importantly, scores of gilt-laden churches that became showcases for Minas' astounding wealth. Spurred by so much precious ore

Colonial architecture in Minas Gerais

extracted in so short a time, the cities of Ouro Preto, Mariana, São João del Rei, Tiradentes, and Congonhas soon became rampant with plots of political intrigue and piracy. And yet this nucleus of colonial communities also gave rise to some of the country's finest artists and artisans – among them, the sculptor and painter Manoel da Costa Athaide, whose works remain a living masterpiece of the baroque colonial era. During the 18th century, gold leaf became the rage, and the churches of Ouro Preto, in particular, transformed the colonialists' experience of worship. One 18th-century observer remarked that praying in Ouro Preto's Church of Pilar was like talking to God inside a great golden urn.

Beyond their artistic treasures and culinary delights, these historical cities are held dear by modern Brazilians for another reason. It was here that the infamous **Inconfîdencia Mineira**, a conspiracy spearheaded by *Mineiros* in the late 18th century, was first initiated against Portuguese rule. Although a failure in its own time, the rebellion became the ultimate symbol of Brazilian independence, inspiring the colony's successful break with the motherland nearly a century later. Today, it is a rare school child who cannot recite the exciting tale of Tiradentes, the conspiracy's martyred hero. Two hundred years have passed since the heydays of these colonial cities, yet the economic decline of Ouro Preto and Mariana at the end of the mining cycle was actually their architectural salvation. As migrant workers moved on to other areas, it became impracticable to replace the old buildings with more modern ones, as happened in Rio. The decisive act for preserving the two cities was the creation in 1937 of what is now known as the **Department of the Ministry of Culture**. Thirty-nine edifices in Ouro Preto and 13 in Mariana, including religious and civil buildings, bridges, fountains, and private houses, were registered as national monuments in the record books, thus providing legal protection and a permanent guarantee of technical assistance for their conservation. In 1980 UNESCO bestowed the title of **Cultural Heritage of Mankind** upon the city of Ouro Preto.

> **UP CLOSE TIP:** *A substantial tour of the major historical cities should take about three or four days, including a day or two in Ouro Preto and Mariana, and two days in São João del Rei, Tiradentes, and Congonhas. An extra three to four days can be spent visiting Diamantina and Serro, staying at charming pousadas while pursuing fascinating ecological treks.*

# Ouro Preto

Mina's premier historical city, Ouro Preto is a treasure of details – gorgeous mansions, curved windows with wrought-iron frames, grilled baroque balconies, antique street lanterns, and cobblestone streets that meander up and down the steep hillsides. What is so surprising is that such a small town should boast 13 baroque churches, from more modest chapels to grand cathedrals washed in a dazzling gold leaf. Today, the city (pop. 67,000) is a real university town with the bohemian flair that students always bring. Crime is low, and it is perfectly safe to stroll around after dark, but on weekend nights and holidays, it's not uncommon to see young scholars and backpackers strung out drunk on the plazas.

The words *ouro preto*, or black gold, refer to the color of ore first discovered in the area: gold mixed with a dark-tinted palladium. If you are interested in buying precious and semi-precious gems, excellent deals can be found in Ouro Preto; often one-third the cost of gems at the big-name jewelry stores in Rio. The best (and the most expensive) is imperial topaz, mining deposits of which can be found near Saramenha, less than two km. (1¼ miles) from the city's center, as well as in the districts of Rodrigo Silva and Antônio Pereira, about 20 km. (15 miles) away. An extremely rare stone, imperial topaz can only be found here and in the Ural Mountains of the former Soviet Union. Colors range from yellow to champagne to an intense rose tone.

The city has had its share of historical characters, not the least of which is the more recent **Dona Olimpia**, made famous by Milton Nascimento in the song of the same name. Once a young woman renowned for her beauty, she was reputed to have lost her first and only love due to her family's financial demise, then later turned eccentric in old age and greeted tour buses dressed in old-style clothes, muttering about the golden days of Ouro Preto. Some locals claimed she was crazy; others called her brilliant; eventually, a Carnaval School was named after her. Alas, she died in the last few years, but shopkeepers still remember her, and you can discover more information about her in local crafts stores.

A famous portrait of the late Dona Olímpia (by Layon), the beloved eccentric from Ouro Preto.

One eccentric addendum for scientists: The **peripatus**, a prehistoric insect that can be found nowhere else on the planet, has been discovered in the forests surrounding Ouro Preto. A program of conservation has been initiated to protect it.

# History

It's no wonder that the fever for Brazilian independence was first ignited among the *inconfidentes* in Ouro Preto. Ever since its start as a mining camp in the early 18th century, Ouro Preto has witnessed a fever pitch of emotions. Immediately after a *Paulista* adventurer named **Antônio Dias** discovered "black gold" while panning near the Itacolomi Peak, thousands flooded the area, setting up makeshift camps along the Riberão and Carmo streams. By 1711, spurred by the appearance of a now prosperous hamlet, the Portuguese government officially founded the village of Vila Rica de Nossa Senhora do Pilar, the first to be recognized in Minas. The stunning outpouring of gold, the burgeoning population, and a frightening lack of food supplies soon erupted in a series of tumultuous rebellions. Ten years later the **Vila Rica Rebellion** broke out, protesting the exorbitant taxes exacted by the Portuguese. This resulted in the establishment of the **Capitania of Minas**, independent of São Paulo, with its official headquarters housed in Vila Rica.

Between 1735 and 1763, gold production peaked and many of Ouro Preto's fine buildings were put up, including the Governor's Palace and numerous bridges and fountains. By 1780, the city was a spider's web of paved, winding streets, and elegant two-story houses with terraced gardens ebullient with flowers. Inspired by Iberian counter-reformist ideals, the new settlers began to build magnificent baroque churches at the end of nearly every great road.

## National Freedom

The political movement considered by historians to have most profoundly influenced colonial Brazil was the **Inconfidência Mineira** (1788-1792). On its face a protest against royal taxes, it was really a muffled cry for national freedom, modeled after the 1776 rebellion of the North American British colonies. Though the conspiracy was a collusion of many social classes, the only name Brazilians remember today is that of **Tiradentes** (The Tooth-Puller) whose real name was Joaquim José da Silva Xavier, a part-time dentist, mineralogist, low-level militia officer, and engineer whose loner personality earmarked him for martyrdom. Enflamed with republican ideals, Tiradentes was able to inspire a nucleus of supporters. But before action could be taken, one of the participants renounced the others, hoping to have his personal debts rescinded, and the cause was immediately lost. At the conspirators' trial, which became a circus of denials and betrayals, Tiradentes alone admitted full responsibility, even though his defense lawyer tried to prove him insane. While the sentences of his colleagues were commuted to exile, Tiradentes' punishment resounded with Iberian revenge: he was to be hung, drawn, and quartered in public, his salted head posted in Vila Rica "till it rotted" and the other members of his body posted in the neighboring cities where he had preached rebellion. (Fortunately for the townspeople, the skull was stolen by compatriots after a few days and was rumored to have been buried in the hills near the city, supposedly filled with gold dust.) It took a hundred years to redeem Tiradentes' name, but now the Brazilian flag bears the motto of his rebellion: "Freedom – Even Late," a phrase originally from Virgil. In Ouro Preto, the central square today bears not only Tiradentes' name but his statue.

### Architectural History

Religious buildings proliferated in Minas ever since the early days of colonization. At first they were rough little chapels raised alongside the paths leading to the mining zones, where a statue of the patron saint of the expedition was placed. Later, as a group settled into a particular area, a full-fledged chapel was built, with bells hung in eccentric coves. As civil authorities founded the village, another kind of church began to appear – the mother church, a true sign of attained prosperity. Meant to hold large congregations of (white) worshippers, churches such as Conceição and Pilar, with their monumental frontispieces, were impressive calls to worship, framed by two bell towers and filled with an opulent explosion of baroque decor. In Pilar, the refinement of gilt carving is purposefully organized, resulting in one of the most remarkable baroque interiors anywhere.

## A Bird's Eye View

Ouro Preto is situated in the area of the Espinhaço Mountain Range in the metallurgic zone known as the **Ferrous Quadrangle**, one of the most important iron ore sites in the world. It lies 98 km. (about 60 miles) from Belo Horizonte and has approximately 45,000 residents. The climate is characteristic of mountain localities, with temperatures ranging from 25°F to 82°F (leather jackets are good for late fall and winter.) The city's highest point is the **Italocomi Peak** at 5,600 ft.

## Sights

Ouro Preto is a bit difficult to navigate on foot. The following tour is best done with a driver. A guide probably won't tell yo more than I have here. (See *Private Guides* under *Hands-On Ouro Preto*.)

### Capela de Padre Faria Church

Start your tour of Ouro Preto at its birthplace, built in 1701 by the first *bandeirantes* and the expedition's priest named Padre Faria, who upon seeing the first flow of golden ore immediately opened his own mines. When the Portuguese authorities in Lisbon soon imposed a new tax (called the Royal Fifth, requiring all gold dust to be minted into bars and taxed 20%), Padre Faria decided not to pay. Instead, he petitioned the Vatican to receive his church under direct subordination and, from that point on, never paid one cent to the royal coffers. Nor did he stick around to manage his flock; when the mines ran dry, Father Faria mysteriously disappeared – obviously, with gold – for the rest of his life.

The church's unpretentious facade in Jesuit style contrasts with the gold-leaf decor inside, though not all followers pray before images of Our Lady of the Rosary and Our Lady of the Good Deliverance. Especially characteristic of the region is the image of Christ as Our Lady of the Green Cane, a red-caped saviour holding a stalk of sugarcane – a sacred symbol of the state. If you look closely at some of the frescoes, the foyer's fountain and the columns over the door, you'll discover Indian motifs – a sign that the priests working with Padre Faria had probably been in contact with Indian missions. During the inauguration of Brasília, the church's bell was taken to the new capital to be rung at the first solemn mass. Mass is held every Sun. at 6 p.m. Visiting hours: 8 a.m.-noon daily.

## Igreja de Nossa Senhora do Rosário dos Pretos

Poorer in decor but certainly not in spirit is **Our Lady of the Rosary of the Blacks**, also called St. Efigênia. During the 17th and 18th centuries, the Portuguese engaged in rabid slave trade with the countries of Angola and Guinea, sometimes buying entire conquered tribes from African chiefs. In the early 1730s, the Portuguese sold one such tribe, including their chief, to gold miners in Ouro Preto, but his subjects eventually bought back his freedom by hiding bits of stolen gold dust in their hair. Once freed, the chief, Chico Rei, fortuitously discovered the richest gold mine in Ouro Preto and started buying back his tribe one by one, eventually founding the first black community. Constructed between 1738 and 1745, this church remains a symbol of the tribe's African unity; note the non-Brazilian, very African elephant on one of the frescoes. Over the main altar the ceiling painting features not only a black Pope but also two black saints – Benedictine and Antônio Donato (though their features appear white). The Madonna atop the front portal is attributed to Aleijadinho. The door's red panes of glass are all new, except the dark tinted portion, which is original (notice how crystal clear it is.) Visiting hours: Tues.-Sun., 8 a.m.-noon.

## House of Pirata Vira-e-saia

Nearby on Rua Santa Efigênia is this house, now reputed to be haunted. During the 18th century it was owned by a rich Portuguese merchant, whose undercover troop of bandits continually ambushed the Portuguese convoys laden with gold. Vira-e-saia managed to infiltrate the mint house with one of his agents, who conveyed which ship was holding the real cargo by turning the image of Our Lady in the nearby oratory to the right direction. After some major coups, the agent was eventually discovered and tortured, the pirate's daughters violated in front of their father and the entire family killed. It's said the nearby church was built at the end of the 18th century to ward off lingering bad spirits. Across the street from the house, the oratory with the cross can still be seen, but the image of Our Lady has been destroyed.

## Praça de Marília

The nearby Praça de Marília is also laden with romantic intrigue. The poetically inclined **Tomás Antônio Gonzaga**, one of the leaders of the *Inconfidentes* (and also Chief Justice in Ouro Preto) used to meet the betrothed Marilia do Dirceu at the fountain in this square (now called Fonte de Marília). Whether young Marília had been involved in the conspiracy was never determined, but after her lover was arrested, she chose never to marry. The poetry he wrote to her is now considered some of the best literary examples of the colonial period.

## São Francisco de Assis Church

This pretty church (1765) is a tribute to the fortitude and artistic determination of Aleijadinho, whose body by that time had become so debilitated that his slave assistants had to tie his instruments to his hands and carry him on their backs. The church, which he designed, was his last and greatest achievement. All the carvings on the main altar, including the angel on the ceiling supporting a huge crystal candelabra, are his; he actually sculpted the figures of Saint Louis and Saint Francis, which is why they are so precious. In the back room is a magnificent fountain that took him three years to complete. The ceiling painting (1802-1812) is the work of Manoel da Costa Athaide – a trompe l'oeil effect showing Our Lady of the Assumption. Visiting hours: 8-11:30 a.m. and 1:30-5 p.m. The

The 18th-century São Francisco de Assis.
*Photo by Stephen Geller Katz.*

fee is minimal; you may also use the ticket from the Aleijadinho Museum.

## Matriz de Nossa Senhora da Conceição de Antônio Dias (Museu Aleijadinho)

Located on the other side of the fountain, this is the largest church in Ouro Preto, with eight lateral altars combined with fat-cheeked cherubs, suspended gold grapes, and winged angels. The architecture of the church is attributed to Aleijadinho's father; his famous son lies buried at the feet of the altar of Our Lady of Good Death, shown lying in her white robes in the sculpted sepulchre. Down some rickety stairs (in what used to be the crypt) is the Aleijadinho Museum (you'll have to stash cameras and bags in the provided lockers; entrance fee is minimal). In the first room are precious objects taken from the old church, such as ornate incense burners, bells, and pure gold chalices of inestimable value. A 17th-century crucified Christ in ivory is considered to be an example of anatomical perfection. Attributed to Aleijadinho is the sculpted figure of São Francisco de Paula and also the crucified Christ on the Cross, the latter a curious historical commentary. A friend of Tiradentes, Aleijadinho carved the sign of a rope and blood on Christ's neck to commemorate Tiradentes' martyred death through hanging. Visiting hours: 8:30-11:30 a.m. and 1:30-5 p.m.

## Matriz de Nossa Senhor do Pilar

The second richest in Brazil, this church has over 1,000 pounds of gold (the first is São Francisco in Salvador). Constructed in 1728-1733, it was inaugurated with a month of magnificent processions, led by nobles and their slaves masquerading in Greek costumes. The main artists responsible were the Portuguese Antônio Francisco Pombal (to whom the general idea of the church's decoration is attributed) and the sculptor Francisco Xavier de Brito, considered one of the possible teachers of Aleijadinho. The four cherubs with their feet dangling over the altar are the zenith of baroque art; their very cellulite seems to be made from solid gold. The ceiling looks curved, but is actually an optical illusion achieved through artistry. Look high up on the balcony in front of the altar and you'll see the carved feet of a human being dangling over the edge. During Holy Week, the statue of the Lady with a dagger in her heart is taken in procession to Our Lady of Mercy Church, while the figure of Christ is carried on Thurs. to the main square in replication of the Via Cruxis. In the back room, the sacristy boasts an amazing chest of drawers made entirely from one piece of jacaranda wood. Visiting hours: Tues.-Sun. noon-5 p.m., minimal fee.

> **UP CLOSE TIP:** *Beside the church is the* **Native Photo de Epoca,** *where the photographer Renato Castelfranchi will take photos of you in an atmospheric courtyard dressed in historical costumes. A bit overpriced, but entertaining for those trying to recapture past lives.*

## The Mint

Taking a right, turn up Rua Rodolfo Bretos and around into Rua São José (also called Rua Tiradentes), where you'll find lots of bars and restaurants for a needed breather. Cross the small stone bridge to the Casa de Fundação (The Mint), also known as the Casa dos Contos, which was used in the 18th century as a government bureau for collecting the royal tax. Constructed in 1787, it was one of the most luxurious manor houses of its time, originally the private residence of João Rodrigues de Macedo, a senior official of the Portuguese administration and one of the richest men in Brazil. Later, it was used as a guesthouse for VIPs; notice the refinement of its upper rooms, whose ceilings are decorated with rococo paintings.

## Teatro Municipal Da Ouro Preto
## (Casa Da Opera)

Inaugurated in 1769, this is the oldest public theater in Latin America to remain in continual use. Both emperors, Peter I and II, attended performances here, sitting in the royal box surrounded by nobles. The acoustics are wonderful and, if you can manage to hop on stage, you'll get an intimate perspective from the performer's eye. Check out the stone floor dressing rooms downstairs. Hours: 1-5 p.m.

## Praça Tiradentes

Adorning the Praça Tiradentes is the statue of Minas' first and premier martyr, Tiradentes. On one side of the square is the **Museu da Inconfîdencia** (Museum of the Inconfídentes) which was once both the former jail (1st floor) and the municipal chamber (2nd floor). All the remains of the exiled conspirators were brought back and buried here (some were collected from as far away as Africa). Also in the museum are fine examples of sacred art, systems of illumination, vehicles of transport, and artisanry. The backroom shows documents from the conspiracy, including the original death sentence of Tiradentes by the Queen of Portugal. Also here are two of the original pieces of wood from his gallows, as well as some of his dental equipment. On your way out, notice the green iron door and double grills of the former prison windows – no one ever escaped.

## Igreja De Nossa Senhora Do Carmo

Next door to the museum is one of the finest churches in Ouro Preto, designed by Antônio Francisco Lisboa, the father of Aleijadinho, who took over supervision after the former died in 1766. For over 40 years, Aleijadinho fiddled with the decoration, some of which, such as the baptismal font in the sacristy, rate as baroque masterpieces. Attached to the church is a museum of impressively displayed sacred art, housed in a recently restored mansion. Hours: 8-11:30 a.m. and 1-5 p.m.

## School of Mines & Metallurgy

In the other side of Praça Tiradentes is the former Governor's Palace, now the School of Mines and Metallurgy of the University of Ouro Preto – an impressive building, with the appearance of a fort. Young people from all over Brazil come here to study; you'll see motorbikes leaning against the walls, one of the many icons of modern *Mineiro* culture.

## Museu De Mineralogia Da Escola
## De Minas

Adjacent to the university, the museum is not just for mineralogists, but anyone interested in precious and semi-precious stones, crystals and rare rock formations. Tours usually visit only the first floor, but scientific-minded persons should also head for the second floor, which has over 23,000 samples of minerals, including imperial topaz. Visiting hours: noon-5 p.m., small fee.

## Boca Da Mina

Opened in 1702, this gold mine formerly belonged to two Portuguese brothers who had no relationship to Chico Rei; nevertheless, it's often referred to today as Mina do Chico Rei. In 100 years of exploration, more than 6,000 tons of gold have been extracted. Today you can walk through some of the remains, then take a bit of lunch or early dinner at the adjacent restaurant. The present owner of the complex – a feisty 78-year-old local named Dona Marazinha – has lived in the adjacent house for over 50 years. A small boutique of crystals and pottery is also on premises. Visiting hours: The mine is opened 7 a.m.-6 p.m.; restaurant hours are noon-6 p.m.

# Where To Stay

Accommodations in Ouro Preto run from colonial elegance to the bare-bones rooms of a fraternity house. Moderate-priced *pousadas*, surrounded by tropical vegetation and forests, can be so inviting you might want to stay a few extra days. Good discounts can be found in low season, particularly at family-run *pousadas*. See page 26 for price chart.

### Solar Do Rosário

*Rua Getúlio Vargas, 270;* ☎ *(31) 551-5200.*

Now fully completed, this former colonial mansion – once a drugstore, then a private residence in the 19th century – has been lovingly transformed into the most luxurious accommodation in the city, retaining its baroque colonial facade. All the finishing material was extracted from the area, such as pink quartzite floors that appear gold when polished. Every detail, from the flowered covered seats in the dining room to the frosted windows, reflects impeccable taste. Ingeniously designed as an intimate inn meant to be strolled through, the hotel boasts a Scotch bar made cozy by a raw rock wall, wood-beam floors and soft jazzy music. The daylight sun enlivens the finished wood staircase, from where the views of the church next door are magnificent. An indoor courtyard captures the leisure of days gone by.

Tapestry bedspreads and gorgeous bathrooms mark the apartments; deluxe rooms are significantly larger, some even have fireplaces. One corner suite has a heart-breaking view of the church. Other luxuries include air conditioning, heat, cable TV with CNN, hairdryer, bidet, and chocolates at bedtime. The tea salon exhibits porcelain and antique bureaus from the hotel's heyday. A meeting room for 100 persons and a garage make this a dream location for conventions. A secret underground passageway, built in the 17th century to connect the mine with São Francisco de Paula church, is still evident. Guests retain special privileges to use the nearby private golf course. **Le Coq d'Or**, the hotel's restaurant, serves French and regional cuisine that rivals the best in the state and maybe Brazil. (See under *Where To Eat.*) *Expensive. All cards.*

### Pousada do Mondego

*Largo de Coimbra, 38;* ☎ *(31) 551-2040, fax 551-3094.*

This charming two-story *pousada* manages to be historical, attractive, and comfortable all at the same time. And the location can't be beat – right off Praça Tiradentes, overlooking the São Francisco church. The scent of pine wafts through the small, but inviting lobby, where a restaurant is being built. The rooms, immaculately clean, are filled with colonial-style furniture; fine art adorns the corridors. Ask for rooms with a balcony; the attic apartment with its triangular roof is quirky, but good for three short people who don't need a view. All rooms have color TV and mini-bar. *18 apts, 2 suites. Expensive. All cards.*

### Estralagem das Minas Gerais

*Rod. Dos Inconfidentes, km. 87 (Road to Belo Horizonte);*
☎ *(31) 551-2122, fax 551-2709.*

Long the most elaborate resort complex in the city, this hotel combines *caseira* (homey) charm with top-notch efficiency. The only problem is its location – about five miles outside Ouro Preto, on a hill overlooking the city.

There's little difference between the deluxe and standard – all are spacious, with color TV, mini-bar, but no heat. Gardens are lovely to stroll through, the pool is enormous, the tennis courts playable, and the wood-beamed dining room extremely attractive. Chalets are great for families of three or four; some come with jacuzzi and fireplace. Lining the hotel's hallways are local paintings and sculptures for sale. Handicapped facilities available. *30 apts, 12 chalets. Expensive. All cards.*

### Pousada Solar das Lajes

*Rua Conselheiro Quintiliano, 604;* ☎ *(31) 551-3388, fax 551-1116.*

Nationally acclaimed sculptor Pedro Correia de Araújo has reconstructed this rustic *pousada* around the original colonial walls of an 18th-century estate; the result is an unusual blend of nature and natural resources that provides a calm, quiet retreat from the tourist hubbub. An easy 10-minute walk from downtown, the hotel is reached via a stone path and surrounded by overgrown gardens with at least 80 different kinds of fruit trees. A number of the rooms are old slave quarters; some even have their stone window seats intact, from where you can contemplate verdant fields. An outdoor pool, which Pedro made himself, overlooks the city. Many of the rooms sport antique beds and old lanterns; Pedro's fascinating sculptures adorn the grounds. Just meeting the owner is a trip, an innovative genius who speaks heavily accented English and is constantly puttering with the house. *13 apts. Moderate. V*

## Quinta dos Barões

*Rua Pandiá Calógeras, 474 (Barra);* ☎ *(31) 551-1056, fax 551-1942. Reservations:* ☎ *(31) 441-1623 in Belo Horizonte.*

Formerly the first German consulate, this 300-year-old house has a long and sensational past. The present owner, descended from one of the *Inconfidentes,* will eagerly show you photos and prints from the Second Empire; just one look at his enormous antique headboards, wood-carved desks and shuttered windows will send you reeling back in time. The bathrooms were originally used as alcoves to lock up the master's virgin daughters. The view from the four-star rooms, across grassy knolls, is spectacular; from the lobby you can see the ruins of the original stone house. A fireplace is being constructed in the cave-like dining room. Apartments do not have heat or air conditioning. Walking to the city will be difficult from here, but across the street is a handmade bedspread factory. *7 apts. Moderate. All cards.*

## Hotel Priskar da Barra

*Rua Antônio Martins, 98;* ☎ *(31) 551-2666, fax 551-1786.*

Brightly polished wooden floors add appeal to the apartments in this two-story hotel about a 15-minute walk uphill from the city. Families will particularly enjoy the enormous pool and the children's pool. A romantic option is the wedding suite, with chiffon curtains and a lace-covered table and couch in an extra room. All rooms come with a color TV, great mini-bar, and radio, but no heat or air conditioning; some rooms have fans. *17 apts, 4 suites. Moderate. All cards.*

## Grand Hotel

*Rua Sen. Rocha Lagoa, 164;* ☎ *(31) 551-1488, fax 551-1612.*

When the state government ceremonially transfers to Ouro Preto on April 21, the governor stays at this traditional hotel, whose glass-enclosed lobby looks out over the city's rooftops. Unfortunately, the Niemeyer-designed facade, the only modern one in the city, is a real blight in contrast to the truly glorious colonial houses down the street. The restaurant, however, is excellent, supervised by the oldest and most famous chef in the city. The furniture in the small standards is more old than old-fashioned, but the bathrooms are clean. Suites with balconies overlooking the most preserved part of Ouro Preto are exceedingly desirable. Before gambling was banned, the hotel labored as a casino and still exudes a little of that swashbuckling ambiance. The lush grounds were designed by Burle Marx; there is no pool. Across the street is the Old Mint House, where gold was melted down for taxes and where one of the *Inconfidentes* committed suicide. Children under five stay free. *35 apts. Moderate. All cards.*

## Luxor Pousada

*Praça Antônio Dias/Rua Dr. Alfredo Baeta, 10;* ☎ *and fax (31) 551-2244.*

This 16-room *pousada* occupies an old colonial mansion, with an inner courtyard that nearly suggests a monastery. The location, across the street from the glorious Matriz de Nossa Senhora da Conceição, is prime, and you can safely walk home from the center at all hours. Rooms are colonial style and extraordinarily comfortable; odd paintings chalked on the wall suggest a strange hippiness. The most wonderful rooms are the suites, particularly the "A" suites, with two rooms, hardwood floors, huge antique beds, and snug comforters. A fireplace in the salon makes a cozy nook, and the gourmet restaurant is considered one of the best in the city. *16 rooms. Moderate-expensive. All cards.*

### Hotel Casa Grande Pousada

*Rua Consellheiro Quintiliano, 96;* ☎ *(31) 551-4314.*

One of my Deep Throats, Bonnie Kassel, recommends this new, less expensive *pousada* that is "immaculately clean, serves a wonderful buffet breakfast, and has a real elegance." It's a five-minute walk from *centro. About $65 a night for a double. Moderate. All cards.*

### Hospedaria Antiga

*Rua Xavier da Veiga, 1113;* ☎ *(31) 551-2203.*

Young backpackers tend to stay at this former public archive owned by the original family. The style reminds me of an old highway chalet, with rough red stucco walls matched by even rougher furniture. Bathrooms are minimal and not always clean, but huge shuttered windows overlook verdant gardens. Rooms can hold one, two, or three beds. There are no TVs, but some rooms have mini-bars. *16 apts. Inexpensive. All cards.*

### Pousada Galeria Panorama Barroco

*Conselheiro Quintiliano, 722;* ☎ *(31) 551-2582.*

Located next door to the Solar, this could be your home away from home, if you're into New Age, no nukes, eco-treks, crystals, and doing your own laundry. The very personable David Peterkin (an American) and his Brazilian wife, Lucia, run this traditional *pousada*, where every room has its own motif. The two bathrooms are shared. The lobby, jam-packed with crystals, jewelry, and objets d'art from all over the world, does nothing to dispel the hippie feel, and Lucia even grinds her own coffee, which she buys south of Minas. David, an anthropologist and archaeologist, leads excursions to Congonhas, the imperial topaz mines, and any destination you can concoct outside the city limits in a four-wheel jeep (check fees on arrival). At night he pulls out videos for the guests and even sets up a telescope for stargazing. From among the international set that descends here, you're sure to make a lifelong friend. *Inexpensive. No cards.*

### Pousado do Pilar

*Rua Benedito Valadares, 231;* ☎ *(31) 551-2422, fax (31) 551-1468.*

A good budget idea, this colonial-style house on a side street near the Pilar Church offers simple but clean rooms with a small shower and fridge. Some rooms share a bathroom. Breakfast is included, and the restaurant turns into a pizzaria for other meals (pizzas served in soapstone tins, come "really hot," I was told). Next door is Milagre dos Minas, a tiny store for soapstone figurines. *Inexpensive. All cards.*

## Pousada Ouro Preto

*Largo Musicista José dos Anjos Casta, 72;* ☎ *(31) 551-3081.*

A good budget deal, this tiny *pousada* truly has one of the most beautiful views in the city, but getting there will be rough, and you'll need a taxi up the steep hill. The owner has the best idea – he scoots around on a moped, and suggests clients drink on his terrace at night (there is no way you could find your way back here from the city if you were the slightest tipsy).

Rooms are simple but have a certain rural charm. Get as large a room as possible; the most private are in the courtyard. The breakfast room is one long wood table where you make friends fast. Reserve at the beginning of Jan. for Carnaval. *Inexpensive. All cards.*

## Albergue da Juventude

*Rua das Mercês, 136;* ☎ *551-3170.*

This youth hostel is the annex to a gym, with bunk beds (seven to a room), kitchen, and a place to wash clothes.

# Where To Eat

See page 26 for price chart.

## Le Coq D'Or

*Hotel Solar do Rosário; Rua Getúlio Vagas, 270;* ☎ *(31) 551-1032.*

If you want to eat some of the finest cuisine in the state, if not Brazil, come to the Coq d'Or, a jewel in the crown of this beautiful new hotel. Decor is gracious and comfortably elegant, and prices for lunch and dinner are phenomenally low (half the price for the same quality in Belo Horizonte). The French chef is Laurent, one of the most famous in the country, who devises two daily specials, ranging from filet of beef to risotto with lobster; a glazed duck we ate was superb. The dessert cart was impressive – not only creatively designed (the color of some deserts matched the napkins), but also mouth-watering. The *torta jabuticaba* – a torte made from an exotic tropical fruit – is the best dessert I've ever eaten in Brazil. Coffee is served with plates of delicate chocolates and fresh-baked cookies, the leftovers of which I surreptitiously stole away with me. Reserve in high season. *Moderate. All cards.*

## Acaso

*Largo do Rosario, 85;* ☎ *(31) 551-2397.*

Romantic dining at its most exquisite – this underground grotto boasts raw rock walls, enormously high ceilings, intimate jungle-like coves, and a candle-washed salon. If you come for drinks and *tira gostos* (hors d'oeuvres), you can eat enough to fill up, but the one full dinner offered is also good – *filet com batata flambada* (steak with flambéed potatoes). *Bamba de couve* – a delicious soup with *milho* (a grain) makes a delicious warmer on a cool night. *Moderate. All cards.*

### Restaurante Chafariz

*Rua São José, 167;* ☎ *(31) 551-2828. 11 a.m.-3 p.m., 7-10:30 p.m., closed Mon.*

Located on a charming narrow street (which is actually the main commercial way), Chafariz has been a tradition since 1929. It offers excellent typical dishes, such as *frango ao molho pardo* (chicken in its own blood), as well as imaginatively cooked steaks. The self-service lunch buffet is a fine bet, and will last you the whole day. The house is where the famous poet Alphonsus de Guimarães died in 1930. During holidays, you'll need reservations. *Moderate. No cards.*

### Casa do Ouvidor

*Rua Direita, 42;* ☎ *551-2142. 11 a.m.-3 p.m., 7:30-10 p.m.*

Considered one of the top kitchens in Ouro Preto, the Ouvidor exudes colonial simplicity, with shutters open to the fresh breeze. The menu, in English and Portuguese, features dishes such as *tutu á Mineira* (roasted pork loin with mashed beans, boiled eggs, and pork sausage), *feijão tropeiro* (beans mixed with manioc flour, fried egg, pork loin, and sausage), and *frango com quiabo* (chicken with okra). The soups are excellent and the filets are simple, but well cooked. Desserts include homemade sweets and preserves, and especially ice cream. *Moderate. All cards.*

### Grand Hotel Restaurant

*Rua Sen. Rocha Lagoa, 164;* ☎ *551-1488.*

The restaurant of this old-fashioned hotel is all modern elegance in a cool salmon-and-gray decor. The chef, the oldest in the city, is famous for his regional dishes, especially the *bamba de couve*, a delicious cornmeal porridge with finely chopped kale and pieces of pork loin, and *macarronnda mineira*, macaroni served with baked sausage. For dessert try the *goiabada com quiejo*, an intensely sweet jelly-like paste of guava served with a wedge of sour Mineiro cheese. *Moderate. All cards.*

### Calabouço

*Rua Conde de Bobadela, 132;* ☎ *551-1222.*
*11 a.m.-3:30 p.m., 6:30-11 p.m. Sun. 11 a.m.-3:30 p.m.*

Located off Praça Tiradentes, this atmospheric eatery looks like an underground cave, with its rough brick walls and wooden tables; an interesting record collection from avant-garde jazz to Elis Regina plays all night. The simple menu features well-seasoned steaks, but the joint's greatest virtue is that it serves dinner starting at 7 p.m. *Moderate. No cards.*

### Relicário 1800

*Praça Tiradentes, 64;* ☎ *551-2855. Opens at 11 a.m.*

The owner, a private French teacher in Ouro Preto, has ebulliently decorated this centrally located eatery with cedar sculptures and local artwork (the name means "the place where you keep relics"). For some reason not yet understood, guests receive a surprise wooden spoon. A 20-year tradition on the square, the menu features typical dishes and beef and chicken. During vacations and weekends, call for reservations. *Moderate. All cards.*

### Restaurante & Pizzeria Casa Nova

*Praça Tiradentes, 84;* ☎ *551-2407. 11 a.m.-3 p.m.*

Not just 14 kinds of pizza, but steaks and traditional dishes are served at this informal eatery off the main square. Sat. night features live classical guitar starting at 8:30 p.m. English spoken. *Moderate. All cards.*

### Restaurante e Pizzaria Canto de Minas

*Rua Direita, 94;* ☎ *(31) 551-4983.*

Regional cuisine with live music.

### Beijinho Doce

*Rua Conde de Bobadela, 134 (Centro).*

Tiny bakery for sweets, small cakes, and salty delicacies. *Inexpensive. No cards.*

# Nightlife

Shows, theater plays, and musical performances occur frequently. A schedule of events is always posted at the Tourist Information Office, at the bus station, and the Central Reception Office, at Praça Tiradentes, 41.

There are numerous bars, where you might stumble on an improvised chorus with guitar accompaniment. I once happened on a wonderful impromptu group-sing of old Brazilian tunes outside the Igreja do Rosário under the moonlight. The best bar to hang out for the evening is **Acaso** (see above, under *Where To Eat*).

# Shopping

## Crafts

Ouro Preto is a magnet for folk art and crafts of the region. Cheaper souvenirs can be found around **Praça Tiradentes, Rua Direita, Rua São José, Largo de Coimbra**, and **Rua Claúdio Manoel**. The best bet is just to stroll around the city and buy on impulse. Do bargain in outdoor markets.

### Bureau d'Art

*Largo do Rosário 41. 10 a.m.-8 p.m.*

The most interesting crafts and antique store in the city, with unusual folk art and modern renditions. Across the street from the Hotel Solar do Rosário.

## Seleiro

*Rua Direita, 191;* ☎ *551-1774. 9 a.m.-7 p.m.*

Craftwork in soapstone and ceramics. Articles in pewter. Oil paintings.

## Jirau

*Rua Direita, 122;* ☎ *551-3135. Mon.-Sat. 8 a.m.-6 p.m.*

Brazilian fashion and exclusive T-shirts with images of Ouro Preto.

# Jewelry

### Brazil Gemas

*Praça Tiradentes, 74;* ☎ *551-2976.*

Ouro Preto is full of jewelry stores: shop around comparing prices. I've found the most reliable in price and quality to be Brazil Gemas. Their specialty is imperial topaz. Rings are set in 18-karat gold and take about two hours to custom-make. Raw amethysts are excellent, as are the emeralds, which run $100-$2,000 per karat. Prices are about one-third the price of H. Stern in Rio. *All cards.*

# Sweets

### Toca

*Rua Direita, 131. 10 a.m.-9 p.m.*

Great for stocking up on local goodies, such as homemade liquors, *pão de queijo* (cheese bread), and dazzling *salgadinhos* (small salty appetizers). The chocolate mousse and cheesecake will fit into your hotel room's fridge.

### Licor Caseiro de Jabuticaba

*Rua São José, 165;* ☎ *551-1011. 10 a.m.-6 p.m.*

Liqueurs, jellies, and homemade condiments by a talented local, Milton Trópia – all free of chemicals.

# Hands-On Ouro Preto

## Arrival/Departure

The *rodoviária* (**bus station**) is at Rua Pe. Rolim, 661; ☎ 551-1081. Eleven buses leave daily from Belo Horizonte for Ouro Preto about every two hours. Traffic is heavy, so book your return ticket as early as possible, especially on weekends and holidays. Buses are also available from Rio, São Paulo, and Mariana, among others.

### Beyond Ouro Preto

Direct **buses** from Ouro Preto to Congonhas are available at 2 and 3:30 p.m. daily, as well as to Mariana (every half-hour). **Hitchhiking** is relatively safe in this part of the country, and you may find a college student who doesn't mind a rider on the back of his moped.

## Money Exchange

**Banco do Brazil**
Rua São José, 195; . . . . . . . . . . . . . . . . . . . . . . . . . . .   ☎ 551-2663
Rates are poor; it's better to exchange in Belo Horizonte.

## Post Office

The post office is across from the Hotel Miranda, on Rua Direita.

## Private Guides

Official English-speaking guides may be hired through the **Tourist Information Office,** Praça Tiradentes, 41; ☎ *551-2655.* One reliable guide is **Cássio A. Antunes** (8 a.m.-6 p.m.); it's considered polite to provide lunch for the guide. A private guide with taxi can be hired, or a private guide who drives – if you really want to see the city, it's best to be driven. The entire city by car can be seen in two or three hours, but leave more time for leisurely strolling and shopping.

## Tourist Information Office

The office is at Praça Tiradentes, 41. Here, you can obtain information in English about sites, guides, hotels, *pousadas,* and alternative accommodations, such as college fraternities, called *repúblicas.* Also check the booth at the bus station, ☎ *551-2501.*

## Travel Agency

**Golden Tour**
Rua São José, 215, loja 403 . . . . . . . . . . . . . . . . . . . . . .   ☎ 551-1706.
The owner is the guide and speaks English fluently.

## When To Go

**JANUARY 1: Feast of Our Lady of the Rosary,** celebrated at the Church of N.S. da Conceição, features a rare exhibition of *congado,* a ceremonial 18th-century dance introduced by slaves from the Congo.

**FEBRUARY 1: Carnaval** takes place down the atmospheric streets and squares, with pageants, samba schools, and displays of the traditional figure of Sé Pereira by the Ouro Preto Jockey Club, the oldest Carnaval society in Brazil (1867).

**MARCH: Holy Week** is particularly beautiful, with processions and ceremonies reenacting Christ's martyrdom.

**APRIL 16-20: Inconfidência Week,** with various artistic programs, culminates on April 21, **Tiradentes Day,** when the state capital is symbolically transferred to Ouro Preto.

**MAY 2-4: Feast of the Holy Cross** is an old Minas tradition held on the bridge of Antônio Dias, also known as Marília's Bridge, with fairs, band concerts, fireworks, and free distribution of fried peanuts.

**JULY 1-7: Anniversary of Ouro Preto.**

**AUGUST 15-22: Folklore Week**, with dance and music groups, local foods, and handicrafts.

**SEPTEMBER 7: Independence Day** (and the preceding week) is celebrated with popular shows and fireworks on the main square.

**SEPTEMBER 17-23: Horsemanship Jousts.**

**NOVEMBER 14-21: Aleijadinho Week.**

# Mariana

Ouro Preto, the political capital of colonial Brazil, and Mariana, the religious capital – two sister cities – are only 7½ miles from each other, so close that 18th-century power-brokers thought they might end up merging their futures together. While the cities remain separate entities today, they did reach an interchange of roles in centuries past, when Portuguese governors installed their headquarters in the less tumultuous Mariana during political rebellions. In reverse, the 18th-century bishop Dom Frei Domingos often fled to Ouro Preto, escaping political pressures of his own chapter. He returned to Mariana only for important religious festivals.

While Ouro Preto is extremely hilly and uneven, basically situated on three hills separated by valleys, Mariana is built on smoothly sloping land suitable for building squares and gardens. Discovered July 16, 1696 by *bandeirantes* from São Paulo searching for gold along the banks of the Riberão do Carmo, the villa was officially dubbed **Nossa Senhora do Carmo** in 1711. In 1743, the king of Portugal dispatched his architect José Fernandes Pinto de Alpoim to plan the urban design of the first official episcopal headquarters and capital of Minas. Two years later the name was changed to Mariana, after the queen Dona Maria Ana of Austria, wife of Dom João V.

## History

Today, time seems to have stopped in this historical town where little has changed since the colonial era. Even the cobblestone streets, models of straightness, date back to the 18th century. Two hundred years ago, horses came to refuel at what is now the principal plaza, Praça Gomes Freire. (Note the iron gate around the pond, which is in the shape of a horseshoe.) It's a lovely place to watch the town walk by and listen to local music groups during festivals. The fountains around the city were also built in the 18th century (prior to indoor sinks!) and served as a meeting point for townswomen; legend has it that slaves often hid gold in their hair and washed it out at these fountains.

Mariana's quiet charm and historical grace has attracted a subculture of artists, musicians, and poets who lend a bohemian flair to the city. Much of their craftwork, particularly wood-carved doors and furniture, approaches the mastery of ages past. Among the most famous artists who welcome visitors to their studios are the sculptor **Alvaro Madeira**, the painter **Zizi Sapateiro**, and the portrait artist **Elias Layon**. A must-hear are the organ performances of **Elisa Freixo**, artist-in-residence at the cathedral. Nothing can bring alive colonial history more than the marvelous architectonic strains of Bach or Buxtehude played in this gold-washed baroque cathedral.

# Sights

**UP CLOSE TIP:** *Avoid Mondays when all churches are closed for cleaning.*

## Igreja de São Pedro dos Clérigos

*Largo São Pedro. Tues.-Sun noon-6 p.m.*

Rumors of ghosts and demons so abounded during the construction of this 18th-century church that the workers refused to finish it, despite its daring curvilinear architecture. Some say a priest was mysteriously assassinated during the construction; others believe that ghosts were stealing the building material. Only in the last four or five years has it begun to function as a church. Constructed around 1780, the magnificent jacaranda altar is worth a look. From here, you can see the cross planted on the nearby hill, put there to destroy the demons.

## Seminário de São José

The seminary was constructed in 1935 for Dom Helvécio and his secular students. In the steps leading to the front door, you'll see bits of imperial topaz that were embedded in the bricks. (Sadly, they have no real value!) Inside, the chapel boasts an extraordinary portrait by Pedro Gentillo of Dom Helvécio in the "Big Brother" style; no matter where you go, Dom Pedro's eyes will follow you around. Imagine how the painting must have inspired terror in his young impressionable scholars.

## Praça João Pinheiro

Considered the most important plaza in Minas, the square dates back to the 18th century, when it housed the public prison; now it's the mayor's office. The clock under the bell tower always rests at 9 a.m. because that's the time the councilmen open up their doors for business. It was also here that slaves who escaped from their masters were severely punished in public.

## Igreja de São Francisco de Assis

*8 a.m.-noon, 1-4 p.m.*

This church with green doors was built from 1763-1794. In Mariana during the 18th century, the *Irmandades* (or brotherhoods who venerated a certain saint) nearly went mad with competitive fervor, going so far as to build two churches directly across from each other. Aleijadinho was contracted to do the sculptures on the doors of this church (the first one built), but his true masterpieces are the vestry's two ceiling panels, which illustrate in chronological order two different moments of the same vision of St. Francis. The church is most notable for its suspended St. Francis above the multi-tiered altar ascending on red ribbons up to Christ. Check out the ceiling painting of St. Francis holding the cross; the eyes of the skull next to him will follow you around the room. The hair on the Christ statue is natural, symbolizing that the hair and nails of a saint will never disintegrate.

## Igreja Nossa Senhora do Carmo

*8 a.m.-5 p.m.*

Across the grassy square from the Igreja de São Francisco de Assis, this church was constructed in 1784 to display an even more powerful facade to the public. Aleijadinho was commissioned to sculpt the cherubs over the door, considered one of the most beautiful portals in Mariana. The towers in the form of a medieval castle and the balconies with lacework sculpted in soapstone all add to the church's charm.

## Museu Arquidiocesano de Arte Sacra de Mariana

*Rua Frei Durão, 49. Tues.-Sun. 9 a.m.-noon, 1-5 p.m. Fee is minimal.*

This is the second most complete sacred art museum in Brazil (the first is Museu do Carmo in Salvador). A salon of extremely fine paintings features works by Aleijadinho and his contemporaries; an extraordinary rendering of the Madonna in her purest essence has an unforgettable face. The second floor features sculptures by Aleijadinho, many completed after he lost the use of most of his fingers. Sacred music manuscripts, mostly performed by black slaves, are also on display. The Fonte de Samaritana in the foyer is a soapstone sculpture by Aleijadinho. Tradition has it that you must close your eyes, turn your back to the fountain, make a wish, then throw a coin. If the coin goes in the fountain, your wish will come true.

## Igreja de Nossa Senhora da Asunção

Across the street from the museum is the largest and oldest cathedral in Minas, as well as the richest in artwork. It's also called **Sé**, or just Cathedral. Constructed between 1709 and 1750, the church was the beloved labor of Aleijadinho's father and José Pereira Aroura, who fashioned one of the most beautiful *paraventos* in the state (the door in front of the real door, which keeps the wind out). Unfortunately, the church is left dark most of the time to preserve the art, but if you stand at the altar and look back to the front door, you'll notice how the columns incline on either side, representing Noah's Ark. The 1701 Schnitger-made organ is spectacular, a gift to the bishop of Mariana from Dom João V, and thrilling concerts are given on request by the artist-in-residence, Elisa Freixa. Hopefully, you will be lucky enough at least to hear her practice (usually in the afternoons). Lights are turned on from 6 p.m.-8:30 p.m. for mass.

To the left of the church is Rua Direita (usually to the right of a cathedral, but reversed in Mariana), the main street of the city. At No. 50, a former residence of the governor of Minas has been transformed into a museum featuring furnishings from the 18th century. The balconies are the only ones in the world made out of soapstone.

> **UP CLOSE TIP:** *The time to hang out on Praça Claudio Manoel in front of the church is around 4 p.m., when school lets out and children of all ages fill up the square.*

# Excursions

## Mina da Passagem

*On the way to Mariana,* ☎ *557-1255. 9 a.m.-6 p.m.*
*Fee is about $7 for adults, slightly less for children.*

Some have called it a tourist trap, but I thoroughly enjoyed my visit to Mina da Passagem, the oldest gold mine in Brazil. Begun in 1779, the mine was first owned by a German baron; up to 1880, slaves worked here under strenuous conditions, many of them dying while underground. (In fact, psychics in deep meditation have witnessed spirits here.) After producing over 35,000 kilograms of gold, the mine became defunct and is now open only to tourists. A trolley without seat belts (hang on!) slowly takes you down the seven-mile tunnel to the main gallery, where you can witness different layers of quartz, black tourmaline, graphite, and pyrite, which resembles false gold. The shrine you will see is for Santa Barbara, the patroness of all mines – an ironic statement, since women, considered the epitome of bad luck, were never allowed underground. Before you leave, it's traditional to leave the saint a few coins, or even some lipstick, which she adores. The mine is said to have a relation to Chico Rei, the tribal chief whose freedom was bought by his former subjects working as slaves in this mine. It's most likely that some of the gold extracted from this mine can be found today in the Efigênia Church in Ouro Preto.

> **UP CLOSE TIP:** *The 40-minute trip is not strenuous, and the atmosphere is cold and humid, but those prone to claustrophobia should probably skip it. Anyone into crystals and the power of rocks will find the atmosphere delightful. Visitors are even allowed to take a piece of quartz home, but be careful not to cut yourself. Happily, there are no bats here since they only like natural grottoes. Make sure you wear tennis shoes.*

## Vila Brumado

About 24 minutes from Mariana, over a rocky dirt road, lies Vila Brumado – a primitive, near-magical village, whose 8,000 residents are nearly all artists. Children learn the craftwork from their fathers starting at the age of five or six; among their artisanry skills are sculpting, straw work, embroidery, and pottery. A small but feisty waterfall may be visited, alongside which is a makeshift restaurant (weekends only); better to take your own picnic lunch. If you hire a car in Mariana (or Ouro Preto), you'll be able to visit the private homes of artists and view their simple lifestyles up close. This is a village where horses are still hitched in front of houses and most children run around barefoot. Some families even use water to make electricity.

### Adão de Lourdes Cassiano

*Rua Firminho Ulhôa, 233; ☎ 557-2052.*

Forty-eight years old, Adãohas been working 21 years as a sculptor, and his specialty is stunning two-tiered nativity scenes carved out of single cedar tree trunks. A rare tranquility and joy exudes from the eyes of this extraordinarily simple man whose work sells well in Germany. He and his nephews work day and night to finish pieces that run about $1,200 each.

### Artur Pereira

*Rua das Flores, 139.*

One of the best known wood sculptors in the region, Artur lives in a simple home that defies his international success. His specialties are strong animal figures – quartets of birds and large lions that serve as chairs.

# Where To Stay

It's preferable to stay in Ouro Preto if you are visiting Mariana, but there are a few options. See page 26 for price chart.

### Pousada Typographia

*Praça Gomes Freire, 220; ☎ (31) 557-1577; fax 557-1311.*

Across from Praça Gomes Freire, this is the prettiest *pousada* in town, in a restored 18th-century mansion. The owners were the first family to own a printing firm in Mariana, and their 1730 printing machine adorns the lobby. Guests eat off silver inherited through generations and many of the family's porcelain and pottery are displayed. Simple but elegant wood furniture enhances the apartments, all of which look out onto the square or historical back streets. Bathrooms are impeccable. Reserve. *20 apts. Moderate. No cards.*

### Hotel Central

*Rua Frei Durão, 8; ☎ (31) 557-1630.*

Cheapest rooms in the city, but only a last-ditch option. You pay extra for use of the bath and TV. No breakfast, but coffee is served from 7:15 to 9 a.m. *Inexpensive. All cards.*

# Where To Eat

See page 26 for price chart.

### Tambaú

*Rua João Pinheiro, 26; ☎ 557-1406. 6:30-10:30 p.m.; Sat., Sun. and holidays 11 a.m.-midnight.*

One of Mariana's best restaurants off Praça Gomes Freire, this house was the first palace of the governor of Minas in 1720. *Frango com quiabo* (chicken with okra) is good, as are all the local dishes. *Inexpensive-moderate. All cards.*

### Alvorada

*Rua Jorge Marques, 101; ☎ 557-1323. 11 a.m.-10 p.m.*

Three minutes by car from centro, this *churrascaria* is hardly homey with its aluminum roof, but it's the only one in town. Try the local plates. Specialties include banana splits. *Inexpensive. All cards.*

### Portão da Praça.

*Off the Praça Gomes Freire.*

Twelve tables and a waterfall (!) make this former 18th-century gold house a cozy lunch spot. *Moderate. All cards.*

### Free Lanches

*Rua Frei Durão, 108.*

Ice creams, sweets, fresh tropical juices, all homemade. Near the museum. *Inexpensive. No cards.*

# Nightlife

### Minas Adega & Bar

*Rua Direita, 92.*

Live music, cheese, wine and cocktails.

# Shopping

Sculptures in soapstone, semi-precious stones, and other regional souvenirs can be found in the stores downtown.

### Artist Studios Atelier Gamarano

*Travessa São Francisco, 22;* ☎ *557-1835.*

The artist Ladim shows his wood sculptures, doors, bureaus, and furniture. He will mail to the US.

### Atelier Alvaro

*Praça da Sé, 164;* ☎ *557-2093.*

Doors, panels, wood carvings, and sculptures.

### Zizi Sapateiro

*Rua Santana, 52;* ☎ *557-1139.*

A former shoemaker is one of Mariana's true *figuras*. After a lifetime cobbling, he started painting local scenes in a primitive style and became an overnight success; today he's one of the most important artists in Minas. Paintings run from $300 to $500, up to $3,000. His son also paints and sells under the name Tumão.

### Layon

*Rua Direita, 19 A.;* ☎ *557-2081. 9 a.m.-6 p.m.*

The city's best classical trained artist, Elias Layon is famous for his near-Rembrandt portraits, which take about a month to complete. Of Jewish descent, Layon has a stellar sense of humor about living in such a Catholic-dominated region. Ask for his calling card – he might paint it.

### Artesanato Tia Marta

*Rua Direita, 8;* ☎ *557-1716.*

The house for homemade liqueurs; the specialty is *Pétalas de Rosas*, topped with a little knit hat. Ask to taste some; the *jabuticaba* is superb.

# Hands-On Mariana

## Arrival

**Cars** (with guides) may be hired in Ouro Preto through the Tourist Information Center.

**Buses** for Mariana leave from Praça Tiradentes in Ouro Preto every half-hour. Buses from Belo Horizonte to Mariana take about 2¼ hours.

**Taxis** from Ouro Preto run about $15-20, but do try bargaining.

## Climate

Only 15 minutes from Ouro Preto, Mariana is, nevertheless, slightly warmer. Your ears will pop as you descend to the valley.

## City Transportation

Taxis:  Praça JFK, ☎ 557-1355 and Praça Tancredo Neves, ☎ 557-1872.

## Private Guide

An excellent guide in Mariana, although he does not speak English, is **João Orestes**, Rua Anibal Walter, 105; ☎ 557-1533. Other guides may be hired through the Tourist Information Center.

## Tourist Information

The bus from Ouro Preto makes its first stop in Mariana at the Tourist Center called **Deturce** (Terminal Turístico Manoel da Costa Athaíde), Praça Tancredo Neves, ☎ 557-1122, *ext. 225*, Tues.-Sat. noon-5:30 p.m., where you can pick up brochures and information in English. The office has a bar, restroom, and artisan store that sells interesting T-shirts with *Mineiro* themes. A great buy are the records of Elisa Freixo, the organist of the cathedral. Private tours can also be arranged here.

## Travel Agency

**OPM Empreendementos**
Rua Eugênio Eduardo Rapallo, 192 (Passagem de Mariana); ☎ 557-1255, can make arrangements to see the mine.

## When To Go

**JULY 16: Birthday of the city and state**, celebrated by numerous singing groups.

**MARCH-APRIL: Holy Week** is celebrated with dramatic theatrical processions led by the bishop in historical clothes and special organ recitals.

# São João del Rei

Of all the historical cities, São João del Rei is the one that lives and breathes a sincere religiosity all year. From dawn till dusk, the air is marked by the "language of the bells," an 18th-century tradition that announces the birth and death of its citizens through the pealing of the church carillons. (Through the number of tolls, the town learns the sex of a newly born baby or whether the deceased was a man, woman, priest, or nun.) **Holy Week** is particularly special in São João, with solemn high masses held in every church and full orchestras performing traditional baroque music. Throughout the holy season, processions of saints file through the streets, accompanied by the clamoring of church bells and the swinging incense of the priests.

São João del Rei is also the birthplace of two of Brazil's most important heroes – **Tiradentes**, who died a martyr's death as leader of the

**Inconfidência Mineira**, and **Tancredo Neves**, who died in 1985 shortly after winning the country's first civilian presidential election ending 20 years of military rule. A savvy politician, Neves (who was called Tancredo by his constituents) was also a visionary, and his sudden death affected Brazilians as deeply as did the loss of JFK in the States. In 1986, a memorial museum was established by his widow to convey the deep strain of humanitarianism that ran through his personal and professional life. Since Tiradentes and Tancredo died on the same day (a fact replete with mystical symbolism), Tiradentes Day in São João del Rei is a heavy-laden commemoration, with a high mass held in the Igreja de São Francisco and a special service at Tancredo's graves.

The best time to visit São João is on Fri., Sat., and Sun., when you can ride the **Maria Fumaça**, an authentic steam engine that travels to Tiradentes. Secular festivities throughout the year also have a particular São João flair. **Festa Junina** (most often held in June and sometimes July) is a country-style party when everyone dresses up as yokels and celebrates a mock wedding with a pregnant bride. **Carnaval** lasts for four days, with four samba schools and *blocos* making their way through the colonial streets, capped by a uniquely provincial climax: At 5 a.m. on the last day, everyone piles out to the street in their bedclothes and revels till the sun rises.

## History

*Bandeirantes* from São Paulo first discovered gold in the hills that surround São João del Rei in 1705. The village was first known as **Nossa Senhora do Pilar**, gaining its present name in 1713, in honor of Dom João V of Portugal. Through the development of the **gold industry** as well as *agropecuária* (the combination of agriculture and stock-raising), the village was transformed into a bustling market city, thriving to this day. The city became more famous after the death of Tancredo Neves; on the day of his burial, so many wanted to attend that the "doors" of the city finally had to be closed because the streets couldn't hold any more people.

## A Bird's Eye View

With its present population of over 80,000, São João del Rei has been able to expand into urban modernity without encroaching on its colonial area. Cut in half by the São João River, the two parts of the city are joined by two 18th-century stone bridges, the **Ponte da Cadeia**, in front of the Hotel Porto Real, and the **Ponte do Rosário**. The latter leads into the commercial zone, where cars vie with horse-drawn carts arriving laden with goods from the countryside. Behind this commercial zone is the main colonial nucleus full of finely wrought baroque churches, flowering courtyards, and winding cobblestone streets. While **Rua Arthur Bernardes** is the main street of the old city, **Rua Santo Antônio** is one of the most picturesque, with each house a different colonial color. Some parts of the street are so narrow that you'll often see cars backing up to let the other one through. Building regulations are strict: when the new owner of a house with an inclined wall destroyed it, the patrimony committee made him rebuild the wall. In front of FUNREI, the city's university, you can see a fine example of a pau brazil tree, running with the red sap that was used as paint in baroque churches.

> **UP CLOSE TIP:** *Driving into São João del Rei from Belo Horizonte, all sweet fanatics should stop at the city of* **Lagoa Dourada** *at the Fabricado pela Glória for the freshest rocambole in Minas. A specialty of the state, rocambole is a type of orange-loaf cake filled with the finest layer of creme de leite. It can be bought in slices at restaurants, but at this bakery, it comes so fresh it literally melts in your mouth.*

## Sights

### Igreja de São Francisco de Assis

*Praça Frei Orlando. Tues.-Sun. 8 a.m.-noon and 1:30-8 p.m.*

Built in 1774, this church, overlooking a wide square with towering palms, is one of the town's most attractive, a true feat of architectural design. One only needs to see the main sanctuary from the choir loft to appreciate the extraordinary engineering it took to create such side arches. While Aleijadinho carved some intricate decorations on the side chapels, it was one of his students who was responsible for the glorious carvings of the main interior. Although they look alike, the altars are masterpieces of subtlety and you must look closely to appreciate the fine differences, each one telling its own story. Originally, all the carvings were intended to be covered in gold leaf, but the mines ran dry before the task could be completed; after some time, even the original white base coat was removed to show the raw wood. On either side of the front door are fantastic sculptures; lean against the front door and look up into the eyes of Christ. Supported fiercely by the Third Order of São Francisco, a lay community, the church is now in the throes of controversy as the order fights against modernists who want to change the traditional baroque music and ritual. (I had the privilege of attending mass on Tiradentes Day, a baroque-influenced ritual so rich in theater, crashing organ chords, and incense that it left me in tears.) In the cemetery behind the church lies the **grave of Tancredo Neves**, a point of homage among some Brazilians who view him as a saint. (Notice the various ex-votos and plaques thanking him for "graces granted.") On the black marble tombstone reads the epitaph taken from one of his speeches, "My beloved land, you have my bones which shall be the last identification of my being to this blessed place," indicating his total, near-religious dedication to his country. On Tiradentes Day, a special service is held graveside, attended by local politicians, his wife Risoleta, and their many children and grandchildren.

## Memorial Tancredo Neves

*Rua Padre José Maria Xavier, 7. 9 a.m.-5 p.m. Sat., Sun., and holidays.*
*Entrance fee is minimal.*

Anyone interested in the heart and soul of Brazilian history must visit this memorial museum commemorating the private life and professional career of Tancredo Neves through photos, newspaper clippings, and personal effects. Most moving is the room memorializing Neves' death, accompanied by the voice of Milton Nascimento singing *Coração de Estudante* (Student Heart), his song that became synonymous with the death of Tancredo by rallying the nation's spirit. A film in Portuguese shows thousands crowding the streets of São Paulo as Tancredo's body was flown to Brasília for burial, then carried in procession through São João to its final resting place. When the country first learned of the politician's untimely demise, many went into shock (some were even felled by fatal heart attacks), forcing Tancredo's wife, Risoleta, to address the nation and urge them to calm down. Captured on film, her incredible courage and extension of love to the nation produced an amazing reversal in the nation's mood, helping the new regime under Sarney to take root.

## Museu Regional do SPHAN

*Praça Severiano Resende. Tues.-Sun. 12:30-5:30 p.m. Fee is minimal.*

Housed in a rare colonial-style mansion, this fine museum features treasures from the region, such as antique carriages, exquisite wood-carved headboards, and a strange collection of life-sized Greek muses in the garden. An 18th-century ceiling painting with people in typical clothes of the time is extraordinary; it was found by accident when the house was being destroyed. Don't miss the gramophones that actually recorded and played music in the 19th century.

## Igreja de Nossa Senhora do Rosário

*Largo do Rosário.*

This small church (1719) boasts marvelous white walls and columns strewn with colorful angels peeping over the altar, which resemble a huge wedding cake.

❖ **GETTING HERE:** *From the museum, walk down Beco da Rameira and turn left to Praça Embaixador Gastão da Cunha.*

Next door is Solar dos Neves, the family residence of the Neves clan for over 200 years, and Tancredo's birthplace. Visitors aren't allowed inside, but you can enjoy the lovely blue and white shutters dripping with red flowers.

## Museu de Arte Sacra

*Praça Embaixador Gastão da Cunha, 8;* ☎ *371-4742.*
*Tues.-Sat. 8 a.m.-5 p.m.; minimal fee.*

Down the same street as the church, this sacred arts museum is also housed in a finely restored mansion. The collection of sacred art is small but interesting, with music manuscripts dating back to the 18th century, when liturgical orchestras were mostly peopled by slaves. Elaborate raiments, oratorios, and sculptures are here, but the most riveting is the nearly life-sized mannequin of **Senhor dos Passos com Cruz** (Lord of the Steps with the Cross); if you look under his robes, you'll see that only his hands, face, and feet are sculpted.

## Igreja de Nossa Senhora de Pilar

*Rua Getúio Vargas;* ☎ *371-2568. Tues.-Sun. 7-11 a.m., 2-4 p.m.*

Nearly next door is the church, which was closed for repairs when I visited, but if you have a moment, step in. Some have called this gold-engulfed church (1721) one of the most beautiful in Brazil.

## Igreja de Nossa Senhora do Carmo

Of lesser interest across the Largo do Rosário is this small church. In the nave are statues, some with long flowing hair that appear startlingly real. Note the little painted cherub faces popping out of the baroque wall.

# Excursions

## Maria Fumaça Train To Tiradentes

The chic way to reach Tiradentes from São João del Rei is to hop a ride on the 19th-century steam train **Maria Fumaça**, or Smoky Maria. Inaugurated in 1881 by Dom Pedro II, this spit-and-polish *trenzinho* (little train) is entirely authentic, all the way down to its hissing stack, wood pew seats, and friendly conductor who loves to blow the whistle. The 30-minute scenic trip winds around the most exquisite pastoral landscapes in Minas – golden fields, sparkling lakes, and the fits and starts of the Rio Grande River as it snakes along the slopes of the Serra de Tiradentes. If you sit close to the front on the left side of the train (coming from São João), you'll be able to look behind you on the curves and see the end of the train (a particular thrill suggested by my guide). Even more fun is to hang out the window and wave at all the locals who come to greet the train four times a day. One of the first railroad lines in Brazil, built to accommodate the burgeoning textile industry, the route lost its commercial value when the highway was completed, but it was later revived as a tourist attraction and cultural patrimony. Unfortunately, ex-President Collor gave little priority to the preservation of culture and continually threatened to close down the train. Ride it while you can.

Arrive early at the Estação Ferroviária in São João to browse through the Museum of Transport in the lobby. Besides great old steam engines, there are fascinating photos of the interiors of the original cars. The train from São João leaves for Tiradentes at 10 a.m. and 2:15 p.m., and returns at 1 and 5 p.m. on Fri., Sat., Sun., and holidays only. (From Dec.-Feb. and July, the train runs daily.) For information, ☎ 371-2888. If you want to stay longer in Tiradentes, note that local buses leave regularly for São João.

## Pewter Factory

### John Somers

*Av. Leite de Castro, 1150;* ☎ *371-4422. Mon.-Sat. 9 a.m.-6 p.m., Sun. 10 a.m.-6 p.m.*

In 1981 the wreckage of the *Utrecht*, a 17th-century Dutch frigate in the service of the West Indies Company, was found off the island of Itaparica in Salvador, Bahia. Sunk during a battle with Portuguese fleets, the 300-year-old ship was laden with goods, all of which had rotted away with the exception of non-organic and non-ferrous items, such as brass, bronze, stone, and above all, pewter. The recovered goods represent the largest collection of pewter from a datable source, including kitchen utensils, officers' tools and an entire surgeon's kit. John Somers spent nearly five years cataloguing, restoring and reproducing these designs, many of which are now offered for sale in finely wrought copies. Candlesticks, tea services, trays, picture frames, utensils and goblets make excellent gifts that are so sturdy they will definitely outlive you. A museum displays some of the original items, and modern designs inspired by the booty.

## Mineral Springs & Spa

### Agua Santa

*Avenida Pres. Castelo Branco;* ☎ *371-3855. Tues.-Sun., 8 a.m.-5 p.m.*

The health complex, six miles from the city, is with a mineral-water springs is run by the owners of the Cantina do Italo in São João. Guests can dive into two swimming pools full of mineral water, enjoy exercise classes out of doors, or indulge in water massage. The water, which comes straight from the serra, is highly recommended for good health. There's a minimal fee to enter; you can drink all the water you want free.

# Where To Stay

See page 26 for price chart.

### Porto Real

*Avenida Eduardo Magalhães, 254;* ☎ *and fax (32) 371-7000.*

The city's main hotel, with rooms of simple elegance and corridors that have the air of a monastery. Restaurant serves *feijoada* on Sat. *32 apts. Moderate. All cards.*

## Pousada Casarão

*Rua Ribeiro Bastos, 94; ☎ (32) 371-7447.*

A charming estate in typical colonial style, this 15-room *pousada* is the epitome of homeyness. Rooms feature antique furniture and carved headboards; hammocks hang in the courtyard. From the front door, there's a spectacular view of São Francisco Church. There's also an outdoor pool. The husband of the gregarious owner is a doctor, so if you get sick, you're safe. The restaurant serves only breakfast, but during Holy Week and Carnaval, dinner is also available. Reserve three months before holidays. *17 apts. Inexpensive. All cards.*

# Where To Eat

See page 26 for price chart.

## Quinta do Ouro

*Praça Severiano de Resende, 4; ☎ 371-7577. 11 a.m.-11 p.m.*

Packed on Sun. after church, this colonial-style restaurant overlooking the city's river, Córrego do Lenheiro, is situated on the side of the Historical Museum. Not surprising, then, that the best dish is the *medalhão à Inconfidentes* (steak, bacon, sauce, mushrooms, and fries) – named in honor of the *Mineiro* rebels, who tried to defeat the Portuguese. Steak au poivre is large and tender, and pastas are interesting, but leave room for the *abóbora com coco*, a delicious caramel-like pudding topped with shredded coconut. After dining, stroll through the surrounding narrow streets full of antique grillwork and traditional wood shutters. *Moderate. No cards.*

## Cantina do Italo

*Rua Min. Gabriel Passos, 317; ☎ 371-2862. 11 a.m.-midnight.*

A typical Italian cantina with pastas, pizzas, and excellent fried trout. Don't pass up the pizza topped with chicken and a creamy cheese.

## Sinhazinha

*Praça São Francisco, 38; ☎ 371-1754. Weekdays 1 p.m.-6 p.m., weekends 8 a.m.-10 p.m.*

A warm, cozy mini-teahouse right in front of the São Francisco Church, with five tables and loads of homemade *doces* and *salgadinhos*.

## Doces Caseiros

*Praça Embaixador Gastão da Cunha, 71.*

Across the street from the house is a necessary pitstop, to stock up on *Mineiro* sweets made by a local couple. But don't walk out without trying the *cajuzinho*, a kind of cashew butter roll.

## Shopping

Folkloric crafts in wood, soapstone, and crochet as well as colonial furniture can be found throughout the city. On Sun. and holidays, visit the **Feira Livre de Artesanato** on Rua Ribeira Bastos, beside the Igreja São Francisco de Assis, from 6 a.m.-6 p.m. for local crafts.

# Hands-On São João Del Rei

### Arrival

**Buses** to São João del Rei run regularly from Belo Horizonte. On Fri. and Sun. they tend to fill quickly, so buy your ticket in advance. Buses also go to Congonhas from Ouro Preto, from where you can catch an evening connection to São João del Rei. For more information, ☎ 371-5617.

From the *rodoviária*, take a local bus to the Terminal Turístico, Praça Dr. Antônio Viegas; ☎ 371-3522, *ext.* 232 (6 a.m.-6 p.m.) in the center of town. The stop is on the opposite side of the street from the main entrance. At the terminal, you'll find a free brochure with a map of the city.

### Money Exchange

It's best to exchange money in a larger city, such as Belo Horizonte or Rio, before arriving.

### Tourist Information

**Terminal Turístico**
Praça Dr. Antônio Viegas
☎ 371-3522, ext. 232 and 229.
Hours: 6 a.m.-6 p.m.

### When To Go

**SEPTEMBER 7: Independence Day.** Celebrating Brazil's freedom from Portugal with parades.
**FEBRUARY: Carnaval.**
**JUNE 24: Festa Juninas.**
**MARCH-APRIL: Holy Week.**
**APRIL 21: Tiradentes Day.**

# Tiradentes

Cut through by the São José River, Tiradentes is a sleepy village with no major attractions, except for a universe of great photo ops. Less preserved than Parati and boasting a population of only about 7,000, Tiradentes, nevertheless, has more natural charm: flowers falling nonchalantly over doorways, dilapidated shutters, narrow cobblestone alleyways that lead to one perfect antique street lamp. Even the Church of São Antônio seems to transform itself magically when seen from different angles and in different lights. Founded around 1702, the community was soon outpaced by São João del Rei, but today remains a weekend escape for *cariocas* in particular, who love to come and shiver in June and July. Many soap operas and movies are filmed here, and you're likely to stumble across some famous actors and *artistas* dining in the local restaurants. As you walk through the town, notice the wave-like roofs, called *eiras*, on many houses; the number of waves used to indicate how rich the owners were. The separated cobblestone bricks in the street were known as *solteironas* (or spinsters) – certainly a commentary on the social status of unmarried colonial women. Around the **Praça das Mercês** are numerous silver shops, featuring craftwork made in Tiradentes. Though I can't vouch for the authenticity, I did see "real silver" necklaces being offered for unbelievable prices.

An ecological preserve, the **Serra de Tiradentes** can best be seen from the Maria Fumaça train that runs between Tiradentes and São João del Rei (see *São João del Rei, Sights*, above). Wild orchids grow profusely in the gently rolling hills, and numerous waterfalls attract bathers in the summer. If you look closely, you may see wild monkeys roaming around.

A mandatory pilgrimage must be made to the city's famous soapstone **Chafariz de São José**, or Fountain of Saint Joseph, dating back to 1749. Two centuries ago, women and slaves brought their ceramic bowls here to fill with water that came from the hill above, flowing through 1,700 feet of natural stone tubing. Since then, the fountains have given birth to many legends. For instance, if you want to get married, drink from the middle one. If you want to stay single or get divorced, drink from the one on the left. Today, women still come to wash their clothes in the natural spring water and dry them on the grassy knoll above.

Up the hill is the **Matriz de São Antônio de Pádua**, the second richest church in Brazil with over 482 kilograms of gold. Built in 1710, the riotously golden church was mostly funded by local residents who were promised a great seat in heaven by the parish's priests. The Arabic-styled ceiling over the altar features female angels on the left and male angels on the right, indicating to the congregation where the sexes should sit. One of the church's greatest treasures is the German slide organ that dates back to 1798, an instrument that few can play; there are only two like it in Brazil. The red paint used here is taken from the pau brazil tree (the red sap is mixed with egg white). Note the mystical figures sitting in front of the choir loft, supporting so many things that they look exhausted and sad. The intriguing sundial in the courtyard was built between 1710 and 1730. The adjacent cemetery was certainly built after the 18th century, because prior to that time, people were buried under the floor of churches, marked here by numbers on the stone tablets.

On the right of the church is the **Museu Padre Toledo**, Rua Pe. Toledo, 190. Hours: 9 a.m.-5 p.m. It was established on the site where Tiradentes lived between the ages of nine and 11. The present building (restored in 1835 and 1991) was the former residence of Padre Toledo, a participant in the Inconfidentes Conspiracy, who also housed daughters of important families, ostensibly to protect their virtue. (Brazilian history is rampant with stories of wayward priests who indoctrinated their young charges into the ways of the world, unbeknownst to their parents.) The richly decorated house seems to suggest that the priest was well paid for his services; on display are antique beds, porcelain collections, and excellent artwork, including ceiling paintings whose religious content is hard to detect.

**UP CLOSE TIP:** *There are two orchestras here that play only locally composed repertoire from the colonial era to the present. Ask around about any scheduled performances.*

# Where To Stay

See page 26 for price chart.

### Solar da Ponte

*Praça das Mercés;* ☎ *(32) 355-255, fax 355-1201.*

This unusual *pousada* is nearly a shrine to the lost arts and crafts that once made São João a thriving community. The owner, John Francis Parson (a Brit), and his Brazilian wife, Ana Maria, a university art professor, deeply researched 18th- and 19th-century techniques to recreate as authentically as possible original *Mineiro* designs, even down to the door handles. All the ironwork was made by local craftsmen and the nails were specially forged for the hotel. None of the rooms have TVs, phone or mini-bar, but they are masterpieces of rustic elegance – part of a living museum where even the flower pots are carefully crafted. Instead of a garden, a natural forest surrounds the outdoor pool; afternoon tea (included in the rate with breakfast) may be taken in a special salon with exquisitely carved tables. The owner's two horses may be used on weekends, but if you stay here, you'll need to rent a car. Rumor is, Brazilians who don't have "connections" can't get a reservation, but I can't imagine that applies to foreigners. Do reserve in advance. *14 apts. Expensive. All cards.*

### Pousada Richard Roth

*Rua Padre Toledo, 104;* ☎ *365-1255.*

Eight sophisticated rooms featuring fine antiques. No children under 12. *Expensive. All cards.*

### Pousada das Artes

*Rua S. Francisco de Paula, 86;* ☎ *(32) 355-1109.*

An old colonial building, well preserved and decorated with paintings from the historical era. Also functions as a gallery for artists. *Inexpensive.*

### Vila Real

*Rua Antônio Teixeira de Carvalho, 127;* ☎ *355-1292.*

Six apartments in a colonial style house. Rooms on the second floor have a fantastic view of the city. *Inexpensive.*

# Where To Eat

See page 26 for price chart.

### Taberna do Padre Toledo

*Rua Direita, 202;* ☎ *355-1222. 11 a.m.-4 p.m., 6:30 p.m.-10 p.m.*

Good regional specialties and chairbacks that are in the shape of baroque pineapples at this eatery near the Museu Padre Toledo. *Moderate. No cards.*

### Donatello

*Rua Direita, 202;* ☎ *355-1176. Tues.-Fri. 11:30 a.m.-11 p.m.*
*Sat. and Sun. 11:30 a.m.-midnight; closed Mon.*

Whenever they're filming in the area, artists and actors descend on this special Italian cantina – maybe it's the handpainted ceiling typical of the city's style before the neoclassics washed everything over. Or maybe it's the sensuous cuisine, like the Agnolotti 1790 – green and white pasta filled with ricotta, raisins, and walnuts, and drowned in white cream and bubbling hot cheese. Two can eat a big plate of lasagna and pizzas arrive with a light graceful crust. The *tábua de quiejo* – a plate of local cheeses and cold meats – is a steal. *Moderate.*

### Bar Aluarte

*Largo do O, 1;* ☎ *355-1202.*

The fact that owners Pedro and Marci Roos met in Tiradentes as tourists and threw their lot together reflects their warm personalities. They designed everything here, from the lights to the wood tables to the woven rugs on the ceiling. Thirty-something Marci makes the wholewheat pizzas while Pedro tends drinks such as the *vaca profana* (profane cow) with vodka, grapes, and condensed milk. Drifting from their excellent sound system are international tapes they've picked up on their world travels; live music happens on holidays and special weekends. Next door, they also own the Aluarte restaurant, and behind is a little hotel with four bedrooms, each with its own garden and fireplace.

# Shopping

### Casa da Prata

*Largo das Forras, 4,* ☎ *355-1343.*

Silver shop.

### Richard's Antiques

*Rua Direita, 224;* ☎ *555-1333.*

Located near the Aluarte Bar, this antique store features fine colonial furniture in Mineiro, English, and European styles. The owner is a tall, chic, black man who inherited the store from his adopted white family.

## Hands-On Tiradentes

### Arrival

**Buses** arrive only from São João del Rei (see above). The Maria Fumaça **historical train** goes to São João del Rei from Tiradentes Tues.-Sun. and holidays at 1 and 5 p.m.

### City Tour

The best way to see the city is to rent a horse or a horse-and-carriage when you arrive at the train station.

### Climate

Highs in January are 82°F, lows 76°F. In July highs reach 75°F, lows 53°F.

### Tourist Information

**Secretaria de Turismo e Meio Ambiente**
Rua Resende Costa, 71 ...................... ☎ 335-1212
Closed on weekends.

# Congonhas

Reposing tranquilly on the hillside as though swept up by the gold rush, then brutally abandoned once the adventure was over, is the small town of Congonhas do Campo. This town would have long been forgotten if not for a series of mystical and artistic events that transformed it into one of the greatest showcases of baroque art. Here, on this quiet, hidden hill, the tortured soul of Aleijadinho was able to find the peace he needed to create what would become his last and most impressive achievement – the 12 soapstone Prophets and the Six Stations of the Cross that adorn the courtyard of the Basílica do Senhor Bom Jesus de Matosinhos. For the previous 38 years Aleijadinho had worked on numerous and varied projects throughout Minas; finally, at the age of 58 he accepted the commission that would not only become his deepest labor of love but testimony to his Christ-like suffering. Today, pilgrims from all over Brazil converge on the site, particularly during Holy Week, when highly theatrical re-enactments of the Calvary are performed with over 200 characters dressed in Biblical costume. During the rest of the year, most tourists visit Congonhas in a day trip from Belo Horizonte or Ouro Preto.

## History

The mysticism that surrounds Aleijadinho's masterworks in Congonhas dates as far back as the origins of the church – the site of which even today inspires numerous miraculous healings. The church itself began as the answer to a prayer of Feliciano Mendes, a Portuguese settler who had journeyed to Minas in the early 18th century in hopes of fortune. Befelled by a seemingly fatal illness, he was spared from death by fervent prayer and vowed to devote his life to Senhor Bom Jesus, collecting alms as a beggar for a small oratory. Later, he begged the ecclesiastical authorities to allow him to convert his mere cross into a chapel. Hearing of his miracle, pilgrims from all over Minas journeyed to the site, donating their pigs, cows, horses, and dowries for the construction. By 1777, after Mendes was dead and long forgotten, the church had become a reality.

Accepting the commission 20 years later, Aleijadinho, aided by numerous slave assistants, completed the 66 cedar-wood images of the Six Stations of the Cross between Aug. 1, 1796 and Dec. 31, 1799; it would take another five years to finish the 12 life-sized Prophets. Much of the initial work of carving down the huge slabs of soapstone and wood was taken care of by assistants; Aleijadinho was said to have applied himself only to the general vision and the details: quirks of design that can be seen throughout his life's work, such as the large, nearly Oriental eyelids, the elongated fingers with square nails, the cleft chins divided into two sections, the high eyebrows connecting in a continuous line with the nose, and the sinuously curving liplines. Despite the fact that Aleijadinho's illness by the time of this project had almost completely debilitated him, the artistic excellence displayed in these works cannot be faulted.

## A Bird's Eye View

As a rather unattractive industrial city, Congonhas itself has little to offer in the way of attractions, besides Aleijadinho's masterworks and a waterfall park. About 84% of the city's 65,000 residents work in the iron industry. The name Congonhas comes from a plant found in the countryside that makes a tea similar to *maté herva*, and can be used also as a tranquilizer. Photos of Congonhas from the 1930s can be seen inside the Cultural Office near the church, along with pictures of Congonhas' sister city, Matosinhos, in Portugal. A famous **Festival of Song** is held annually in the city, with stars as big as Milton Nascimento performing outdoors to thousands of fans. Many theater, dance, and sacred choir groups also present programs.

### ALEIJADINHO
#### The Artist's Life

Much of the personal history of perhaps Brazil's greatest artist lies in obscurity, as much a victim of hyperbole as rumor. What has never been contested is the skill and devotion of Antônio Francisco Lisboa, nicknamed Aleijadinho (the Little Cripple). The mulatto, Brazilian-born sculptor was able to claim direct ties to the baroque Iberian tradition; his father, Manuel Francisco Lisboa, a well-trained carpenter, had come to Brazil straight from Portugal during the heady days of the gold rush and had quickly developed into a master builder and architect. The young Antônio, the result of an illegitimate liaison with a Negro slave, was fortunate enough to be accepted and raised by his father; indeed, most of his skills were absorbed through osmosis as he hung about his father's projects. Although Aleijadinho received no formal education, he was fiercely dedicated to the Bible and to the study of anatomy, both of which deeply influenced his artistry. Up to the time he was 39, he lived a bon vivant life, until he was struck with a crippling disease (some say leprosy, others venereal disease) that progressively deteriorated his body and tortured his spirit – a particularly gruesome fate for one so compelled to create with his hands. As Aleijadinho lost fingers and toes, he was reduced to working on his knees, and as self-hatred and self-consciousness festered, he started to work behind tarpaulins, arising for work before dawn and returning late at night to avoid being seen by curious crowds. Like Beethoven, who was felled by deafness late in life, Aleijadinho developed a fanatic's commitment to his art that increased in the same increments that his body inhibited it. His three talented slaves, whom he had trained as assistants, were the only people allowed near him, carrying him on their backs and weathering his foul temper. It was rumored that he even asked them to break his fingers with his own mallets when the pain became too much to bear.

Although Aleijadinho showed a preference to soapstone from his very first work, the Church of St. Francis in Ouro Preto, he remained loyal to this soft bluish variety of stealite until his death, possibly because, like his favored cedar, it was the easiest to manipulate in his condition. At the age of 58, he began what would be considered his greatest ensemble, the Stations of the Cross and The Prophets, which he was able to complete only by having his assistants strap tools to his wrists. At the age of 76, so debilitated that he could not rise from bed, he retired to the house of his daughter-in-law in Ouro Preto, having been abandoned by his last disciple and extremely bitter over unpaid commissions. He died nearly forgotten.

## Sights

### The Stations Of The Cross

The best way to visit Aleijadinho's shrine is with the reverence of an 18th-century pilgrim, starting at the base of the hill and passing through the Stations of the Cross on the way up to the Basílica. Studying the tableaus at extremely close range will be difficult as grills keep the public from entering or touching the figures. Although Aleijadinho remained loyal to the baroque tradition, his figures are all infused with a vivid physicality that is at times almost frightening. The Roman soldiers, especially, boast markedly ferocious features, in contrast to the stiff jointless bodies of the Jewish disciples and the always reverentially carved figure of Christ. After being shaped by Aleijadinho and his assistants, all the figures were painted by Manoel da Costa Athaíde, one of the period's greatest artists, who used natural paints mixed from ox blood, egg whites, crushed flowers, and vegetable dye.

As displayed in these tableaus, Aleijadinho's genius lay not only in his technical skill, but in his ability to infuse the Calvary saga with his own political views (decidedly pro-independence) through the minute manipulation of details.

- ☐ **Tableau #1** re-enacts the Last Supper, with a decidedly Oriental-lidded Jesus (an influence from the Portuguese colony in Macau, China). Remarkable are the passionate gestures of the figures, infused with the contorted energy of real-life devotees – a religious fervor that is not to be underestimated in Brazil. In fact, during a festival in recent years, fanatics actually shot the figure of Judas with a gun, hence his pockmarked face.

- ☐ **Tableau #2** shows Jesus in the Garden of Gethsemane with the sleeping apostles; that's the angel Gabriel hanging in suspension.

- ☐ **Tableau #3** shows Judas betraying Jesus to the Romans. Most notable is Jesus' bloody ear, and the hand cut off a Roman soldier by Peter.

- ☐ **Tableau #4** shows the Flagellation and the moment the crown of thorns was placed on Jesus' head. Note the ankle boots worn by all the Roman soldiers (a style fashionable with the Portuguese authorities at the time); the apostles always appear barefoot (a subtle commentary on the impoverished status of the Brazilian colonists). In this scene, particularly, the flowing movement created by Aleijadinho out of solid wood is truly stunning.

- ☐ **Tableau #5**, symbolizing the Calvary, shows Jesus carrying an enormous cross surrounded by Romans and the jester of the court. Here again, Aleijadinho has placed the mark of Tiradentes on Jesus' throat (the trickle of blood represents the *Mineiro*'s death by hanging), not a small hint of where the artist's true political sentiments lay.

- ☐ **Tableau #6** shows the Romans hammering the nails into Jesus' body, surrounded by other thieves. Most interesting is that Mary Magdalene is dressed as a typical Portuguese woman, much older and stockier than the traditional lithe representations.

## The Prophets

As you climb the soapstone-brick path up the hill, Aleijadinho's 12 Prophets in the courtyard of the church seem to be engaged in a slow-motion ballet, their stone beards wafting in the wind. Meant to be viewed from afar, the statues look life-sized from the street, but in reality are much smaller and short-legged. Despite their fragility, they stand pondering man's condition with a remarkable robustness; the poet Carlos Drummond de Andrade once remarked that they even seem to be expressing the epitome of the Mineiro personality – moody, taciturn, melancholy, and messianic. Though they stand with great dignity as separate beings, from a distance there seems to be a mystical unity tying them together. A researcher recently discovered that the impassioned ensemble, made some years after the conspiracy, actually corresponds to the rebels of Tiradentes' Inconfidência Conspiracy. Jonas, with his heavy expression of death – vacant eyes and slack-jawed mouth – is thought to be Tiradentes; Amos, the artist's representation of himself. Critics consider the statue of Daniel, carved from one piece of stone, to be the best. Sadly, a few of the statues have had their hands cut off by defilers, and now it is expressly forbidden to touch them.

Two of the Twelve Prophets sculpted by Aleijadinho, Brazil's greatest artist.

## The Basilica

After seeing these riveting pieces of art, you may find the Basílica de Bom Jesus de Matosinhos slightly less impressive. A Greek influence may be seen in the columns, while an Oriental flair characterizes the dragons from whose mouths hang chandeliers. The stained-glass windows are particularly beautiful for the shadows they cast on the altar and pews. Only four of the reliquaries on the altar are by Aleijadinho. Housed in a glass on the altar is the original effigy of the dead Christ that Mendes brought from his hometown of Braga, Portugal, on whose basilica this church was based. Of particular interest is the **Milagro Room**, next to the church, full of very old ex-votos and offerings from those who have received healings and miracles. The collection is a tribute to the power of Aleijadinho's art. Most intriguing are the many photos of weddings; the couples shown either resolved their problems through marrying or were at least saved from divorce. You'll see lots of wax heads and arm casts; many of the really old ex-votos, dating back to the early 18th century, record dramatic escapes from fires, raging bulls, and coach crashes. The guards will be happy to open the room for you – if they aren't at lunch.

> **UP CLOSE TIP:** *Many marriages take place in the church; hopefully you'll be lucky enough to catch one. If you want to walk downtown, it's only about 15 minutes away.*

### Parque da Cachoeira

*Bairro da Praia;* ☎ *731-1911.*

An ecological park of over 55 acres, this "waterfall resort" about 15 minutes from the city has a number of barbecue sites, hiking trails, sports fields, and a decent restaurant and snack bar. On Sat., eco-programs are held for kids. A natural pool is available and camping areas may be rented quite cheaply.

# Where To Stay

See page 26 for price chart.

### Colonial Hotel

*Praça da Basílica, 76;* ☎ *(31) 731-1834.*

Located across from the Prophet's Rooms, this tiny two-star features antique furniture and bedspreads. An outdoor pool and children's pool overlooks the city. *12 apts. Inexpensive. No cards.*

### Newton Hotel

*Avenida Júlia Kubitschek, 54,* ☎ *(31) 731-1352, fax 731-2789.*

Located downtown on the main street, the rooms here are very simple and clean, with TV, but no mini-bar, heat, or air conditioning. Most tourists prefer to stay closer to the church. *39 apts. Inexpensive. No cards.*

# Where To Eat

See page 26 for price chart.

### Cova do Daniel

*Hotel Colonial, Praça do Santuário, 76, Basílica;* ☎ *731-1834. 11 a.m.-6 p.m.*

Located next to Bom Jesus, this blue-and-white colonial house serves solid regional cuisine, such as *Tutu à Mineira*. There are several private coves for lingering, including one completely strange optical illusion. *Moderate. No cards.*

## D'jan Churrascaria

*Rua Mário Pereira, 48;* ☎ *731-1534. 11 a.m.-midnight.*

Connected to the Hotel Casarão, this is a decent steakhouse with 12 cold dishes, eight hot plates, and desserts for a reasonable price. *Inexpensive. V.*

# Shopping

## Bel-Artes

*Praça do Santuário, Basílica, 27;* ☎ *731-1832.*

Of the several souvenir shops near the church, this one has some of the best collections. Soapstone statues of the Madonna are lovely, but be careful packing them; they break easily. Crocheted and embroidered linen make good gifts.

# Hands-On Congonhas

## Arrivals

The **bus station** is on Av. Júlia Kubitschek, 1982; ☎ *731-1386/1039.* Buses from Belo Horizonte run six times a day; best to buy your return tickets as soon as possible. From São João del Rei, take the São João del Rei-Belo Horizonte bus and get off at Muritinho; from there, you take a local bus (about every half-hour) into Congonhas. To reach Ouro Preto from Congonhas, either go via Belo Horizonte, or take the local bus to Muritinho or Conselheiro Lafaiete and change to a bus for Ouro Preto via Itabirito. For more information, ☎ *731-1727.*

## Climate

Temperatures range from 61°F to 74°F, plummeting as low as 46°F in winter.

## Tourist Information

**The Cultural Office,** opposite the church, will provide you with a few brochures. Guides always seem to be hanging about to explain the Steps and the Prophets of Aleijadinho, but don't count on superlative English. It's easy enough to escort yourself through the area, but you need to ask at the Cultural Center for permission to enter the chapel surrounding the Basílica. A policeman will accompany you.

## Travel Agency

**Unitour**
Rua Tupis, 171; ☎ *201-7144.*
Located in Belo Horizonte, this agency can arrange day trips to Congonhas with transportation originating in a variety of historical cities.

## When To Go

**Carnaval** is celebrated in the center of the city with four schools.

**Holy Week** re-enacts the Via Cruxis in an emotional, dramatic procession, supported by 200 local actors dressed in Biblical costumes during Easter week.

**JUNE: Congado Festival** with folkloric groups, African dances, and local foods.

**AUGUST: Cultural Week** commemorates the life and death of Aleijadinho.

**SEPTEMBER 7-14: Jubilee of Bom Jesus de Matosinhos.**

**OCTOBER: Song Festival.**

**DECEMBER 17: City's birthday.**

# Diamantina

For those who have Minas Gerais in their veins, an inspiring ecological/historical adventure can be had by exploring the complex of the four neighboring villages of Diamantina, Serro, Milho Verde, and São Gonçales.

The historical city of Diamantina won the heart of singer/composer Milton Nascimento and his lyricist Fernando Brant when they not only composed a song about it, but featured a line drawing of the town on one of their early albums. It's easy to see their inspiration – against the backdrop of a purple-cast mountain range, the city hugs the steep side of a dramatic rocky valley, its colonial center still perfectly preserved from the 18th and 19th centuries when it was one of the most thriving mercantile and cultural centers of the state. While there are no churches that rival those of Ouro Preto, the overall ambiance is as charming as a toy city, with cobblestone streets rarely big enough for two cars that wind around colorful colonial houses.

Located about five hours (bus or car) from Belo Horizonte, Diamantina lies on the border of the Espinaço highlands, a drive you should take during the day since the variety of landscapes is stunning. It's here you will truly feel the soul of Minas – rust-colored escarpments, stunted shrubs and savannah, the bright yellows and the purples of the regional ipê trees contrasting against the greens and browns of cacti. As you reach the upland plateau, a stark moonscape of strange rock figures leads to coves where some of the most beautiful waterfalls in the country can be found. It is a topography of constant surprise.

Romance still lingers in Diamantina, particularly at night when the flower Dama da Noite (Lady of the Night) perfumes the air with its heady scent. If you wander around the town, you're sure to hear some old-fashioned *serestas* (country songs) in tiny bars or even in the parlors of some homes. Diamantina *serestas* are famous throughout Brazil, and on moonlit nights you might find a lone *seresteiro* with his guitar, or even a whole band, serenading the street. If a door is open and you hear music, peek in and enter – you'll probably be most welcomed at these spontaneous country jams.

The best itinerary for this region is to spend one night in Diamantina, one night in Serro, and more than a few days at the Pousada do 5 Amigos in São Gonçalo (see below) to pursue eco-treks. (Believe me, you will never want to leave.) The next best plan is to rent or buy a house in Milho Verde, stock up on *cachaça*, and never be seen again.

---

## VP CLOSE ADVENTVRE from the author

My dearest memory of this region was stumbling upon such a party, whose plaintive singing was led by a middle-aged woman with a heart of gold, a voice of honey, and the most natural phrasing I have ever heard. Two men accompanied her on an accordion and a tiny guitar (*cavaquinho*) while everyone else sat around card tables slugging beer and joining in on the chorus. As I sat mesmerized in a corner, it seemed as if the group were pulling these songs out of some collective unconscious, and my only regret was that I did not have my tape recorder handy. Later, I found out this simple soul was actually an educated voice teacher at the local music school – and could sing opera!

---

# History

A baby of the gold rush, Diamantina was born in 1713 and baptized **Arraial do Tijuco**. In only short seven years, the population exploded when not only gold but diamonds were discovered in the surrounding hills. In 1729 the Crown laid claim to the region in the face of marauding *Paulistas*, initiating a predatory exploration until 1845. By the time the city was renamed Diamantina in 1831, grand fortunes had been won (and some already lost), and the city soon developed as a leader in music and theatre, attracting the elite of Minas.

Today the diamond rush has long since peaked, and the Jequitinhonha Valley, though rich in artistic output, is now one of the poorest per capita in Brazil. Five years ago, there were 20,000 *garimpeiros*, today only about 2-3,000 eke out a bare existence as gold miners. With minerals now in sad depletion, the city is turning to tourism as its only salvation; due to its isolation, however, it still remains untainted by commercialism. But the city does know how to party (the result of a substantial young population) and outdoor dances with ear-shattering acoustics are often held in the main square in front of the cathedral.

**UP CLOSE TIP:** *The area is rife with stories of UFO sightings; the city is apparently sitting on piles of crystals, and lots of psychics report hearing the ghosts of slaves lamenting. One legend says they congregate for spiritual meetings here. Another story I heard was about a man in recent years who discovered a circle of stones at a "nearby" (i.e., yet to be determined) location and was unable to leave without help because the energy had made his feet stick to the ground. Also, ask around for Saké,* *a black street dweller, well-respected by the general population, who claims to be an extraterrestrial.*

## Sights

The colonial city is filled with architecture showing an Arabian influence that came from Portugal – particularly in the trellises of balconies where young women greeted their visitors. Check out the house of the **Biblioteca Antônio Torres** on Rua da Quintanda, 48.

### Beco do Mota

For hundreds of years, this steep cobbletone street in the center of the city was famous for its red-light district – right up to the 1960s when its colorful denizens were finally expelled by local families. Today, there are lots of bars and good photo ops to be enjoyed. At the end of the street is a plaque with lyrics from Milton Nascimento's song *Clareia no noite*.

### Casa de Chica da Silva

*Praça Lobo de Mesquita, 266.*

One of the most interesting colonial constructions in Minas, this house was the site of perhaps the biggest romances in Brazil's history. Between 1763 and 1771, the rich diamond contractor João Fernandes de Oliveira lived here openly with his beloved, a beautiful slave named Chica da Silva, who bore him numerous children and defied cultural mores; annexed to the house is a small chapel he built especially for her use. Today, the house, finally restored, is used for cultural activities.

### Mercado Municipal

*Praça do Guaicuí.*

Diamantina served as the primary trading place for the entire Jequitinhonha Valley, and its 19th-century market, a block down from the cathedral, is an intriguing wood structure whose antique arches were copied by Oscar Niemeyer for the presidential palace in Brasília. Mules still transport goods to the market stalls, today laden with regional cheese, sausage, raw sugar, and blocks of salt. For arts and crafts, look in *Shopping*, below.

### Casa de JK

*Rua São Francisco, 241. Tues.-Sun. noon-5:30 p.m.*

This simple house, now decorated with photos and other memorabilia, is where Juscelino Kubitschek, the most famous president of modern Brazil, passed the first 17 years of his life. The son of poor Czech immigrants, JK (as he was known) grew from these very humble beginnings to become not only a beloved physician, but the spiritual architect of the new capital of

Brasília (see *Brasília* chapter). More photographs and clippings can be found at **Te Casa e Cultura** on Praça Antônio Eulálio.

## Museu do Diamantina

*Tues.-Sun. noon-5:30 p.m.*

One of the homiest museums in Brazil, this 18th-century house was originally the residence of Padre Rolim, a priest and one of the original members so the Inconfidencia Rebellion. A browse through will transport you back to the daily life of Diamantina in its gold heydays, when money was stashed in huge cast-iron English safes, and slaves were whipped with chains, then branded with the mark of the master (an unnerving display of instruments). Ancient photos of locals, the odd top hat, colonial hair-curlers, and a vast array of domestic tools complete the picture.

A more extensive list of sights written in English is available at the **Secretaria Municipal de Cultura e Turismo**, Praça Antônio Elálio, 53; ☎ *(38) 531-1636*, fax *(38) 531-1857*.

# Excursions

## Caminho dos Escravos (Road of the Slaves)

Running from Medonha to Diamantina, this hand-built road made of stones and boulders has been partially restored and offers the best view of the city. Originally it was 20 km. long (12½ miles), connecting Diamantina with the rest of the state. Today you can only see a fraction of it, but one look will impress upon you the horror of being a slave during the colonial era.

❖ **GETTING HERE:** *Take km 584 to BR-367, then go four km. farther.*

## A Gruta do Salitre

One of the most magical places in Brazil! Reached by stone steps that lead to an Alice-in-Wonderland arena, this undergound grotto looks like something between a beach and a rainforest – the epitome of magical realism. Wet, cool, and vibrationally alive, the grotto invites all sorts of strange happenings: weird birds sweep down overhead, tropical trees grow out of rocks, and bats thump in dark corners. Special permission is required to visit the caves in the back, but the main space is perfect for meditation or romantic picnic lunches. Plan to spend hours just staring. The grotto, well known by locals, is accessed from a dirt road about seven km. (4.3 miles) from the center of Diamantina.

## Fábrica de Tecidos Biribiri

Inaugurated in 1876, this former plantation had been reconstructed in recent times as a self-sustaining community and factory for the production of material. Today it's all but abandoned, except for about six families who inhabit the still impressive blue-and-white colonial houses. Goats and cows graze the land, and a quaint church recalls a lost era of devotion. The city is named for a local fish.

## Waterfalls

Millions of years ago the sea came this far inland, forming weathered rocks and towering waterfalls. In most cases, torturous dirt roads are the only way to reach the waterfalls, of which the easiest to access are **Sentinela** and **Cristais**. Others to explore include: Três Quedas, Véu da Noiva, Quebrada, Piscininha and das Fadas. You will most likely need to hire a private guide/car to reach them. A full day or two can be spent exploring.

# Where To Stay

See page 26 for price chart.

### Pousada do Garimpo

*Rua Juiz de Fora. 1265; ☎ 931-2523, fax 931-2316;*
*reservations in Belo Horizonte ☎ (31) 335-7468.*

A well-kept *pousada* with a cozy ambiance, but a hefty walk from the center of town. The traditional ceilings of bamboo are the same as those found in old *Mineiro* houses. The balcony of the restaurant overlooks the countryside. Rooms feature color TV, fridge, and telephone. *40 apts. Moderate. All cards.*

### Dália Hotel Pousada

*Praça Juscelino Kubitschek, 25; ☎ 931-1477.*

Cheaper than the Pousada do Garimpo, this is the most stylish inn within the city, with wood-beam ceilings, antique lamps, ancient wood shutters, and a breakfast room filled with religious tapestries. Rooms offer fridge, telephone, and TV. It's located in the center of the historical area next door to the Restaurante Chica da Silva. *28 apts. Inexpensive. All cards.*

### Jardim da Serra

*Rua das Rosas 65; ☎ (38) 531-1607.*

Perched on a hill, this is one of the area's most charming *pousadas*, tastefully filled with antiques. The best suite has a double bed and carved headboards. The only TV is in the lobby. Breakfast is taken on an outdoor flower-strewn terrace overlooking the city. Private chalets resemble tiny colonial-style homes. *Inexpensive. All cards.*

# Where To Eat

Diamantina is not a culinary oasis; most people get tired of eating after two days. See page 26 for price chart.

### Churrascararia Espeto de Praia

*Beco da Pena, 30 (centro);* ☎ *(38) 531-1057.*

If you are in the mood for grilled meat, this is your best choice, though don't expect the quality of Rio. *Inexpensive. No cards.*

### Restaurante de Raimundo Sem Braço

*Rua José Anacleto Alves, BR259, km. 588 (exit to Gouvêa);* ☎ *531-2284.*
*Mon. 11 a.m.-1 p.m., Tues.-Sat. 11 a.m.-11 p.m., Sun. 11 a.m.-5 p.m.*

Everyone seems to come into this tent-like restaurant with a smile; maybe it's the precious light that filters through the walls made of pindaiba tree trunks. One hard-to-find specialty here is *feijão ferrado* – a semi-stew of bean, tomatoes, onions, greens, and rice – a light *feijoada*. Sometimes the cook even whips up *coelho* (rabbit). Raimundo, the porky owner, has one arm – hence the name. *Inexpensive. All cards.*

### Casa Velha Restaurante

*Rua Macau do Meio, 250 (centro);* ☎ *931-3538.*
*Self-service lunch 11 a.m.-4 p.m., Tues.-Sun., and dinner.*

Colonial-style home with wood-beam floors, antiques, and local artwork on walls, walking distance from downtown. Pizzas are filling, chicken soup excellent on a cold day. *Inexpensive. All cards.*

# Shopping

*Tapetes dos arraiolos*, a type of hand-woven rug, are typical of the region, brought to Brazil via the Arabs in Portugal. Also look for crafts made of soapstone, straw, wood, raw cotton clothing, and ceramics.

### CARDI-Cooperativa Artesanal Regional de Diamantina

*Rua das Bicas, 115;* ☎ *931-1100.*

Interesting regional crafts sold by a cooperative of 5,000 artists from the valley of Jequitinhonha.

### Diamantina Tapetes Arraiolo

*Rua do Burgalhau, 275-A;* ☎ *531-2664.*

Master store for rugs of the region.

### Reliquias do Vale Atesanato

*Rua Macando Meio, 40,* ☎ *931-1627.*

Crafts of the city, including straw dolls, angels, rugs, and paintings of local scenes.

### Drogaria Diamantina

*Praça Corrêa Rabelo, 109;* ☎ *531-1275.*

This drugstore (*drogaria*) is across from the cathedral, where you can buy film and other personal sundries.

> **UP CLOSE TIP:** *For the bargain hunter as well as the merely curious: visit the home-style studio of lapidarian* **Geraldo Baracho**, *Trav. Dom Joaquim, 25, who is a master at converting rough precious and semi-precious stones into polished jewels. Inside, he'll show you how he works his old-fashioned artisanry; out back he keeps a most unusual orchid garden with specimens he pulls from the countryside. Do ask to see his unusual mosquito repellant – a tradition in Minas – which is usually hanging from his ceiling: a condom-like bag full of water!*

### Reliquias do Vale

*Rua Macau do Meio, 401;* ☎ *531-1627. 8 a.m.-6 p.m., Sun. 8 a.m.-1 p.m.*

This is the city's most stylish crafts store, located near the Hotel Tijuco downtown. Embroidered hand towels, linens, magnificent water jugs in the shape of women, regional figurines, line drawings of the city, and jars of marinated carrots and pimentos.

# Hands-On Diamantina

## Arrival

Diamantina is reachable from Belo Horizonte (285 km./177 miles) by bus (five daily). For a schedule contact: **Viação Passaro Verde, Ltd.**, Rua as Biquinhas 151; ☎ *931-1758.*

By car from Belo Horizonte, take BRT-040 for 114 km./70 miles, and then BR-135 to Curvelo (50 km./31 miles) and BR-259 for 128 km./80 miles. The most picturesque trail from Belo is MG-010, which crosses the Serra do Cipó, passing through Conceição do Mato Dentro, Serro and the tiny towns of Milho Verde and São Gonçalo until Diamantina. (Do note that for 195 km./121 miles, the road is dirt, winding and not well kept.) Ouro Preto is 373 km./232 miles away, reachable by bus.

## Money Exchange

**Banco do Brasil S.A.**
Praça Conselheiro Mata, 23.................... ☎ 931-1503
**Banco do Brasil**
Praça Conselheiro Mata, 23.................... ☎ 531-1175

## Post Office

**Correio** (post office)
Rua da Quintanda, 31 (centro) ................ ☎ 931-1631

## Private Guide

**Vandersom Morette Silva,** Rua da Liberdade, 83. Although Vandersom can't speak English, this fine young man made a good guide for me. He can be contacted through the Tourist Office (see below).

## Telephone

There is a public telephone at **Praça JK,** Largo Dom João, 153.

## Tourist Information

**Departamento de Turismo de Prefeitura**
Praça Antonio Eulálio, 57 . . . . . . . . . . . . . . . . . . . . .   ☎ 931-1769
**Casa da Cultura**
Praça Antônio Eulálio, 53 . . . . . . . . . . . . . . . . . . . .   ☎ 531-1636
Weekdays, 8 a.m.-6 p.m., Sat. and holidays 9 a.m.-5 p.m., Sun. 8 a.m.-noon.

## What To Wear

Nights can get cold, days misty and cool, so take a sweater or jacket.

## When To Go

**Carnaval** is a true street affair in Diamantina, when the city is transformed into a great spectacle of costumes and confetti. Great parades of revelers (samba schools and *blocos*) parade down the street and tiny lanes, singing at the top of their lungs. Many considered Diamantina's Carnaval to be one of the best in Brazil.

During **Holy Week** the Passion of the Christ is re-enacted with enormous devotion in the town's squares and streets. On Palm Sunday devotees carry fragrant branches through the city.

The **Festa do Rosário** takes place between Sept. and Oct.

Fifty days after Easter is the **Festa do Divino**, a tradition since 1864, initiated by a novena prayer and ending with the Holy Ghost's Empire procession through the streets.

The **Seresta National Day** in Diamantina is Sept. 12, a tribute to Juscelino Kubitschek's birthday and celebrated with strolling troubadours.

# Serro

One hour from Diamantina along a scenic highway lies the historical town of Serro. The drive here is entrancing: around green-carpeted mountains, through cloud patches lying low on the hillsides, past stray cows and over rivers inundated with gravel and sand – the latter the tell-tale sign of the presence of goldminers. Best of all, Serro is a city still at odds with modernization. Even in the city proper, you may find horses hitched up next to stores that sell modern washing machines. And it was here in Serro, outside the Igreja Matriz, that I first saw what passes as a bus for the interior: actually an open-air truck that fills up quickly with locals (not to worry – it's *not* the kind of bus you will take to get here!)

With only 20,000 people, Serro has developed a strange connection to the States, and you are hard pressed to find a family where at least one member has not gone to live and work for a time in the States. (At least 4,000 residents have.) This does not mean that many people speak English, but you will at least find a love of Americans and a nostalgia for, of all places, Hyannis, Massachusetts. (This is a good place to bring pictures from home.)

Politically, Serro is one of the most progressive towns in the region. The last mayor is known as one of the most honest in the state and regularly supplies educational opportunities for children who live in the countryside. UNICEF has also provided a free medical center for the poor, which you can see in action next to the Prefeitura.

Overriding Serro's historical charms (not as profuse as Ouro Preto) is the city's proximity to fascinating ecological excursions, including mountain trekking and bathing in waterfalls. As for festivals, Serro boasts some of the most traditional in the state, including the **Festa do Rosário** in the first weekend of July, in which large religious mannequins are carried through the streets. And don't leave here without buying fresh slabs of *quiejo do serro* – the most famous cheese of Minas – made in Serro.

## Sights

### Chacara do Barão do Serro

*Rua Santa Teresa. 8-11:30 a.m., 2-5:30 p.m.*

Erected in the second half of the 19th century, this "Big House" was formerly the residence of one Baron José Ferreira Rabelo. The charm of this estate, now opened as the Center for Cultural Activities, is impressive as a model of how masters and slaves interacted. Most intriguing is the secret 22-km. (13½-mile) tunnel in the backyard, barely big enough for one, through which slaves tried to escape; it was a chilling experience to step inside a few feet to feel the wet, clammy vibrations. The windows of the *senzala*, or slave quarters, are much smaller than those of the master's quarters; the remains of a stone bath served by a water font and stone aqueduct can be seen. A characteristic of such regional houses is that they look impressive from both the front and the back. Outside the grounds is a huge cauldron that commemorates the kettles carried by the *tropeiros* for cooking.

### Sobrado da Prefeitura Municipal

This charming house, now the mayor's office, was built in the last quarter of the 19th century to host the Emperor Dom Pedro II during a visit to Serro.

## Casa das Otoni

*Praça Cristiano Otoni. 8-11:30 a.m., 2-5:30 p.m.*

Probably constructed in the 18th century, this house was the residence of the family of Teófilo Otoni, a journalist, politican, and leader of the Liberal Revolution of 1842. Paintings and drawings from the times, as well as kitchen instruments and firearms, hold some interest. The church next door may still be in the midst of renovation, but is impressive for its wall paintings and bright ceiling murals.

## Igreja de Nossa Senhora do Rosário

*Praça do Rosário.*

Constructed in the first half of the 18th century, this church is notable for its turquoise altar and blood-dripping Jesus affixed to a huge wooden cross against a simple white-beamed ceiling. The bell is the original one from the 18th century.

## Matriz de Nossa Senhora da Conceição

*Praça Getúlio Vargas.*

Dedicated to Saint Anthony, this is the mother church of Serro, dating back to 1776. The multitiered altar is dominated by a huge Madonna surrounded by sculptured cherubs, biblical figures, and saints. Don't miss the ceiling paintings, completed in 1872-73. The huge guardian angels in front of the pews are dressed as Portuguese. Mass is held continually on Sun.; Dec. 8 is the church's special holiday.

# Excursions

The most interesting excursions from Serro are eco-trips to numerous waterfalls, natural pools, and rock formations. One of the best waterfalls is **Lageado,** on the road to São Gonçalo do Rio das Pedras, in the district of Milho Verde. (You can also camp here.) The road here is simply magical, with towering palms, shrubbery lining the way, the next curve never apparent, yet each bend opening a new view. About 20-25 miles from Serro, we passed through a small village of abandoned shacks which fill up during festivals. From here, you can climb up a circle of huge boulders to view the impressive expanse of countryside. The rock circle seems to emit strong vibrations and is good for meditating – or, as some locals privately confessed to me, primal screaming.

At **Fazenda de Malheiros**, a fine waterfall, natural pool, and rock formation is five miles from Serro on the way to Conceição do Mato Dentro.

Other waterfalls inside the city limits that are good for bathing include **Fumaça, Agua Santa**, and **Ponte de Pedra**.

**Pico do Itambé** is a 1¼-mile-high peak, which takes about five hours to climb. Camping overnight is allowed here.

# Where To Stay & Eat

See page 26 for price chart.

## Pousado Vila do Principe

*Rua Antônio Honório Pires, 38;* ☎ *941-1485.*

Monastery-like ceilings add atmosphere to this inn down the street from the Santa Rita church. Rooms on the street are noisy, but the view is pure small town Brazil. Roosters make an incredible ruckus at dawn. *10 apts. Inexpensive. All cards.*

## Restaurante Itacoloni.

*Praça João Pinheiro, 20;* ☎ *941-1227. 11 a.m.-midnight.*

Near the mayor's office, this simple restaurant offers regional cuisine commandeered by the family of Dona Lucinha, one of Minas' premier culinary forces. (See her restaurants in Belo Horizonte and São Paulo.) *Prato feitos* (prepared dish of the day) are great bargains for about $3. *Inexpensive. No cards.*

# Shopping

Crafts of the region are limited to soapstone, wood, and ceramics. The best buy is the cheese called *quiejo do serro*, the tastiest in Minas. There is a **Stone Factory**, which is fascinating for its water jugs and politically incorrect sculptures.

# Hands-On Serro

## Guide/Driver

An excellent driver is **Geraldo Quirino Gatardo,** Rua Sinval Lins, no. 398; Serro, 19, who has a lovely personality, but no English. Contact him through the Prefeitura's office and negotiate on the spot. A good trip is to travel from Diamantina to Serro to see the waterfalls. You will need a driver in Diamantina who knows the dangerous route to Milho Verde.

## Tourist Information

Tourist information is available at **Casa da Cultura**, annex to the Biblioteca Municipal, Beco do Pe. Almeida; ☎ *941-1255*; and **Casa dos Otoni**, Praça Cristiano Otoni, bairro da Praia; ☎ *941-1448*.

## Travel Agency

**Santa Rita Turismo**
Rua Tupis, 25, loja 230 (downtown) . . . . . . . . . . ☎ (71) 212-1196

### When To Go

The **Festa do Rosário de Serro** is held in the first weekend of July, with masses, processions, and regional food and dance. The **Festa do Divino** takes place in May. The city's **patron saint** is celebrated on Dec. 8.

# Milho Verde & São Gonçalo

About a 20-minute drive from Serro are the districts of Milho Verde and São Gonçalo das Pedras, at one time villages of commercial importance in the passage of gold to Serro and Diamantina. Today they are outposts of primitivity, and jumping-off points for exciting excursions to waterfalls and mountain treks. (São Gonçalo is actually a little larger than Serro, though it seems smaller and more spread out.) Most people come to visit on weekends and festivals.

Off the highway toward Diamantina, over a dirt road that winds through lush countryside, lies Milho Verde, a tiny village of 1,354 people (urban and rural), living, as it seemed to me, at the edge of the world. The smell of wood fires permeates the air; unusual rock formations suggest an other-wordly presence. Indeed this isolated community did belong to another world – when the first diamonds in Minas were discovered here by *bandeirantes*. During the gold rush of the 18th century, the area used to be part of a military region and visitors were interned for 24 hours to make certain they had not swallowed any precious jewels (you figure it out!).

Today, the small colonial-style houses are inhabited by the ancestors of the former *garimpos* who, having had their trade taken from them (it's prohibited today), know little else to do. They know only how to plant banana and milho, which is what their own ancestors planted as far back as 1700. Eventually even the Portuguese abandoned their slaves here.

The community today is being given new life by a visionary young Brazilian woman Margot de Mirá, who fell in love with the area and bought her own house "only on heart." Five years ago she began documenting the town's social history and has started a group to protect the environment. Today she and her Italian boyfriend lead an idyllic life; when asked what they do for fun in this one-bar town (their bar!), she replied: "We visit waterfalls, go on walks, talk to people, and be creative without TV."

> **UP CLOSE TIP:** *UFOs are sighted here all the time. Locals call it the Mae d'Ouro, mother of gold. The experience is understandable since the nighttime stars are so close they seem as if they are falling down on you. And the road here is eery at night.*

## Sights

In Milho Verde there is one lone church in a grassy field. The main hot spot (the only one?!) is the **Pescoco Bar**, across the road (enter through the little gate) owned by Mirá, complete with pool table and an incredible view of the city. In São Gonçalo there is an interesting rug coop, open Mon.-Fri., 9 a.m.-4 p.m., where you can see local women weaving.

# Where To Stay

There are actually two *pousadas* in Milho Verde and two stores to buy food. The best place to stay in the region, however, is **Pousada dos Refugios 5 Amigos** in São Gonçalo (see below). See page 26 for price chart.

## Pousada Morais

*Rua Direita, 76;* ☎ *(38) 531-2007 (Milho Verde).*

The best of two is this very simple inn, with cement floors, tile walls, air conditioning, and lots of cheerful greenery. Showers and toilets are communal. Dinner is served at a long wooden table. The rate (about $14) includes all three meals. *Inexpensive. V.*

## Pousada dos Refugios 5 Amigos.

*Lg. Félix Antônio (district of São, Gonçalo do Rio das Pedras, 32 km. fax/phone* ☎ *(38) 531-2510.*

A German-born professor of philosophy who fell in love with Brazil (like all of us!) finally decided to live out his dream in this tiny town. More Brazilian than most Brazilians, he has learned to make his own traditional breads, cheese, and jams; vegetables are grown right in his garden and cooked over a wood fire. He even works a sugarcane mill. The main house is colonial style; the owner lives across the street in a more modern construction, where he also rents out rooms. The sunken living room is devoid of TV or stereo because he believes in making his guests learn the art of conversation. Books are everywhere. Bathrooms are clean, but shared; when it rains here, the phone doesn't work. Guests come from Iceland, Indonesia, Nepal, Israel, South Africa – just by word of mouth. Excursions are arranged to Serro, nearby waterfalls and mountain trekking. From the food, to the rooms, to the treks, this might well be the most charming *pousada* in Brazil. "My suffering in Europe finished the moment I came here," the owner claims. Yours might, too. And rates, which include lunch and dinner, are unbelievably low – about $17, seven-day packages a few dollars less. *Inexpensive.*

## Pousada do Japão

*District of São Gonçalo do Rio das Pedras;* ☎ *531-2510.*

An attractive inn with six rooms and a totally charming lobby/dining room/lounge filled with the smells of a wood-burning stove. No air conditioning, but the second-floor rooms boast renovated wood floors, natural wood-beam beds, and windows that open to a glorious view. The best room is on the corner (*quarto das esquina*). The bathroom is shared. The owner will pick you up at the bus stop if you notify in advance: otherwise it's a very long walk. *Inexpensive.*

## Hanɔs-On Milho Verɔe & São Gonçalo

### Arrival

**Buses** leave Belo Horizonte at 9 a.m. and arrive at 2:30 p.m. There is also a 3 p.m. bus. The busline **VAU** goes (officially) to Milho Verde, but will drop you off elsewhere if you ask. The trip takes about 1½ hours. Ask to sit on the left side of the bus for the view.

# Caraça

Tucked like a bird's nest inside a foresty national park (O Parque Natural do Caraça), 120 km./75 miles from Belo Horizonte, is the tiny village of Caraça, once home to a famous college which has since been turned into a very home-style *pousada*. What attracts visitors to this 19th-century college is a startling nightly phenomenon: the appearance of wild wolves who, after 12 years, have learned not to be afraid of humans and come stealthily up the steps of the 18th-century Matriz de Santo Antônio church around 9 p.m. to pick over the remains of dinner. Once you overcome your fear, it is thrilling to be mere feet away from these wild animals! You do have to keep quiet, however; one story goes that a group of 80 Japanese tourists (with two cameras each) sent the wolves packing. The wolves don't seem to mind light of flash bulbs, but the loud clicking of camera shutters scares them. Another strange phenomenon to witness in this area are UFOs; I saw one myself, hovering in the sky, zigzagging about in non-airplane fashion, then strangely dissolving. Locals seem to be very used to this stuff, and I even heard one story about a local woman who had a strange piece of unidentified metal removed from her brain during an operation to cure her headaches (she had sighted a UFO some months earlier). Ask around if you have interest.

Caraça is also great for trekking and horseback riding. Rooms (about $65-75 for a double) in the *pousada* are simple and clean, decorated with wood floors, blue shutters, and straw-braided ceilings. Three meals a day are served, and silence is required after 10 p.m. The old local priest, Padre Tobias, is quite outgoing, gives a lively mass, and even feeds the wolves by hand. Daily, an old geezer in a gold cap strolls the grounds calling all to mass with a ringing bell. During Holy Week, the statue of Jesus is paraded through the cobbled streets of the tiny village. June 13 is the town's birthday, celebrated with a big party. But the biggest thing to do here is nothing. A sign at the gate of the park reads "You are entering Paradise."

❖ **GETTING HERE:** *Buses go to Caraça from Belo Horizonte. The city is accessed from Belo Horizonte on BR 381/262, in the direction of Governador Valadres.*

For information about lodging, contact **Hospedaria do Caraça** (parque), Seminário do Caraça, 26 km; (101) PS 1 Caraça. Several tourist agencies in Belo Horizonte handle packages to Caraça. For more information, contact the city tourist board **Belotur** in Belo Horizonte, Rua Paraiba, 330, 19th floor; ☎ *220-1310.*

# THE SPA TOWNS

A collection of towns, collectively known as **Circuito das Aguas** (or Water Circuit) lends an aura of mysticism to the south of Minas. Tucked into hilly countryside favored by cool temperatures and dry air, the best of these spa towns, including São Lourenço, Caxambu, and Poços de Caldas, have been constructed around mineral water springs that are reputed to have healing qualities. In high season, activity at the hydromineral parks resembles something between a Catskills resort and *Death in Venice*, as visitors, both young and old, faithfully fill up their tin cups at various fountains. A stay in these peaceful, crime-free towns is a relaxing, if not possibly miraculous, way to experience the interior of the state.

This region has attracted all sorts of spiritual groups convinced that the end of the world is near; many believe that this area will be one of the few to withstand the rages of Judgment Day. One such town, **São Tomé das Letras**, has also become known nationwide as a major landing area for UFOs. About a half-hour away, in Carmo da Cachoeira, is the **Fazenda Figueira**, a devoted spiritual community founded by Trigueirinho, a famous author and former film director who is well known for his contact with extraterrestrials.

## São Lourenço

## Sights

### Parque Dos Fontes

☎ *331-1940*

São Lourenço's **water park** could pass as something straight out of Albert Brooks' version of Heaven. Built around a gleaming lake, the landscaped acres are flanked by woody hills and dominated by elaborate Art Deco fountains bursting with six different kinds of mineral water. The green-and-white **Hydrotherapy Center**, the *Balneário*, looks like a huge sacred temple, hosting some 500,000 people a year who take advantage of the special mineral baths, energetic water massages, and body therapies. It's open from 8:30 a.m. to noon and 2:30 to 4:50 p.m. daily, with separate facilities for men and women. During high season, you should make an appointment for a private bath or massage as soon as you arrive.

Anyone may drink from the individual fountains, but if you are going to do it seriously, you should probably have a medical consultation, available through the park's clinic. There are six types of waters: *bicarbonatadas sódicas* for kidney problems, gastrointestinal disturbances, hepatitis, arthritis, and gout; *magnesiana* for ulcers and hepatitis; *alcalina* for peptic ulcers and stimulation of the nervous system; *ferruginosa* for anorexia and anemia; *carbo-gasosa* for digestion and renal problems; and *sulfurosa laxativa* for chronic ulcers, diabetes, and allergies. To get the full effect, you should drink the water for 21-30 days. What you shouldn't do is drink too much at one time or mix too many different waters on the same day. (Otherwise, you'll find your body "cleansing" itself at a turbulent rate!) Inside the park you can only take home two-three liters (after two days it loses its potency), but you can fill up free outside the park at the fount at Vila Ramon.

After getting your fill of water, stop by the grotto of **Nossa Senhora dos Remedios** (Our Lady of the Remedies), strewn with plaques and flowers and even plastic limbs, to thank her for your healing. Near the grotto is a magnificent example of a pau brazil tree. If you're feeling energetic, you can jog around the perimeter of the park or rent paddleboats, kayaks, or canoes to traverse the lake. There are boutiques, crystal stores, and metaphysical bookstores, as well as a restaurant and luncheonette. In **Parque II** (adjacent to the main park), you can rent bikes and take baths in mineral water. There are also two tubes of mineral gas, which you bend down and inhale (it's reported to be good for colds).

## Aldeia Vela Verde

A half-block from the park is a series of chalets with all kinds of artisanry for sale, such as crocheted clothes, straw purses, and handmade sweaters. If you're paying in cash, ask for a discount.

## Templo da Euboise

*Avenida Getúlio Vargas, 481. Sun. 4-6 p.m.*

Founded in 1949 by the spiritualists Henrique José de Souza and his wife, Helena, this Greek-style temple is the center for an interfaith organization dedicated to universal wisdom. Around the turn of the century, the founder, during travels in India at the age of 16, became initiated into a Buddhist monastery in Ladakh, hidden in the Himalayas. The essence of Euboise is the search for perfection according to the triad *bem-bom-belo*, and the sublimation of imperfections through yoga. The temple's adepts participate in an ongoing spiritual practice, closed to visitors except on Sun., when they are received between 2 and 4 p.m. In front of the temple is a plaza that visitors are invited to circle upon arrival and departure to "receive the energy." It's been said that when President John F. Kennedy died, a group at the temple held a seance and claimed his bust appeared. Members of the organization feel that the land in this region is sacred and will survive the end of the world. On Feb. 20-25, the temple receives thousands of adepts and curiosity-seekers for cultural events, theaters, debates, and conferences.

# Where To Stay

See page 26 for price chart.

## Hotel Brazil

*Al. João Lage, 87;* ☎ *(35) 332-1313; fax 331-1536.*

This is the town's luxury hotel, though not on the scale of a five-star. The presidential suite has a fantastic veranda overlooking the park, and handicap facilities are also available. Some suites even have hydromassage. There is an indoor pool as well as a fountain and bath of mineral water outdoors. *145 apts. Moderate. All cards.*

## Hotel Primus

*Rua Cel. José Justino, 681;* ☎ *(35) 332-3232; fax 332-4100.*

Standards are clean and spacious, deluxe rooms are even larger with an anterior room. An octagonal, indoor heated pool and an outdoor pool and sauna add to the diversions. Nice buffets with fresh vegetables are good for dieters. *129 apts. Moderate. All cards.*

## Fazenda Emboaba

*Rua Cel. Jorge Amado, 350 (Solar dos Lagos);* ☎ *(35) 332-4600, fax 332-4392.*

This country estate, constructed around beautiful rolling hills outside the city, is a remarkable place to relax into nature. Extremely spacious rooms with burnt-orange jacaranda furniture and glass doors look out onto beautiful vistas; ask for the ones with wooden floors. An elegant lobby with grand piano and oriental rugs adds allure to the rustic charm. Pigs and cows roam the grounds (you're invited to milk them!) and horses are available for riding. A separate building holds a theater, screening room, and convention salons. There are also outdoor tennis courts, soccer fields, luxuriant gardens, sauna, massage, and discounts for groups. Cars are provided to the mineral park or you may walk the route in 20 minutes. *20 apts. Moderate. All cards.*

# Where To Eat

See page 26 for price chart.

## Le Sapê

*Avenida Comendador Costa, 589;* ☎ *331-1142. 11 a.m.-midnight.*

This open-air eatery with a high-beam roof is the city's best – made cozy in winter by a roaring fireplace. Fondues, pizzas, and regional dishes. *Moderate. No cards.*

**Mamma Mia**

*Avenida Cel. José Justino, 674;* ☎ *331-3242. 12 p.m.-2 p.m., 6 p.m.-midnight.*
Famous for pizzas.

# Shopping

For **crafts**, try the mini-shopping mall, **Centro de Artesanato,** on Rua Wenceslau Bráz for handmade baskets of *palha* (straw) and crochet bedspreads and sweaters. In front of the **Parque da Aguas**, you can find crystals, sweets, and liquers.

Sweet-toothed travelers should stop at **Chocarte**, Rua Wenceslau Bráz, 71 (8 a.m.-9 p.m.) to stock up on locally made chocolates and fruit-flavored liqueurs. A regional favorite is *pé de moleque*, a type of peanut brittle.

# Hands-On São Lourenço

## Arrival

São Lourenço is three hours from Rio by car (five by bus); five hours from Belo Horizonte (eight by bus) and four hours from São Paulo (six by bus). The *rodoviária* (☎ *331-1204/1153*) is half a block from the main street, Avenida Dom Pedro II, where you'll find lots of hotels, bars, and restaurants. Buses to Caxambu leave at 7 a.m., 10 a.m., 2 p.m., 3:50 p.m. and 6 p.m.

## Car Rental

**Interlocadora** . . . . . . . . . . . . . . . . . . . . . . . . . . . . . ☎ 332-3100

## City Transportation

**Taxi Brasil** . . . . . . . . . . . . . . . . . . . . . . . . . . . . . . ☎ 331-2650
**City Taxis** . . . . . . . . . . . . . . . . . . . . . . . . . . . . . . . ☎ 331-1354

## Climate

Temperatures range from 55°F to 71°F – a typical European climate conducive to deep breathing and relaxation.

## Goat Rides

Children will adore riding around the park on a goat near Praça Brasil. Look for the goat herd near the tourism kiosk.

## Horses

City tours in a horse-and-buggy (for three persons) can be taken from the corner of Avenida Getúlio Vargas and Avenida Comendador Costa.

## Tourist Information

Brochures and folders can be picked up at the tourism kiosk on Praça Brasil, ☎ 332-4455. Hours: 8-11 a.m., 1-6 p.m. in the center of the city.

# Caxambu

Although slightly smaller than São Lourenço, Caxambu is a much more interesting spa town to settle into (although the two cities, a mere 19 miles apart, are so close, you might as well pay a visit to both). The first spring was founded in 1814, attracting hordes of 19th-century visitors who believed the water had powers to cure. The reputation of the springs soared when Princesa Isabel, daughter of the emperor Dom Pedro II, cured her sterility from the font now bearing her name (a combination of alkaline gas and iron, also indicated for anemia). In gratitude, she built a small gothic chapel, **Igreja de Santa Isabel de Hungria**, which still stands today, overlooking the springs. Today, **O Parque das Aguas** is owned by the mayor's office, although the water is made available through the Superágua Company, responsible for the bottling and commercialization of over 200,000 liters of mineral water daily. The park itself is a Victorian oasis of tranquility, a veritable paradise where you can stroll and sip water at leisure, indulge in hydrotherapy baths, or engage in more invigorating exercise around the shimmering lakes.

Situated on the plateau of Mantiqueira, Caxambu is reachable over good asphalted roads, about 222 miles from Belo Horizonte, 144 miles from Rio, and 167 miles from São Paulo. The area, built on several hills (the highest of which holds a commanding figure of Christ), is dominated by coffee plantations and cattle ranches; among the unusual animals bred here is the Manga-Larga Marchador, a trotting horse excellent for long rides. A visit to nearby *fazendas* (farms) is an excellent way to experience the countryside. In Sept., fishermen can head for a city-subsidized trout farm and fish by the kilo. As with all the cities of the interior of Minas, the people of Caxambu get up early and go to bed early. After dinner, before sleeping, it's become traditional to take a turn around the principal plaza, close to the park, where there is a Belgian-style bandstand dating back to the last century. If gambling is reinstated in Brazil, Caxambu might reclaim some of its past glories, when the city was a magnet for high rollers and politicians who filled the hotel's ornamental salons. Today, the city is as peaceful as they come in Brazil; violence is unheard of and the street cleaners still sweep the roads with huge tree branches.

# Sights

## Parque Das Aguas

The "Park of Waters" in Caxambu is not just a plot of land for consuming mineral water; it's an entire entertainment complex designed to heal the body, mind, and spirit. Just strolling about the immaculately tended grounds and breathing in the fresh air rich with the scent of pines and flowers invigorates one's soul. Built at the turn of the century, the 11 fountains with various kinds of mineral water are constructed in attractively designed Art Nouveau pavilions with steps leading up to the fount; the dramatic effect leaves you with the impression that you are drinking from the lips of the gods. If you are using the waters medicinally, however, you should request a medical consultation (not free) that will direct you to the proper founts. In truth, a few of the names of the waters can be misleading. Many people imagine that Fonte Beleza is for beauty treatments, but the name actually came about because so many people gasped *Que beleza* (how beautiful) upon seeing the lovely fountain. The Ernestina Guedes fountain must have a good story behind it, but I don't know it; today it's used for hemorrhoids. Particularly impressive is the Dom Pedro, with its replica of the crown of the monarch.

The **Balneário** is open 8:30 a.m.-5 p.m. With its magnificent painted tile floor, this spot will take you back centuries – that is, if you ever were a royal receiving a bath from your servants. The body doche (*ducha*) I opted for involved a very muscular lady shooting a heavy stream of warm water at my naked body for 10 very long minutes (at least I had remembered to request *não frio* or "not cold"). Fortunately, that torture was followed by a relaxing, warm bubble bath with exotic minerals. Many other kinds of water therapies are also available. Men and women are separated in the bathhouse, but don't expect anyone to understand English. In fact, make sure you have the phrases *muito frio* (too cold) and *muito quente* (too hot) down pat before you start. There is also a beauty salon for women, where you can buy special shampoos and cleansers.

If getting cleansed like a duchess starts to get boring, you can always choose to paddleboat around the man-made lake or ride the newly installed ski-lift – an exciting feet-dangling jaunt over verdant hills. Don't miss the ingenious children's playground, built by the architect José Tabacow, whose outdoor learning games are gargantuan-sized, like the slide in the shape of a sundial and a huge iron musical scale that you can actually play. A major attraction that everyone seems to love is the natural geyser, which explodes every three hours. The hilltop restaurant, with its castle-like turrets and a huge Coke bottle, is the epitome of Brazilian kitsch, but the food is passable. Water fanatics can take a look at the **Superágua Factory,** where the famous Caxambu water is bottled.

> **UP CLOSE TIP:** *Park hours are 7 a.m.-6 p.m. The entrance fee is about 50 cents, a little more on weekends. Bring your own cup or buy a plastic one for about 75 cents.*

## Trout Farm

Owned by the *prefeitura* (mayor's office), this *criação de trutas*, in front of a rich forested reserve, was established to breed trout. In Feb., up to 20,000 trouts are spawned; in Sept. there is the **Festival of Trouts**, where you may come to fish at dawn. Visitors pay by the kilos caught, and the money is given to a fund for poor children. This dam used to be a water reservoir for the city, but was turned into an ecological preserve with a social vision. On the nearby hillsides, you can see strange orange mounds that resemble the stone formations at Stonehenge, but are actually the dirt homes of *cupin*, a kind of termite local to the region.

## Horta Florestal

This conservation program funded by the government outside the city, grows trees for city dwellers who would like to replant them in front of their homes. About five people a day come to take home free saplings. Anyone interested in Brazilian greenery will appreciate the 50 types of trees. Unfortunately, US customs prohibits the transport of live plants. (A horse-and-buggy ride in front of the Hotel Glória will transport you there and back.)

# Excursions

Many horse trails lead out to *fazendas*, country farms, such as Fazenda Santa Helena, the most famous. Call the Secretary of Tourism for more information, ☎ 341-1136.

Only 54 km./34 miles from Caxambu, the tiny village of São Tomé das Letras makes an unforgettable, if eerie day-excursion (see below).

# Where To Stay

See page 26 for price chart.

## Hotel Glória

*Avenida Camilio Soares, 590; ☎ and fax (35) 341-3000.*

One of the city's premier hotels, well situated across from the park, the Glória was inaugurated in 1946. A massive dining hall with antique chandeliers serves three meals a day on real silver plates and fine crystal goblets. Dark wood furniture and enormous old-style lounges give the feel of an old-country hunting lodge. Bathrooms have been reformed in marble. All rooms have color TVs, some have air conditioning, and a few of the suites have hydromassage. The property is perfect for those who want the feel of a *pousada* with the efficiency of a hotel. *119 apts. Moderate. All cards.*

## Palace Hotel

*Rua Dr. Viotti, 567; ☎ (35) 341-3344; fax 341-3131.*

This comfortable, old-fashioned hotel (inaugurated in 1894) is not unlike a Catskills resort, with an upright piano played from the balcony during meals. Multi-course meals are excellent here; à la carte choices include a cold buffet of chicken, roast beef, and fresh vegetables every night. A charming antique sink graces the dining room for washing your hands before eating. During high season, the **Katacumba nightclub** is one of the few places to swing in town; a screening room also is available. The rooms are graced with antique bureaus and headboards, complementing the original Art Deco light fixtures in the hall. Outside, a horse and buggy awaits riders. *Expensive. All cards.*

### Hotel Marques

*Rua Oliveira Mafra, 223; ☎ (35) 341-1013.*

Something between a funky rooming house and an old folks' home, the Marques actually has a perfectly respectable clientele, and some of the lowest rates in town. The reception area has two TVs, and the food is reputed to be good (three meals included). All rooms have tubs. *46 apts. Inexpensive. No cards.*

# Where To Eat

Most hotels offer three meals included in the room rate, so dining out is usually partaken of only by residents. However, the restaurant listed below is so good it's worth wasting your meal ticket at least once, if not a couple of times. See page 26 for price chart.

### La Forelle

*BR-354 p/Pouso Alto, km. 657; ☎ 341-1961. 7 p.m.-midnight.*

Danish cuisine at its heartiest – and with an authentic bloodline. Owner Antônio Godtfredsen's father, an early immigrant in the 1920s, was the first to make blue cheese in South America. Only about 30 Scandinavians are left of this once-thriving community of milk farmers and cheesemakers, but some of their secrets can still be tasted here, as in the filet mignon with roquefort – the best I have ever eaten. The menu is colossal, from smoked salmon with mushroom-spiked scrambled eggs to delicious pâtés with homemade bread and all kinds of fondues. The specialty is smoked trout with almond sauce, but unforgettable is the *peito de frango empanado* (chicken breast pie) in curry sauce. The homemade apple pie is tender, crispy and creamy, all at once. Reservations are absolutely necessary; be sure you sit Senhor Antônio down for some stories from the old days. *Expensive. All cards.*

### Agostini

*Rua João Constantino, 48 (Centro); ☎ 341-1120.*

Pleasant surroundings illuminated by candles and reliable air conditioning. Open for dinner only. *Inexpensive.*

> **UP CLOSE TIP:** *Scandinavian cheeses, gruyere, roquefort, and parmesan, can be bought at* **Sobradino Laticínio**, *Avenida Gabriel Fernandes. The label "Skandia" is the best from the area.*

# Nightlife

During high season check out the Katacumba nightclub in the **Palace Hotel**, the nightclub in **Hotel Glória**, and **Overnight** on Praça 15 de Setembro. **La Nave 307**, Rua João Pinheiro, 307, is a young hangout for pizza and beer from 7:30 p.m. onward.

# Shopping

Among souvenirs to buy in the center of the city are handmade crochet objects, handmade rugs, intriguing T-shirts, bamboo purses, and homemade liqueur.

On the way back from the trout farm, stop at **Doces Imperial Rod.**, BR 354, km. 92; ☎ *341-2691*, for sweets, *balas de leite com mel* (juicy caramels), *doce de leite*, canned fruits, and fruit liqueurs. Prices are a little cheaper here because this is the factory. For stylish sweats and T-shirts, try **W. R. Confecções**, Avenida Dom Pedro II, 538; ☎ *331-2784*.

# Hands-On Caxambu

### Arrival

**Buses** from Rio run on the Viação Cidade do Aço line twice a day, four times on Fri. From Belo Horizonte, buses on the Viação ENSA line run two times a day, four on Fri. and Sat. From São Paulo, the Resen Sense line runs five times daily. Buses to and from São Lourenço run six times a day. In high season (Dec.-Feb. and July) and holidays, you should buy your tickets for the big cities 10 days in advance. Other times, buy one-three days in advance.

### City Tour

Horse-drawn carriages can be hired in front of the Hotel Glória to go to Horta Florestal.

### Tourist Information

Visit the **Secretary of Tourism** office at the white kiosk on Praça 16 de Setembro. Hours: Mon.-Fri. 9am.-noon, 2-6 p.m.

### When To Go

**JANUARY: National Motorbike Competition.**
**JULY: Rock na Rua** (Street Rock) festival features new Brazilian bands on the third weekend.
**MAY: Video Festival** featuring new works.

# São Tomé das Letras

São Tomé das Letras must be the strangest town in the whole world. Isolated in the middle of a granite mountain, the village is about 500 feet above sea level, yet a strange smell of sea pervades the air. Just getting to the town – over an incredibly rocky road – may prove daunting, but the moment you approach, you'll begin to feel an unmistakable shift in the atmosphere – a kind of eerie timelessness promoted by its glassy-eyed inhabitants, who look as though they've just been defrosted from Woodstock. Most of the 7,500 residents live in eccentric stone houses they have made themselves, though many of the dwellings look to be somewhere between half-constructed and fully abandoned. Despite its primitive lifestyle, São Tomé has received enormous Brazilian TV coverage since it is considered one of the prime locations for sighting *discos voadores*, or flying saucers. In fact, an apparently sane gentlemen named Tatá, the owner of a small *pousada*, claimed in an interview with me that he has seen and talked to arriving extraterrestrials for the last 30 years. In general, the residents of São Tomé, many of whom have been mystically guided to settle here, believe that the civilization of a new world will be founded in the area in the year 2005. Located in the sand-based village are over 30 holes, one of which is believed to lead directly to a thriving civilization located at the center of the earth. (My one travel precaution: think twice if anyone tries to sell you a ride on a space ship.)

Mysticism has been a part of the city since its origins. According to one legend, a runaway slave from a baron's farm in Campo Grande had been hiding in a cave when he discovered an image of São Tomé. The saint appeared to the slave, asking him to return to his master, present the image, then build a chapel close to the cave. With great courage, the slave did as he was asked and was not only not punished, but freed as promised. The phrase *das letras* or "of the letters," refers to the indecipherable hieroglyphics that were discovered on the cave wall. Some say ancient Phoenicians wrote them; others claim it was descendants of Atlantis, who lived in a subterranean city of the cave called Gruta do Carimbado. Another popular legend claims there's an underground tunnel that runs between São Tomé, Brasília, and Machu Picchu in Peru, forming a sacred triangle. In more recent years, hippies, healers, and psychics have moved here, as well as some very strange creatures who actually look like extraterrestrials getting accustomed to human forms (seriously). A few handicrafts are sold, particularly miniatures of the locals' stone houses, all of which resemble some kind of architecture from outer space.

The quartzite sites are fascinating to see (some people still chip away at them for a modest livelihood), and anyone sensitive to rock formations and crystals will find their energy both invigorating and strangely unsettling.

Despite (or because of) its oddities, the city lives mostly on tourism, though the infrastructure is minute. There are only 35 telephones, a first aid center with a doctor once a week, one bank, one pharmacy, one supermarket, two small inns, five restaurants, and 12 bars. If you're game, you might be able to rent a hammock in a private home.

# Excursions

If you have a car and driver, it's worth a visit to the following waterfalls: **Veu de Noiva, do Flávio** and **da Euboise**. One of the most beautiful areas in the region is **Vale das Borboletas** (exit to Tres Coraçõe, access to the left, three km./1.8 miles) overrun with hundreds of colored butterflies during the spring. Fascinating treks can be made to several caverns in the region, including the most mystical, **Gruta do Carimbado,** which is said to have a connection with Macchu Pichu in Peru. **Gruta do Triangulo,** with its beautiful view of the mountains, is considered to have "high spiritual vibes" by locals.

Guides can be contacted inside the Igreja Matriz in São Tomé. Make sure you are equipped with your own bottled water, ropes, flashlight, and medical kit, etc.

# Where To Stay

See page 26 for price chart.

### Pousada do Tatá

*Praça do Rosário, 25;* ☎ *237-1248.*

Oriental owner Luiz Noronha, otherwise known as Tatá, calls himself an *arqueologia mística,* mystic archeologist. He owns the simplest of *pousadas* (only two rooms) and an even simpler restaurant, whose walls are plastered with his media coverage over the years. One room runs about $10. To contact him, call the São Tomé operator (area code 201) and leave a message. *Inexpensive. No cards.*

### Hospedaria dos Sonhos

*R. Gabriel Luiz Alves, 11;* ☎ *237-1235.*

Small, modest apartments; the best ones are in the front, with a veranda. *Inexpensive. No cards.*

### Paraisa

*Rua Marceonílio Ribeiro Costa, 33.*

Livable rooms with excellent views of the valley. *Inexpensive. No cards.*

# Where To Eat

During low season few restaurants are open at night. Ask in advance so you don't go hungry. See page 26 for price chart.

### Castelo de Cristal

*Praça Gétulio Vargas, 16.*

Three small salons, with stone tables and mystically minded decor. Live music during high season. All three meals served. *Inexpensive. No cards.*

### Néctar

*Praça Barão de Alfenas, 35 (Centro).*

The simplest of locales, where everybody goes for breakfast. *Inexpensive.*

### Das Magas

*Rua Camilo Rios, 2;* ☎ *237-1240.*

An old house typical of the region offers cuisine of Minas. *Inexpensive. No cards.*

# Shopping

**Pedra Mística Atelier**, Praça Central, sells crystals and sweets. **Vendinha das Gnomos** offers an excellent bag of natural homemade granola.

# Hands-On Sao Tomé Das Letras

## Arrival

São Tomé is 195 miles from Belo Horizonte, and 20 miles from Tres Corações. If driving, take the road that links Caxambu to Juiz de Fora. About 10 km./6.2 miles after you leave Caxambu, turn left and take a gravel road 50 km. (31 miles), or about one hour. Pay attention, because there is only one very small sign on the road. Buses arrive and depart about three times a week from Três Corações.

# THE STATE OF SÃO PAULO

## São Paulo City

Think of the city of São Paulo as the Brazilian Big Apple, only sweeter. With 15 million people, São Paulo rates as the third largest city in the world, complete with all the problems of an ever-burgeoning metropolis – skyscrapers, traffic jams, slums, pollution, and noise. But there is also a certain kind of charm in the residents of the city (called *Paulistanos*) that somehow makes these problems seem less imposing. Taxi drivers are honest (*mais ou menos*), waiters gracious, and shopgirls – always pretty – remain irrepressibly helpful.

Finally, it's home to the largest industrial complex in Latin America and accounts for about half of Brazil's federal taxes. Whatever is modern in Brazil can be found in São Paulo, South America' largest city and home to the world's second largest commodity exchange (after Chicago's). A dominant political force, *Paulistanos* like to say they work for the rest of Brazil. And they love to talk in industrial percentages. The state of São Paulo (of which the city is capital) produces 40% of the Brazilian gross national product, (including 62% of the country's sugar, 33% of coffee and 50% of fruit exports), all the while utilizing 60% of the available electrical energy. The city's 64,000 industries correspond to 50% of the country's total industrial output. With 70% of the country's wealth passing through **Avenida Paulista**, the banking center of the country, São Paulo, for all its hard-driving activity, almost seems like its own country.

And indeed, if it were its own country, it would be in a deep mess. The government of the state that likes to call itself "the locomotive of Brazil" is $50 billion in debt, partially due to politically motivated state spending before elections – extravagant gestures that have thrown **Banespa**, the state bank, into deep arrears. (The state government is supposed to be paying 20 million dollars a month to Banespa in interest alone for its accumulated debt of $30 billion.) And yet dozens of foreign investments totalling $7.6 billion are already scheduled for São Paulo state in the next two years. They include a $100 million factory for Compaq, an $850 million commitment from Volkswagen, and a $2.2 billion expansion project by General Motors of Brazil.

But there is much more to the city than skyscrapers and industry. Over 1,600 events are held in São Paulo city *daily*. The **São Paulo Convention and Visitors Bureau** actively competes on the international market to host conventions, seminars, and exhibitions from fields as diverse as medicine, arts, science, and commerce. Whatever intellectual currents occur in Brazil are often forged first in São Paulo; the hearts of the theater, film, and literary worlds are all firmly established here. Certainly the best medical care is here, as are the country's finest museums. As one *Paulistano* said to this transplanted New Yorker (and without a trace of irony!), "If you can make it in São Paulo, you can make it anywhere in Brazil."

These days it may be hard to find a hotel room in São Paulo. American, European, and Japanese investors are flocking in droves to the city to take advantage of the recent trade opening which has seen the arrival of American computers, American junk food, and American savvy. In any of the top hotels, particularly the **Transamérica**, the city's only resort hotel, you can easily eavesdrop on conversations devoted to the latest in international finance.

One of the major attractions of the city is its diverse ethnicity. During the 19th century, as slavery was abolished, immigrants from Italy, Germany, France, and Japan, among others, converged on the area, forming strong communities and forging distinctive cultures. Today, the Italian neighborhood of **Bexiga**, the Japanese **Liberdade**, and various Arab, Jewish and Korean communities provide colorful backdrops in a city that hardly seems to belong to a tropical country.

## 3,000 Restaurants & 3,500 Bars

If you need one good reason to go to São Paulo, *go to eat*. The syncretic mix of cultures has produced some of the most **cosmopolitan menus** in Brazil, as well as masterful chefs. With its 3,000 restaurants and 3,500 bars, São Paulo is a city where you can find an excellent dinner at 4 in the morning. While *Paulistanos* flee the city on the weekend, 70% of other states come here just for the nightlife. Fri. is the hub of the weekend; clubs and bars often stay open till the last client leaves.

Of course, being 43 miles inland, São Paulo can hardly compare to Rio in terms of natural wonders. Yet, in its own way the city benefits from a privileged location. Two beach cities, **Guarujá** and **Santos**, are just an hour away. And if *Paulistanos* want to shiver in a foresty highland, they can head to **Campos do Jordão**, the Aspen of Brazil's eastern coast (with ski-lifts, but no snow).

## History

The sprawling metropolis of São Paulo began in 1555 as a tiny **Jesuit mission** established along the Tietê River to convert the Tupí-Guaraní Indians. Eventually, the modest station grew into a trading post, around which a new settlement was founded. The true heroes of colonial expansion in São Paulo state, however, were the daring bands of expeditioners, called *bandeirantes*, who plunged into the interior seeking wealth and power, runaway slaves, precious metals, and new territory in the name of the crown. These *bandeirantes* were romantic figures, traveling immense distances by foot and canoe as they opened new routes of communication and became wealthy landowners themselves. Though not a few of them were themselves rogues and runaway criminals, their single-minded determination and hard-driving persistence became traits that were forged deeply in the personality of the modern *Paulistanos* – if stereotypes are to be believed.

In 1711, São Paulo officially became a city. The sleepy provincial town was jolted into prominence at the end of the 19th century as the coffee cycle took hold and railway expansion throughout the Paulista Plateau transformed the city into the most important center of the province. Enormous **coffee plantations**, called *fazendas*, swept over the area, creating power and wealth for its owners and scores of job opportunities for the lower class. **Dumont**, the most famous coffee farm at the end of the 19th century, was practically a city in itself, with 13,000 acres of coffee fields and 5,000 live-in employees. When slavery was abolished in 1881, waves of immigrants descended on the plantations, offering a cheap form of labor. **Italians** were the first to arrive, followed by a boatload of 781 **Japanese** in 1808. Dreaming of making a little money, then returning to their homeland, the Japanese were spurred on by agricultural conquests; by the second generation, they had progressed from working the fields to selling produce. Today, some of the largest industries are owned by Japanese descendants.

São Paulo's **industrial boom** began in the 20th century, gaining extraordinary proportions after World War II. Factories cropped up, invading the lowlands and attracting more immigrants, who began to change the economic and cultural face of the city. **Jews** of Eastern European origin came to Brazil as itinerant peddlars and flocked to **Bom Retiro**, a

A banana face in the countryside of São Paulo.

*bairro* (district) near the Luz train station. As they gathered economic power they moved the limits of the city even farther south, while **Koreans** – São Paulo's latest immigrants – moved in behind them. **Arabs** also started arriving in the early 20th century from Syria and Lebanon, bringing with them strong religious ties (divided equally between Muslims and Christians), as well as a penchant for excellent sweets and spicy cuisines (all of which can be found in the *bairro* around Rua 25 de Marco).

---

# A Bird's Eye View

---

*Paulistanos* have adopted the slogan "São Paulo cannot stop" for good reason. At present, the city covers over 2,000 square km., an area three times the size of Paris, but its outskirts are still snaking southward. The traditional heart of the city lies around **Praça da Sé**, an enormous concrete plaza throbbing with activity during the day and dominated by the **Catedral Metropolitana**, a towering neo-Gothic structure completed in 1954. Opposite the cathedral along Rua Boa Vista is the **Pátio do Colégio**, one of the few historical sites left in São Paulo, housing the first college and chapel of the Jesuit mission. Also located here is the home of the infamous **Marquesa de Santos**, mistress of Emperor Pedro I. North of Praça da Sé on Avenida Tiradentes 676 is the **Igreja e Convento da Luz** (Church and Convent of Light) an 18th-century Franciscan monastery that today houses the **Museu de Arte Sacra** (Museum of Sacred Art).

The hub of the commercial district is **Avenida Paulista**, home to scores of companies and banks, including Bank of Tokyo, Bradesco, and Banco do Brazil. Just a drive down the avenue will take you past some of the most exotic buildings in the world, from Citibank, a study in curves and angles, to Banco Sumitomo Brasileiro, which defies gravity. Here also you can see beautifully restored colonial houses nearly squashed between towering skyscrapers. South of the commercial district, straddling Rua 13 de Maio, is **Bela Vista**, also known as Bexiga (São Paulo's Little Italy), where you can find hundreds of Italian cantinas and excellent pizzerias. South of Praça da Sé is the Japanese district of **Liberdade**, through which runs its main street, Rua Galvão Bueno. In the north of the city, **Bom Retiro** received the first Arab immigrants, though it is in the *bairro* of **Pacaembu** that Arabs and Jews continue to live together in harmony as they have for years. A number of the finer hotels, such as the Maksoud Plaza and the Crown Plaza, are located in **Cerqueira César**, west of Bela Vista. Going south from Cerqueira César, you'll find the **Parque Ibirapuera**. Full of fine bars and boutiques, **Jardins** is an elite neighborhood where magnates of industry live; the area between Estados Unidos and Faria Lima streets are now being zoned to ensure that only houses will be built. One of the nicest neighborhoods to browse through by car is **Morumbí**, the site of fabulous mansions and an extravagant shopping mall by the same name.

## Sights

### Liberdade: Japan Town

The home of the Japanese community in São Paulo, Liberdade is a colorful neighborhood full of exotic sushi bars, native boutiques and narrow cobblestone streets. The red oriental arches overhanging Rua Galvão Bueno, the main street – a symbol of the neighborhood – add an exotic flavor. The best time to visit is during one of the four Japanese festivals. On Dec. 31, during the **New Year's Festival**, riceballs, eaten for good will, are distributed free of charge to all visitors during the street fair. The celebration of the **Buddha's Birthday** in Jan. includes a procession of a statue of the Buddha carried by children dressed in ceremonial robes. During the **Festival of the Stars** (second Sat. in June), personal wishes are written on a piece of paper and attached to a stick of bamboo. Perhaps the most colorful event is the **Oriental Festival** (first Sat. in Dec.), when the streets fill with people singing and dancing folkloric tunes in traditional costumes.

Every Sun. throughout the year, an **Oriental Fair** is held in the main square from 10 a.m. to 7 p.m., with vendors hawking plants, ceramics, crafts, and typical sweets.

The **Nikkey Palace Hotel** also organizes Japanese events throughout the year. Located on Rua Tomáz Gonzaga, **Marwyama** is the largest folklore and jewelry store in the neighborhood, with precious stones considerably cheaper than those at H. Stern. For the area's best Japanese restaurants, see under *Restaurants*. For more about shopping in Liberdade, see under *Shopping*.

# Other Sights

## Butantã Institute

*Avenida Vital Brazil, 1500 Butantã;* ☎ *211-8211. Daily 8 a.m.-5 p.m., closed Mon. Fee about $2.*

Snake buffs will love the numerous displays of Amazon serpents, spiders, and scorpions at this research center, famous for its anti-venom serums. The bus "Butantã" runs from Praça da República.

## Exotiquarium

*Morumbí Shopping Mall. Daily 10 a.m.-10 p.m.*

Rumored to be the largest aquarium in South America, it is surely the most exotic for a shopping mall. It even boasts a pink river dolphin. Once in the mall, you can eat, bowl, ice-skate, or shop.

## Zoological Gardens

*Av. Miguel Stéfano, 4241 (Agua Funda);* ☎ *276-0811. 9 a.m.-5 p.m.*

Ranking among the 10 largest and best equipped in the world, this zoo boasts over 2,500 animals and 130 species from lions, tigers, and monkeys to waterfowl and a nest of leaf-cutting ants in their natural environs. The gardens are well cultivated, and there are numerous snack bars.

## Playcenter

*Rua Dr. Rubens Meirelles, 380 Barra Funda;* ☎ *826-9511. Tues.-Fri. 2 p.m.-10 p.m., Sat. 2 p.m.-11 p.m., Sun. 10 a.m.-10 p.m.*

Even *Paulistanos* in business suits talk wistfully about the largest amusement park in South America; many adults play hooky to enjoy the dozens of rides scattered over the 45 acres. The park also includes restaurants, snack bars, a 180° movie screen, and cable car.

## Jaraguá Peak

*Via Anhaguera, km. 18.*

Located in the State Park of Jaraguá in two square miles of green forest, the peak is 1,135 meters high (3,723 feet) and offers an excellent panoramic view of the city. Easy treks can be made around a paved track, and there are numerous lakes for scenic picnicking.

## Simba Safari

*Avenida do Cursinho, 6338 (V. Morães); ☎ 846-6249. Tues.-Fri. 10 a.m.-4:45 p.m., Sat., Sun., and holidays 9 a.m.-5 p.m.*

A strange sight in a cosmopolitan city, but wild lions, camels, zebras, and monkeys do roam this 25-acre park, at peace in their natural habitats. Visitors are admitted for the safari-like tours in their own cars, or they may rent one. There's also a cafeteria and playground.

## The Waves

*Avenida Guido Caloi, 25; ☎ 521-8666.*

Landscaped by Roberto Burle Marx, the first aquatic park in São Paulo was inaugurated in 1991 and is geared for irresistible fun. Main attractions are the swimming pools (with waves à la Wet 'n' Wild), illuminated fountains, jet-streams, and water slides. There's also a sauna and an artificial solarium.

## Ibirapuera Park

Joggers should head straight for S.P.'s biggest park, designed by Oscar Niemeyer and landscape artist Roberto Burle Marx. Dominating the grounds are four lakes, a plant nursery, and a Japanese pavilion with a replica of the Kyoto Imperial Palace. The **Museum of Contemporary Art** is also located here, as is the **Museum of Modern Art** (MAM), the **Aeronáutica Museum**, featuring the Santos Dumont airplane, and the **Folklore Museum**. The **Planetarium** presents shows at 4 and 6 p.m. weekends and holidays.

❖ **GETTING HERE:** *Take the Monções bus 675-C from the Ana Rosa metro station to the park.*

## Museums

### Museum de Arte de São Paulo

*Avenida Paulista, 1578. Tues.-Fri. 1-6 p.m., Sat. and Sun. 2-6 p.m.*

One of the finest art collections in Brazil, MASP has an impressive exhibition of masterpieces, including works by Rembrandt, Rubens, Renoir, Toulouse-Lautrec, and Raphael. The foremost Brazilian artists and sculptors are also represented. The building itself – a unique elevated rectangle supported by two bright red panels split through the middle – has been often cited for architectural achievement.

### Fundação Maria Luiza and Oscar Americano

*Avenida Morumbí, 3700; ☎ 842-0077. Tues.-Sun. 10 a.m.-5 p.m.*

Opposite the Palácio dos Bandeirantes (the seat of the state government), this museum is the former home of the industrialist Oscar Americano and shows just how the elite of Brazil have spent some of their riches. Important works of the famous Brazilian painters Di Calvacanti and Portinari are on display, as well as fine furnishings and memorabilia of the Brazilian royal family.

## Casa do Bandeirante (Pioneer House)

*Praça Monteiro Lobato;* ☎ *211-0920. Tues.-Fri. 10:30 a.m.-5 p.m.,*
*Sat. and Sun. 9 a.m.-5 p.m.*

This living museum recreates the traditionally rustic homestead of *bandeirantes*, those 18th-century pioneers by whose courageous efforts the interior of São Paulo was settled.

## Casa do Sertanista

*Avenida Prof. Francisco Morato, 2200 (Caxingui);* ☎ *211-5341.*

Exhibitions of Indian folklore and handicrafts under the direction of the famed Indian researcher Orlando Villas Boas.

## Museu da Imagem e do Som

*Avenida Europa, 158. Tues.-Sun. 2 p.m.-10 p.m.*

Ongoing photo exhibitions and a back archive of Brazilian film, video, and music that may be rented by the public.

## Memorial da América Latina

*Av. Mário de Andrade, 664, next to the Barra Funda metro station. 9 a.m.-9 p.m.*

Designed by Oscar Niemeyer to commemorate the solidarity of Latin America, this oddly shaped memorial resembles three lumps of chocolate ice cream with a splash of whipped cream on top. In the nearby museum complex is a spectacular array of Latin American crafts, a photo library, books, magazines, films from the continent, and a restaurant. During the weekends, drop by for free concerts by Brazilian and Latin musicians.

## Museu Lasar Segall

*Rua Afonso Celso, 362 (V. Mariana);* ☎ *574-7322. Tues., Wed., Thurs. and Sun.*
*2:30 p.m.-6:30 p.m.; Fri.-Sat. 2:30- p.m.-8 p.m.*

More than 1,700 works by Segall, including paintings, drawings, engravings, and sculptures shown in temporary exhibitions. Good library and cinema.

## Free Events

## Memorial da América Latina

*Rua Mario de Andrade, 664 (Barra Funda);* ☎ *823-9611.*

Pop musicians from different countries perform on weekends at this large square designed by Oscar Niemeyer. Don't miss the Pavilhão da Criatividade, a fine showcase of Latin-American handicraft.

## Mosteiro de São Bento

*Largo de São Bento (downtown);* ☎ *228-3633.*

Exquisite Gregorian chants are sung by the monks of this famous church at the 10 a.m. Sun. mass.

# Excursions

São Paulo was built on a plateau. However, a mere one hour (at the most three) by car on well-maintained roads can bring you to some of the prettiest beaches on the northern shore: Pernambuco in Guarujá, Sahy and Camburi, in São Sebastian. These trips are fine leisure options, particularly in off-season (Mar.-Dec.). Other scenic destinations include:

## Aldeia da Serra

A scenic sightseeing drive to a settlement built in colonial style. You'll find a church, bandstand, rental horses, helicopter rides, and two good restaurants.

❖ **GETTING HERE:** *Access road on km. 3 of Castelo Branco Highway, at the Jandira intersection.*

## Atlantic Forest

☎ *702-1100.*

An easy and enjoyable train ride through some of the last remaining vestiges of the Atlantic rainforest leaves every Sat. at 8:30 a.m. from Luz Station on its way to Santos, where you can enjoy the now-revived beaches.

## Embu

On Sun. there is a street fair with handicrafts and foods. Good place to buy old-fashion furniture. (For more Street Fairs see under *Shopping*, below.

❖ **GETTING HERE:** *Access road on km. 29 of Régis Bitencourt Highway.*

## Horto Florestal

*Rua do Horto, 931 (Tremembé);* ☎ *952-8555. Daily 8 a.m.-5:30 p.m.*

Beautiful area to picnic with gardens, playgrounds, and lakes.

## Paranapiacaba

☎ *702-1100.*

A train ride between the Luz Station and the English railway settlement built at the turn of the century, located in the beautiful Serra do Mar Mountains.

## Serra da Cantareira

Relish the lovely landscape and the fresh country air, so near the city. Rest at the comfortable Chalé restaurant, located high up on the mountain.

❖ **GETTING HERE:** *Use Avenida Cruzeiro do Sul, in the east part of the city.*

## Solo Sagrado

About an hour's drive from São Paulo lies one of the most remarkable ecological parks in Brazil. Built around a lovely reservoir, this 80-acre park is called Solo Sagrado, meaning "Sacred Grounds." It was built by the **Igreja Messiânica Mundial do Brasil** (or Johrei Fellowship, as it is known in the United States), an international spiritual organization dedicated to healing. Founded by Mochiti Okada, an enlightened Japanese master, during the 30s and 40s, the worldwide organization is deeply committed to creating what it calls "prototypes for Paradise on Earth" – in this case, a park sensitively designed to reflect the natural balance and healing powers innate to Mother Earth. The park, which was inaugurated in Nov. 1995, is now open to the general public who come to revel in the tropically designed landscapes as well as partake in the healing practice of love and prayer. Visitors are invited to stay for the day or longer (preference, of course, is given to members); the simple, but impeccably clean dormitory-style rooms run about $5 a night, including food. Spiritual service may be offered in the form of kitchen help, ground maintenance, or practicing the healing technique. There are many paths for easy trekking as well as seated areas for meditation; the views are fantastic. I visited in mid-1994 during construction and again during the moving inauguration (which included speeches by both the mayor and governor of São Paulo and was covered by four TV news channels); even then a deep sense of peace and sacredness was already in evidence. If you would like to visit, it is best to contact the main headquarters in São Paulo to arrange a visit. Igreja Messianica Mundial do Brasil, Rua Morgado de Mateus, 77 (Vila Mariana), 04015-050; ☎ *(11) 574-0800.*

# Where To Stay

São Paulo hotels are primarily geared for executives. The high and low season in São Paulo is nearly the opposite from that of Rio. Low season runs from Dec. to Feb. (including July, which is school vacation). Active months, when rates are usually the highest, are Aug.-Nov. Rates given here are usually the highest charged; negotiate for good deals during periods of low activity.

Your best bets are the luxurious apart-hotels, whose rooms resemble high-class apartments, equipped with fully stocked kitchens and marvelous decor. Rates are usually much lower than comparable five-star hotels, and all you forego are the bevy of restaurants, hair salons, and boutiques that crowd the lobbies of the larger hotels. See page 26 for price chart.

## Five-Star Hotels

### Maksoud Plaza

*Al. Campinas, 150 (Bela Vista);* ☎ *(11) 253-4411; fax 253-4541;*
*reservations, toll-free (22) 800-1155.*

A marvelous oasis from the city snarls, the Maksoud is one of the best-run hotels in São Paulo. The vine-entwined lobby, which has been compared to the Contemporary Hotel in Walt Disney World, is an extravaganza of dining areas and elite shops, calmed by the constant rush of waterfalls. Not a place for screaming kids, the hotel attracts guests like David Rockefeller and Henry Kissinger, who enjoy the $1,200-a-day Presidential Suite. Handsome international businessmen roam the lobby.

Rooms are built in circular fashion around an open lobby; management has been known to drop watermelons from the 21st floor just to test security's reactions. Music seems to be everywhere. At the 150 Club, jazz greats such as Earl Hines and Carmen McRae perform regularly to packed houses; *chorinhos* can be heard in the Batidas e Petiscos Bar, soft jazz with a renowned trumpeter in the Trianon Bar and classical concerts Weds.-Sun. in the theater. The five restaurants are all top class: a Scandinavian buffet, a Japanese sushi bar, a barbecue grill, a gourmet pizzeria, and a five-star French gourmet. Society ladies take afternoon tea in the atrium, serenaded by chamber music, and cultural events, seminars, and sneak previews are held in the theater.

Standard rooms, attractively appointed with modern art, boast electronic controls, blackout curtains, mini-bar, makeup mirror, bathroom phone, and shower/tubs. Special Trinitron TVs offer 120 channels with in-house video. Japanese breakfast is available, as are special secretarial services. Most important, the management is intimately involved with the personal needs of each client; a computerized system records all personal requests in case of return visits. In its relentless pursuit of novel entertainment, the hotel has even hosted cowmilking contests in the lobby. Do note that breakfast is not included, but the water in the frigobar is free. *416 apts. Very expensive. All cards.*

## Caesar Park

*Rua Augusta, 1508 (Cerqueira César);* ☎ *(11) 253-6622; fax 288-6146.*

One block from Paulistano Avenida, the commercial heart of downtown, the Caesar Park caters to captains of industry and top-level execs with special needs. Long a favorite among Japanese clientele who appreciate the exquisite decor, the hotel, part of the Westin chain, is now actively seeking the American market, particularly women traveling alone. Every nook and cranny of the hotel is impeccably appointed, including the walnut-walled, British-style pub with live music nightly. Special gastronomic festivals add excitement; *feijoada* is served Weds., and the Japanese restaurant is considered the best in the city.

Bedrooms all have scales, hairdryers, makeup mirrors, and safes. Japanese-style apartments, equipped with futons, low tables, and bamboo screens, have become the rage among honeymooners. There's also a small gym, sauna, outdoor pool, and masseur. *177 apts. Very expensive. All cards.*

## Sheraton Mofarrej & Towers

*Al. Santos, 1437 (Cerqueira César);* ☎ *(11) 253-5544; fax 289-8670.*

From the gold sculptures to the gold elevators to the black marble floors covered in priceless Oriental rugs, the Sheraton's lobby looks like an Arabian palace. A veritable wonder, the Presidential suite takes up the entire 22nd floor. The Vivaldi restaurant boasts a stunning wraparound view of the city. The coffee shop is a study in waterfalls.

All bedrooms come equipped with hairdryers, scales, special mirrors, and safes. The outdoor pool is decorated like a tropical jungle, and the indoor pool is bordered by fine wooden floors. Equipped with a masseur, the health club also offers weight-training and dry sauna. *244 apts. Very expensive. All cards.*

## São Paulo Hilton

*Avenida Ipiranga, 165 (Centro);* ☎ *(11) 256-0033; fax 257-3137.*

This circular, 33-story hotel boasts the fine service and attractive decor of Hiltons worldwide. Many execs come just to breakfast in the appealing coffee shop, which serves a groaning buffet. The top three executive floors require a special key, and VIP guests may take their breakfast and cocktails in a private lounge serviced by bilingual receptionists from 7 a.m.-10 p.m. A full array of gourmet restaurants and intimate bars make socializing pleasant and an adjacent shopping arcade serves all needs.

Individual rooms are spacious, with extremely comfortable beds. There's also a steam room and pool. The only drawback is the hotel's location in the old section of downtown, now a magnet for sleazy characters, prostitutes and transvestites, who stroll the surrounding streets after the sun goes down. To be safe, don't walk around the area at night and always take taxis. *380 apts. Very expensive. All cards.*

## Grand Hotel Ca' d'Oro

*Rua Augusta, 129 (Centro);* ☎ *(11) 256-8011; fax 231-0359.*

This hotel oozes with old-world charm, the kind appreciated by clients like the King of Spain. Owned by a traditional Italian family for the last 38 years, the hotel actually resembles a small village, with a maze of corridors that connect the original building to the newer annex. Standards in the old building must rate as the largest in São Paulo, but the tradeoff is out-of-date furniture, which leaves a heavy impression. Lunch buffets look out onto the pool, with its barbecue area and playground. A second pool is located rooftop. To complete the patriarchal touch, there's a snooker room, a reading room, and the top-class Ca D'Oro restaurant, one of the few city eateries where a tie is important. Sauna, gym, and hair salon are available, but the most-favored meeting place is the lounge, where guests have been known to fight for space in front of the wood-burning fireplace. *290 apts. Expensive. All cards.*

## Crowne Plaza

*Rua Frei Caneca, 1360 (Cerqueira César);* ☎ *(11) 284-1144; fax 251-3121.*

Only five years old, the Crowne Plaza boasts the highest occupancy in the city. The American Airlines crew on the São Paulo-Miami flight stays here, and for good reason – the gym is excellent, the rooms spacious, and the lunch buffet, with its huge grill of shrimp, fish, and paella, looks inviting. Located not far from Paulistano Avenida, the hotel is also within sneezing distance of 10 international banks. The lobby sports a fantastic view of the garden, which creates a haunting optical illusion. Fri. nights, a jam session with visiting musicians draws crowds in the hotel's new cultural center. On Weds. and Sat. *feijoada* buffets are served.

Most standards have queen-sized beds; all have tubs, large mirrors, hairdryers, and safes. An extensive gym is equipped with free weights, bikes, saunas, and a small Jacuzzi. A concierge floor serves private breakfast for VIP clients, as well as a free bar and secretarial service. Nonsmoking floor. *223 apts. Expensive. All cards.*

## Four-Star Hotels

### Nikkey Palace

*Rua Galvão Bueno, 425; ☎ (11) 270-8511; fax 270-6614.*

In the heart of the Japanese district, this hotel is the place to be during the Japanese festivals (including New Year's Eve and Buddha's birthday), when the neighboring streets are filled with parades and festivities. About 70% of the clientele are Japanese, who enjoy the optional Japanese breakfast of rice, soy sauce, soup, and fish. The furniture also suits Japanese needs – low and sedate (although some pieces look a bit worn). The best deal is for the junior suites, about twice as large as a five-star double, for the same price. The Japanese restaurant in the basement is the largest in the city. The men-only sauna, frequented by yuppies and a variety of artists, was ranked the best in São Paulo by *Playboy* magazine. Shiatzu for both men and women is available Tues.-Sat. Recent renovations extend the capacity of the hotel. *95 apts. Moderate-expensive. All cards.*

### Eldorado Boulevard

*Avenida São Luis, 234 (Centro); ☎ and fax (11) 214-1833.*

International execs, mostly from the U.S. and Argentina, populate the Eldorado, located downtown. The 24-hour coffee shop is frequented by TV and theater actors, usually after midnight. Rooms are more serviceable than luscious, with color TV and mini-bar; some rooms have tubs. The exec floor is not substantially nicer, but VIP service does include fruit bowls, shoeshines, and robes. Suites have a living room, dressing room, and a large bath, plus an outdoor veranda; 11th floor is nonsmoking. An international restaurant and self-service buffet, plus a bar, round out the culinary needs. *157 apts. Expensive. All cards.*

### Fortune Residence and Executive Service

*Rua Haddock Lobo, 804 (Jardins); ☎ (11) 853-9511; fax 853-1139.*

This apart-hotel is considered the best in São Paulo. Though the two-room apartments are owned by individual investors, an excellent management supervises the 42 apartments and provides security and maid service. The living room is extremely classy, though the bedroom is small. A balcony provides additional space. Complimentary breakfast is served in the coffee shop, as well as light meals and snacks. There is also a pool, gym, and sauna. A full set of kitchen utensils is available on request. Other services include:

110 volts, central air conditioning, and convention room. Children up to 12 stay free. *Expensive. All cards.*

## Trianon Hotel

*Alameda Casa Branca, 363 (Jardins);* ☎ *(11) 283-0066, fax (11) 283-0181.*

Businessmen wanting a good deal can find one in this four-star just a few blocks from the commercial hub on Avenida Paulista, including the Modern Art Museum, theaters, and shopping malls. Nearby is also the Trianon Park, famed for its greenery.

Apartments are clean, with furniture reminiscent of the 60s, though not luxurious. There's also a swimming pool, solarium, and panoramic bar. The dining room/breakfast room is small but charming. *Moderate. All cards.*

## Three-Star Hotels

## Cambridge

*Av. 9 de Julho, 216;* ☎ *(11) 239-0399.*

One of the most traditional hotels in the city, this three-star even boasts a quiet charm, with a bar that actually attracts some VIPs. Apartments are air conditioned, come with TV, radio, fridge; restaurant on premises. *114 apts. Moderate. All cards.*

## Excelsior Hotel

*Avenida Ipiranga, 770;* ☎ *(11) 222-7377; fax 222-8369.*

A complex of 180 simple apartments with phone, air conditioning, and TV. There's also a coffee shop, bar, and barbershop. *180 apts. Moderate. All cards.*

## Carillon Plaza

*Rua Bela Cintra, 652;* ☎ *(11) 257-9233.*

Small but inviting, this hotel is a good choice for reasonable rates. The air-conditioned rooms come with phone, TV, fridge, and radio. Pool and parking available. *Moderate. All cards.*

## Fuji Palace

*Largo da Pólvora, 120 (Liberdade);* ☎ *(11) 278-7466; fax 279-9041.*

This adequate hotel is in the Japanese district, where you can enjoy the streetside atmosphere and excellent cuisine. Rooms include mini-bar, TV, phone, and air conditioning. *77 apts. Moderate. No cards.*

## Two-Star Hotels

## Esplanada Hotel

*Largo do Arouche, 414;* ☎ *(11) 220-5711.*

Modest but clean apartments located downtown with mini-bar, air conditioning, and TV. *48 apts. Inexpensive. No cards.*

## Regência

*Avenida São João, 1523;* ☎ *(11) 220-9611.*

As simple as they come without getting seedy. Rooms have phone, radio, TV, and mini-bar. *49 apts. Inexpensive. No cards.*

# Where To Eat

São Paulo is the culinary capital of South America. Eating well is the way *Paulistanos* like to spend their hard-earned paychecks, and they do it in fabulous surroundings; this is a town where the bathrooms of some five-star restaurants are as beautiful as the dining rooms. Quality is the rage here, and there's an endless list of options: from Scandinavian buffets to wienerschnitzel to the tiniest portions of nouvelle cuisine, with every ethnic group represented. Like clothes and music, restaurants in São Paulo are subject to the cruel winds of trendiness (*Paulistanos* are known to be incredibly fickle), but the restaurants I've listed here tend to make the best lists every year. Dinner service starts no earlier than 8 p.m., but restaurants don't reach their peak service till after 11 p.m. Dress can be surprisingly casual, although the only night businessmen don't need to wear a tie is Sat. (You must, however, always wear one at the Jockey Club and at the restaurant Cuisine du Soleil at the Maksoud Plaza.) Restaurant rows include **Rua Haddock Lobo** and **Rua 13 de Maio** in the Italian district. Arabian restaurants are located along Rua 25 de Março. See page 26 for price chart.

> **UP CLOSE TIP:** *Stiff fines are imposed on restaurants and bars in São Paulo allowing clientele to smoke. Smokers can also receive a fine. However, many restaurants offer verandas for those in need of a puff. Do ask before you light up.*

## Brazilian

### Abril em Portugal

*Rua Caio Prado, 47 (Consolação);* ☎ *256-5160. 8 p.m.-last client, closed Sun.*

Portugal in April (as the name says) is what this restaurant recreates – from the Portuguese-inspired panels and ceramic tiles to the Iberian cuisine. Add strolling guitarists and some of the best *fado* singers in the city. *Moderate. No cards.*

### Bacalhau do Rei

*Avenida Moaci, 279 (Moema);* ☎ *533-4318. Daily 11 a.m.-midnight, Sun. 11 a.m.-5 p.m., closed Mon.*

Near the Central Market, this is the leading eatery for Portuguese-style codfish. Stained-glass windows from the 1930s adorn the walls. *Moderate. D, MC.*

## Bargaço

*Rua Oscar Freire, 1189 (Jardim Paulista);* ☎ *835-5058. Mon.-Fri., noon-3 p.m.,*
*7 p.m.-midnight (Fri. until dawn); Sat. noon-4 p.m., 7 p.m.-2 a.m.;*
*Sun. noon-11 p.m.*

Bahian cuisine from the city of Salvador, and the famed restaurant of the
same name, featuring seafood like *bobo de camarão* (shrimp in a thick sauce).
*Moderate. All cards.*

## Bolinha

*Av. Cidade Jardim, 53 (Jardim Europa);* ☎ *852-9526. Daily 11 a.m.-1 a.m.*

Best *feijoada* in São Paulo in a modest environs. *Expensive. All cards.*

## Dona Lucinha

*Av. dos Chibards, 399 (Moema);* ☎ *549-2050. Mon.-Fri. noon-3 p.m.,*
*8 p.m.-midnight. Sat. 4:30 p.m.-midnight. Sun. till 5 p.m.*

Typical cuisine from the state of Minas Gerais by one of its foremost chefs,
served buffet-style. The cuisine is heavy on the digestive tract, but worth
the trouble. *All cards. Moderate.*

## O Profeta

*Rua dos Aicás, 40 (Indianópolis);* ☎ *549-5311. Daily noon-1 a.m.*

Typical Brazilian food with a *Mineiro* swing – that heavy but delicious fare
from the state of Minas Gerais. The waiters dress as monks, hence the name
The Prophet, but live music cuts through any signs of encroaching piety.
*Moderate. All cards.*

## Star City

*Rua Frederico Abranches, 453 (Santa Cecília);* ☎ *220-2044.*
*Daily 11 a.m.-11 p.m., Sat. until 6 p.m., closed Sun.*

Those looking for "real" Brazilian food should try this ancient São Paulo
address known for its honest *feijoada* served buffet-style. Lighter appetites
can go for the special stuffed trout called *truta empanada. Moderate.*

## Tambaqui Grill

*Rua Santo Amaro, 15 ( downtown);* ☎ *37-8745. 10 a.m.-9 p.m., Sun. until 5 p.m.*

Tasty Amazonian fish called *tambaqui* is the hurrah here, grilled or cooked
stew-like. Other excellent dishes from the Northeast are *pato no tucupi*
(duck) and *tacacá*, made with dried shrimps. Don't miss the unique
Amazonian juices made from *cupuaçu* and *açai. Moderate.*

## Churrascaria

### Baby Beef Paes Mendonça

*Avenida Nações Unidas, 16741 (Morumbí);* ☎ *843-7829.*
*Daily 6:30 p.m.-1 a.m.; weekends 11:45 a.m.-2 a.m.*

Always a reliable, and sometimes excellent steakhouse situated near the Morumbí Shopping Center, next to Carrefour, a gargantuan-sized supermarket where the clerks wear rollerskates and very short skirts. *Moderate. All cards.*

### Esplanada Grill

*Rua Haddock Lobo, 1682 (Cerqueira César);* ☎ *881-3199.*
*Daily, noon-3:30 p.m., 7 p.m.-1:30 a.m.*

The young, hip, and restless attend this steakery right next to the classier restaurant Fasano. That means who's who at the next table is more important than what's on your plate. *Moderate. MC, D.*

### The Place

*Rua Haddock Lobo, 1550 (Cerqueira César);* ☎ *282-5800.*
*Daily, 11:30 a.m.-1:30 a.m.*

The place you must visit at least three times: once for drinks, once for dinner and once for dessert. Start with complimentary hors d'oeuvres in the plush, carriagehouse bar – a tiny feast of mini-pizzas, nuts, and croquettes. Dinners (including a huge self-serve salad buffet) are prepared tableside; don't miss the house rice, sautéed with onions, crispy sliced potatoes, and oven-fried eggs. Fish like the *truta à jardineira* (trout) is favorably seasoned, but the grilled beefs are also superb, and the carpaccio with cheese strips, onions, and toast is out of this world. Desserts, such as papaya and chocolate mousses, are worth their own trip. Reservations recommended. *Expensive. All cards.*

## Fast Food

### America

*Rua Alameda Santos 957;* ☎ *289-7900. Noon-2 a.m.*

A natural fast-food joint, small and inexpensive, frequented by businessmen on fast lunches. Two blocks from the Maksoud Plaza (there's also one in Morumbi Shopping Center). Good hamburgers, salads, and natural foods. *Inexpensive.*

# French

### Roanne

*Rua Henrique Martins, 631 (Jardim. Paulista);* ☎ *887-4516. 7:30 p.m.-1:30 a.m. Closed Sun.*

The Dijon chef Emmanoel Bassoleil, who learned his trade from Troisgros in Roanne, France, has won the hearts of *Paulistanos* for such unusual pairings as ravioli with duck and dried mushrooms, and shrimp with shitake mushrooms cooked oriental-style. In 1994, he was named São Paulo's chef of the year, not an easy appellation to garner in a city of superb international chefs. *Expensive. AE, MC.*

### La Casserole

*Largo do Arouche, 346;* ☎ *220-6283. Noon-3 p.m., 7 p.m.-midnight, Sat. till 1 a.m.*

French peasant cooking as cozy as a warm iron pot. Walnut-carved chandeliers and blowups of Notre Dame enhance the continental ambiance of this very old, very established restaurant, once featured in *Gourmet* magazine. *Inexpensive-moderate. All cards.*

### Le Bistingo

*Al. Franca, 580 (Cerqueira César),* ☎ *289-3010. Tues.-Fri. noon-3 p.m., 7-12 p.m.; Sat. 7 p.m.-1 a.m.; Sun. noon-4 p.m., 7 p.m.-11 p.m.; closed Mon.*

One of the city's best French restaurants, Bistingo is patterned after the original in Paris – candlelit elegance and private banquettes. Specialties are fish, particularly poached haddock with roquefort, and grilled shrimp with apples. Lunch is usually packed, and you'll also need a reservation on weekends, when the wait can be at least a half-hour. *Expensive. No cards.*

### Chamonix

*Rua Pamplona, 1446 (Jardim Paulista);* ☎ *884-7664. 7 p.m.-2 a.m., closed Sun.*

One of the most romantic and charming locales in the city for *fondue deverão*, a delicious mix of seafood with five different kinds of sauces. *Moderate. All cards.*

# German

### Arnold's Naschbar

*Rua Pereira Leite, 98;* ☎ *256-5648. Mon.-Sat. 6 p.m.-midnight; closed Sun.*

One of the best German eateries in the city, with a romantic ambiance and generous portions of trout, *picanha,* and stuffed chicken breasts. *Moderate. No cards.*

# International

## Ouro Velho Jardins

*Al. Jaú, 1617 (Cerqueira César);* ☎ *881-0271. Daily noon-3 p.m., 7 p.m.-midnight.*

For the last 27 years, Senhor Bené and his family have been dedicated to quality at this elegant French-style bistro (the name means "Old Gold"). The menu is small but finely executed, with the house Chateaubriand a clear winner. *Feijoada* is served on Sat. The flurry of waiters around each table makes you feel as though you're at a private party, and the clientele is always upper-crust. *Expensive. All cards.*

## Moraes

*Praça Júlio de Mesquita, 175;* ☎ *221-8066. Daily 11 a.m.-2 a.m.*

A favorite dive of chef Massimo Ferrari, who raves about the fabulous steak grilled in garlic and oil. You may have to shoo away the pimps and prostitutes, but that's part of the charm. *Inexpensive. MC, D.*

# Italian

## Ca' D'Oro

*(Grande Hotel Ca' D'Oro) Rua Augusta, 129;* ☎ *256-8011. Daily noon-2:30 p.m., 7:30 p.m.-1 a.m.; Sun. noon-3 p.m.*

The John Houseman of restaurants: where the waiters are humorless, but the service is faultless and the northern Italian cuisine served under antique chandeliers and favored by heads of state is exceptional. Pasta melted with four cheeses is a sensual explosion, as is the traditional *casconcelli bergamasca*, sweet-and-sour ravioli plumped with various meats, raisins, and a splash of Amaretto. The best dessert is the *torroncina*, ice cream loaded with peanuts and caramel. Reservations recommended. *Very expensive. All cards.*

## Cantina Balilla

*Rua do Gasômetro, 332 (Brás);* ☎ *228-8282. Daily 11 a.m.-2 a.m.*

Small, old-fashioned, and humble with superb Italian food at moderate prices. Live music. *Moderate. All cards.*

## Fasano

*Rua Haddock Lobo, 1644 (Cerqueira César);* ☎ *852-4000.*
*Daily noon-3 p.m., 7:30 p.m.-1 a.m., Sun. noon-6 p.m.*

The late Italian-born Victor Fasano served Eisenhower and Dietrich. Forty years later in 1991, his grandchildren revived his top-class eatery in a spectacularly remodeled mansion. Service is something from an MGM movie: waiters love to remove silver covers with a musical flourish. Unfortunately, the portions, though beautifully arranged, are so small they are almost laughable. Still, the *tortelloni di zucca* is impressive, as is the tangy passion fruit mousse with a blueberry sauce. Ask to tour the wine cellar, one of the best in the city. No ties necessary, but the ambiance is classy. Reserve. *Very expensive. All cards.*

## Mássimo

*Al. Santos, 1826 (Cerqueira César);* ☎ *284-0311. Daily 11:30 a.m.-3 p.m., 7:30 a.m.-midnight.*

If Mássimo were the only reason to come to São Paulo, it would be enough. Mássimo Ferrari is considered by any knowledgeable gourmet as the city's finest chef/owner, and everything about his top-class eatery bespeaks his unforgettable personality – passionate, tender, yet full of great humor. An Italian-Brazilian, Mássimo learned to cook in his mother's kitchen when he was nine; today, his repertoire of over 800 dishes has brought him a world-class rep. If he has any philosophy, it is to mine the simplicity of food by exploiting its natural sensuality. And even the decor is sensuous, from the enormous arrangements of poinsettias and luxurious table settings to the Versailles-like bathrooms. The feast Mássimo cooked me was a dream: velvety cream-filled *gnocchis*, perfectly grilled goatlegs, and *picanha*, exquisitely baked trout with shrimp sauce, finely herbed wild rice and ratatouille – every dish, accompanied by a specially picked wine, was a wonder of subtle flavors and spices. The couvert alone – plates of freshly baked croissants, breads, sweet butters, and pâté – was an embarrassment of riches. Only a small percentage of Brazilians can afford the stiff prices, but no traveling gourmet should pass up the opportunity to dine here or just come for drinks and dessert. The Brazilian guitarist in the plush bar is superb. The night isn't over, however, until Mássimo bounds out of the kitchen, pulls up his suspenders, and shrugs, "Simple, very simple." *Very expensive. Credit cards not usually accepted.*

## Mezzaluna

*Rua Bela Cintra, 2231 (Jardim Paulista);* ☎ *881-8633. Noon-3:30 p.m., 7 p.m.-2 a.m.*
Live music and good Italian food at affordable prices. *Moderate. No cards.*

## Famiglia Mancini

*Rua Avanhandava, 81;* ☎ *256-4320.*
A typical boisterous Italian cantina that's garnered a great name for *gnocchi bolonesa.* Appetizers are tasty but can wrack up a bill. Huge lines on the weekends. *Moderate. All cards.*

## Japanese

The best Japanese restaurants with the most reasonable prices are located on **Rua Tomás Gonzaga** in Liberdade, the Japanese district. Service is friendly, if inscrutable; you'll be lucky to find waiters who speak Portuguese, let alone English. The street action in Liberdade alone is worth the trek, especially at night, when Japanese lanterns illuminate the sidewalks.

## Suntory

*Al. Campinas, 600 (Cerqueira César);* ☎ *283-2455. Noon-2:15 p.m.,*
*7 p.m.-11:45 p.m., Sat. 7 p.m.-12:45 a.m., closed Sun.*

Considered the best Japanese restaurant in São Paulo, with superior sushi
and sashimi, and even *shabu shabu*, a type of Japanese fondue. *Very*
*expensive. All cards.*

## Gombe

*Rua Tomás Gonzaga, 22A (Liberdade);* ☎ *279-8499.*
*Daily 11:30 a.m.-2 p.m., 6 p.m.-midnight, closed Sun.*

The menu is in Japanese, but the waiters understand "sushi," "sashimi" and
"yakitori" in any accent. Look for the rustic Japanese country design next
to the Casa Ono bookstore. *Moderate. All cards.*

## Mariko (Caesar Park Hotel)

*Rua Augusta, 1508;* ☎ *285-6622.*

Superlative cuisine at top-dollar prices in one of the most elegant hotels in
the city. The restaurant itself is more casual. *Expensive. All cards.*

## Hidetaka Kanazawa

*Rua Galvão Bueno, 378;* ☎ *270-1801.*

Not a restaurant, but a takeout counter in the Japanese district of Liberdade,
selling all kinds of Japanese sweets and confections. *Inexpensive. No cards.*

# Jewish

## Shoshi Deli Show

*Rua Correia de Melo, 206 (Bom Retiro);* ☎ *228-4774. Daily 9 a.m.-6 p.m.,*
*Sat. till 3:30 p.m., closed Sun.*

An Israeli couple supervises the Rumanian Jewish kitchen here, with such
specialties as *ikra* (pasta with eggs and fish). Fresh salads offer lighter fare.
*Inexpensive. No cards.*

## Z Deli

*Al. Santos, 1518 (Cerqueira César);* ☎ *285-6509.*
*Daily 7 a.m.-7 p.m., Sat. 6 p.m.-midnight, closed Sun.*

Kosher food and deli-style goodies, herring with *creme de leite*, and quiches
stuffed with cheese, salmon, mushrooms, and leeks. *Inexpensive. No cards.*

## Cecília

*Rua Correia de Melo, 1; dos Bandeirantes, 112 (Bom Retiro);* ☎ *228-9174.*
*Daily 11:30 a.m.-3:30 p.m., closed Mon.*

Cecília had to move after seven years to accommodate the growing bevy of
fans who clamor for her gefilte fish, kreplach, and marinated herring with
homemade mayonnaise and onions. Delicious desserts include fruit

compotes and ricotta and apple tarts. The surrounding neighborhood is known for its wholesale houses. *Moderate. All cards.*

## Portuguese

### Antiquarius

*Al. Lorena, 1884 (Cerqueira César);* ☎ *282-3015. Noon-3 p.m., 7 p.m.-1 a.m., weekends and holidays noon-1 a.m., closed Mon.*

The well-wrought son of the famous restaurant in Rio – the *Paulistano* version here offers equally outstanding delicacies from Portugal. The couvert is excellent, as are the desserts. The environs are luxurious. *Expensive. All cards.*

### Marquês de Marialva

*Rua Haddock Lobo 1583 (Jardim Paulista);* ☎ *852-1805. Daily noon-3 p.m., 7 p.m.-1 a.m.; Fri. and Sat. until 1:30 a.m. Sat. and Sun. lunch until 4:30 p.m.; Sun., dinner until midnight. Closed Mon.*

Elegant, with excellent service, this is one of the most authentic Portuguese kitchens in the city. Try the imported grains from Portugal, or the beans with three types of pork sausage. Fish and shrimp dishes are also notable. *Expensive. All cards.*

## Pizza

### La Brasserie

*(Maksoud Plaza Hotel) Al. Campinas, 150;* ☎ *251-2233.*

A late-night hangout open around the clock, with gourmet pizzas (try the one with escargot). *Moderate. All cards.*

### Cristal

*Rua Arthur Ramos, 551;* ☎ *211-0828. Daily 7 p.m.-1:30 a.m.; Fri. and Sat. till 2 a.m.*

The pizzeria most frequented by famous people, who adore the fine crusts and salad bar. You can also order grilled meats. *Moderate. No cards.*

### Michelluccio

*Rua da Consolação, 2396;* ☎ *256-5677 and Avenida Pompéia, 600. Daily 5 p.m.-1 a.m.; Fri., Sat. and Sun. until 3 a.m.*

An unabashed favorite in the city for its thick-crusted pizzas and creative toppings. *Inexpensive. All cards.*

## Panoramic Views

### Terraço Itália

*Ave. Ipiranga, 344 (Edifício Itália, across from the Hilton, 41st and 42nd floors);*
☎ *257-6566. Daily noon-2 a.m., dinner at 8:30 p.m., dancing at 9:30 p.m.*

São Paulo from the 41st floor is the place where rich *Paulistanos* drag out-of-towners whom they want to impress. The view is awesome; unfortunately, the international cuisine is somewhat lackluster. Better to nurse a cocktail in the wonderful leather-and-wood bar, or boogie on the dance floor to a live band. If you do choose to eat, you'll find the waiters impeccable, and your dinner can be prepared by the time you are seated. Filet mignon comes with herbs and Madeira sauce; the trout with a serviceable cream sauce. I was here in a brilliant rain-and-lightning storm, which, despite not one square inch of view, was still wildly exciting. Reserve. *Very expensive. All cards.*

## Sandwiches

### La Cave

*Rua Clodomiro Amazonas, 77 (Itaim Bibi);* ☎ *829-0859.*
*Daily 10 a.m.-midnight, closed Sun.*

Excellent for sandwiches, with 15 types of rolls, 12 kinds of Italian breads, and a cornucopia of fillings. Try the La Cave: ham, buffalo cheese, and artichoke hearts on a baguette. *Inexpensive. No cards.*

## Scandinavian

### Viking

*(Maksoud Plaza Hotel) Al. Campinas, 150 (Bela Vista);* ☎ *253-4411. Weekdays, noon-2:30 p.m., 7 p.m.-midnight; Sat. 7 p.m.-1 a.m.; closed Sun.*

This fabulous Scandinavian buffet (for lunch only) offers smoked salmon, cold salads, liver pâté, and steak tartare. *Very expensive. All cards.*

## Vegetarian

### Salad's

*Avenida Brig. Faria Lima, 1191 (Shopping Center Iguatemí);* ☎ *210-2277. Mon.-Fri. noon-3:30 p.m., 7 p.m.-10:30 p.m.; Sat. and Sun. noon-5:30 p.m.*

Flowered wallpaper, wicker dividers, and faux blue skies make a light and airy ambiance for chic salad eaters. A different buffet of 12 salads is offered daily – Weds. is devoted to fish salads. Stunning desserts come in big tulip glasses: the *torta de Belmont*, topped with whipped cream and fudge sauce, is superb; the coconut ice cream is the best in the city. On Sats. they are packed with shoppers from Iguatemí Mall next door, so make a reservation. *Expensive. No cards.*

### Cheiro Verde

*Rua Peixoto Gomide, 1413 (Cerqueira César); ☎ 289-6853.*
*Daily noon-3 p.m., 7 p.m.-11 p.m. (later on Sat.).*

You'll love the natural wood tables in this tiny house. Excellent is the Primavera, a brown-rice casserole with castanhas, raisins, and cooked vegetables. A bulletin board with holistic and spiritually oriented activities adorns the front hallway. *Moderate. No cards.*

### Associação Macrobiótica

*Rua Bela Cintra, 1235 (Cerqueira César); ☎ 282-8831.*
*Daily, 11 a.m.-2:30 p.m., 5:30 p.m.-7:45 p.m., closed Sat. and Sun.*

A fixed menu of brown rice, cereals, vegetables, and fish. *Moderate. No cards.*

### Sattva

*Rua da Consolação, 3140 (Cerqueira César); ☎ 883-6237.*
*Mon.-Fri. noon-3:30 p.m., Sat. noon-4 p.m., 7 -9 p.m.*

Natural food menu with a *prato o dia* (plate of the day) accompanied by juice and dessert for a fixed price. Good value. *Inexpensive. No cards.*

## Teahouses

### As Noviças

*Avenida Cotovia, 205 (Moema); ☎ 533-0692. Daily 3 p.m.-11 p.m.*

Take tea in this convent-styled teahouse with piped-in Gregorian chants and handsome waiters dressed like friars. A fixed-price meal includes 63 kinds of delicacies, plus excellent hot chocolate, tea, or *café com leite*. *Moderate. All cards.*

## Twenty-four Hours

### Café Brasserie Belavista

*Alameda Campinas, 150; ☎ 251-2233.*

A great place to collapse, this café in the gorgeous Maksoud Plaza Hotel is sometimes busier at 4 a.m. than it is all day. You'll find fast-cooked food and pizzas, as well as an excellent tea served daily from 3-6 p.m. *Moderate. All cards.*

### Fran's Café

*Avenida Ipiranga, 354, Edifício Itália.*

This little bar serves coffee, cakes, and cookies day or night. *Inexpensive. No cards.*

# Nightlife

## Bars With Live Music/Jazz Clubs

### Tom Brazil

*Rua das Olimpiades, 56;* ☎ *820-2326.*

A new showplace for the best of *música popular brasileiro* (MPB). Drinks and food are served before, during, and after the show.

### Café Sociate

*Rua Treze de Maio, 46 (Bela Vista);* ☎ *259-6562. Daily 6 p.m.-2 a.m. or last client.*

An elegant bar on the noisiest corner of the neighborhood of Bela Vista offers a delectable daily array of music, from MPB to samba to Sat. night's *chorinhos* and *forrós*. *All cards.*

### Clyde's

*Rua da Mata, 70 (Itaim Bibi);* ☎ *883-0300. Daily 6 p.m.-last client, starts at 10 p.m. on Sat.*

Excellent live music at this club known as a place for elegant, but daring singles – as per the favored drink *divida externa* (tequila, rum, vodka, gin, curaçao, Triple Sec, and Coke). *All cards.*

### Café Piu-Piu

*Rua Treze de Maio, 134 (Bela Vista);* ☎ *250-8066. Tues.-Sun. 10 a.m.-4 p.m.*

A comfortable, enticing café to hear all kinds of music. Tues. features jazz and *bossa*, Weds. reggae, Thurs. blues, and Fri. and Sat. an eclectic band that flows freely from rock to classical. *Inexpensive. No cards.*

### Café Teatro Opus 2004

*Rua Pamplona, 1187;* ☎ *884-9086. Daily 8 p.m.-last client, closed Sun., Mon. and Weds.*

One of the best clubs for all kinds of music. Tues. is blues night, Thurs. jazz, Fri. and Sat. are covered by excellent house bands. Shows start at 10 p.m. *Inexpensive. All cards.*

### Chariot

*(Caesar Park Hotel) Rua Augusta, 1508;* ☎ *285-6622. Daily 11:30 a.m.-2 a.m.*

The best hotel bar in São Paulo – elegant, calm, with the feel of a plush English pub. Mon.-Sat. 8 p.m.-midnight, a fine local pianist plays classical American music, jazz and MPB. *Moderate. All cards.*

## Nightclubs

Nightclub hopping in São Paulo can be as easy as strolling down Rua Franz Schubert. During the day this tiny street doesn't look like much, but at night, it transforms into Tin Party Alley, with six major nightclubs. Like the party babes of Rio, *Paulistanos* start living it up late and don't go home until dawn (the difference is, *Paulistanos* get up in the morning!). The dress code aims towards the provocative; for women, short skirts are de rigueur. One tip: some clubs require loads of attitude, others just a penchant for down-home fun.

## Gallery

*Rua Haddock Lobo, 1626;* ☎ *881-8833. Tues.-Sat. 8 p.m.-2 a.m.*

The ultimate in snobbery, with a reception desk manned by David Bowie-like androids. The restaurant/nightclub belongs to Victor Olivia and the decorator Uza da Pau, who has pitted real Italian sculptures against Aubusson tapestries and baroque candelabras. Clients of five-star hotels receive special passes to grace the hallowed halls. Live jazz in the lush piano bar. Best to go on Tues. and Weds. when the disco is free and the piano bar drops its minimum. A block away is **The Place** restaurant. *Very expensive. All cards.*

## Cotton Club

*Rua Franz Schubert, 59;* ☎ *814-0515. Tues.-Sat. 9:30 p.m.-last client, peaks after 11:30 p.m.*

With rustic wood pews downstairs and a flashdance disco upstairs, this cavern-like club caters to the 25-35 crowd and offers the best blues, jazz, and rock in the city. Three different types of bands play nightly. Tues. night's Chippendale-type striptease for women only attracts the elite of São Paulo. Cover and drink minimum. *Moderate. All cards.*

## Stardust

*Rua Franz Schubert, 135;* ☎ *210-5283. Daily 9:30 p.m.-4 a.m.*

Some tourists might find this dinner and dancing club corny, but owner Alan Gordon's *joie de vivre* can't be faulted. Russian-Jewish by way of Shanghai, Gordon fronts an indefatigable New Orleans-style band and shmoozes with customers between sets. *Moderate. All cards.*

## Tramp

*Rua Franz Schubert, 159;* ☎ *210-9093. Daily 8 p.m.-last client.*

Since Brazilians go to clubs as prelude to more intimate doings, this elite private club for the 25-40 set rates as perfect foreplay. Prospective members are scrutinized, but tourists, if they call ahead, are welcome inside for a drink. The piano bar is pink, mauve, and cushy; the dance floor hot. *Moderate. All cards.*

## Crowne Plaza Theatre

*Crowne Plaza Hotel, Rua Frei Caneca, 1360 (Cerqueira César);* ☎ *284-1144. Daily midnight-4 a.m.*

Fri. night jam sessions are held here in the hotel's new cultural center, where the week's featured musicians invite their friends for a *canja* (the word actually means chicken soup, but refers to the time when musicians played just for their soup). Cover is $10. Reserve. *Moderate. All cards.*

## Resume da Opera

*Av. Rebouças, 3970;* ☎ *211-2411. Tues.-Fri., 10 p.m.-last client, Sat. 4 p.m.-9 p.m., 10-last client, Sun. 5 p.m.-10 p.m.*

The brainchild of Brazilian nightclub wizard Ricardo Amaral, famous in Rio for the club of the same name. Sure to meet the rich, famous, and terminally stuck-up.

## Balafon

*Rua Sergipe, 160 (Higienópolis);* ☎ *259-8341. 10:30 p.m.-last client, Sun.6 p.m.-midnight.*

The most exotic of world music reigns in this new club for dancing. Thurs. nights feature a traditional *capoeira* show.

## Vektra

*Rua Martiniano de Carvalho, 256/262 (Bela Vista);* ☎ *284-5870.*

Ensconced in a historical house now pronounced a patrimony, this dance club gives way to jungle, underground, 60s, and *axé* music, that boisterous samba-reggae sounds from Bahia. Thurs. women get in free and everyone drinks beer on the house. Fri. and Sun. are reggae nights.

# Samba Shows

## Palladium

*(Shopping Center Eldorado, 3rd fl.) Avenida Rebouças, 3970;* ☎ *814-9461.*

Carnaval-based extravaganzas featuring dancing fast-moving sambas. *Moderate. All cards.*

## Plataforma 1

*Avenida Paulista, 412 (Cerqueira César);* ☎ *289-5238.*

*Mulatas* in string bikinis, *capoeira* artists, folkloric music, and cheeky masters of ceremonies create this samba extravaganza complete with elaborate Carnaval costumes. *Moderate. All cards.*

## Carioca Club

*Rua Cardeal Arcoverde, 2899;* ☎ *212-3782.*

A barn-like spot in the Pinheiros district serving those who want to pig out on samba. Local groups play Tues.-Thurs. Fri. and Sat. samba schools from Rio preset shows at 11 p.m. with a house band playing before that for dancing.

## O Guarani

*Av. João Carlos da Silva Borges, 80-A; ☎ 524-7428. Tues.-Sat., open at 6 p.m., shows on Thurs., Fri., and Sat.*

To get a real whiff of Latin American culture, reserve a seat at this buffet of local and international foods, with a folklore show that includes drums, fire, and the primitive weapon called *boleadeira*.

# Gay São Paulo

Gays tend to frequent the sauna in the Hilton. Other gay bars and shows include:

## Clube Massivo

*Al. Itú (Jardins); ☎ 883-7505.*

Best to go on Thurs.

## Rave

*Rua Bela Cintra, 1900; ☎ 883-2133. Daily, opening around 11:30p.m.*

Club for dancing with restaurant and snack bar in a good neighborhood of Jardims. Strip shows nightly.

## Gents' Theater House

*Av. Ibirapueraa, 1911; ☎ 572-8227. 11:30 p.m.-last client.*

Older clientele frequent this club, which has a restaurant and snack bar. Sun. is the night to go.

## Zoe

*Rua Oscar Freire, 1225 (Jardins); ☎ 852-8596.*

Modern club with three different bars.

# Shopping

Despite the fact that *Paulistanos* who can afford it prefer to fly to New York to shop (since it is now cheaper than shopping in Brazil!), there are numerous options in São Paulo. The major shopping streets include: **Rua Augusta** (once the most chic area of town, now lined with small high-class boutiques); stores on the side streets of **Rua Oscar Freire, Europa, Alameda Lorena,** and **Doutor Melo Alves); Avenida Cidade Jardim** (South Zone); **Rua João Cachoeira** (cheap goods, near the end of Ave. 9 de Julho); **Rua 25 de Março** (downtown, famous for its wholesale trade); **Rua Joli** in Bras (fabrics); and **Rua Silveira Martina** (perfumes and cosmetics). **Rua Maracatins** is full of stores and boutiques selling clothes and shoes at wholesale prices. The best buys are leather goods. In a chic district of the South Zone, the street **Alameda Gabriela** has transformed itself into the most modern interior design showcase in Brazil. Here, all styles of antiques, oriental carpets, porcelain, and wall furnishings can be found. The most complete shopping area for electronics is on **Rua Santa Ifigência** in the central zone district of Luz.

## Native Handicrafts

### Artindia

*Rua Augusta, 1371, #119 (Cerqueira César);* ☎ *883-2102.*

Native indigenous crafts made out of feathers, wood, and ceramics.

### Casa do Amazonas

*Avenida São Luis, 187, store 14;* ☎ *258-9727.*

A large variety of authentic indigenous art, specializing in *arte plumária* – extravagant headdresses and sculptures made out of exotic bird feathers.

### SUTACO

*Av. Duduque de Caxias (downtown);* ☎ *222-5777.*

This cooperative of artisans promotes the handicrafts of the state of São Paulo. A permanent exhibit is on display at their store.

### Galeria de Arte Brasileira

*Rua Al. Lorna, 2163;* ☎ *853-8769.*

A one-stop souvenir store selling Bahian and *candomblé* dolls, Indian baskets, *carajá* (fertility dolls), hand-carved wooden necklaces, T-shirts, native lace crafts, and *balangandãs* (traditional silver bracelets worn by slaves).

## Stones

### Park-Pedras

*Rua Augusta, 1523;* ☎ *288-0819.*

Large selection of precious and semi-precious stones from the mines of Minas, with an adjoining factory that makes jewelry.

## Street Fairs

### Hippie Fair (Arte e Artesanato)

*Praça da República. Sun. 8 a.m.-1 p.m.*

A grand open-air bazaar of sweets, music, and handmade crafts.

### Oriental Fair (Artesanato Oriental)

*Praça da Liberdade. Sun. 8 a.m.-6 p.m.*

Oriental handicrafts fair held around the entrance to the subway station.

## MASP Antique Fair

*Avenida Paulista, 1578. Sun. 9 a.m.-5 p.m.*

The antique fair of the Modern Museum of Art is held in the open area beneath the museum.

## Flower Market

*Praça Charles Miller. Sun.*

A wonderful profusion of exotic and common flowers.

## Embu

*Sun. 9 a.m.-6 p.m. Located 27 km. from the city.*

This colonial town has been transformed into an arts and crafts center – a kind of artistic Woodstock. Sun. features a renowned fair. Take bus #056 from the Conceição metro station or #179-S from the Tietê *rodoviária;* the trip takes about an hour one way.

# In Liberdade

## Minikimono

*Rua Galvão Bueno, 22 (Liberdade);* ☎ *278-0322.*

Liberdade is filled with antique and jewelry stores. This is one of the better clothes stores, with silk robes and complete Ninja outfits for kids.

# Shopping Malls

## Shopping Center Iguatemi

*Avenida Brigadeiro Faria Lima, 1191;* ☎ *210-1333.*

This is considered the best shopping mall in town and is a hangout for teens on the weekends. There are five cinemas, a bank, and a post office. At **Lojas Americanas** you can find Woolworth's-type items. Also try **Bruno Minelli** (men's), **Hi-Fi** (music), **Petistil** (stylish children's wear), **Joge** (lingerie), **Victor Hugo** (leather), **Bicho da Seda** (chic linen suits), **Boat** (punk), **Sidewalk** (teen's), **Maria Bonita** (best for chic women's clothes), and **Rose Benedetti** (internationally known for costume jewelry). The third floor is a food pavilion with pizzas, hot dogs, burgers, ice cream, and exquisite cakes.

## Shopping Center Morumbi

*Avenida Roque Petroni Jr., 1089;* ☎ *533-2444.*

One of the most famed malls in Brazil, with an ice-skating rink, exotic aquarium, video game room, bowling, gourmet foods center, and even a lost-and-found center for kids. The most stylish stores in Brazil have branches here.

# Hands-On São Paulo

## Climate

From Dec. to Feb., temperatures can reach 90°F. Between June and Aug., cold waves can plummet as low as freezing, but only for a few days. Lots of rainfall is received between Jan. and Mar., when it's quite hot and humid. July days are beautiful.

## Communications

### Language

English is spoken at top travel agencies, all five-star hotels, better restaurants, at a few downtown shops, and in some shopping malls.

### Mail

The main office is at Av. São João, s/n(downtown); ☎ 831-5522. Hours: 8 a.m.-8 p.m. Other branches are at **Correio Central**, Praça do Correio; ☎ 831-5222; and **Correio Central**, Praça do Correio; ☎ 831-5222. There are branches throughout the city. **DHL (WorldWide Express)**, Rua Periquito, 236 (Indianópolis); ☎ 542-2722, delivers parcels and documents door-to-door from Brazil to 177 countries worldwide.

### Newspapers

The major newspapers are *O Estado de São Paulo* and *A Folha da Tarde*. Hotel newsstands usually sell international editions of *Time* and *Newsweek*, as well as the *International Herald Tribune*.

## Consulates

**American Consulate**
General Rua Padre João Manuel 933 . . . . . . . . . . .  ☎ 881-7917
**Canadian Consulate General**
Avenida Paulista 1106, 5th floor . . . . . . . . . . . . . .  ☎ 287-2122
**British Consulate General**
Avenida Paulista 1938, 7th floor . . . . . . . . . . . . . .  ☎ 287-7722

## Emergencies

### Important Telephone Numbers

**Police** . . . . . . . . . . . . . . . . . . . . . . . . . . . . . . . . . . . .  ☎ 190
**Special police for foreign visitors** . . . . . . . . . . . .  ☎ 251-1733
**Drugstores on duty** . . . . . . . . . . . . . . . . . . . . . . . . .  ☎ 136

## Medical Emergencies

Medical attention in São Paulo should be the best in the country.

**Albert Einstein** (hospital)
Av. Albert Einstein 627 ..................... ☎ 845-1145
Emergencies answered by ambulance and helicopter.
**Beneficência Portuguesa**
Rua Maestro Cardim, 769 ................... ☎ 253-5022

## Pharmacies

**24-hour information line** ................... ☎ 136
**Droga Raia**
Rua Augusto, 2455 ........................ ☎ 881-0065
Av. São Luis, 39........................... ☎ 259-1531
**Droagaria SP**
Av. Paulista, 2103 ........................ ☎ 251-0206

## Money Exchange

Currency can be exchanged at the São Paulo International Airport (Guarulhos) and at banks throughout the city. Look for travel agencies marked *câmbio* along **Avenida São Luiz** (downtown), near the **Praça da República**, on **Avenida Paulista** (Jardins area), and in the **Iguatemí shopping center.**

Major hotels will exchange money and traveler's checks, but beware: the rate you will receive for the dollar at a hotel will probably be lower than the tourist dollar.

## Tourist Offices & Information

Ample information in English is available at tourist information booths located at **Praça da República, Teatro Municipal, Praça da Sé, Praça da Liberdade** (downtown), and the **Ibirapuera, Morumbí,** and **Iguatemí shopping malls**. For weekly events, shows, and trendy clubs, pick up a copy of *Veja São Paulo*, part of the weekly magazine *Veja*. The English publications *Where* and *São Paulo This Month* also give good tips and are available at most hotels.

**São Paulo Convention and Visitors Bureau**, Rua Alameda Campinas, 646, 5th floor; ☎ *289-9397*, offers a wealth of booklets, brochures, and maps. Make sure you ask for their publication, *The Best Restaurants in São Paulo*.

**Anhembi Turismo e Eventos da Cidade de São Paulo**, ☎ *267-2122;* fax *267-0191*, provides travel and leisure information via a 3,500 videotext system that can be found in booths strategically situated throughout the city. Anhembi, the official travel bureau of the city of São Paulo, responds to inquiries by phone.

**Tourist Support Agency**, Av. São Luis, 115 (downtown); ☎ *231-0044*, provides policemen who assist tourists in English, French and Spanish from 8 a.m.-8 p.m.

## Tourist Police

**DEATUR** (Special Police for Tourists), Av. São Luis, 115; ☎ *214-0209*, and at Anhembi Park, ☎ *267-0122*.

Tourist Police are on duty from 8 a.m.-8 p.m. **CEPOL** (the Civil Police), ☎ *227-2569*, or *147*, are also available to provide assistance at any hour to travelers.

**Tourist Support Agency**, Av. São Luis, 115 (downtown); ☎ *231-0044*, provides policemen who assist tourists in English, French and Spanish from 8 a.m.-8 p.m.

## Safety

Among the 500,000 foreigners living in São Paulo you'll be less conspicuous as a tourist than in Rio. Most *Paulistanos*, even if they don't speak English, will try to be helpful, though do take the common precautions of securing your wallet and purse and leaving your real jewelry at home. A team of 50 elite police speak English and have lessened the force of *trombadinhas* (kids who snatch purses). Areas to avoid: downtown, particularly at night.

## Air Transportation

---

### Airlines Serving São Paulo

| | |
|---|---|
| **Aerolinas Argentinas**...................... | ☎ 214-4233 |
| ........................................... | or 214-6022 |
| **American Airlines** ......................... | ☎ 214-4000 |
| **Air France**................................ | ☎ 288-6577 |
| **Canadian Airlines International** ............ | ☎ 259-9066 |
| **VASP**..................................... | ☎ 536-5055 |
| **Varig** ..................................... | ☎ 520-3922 |

---

### International Arrival

This is the main airport for domestic and international flights, variously called **Guarulhos** or **Cumbique**, located about 19 miles from downtown. All international flights arrive here. Check the weather report because the airport often closes due to inclement conditions. Top execs in a hurry usually take a helicopter shuttle to Congonhas airport (see below). Executive buses also depart about every 45 minutes, stopping at major hotels; a special one goes direct to Congonhas. Tickets are bought at the airport. (I have split taxis with strangers to good effect, though I have heard stories of riders getting ripped off.)

### Domestic Arrival

Called **Congonhas**, this domestic airport is in the southern region of the city. Airlines connect Congonhas to the downtown airports of Belo Horizonte, Curitiba and Rio de Janeiro. Regional airlines and charter companies also use this airport. Transportation to Guarulhos (see above) can be made by helicopter (best for avoiding traffic), executive bus or taxi.

**Varig-Cruzeiro/Vasp/Transbrasil,** ☎ *534-0216,* offer a joint operation of shuttle flights every 30 minutes on a first-come, first-served basis; it flies into Congonhas. Flights between Rio-São Paulo are also served by **Rio Sul,** ☎ *240-3044* and **TAM,** ☎ *577-7711.* If you need to switch to an international flight at Garulhos, or other flights in Brazil, a shuttle connects the two airports.

### From The Airport

**Taxis** from the international airport to the city run over $30; you might find someone to share a taxi with at the taxi stand, but be careful – I've heard sometimes it's a scam to steal your luggage (though nothing ever happened to me). Air-conditioned **buses**, available at the airport, stop at major four- and five-star hotels; they run about $6. Buy the ticket in the lobby after you depart from customs.

### Points Beyond São Paulo

Direct flights are available to other Brazilian cities from Guarulhos. Among others, these include: Manaus (4 hours); Salvador (2 hours); Brasília (90 minutes); Belo Horizonte (90 minutes); and Iguaçu Falls (90 minutes).

## Bus Transportation

Buses arrive in São Paulo from all points in Brazil. São Paulo can be reached by bus from Rio. The trip takes about seven hours, with rest stops at two-hour intervals. The scenic route along the seashore on the Rio-Santos Highway is a lovely, relaxing way to see the coastline and backroad villages, but the buses are not air conditioned. Express buses, which are air-conditioned, also run frequently between Rio and São Paulo.

## Train Transportation

Passengers can sleep soundly on the new luxury **Silver Train**, which travels overnight between Rio de Janeiro and São Paulo (about 170 miles). Plush, air-conditioned suites, two meals, and hotel shuttle service are included in the $300 round-trip fare. Reservations: ☎ *800-544-5503.*

## Car Rental

Several rental agencies at the airport are open after regular business hours. Companies include **Avis,** ☎ *258-8833;* and **Localiza,** ☎ *533-2133.*

## City Transportation

Unless you're becoming a native, forgo the bus system and splurge on taxis. They're safer, faster, and a lot less taxing on the nerves.

### Taxis

Most hotels offer luxury taxi service, paged by your concierge. Cheaper rates can be had from **radio taxis,** ☎ *251-1733.* Taxis hailed in the street are the least expensive.

**Alô Taxi,** ☎ *229-7688,* offers service 24 hours a day with normal rates. You might be able to squeeze a discount to Garulhos from **Guarucoop,** ☎ *940-7070.* White and blue taxis serve Guarulhos only. For service to Santos and Guarujá, call **Expresso Luxo,** ☎ *223-5161.*

### Buses

For bus service to the **International Airport,** ☎ *221-9103.* The major bus station is the **Terminal Rodoviário do Tietê**, Avenida Cruzeiro do Sul 1800; ☎ *235-0322.* A second terminal is **Terminal Rodoviário do Jabaquara**, Rua Jequitibá, ☎ *577-0872.*

## Travel Agencies

The **American Express** office is in the Hotel Sheraton Mofarrej Rua Al. Santos, 1437; ☎ *284-6622.*

**Receptur,** Avenida Ipiranga, 104 (Downtown); ☎ *259-4066.*

**City Tour**, Anhembi Turismo, Av. Olavo Fontoura, 1209, Pq. do Anhembi, Dept. de Turismo, ☎ *(11) 267-2122, ramal 627.* Weekend excursions offer several different itineraries to take in the sights of the city.

## What To Wear

São Paulo is a serious business town. *Paulistanos* wear suits on most occasions; for men, ties are common, and even women tend to wear suits, though they are usually short, sexy, and brightly colored. Outside the business environment, casual wear should be directed toward the season. A jacket (leather is good) is needed during the winter months, but shorts are fine for casual excursions during the summer. Always take an umbrella, especially between Dec. and Mar.

# Guarujá

When the pollution and the summer sun get too intense, *Paulistanos* head for the seaside resort of Guarujá, only an hour away. Like *cariocas*, the residents of Guarajá are sunworshippers, and not especially work-oriented. For years, high-class *Paulistanos* have enjoyed beautiful beachside homes in private neighborhoods called *condomínios*. In 1989, a new highway from Anchieta Isle made the two cities more accessible, opening up the resort to an even greater stream of vacationers. During high season (Dec.-Carnaval and July, when the population of 200,000 nearly doubles), it's almost impossible to find a room without a reservation.

A few beaches in Guarujá have been officially declared polluted. **Asturias Beach**, however, is good for swimming. **Tombo Beach** is excellent for surfing. The **Jequiti-mar Beach** (where the resort of the same name is located) is considered the safest. Two km. north of the resort is a beach where fishing boats land with the day's catch; the best seafood restaurants are located here.

The city's main beach is **Pitangueiras**, full of sidewalk cafés, bars, and luncheonettes. As at most of Guarujá's beaches, however, the undertow here is strong and bathers must take care. A dramatic view of the shoreline can be seen from in front of the **Gávea Hotel**, where you can enjoy a tropical drink and watch the sun set. **Terraço**, next to Escat Video on Pitangueiras Beach, is also an in-spot for a cool drink. For about $5, you can rent a horse and carriage and mosey through the town.

Somewhat gloomy in low season (not to mention cold and windy), Guarujá is valiantly trying to make the island profitable year-round. In Aug. 1991 the city sponsored the International Folklore Festival, an event that may become annual. To avoid the seasonal crunch, the best time to come is during May.

A blue-and-white ferry to the city of Santos (the most important port in Brazil and another holiday resort) looks a bit scrappy, but is actually very safe. The trip takes only five minutes.

## Where To Stay

See page 26 for price chart.

### Jequitimar Hotel and Spa Ala Szerman

*Avenida Marjory Prado, 1100 (praia de Pernambuco);* ☎ *(132) 53-3111.*

Eight km. from Guarujá, on the road to Bertioga, is this extremely attractive resort right on its own beach. The swimming and boating are excellent and fishing grounds are good. Accommodations are chalets of varying size. Many rich Brazilians come to take advantage of the spa facilities, which include aerobics, watersports, and cellulite and massage treatments. A gourmet diet menu is served to spa participants in a salon separate from the main dining room. Two nightclubs keep the after-dark action hot. *68 apts. Very expensive. All cards.*

### Casa Grande

*Avenida Miguel Stefano, 999 (praia da Enseada);* ☎ *(132) 86-2223.*
*Reservations: São Paulo (11) 282-4277.*

Cannons in the lobby of this five-star white *fazenda* (farm) recall a 19th-century plantation. The magnificent glass lobby is built around tropical gardens that tower toward the heavens; in fact, the entire grounds are exquisitely landscaped. The arrangement of the inner courtyard and pool resembles a Caribbean resort. Music continually wafts through the grounds, vying with the crashing sound of waves. A full pleasure center includes the circular pool, lighted tennis courts, a sauna, an exercise bike, racquet games, and weight equipment. A festive American-style snack bar and an international restaurant offer fine cuisine; you can even nosh on oysters and crab claws while in the pool.

Suites, some of which have verandas, are stunningly decorated, with two double white beds, large bath, and living room. Standards are small, with no view; most worthwhile are the deluxe rooms, overlooking the garden courtyard, with an extra small room holding a couch and table. *162 apts. Expensive. All cards.*

## Delphin

*Avenida Miguel Stefano, 1295 (praia da Enseada),* ☎ *(132) 86-2111, fax 86-6844. Reservations: São Paulo (11) 259-6100.*

The Delphin has been called the camping club for Argentines, who tend to travel in large, noisy groups. A leather-and-walnut decor offsets the nautical antiques in the lobby. The pool is not particularly pretty, but guests can saunter to the beach, where they will be plied with drinks, natural straw umbrellas, and plastic chairs. Double deluxe rooms have no view; standards have no real window. The best bet, particularly for four, is the garden suite, with its own balcony, looking out on a wondrous tropical view. A nightclub rocks during summer. *114 apts. Moderate. All cards.*

## Strand Hotel

*Avenida Prestes Maia, 385 (praia do Tombo);* ☎ *(132) 54-2822.*

This three-floor hotel doesn't believe in frills, let alone exciting decoration, but it is spacious, breezy and a good budget option, especially for families. There is no air conditioning, but well-placed fans and large open windows set up a breeze if the door is left open. The large pool and tennis courts are unusual for a small hotel; unfortunately, the TV room looks like an old folk's home and the corridors have a dark feel. Children up to five stay free; if you book at least seven days, you'll receive a 40% discount. Breakfast not included. *42 apts. Moderate. All cards.*

# Where To Eat

See page 26 for price chart.

## Il Faro

*(Il Faro Hotel) Rua Iracema, 38 Enseada;* ☎ *53-9305. Daily noon-midnight.*

*Paulistanos* love this homey Italian cantina with its white stucco arches and pictures of Venice. Over 50 pastas are available. Fish cooked in red tiles (the ones on the roof!) are specialties, and the *camarões Afrikana* in garlic sauce is excellent. For dessert, try the *torta da casa*, a chocolate brownie-like cake dotted through with almonds and splashed with whiskey. The owner, an Italian immigrant, loves to shmooze, and even the head waiter speaks English, French, and Spanish. *Moderate. All cards.*

### Strand

*Avenida Prestes Maia, 385;* ☎ *86-6734.*

Best *chopp* in town at this German bierhouse at the Strand Hotel, where the presidents of Volkswagen and Hertz hang out. The menu is in German and Portuguese. The best dish is sausage with sauerkraut, wienerschnitzel, and bratwurst. *Inexpensive. All cards.*

### Picanha's

*Avenida Santos Dumont, 825,* ☎ *552-947. Daily noon-2 a.m.*

Four blocks from downtown, this *churrascaria/rodízio* across from the bus station looks like a cross between a ranch and a cathedral, but the *cachaça* is free. If you have to wait for a table, you even get free drinks and hors d'oeuvres. A self-service salad bar is included; dessert is extra. Live music nightly. *Moderate. All cards.*

### Alcide's

*Avenida Dom Pedro I, 398.*

Every dish at this boisterous ranchhouse looks superb. Alcide, the owner, names his creations after his friends; even his wife Matilda got a shrimp dish laden with apples and cream. Big enough for two, Mignon Alcide's looks like a huge corn dog, but is actually a superb steak stuffed with cheese and bacon and wrapped in a hot crust. During summer, up to 50 people wait a half-hour to eat, so avoid peak hours between 2 p.m.-4:30 p.m. and after 8 p.m. Local artists show on the walls. *Moderate. All cards.*

### Restaurante do Joca

*Estrada de Bertioga, km. 14 (Cachoeira).*

This open-air eatery near the pier serves the best stuffed crabs in the city. The fried bananas are perfect. *Moderate. No cards.*

### Boi Branco

*Av. Dom Pedro I;* ☎ *51-9207.*

An excellent steakhouse.

# Nightlife

Young adults head for **Terraço**, at the corner of Rua Petrópolis and Av. Marechal, for *chopp*, milkshakes, burgers, and pizzas. Near the Gávea Hotel, **Aquarius Boite** is the city's disco, where the average age is 25. Be prepared for strobes, deafening volume, and a DJ who keeps the American rock, samba and reggae loud. From the parking lot is a great view of Enseada Beach.

## Shopping

**Guarujá Center Shopping**, off Pitangueiras Beach, is an indoor mini-mall, with merchandise at least 15% more expensive than in São Paulo. For souvenirs, flowers, crystals, and local artisanry, try **Le Petit Trianon**, Rua Petrópolis, 15 Pitangueiras Beach. **Centro Cultural de Guarujá**, Rua Petrópolis, 7, upstairs from Escot Video is owned by the artist Ortega, whose work mostly lines the walls. He also excels in Miró and Picasso replicas. The city's only **cinema** is located on Rua Mario Ribeiro, across the street from the shopping center. The **drugstore** Droga Raia is next door to the cinema.

## Hands-On Guarujá

### Arrival

**Buses** run continuously throughout the day to Guarujá from São Paulo. For information, ☎ *386-2325.*

A five-minute **ferry** traverses the bay between Guarujá and Santos. For details, ☎ *236-3399.*

### Excursions

Schooners may be rented for a six-hour trip to the beach of Iporanga, passing by the islands and strands north of the city. Call ☎ *354-1458.*

### Money Exchange

**Bradesco**
Rua Dom Pedro I,1015 (Praia da Enseada)

# Santos

A mere 65 km. from São Paulo, the city of Santos is a miracle in progress. Six years ago, when I researched the first edition of this guide, nobody wanted to go to Santos. The port city had some of the worst slums in Brazil, the bay was so polluted you couldn't swim, and the beaches were so filthy you couldn't even walk on them. Plus, the metropolitain area was found to have the highest AIDS rate in the country – hardly a paradise for tourists. Back then, the only thing the half-million inhabitants could be proud of was Pelé, the world-champion soccer player who brought his home team of Santos to international prominence many times over.

What turned things around for Santos in 1989 was that that a leftist city government took power in a country run by rightists. Dedicated to improving the lot of the people and their environment, the young followers of Mayor Thelma de Souza pushed up their shirtsleeves and got to work.

Through research, it was discovered that the illicit channeling of sewage into the drainage canals that have criss-crossed the city since the beginning of the century was the main culprit. A program to locate these outlets and the installaion of locks to prevent canal water from reaching the beach eventually allowed the city to reopen its beaches. Environmental activity also extended to citywide recycling programs, preservation of forest areas, and the restructing of *favelas*. To combat the AIDS epidemic, Santos initated a massive education and prevention program, which has become the leading model for other cities. Even psychiatric hospitals, which had at one time resembled Nazi concentration camps, were invaded and restructured; a group of former patients now even run their own radio program called "Tantam" (slang for crazy) and produce and sell their own line of T-shirts, belts, shoes, and diaries.

Today, no one is claiming that Santos has become a Caribbean paradise, but it is, nevertheless, a fascinating place to visit. Kiosks and ebullient gardens line the beach drag; the historical center recalls the city's heyday as a coffee port; and the ecological treks within easy access are among the most interesting in the region. And those interested in "social tourism" should not miss an opportunity to visit the Dique project, a slum in public renovation, whose sights and sounds will leave haunting impressions.

# History

Tourism in Santos started in 1895, when the International Hotel was built. In 1912 an engineer named Brito constructed seven channels that crossed the city. During the 20s and 30s the seaside and beach areas started to become populated, especially when coffee barons and important farmers built lots of big houses. In 1936 a garden seven km. long was planted along the beach, considered the longest seaside garden in the world. In 1940s Santos was the most important tourist destination in Brazil, with casinos, glamorous restaurants, and a thriving coffee port. In 1936, however, the federal government delegalized casinos. In 1964 the city was declared an international security area and thus prohibited from electing its own mayor; the status eventually led the area into environmental demise. During the 60s, the coffee market, which had been Santos' main source of income, moved to São Paulo. By 1973, scientific organizations noticed that the beaches were polluted, hammering the last nails into the coffin.

It's fortunate not only for the city but for tourists that ecotourism programs began in 1994. Tourism has now become the second most important activity.

# A Bird's Eye View

Santos has seven km. of beaches for leisure; the rest are occupied by the port. They are totally urbanized and exude an old-world elegance that reminded me of the strands in Nice, France. **Rua Ana Costa** is one of the main beach avenues, lined with century-old trees where the cinemas and restaurants are located. A garden of lilies bloom in Sept. and Oct., leaving the strand awash with yellow blossoms.

As a result of the city's recuperation program, six posts have been established along the beach drag to serve bathers and tourists: #1–Beach guard; #2–School for sports; #3–*Policlinica* (medical assistance); #4–Cinearte (38-seat movie house for showing only art films; #5–Library for comic books; #6–Library.

The **bus station** (*rodoviária*) is located at Praça das Andradas, within walking distance of the city center. The beaches of Santos are reached by bus from Praça Mauá, about a 20-minute trip.

# Sights

## Aquário Municipal

*Av. Bartolomeu de Gusmão (Ponta da Praia);* ☎ *236-9996. Tues.-Sun. 8 a.m.-8 p.m.*

The city's aquarium has 90 species in over 42 tanks. One of the prize joys is a 20-year-old sea lion discovered off the Brazilian coast.

## Orquidário Municipal de Santos

*Praça Washington (José Menio);* ☎ *237-6970, fax 234-3864.*
*Hours: 8 a.m.-6 p.m. Tues.-Sun. (every day in Jan., Feb., and July).*

This zoo/botanical park is a lovely shaded oasis, with over 6,000 specimens of orchids, many from the Atlantic Forest. There are also fruit and medicinal trees, including rare species like the *pau-brazil, embaúba, ipê roxo,* and *pau-ferro.* Peacocks, monkeys, *guarás* (foxes), and rare tropical birds roam the grounds.

## Bolsa Oficial do Café

*Rua XV de Novembri, 95;* ☎ *234-5734. Mon.-Fri. 8 a.m.-11 a.m. and 1 p.m.-5 p.m.*

The smell of coffee beans still lingers in this city's official coffee market. Inaugurated in 1922, this eclectically styled building with a beautiful interior features three frescoes of Benedicto Calixto recalling the history of Santos; a stained-glass window on the roof shows Anhanguera's legend.

## Santa Catarina Hillock

*Rua Visconde do Rio Branco;* ☎ *235-6021. Hours: Mon.-Fri. 8 a.m.-6 p.m.*

A beloved landmark of the city, this hillock was originally the Santa Catarina de Alexandria Chapel, constructed between 1591 and 1630. Between 1880 and 1884, Dr. João Eboli, an Italian doctor, built a house on the remains of the hillock; the city government restored it in 1992.

## Our Lady of Monte Serrat

*Monsenhor Moreira Pathway;* ☎ *235-2295. Hours: 8 a.m.-7:45 p.m.*

This shrine was originally built in 1603 to shelter the image of the patron saint of Santos. On the saint's feast day, great processions of devotees climb the 415 steps. It's easier, however, to take the charming funicular railway to see the church, the small village and a panoramic vista of the city and port. The train runs about every half-hour.

## Igreja de Santo Antônio do Valongo

*Largo Marquês de Monte Alegre;* ☎ *235-6681. Tues.-Sat. 3 p.m.-7 p.m.,*
*Sun. 8 a.m.-7:30 p.m.*

Constructed around 1640, this baroque church boasts a facade considered one of the most beautiful masterpieces of the 18th century. The building houses a Franciscan monastery.

## Largo of Marquês de Monte Alegre Ferroviaria

*Av. Ana Costa, 240 (Campo Grande);* ☎ *235-1220.*

This railway station was inaugurated in Feb., 1867 when its first train pulled into the station with a steam locomotive.

# Excursions

## Fazenda Cabucu

Once an operating banana farm, this estate off the Rio-Santos Highway is now used for ecotourism, offering an interesting (easy) walk through a forest in recovery. An Alice-in-Wonderland path leads inside a dense forest full of samambaia trees and bromeliads; look for ancient mango trees and heliconias – epiphytes with bright red curves. A fantastic waterfall and outcropping of rock awaits you at the end of the trek. You must wear mosquito repellant (citronella is best) or you will regret it dearly.

## Laje de Santos

The marine park of Santos sits 45 km. off the coast and is considered one of the best diving areas in Brazil. Actually, it is just a rock in the middle of the ocean, surrounded by many sunken boats and schools of fish. Visibility ranges from 60-130 feet. Make reservations for a day-trip diving excursion through travel agencies listed under *Hands-On Santos*, below.

## Itatinga Village/Itatinga Tracks

Since 1919 when the Santos Docks Company installed a dam and mill, the Itatinga River, which begins at Serra do Mar, has supplied hydroelectric power for the region. ("Itatinga" in Tupi-Guarani language means "white rock," referring to the color of the rocks in the river.) In 1920 Itatinga Village (in typically British style) was formed for the maintenance staff – 70 houses, school, bakery, soccer club, and a chapel. The villagers still maintain close contact with nature, and several trails have been preserved, showing the three ecological systems. Five different trails take you over brooklets, past waterfalls, through sandbanks and hillside forest filled with bromeliads and small animals. The most difficult trek (three hours) leads six km. to the top of the 2,500-foot mountain, where you are rewarded with a stunning view of the Itatinga and Itapunha rivers, the vegetation and the sea.

❖ **GETTING HERE:** *19 miles from Santos, take BR-101 (Rio-Santos) road, including a three-minute crossing by boat and 4½ miles by street car. Or, by boat in a three-hour trip by Estuario Channel and Itapanhau River and the same distance by street car. Trips must be arranged through travel agencies (see under Hands-On Santos).*

## O Dique

Not a trip for everyone, but a visit to O Dique, probably *the* worse *favela* slum that has ever existed in Brazil, is a very privileged experience. A result of the lack of housing space in Santos, this community of shacks built on stilts grew up on the edge of the river facing the garbage dump. When the river rose, so did the garbage, right into their front doors; a sudden rainfall could send one's entire belongings skidding into the river. Moved by the horrendous plight of these squatters, the leftist government devised a program to temporarily house the dwellers (in groups) elsewhere, while new, more secure cement housing was built in a neighborhood layout. Today, more than half the program has been completed, so it is inspiring to see the before-and-after pictures. Through the eyes of the middle class, the new housing still looks like slums, but the vast improvement has profoundly changed the lives of the inhabitants on all levels, thanks to the presence of psychologists and social workers. As one dweller told a psychologist after living in her new abode for a few months: "It's only now that we are slowly learning to feel what it means to be a human being."

To visit the project, contact the **Tourist Board of Santos, (SICTUR),** Rua Carvalho de Mendonça, 247; ☎ *233-3844, fax 234-3864.*

## Schooner Trips

Excursions on schooners (called *catraias*) may be taken to the port of Santos, the island of Urubuqueçaba, and Morro da Bahia, as well as the Bertioga Channel (to view the mangrove system). Boats leave from Ponte dos Práticos, Ponta da Praia, daily starting at 10 a.m. For more information, contact the travel agencies (see *Hands-On Santos*).

# Where To Stay

See page 26 for price chart.

## Parque Balneário Hotel

*Av. Ana Costa, 535;* ☎ *(013) 289-5700, fax 284-0475.*

A bit scruffy for a five-star hotel, but the breakfast buffet is mammoth and the location, near shopping and nightlife, is excellent. Bathrooms are not luxurious and amenities are minimal. Some rooms look out on the ocean a block away. *Expensive. All cards.*

## Mendes Plaza Hotel

*Av. Mal. Floriano Peixoto, 42;* ☎ *(013) 289-4243, fax 284-8253.*

More modern than the Parque Balneário, this five-star even offers a special deluxe floor with its own meeting areas. Standards are large, with healthy-sized marble baths. The rooftop pool has plenty of sunning space. Breakfast and dinner are served in a tiled area off the pool. *104 apts. Moderate-expensive. All cards.*

## Mendes Panorama Hotel

*Rua Euclides da Cunha, 7;* ☎ *(013) 289-2627, fax 284-8253.*

Connected to the Mendes Plaza above, this three-star is about $50 less per apartment; rooms are only slightly smaller and you have no use of the pool, courts, or sauna. It's occupied all year long; reserve at least 15 days in advance. *Moderate. All cards.*

## Hotel Avenida Palace

*Av. Pres. Wilson, 10;* ☎ *and fax (013) 289-3555.*

For tight budgets, this 70-year-old two-star hotel offers clean rooms with not much style. *Inexpensive. All cards.*

# Where To Eat

Lots of bars, rstaurants, and pizzerias can be found along the beach on **Rua 223 Vicente de Carvalho**. See page 26 for price chart.

## Cibus

*Av. Vicente de Carvalho, 1 (Roqueiro);* ☎ *233-3795.*

In one of city's best restaurants, where you can dine in air-conditioned comfort, across from Posto 5, with views to the ocean. Delicious bowls of garlic breads precede dishes cooked tableside with great style. Chateaubriand for two is reasonably priced. Try the papaya mousse for dessert. *Moderate. All cards.*

### Bar da Praia

*Posto #4. Hours: open at 6 p.m.*

Outdoor garden across from the Cine Arte, with troll-like chairs and tree-trunk tables on a tree-shaded porch. Sandwiches, grilled chicken, and beef, pastas. Live jazz Tues.-Sun. after 10 p.m. – sometimes. *Inexpensive-moderate. All cards.*

### Restaurante Roma

*Rua Frei Gaspar, 46; ☎ 235-3006. Hours: 11 a.m.-3 p.m., lunch only.*

Situated downtown, this sturdy warhorse offers Italian specialties in hearty portions. Waiters seem to belong in Brooklyn. *Inexpensive. All cards.*

### Point 44

*Rua Jorge Tibiriça, 44; ☎ 4-4069. Hours: weekdays for lunch, at night only hors d'oeuvres and snacks.*

Cathedral-like feeling lends a casual elegance to this plant-strewn restaurant. Fine hot and cold lunch buffets, where the pastas are homemade. *All cards.*

### Leopardi Restaurante e Pizzeria

*Av. Dr. Bernardini de Campos, 626; ☎ 225-4241. Hours: 6 p.m.-last client, Sat., Sun., and holidays 11 a.m.-last client.*

Intriguing pastas and pizzas cooked in wood ovens somehow feel romantic in this charming house decorated colonial-style. The restaurant will even deliver. *Moderate. All cards.*

# Nightlife

During the summer, music programs are scheduled nightly on the beach. Bars and discos cater to the young, but sometimes there are special nights for the middle-aged (particularly single women!).

### Reggae Night

*Av. Antonio Manoel de Carvalho, 1747; ☎ 239-5320. Tues.-Sun. 9 p.m. on.*

A dance club located in the hills with a wonderful view of the city.

### Lofty Discoteca

*Av. Ana Costa, 554; ☎ 284-5920.*

Across from the Balneário Hotel, this is a hot spot with the younger set.

# Shopping

The masses shop downtown, near City Hall, in a maze of streets with tiny stores brimming over with goods and appliances.

More sophisticated clothes are found in shopping malls; one next door to the Parque Balneário Hotel. **Miramar Shopping** connects the two Mendes hotels: three levels, with modern stores, including Mesbla, the department store and lots of snack bars.

### Crafts Fair

*Av. Vincente de Carvalho, Channel #4, in the Fonte Luminosa do Boqueirão. Hours: Sat. 2 p.m.-10 p.m.*

### Crafts Fair

*Praça Caio Ribeiro Moraes Silva, next to Sesc. Hours: Sun. 2 p.m.-10 p.m.*

Good buys are kangas, embroidered foods, *Bahianas* selling *acarajé*, Japanese-style tempura.

# Hands-On Santos

## Airlines

Shuttle flights run between São Paulo and Santos.

**Varig Cruzeiro**
Rua Ruachuelo, 103 . . . . . . . . . . . . . . . . . . . . . . . .    ☎ 232-1114
International reservations . . . . . . . . . . . . . . . . . . . .    ☎ 0800-997-000
**VASP**
Rua Riachuelo, 101 . . . . . . . . . . . . . . . . . . . . . . . .    ☎ 232-9511

## Bus

**Praça dos Andradas** (Valongo). . . . . . . . . . . . . . . .    ☎ 235-3719

## Ferry

**Ponta da Praia** (five-min. crossing to Guarujá). .    ☎ 236-3399

## Tourist Information

**Secretaria de Turismo** (SICTUR), Rua Carvalho de Mendonça, 247; ☎ *233-3844*, fax *234-3864*. Some brochures in English are available.

## Travel Agency

**Harpyia Serviços Ambiente**
Rua Vergueiro Steidel, 94 . . . . . . . . . . . . . . . . . . . .    ☎ 227-2000
Good for eco-excursions.
**Indaiá Turismo**
Av. Ana Costa, 493; 2nd floor . . . . . . . . . . . . . . . . .    ☎ 289-4849
Good for city tours.

## When To Go

Don't miss the **Plain Chant Chorus** every second Sun. of the month at 11 a.m. at the **Igreja do Carmo**.

**JANUARY 26: Birthday of Santos**. Shows fireworks contests, sports.

**FEBRUARY:** Carnaval bands parade along the downtown streets.

**JULY: Cidade Juninas**. A typical Brazilian party at José Menino Beach. Each night in July there is a show with restaurants set in a circle around the state. Afterwards people go to the Amusement Park Clube Play Center.

**SEPTEMBER 8: Feasts of Our Lady of Monte Serrat** (patron saint of Santos). Outdoor mass in front of the Cathedral with processions along downtown streets on top of the Monte Serrat Hill.

**NOVEMBER: North/Northeast Festival**. Music, food, and regional drinks.

**All Saint's Day** (first week of Nov.). Celebrated with cultural and artistic activities at Santa Catarina Hillock.

**DECEMBER:** Christmas nativity scenes with theater and dance are held at Praça Mauá.

# SANTA CATARINA

Santa Catarina is both the name of a state in southern Brazil and the name of a connecting island, **Florianópolis**, where the state capital of the same name is situated (a point of continuing confusion even for Brazilians). Like other parts of southern Brazil, the state of Santa Catarina boasts a decided European flair, thanks to the millions of immigrants since the 18th century who have been attracted by the cool temperatures and fertile hills. Today, Santa Catarina's population is made up of three distinct ethnic groups: **Germans**, the first to settle, who contributed both their intellectual and industrial acumen; **Italians**, who still toil the land as farmers; and **Azoreans** (from the Azores off Portugal), who populate quaint fishing villages that haven't changed in centuries. Interestingly, this syncretic mix of European cultures has created one of the most hospitable social structures in Brazil; foreigners constantly remark about the warm welcomes received in this region. Cities, such as **Blumenau** and **Joinville,** have hung onto their cultural traditions mostly through large German folk festivals and historical renovations, but in smaller towns, such as the isolated **Pomerode** (19 miles north of Blumenau), 80% of the residents still speak German fluently. The tiny village of **Treze Tilias** (founded by Austrians and recently delivered from obscurity by a TV soap opera) still looks as though it has been transplanted from an Alpine village.

The **coastal drive** from Blumenau to Florianópolis is one of the most beautiful in the country, lined with rolling green hills, grazing cattle, and quaint colorful houses in einxaimel (German) style. The main highway, **BR 101,** is uncommonly hazardous because crazy drivers tend to crisscross in front of each other with a vengeance, but the superb view of the primitive, undeveloped beaches is worth the risk.

So many mystical legends surround the history of Santa Catarina Island that it has been dubbed **Ilha das Bruxas** (Island of the Witches). Most of the prevailing myths have something to do with beautiful, powerful women (i.e., witches!) who lure "innocent" fishermen to their doom. Many say that the old Azorean women who spend their days making lacework in the northern fishing villages are full of power. Perhaps it's no coincidence Florianópolis has recently been hosting an annual New Age convention, which brings together the best astrologers, Tarot readers, crystal vendors, and healers from all over Brazil during Aug.

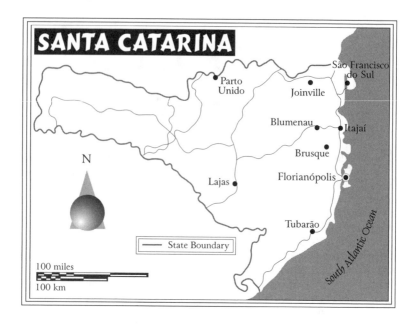

# Florianópolis

Florianópolis is the perfect place to escape from the social-climbing pressures and high prices of more upwardly mobile beaches, such as Ipanema and Copacabana in Rio. Joined to the mainland by two bridges, Florianópolis doesn't stand out as a city in itself; instead, tourists head straight for the 42 beaches that dot the 25-mile-long island. Since it has not been subjected to industrial development, the city has little, if any, pollution, and the beaches remain pristine. The island and mainland is served by excellent bus service, but a car will be necessary if you want to investigate the more remote beaches and fishing villages.

## Beaches

The northwestern side of the island, with its relatively calm seas, is best for swimming. The best restaurants and hotels are located at **Praia Canasvieiras**, but during high season it's sure to be packed with fashionable beachcombers, many from the neighboring countries of Uruguay and Argentina. **Praia Juerê Beach**, which attracts families to its calm waters, is usually full of sailboats. Between Jurerê and Daniela beaches, a series of coves tucked under the road is well worth investigating. Around the **Lagoa da Conceição**, a large saltwater lagoon, you'll find many simple restaurants specializing in seafood, with open-air verandas looking out onto the sea. Here you can rent canoes, labeled *Barco para Passeio*, to row around the lake with a guide ($6 per half-hour). At the entrance to the lagoon, **Barra da**

**Lagoa** remains a colony of Azorean fishermen who continue their daily seawork oblivious to the onslaught of tourists piling into the tiny bars and restaurants. It's here you might see fish hanging from an iron pole for sale. Unfortunately, several years ago, an eco-disaster occurred here when millions of sardines suddenly died. The eco-park near Barra is called **Parque da Florestal Rio Vermelho.**

Unless you are an expert swimmer, avoid the eastern shore since the rough undercurrents can be deadly. **Praia da Joaquina,** however, makes an excellent beach for surfing (the national championships are held here each Jan.). The road to this beach, filled with hilly green areas and small quaint houses, is as exotic as the shoreline itself; cows graze near *peixarias*, and makeshift stalls sell fresh fish. For strolling, **Praia do Campeche** (which connects to Joaquina) has the rep for being the most beautiful beach, but be careful with the torturous undertow.

> **UP CLOSE TIP:** *Wait to do your shopping till you get to the airport, where there is an excellent mall of shops, especially a great T-shirt store called* **Textil & Co.** *Also, if you love seeing planes take off, get to the airport early and watch from under an outdoor shelter.*

# Sights

Start a short city tour at what is the **former waterfront,** where you'll find the two ocher-colored **municipal market custom houses** (*Alfândega*) buildings. Here you'll find crafts stalls, an artisanry store associated with the Ministry of Labor, an art gallery, and the **Museu de História de Arte.** From here, gear yourself for a steep walk to the Praia de Fora (the "new town") on the city's main square, called **Praça XV de Novembro.** On one side of the square is the 18th-century **Palácio Cruz e Souza,** with its impressive pink facade. Inside is the **Historical Museum of Santa Catarina** (see below).

## Museu Histórico de Santa Catarina

*Praça 15 de Novembro, 227;* ☎ *221-3000.*
*Tues.-Fri. 10 a.m.-7 p.m., Sat. and Sun. 1 p.m.-7 p.m.*

The 19th-century decor of the exterior is more compelling than the exhibits inside, but historians might find interest in the antique guns, swords, and scrolls.

## Igreja de Nossa Senhora do Rosário

This church is the last remaining architecture from the colonial era; some of the original Portuguese baroque decoration is still in evidence. It is best approached by a flight of steep steps from Rua Marechal Guilherme.

## Museu de Antropólogia

*Campus Universitário (Trindade);* ☎ *234-1000. Mon.-Sat. 9 p.m.-noon, 1 p.m.-5 p.m.*

This museum, about 20 minutes by bus from downtown, offers a modest collection of native crafts and artifacts hewn by the state's nearly extinct Indian tribes – Kaingang and Okleng.

## Museu de Art de Santa Catarina

*Tues.-Fri. 9 a.m.-noon, 1 p.m.-9 p.m. Sat. and Sun. 5 p.m.-10 p.m.*

The official art museum of the state, located in the Centro Integrado de Cultur (take the buses marked "Agronômica"). Exhibits feature work by local and national artists. There's also a cinema showing art films.

# Where To Stay

If you're coming for beach time, avoid staying in the city of Florianópolis and head for the chalets and *pousadas* along the various beaches of Santa Catarina Island. Note that many hotels close for low season (Apr.-Nov.), as do some restaurants. See page 26 for price chart.

## Hotel Diplomata

*Avenida Dr. Paulo Fontes, 1210 (Centro);* ☎ *(481) 224-4455.*

The best executive hotel downtown is, unfortunately, a half-hour from the beach. This four-star supplies its own transfer to the beach, however, as well as private cabanas and shower facilities. Noise from the highway can be severe at night, so ask for a room on the side without traffic. Service is top class; an elegant dining room for dinner and a three-course breakfast is luxurious. *90 rooms. Expensive. All cards.*

## Jurerê Praia Hotel

*Al. César Nascimento, 200 (Praia de Jurerê), 25 km.;* ☎ *(481) 282-1108,*
*fax 284-1311.*

These black-and-white, avant-garde-looking chalets might look better in Brasília, but the complex (on a well-preserved beach) is excellent for families. The smallest cabana ($40) holds two persons; the large fits four nicely. The apartment-like houses have a bedroom, dining room, patio with grill, and full kitchen, and guests can take advantage of the pool and resort-like grounds: perfect environs for total relaxation. Reserve 30 days in advance; special weekly rates available. *58 chalets. Moderate-expensive. All cards.*

## Ponta das Canas Praia

*Av. Dep. Fernando Viegas, 560;* ☎ *284-1311.*

This low-key, three-star resort with a tropical backyard is packed with grass huts for dining and relaxing. A modest spa from Nov.-Apr. offers eco-walks, tennis, volleyball, scuba, windsurfing, and bicycling. Boat trips can also be taken to the nearby ruins. The homey restaurant overlooking the sea serves wonderful grilled shrimp. Other restaurants serving native dishes and bars are within walking distance. Ask for a room with a view. Singles run $42, doubles $54. *55 apts. Moderate. All cards.*

## Cris Hotel

*Praia da Joaquina, 17 km.;* ☎ *(481) 32-0380, fax 232-0075.*

A decent budget hotel on the beach of Joaquina, with air conditioning and mini-bars. *68 apts. Moderate. No cards.*

# Where To Eat

The most sophisticated restaurants are downtown, but if you're beachside, go for fish, particularly steamed or grilled just off the boat. In the area of **Beira-Mar Norte** (in the north of the city near the Hercilio Luz Bridge), you'll find several notable restaurants, such as **Moçambique** (seafood), **Pizzaria Don Pepe** (pizza), and **Restaurante Kaffa** (Lebanese). See page 26 for price chart.

## Cantábria

*Est. Geral da Joaquina, 17 km;* ☎ *232-0235. Call for hours.*

The best place to sample the traditional Spanish cuisine of the island. *Moderate. All cards.*

## Martim Pescador

*Beco do Surfista (estr. da Joaquina), 17.5 km;* ☎ *232-0660. Noon-3 p.m., 8 p.m.-12:30 a.m., Sat. noon-6 p.m., closed Sun.*

One of the best places for fish. Try the *moqueca de garoupa* (grouper) or the *lula recheado* (stuffed squid). *Moderate. All cards.*

## Andrinus

*Rua Geral da Lagoa da Conceição, 14;* ☎ *232-0153. Daily 11 a.m.-11 p.m.*

This simple seaside establishment, adorned with paintings of local fishermen, serves a shrimp buffet. A veritable steal. *Moderate. No cards.*

## Ataliba

*Av. Me. Irineu Bornhausen, 5050 (Agroonômica);* ☎ *234-00990. 11 a.m.-3 p.m, 7 p.m.-11 p.m., Sun. 11 a.m.-4 p.m.*

Best *rodízio* steakhouse in the city – all you can eat for a fixed price. *Moderate. All cards.*

### Bierplatz

*Av. Rubens de Arruda Ramos;* ☎ *228-0099.*

A typical German-style restaurant that offers café colonial, a buffet (40 items) of teas, wines, cheeses and sweets. Live German music Wed.-Sat. *Inexpensive. All cards.*

### Mar Massas

*Rua Rita Lourenço Silveira, 97 (Lagoa da Conceição), 14 km.;* ☎ *232-0890. 7 p.m.-1 a.m., Sun. noon-6 p.m. Apr.-Nov.*

The rustic ambiance of this restaurant makes the fine pastas seem like true artistry. *Inexpensive. All cards.*

### Armação Ilimitada

*SC-406 (Praia da Armação). Daily 10:30 a.m.-1 a.m.*

Interesting pizza with live music and wine. Located on Armação Beach. *Inexpensive. All cards.*

# Nightlife

Most bars on the island feature live music; the hottest action centers around the avenue **Beira Mar Norte** (known as *Avenida Rubens de Arruda Ramos*), which runs north of the city beginning at the Hercilio Luz Bridge. Ask when you arrive since bars fall fast in and out of fashion. **Bar do Erico**, near Mole and Joaquina beaches, has a hot spot bar with live MPB.

# Hands-On Florianópolis

## Money Exchange

**Banco do Brazil,** Praça XV de Novembro, 20
**BESC**, Rua Jerônimo Coelho, 183

## Tourist Information

Tourist information can be found at Praça 15 de Novembro; ☎ *224-0024;* and at the train station, ☎ *224-2777*, ext. 15.

## Transportation

### Arrival

**Flights** run daily from Porto Alegre and São Paulo. **Buses** are available from Porto Alegre, São Paulo, Brasília, Curitiba, Blumenau and Joinville.

| | |
|---|---|
| **Varig/Cruzeiro/Rio Sul** | ☎ 236-1121 |
| **VASP** | ☎ 236-1394 |
| **Transbrasil** | ☎ 236-1229 |

## Car Rental

Avis . . . . . . . . . . . . . . . . . . . . . . . . . . . . . . . . . . . . . . . ☎ 236-1426
Interlocadora . . . . . . . . . . . . . . . . . . . . . . . . . . . . . . ☎ 236-1278

## Hitching

Hitching is probably safer here than anywhere else in Brazil. Locals are so friendly that you won't have to wait long for a pickup.

## Taxis

Air Taxis (TAF) . . . . . . . . . . . . . . . . . . . . . . . . . . . . ☎ 236-1311
Taxi . . . . . . . . . . . . . . . . . . . . . . . . . . . . . . . . . . . . . . . ☎ 197

## When To Go

Dec.-May is the best time for the beach (though foreigners may enjoy the less crowded strands during Nov., Mar., Apr. and May). June-Nov. is colder, with a delightful wind, but you will need a jacket, and the beachcombing might be chilly.

The Festival of Shrimp is held in Jan., National Surfing Championships the last week in Jan. Semana de Florianópolis, a week-long festival of folkloric music and dance, is held during the last week of Mar. The Rodeio Crioulo (rodeo) takes place in July.

# Joinville

Joinville and its neighboring sister Blumenau carry on a good-natured competition over which city is more hospitable to tourists. Located in the valley, Joinville (population: 343,000) welcomes guests with large bouquets of flowers, but the German-descended residents of both cities seem to party equally hard, downing about the same amount of beer. Joinville was settled on land that was originally given as a dowry to the Prince of Joinville upon his marriage to the daughter of the Portuguese Emperor Pedro I and his consort Dona Leopoldina of Austria. In 1851, under a deal with Hamburg lumber companies, nearly 200 German, Swiss, and Norwegians descended on the 43 square miles of virgin forest. Attracting more immigrants throughout the century, the city grew into the state's foremost industrial center. Today, Joinville, known as Cidade das Flores (City of Flowers), is made for leisurely browsing. Streets are impeccably clean and filled with bicycles (cycling is a city-wide pastime). And much of the architecture remains staunchly German; according to a recent law, new banks and shops do not have to pay taxes if they build in the einxaimel style. The well-kept parks are all maintained individually through the patronship of various industries, who take active interest in the upkeep of the city. Enjoying an enviable location, Joinville is a half-hour both from the beach and the *serra* (mountain range).

In July the city is transformed by the biggest **dance festival** in Latin America (fourth largest in the world), attended by international teachers and graced by performances (from flamenco to ballet) in open plazas, factories, and theaters. One local *figura* (a real character) who can be enjoyed throughout the year is **Alberto Holdereger**, a lawyer turned singer, whose near-Pavarotti voice and girth nightly turns up at local restaurants, bars and festivals.

## Sights

The majority of German-style houses are concentrated along the cobblestone street, **Rua 15 de Novembro**. Artisan and produce stores line the main street, **Rua Princesa Isabel**, which runs parallel to Rua 15 de Novembro and Rua 9 de Março.

### Museu Nacional de Imigração e Colonização

*Rua Rio Branco, 229; ☎ 22-4485. Tues.-Fri. 9 a.m.-6 p.m.;*
*Sat. and Sun. 9 a.m.-noon, 2 p.m.-6 p.m.*

The most interesting historical stop, this was once the palace of the Prince of Joinville, who never returned to Brazil to inhabit it. The building has since been turned into a museum honoring the history of the German immigrants in the region. The excellent exhibition displays 19th-century sewing machines, old Victrolas, clocks, military uniforms, and complete furnished salons from the Imperial era. Most compelling is a 19th-century barnhouse complete with period equipment. The palm trees lining the courtyard in front of the museum were actually grown from seedlings taken from the royal palms in Rio's Botanical Gardens.

### Museu Arquelógico de Sambaqui

*Rua Dona Francisca, 600; ☎ 22-0144. Tues.-Fri. 9 a.m.-noon;*
*Sat. and Sun. 9 a.m.-noon, 2 p.m.-6 p.m.*

Donated by an amateur archaeologist, the Indian artifacts displayed here includes ceramics from the Tupí-Guarani Indians, 4,000-year-old sculptures of whales, and special arrows developed only by Indians in this area to kill animals without drawing blood. The staff speaks English and will even help you to carve a tiny indenture Indian-style into a stone with a mere piece of flint. (You could be there all day.)

### Catedral São Francisco Xavier

*Rua do Principe.*

The 15-year-old cathedral is ultramodern, with circular stained-glass windows depicting the history of Joinville. One of the best examples of German architecture is the old train station (1910), with its steepled orange brick roof and chocolate-brown windows.

## Cemitério do Imigrante
## (Immigrant's Cemetery)

Perched on a hillside with a panoramic view of the city, the cemetery is interesting for a walk through its ancient tombstones. It has now been preserved as a national patrimony.

# Excursions

Visitors shouldn't miss **Joinvilândia**, an entertainment complex with a restaurant, chocolate factory, and artisan shop, 10 minutes from the city on BR-101. At the restaurant **Moinho da Oma**, you can feast on colorful dishes such as purple cabbage, bright yellow sauerkraut, green lettuce, and golden-brown sausage. (The loud music might be insufferable, but where else can you hear Bizet's *Toreador Song* played by an oom-pah band?) After dining, take a scrumptious tour of the chocolate factory (they give out free samples!) and check out the sculptured erotic chocolates for sale. The creative entrepreneur, Laércio Beckhauser, started the factory as a small kitchen and watched it grow into one of the best success stories in Brazil. Ask if his Oma Farm has opened, an old private estate, now an ecological farm.

# Where To Stay

See page 26 for price chart.

### Tannenhof

*Rua Visconde de Taunay, 340; ☎ and fax (474) 322-8011.*

The town pride, this pretty German-style high-rise is a homey but elegant meeting place for the elite. The German-print curtains in the bright, white apartments and the folkloric bathroom tile lend a touch of the motherland. Standards have no heat, but all rooms have air conditioning and color TV. Almost all rooms have grilled verandas. A panoramic restaurant serves excellent buffets and offers live music nightly. *103 apts. Moderate. All cards.*

### Anthurium Parque Hotel

*Rua São José, 226; fax and ☎ (474) 433-6299.*

This small German-style guesthouse boasts old-world furniture and blue-and-white shutters, but the beds feel like bricks. An eggplant-shaped pool is offset by landscaped gardens and swings. Breakfast includes sumptuous chocolate cakes and strudels. *49 apts. Moderate. All cards.*

### Ideal

*R. Jerónimo Coelho, 98; ☎ 22-3660.*

These budget accommodations are modest but clean. Near the bus station. No air conditioning, only fans. *Inexpensive. No cards.*

# Where To Eat

## Tannenhof

*Rua Visconde de Taunay, 340;* ☎ *433-8011. Noon-3 p.m., 7-10 p.m., closed Sun.*

Live music. A substantial buffet, but specialties are renowned, such as shrimps flambéed with cherries and typically regional plates of duck and sausage. *Moderate. No cards.*

## Bierkeller

*Rua 15 de Novembro, 497;* ☎ *422-1360. 11 a.m.-3 p.m., 6 p.m.-11 p.m.*

Sit on wood benches under antelope horns and savor the typical German plates like *marreco com repolho roxo* (goose with purple lettuce) and bratwurst with sauerkraut. Oom-pah music and dark beer round out the picture. *Inexpensive. No cards.*

## Churrascaria Ataliba

*Rua 15 de Novembro/BR 101 (Expoville);* ☎ *22-1870. Daily 11 a.m.-3 p.m., 6 p.m.-11 p.m., Sun. 11 a.m.-4 p.m.*

Ataliba is always a good name in the South for *rodízio*-style beef. One moderate price includes hot dishes, 42 salads – enough for any vegetarian – and 10 desserts. Children can fish in the nearby lake. *Moderate. No cards.*

## Brunkow

*9 de Março, 607 (Centro). 11:30 a.m.-2 a.m.; on Sun. only the bakery is open.*

The oldest and most traditional *confeitaria* (sweet shop) in the city, famous for its sweets, homemade bread, and banana cake. *Inexpensive. No cards.*

# Nightlife

The most beautiful pub is **Chopperia Sop**. Or try **Escotilha** (open only at night), where the waiters are dressed as sailors.

# Shopping

**Centro Commercial** is a shopping mall selling local products, such as lace at **Lepper** and porcelain at **Porzellanhaus**. Also try **Artesanato da Terra**, where you can buy your very own Fritz and Frieda dolls (symbols of the German influence), as well as attractive carved-wood cars.

At **Chocolate Caseiro Germânico**, you'll find a variety of homemade chocolates, German hats, and *cachaça* in porcelain bottles.

The **Crafts Fair** is held the second Sat. of each month at Praça Nereu Ramos.

**UP CLOSE TIP:** *Antartica cerveja (beer), made in Joinville, is considered the best in Brazil (due to the city's high water quality). Ask for it throughout the country.*

## Hands-On Joinville

### Arrival

Seven **flights** run daily from São Paulo and Rio. **Bus service** from neighboring cities is excellent, with hourly departures to Blumenau (2 hours), Florianópolis (3 hours), and Curitiba (2½ hours). Seven buses leave daily for São Paulo (9 hours), one bus leaves daily for Rio (15 hours), and two head to Porto Alegre (10 hours).

### Car Rental

Localiza National . . . . . . . . . . . . . . . . . . . . . . . . . . . ☎ 33-9393

### Tourist Information

**Pórtico**
Rua 15 de Novembro/BR-101 . . . . . . . . . . . . . . . . ☎ 22-8177
**Secretary of Tourism**
Praça Nereu Ramos, 372. . . . . . . . . . . . . . . . . . . . . ☎ 33-1437

### Travel Agency

**Adinco Turismo**
Rua 9 de Marco, 857 . . . . . . . . . . . . . . . . . . . . . . . ☎ 22-1115
**Tivoli Agência de Viagens**
Rua Princesa Isabel, 374 . . . . . . . . . . . . . . . . . . . . ☎ 22-3244

### When To Go

Orchid-lovers will adore the 10-day **Festa das Flores**, held during the second half of Nov. to the accompaniment of German folkmusic, dance, food, and beer. **Semana de Joinville** is a week-long festival in Mar. featuring traditional foods, folkloric dance, and music. **Oktoberfest** in nearby Blumenau takes place in Oct.

# Blumenau

Oom-pah music, blonde hair, and blue eyes fill the sparkling clean streets of Blumenau, a city of proud German origin picturesquely perched on the banks of the Itajaí River. The city of approximately 213,000 people was founded in 1859 by Dr. Hermann Blumenau, whose descendants still live in the area and run a charming *pousada*. Scores of German immigrants followed Dr. Blumenau, as did a wave of Italians; it was only well into this century that the residents even felt compelled to learn Portuguese, so isolated were they by poor river connections.

Today, whatever German traditions remain here are as much a touristic device as true nostalgia for roots, but the locals are so cheerful they make the *gemütlichkeit* work. Local German bands perform nightly at the **Biergarten**, the city's main entertainment complex in the Praça Hercilio Luz, and numerous restaurants offer choice German cuisine. However, the main German event is the **Oktoberfest**, which attracts over a million visitors each year.

The most traditional band in Blumenau plays German oom-pah music every weekend.

Nearly destroyed by several tragic floods, the city began celebrating Oktoberfest on a city-wide basis in 1984 to recoup financial losses and reinvigorate the people. The first festival, 17 days long, was a smashing success, and now visitors from all over Latin America come to swill beer, eat wienerschnitzel and spätzle, and cart home German crafts and crystal. Called the "second party in Brazil next to Carnaval," Oktoberfest is actually a much more organized event, even suitable for children. As part of a long-running tradition, local seamstresses create costumes free of charge for visitors and shoemakers cobble traditional footwear. Contests of swigging beer from large glass tubes are a continuous day-to-night diversion, and when a reveler gets too drunk, the police graciously escort him or her home. During the week, two parades are held down the main street and a food fair takes place in the pavilion. To make liquid consumption easy on the revelers, *chopp* is distributed by bierwagens free of charge throughout the downtown area. Hotel reservations must be made at least six months in advance. If you want to stay with a German family, write: **Secretaria de Turismo de Blumenau,** Rua Alberto Stein, s/no. Bairro da Velha, Blumenau, Santa Catarina, Brazil.

> **UP CLOSE TIP:** *Fritz and Frieda – a short, dumpy German man with with wire-rim glasses and his much taller, blonde pig-tailed girlfriend – are the official mascots of the city. During Oktoberfest, the custom is to pin as many medallions, broaches, and feathers on your green-felt Alps cap as you can. The height of Oktoberfest chic, however, is a drinking cup that involves a ridiculous contraption of two cups with connecting tubes that run straight into your mouth. Perhaps the most oft-repeated phase during the festival is* Wir trinken unser Bier *("we drink our beer").*

## Sights

**Fundação Casa Doutor Blumenau** (Alameda Duque de Caxias, 64). This library and museum catalogues the history of Blumenau; the display of clothes worn by the first immigrants is worth the visit. Closed weekends.

An ecological park, **Spitzkopf**, adorned with picturesque waterfalls and walking trails, is a lovely place to stroll through.

The chic street of the city, **Alameda Rio Branco**, is full of German-styled mansions and restaurants teeming with people, especially on the weekends.

## Where To Stay

See page 26 for price chart.

### Viena Park Hotel

*Rua Herman Huscher, 670 (Vila Formosa); fax and* ☎ *(473) 326-8888.*

Almost resort-like, this moderate-sized five-star has the feel of a privileged private home. The incredible suite has two jacuzzis, one of which sits on an outdoor veranda. An elegant restaurant serves German specialties, and the bar is well known for its fruit cocktails. Guests completely fill the hotel during Oktoberfest and Dec.-Feb., taking advantage of the tennis courts, saunas, and poolside *churrascaria. Expensive. All cards.*

### Hotel Cristina Blumenau

*R. Paraiba, 380;* ☎ *(473) 322-1198.*

A two-story German-style house owned by Cristina Blumenau, the daughter of the city's founder Herr Otto Blumenau, conveniently located near the Oktoberfest Pavilion. Breakfast (included) is served in a charming salon with white curtains and bright tablecloths. Rooms come with air conditioning and TV; there's also a homey living room with TV and guests may use the kitchen. Ask for a larger room in the old house. Reservations required. *20 apts, no elevator. Inexpensive. No cards.*

# Where To Eat

See page 26 for price chart.

## Ataliba

*Rua Alberto Stein (Proeb);* ☎ *322-5088. 11 a.m.-3 p.m., 7 p.m.-10 p.m.;*
*Sun. 11 a.m.-3 p.m.*

Best *rodízio*-style steakhouse in town, with live music. *Moderate. No cards.*

## Himmelblau Palace

*(Hotel) Rua 7 de Setembro, 1415;* ☎ *326-5800. 4 p.m.-8 p.m., closed Dec.-Feb.*

Breakfast is excellent, with hearty German cakes, quiche, scrambled eggs, ham and sausage, and fried bananas with cinnamon. Excellent café colonial. *Moderate. No cards.*

## German

German delicacies are everywhere here – from Hungarian goulash to pig knuckles (*eisbein*) and sauerkraut. Do try the café colonial, a traditional southern tea served from noon to 5 p.m. It includes a luscious buffet of cakes, breads, sausages, apple strudel, chees,e and jellies that can pass as your one meal of the day. An excellent one is held at the Himmelblau Palace Hotel.

## Frohsinn

*Morro do Aipim, 1 km. (acesso pela Rua Itajaí);* ☎ *322-2137.*
*Daily noon.-2:30 p.m., 6 p.m.-midnight., Sun. 11 a.m.-2:30 p.m.*

Tucked on a hillside, this large wood-beam chalet looks out onto the River-Itajaí-Açu. Long lines of patrons wait patiently for the excellent Hungarian goulash with spätzle, smoked salmon, and Viennese sausage. Excellent fondue. *Moderate. No cards.*

## Le Bon Gourmet

*Rua 7 de Setembro, 818 (Hotel Plaza);* ☎ *326-1277. Daily 11:30 a.m.-2 p.m.,*
*7 p.m.-11 p.m.*

Blumenau's top-class French eatery happily ensconced at the Plaza Hering Hotel. *Moderate-expensive. All cards.*

## Confeitaria Cafehaus Glória

*(Hotel Glória) Rua 7 de Setembro, 954;* ☎ *322-6942. Daily 3-8 p.m.*

Stained-glass windows, German tableaus, and a fabulous spread make café colonial (tea) at this coffee house a must. Gorge on bread, pâté, cheese, sweets, sausage, and even omelettes. *Inexpensive. No cards.*

### Cavalinho Branco

*Alameda Rio Branco, 165; ☎ 322-4300. Daily 11 a.m.-midnight.*

At the city's best German restaurant, housed in a stunning mansion, fill up on pig knuckles and sauerkraut, roast duck à la Hamburg, apple strudel, and schnitzel. *Inexpensive. AE, V.*

# Nightlife

### Blumenau Biergarten Restaurante

*Tues.-Sun., 11 a.m.-last client.*

This entertainment complex is located in a woody park, complete with restaurant, beer garden, shops, and loud German bands on Sun. at 5 p.m.

### Teatro Carlos Gomes

Check to see if the Orquestra de Câmara de Blumenau, a big success in Europe, is playing here. There are also frequent performances of ballet and theater.

### Avenida Beira Rio

Nighttime activity centers along this street, where three adjacent *chopparias* – **Tunza, Casinha,** and **Bude** (the most famous) – play loud Brazilian rock and serve *chopp* in German steins.

### Bar Kriado

*Rua Alwin Schraeder, 137.*

Live Brazilian music can be heard here Mon.-Fri., starting at 5 p.m. On the outside wall, you can see how high the floods came in 1983 and 1984.

### Baturité Disco

Across the street from Cavalinho Branco restaurant on Avenida Alameda Rio Branco is the disco, which opens at 11 p.m. but doesn't start rolling until 1 a.m., Fri., Sat., and Sun.

# Shopping

Blumenau is famous for its **hand-blown crystal.** Two excellent labels are Cristal Blumenau and Hering, both available at **Moellman** (on the main street), a white-and-brown German house that looks like a carved piece of chocolate. Other excellent buys are the **porcelain** and **china** made by Porcelana Schmidt. Delicious homemade **honey breads** (*honigschnitten*) can be found at **Adega Montenegro,** Rua Dr. Amadeu da Luz, 226, where you can also stock up on **Bavarian chocolates** (Blumenaier Scholoade is the best) and 100% **pure malt whiskey** called Barrilete in beautifully designed cases. Also available are **German wines** made in the region; the best is Richburg Riesling 1989, a dry white wine.

The biggest department store is Lojas Hering, where you can buy **German-dressed dolls**, special drinking helmets, green felt hats, and red suspenders for Oktoberfest. **Homemade jams** are also special buys as are unusual handmade **Christmas tree decorations**. A cheap lunch can be found upstairs.

## Hands-On Blumenau

### Arrival

You will have to fly to Florianópolis and take a bus to Blumenau. Hourly **bus service** is available from Florianópolis, Joinville, and Itajaí, plus frequent service to Curitiba, São Paulo, Foz do Iguaçu, and western Santa Catarina. The *rodoviária* (bus station) is about five miles from the center of town; take the Cidade Jardim bus from downtown.

### Money Exchange

**Vale do Hajaí Turismo e Câmbio**
Avenida Beira Rio, 167.

### Tourist Office

The tourist office is located at Rua 15 de Novembro, 420. Brochures, maps and friendly assistance. Some English.

### When To Go

Besides Oktoberfest, other reasons to go to Blumenau are: **Festa do Cavalo**, a rodeo held Apr. 1-14; **Semana de Blumenau** starting Sept. 2, with traditional foods, dance, and music; and the **Blumenau Marathon** on the last Sun. of July. A **festival of music** also takes place in July.

# Camboriú

Once called the Copacabana of southern Brazil, Camboriú has lost its ultra-elite rep as the south's best beach spa, but thousands of tourists still descend on the high-rise hotels, high-gear nightclubs, and eight mini-beaches, where cows still graze. Good hotel rates can be found when the value of Argentine currency drops in relation to the *cruzeiro*, since the city is a destination for Argentine vacationers. The first nude beach in the south is here at **Praia do Pino**. Around **Camboriú Bay** you can swim out 300 feet in waist-level water. Along the main beach drag, **Avenida Brazil**, you'll find special truck-like buses to transport you along the strand. Two or three times a day, fishermen pull in their nets, and you can buy their catch right off the boats. International **surfing** competitions are held once a year. **Barra de Camboriú**, a small fishing village across the bay, can be visited by canoe or car, and schooners may be rented at Praia Laranjeiras.

# Sights

The drive from Blumenau to Florianópolis, which heads through Camboriú, passes some of the most beautiful farms in Brazil. Gaspar, about 1½ hours from Florianópolis, has an immense cathedral that looks from the highway like a story-book palace.

## Parque da Santur

*BR-101, km. 137;* ☎ *66-0033.*

A major tourist complex, the park offers a mini-zoo, mini-farm, train rides, aquarium and *tortarugário* (turtle farm), bird and reptile museum, and restaurants with Italian and German foods.

# Where To Stay

See page 26 for price chart.

## Marambaia Cassino Hotel

*Avenida Atlântica, 300;* ☎ *(473) 367-4099; fax 367-4302.*

This four-star is the city's principal luxury hotel. The adult and children's pool is surrounded by tropical gardens and rooms are sleekly furnished. The circular floors open onto a plant-strewn lobby. *111 apts. Expensive. All cards.*

## Rieger Apart Hotel Residence

*Rua 701 N, 162/188;* ☎ *(473) 367-2887, fax 367-2404.*

Something between a hotel and a private apartment complex, this apart hotel offers attractively appointed one- , two- , and three-bedroom apartments equipped with full kitchens. A thermal pool is being constructed, and guests may also enjoy a wet and dry sauna, a spa, and convention facilities. The location is prime, a block from the morning market where food and fruits are sold. Make reservation in July for Jan. *108 apts. Moderate. All cards.*

# Where To Eat

See page 26 for price chart.

## Moenda Calamares

*Avenida Atlântica, 5340;* ☎ *367-2587. 11 a.m.-3 p.m., 6 p.m.-midnight.*

Good seafood and *picanha na brasa* (steak served on a grill). *Moderate. No cards.*

### Macarronada Italiana

*Rua Dom Alfonso, 230 (V. Real);* ☎ *367-0788. Daily 11 a.m.-4 p.m.,*
*6:30 p.m.-11:30 p.m. Closed Mon.*

Lasagna, pizza, and pastas.

# Nightlife

All the best nightclubs are located on the **South Bay**. Try **Whiskadão** (Big
Whiskey), and **Mario's**, a show of samba and transvestites on Rua
Florianópolis.

# Hands-On Camboriú

## Arrival

Daily **flights** come from Rio, São Paulo, Curitiba, and Porto Alegre. The
airport is 12 km. from the city on BR-101. Daily **bus** connections are
available to all surrounding cities.

## Car Rental

**LocaSul**
Rua 15 de Novembro . . . . . . . . . . . . . . . . . . . . . . .   ☎ 367-1077

## Tourist Information

**Secretaria do Turismo**
Av. do Estado, 504 . . . . . . . . . . . . . . . . . . . . . . . .   ☎ 367-4422
. . . . . . . . . . . . . . . . . . . . . . . . . . . . . . . . . . . . . . . .   ext. 241

## When To Go

Sept.-Apr. is the prime beach time.

# IGUAÇU FALLS

Niagara Falls has been called a "trickle in God's mind" compared to the torrential thunder of Iguaçu Falls, the second most important tourist site in Brazil. Rising from a modest stream that originates near Curitiba (the capital of Paraná state), the Iguaçu River inches its way westward over a 745-mile journey, slowly coalescing its tributaries and small streams until – just before it merges with the great Paraná River – it plunges passionately over a 2624-ft.-high cliff. What makes such a spectacular view is not just one cataract, but 275 interlinking ones that form a horseshoe torrent around the semi-circular cliff. Throughout the day, rainbows explode over the shimmering torrents, tropical birds fly overhead, and fish can be glimpsed struggling against the white crashing foam. Given its near-mystical beauty, it's no wonder that recent "spiritual-discovery tours" of South America have included the falls as a "power spot" destination.

The colossal downpour of Iguaçu Falls, viewed from a helicopter.

The falls were first discovered in 1525 by the Spanish explorer **Alvaro Nunes Cabeza de Vaca**, who had fallen into disgrace at the court for not having brought back substantial riches from his Mississippi River treks. Appointed the Royal Overseer for the Jesuit-founded colonies along the Paraguay River, he quickly became bored and set off to explore the mouth of the Iguaçu River. When he first heard the terrifying roar of the currents, he immediately disembarked and set off on foot to confront the vision face to face. Unfortunately, Vaca was in such disrepute back home that no one at the Spanish court cared to hear of his marvelous discovery.

Numerous legends of the falls are now part of the folkloric tradition. In general, they have to do with a young boy and girl from the Caigangue tribe, who once inhabited this region. The most romantic story involves Tarobá, a beautiful, but sightless young girl who inspires her lover Naipí to sacrifice himself to the gods so that she might see. As the story goes, Naipí is swallowed up by the crashing of rocks at the very moment Tarobá regains her vision, thus making her the first person to catch sight of the newly created falls. Of course, Tarobá's restored eyesight was hardly recompense for her lost love, but it's said you can still hear her dead lover crying "Tarobá, Tarobá" under the sound of the falls.

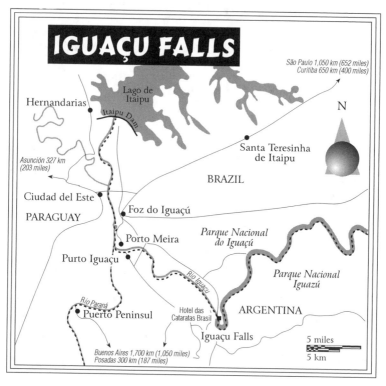

# The Brazilian Side

Part of a national park ostensibly protected by environmental guidelines, the falls are near the towns of Foz do Iguaçu in Brazil, Puerto Iguazú in Argentina, and Ciudad Presidente Stroessner in Paraguay. With a population of 200,000, Foz do Iguaçu has enjoyed a major expansion following the construction of the **Itaipu Dam**, the world's largest hydroelectric station. Beyond visiting the waterfalls, many Brazilians come to the tri-city area to take advantage of the cheap shopping in Paraguay;

American travelers, however, usually find the quality of merchandise suspicious, if not outright damaged.

The falls can be viewed both from the Brazilian side and from the Argentine side – a combination that provides both a panoramic and more detailed perspective. Just from the Brazilian side, there are at least three ways to experience the falls, and if you can accomplish all three in your visit, you'll have had a holographic view of one of nature's most fantastic achievements. For a leisurely visit, plan two days; otherwise you can get a cursory view by arriving early in the morning and departing at night.

## By Foot

The easiest (and cheapest) way to see the falls is to walk around the visitor's walkway. The lovely stone path that snakes around the side of a woody cliff gives you various viewing platforms. You may be lucky enough to receive a visit from the park's resident *coatis* (pronounced kwa-CHEESE) – racoon-like fellows who are smarter than cats and will even eat seeds right out of your hand. But be careful: I once witnessed an exciting *coati* catfight (over some candy) that inspired packs of them to come squealing angrily out of the woods. The shimmering noise you may hear under the roar of the falls is the rhythmic beating of hundreds of *cigarra* wings – a grasshopper-like insect that fills the air with its powerful song, then dies.

At the end of the walkway, a small elevator will take you to the top level, where there is a souvenir shop and an observation point to view the top plateau of the Iguaçu River. It's here that you can get close enough to feel the spray. In cold weather, a light raincoat may be helpful, but in hot weather, why not wear a bathing suit and a pair of shorts and enjoy it?

## By Air

**Helicopter rides** give you a spectacular view of the rocky plateaus from above – a kind of geological tour seen from an astronaut's eyes. The price is steep (probably more than $40 for 5-7 minutes, and $150 for 25 minutes; the latter includes the city, the dam, and the falls), but the trip is worth it and not unduly discomforting. Ecologists, however, have been complaining that the noise of the helicopters is seriously disturbing the forest animals, who have sought refuge deeper inside the woods. **Helisul Taxi Aeréo**, Rodoviária Cataratas, km. 6.5, can be found outside on the roadway; no reservations are necessary, though there may be a slight wait. Also, try **Edra Helicópteros**, Avenida Cataratas, km. 18; ☎ 74-5022.

## By Water

The **Macuco Boat Safari**, located inside the national park, is the brainchild of a native Chicagoan, Peter George, who discovered this eco-trek only six years ago and has been delighting unsuspecting tourists ever since. A rocky

10-minute jeep ride carries you through a tropical forest where you may see (only in the very early morning) monkeys, pumas, javelins, and pigs. The trail leads past the beautiful waterfall of the São José River (a hearty trek over narrow trails and log bridges) to the dock, where hundreds of multicolored butterflies will swarm over you, lighting on your face and hands, as you wait for the boat to arrive. Shortly, you'll pile into an aluminum motorized canoe, complete with life jackets, and head for the series of falls called "The Three Musketeers."

What starts out as a peaceful float suddenly turns wildly exciting as the rapids churn faster and the magnificent falls come into focus – a voluminous spray of steam and foam falling like pure energy from the azure-blue heavens. In June and July, when the river is higher, you can even go closer to the falls, but no matter the proximity, the trip will make you feel like one of those 17th-century *bandeirantes* who scoured the jungles of Brazil looking for treasure. At the same time, it's not difficult to sense the fragility of these natural resources and how necessary it is to preserve them as we head for the 21st century. On the way back, the guide will no doubt point out the various kinds of jungle trees, particularly the palm, from where the delicious palmitos (palm hearts) are obtained. (It was here that I first learned that palm trees, which take 15 years to mature, die when the palmito is cut – enough to make me boycott my own consumption of them.)

Between Nov. and Dec., you will be blessed with the sight of thousands of butterflies being born; during Sept. and Oct., white and yellow wild orchids burst into bloom.

Other fascinating eco-tours are offered by this same company, including alligator hunting, dourado fishing (best in Oct. and Nov.), and vigorous half-day walking tours. Boats can also be rented by the hour or day and outfitted with scientific equipment and specialized guides. For more information, contact **Ilha do Sol Turismo e Navegação,** Rua Lima, 509 (Beverly Falls Parque); ☎ 74-4244.

❖ **GETTING HERE:** *If you are staying at the Hotel das Cataratas, all you need do is cross the street and walk down the paved stairway to a mile-long cliffside path leading to the waterfalls. Other hotels may supply a transfer to the entrance, but a private guide on the Brazilian side is not really necessary. Buses from the local bus terminal downtown (Avenida Juscelino Kubitschek) run every half-hour from 8 a.m.-6 p.m., including holidays and Sun., dropping you off at the road above the stairway. The fee is minimal. Cars may also be rented at the airport from three agencies.*

# The Argentine Side

For many, the Argentine side of the falls is the most impressive; the maze of catwalks and footpaths get much closer to the waterfall. Getting there takes a little more effort, though.

❖ **GETTING HERE:** *The easiest way is to join an organized tour. Or you can take a bus to Puerto Iguazú, which departs from the* *main bus terminal every half-hour from 7 a.m.-9 p.m. daily. Entering the park will cost about $1; ask for a map. A trail called* **Circuito Inferior,** *which starts at the Visitor's Center, will allow you to revel in the beauty of the falls for about two hours. The most impressive sight is the* **Garganta del Diablo** *(Devil's Throat) at Puerto Canoas, a conjunction of 14 separate falls that combine to form the world's most voluminous single waterfall in terms of flow per second.*

If you do not stay longer than one day, you will not need a visa, but check with the Argentine consulate to be certain. In any case, it's a good idea to take your passport as identification.

# Other Sights

## Itaipu Dam

If Iguaçu Falls is a natural-born beauty, Itaipu Dam is a facelift. A man-made harness of water power that cost over US $9 billion (plus another $15 billion in financial charges), Itaipu is considered by the Brazilian government as one of their greatest industrial achievements. Indeed, its 18 turbines, now fully operating, provide the country with one-third of its electrical power, but at an ecological cost that is only now being truly fathomed. The name Itaipu means "Singing Rock" in the language of the Guarani, an Indian tribe who would have been appalled by the climatic changes and fauna redistribution resulting from the dam's razing of over 869 miles of tropical forest. Ironically, Itaipu was also the name of a small island that has long since disappeared due to the dam's construction. Also destroyed was **Sete Quedas** (Seven Falls), a magnificent waterfall once rated by the *Guinness Book of World Records* as the greatest in the world.

Eager to offset controversy, the Visitor's Center presents a slick, pro-dam documentary that obscures these issues and instead shows the immense challenges faced by the construction team (8 a.m., 9 a.m., 10 a.m., 2 p.m., 3 p.m., 4 p.m.). Free guided tours, which leave from the Visitor's Center at 8:30 a.m., 10:30 a.m., 2:30 p.m., and 4:30 p.m. from Mon. to Sat., are diverting, though not as enjoyable as spending more time in the forest or at the falls. Technical visits by scientists and engineers may be arranged two to three days in advance, and are much more interesting than the group tours, including a guided tour of the plant and the impressive spillways. This kind of tour, however, is not recommended for children, who might push an important button and shut down electricity from here to Rio de Janeiro.

❖ **GETTING HERE:** *To reach the Visitor's Center of Itaipu Dam, take a bus from the main bus terminal; they leave hourly.*

## Ecomuseum de Itaipu

*Av. Tancredo Neves, by Rodovia Tancredo Neves, near the Itaipu Binacional Gate. Tues.-Sat. 9 a.m.-11:30 a.m., 2-5 p.m.*

Inaugurated in 1987, this ecologically oriented museum pays homage to the region's flora and fauna in artistically mounted displays. Indigenous crafts and tools from the pre-Columbian and colonial eras are also represented. This museum is usually included on the tour of Itaipu Dam.

# Where To Stay

See page 26 for price chart.

## Hotel Bourbon

*Rodovia das Cataratas, km. 2.5; ☎ (456) 23-1313, fax 74-1110.*

The Bourbon is a full-scale resort hotel with enough diversions to convince you to stay longer than the usual one day. The sweet smell of tropical flowers and the calming rush of a tiny waterfall pervade the lobby. The sprawling grounds still retain the feel of an intimate estate or tropical country club; most attractive is the large circular pool surrounded by exquisitely landscaped gardens.

Organized leisure activities include gymnastics, walking, tennis, soccer and leisure programs for children who cavort around with *Mickey Ratão* (Mickey Mouse). A mini-spa with dry and wet sauna, jacuzzi and massage are available. An elegant à la carte dining room overlooks the pool; lunch and dinner buffets are served daily, with a poolside barbecue on Sat. Rooms are plush, with views of the landscaped garden; the only difference between the deluxe and standard is the makeup mirror in the bathroom. The Bourbon is also walking distance to the Rafain Churrascaria, 2 km. from downtown. *180 apts. Expensive. All cards.*

## Hotel das Cataratas

*Rodovia das Cataratas, km. 28; ☎ (455) 23-2266; fax 74-1688.*

The impressive, colonial-style Das Cataratas has gained a popular reputation since it is the only Brazilian hotel that offers a view of the falls. Unfortunately, this reputation is misleading. Even though the falls are an easy walk across the street, the view from the apartments is some distance away and often obscured by trees. Moreover, you cannot confirm a room with a view in advance, and must accept whatever is available on arrival. The alternative view, of the tropically landscaped backyard, may actually be preferable, since a variety of animals, including ostriches and emus, stroll around at will.

Rooms are spacious, furnished in the rich carved woodwork of the colonial period. Breakfast is served from 4 a.m.-10 a.m. to accommodate guests departing on early-morning flights. A barbecue buffet is served poolside for lunch and dinner, with music nightly. Tennis courts and game room round out the sports. Varig handles all reservations for the hotel, since it is full owner. If you are interested in an apartment with a view of the falls, book a luxe room and take your chances. *206 apts. Moderate. All cards.*

## Hotel Carimã

*Rodovia das Cataratas, km. 10;* ☎ *(455) 23-1818, fax 74-3531.*

Located on the Rodovia das Cataratas, this four-star hacienda-style hotel is a mere 10 minutes from the airport. Modern sculptures dominate the large lobby, as well as a travel agency that can arrange tours of the area. A huge, unusually shaped pool is accompanied by a children's pool. Two restaurants include a *churrascaria* and a coffee shop for sandwiches and drinks. Simply furnished, standards differ from the superior and deluxe only in size, and the amount of food in the mini-bar. Children in the same room as their parents pay half-price. *421 apts. Moderate-expensive. All cards.*

## Continental Inn

*Avenida Paraná, 1089;* ☎ *and fax (455) 74-4122.*

Teenagers, Argentines, and engineers from Itaipu Dam stay at this nicely appointed three-star with an outdoor pool overlooking the city. No restaurant, just a coffee shop that serves breakfast. Six blocks from the center of downtown, the hotel prides itself on its calm atmosphere. Tropical drinks may be nursed on a circular outdoor veranda. *66 apts. Moderate. All cards.*

## Recanto Park Hotel

*Avenida Costa e Silva, 3500;* ☎ *and fax (455) 22-3000.*

The best medium-priced option, the soothing Recanto Park opened in 1991. Perfect for families, it's a favorite among Argentines, Uruguayans, and Germans. Pleasantly furnished apartments are all air conditioned and come with small verandas. No real difference exists between standards and deluxes, except for some minor decorations. Suites, with a couch bed, can accommodate up to five persons. Presently, there is a path for walking and jogging, and a gym is planned for the future. The restaurant serves only breakfast. Children up to age five stay free. *72 apts. Moderate. All cards.*

## Colina

*Rua Paço da Pátria, 1343;* ☎ *574-5712.*

Close to the bus stations, the apartments here are modern but simple. A good budget alternative, especially for those who don't plan to spend the night (half-day rates available for about $10). *Inexpensive. No cards.*

## Cisne

*Avenida Brazil, 144;* ☎ *74-2488.*

Located across the street from the Centro Gastronômico in the hubbub of downtown, this two-star has minimally decorated rooms and a simple, but dear coffee shop. All rooms are air conditioned, with small desks, tiny bathrooms, and even tinier closets. Only the deluxe have TVs. There's no elevator. *27 apts. Inexpensive. All cards.*

### Fazenda-Escola Picuí do Sul

*Near the highway to Santa Rosa of Ocuí, São Miguel. 54 km. from Foz do Iguaçua;* ☎ *565-1641.*

An unusual way to experience this region would be to stay at this youth hostel, situated 54 km./33.5 miles from Foz, on an old farm that now functions as an agriculture school. Two houses host 10 persons, with kitchen facilities included. The main building houses up to 60 persons. Bathrooms are communal. A 6-km./3.7-mile artifical beach is nearby. Groups of more than four persons can be picked up at the bus station, if arranged in advance. *Inexpensive. No cards.*

# Where To Eat

Since most tourists rarely stay longer than a day or two in Foz, the city has not developed into a culinary oasis. The Arabian community has contributed some provocative cuisine, and there is at least one fine steakhouse, **Búfalo Branco**. Noshers should head for the **Gastronomic Center** downtown. Excellent meals can also be found at the **Bourbon** and **San Rafael hotels.**

### Rafain

*Rodovia das Cataratas, km. 6.5,* ☎ *74-2720. 11 a.m.-4 p.m., 6 p.m.-midnight.*

Built as a huge barn seating 1,200, this *churrascaria* has no air conditioning, so pray for a cool wind. The buffet includes a self-serve salad bar, dessert buffet, and all the meat you can eat. Latin American music starts at 9 p.m.; by 9:30, a Paraguayan troupe of women are dancing with bottles. Not the greatest cuts of beef, but you can go up to the grill and choose what you want. During high season, come early (by 8 p.m.) to avoid the rush. *Inexpensive. No cards.*

### Centro Gastronômico Rafain

*Avenida Brasil, 157,* ☎ *74-5050.*

There aren't any 24-hour restaurants in Foz, but this gastronomic complex downtown is a fun place to hang until 3 or 4 a.m. Owned by the Rafain family, one of the city's most powerful hoteliers, the outdoor bazaar features pizza, pastries, ice cream, and meat pies at individual stalls; indoors, a charming air-conditioned teahouse serves more sophisticated fare. The lunch buffet is downtown's best bet, with seven cold salads, two cold meats, lasagna, fish, and pasta, as well as the ubiquitous rice and beans. In high season, samba shows erupt in the outdoor plaza around 9 p.m.; while you're watching, try out the incredible sweet called a "Balloon." *Moderate. No cards.*

### Churrascaria Búfalo Branco

*Rua Rebouças, 550;* ☎ *74-5115. Noon-11 p.m.*

Head here for the best steaks in Foz – an elegant eatery in one of the ritzier districts. Waiters wear tuxes (though you don't need a tie), and the chefs cook your order from scratch. A cold buffet of salads includes Arabian eggplant and potato salad. The dessert cart is spectacular. *Moderate. All cards.*

### Abaeté

*Rua Almirante Barroso, 893 (Galeria Viela),* ☎ *74-3084.*
*11 a.m.-3 p.m., 7:30 p.m.-midnight.*

Next door to Al Manara restaurant in the same shopping gallery, Abaeté offers international cuisine at candlelit tables. Codfish, paella, and a full array of chicken and steak are cooked with an Arabian flair. *Moderate. No cards.*

### Du Cheff Restaurante

*Rua Almirante Barroso, 683;* ☎ *74-3311.*

Situated in the San Rafael Hotel in the downtown district, this international eatery serves a full menu of chicken, beef, and pasta, with tasty specialties like the *pato ao vino* (duck in wine sauce) and fish dishes such as *surubi ao tartare*. From the road you can see Ciudad del Este and the skyscrapers of Paraguay. *Moderate. All cards.*

### Al Manara

*Rua Almirante Barroso, 893 (Galeria Viela);* ☎ *72-1112.*
*11 a.m.-3 p.m., 7-11:30 p.m.*

Drawing on the substantial Arabic population in Foz, this small but homey Arabian restaurant serves Middle Eastern delicacies *rodízio*-style. Dine on 13 dishes, including hummus, babaganoush, falafal, kafta (meat), yogurt, and sweet dessert. *Moderate. No cards.*

### Pizza D'Oro

*Avenida Jorge Schmmepfeng, 500;* ☎ *72-1961. 7 p.m.-5 a.m.*

When the last bus from the national park leaves at 7 p.m., head for this pizzeria, where the waiters dress in tuxes and you can dance til 5 a.m. Two to three people can fill up on 13 kinds of pizza. Beef, chicken, pasta, salads, fish, and desserts are also available. The artistic cover (under a dollar) includes live rock, blues, and Brazilian folk. *Inexpensive. No cards.*

# Nightlife

A **folkloric show** is held at the **Rafain Churrascaria** (see above). **Disco** dancing can be found at **Whiskadão**, Rua Almirante Barroso, 763, which turns frisky on the weekends. On a clear night, hang outside at the **Gastronomic Center**, where samba bands start blasting around 10 p.m.

### Oba Oba Samba Rio Rafain Samba Foz Nightclub

*Rodovia das Cataratas, km. 6.5;* ☎ *74-2720. Daily from 10:30 p.m.*

Iguaçu's version of the typical Rio samba extravaganza, with beautiful mulatta showgirls in glittery bikinis and over 40 folkloric singers and dancers. Visitors are encouraged to join in. *Moderate. No cards.*

### China

*Av. Das Cataratas, 1230;* ☎ *574-1314.*

Self-service Chinese buffet, including fruit and desserts. A good budget idea to fill up. *Inexpensive. No cards.*

# Shopping

### Artesanato Chocolates

*Três Fronteiras, km. 11.*

If you're traveling by car, stop by this enormous souvenir shop with trays of jewelry, machetes in leather cases, leather gun holsters *gaúcho*-style, and a chocolate shop that must be inhaled to be believed. Also available is **Café Iguaçu**, a coffee exported throughout the country and famous for its *cafezinho* blend.

# Hands-On Foz do Iguaçu

## Arrival

Many people arrive in Iguaçu in the morning and leave the same night. This makes for a full day and can be strenuous, particularly if you are city-hopping on a three-week air pass. On the other hand, nightlife is slim, and anything more than a handful of good restaurants is hard to find. You could extend your trip by crossing the border to shop in Paraguay, visiting the Argentine side of the falls, or taking a more involved eco-trip.

### Air

**Varig/Cruzeiro**, Avenida Brazil, 82, ☎ *174-3344;* **VASP,** ☎ *74-2999;* and **Transbrasil,** ☎ *272-4669,* all fly into the city's international airport, with good connections to and from all major Brazilian cities. The airport is 18 km./11 miles from downtown (about $15 by taxi). The bus from the airport to town ("Dois Irmãos") does not accommodate large pieces of luggage.

### Bus

The *rodoviária* is at Av. Brazil, 99, behind Hotel Foz do Iguaçu; ☎ *73-1525.* If you're prepared for long bus rides, you can embark from Curitiba (9-11 hours), Porto Alegre (16 hours) or São Paulo (15 hours). Direct buses from Rio take about 22 hours. Air-conditioned express buses on the Pluma line are suitable for sleeping and cost twice as much.

## Climate

Highs in January run 90°F, lows 68°F. In July, temperatures range from 46°F to 75°F.

## Consulates

If you plan to spend the night in either Argentina or Paraguay, you will need a visa and must pass through immigration procedures on either side of the Ponte Presidente Tancredo Neves, the bridge that spans the Iguaçu River between the two countries.

**Argentina**
Rua Dom Pedro, I, 28 . . . . . . . . . . . . . . . . . . . . . . . ☎ 74-2877
**Paraguay**
Rua Bartolomeo de Gusmão, 777 . . . . . . . . . . . . . ☎ 72-1169

## Money Exchange

Good rates can be found at the airport exchange house. In the city, try **Casa Jerusalem**, Avenida Brazil, 1055. If you're planning to visit Argentina, it's a good idea to have a handful of Argentine currency for bus fare, food, and park fees (*cruzeiros* are accepted, but at a low rate).

## Travel Agencies

Most good hotels will arrange tours of the falls and special excursions. A good travel agency that also exchanges money is **Bomcâmbio**, Avenida Juscelino Kubitschek, 565; ☎ *74-1100.*

### Rafain Turismo

*Avenida Olimpio Rafagnin, BR 227;* ☎ *73-3434.*

This is the city's leading travel agency – the family owns a nightclub, three hotels, and a gastronomic center.

## Tourist Information

### Foztur

*Rua Almirante Barroso, 1065;* ☎ *74-2196.*

The official tourist board, this office can supply information in English. For information by phone, ☎ *139.*

## Tourist Booths

Booths are located at the airport. In Puerto Iguazú, Argentina, an information booth is on Praça Almirante Tamandaré, 64.

# When To Go

Between Apr. and July, the rainy season plumps the volume of the falls to their full peak, but the sky is often overcast and you will surely need a jacket to protect against the chilly air. In Mar., at the end of the dry season when the falls reach their lowest ebb, the weather can approach the uncomfortably humid, and mosquitos abound.

In years past, due to drought, the falls have been known to dry up altogether or, as in 1983, flood the area to such an extent that several spectator catwalks were destroyed. Whatever the time of year, do check the water conditions in advance, or you may be sorely disappointed.

## Time of Day

It's difficult to suggest the best time of day to see the falls. In early morning, the mist rises mysteriously to meet the tumultuous waters, and at sunset the play of orange and pink lights over the water is magical. It's under a bright sun, however, that the full majesty and volume of the falls can be experienced, especially if you want to take clear photographs. The best timw to visit the park is during the week when the crowds are less.

# RIO GRANDE DO SUL

Consider Rio Grande do Sul the Texas of Brazil. The southernmost state, bordered by Argentina in the west and Uruguay in the south, Rio Grande do Sul is steeped in a powerful cowboy culture shared by the *pampas* of all three countries – that vast territory of cattle-grazing grasslands that provides the best beef in South America. Like Texans, natives of Rio Grande do Sul (called *gaúchos*) have evinced a fierce pride in their culture and region, forced as they were to defend their borders without the help of the central government (who tended to ignore them for centuries). When **Getúlio Vargas,** the state's most famous resident, seized national power in 1930 through a coup d'etat, the country perked up to Rio Grande's existence. Since then, it has developed into one of the most educated regions in the country, and is definitely the most picturesque.

The state has a deep love for land and roots, and in both cases the profile is extremely diverse – apparent not only in the ethnic mix of the people, but

in the topography as well. Blue-eyed blonds and dark swarthy looks reflect the region's deep **European heritage**, mixing Portuguese, Spanish, German, and Italian-descended Brazilians. Towns such as Gramado and Canela, with their German chalets and mountainous vistas, appear to have been transplanted from the Alps, and in the wine country of Garibaldi and Bento Gonçalves, you can still find families that speak their native Italian and use the winery techniques of their homeland. Topographically, the landscape changes dramatically from secluded beaches along the coast to the **Serra Gaucha**, a mountainous plateau 40 miles inland, where the only snowfall in Brazil can be found. Perfect for trekkers and equestrians, the Serra's green valleys, rolling hills, and pine forests make a spectacular backdrop for massive waterfalls and death-defying canyons. **Itaimbezinho Canyon**, some 2,200 feet deep, four miles long and, in some places, a mile wide, is the largest in South America. At the most southern point of the state, the shoreline, dominated by the resort city of Torres, remains legendary for its craggy rock formations and the mysterious stories they have inspired.

# Culture

## Gaúcho

A *gaúcho* sips *chimarrão* in a typical saloon.

The term *gaúcho* (gow-OO-shoo) refers to the culture and figure of the macho Brazilian cowboy, a colorfully dressed character who still survives authentically in the smaller towns of the extreme south. In the larger cities, *gaúcho* dress is often worn at festivals and special parties; the suede chaps, red kerchief, and black baggy pants tucked into knee-high boots usually require a large-shouldered frame to look appropriately virile, but these days girls and young women have appropriated the voluminous pants as street fashion, wearing them with tightly fitting turtlenecks. Recently, the South's version of country music, particularly accordion folk tunes, has peaked the interest of youths, who are now returning to their roots for inspiration. Recent TV soap operas have further helped to revitalize this cowboy culture, already replete with rodeos, contests of skill, colorful aphorisms, and romantic traditions.

Traditional *gaúcho* schools, like the one in São Francisco, maintain traditions by teaching young people the unique dances and music of the culture. Professional shows of dancing *gaúchos*, with their high-flying spurs and lasso twirling, can often be more exciting than Spanish flamenco. Country dancing, couple-style, is also charming and can be seen in shows presented at some large steakhouses. To truly enter the cowboy culture of Brazil, however, you should sign up for the kind of equestrian Wild West experience Christine Chauvin describes below.

## UP CLOSE ADVENTURE from Christine Chauvin "Riding the Life of a Gaúcho"

"... After our first day riding across the coastal plain to the base of the *serra* (mountain range), we finally take on the services of a local guide. Mounting our spare criollo horse, he leads us up a narrow and very steep path, through remnants of the Atlantic rainforest, until the terrain becomes so rocky and steep that we have to dismount and continue on foot. The horses are set free and go ahead of us. It's a tough climb and we stop often to catch our breath. Finally, we reach a clearing where we find the horses grazing, then remount and climb another hundred yards or so. Suddenly we are on the *serra*, 3,000 feet above sea level. A strong wind blows over the vast *pampas* before us. We resume our ride across cattle-grazing prairie, through woods, up and down hills, and never once encounter another human. Late in the afternoon, we reach the *fazenda* (farm) that will be our home for the next couple of nights. Dante, the owner, greets us, surrounded by his three-generation family.

The next couple of days are spent riding over this majestic countryside. Everything is lusciously green, the rivers gorged with water. One day, as we race to the top of a mound, we pull up to admire the breathtaking view of a waterfall, the Passo do S, so-named after the shallow underwater path in the shape of an S that is used to cross the river just above the fall. It is a spectacular sight, the water cascading in tiers before thundering down another 100 feet to the riverbed below.

After a succession of magnificent views, we end our ride on the outskirts of the attractive town of São Francisco Paulo. Our last night is spent at the Pousada Pomar do Cisne Branco (White Swan Inn), locally referred to as Zeze's Place. An entrepreneurial *gaúcho*, Zezé has refurbished his farmhouse into a comfortable inn with eight guest rooms and ensuite bath facilities. The barn is now a rustic banquet hall that's a favorite meeting place for the young people from the traditional *gaúcho* school of São Francisco. These schools, found in most mountain towns, teach music and the traditional dances of the region as well as all the equestrian skills. It was such a treat to dance with these accomplished young men while sampling succulent barbecued meats, sausages, salads, vegetables, and the typical bean and rice stews. I couldn't think of a better way to end a memorable ride."

*(Reprinted with permission from* Travel Log *newsletter. For more information about Christine and her equestrian adventures, see under Specialty Tours in the back of the book.)*

# Chimarrão

At least once during your stay in Rio Grande, you must partake of *chimarrão*, an herbal tea that substitutes in this region for *cafezinho* as the daily caffeine fix. A communal ritual, the making of *chimarrão* from *erva maté* (the raw leaves of a bitter-tasting plant) takes time not only to prepare properly, but to sip gracefully; in 1991 the state government passed a law prohibiting the use of *chimarrão* in public offices because workers were wasting too much time drinking it (in contrast to *cafezinho*, which takes only a few seconds to down). Traditions die hard, however; I once saw a fashionable woman in the airport of Porto Alegre, the state capital, stroll toward her plane, nonchalantly sipping from her *cuia*, the traditional cup made from a gourd. Today, many hotels and inns have *chimarrão* salons, rustically appointed with antique stoves and saddles, where you may experiment in private. Beware, however, that the taste is strong and often impossibly bitter.

### Method for Making Chimarrão

*Chimarrão*, the traditional *gaúcho* tea that originated in Paraguay on the Paraná border, is a sign of hospitality among friends, family, and business partners. If you spend any time in this region, it's almost certain you will be offered some in the form of a communal cup. I cringed at the thought of drinking out of somebody else's cup, but it's considered impolite to refuse. *Gaúchos* claim that the hot water kills any germs.

1. Fill a *cuia* (cup) two-thirds full with *erva maté* (tea leaves).

2. Pack the tea to one side and pour water (warm or cold) up to the slant.

3. Let the *cuia* rest for 5-10 minutes until water is absorbed.

4. Close the tip of the *bomba* (spoon-like straw) and put it in the empty space of the *cuia*.

5. Keep the *cuia* in the support with the *bomba* closed as you put in the hot water. Start serving.

# Porto Alegre

Despite housing more than one million people (three million if we include suburbs), Porto Alegre, the capital of Rio Grande do Sul, still retains its small-town feel. Maybe it's the 19th-century balconies with antique facades that labor next to the towering skyscrapers, or the vendors in horse-drawn carts who collect bottles and garbage in the old sector of downtown. Situated on the eastern bank of the Guaíba River, where five rivers converge to form a freshwater lagoon, the city dates back to 1755, when it was founded as a Portuguese garrison to guard against Spanish invasion. The city did not reach prominence, however, until it became Brazil's largest exporter of commercial meat. Today, the commercial sector is situated on a hill overlooking the residential levels down below.

Most tourists use Porto Alegre as a jumping-off point to tour the more picturesque cities of **Gramado** and **Canela**. There are a few interesting sights, in particular the historical city center, but mostly Porto Alegre is a city to savor some of the **best barbecue** you can find in Brazil. (Maybe the chefs here have a secret since they're so close to the cows...) In any case, the musical traditions of this cowboy culture shouldn't be missed (see under *Where To Eat*). Also, **soccer** reigns supreme in Porto Alegre; residents are fanatics, and their soccer club even won the world championships in 1983. One or two games a week throughout the year are held at Estádio Beira-Rio (except for Jan. and Feb.).

# Sights

Make your first stop at the **Mercado Público**, near Praça XV, which is a replica of Lisbon's Mercado da Figueira; its maze of stalls offers everything from *gaúcho* tea (*erva maté*) to food and handicrafts. On the left of the market is the neo-classical **Palácio Municipal**, the former mayor's office, built between 1898-1904. The influence of Eastern and southern European immigrants between 1880 and 1930 can be seen in various styles of architecture, including a fountain in front of the palace from its once-thriving Spanish community. **Avenida Otavio Rocha** is a sidewalk mall where you'll be able to find *gaúcho* music in the discount bins of record stores.

Porto Alegre's main commercial center is set along **Ruas General Vitorino**, **Senador Salgado Filho** and **das Andradas**, along the sharp-rising slope spiraling from the low-lying center. Here you'll find clothing stores, travel agencies, and banks that will exchange money. Some of the city's oldest architecture (from the 18th and 19th centuries) can be found further up the hill, along **Praça Marechal Deodoro** (known locally as Praça da Matriz), although so many renovations have obscured the original lines. The neo-Renaissance **Catedral Metropolitana**, which took 67 years to complete and wasn't finished until 1986, was built on foundations of a church that dated back to 1772. On the east side of the Praça da Matriz, the fine artistic influence of the Italian community can be seen in the mansion of the **Consulado Italiano**. Two other buildings to check out are the **Teatro São Pedro** (1858) and the **Palácio Piratini** (the fin-de-siecle governor's residence).

**Praia Ipanema** is polluted, but at night the drag is a major hangout for teens, who fill the street with their motorcycles, short skirts, and confident stares.

# Where To Stay

See page 26 for price chart.

### Plaza São Rafael Hotel

*Avenida Alberto Bins, 514 (Centro);* ☎ *(512) 221-6100, fax 221-6883.*

As elegant as you get in Porto Alegre, this five-star is a full-service hotel with outdoor pool, sauna, beauty salon, Varig office, *churrascaria*, gift shop, and *salão de chá* (tea salon). The impressive lobby bustles with execs and famous guests. Ask for an apartment with a view of the water; you'll be able to look down into other people's backyards. The live music in the bar is renowned. *284 apts. Moderate-expensive. All cards.*

### Porto Alegre Ritter

*Lg. Vespasiano Júlio Veppo, 55 (Rodoviária, Centro);*
☎ *(512) 228-4044, fax 228-1610.*

Across the street from the bus station and within walking distance of downtown, this three-star offers the service of a four-star, since you can use the pool, sauna, and restaurants at the hotel next door. Suites are comfortable, though even deluxes have no real decoration. A *chimarrão* salon serves tea. An executive buffet is a pleasant spot to catch a quick, decent lunch at a reasonable price. *107 apts. Moderate. All cards.*

### Terminal Tur

*Lg. Vespasiano Júlio Veppo, 125 (downtown);* ☎ *(512) 27-1656.*

Well situated across from the bus station, this modest two-star offers reasonably adequate rooms for budget prices. *60 apts. Inexpensive. No cards.*

### Colossi II

*Av. Cairu, 340 (Navegantes);* ☎ *343-5970.*

Budget lodgings, but the apartments are reasonably well maintained. Restaurant on premises. *Inexpensive. No cards.*

# Where To Eat

Meat is king in this cowboy country, and restaurants here seem to know just how to grill cuts to perfection. Many, such as **Galpão Crioulo** and **Recanto do Tio Flor**, offer shows featuring the music and dance of the *gaúcho* culture; don't miss your chance. Take caution at night in the city – as in all large urban centers of Brazil. See page 26 for price chart.

### Le Cap Ferrat

*Rua Lucas de Oliveira, 1035 (Bela Vista);* ☎ *330-6059. 8 p.m.-11:30 p.m.*

Definitely the prettiest restaurant in the city – luxurious, discrete, with a creative kitchen featuring six kinds of carpaccio, oysters gratiné, and a delectable *linguado* (flounder) in an orange Cointreau sauce. A romantic bar adds even more tang. *Expensive. No cards.*

## Barranco

*Av. Protásio Alves, 1578 (Auxiliadora) ;* ☎ *343-0717. 10 a.m.-2a.m.*

You might run into regional rock stars at this well-attended, upbeat *churrascaria*, where outdoor tables are situated under 100-year-old trees. Order the specialty, *galinha a Espanhola* (Spanish-style chicken). *Moderate. All cards.*

## Gambrinus

*Av. Borges de Medeiros 89,* ☎ *226-6914. Daily 8 a.m.-9 p.m., except Sun.*

One of the original standbys of the Public Market square (circa 1890s), Gambrinus is the oldest restaurant in the city, with menus that daily cater to the changing tastes of the clients. Fine Brazilian food, with *charque desfiado* (smoked shark) a true winner. *Moderate. No cards.*

## Churrascaria Galpão Crioulo

*Avenida Loureiro da Silva (Parque da Harmonia) (Cidade Baixa);* ☎ *226-8194. Daily 11:30 a.m.-3 p.m., 7:30 p.m.-1 a.m. Shows at 10, 10:30, and 11:15 p.m.*

Rio Grande's most typical barbecue house (*rodízio*-style) housed in a big rowdy barn with a gift shop for *gaúcho* supplies. The 15 rounds of beef (including chicken hearts) are excellent, the folkloric show featuring eight dancers is lively, and the band, with accordion, traps, and electric guitars, booms. *Moderate. All cards.*

## Recanto do Tio Flor

*Av. Getúlio Vargas, 1700 (Menino Deus);* ☎ *233-6512. 11 a.m.-2 p.m., 6 p.m.-1 a.m.*

Owner Alceri Garcia Flores, lovingly nicknamed Uncle Tio, has served the best regional food in Rio Grande for the last 10 years. Every plate is a macho delight, from the *matambre enrolado* (tasty slabs of rib beef with Texas-style sauce) to the *espinha* (juicy backbones that skid around the plate). The home-style joint can get rowdy when the clients start to sing, but the real floor show is wonderful: an attractive quartet who perform everything from elegant salon dances to flamenco-type stomping. The spur and heel competition between the men is thrilling. *Moderate. MC.*

## Chalé da Praça

*Praça XV de Novembro in front of the Largo Glénio Peres;* ☎ *221-6725 (Centro);* ☎ *221-6725. Daily 11 a.m.-11 p.m., except Sun.*

Considered a precious historical monument, this lovely house, located on Praça XV, was originally the city's carriage station and was actually dismantled once and taken to the 1915 International Fair in Buenos Aires. The French and German menu is enormous, including a rabbit specialty and goulash. A perfect oasis in the center of downtown for happy hour, where you can sit on the sidewalk under ancient paneling. *Moderate. No cards.*

### Piacevole

*Rua dos Andrades 1001, lj. 25;* ☎ *228-2632. Daily 11 a.m.-midnight.*
Good price for an all-you-can-eat antipasto buffet in a stylish Roman cantina downtown. Don't miss the afternoon teatime in *gaúcho*-style – shockingly generous – with steamy pots of tea or coffee and more than 50 varieties of sweets and hors d'oeuvres. *Moderate. All cards.*

### Archote

*Rua 24 de Outubro 905;* ☎ *222-6362. 11:30 a.m.-2 p.m.; 7:30 p.m.-11:30 p.m.*
In the best Lusitanian restaurant in the city, the delicious melancholy of Portuguese folksong, called *fado,* fills the air while you dine on authentic Portuguese fare, like the seafood risotto. *Moderate. All cards.*

### Nova Bréscia

*Rua 18 de Novembro 81 (Navegantes);* ☎ *342-3285.*
This is considered one of the best *rodízio*-style barbecue houses in the city. You can also order à la carte in a separate salon. *Inexpensive. No cards.*

### Chopão

*Av. Padre Cacique 891;* ☎ *233-1522. Daily 7 p.m.-1 a.m.*
For regional German delicacies and hefty beers served by cheery waitresses in *fraülein* attire. A staunch oom-pah band plays marches and polkas. *Inexpensive. No cards.*

### Primavera

*Rua Dr. Timôteo 842 (Moinhos de Vento).* ☎ *222-5389.*
*Daily 11:30 a.m.-9p.m, except Sat. night and Sun.*
A pioneer in the city for sophisticated sandwiches modeled from the Argentine and an inexpensive lunch stop. The fantastic cakes and sweets, like the Marta Rocha, are good any time. *Inexpensive. No cards.*

### Ilha Natural

*Rua Andrade Neves, 42, 1st floor;* ☎ *25-0214. Daily 11 a.m.-2:30 p.m.*
Vegetarian cuisine in this meat-oriented culture is difficult to find, but not impossible. Try the buffet of salads, hot dishes, and a variety of desserts. *Inexpensive. No cards.*

### Cantina do Peppe

*Av. Gêtulio Vargas, 273 (Menino Deus);* ☎ *227-5680.*
This rustic Italian cantina offers over 20 items on the menu, with an emphasis on pastas. Good for small budgets and big stomachs. *Inexpensive. No cards.*

## Teahouses

### Bela Vista

*Av. Cristóvão Colombo, 1931 (Floresta);* ☎ *222-7113.*

Don't miss the scrumptious spread for afternoon tea, served in the embarassment-of-riches style called *café colonial. Moderate. All cards.*

# Nightlife

As in most of the larger Brazilian cities, bars are determined by the age, musical taste, and even politics of the clientele. Most of the under-30 crowd venture toward **Avenida Osvaldo Aranha**, near the Parque Farroupilha, where a number of bars are located. Porto Alegre is also a major stop for Brazilian and international stars who give concerts. (On one trip, I even ran into Julio Iglesias, an old interviewee of mine.)

### Arubar

*Av. Goethe 550 (Rio Branco);* ☎ *331-6822. 5 p.m.-2 a.m., except Mon.*

One of the few bars left in Porto Alegre that still exudes the atmosphere of the 70s, frequented by old bohemians, journalists, rock singers, and actresses. *No cards.*

### Blue Jazz

*Rua Aureliano de Figueiredo Pinto, 998 (Cidade de Baixa). 7 p.m.-4 a.m., except Sun. and Mon.*

One of the best places to hear local and national bands leaning toward jazz. The kitchen is best on open sandwiches. *No cards.*

### Gruta Azul

*Rua Farrapos, 1274;* ☎ *22-9380.*

Designed like a dark tropical grotto, this "high-class" dance club is the Brazilian version of "Ten Cents a Dance." Couples and single men come to watch semi-attractive girls without much talent gyrate in leotards and hula skirts to the strains of a live band; afterwards, the clients are invited to flirt. Dinner and drinks are also available. Exactly why I found this famous joint so depressing became crystal-clear when I asked my companion what these girls actually do. "Everything," he said. *Moderate. All cards.*

### Radical

*Av. Guaíba 926;* ☎ *248-3426. Daily 11 a.m.-last client.*

On the edge of the Guaíba River, this in-spot is a country-cowboy-styled bar and restaurant with a mechanical bull, dance floor, and regional specialties. Crowded and ya-hooish. *All cards.*

### Sala Tom Jazz Tom Jobim

*Rua Santo Antônio, 421;* ☎ *225-1229.*

Hear some of the best jazz musicians in the country congregate for jam sessions.

### Clube dos Coroas

*Av. Carlos Barbosa, 1525; (Menino Deus)* ☎ *233-0045.*

An old-fashioned dance hall, with lots of space for boleros, tangos, and the samba-*canção*, a cheek-to-cheek way of doing samba.

### Ocidente

*Rua João Telles, (Mob Fim).*

The in-spot for the counterculture to dance and drink.

# Gay Porto Alegre

### Enigma Privê

*Rua Pinto Bandeira, 485 (Centro).*

Sophisticated and colorful, the Private Enigma has gained the reputation as the "gay temple" in town. Dance to live music.

# Shopping

Porto Alegre is a fount of *gaúcho* artifacts, though most goods can be bought cheaper in Gramado and Canela. One of the best traditional stores is **Invernada Grande**, Rua Senhor dos Passos, 166, Praça Otávio Rocha; ☎ 27-2961, where a cowgirl or boy could go crazy over the knee-high boots, leather capes, voluminous *gaúcho* pants, silver spurs, and finely engraved saddles. **Alchieri**, Rua Voluntários da Pátria, 777; ☎ 225-0473, also features typical arts and crafts. The best shopping mall is **Iguatemí Shopping** in Zona Norte. At the **Museu de Arte** of Rio Grande do Sul Praça da Alfândega (Tues.-Sun. 10 a.m.-5 p.m.) you can pick from a small collection of prints and paintings by local artists.

# Hands-On Porto Alegre

## Arrivals

### Air

The **Salgado Filho International Airport** is eight km. from downtown. **Varig, Transbrasil, VASP,** and **Rio Sul** all fly into Porto Alegre from major Brazilian cities; in fact, Porto Alegre is the stop-over for almost all travel to the South. International flights also arrive from Montevideo, Santiago, and Buenos Aires.

## Subway

A modern sophisticated subway system offers service from the airport to the Mercado Público (Public Market) in the city's center. This is the preferable way to reach the city, unless you go by taxi (about $20).

## Bus

The bus station is at Lg. Vespasiano Júlio Veppo; ☎ 221-7655. For general information, ☎ 145. Buses arrive in Porto Alegre from all over the country.

### Car Rental

Avis . . . . . . . . . . . . . . . . . . . . . . . . . . . . . . . . . . . .   ☎ 342-0400
Localiza . . . . . . . . . . . . . . . . . . . . . . . . . . . . . . . .   ☎ 342-4926

### Climate

Very hot summer (up to 91°F), with winters averaging about 42°F.

### Folklore

To gather more folkloric information, contact the **Gaúcho Tradition Centers**, CTG 35 Avenida Ipiranga, 5200; ☎ *36-0035*.

### Money Exchange

**Banco do Brazil**
Rua Uruguai, 185, 9th floor . . . . . . . . . . . . . . . . . .   ☎ 221-0044
**Exprinter**
Sen. Salgado Filho, 247

### Taxis

**Táxi-Cidade** . . . . . . . . . . . . . . . . . . . . . . . . . . . . .   ☎ 223-1122

### Travel Agency

**Mercatur**
Avenida Salgado Filho, 97 . . . . . . . . . . . . . . . . . . .   ☎ 25-8055
Excursions to the five-city area, wine country tours and money exchange.

### Tourist Information

## CRTUR

*Av. Borges de Medeiros, 1501, 17th floor;* ☎ *228-7377.*

This is the official state tourist board, providing brochures and assistance. Helpful information booths also are located at the airport, Casa de Cultura Maria Quintana and the train station.

## EPATVR

*Travessa do Carmo, 84;* ☎ *25-4744*

This is the official tourist board for the city of Porto Alegre. Information booths are also located at Praça 15 de Novembro; ☎ *21-0220* and at Travessa do Carmo, 84 (Largo dos Açorianos).

## When To Go

During the **Festa dos Navegantes** on Feb. 2, the image of Nossa Senhora dos Navegantes is carried through the streets from the Igreja do Rosário to the Igreja Nossa Senhora dos Navegantes. Festivities include a boat procession through the harbor, barbecues and dances. **Semana Farroupilha**, on Sept. 20, celebrates *gaúcho* traditions.

# Gramado & Canela

A mere 54 miles from Porto Alegre, these two picturesque towns situated high up in the Serra Gaúcha are a favorite among mountain climbers and anyone in need of a good box of chocolates. The Bavarian-styled towns date back to 1875 when the first Italian and German immigrants settled to pursue farming. Today, the einxaimel architecture and impeccably kept gardens are as much touristic attractions as ancestral homage, but the quaint beauty of the area can't be denied. Horses are still tied up in front of traditionally tiled homes, and residents resemble Rip Van Winkle as they walk through the cobblestoned streets sipping tea from traditional *cuias*. During the summer months, the air is fragrant with rose-colored hydrangeas (from which the region, known as Região das Hortências, gets its name). In winter, the cool (if not freezing) air is a refreshing break from the tropical heat.

A rivalry used to exist between these two mini-cities; now they find it more advantageous to unite forces. Gramado still boasts the better hotels, the coziest restaurants and easier access to shopping, but Canela offers the finest in natural wonders, such as the **Parque Estadual do Caracól**. After trekking to some of the country's most fabulous waterfalls, make sure you find a table at a *café colonial*, a traditional teahouse that serves a glorious spread of cakes, cookies, jams, breads, cheeses, hot chocolate and tea.

## Sights In Canela

### Parque Cascata do Caracól

*Located 4½ miles from Canela.*

Sixty-two acres full of mountainous vegetation with a 430-foot waterfall that cascades dramatically down a forested cliff. Within the park there is also a restaurant, crafts fair and playground, as well as camping facilities.

## Vale da Ferradura

Hardy trekkers can walk down a path to the foot of the waterfall, or travel an additional five miles beyond the park to the Vale da Ferradura, with its 1,300-foot canyon, around which the Rio Santa Cruz forms a horseshoe. The vista is particularly lovely at sunset.

## Araucária Multissecular

Don't miss a side trek to the 150-foot-tall pine tree rumored to be between 500 and 700 years old. It takes about eight people to fully embrace the trunk.

## Igreja Nossa Senhora de Lourdes

In the city of Canela, this church is also known as the Catedral de Pedra (Cathedral of Stones) because it's made entirely of basalt rock.

# Sights In Gramado

## Cascata Véu de Noiva

With access from Rua das Hortênsias, the 68-foot waterfall in the middle of dense vegetation is said to resemble a bride's veil.

## Lago Negro

*Rua 25 de Julho 175.*

You can rent rowboats at this beautiful lake surrounded by pines.

## Parque Knorr

Constructed by Oscar Knorr, this park is considered to be the heart of the city, a picturesque place where you can stroll at leisure, smell the flowers, and take photos of the *alegria do jardim* (profuse bushes of red flowers).

## Igreja São Pedro (1943)

In the center of the city, this church is notable for its richly colored stained-glass windows and the 71,000 stones that create the structure.

## Mini Mundo

*Rua Horácio Cardoso; ☎ 286-1334. Tues.-Sun. 1-6 p.m.*

Not just for children, this 8,500-square-foot miniature replica of Frankfurt, Germany, was created by Otto Hopper and his son, Heino, incorporating details from their favorite fairy tales. The marvelous work of art includes a Bavarian-style cathedral, tiny waterfalls, and a real train that choo-choos around the perimeter.

## Gaúcho Culture

Gramado's only museum is owned by a colorful local, Lúcio Petersen, who has spent his life collecting *gaúcho* paraphernalia. Saddles with silver, stirrups, stuffed armadillos, and animal teeth necklaces fill his two-room display house; in the back is a *galpão crioulo*, a rustic room with an antique stove where traditional tea is served.

Ask to see Senhor Lúcio's two horses ("You can't be a real *gaúcho* without horses," he told me), as well as his homemade *cachaça* collection, some bottles of which he just might sell to you. To see the museum, contact the tourist office (see *Hands-On Gramado*).

### Centro Municipal de Cultura

*Rua São Pedro, 369;* ☎ *(54) 286-2522, ramal 25.*

The center holds *gaúcho* dance classes every Tues. from 7:30 p.m.-8:30 p.m.

# Where To Stay

See page 26 for price chart.

### Hotel Serra Azul

*Rua Garibaldi, 152 (Gramado);* ☎ *(54) 286-1082; fax 286-3374.*

Exposed wood-beam ceilings, roaring fireplaces, and excellent service make this five-star hotel both elegant and rustic. Rooms are spacious and equipped with electronic controls, heat, and color TVs. The **Roda de Chimarrão** is a typical *gaúcho* salon for drinking traditional tea and *cachaça*. The excellent location offers easy access to sweater shops and crafts stores. Guests may play at the Gramado Golf Club. *152 apts. Expensive. All cards.*

### Hotel Serrano

*(Parque) Av. das Hortênsias, 1160 (Gramado).* ☎ *(54) 286-1332; fax 286-1639.*

Just 300-odd feet from the center of town, this four-star has its own extensive backyard park. Rustic wooden doors recall the forest outside. Rooms are well-equipped with color TV, video, heat (no air conditioning), and a huge mini-bar. Heated pool and sauna are also available. Dec.-Feb. special activities are arranged for children. There are no elevators, only stairs. The hotel's clothing store is excellent. *84 apts. Expensive. All cards.*

### Laje de Pedra

*Avenida Presidente Kennedy (Canela);* ☎ *(54) 282-1530;*
*fax 282-1532. Reservations in Rio:* ☎ *(21) 224-4798.*

Even if you don't stay at this fabulous mountain resort, do stop by the lobby to check out one of the region's best vistas: a paradise valley around which snakes the River Caí. The hotel even has its own backyard park, including a heated pool set amid the greenery. A *chimarrão* salon is an inviting place to try *gaúcho* tea, or you can spend the evening indulging in wine and cheese in the cave-like restaurant. The hotel's disco is one of the few nightspots in a city where most everyone curls up early before a fireplace. Rooms are rustically appointed; the ones with a view of the valley are worth requesting. *250 apts. Moderate-expensive. All cards.*

### Hotel das Hortênsias

*Rua Bela Vista, 83 (Gramado)* ☎ *(54) 286-1057; fax 286-3138.*

Situated on its own forested estate near the center of town, this exclusive Swiss-style chalet is decorated in fine wood furniture. Ferns drip from the balconies, and the lobby is the picture of comfort, with a roaring fireplace. Rooms are spacious. An indoor pool and sauna complement the rustic feel, but the restaurant only serves breakfast. No children under two years of age. *16 apts. Moderate. No cards.*

### Hotel Pousada das Flores

*Rua Venerável, 267 (Gramado);* ☎ *(54) 286-1841.*

Log wood walls decorate this Bavarian-style chalet with spacious, though austere, rooms that offer heat, but no air conditioning. The small lobby sports a fireplace and the lovely wood furniture of the region. Across the street is the Café Colonial Bela Vista, where you can find a scrumptious afternoon tea; down the road is a fascinating furniture factory. *16 apts. Moderate. No cards.*

### Hosperdaria Andrade

*Avenida Borges de Medeiros, 3585 (Gramado);* ☎ *(54) 286-3356.*

Located 10 minutes from downtown, this newly built hotel boasts simple but clean furnishings. All apartments have color TV, mini-bar and shower, but no heat or air conditioning. Breakfast in a tiny salon is included. *8 apts. Inexpensive. No cards.*

### Hotel Cavalo Branco

*Rua Reinaldo Sperb, 108 (Gramado);* ☎ *and fax (54) 286-1254.*

This is a good option for low-budget travelers and families. Apartments are not air conditioned, but do have a color TV. Suites can sleep five. A heated pool is located on the balcony and there is also a small playground. The restaurant serves only breakfast and snacks at night. *27 apts. Inexpensive. No cards.*

## Spas

### Instituto Balneo e Lodoterápico

*Avenida Borges de Medeiros, 3550 (Gramado);* ☎ *(54) 286-1027.*

This spa offers mud therapies rumored to be excellent for such disorders as rheumatism, infections of the skin, obesity, and impotence, all under medical supervision.

## Kur Hotel

*(Parque/clínica) Rua das Nações Unidas, 533 (Gramado);* ☎ *(54) 286-2133.*

A glorious place to rest, this famous health spa with hotel accommodations features minimum stays of one week. Not just for weight control, the clinic deals under medical supervision with all kinds of illnesses. Lectures on nutrition and psychology accompany 25 types of physical therapy, including herbal baths, massage, compresses, and sauna. Aerobic classes are available, as is a special walking pool. The hotel's store sells excellent herbal shampoos and herbs, as well as *guaraná,* a natural Brazilian stimulant. The Chinese shiatzu I tested was authentic but brutal. *19 apts. Expensive. All cards.*

# Where To Eat

See page 26 for price chart.

## Churrascaria Três Reis

*Avenida Borges de Medeiros, 2713 (Gramado);* ☎ *286-1874.*
*11:30 a.m.-3 p.m., 7 p.m.-midnight.*

Next door to where the Film Festival is held, this intimate *rodízio,* with a fine salad bar, even serves popcorn with their *cafezinho.* Try the soup "Ainho Lini." *Moderate. All cards.*

## St. Hubertus

*Rua da Carriere, 974 (Lago Negro);* ☎ *286-1273. 12 p.m.-2:30 p.m., 6:30-11 p.m. Closed Tues., Mar.-May, and Aug. to Nov.*

This Swiss-style restaurant is considered the best in Gramado. The lace tablecloths and panoramic forested scenery is a great backdrop for delicious fondues. Try some regional wines, such as Almaden, Garibaldi, and Adega Aurora. The hotel of the same name has a different owner, but its 20 apartments are also exceedingly pretty. *Moderate. All cards.*

## Torre

*Av. das Hortênsias, 2174 (Gramado);* ☎ *286-1921. Daily 1-10 p.m.*

Old photos of immigrants and *gaúchos* from the early 1930s line the walls of this traditional teahouse, where the waitresses dress like *fräuleins.* For a fixed price, you'll receive seven plates of sweets, sausage, chicken, polenta, cold cuts, vegetables, jams, and steaming pots of coffee, tea, and chocolate. Downstairs is Lucirene, an excellent knitwear store, and Artesanato, a good crafts store for leather, iron wares, wine, and cheese. *Inexpensive. No cards.*

## Café Colonial Bela Vista

*Av. Das Hortênsias, 3600 (Gramado);* ☎ *286-1036.*

Considered the best colonial in Gramado, with over 60 selections. *Moderate. No cards.*

### Churrascaria Garfo e Bombacha

*Estrada do Caracól, km. 5 (Canela);* ☎ *286-2677. Noon-3 p.m., 8 p.m.-midnight; Sun. noon-4 p.m.*

An excellent self-service *churrascaria* with a *gaúcho* folkloric show. *Moderate. No cards.*

# Shopping

### Sweaters

You'll find over 30 sweater stores in this region; two of the best are: **Malharia Vovó Anita**, Avenida Borges de Medeiros, 2717, next to the Gramado cinema, and **Knitmaage** downtown. Cashmere sweaters from Argentine wool can be found at **Avenida Osvaldo Aranha**, 235; ☎ *282-2223.*

### Gaúcho

The best *gaúcho* clothes can be found at **Dan Mathi Nativa**, where leather jackets, hot pants and vests direct from the factory can be bought. Also try **Kouro Arte,** Avenida das Hortênsias, 3021/1438 and 1835 (Gramado). Quality *gaúcho* boots are sold at **Casa da Bota**, Rua Henrique Muxfeldt, 67.

### Gifts

The largest gift store (with a large variety of *chimarrão* sets and *gaúcho* hats) is **Artesenato Martini,** Avenida das Hortênsias, 5480.

### Wine

For local wines and cheese, try **Casa di Vinho Jolimont,** Avenida Osvaldo Aranha, 370; ☎ *282-1232* (Canela, across from the cinema).

### Furniture

If you have time, visit the fascinating handmade furniture factory **Moveis Serrano Fabrika**, Avenida das Hortênsias, 4070. The sawdust is knee-deep, but the designs are outrageously inventive, like the chair that folds into a ladder and another that turns into an ironing board. An agent in Texas delivers orders to the States.

### Chocolate

The region excels in chocolate. Seventy varieties can be found at **Chocolate Caracol**, Avenida Dom Guanella, 1638/RD 236; ☎ *282-1829.* **Chocolate Caseiro Gramado da Pawer** at Avenida de Hortênsias, 4100, is near the Pousada das Flores. **Chocolate Cogumelo** at Rua Dona Carlinda, 554, ☎ *282-2422,* is best known for its truffles and fruit-filled chocolates in the best European style.

## Hands-On Gramado & Canela

### Arrivals

**Buses** run from Porto Alegre, Canela, Nova Pétropolis, and Torres. The bus station is at Av. Borges de Medeiros, 2100; ☎ *286-1302.*

### Climate

Temperatures in Jan. run from 76° to 104°F; in July 68° to 75°F.

### Car Rental

Sergatur . . . . . . . . . . . . . . . . . . . . . . . . . . . . . . . . .   ☎ 286-2087

### Tourist Information

The tourist office is at Av. das Hortênsias. It's open from 8 a.m.-6 p.m.

### Travel Agencies

**Bella Tur**. . . . . . . . . . . . . . . . . . . . . . . . . . . . . . . .   ☎ 286-2087
**Sergatur** . . . . . . . . . . . . . . . . . . . . . . . . . . . . . . . .   ☎ 286-2087

### When To Visit

A well-attended **film festival** takes place in Aug. The **Festa da Colônia** is in Feb.

# Nova Petrópolis

A half-hour drive from Gramado on the northeast mountain ridges lies Nova Petrópolis, one of the sleepiest, safest cities in all Brazil (the residents don't even lock their car doors!). In the 19th century, Nova Petrópolis was established by German immigrants from the Austro-Hungarian Empire, as well as by Prussians and Bavarians, who maintained their own customs while adopting the *gaúcho* traditions. Because the land so resembled Petrópolis (where the Emperor summered near Rio de Janeiro), the immigrants called their territory "New Petrópolis." Today, the area is considered a model of development for a small landed estate. At 6 a.m., carillon bells start ringing, with a hundred tolls at 6:30 a.m., making it impossible for any normal person to remain sleeping, although the residents claim they don't hear it anymore. Most children speak German at home, and many groups seriously study folkloric dances, particularly for Oktoberfest. Noted for its atmosphere of "nothing going on," the town is a perfect place to rest. Horse-drawn carts still mosey down the avenues and cattle graze contentedly in the tall grassy fields.

**UP CLOSE TIP:** *Do be careful of mosquitoes. They were once considered a widespread problem, but are now only frisky at night in hot weather.*

# Sights

## Parque Aldeia do Imigrante
## (Park of the Immigrant)

The main tourist attraction in Nova Petrópolis is this sprawling forested park that features a reconstructed immigrant village. Peacocks and chickens wander freely around the picturesque lake, where you can swim and rent paddleboats; a beer garden hosts winter and summer festivals. The park is perfect for long, idyllic walks, as well as offering a shopping complex for local crafts.

## Ninho das Aguas

You'll need a guide and jeep to take you over the long rocky road that goes to Ninho das Aguas, one of the best hang-gliding drops in the country. At the platform, you'll find a fantastic view of the countryside.

## Floricultura Ursula

To see the variety of plants grown in the region visit this nursery, which supplies flowers to the region's hotels.

## Recanto Suiço

Don't miss *café colonial* at this eight-table German-style eatery where the owner herself serves the generous tea beneath antique cuckoo clocks and all sorts of knickkacks. *Nata*, a cream-like substance, is exceedingly wonderful on toast with jam; even the butter here comes shaped like flowers.

# Where To Stay

See page 26 for price chart.

### Veraneio Recanto Suiço

*Avenida 15 de Novembro, 2195; fax and ☎ (54) 281-1229.*

German hospitality prevails at this intimate hotel, where you'll feel like you're living with the owners. The apartments are attached to the main house. They are cozy, and some even have their own chalets. *4 suites, 4 chalets, 2 cabanas. Inexpensive. All cards.*

### Hotel Petrópolis

*Rua Cel. Alfredo Steglich, 81; fax and ☎ (54) 281-1091.*

A simple chalet house with a tiny pool, overlooking a mountain view on a picturesque estate. *21 apts, 9 chalets. Inexpensive. No cards.*

## Where To Eat

See page 26 for price chart.

### Colina Verde

*BR-116 Sul (Linha Olinda); ☎ 281-1388. 11:30 a.m.-2 p.m., closed Mon.*

Well-cooked dishes that mix Italian and German influences include soup, cheese, salad, potatoes, chicken, and sauerkraut. *Inexpensive. No cards.*

### Cantina Príncipe di Napoli

*Avenida 15 de Novembro, 832; ☎ 281-1202.*

This brightly colored Italian cantina is strewn with party streamers and graffiti. Try the hearty plates of lasagna. *Inexpensive. No cards.*

## Shopping

The main street of Nova Petrópolis is full of shops that sell sweaters – which is a major product of the region – both handmade and factory-made. One of the best stores is **Christian Malha**. Also try **Art' Elis** for leather briefcases and lace handiwork; **Malharia Beatriz** for needlepoint and sweaters; **Arte & Manha** for interesting children's sweaters; **Salão do Artesanato** for excellent *cachaça* in fruit-filled glass bottles. At **Folklorica**, owner Gessy Deppe makes wonderful German-style clothes, dolls, and dancing shoes; you can even order custom-made dresses.

> **UP CLOSE TIP:** *Don't buy cachaça in the supermarket. The best is homemade; try the Velho Barreiro sold at specialty stores.*

## Hands-On Nova Petrópolis

### Arrival

**Buses** run regularly from Porto Alegre, Canela, and Gramado. The bus station is located at Av. 15 de Novembro, 1577; ☎ *281-1100.*

### Climate

Summers are hot and humid in the valley, up to 85°F; during winter, temperatures can fall to 10°F. Frost is an annual phenomenon and snow can occur now and then. Best months are Apr., May, Sept., Oct., Jan., and Feb.

## Tourist Information

**Secretaria Municipal de Turismo**

Rua Cel. Alfredo Steglich, 95 . . . . . . . . . . . . . . . . .    ☎ (54) 281-1088

## Travel Agency

**Turisflor,** Avenida 15 de Novembro, 1936; ☎ *(54) 281-1107.* Offers one-day tours of Canela and Gramado, as well as Caxias do Sul.

## When To Go

In the last weeks of July, the **Festival de Folclore** features dance groups from all over the world. In the last week of Jan., **Festival de Verão** has German-style bands and traditional foods. **Oktoberfest** takes place in the last week of Oct.

# Torres

Rio Grando do Sul is not particularly noted for its seaside resorts, despite the unbroken 310-mile-long coast visited frequently by Uruguayan tourists. Torres is the one exception; with its mountainous cliffs and raging ocean, it's a dramatic point to visit even in off-season. Getting there is half the beauty: The rolling green hills on the road from Porto Alegre are strangely reminiscent of Texas, except for the *garças* (tiny white birds), who love to perch on the backs of friendly cows. The beach resort is considered one of the cleanest in Brazil, since the waste of the city is not permitted to drain there. The dynamic coastline has given birth to hundreds of legends, and once you glimpse the mysterious rock formations off the cliff, you will understand why the boatmen are inspired to spin such magical yarns. One popular legend tells of a beautiful mermaid who appeared to a fisherman, asked for a comb, then pointed out a fabulous treasure. (Another version claims the fisherman went mad just from the sight of the mermaid and never retrieved the treasure.) In summer the main beaches, such as **Praia Grande**, teem with colorful cabanas and bathers; better to go in Mar. or Nov.

The main street of Torres has the feel of a small rural town. Along the beach drag, however, are houses of such architectural interest that students from all over the country come just to study them.

## Beaches

### Praia da Guarita

The main beach in Torres, Praia da Guarita is a gathering place for elite bathers. Take a walk up over the rocks and stone steps for a magnificent view of the beach and sand dunes. You are not permitted to touch the vegetation, which is part of a microsystem under the supervision of landscaper Roberto Burle Marx, but you may take a walk down to the

**Furnas do Diamante**, one of the most dramatic and raging seas in Brazil. With great care, descend into the grotto and stay all day (pack a lunch bag). Full of mist mixing with foam, the cave has given birth to myriad legends and appears particularly mysterious at full moons. As you walk north along the edge of the cliff the green fields might remind you of Druid country in England. The last descent, Ponte de Portão, sports a cliff with totem-like faces carved naturally into the rock. Photo ops abound.

### Santa Catarina

On the other side of Rio Mampituba is Santa Catarina, where you can see fishermen throw their nets after leaping dolphins have pointed out the schools of fish.

### Parque Estadual de Guarita

You can drive through this ecological park and contemplate the massive beige sand dunes.

# Excursions

## Região dos Alambiques

This area outside the city, where horses still graze in front of houses, is well known for its *cachaças*. Tucked into the nearby hillside is a grotto (*gruta*) famous for its miraculous healings, as well as scads of magnolia trees that lend a delicate feel to the air. Built in 1950 by the parish, the tiny altar at the top of a steep stone stairway still attracts thousands of pilgrims, many of whom climb the stairs on their knees and report miraculous healings.

## Sitio Nirvana Produtos Naturais

On the same dirt road is this brainchild of "immigrants" from the more industrial city of Caxias do Sul, who have become committed to living off the land.

Owners Spalding Rover, a New Age painter, and his wife, Mirtes, run this ecologically minded store, which sells fantastic honey bread, honey drops, natural oatmeal, and tropical-flavored liqueurs packaged in beautiful gift kits. Upstairs is a perfect view of the grotto, as well as their own paradisiacal backyard. Ask to see Spalding's inspirational paintings.

## Adega Don Cido

Beira 101. Delicious cheese and wines can be bought here.

# Where To Stay

See page 26 for price chart.

## Continental Torres

*Rua Plinio Kroeff, 465 (Mampituba);* ☎ *(532) 664-1811; fax 664-1090.*

This five-star hotel offers efficient service and a substantial restaurant. *132 apts. Expensive. All cards.*

## Dunas Praia Hotel

*Praça Mal. Deodoro, 48;* ☎ *(532) 664-1011; fax 64-2080.*

This three-star hotel is made for the beach, just steps away. Breeze from the sea cools the rooms without air conditioning and you can always escape to the verandas. All rooms come with phone, mini-bar, and color TV. The hotel is most likely open only between Dec. and Mar. *59 apts. Inexpensive. All cards.*

## De Rose Palace Hotel

*Avenida Rio Branco, 429;* ☎ *(532) 664-1087; fax 664-3163.*

Super deluxe rooms are nearly suite-like in this moderately priced hotel, where a rooftop restaurant offers a pleasant diversion. All rooms include color TV, phone, and mini-bar, but only some have air conditioning. *51 apts. Inexpensive. All cards.*

> **UP CLOSE TIP:** *Homes and apartments can be rented for 30 days during the summer. Contact the* **Secretary of Tourism,** *Avenida Rio Branco,* ☎ *664-1219.*

# Where To Eat

See page 26 for price chart.

## Restaurante Mirador Praia

*(Dunas Praia Hotel) Praça Mal. Deodoro, 48;* ☎ *664-1011. Noon-3 p.m., 8-11 p.m.*

The restaurant at this three-star hotel far exceeds the quality of the accommodations. Shrimp dishes are a good deal; the *camarão* tropical is a steamy shrimp stew served in a sweet pineapple. *Moderate. All cards.*

## Café Colonial Tia Zilma

*BR-101, km. 11, Porto Côlonia. 8 a.m.-9 p.m.*

A country-style inn located outside the city near Lagoa Itapeva. It is shaded by fig trees dripping with moss – a symbol of Rio Grande do Sul. Through the wood-shuttered windows you can gaze upon grazing cows as you munch on grilled ham and cheese sandwiches, deli goodies, and *torta mesclada* – a thrillingly light coconut cake topped with chocolate sauce. *Moderate. No cards.*

### Restaurante Molhes

*Av. Cristóvão Colombo, 30;* ☎ *664-2229. Daily 11 a.m.-3 p.m., 7 p.m.-midnight.*

A short walk from the Continental Hotel, this restaurant features huge black beetles dive-bombing through the open windows. Nobody offered an explanation, but the fish specialties, like the grilled shrimp, were excellent. *Moderate. AE, MC.*

### Restaurante Parque da Guarita

*Parque da Guarita;* ☎ *664-1056. Mar.-Nov. 10 a.m.-3 p.m., closed Tues.*

The fantastic park surrounding this grass-roofed eatery transforms its simple decorations into casual elegance. In summer the house is teeming with clients clamoring for the *casca de siri* (stuffed crabs). *Tainha* is a large fish from the region, serving two. Afterwards, take a walk around the rocky coves, where crashing waves and provocative rock formations create one of the most beautiful vistas in southern Brazil. *Moderate. No cards.*

### Ravenna

*Avenida Br. do Rio Branco, 117;* ☎ *664-1031. Daily 10 a.m.-4 p.m., 8 p.m.-2 a.m., Mar.-Nov. 7 p.m.-3 a.m.*

Best pizzeria in town *rodízio*-style, with live music. *Moderate. No cards.*

# Shopping

**Artesanato Avila**, Avenida José Bonifácio, 491; ☎ 664-1446, is the place for custom handmade boots; knee-high buffalo suedes are great buys.

# Hands-On Torres

## Arrival

The **bus station** is at Av. José Bonifacio, 524; ☎ 664-1787. Buses run daily from Porto Alegre, and frequently, Florianópolis. There is also a small **airport** at Castelo Branco.

## Climate

Summer temperatures (Dec.-Mar.) average around 75°F and 68°F in winter, making the area the most temperate in the state. May-Aug. is too cold to bathe in the ocean.

## Money Exchange

Money can be exchanged at **Banco do Brasil** and at the **bus station**.

## Tourist Information

**Secretaria de Turismo**
Avenida Rio Branco ......................... ☎ 664-1219

## When To Go

**Festival do Mar** in Nov. features all kinds of sports competitions, kite-flying, sand sculptures, poetry readings and musical shows.

Annual **balloon festivals** occur the first week in May. A **rodeo** takes place in Apr. **Surfing** competitions are held in Feb.

# WINE COUNTRY

North of Gramado and Canela on BR-116 lies the cradle of Italian immigration in Brazil. Wine-making dominates the yearly calendar here, immigrants having discovered extraordinary conditions of soil and climate as far back as the 19th century. The region can be considered a five-city community – consisting of Caxias do Sul, Farroupilha, Garibaldi, Carlos Barbosa, and Bento Gonçalves – all of which can be visited leisurely in a couple of days. (The major sites, including wine-tasting, can be crammed into a one-day tour.) For the most part, the picturesque roads, lined with rolling hills and fertile valleys, are good, except when they're bad and then they're awful.

Customs of the area are extremely conservative. Italian is still spoken at home, Catholic traditions remain strong, and family life is a high priority (women tend to marry young, though they have just recently begun to work outside the home). Accommodations can be found throughout the region, but one of the best (for its central location and park-like estate) is the **Samuara Alfred** (see below).

To reach this region, you can take a bus from Blumenau, Foz do Iguaçu, Porto Alegre, and various other cities in Rio Grande do Sul. Buses also run between the five cities listed below. You might also consider hiring a private car in Porto Alegre (see *Hands-On Porto Alegre*) or organizing a package tour through an agency. (Also see *Tourist Information* under *Hands-On Caxias do Sul*.)

## Caxias do Sul

Following BR-116, via São Vendelino, you'll come upon Caxias do Sul, one of the most industrialized cities in the region. Save your wine-tasting for Garibaldi, but most worthy of a stop here is the **Igreja de São Pelegrino**, Avenida Itália, 50 (Caxias do Sul), which houses an excellent replica of Michelangelo's Pietá, as well as 14 magnificent paintings of the Via Sacra by the Italian master Aldo Locatelli. As life-like as cinema, Locatelli's style uses immaculate detail to express the torment and despair of Jesus' life. The padre of the church, Father Mario B. Pedrotti, is a world-class spirit who loves to show off his church; ask him to show you the neon-lit cross and sepulchre, which electronically rise from the church floor to an electronic recording of *Taps*. Also visit **Ana Rech**, a chic suburb of Caxias, full of excellent Italian cantinas and interesting shops.

# Where To Stay

See page 26 for price chart.

## Samuara Alfreð

*RS-122, km. 69 (Highway to Farroupilha);* ☎*(54) 223-5844; fax 223-5843.*
About an hour from Porto Alegre and 40 minutes from Bento Gonçalves, this resort hotel is perfectly situated for visits to the five-city area. Rooms are large, and mine happened to look out onto one of the most beautiful scenes in Brazil – wooded mountains foreshadowing a duck-filled lake. Heavily forested grounds are excellent for strolling, and families can take full advantage of the large, indoor heated pool, sauna, tennis courts, and soccer field. Small animals seem to be always scurrying about, and one morning there was even a big white rabbit hopping through the breakfast room. A large TV room features wide screens and a roaring fireplace. An interesting game played here is *bocha*, the Latin version of 10-pins. *81 apts. Moderate-expensive. All cards.*

## Bela Vista Parque Hotel

*Avenida Rio Branco, 1965;* ☎ *and fax (54) 283-1177.*
Old-world charm is very much alive at this 50-year-old renovated hotel set on its own forested grounds in Ana Rech, a suburb of 10,000 near Caxias. A cozy bar, heated pool, and living room with fireplace add to the country-style warmth. Spacious doubles with exposed brick walls look out onto the forest. A Sat. buffet serves Italian food. *51 apts. Moderate. No cards.*

# Where To Eat

See page 26 for price chart.

## Cantina ði Walðemar

*Rua Antônio Ribeiro Mendes, 3054 (Santa Catarina);* ☎ *224-1520.*
*11:30 a.m.-2 p.m., 7 p.m.-midnight. No evening hours Apr.-Nov.*
This typical Italian cantina with wood benches and exposed brick walls offers a simple menu, but dinners come with a feast of side dishes, including antipasto, *sopa de capeletti* (chicken soup), salad, and pasta. Try a hearty regional wine, such as Granja União. *Inexpensive. All cards.*

### Roda Pizza Giordani

*Rua Governador R. Silveira, 1268;* ☎ *223-2703. Daily Tues.-Sun. 7 p.m.-11 p.m.*

Best pizza in Caxias, *rodízio* style, with 28 different kinds. The chocolate pizza with *creme de leite* is to die for. After 9 p.m., the joint starts hopping. *Inexpensive. No cards.*

### Belaria

*Rua Mq. do Herval, 1124;* ☎ *223-0100. 11:30 a.m.-2:15 p.m., 7 p.m.-11:30 p.m.*

One of the area's best restaurants, featuring finely prepared meats, such as the filet with camembert sauce.

## Shopping

Fine quality sweaters can be found at **Malhas Celli**, Rua Visconde de Pelotas, 2473; ☎ *(54) 221-3555.*

## Hands-On Caxias do Sul

### Arrival

**Buses** arrive daily from Porto Alegre.

### Climate

Temperatures average around 60°F.

### Tourist Information

For the five-city area, contact **Semtur Rua Alfredo Chaves**; ☎ 222-3344. Booths and information are available at Praça do Centro Administrativo and at the kiosk at Praça Rui Barbosa.

### Travel Agency

**Farrapo Travel** . . . . . . . . . . . . . . . . . . . . . . . . . . . . . ☎ 223-4041

# Farroupilha

Considered the heart of Italian immigration, Farroupilha is most noted today as the wholesale capital for shoes and sweaters. You'll probably need a car and guide to make the factory visits, but you can get a steal on well-crafted boots and department-store quality sweaters. One excellent sweater store is **Malharia Farroupilha,** Rua Treze de Maio, 275; ☎ 543-765. Also notable is the **Sanctuário de Nossa Senhora do Caravaggio**, six km. from downtown. For the last 100 years, at least 500,000 faithfuls have made pilgrimages here during May. On the perimeter of the city is **Parque dos Pinheiros**, 22 hectares of virgin forest sporting a fine restaurant, lake, pools, and sports courts. During the last days of Oct., a traditional *gaúcho* festival called **FEGART** is held.

# Garibaldi

Located in the middle of an exquisite valley, Garibaldi is the champagne capital of the region, responsible for over 96% of the country's production. The city is also the skiing capital of the country (one of the few places where it snows in Brazil, although not consistently). The city takes its name from Guiseppe Garibaldi, an Italian hero who took part in the Farroupilha Revolution, a provincial revolt against the Empire that failed. This is the best place to visit wineries, stroll through vineyards, and indulge in wine-tastings, as listed below.

## Wine-Tasting

### Coop. Vinicola Garibaldi, LTDA

*Avenida Rio Branco, 833;* ☎ *(54) 262-1100. Daily 8-11 a.m., 1:15 p.m.-5 p.m., Sun. 8-11 a.m., 1:15 p.m.-5:15 p.m.*

This winery is notable because it's the only cooperative in the area: 1,650 families of the region make up the ownership and more than 66,000 tons of grapes are harvested yearly. Best buys are the rosé and white wines.

### Maison Forestier

*RS 470, km. 62.2;* ☎ *262-1811. Mon.-Fri. 8:30 a.m.-4:40 p.m., Sat. and Sun. 9 a.m.-4 p.m.*

A classic name, this winery was the first in Brazil to possess its own land. Enter through the long forested driveway reminiscent of *Les Liaisons Dangereuses*, and ask for the guided tour, which includes a fascinating film about the wine-making process. The best labels are the Reserve Forestier and the limited Cabernet Sauvignon; also try Gewürztraminer. Most expensive is the Porte Forestier, which you can only buy here.

### Granja Piccoli

*Rua Lodovico Cavinatto, 1127;* ☎ *221-7744.*

A medium-sized vineyard owned by a single family, where you can walk through the orchards and pluck off the grapes when they're in season (Jan.-Mar.). Take time to wander through the vat room, with its overpowering aroma of wine. Besides nine types of wine, you can buy excellent grape juice and dried apples.

### Peterlongo

*Rua Manoel Peterlongo Filho, 216;* ☎ *262-1355. Mon.-Fri. 8 a.m.-11 a.m.,*
*2 p.m.-5 p.m. (3rd weekend of the month, 9 a.m.-4 p.m.)*

Since 1912, when the Peterlongo family developed the first Brazilian champagne, the sector has represented 70% of the municipal economy. Costumed guides escort you through the underground vats; don't miss the Cave de Bacco, where you can taste samples under electronically lit grapes. Ask for the English brochure.

## Where To Stay

See page 26 for price chart.

### Hotel Cascacurta

*Rua Luis Rogério Casacurta, 510 (Garibaldi);* ☎ *(54) 262-2166, fax 262-2354.*

Folks from Porto Alegre and and São Paulo come to Garibaldi to buy good wines at excellent prices, breathe in the fresh air, and settle into the comfort of this beautifully renovated 12-room chateau. Tastefully decorated apartments have a view to the rolling hills; the elegant restaurant is the best in the region. Upstairs is a cave-like eatery that opens onto landscaped grounds. Reservations are needed one week in advance. *Moderate. No cards.*

# Bento Gonçalves

In the heart of the colonial Italian region lies Bento Gonçalves, situated a little more than a hour by car from Gramado and Canela. The main annual event is the **Festa Nacional do Vinho,** held in the last weeks of July. **Museu Histórico Casa do Imigrante**, Rua Erny Hugo Dreher, located in the high part of the city, is one of the most complete museums in the area, with an archive that includes over 3,000 photos of Italian immigrants. Complete with a skating rink and antiquated trains, the forested **Parque da Fenavinho** sponsors major expositions. Don't miss the **Igreja São Bento**, the second church in the world to be shaped as a wine vat. Built in 1982, the church was constructed by parishioners during a drought year as a petition for rain. As things tend to happen in Brazil, rain poured the minute the church was completed. At the **Igreja do Christo Rei**, enjoy the 100 varieties of roses that are in full bloom Jan.-Mar.

# Wine-Tasting

## Casa Valduga

*Access from RS-470 (68.5 km.);* ☎ *252-4338. Office at Travessa Guaíba, 89;*
☎ *252-2709.*

The French chef Paul Bocuse chose Casa Valduga as the best Cabernet in
Brazil in 1989. The house also gets my vote as the most charming winery in
the region, owned by a first-generation Italian and his two sons. (Their
gnarled and grape-stained hands should alone prove the extent of their
labors.) Combining old-world wisdom with high-tech Brazilian schooling,
the family has come to produce over 120 varieties of grapes that they leave
in homemade vats until they mature. Between Jan. and Mar., visitors may
collect grapes and eat them free of charge, then sit down to a fabulous Italian
buffet lovingly cooked by Mother Valduga, whose homemade cheeses and
salamis are delicious.

Having started with nothing, the Valduga family now sells in bulk only
to five-star properties, such as the Meridien Hotel in Rio, as well as
Mássimo's (the restaurant) in São Paulo, who also orders an exclusive
vinegar. Guests are welcome throughout the week, but should make
reservations in advance for the weekends. Contact the Secretary of Tourism
for a map since the rocky path is often difficult to find.

# Where To Stay

See page 26 for price chart.

## Hotel Dall'Onder

*Rua Erny Hugo Dreher, 197 (Bento Gonçalves).* ☎ *(54) 451-3555.*

The principal four-star in the area boasts seven suites with jacuzzis. Deluxe
apartments are tight, but well appointed, and include color TV, mini-bars,
central heat, and electronic controls. The heated pool and sauna opens onto
gardens, and the wine cavern with fireplace is a cozy place to sample the
best vintages. *150 apts. Moderate. All cards.*

# Where To Eat

See page 26 for price chart.

## Pão e Vinho

*RS-470, km. 68;* ☎ *452-2250. 11 a.m.-2 p.m., 6:30 p.m.-11 p.m., closed Mon.*

The simplest of *bodegas*, but the Italian house plate is an embarrassment of
riches: salami, cheese, pasta, chicken polenta, fried sausage, and salad for
a mere $5. Downstairs, pick up regional salamis, homemade breads, cheese,
and wines. *Inexpensive. No cards.*

## Onder

*Rua Erny Hugo Dreher, 197;* ☎ *252-3555.*

Large Italo-Brazilian families love the hearty plates at this semi-sophisticated restaurant in the Dall'Onder hotel. A *gaúcho* show is offered every Fri., Sat., and Sun., and during the week you may be lucky enough to catch a hilarious choir of senior citizens who act out old Italian songs and tell jokes. *Moderate. All cards.*

# Carlos Barbosa

The only reason to stop in this tiny town between Garibaldi and Bento Gonçalves is the **Tramontina store**, known worldwide for its cutlery, tableware, and garden tools. Sheep graze in front of the factory down the highway. The quality of its utensils is superb and the prices are excellent.

# BRASÍLIA

Oscar Niemeyer, the architect responsible for the construction of Brasília, keenly described the ultramodern capital of Brazil as "the city Juscelino Kubitschek made with unlimited audacity and confidence." Truly, it was overweening chutzpah and daring imagination that built this wildly futuristic city literally in the middle of nowhere. Located on the desolate plateaus of central Brazil, one thousand miles from the coast in the state of Goiás, Brasília sits among the dry arthritic shrubs of the cerrado, looking, with all its circular, pyramidal, and polygonal buildings, just like desert sculpture. Although most visitors arrive by airplane, the oddity of Brasília's location can only truly be appreciated by land. As you drive across the lonely plains of the Central Plateau, you will go hundreds of miles without ever sighting a human – until suddenly, the highway widens, billboards blare out, gigantic modern sculptures pop up like mirages, and at one carefully choreographed moment a 14-lane speedway rears into view. You have arrived in Brasília.

Despite the fact that Brasília has evolved into an efficient city complex since its construction in the late 1950s, it still remains for many a powerful metaphor. For some, it symbolizes Brazil's arrival into the industrial era. For others, it's considered an architectural disaster, a monumental descent into conspicuous consumption, and the megalomania of a populist politician hell-bent on posterity. To a third, underground minority, Brasília is beloved as the capital of the Third Millenium – the focus of mystical and mysterious vibrations that are set to usher in the next one thousand years. As such, I suggest you visit Brasília with three sets of eyes: political, aesthetic, and spiritual. If you only see concrete, you will side on the opinion of Simone de Beauvoir who in 1963 called the city "an elegant monotony." But if you are keen to another sense, you can be inspired not only by the architecture, which seems to thrust into space with a passionate burst, but you'll be able to "grok" the enormous spiritual energy generated by a subculture of religious practitioners. In truth, the architectural meaning of Brasília is as much about space as it is about form. If the steel-and-glass structures seem at first cold to you, stop for a moment and contemplate their edges against the gorgeous ever-changing sky: the blue of day, the pinks and oranges of dusk, the twilight firmament at night. It's been said that 80% of all visitors to Brasília leave wanting to fly, and that's because the majority of Brasília is an awesome expanse of sky.

## History

When you consider the mystical origins of Brasília, it's no wonder that an astronaut was moved to say that the city is "the prettiest sight on Earth from space." Ever since the middle of the 18th century, the idea of transferring the capital from the coast to the center of this uninhabited interior has been the dream of numerous visionaries. Politicians first talked about the idea of a Brazilian inland capital in 1789, and in fact the plan was written into the constitution in 1891. On August 30, 1883, an Italian priest named **Dom João Bosco** had a truly remarkable dream in which he found himself traveling across the Andes to Rio in the company of a celestial guide. In his dream, he noticed mountains, plains, and rich deposits of metals, coal, and oil between the 15 and 16 degree latitude, as well as a wide stretch of land, at the point of which a lake had formed. As he later related, a voice in his dream repeatedly told him that when people came to excavate the mines hidden in the mountains, there would appear a Promised Land, "flowing with milk and honey." Quite intriguing is the fact that the topography in the dream exactly corresponds to that of Brasília, which was constructed between the 15 and 16 degree latitude (the lake referred to is the man-made Lagoa Paranoá, which was built to temper the low humidity). Indeed, it was about 75 years later (or three generations, as Dom João Bosco had predicted) that the vision of a "Promised Land" was realized. Today, a cathedral in homage to Dom João Bosco is one of Brasília's most beautiful churches.

# The Project of JK's Career

It wasn't until the presidency of **Juscelino Kubitschek**, who fueled his campaign with the fiery promise to build a new capital, that the energy to construct Brasília finally connected with the vision. The project became the central, if not all-consuming, project of JK's career. Many were skeptical of the government's ability to build in the middle of a wasteland, but Kubitschek rallied the nation with seductive political goals: By focussing the power of the federal government in Brasília, he claimed that the population of the interior would be stimulated, the capital cleansed of the "negative" international influences it felt in Rio, the federal budget empowered to deter inflation, and the country endowed with a living symbol of modernism. In essence, what the former physician-turned-politician was offering the country was 50 years of economic progress in five – a chance to make leaps of innovation in every area, from housing to transportation, education, commerce, and the social sciences.

## The Drawing Board

At the insistence of **Oscar Niemeyer**, who had already been selected as the principal architect for the project, the federal government in 1957 held a national competition to select a city plan. At first, many thought the winning submission by **Lúcio Costa** was a joke. In contrast to the hundreds of elaborate designs submitted by other contestants, Costa's entry consisted only of five medium-sized cards, some of which were mere sketches of crosses, or two axes on which was superimposed an equilateral triangle. In fact, Costa claimed he had not even planned on entering the competition, but after a long deliberation of the problem, the sign of a cross had popped unbidden into his head. Although some have called the shape of Brasília a plane, a bird, or a dragonfly, Costa described it as the kind of "X" mark you would make in the sand if you were locating a treasure. Despite (or because of) its simplicity, the jury, which included Niemeyer, saw in Costa's plan the thrust and unity required to meet the growth of a capital city. Mystics like to point out that the simple design also has roots in ancient sacred symbols, especially Egyptian hieroglyphics. As Costa envisioned, one axis, called the Eixo Monumental, would constitute the fuselage of the city – the official political and administrative offices – while the other axis would comprise the residential sector.

## Frontier Democracy

Fueled by paper money and international loans and grants, Brasília was built in an extraordinarily short time, pressured by JK's desire to inaugurate the city before he left office. A gold rush atmosphere prevailed. Bulldozers, food, and cement were dropped in by helicopters; migrants from all over Brazil came in hopes of a new life. As architects, administrators, and workers shared the same makeshift houses, bars, and restaurants, a frontier democracy was momentarily enjoyed, what Niemeyer called "a climate of fraternization resulting from identical discomforts." Kubitschek himself came to visit often, staying in a wooden building built in 10 days, called *Catetinho*, or Little Catete (after the Presidential Palace in Rio). To the delight of the *candangos* (or workers), Kubitschek walked around the site without police protection, threw barbecues for the workers, and upon leaving the Presidency even sent each employee of the federal construction company a signed letter of thanks.

In April 1960, exactly three years, one month, and five days after the master plan was revealed, Brasília was inaugurated with 150,000 guests in attendance, including President Eisenhower and Queen Elizabeth. Unfortunately, the 38-ton fireworks salute proved a bit premature. Many of the buildings had to be redone when they collapsed due to hasty construction; road junctions still had to be built; and landscaping in the residential sector was a dream away. The enormous debt – two billion dollars worth – was left in the hands of Kubitschek's successor, **Jânio Quadros**. Most disturbing of all was the fact that the planners had failed to account for the homes of the migrant workers who chose to remain once their jobs were completed. As a result, satellite cities sprung up around the federal district to house the overflow – some of them miserable shanty towns little different from Rio's *favelas*.

## Genius or Joke?

Much of the fun of touring Brasília is trying to guess what shape Niemeyer had in mind when he created various buildings. Although the architect was known for jesting with interviewers, he once claimed that he liked to throw a wadded piece of paper up in the air and used whatever shape it landed in. In truth, Niemeyer had been the leading student of **Le Corbusier**, founder of the modern planned city, whose designs were profoundly based on social philosophy. For his services, Niemeyer accepted only minimal pay (the equivalent of US $300 a month) and, like the other workers, he lived in makeshift accommodations until the project was completed. Because the workload was monumental, he often sketched the basic ideas and left the details to a team of architects and engineers. Politically, Niemeyer had the most socialist of intentions in constructing apartment complexes that were identical and, therefore, classless, but one of his great disappointments regarding Brasília was to discover that utopian societies cannot spring spontaneously from utopian architecture unless the necessary social changes are first initiated.

## Hunger for Suburbia

What is it like to live in Brasília? The term *Brasilite* (Brasilia-itis) was coined by the first generation of migrants, referring to the boredom of living in anonymous, identical apartment houses. Added to that was a deep longing for the hustle and bustle of city life – a tradition in most Brazilian cities, where much of the social and commercial life is played out on the street corner. In fact, it was the people who insisted that shops be put back on the street in contact with the curb. In frustration, many upper-echelon bureaucrats – hungry to display their individuality by negating the modern aesthetic – moved out of the apartment complexes and into their own houses on the other side of the city. If you have time, take a drive around to check out some of the more extraordinary houses: I even saw an igloo-type construction that had been handmade by a Japanese-descended scientist.

*Brasilite* does have its positive side. Despite the impoverished status of satellite towns such as Sobradinho and Planaltina, the standard of life in the federal district is high and the crime rate extremely low. For every four superblocks, there is a church, movie house, police, post box, school, gym, art center, and gas station, and every superblock is walking distance to a small shopping center full of food stores, restaurants, and boutiques. It is expensive to live here (since 60% of what is consumed must be imported), but there is no lack of urban services. Though nightlife is palpable (after all, the city is full of ambitious young politicians), the real activity seems to take place behind closed doors (in Brasília, it's said, everyone's in bed by 10, then goes home at six in the morning). From personal experience, I can say that there is a certain buzz of peacefulness that prevails in the city. Given the opportunity to stay several weeks in a private apartment, I discovered the layman's life here can have a slow, unthreatening rhythm all its own.

# A Bird's Eye View

Although getting around a city that uses only a series of codes and numbers for street names might seem daunting at first, the system is perfectly logical, if hardly poetic. The city is carved into sectors – the residential sector, the hotel sector, the banking and commerce sector, etc. – and their addresses represent the proximity north and south of the Eixo Monumental, or east and west of the other main axis called Eixo Rodoviário. For example, SCN 310 means Sector Commercial North (from the Eixo Monumental) at # 310. Fortunately for the tourist, all the major architecture of Niemeyer (the political buildings) are within walking distance along the Eixo Monumental.

It was Costa's genius that placed the *rodoviária* (bus station) at its most logical point – at the center of the city where the Eixo Monumental and the Eixo Rodoviário meet. Within easy walking distance from the bus station is the **cathedral** and the **National Theater**. About a half-hour walk away are the towers and dome of the **National Congress**. The **Hotel Nacional** is also just a stone's throw from the junction, as are two of the biggest shopping centers, on either side of the *rodoviária*. For a quick overview of the city, there's a circular bus route (bus #106) that gives you a long outer city tour (leaving and departing from the bus station); just be careful to keep your wallet close at hand. Taxis are also plentiful, though they tend not to be cheap in Brasília. The easiest way to see the city is to arrange a professional tour offered by one of the many travel agencies, which may even pick you up at the airport and deliver you back the same day for late-night flights. To see the city during the day and again at night, with the monuments fantastically illuminated against the dark sky, is like seeing two different faces of the moon; if you have the money, you won't be disappointed. A daring way to see Brasília is from the sky – in an ultralight plane. For information, contact the owner, Moacei, at his office, ☎ 223-5506, or at home, ☎ 248-6136.

Most people live in apartment complexes called **Superquadras** – nearly identical blocks of apartments based on the fundamentally utopian premise that the architectural design of Brasília would inspire the development of a classless society. The layout, however, never quite prevented the proliferation of political bribes to obtain choice locations (closer to the center), nor did it keep residents from decorating their apartments with individual style. At least, residential addresses are fairly easy to decipher. For example, SQS 510, bl. 4-209 means Superquadra South (of the Eixo Monumental), *bloco* (block) 4, apartment 209. Sometimes, signs on the street are not clear, so if you're visiting a private apartment, don't feel daunted. Each apartment block has a porter who will be happy to direct you; they're used to even long-time residents getting lost. (My local friends continually drop me off at the wrong address, particularly at night, when the superquadras really do look alike.)

The best view is from the 715-foot **TV tower**, which looms like a steel skeleton over the city. Designed by Lúcio Costa, it's located by the Eixo Monumental, Setor Oeste (West), and can be reached easily from the *rodoviária* (bus #131) or on foot. There's an acceptable restaurant, a bar, and gift shop. On weekends and holidays, a crafts fair is held at the base.

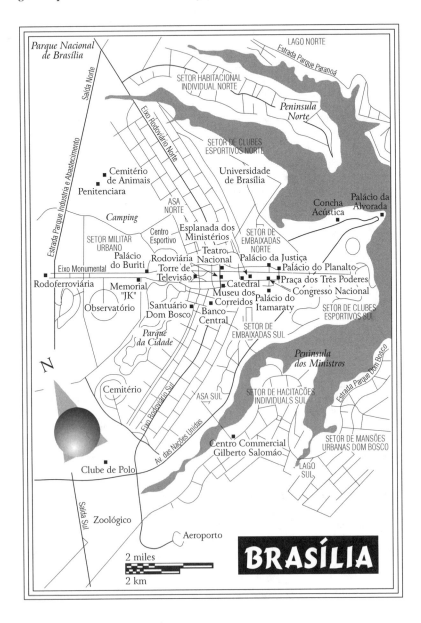

# Political Sights

Many people claim there are two powers in Brasília – one political, the other spiritual. (In fact, a popular joke runs: If there really is so much spiritual power in Brasília, why isn't the government doing a better job? The answer: Imagine what it would be like without it!) In any case, the following tour has been divided into two sectors – to respect the traditional separation of church and state – though, in Brazil that line is often finely drawn.

As envisioned by designer Lúcio Costa, the main political and administrative buildings are located along the horizontal axis of the city. On the eastern tip is the area known as the **Power Plaza Complex**, comprising the National Congress, the Palace of Justice, the Itamarati Palace, the Planalto Palace, the Historical Museum, and the Supreme Court. Dominating the center of this complex is the **Praça dos Três Poderes** (Square of the Three Powers), representing the forces of the Executive, Legislative and Judicial branches.

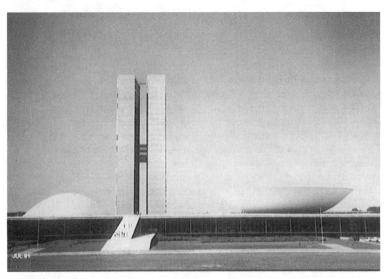

The futuristic National Congress building: the upward-turned bowl is the House of Representatives; the contained dome is the Senate; the towers in between the two hold the offices of the Congressmen.

## Congresso Nacional

*Mon.-Fri. 8 a.m.-noon, 2-5p.m;, Sat. and Sun. 9 a.m.-noon, 2-5:30 p.m.*

This is one of the most well-known landmarks of Brasília. Though Niemeyer would never admit it, many people feel that his downward-turned dome (seating 120) symbolizes the elitist views of the Senate, while the up-raised bowl of the House of Representatives shows its openness to the views of the people. Others claim that the bowl receives inspiration from the heavens while the dome keeps it contained. On Apr. 21, the anniversary of the city, the sun rises exactly in the middle of the office buildings between the dome and the bowl, which house the offices of the Congressmen. These two towers, both 28 stories, were constructed to be the highest buildings in Brasília by mandate of JK. (The law normally permits only 17 stories.) You'll probably see people climbing over the dome, which is officially permitted. Less exhausting tours can be made of the interior of the Congress, but must be scheduled in advance at the **Department of Public Relations, ☎** *31-5107.* English-speaking guides are available.

## Justice Palace

Also designed by Niemeyer, the seat of the Ministry of Justice is famous for its facade of suspended curved platforms from which falls a curtain of water. Some say (though sometimes sarcastically), it serves as a symbol of the "bountiful flow of justice" in the country.

## Itamarati Palace

A fine view of the Justice Palace can be seen from the balcony of this building, designed by Niemeyer, with gardens and pool by Roberto Burle Marx. Here, at the President's palace, heads of state are formally received, first passing by the front courtyard's sculptures of extremely large-hipped women – perhaps a symbol of another kind of Brazilian justice. In the foyer, the first sculpture you'll see is the *Polivolume,* by Ana Maria Vieira, made entirely from aluminum; that the artist invites you to push and pull the movable sculpture into any shape you wish is considered a symbol of the people's power to effect political change. The indoor gardens are full of plants from the Amazon; they do well here in the shadowed light. Upstairs are galleries and salons full of 18th-century furniture and modern and classical art: one particularly intriguing piece is the *Namoradeira* – a three-cushion love seat for a girl, her boyfriend, and her mother. In front of the building, the sculpture entitled *Meteors,* by Bruno Giorgi, represents the continents; it's made from interlocking pieces of marble and at night makes a marvelous reflection in the dark pools. Note that visitors to the palace may not wear short pants. Group tours are given free of charge Mon.-Fri. at 4 p.m. if no foreign heads of state are visiting. No photos are allowed.

## Palácio do Planalto

*Mon.-Fri. 9-10:30 a.m., 3-5 p.m.*

Behind the National Congress, on the north side, this palace houses the President's office, which is not always open to the public. You can, however, enjoy the changing of the guard at 8:30 a.m. and 5:30 p.m. daily. When the President is in town, he ascends the ramp of the Planalto in a ceremonial procession (complete with a band playing the National Anthem) every Tues. at 8:30 a.m. and descends Fri. at 5:30 p.m.

## Panteão da Pátria

Most people don't go inside the National Pantheon, but its external view is riveting; the shape of two doves in flight suggests the sense of unlimited freedom. The building was constructed in honor of former President Tancredo Neves and all the nation's heroes. In 1961, at the request of Kubitschek's wife, the First Lady, Niemeyer built a pigeon house across from the Pantheon. The 250 pigeons that were shipped in are affectionately known as the Brazilian Air Force, roosting during the day on top of the dove-like building. Nearby are the impressive sculptures of two warriors (by the same artist who made the *Meteors* at Itamarati Palace). Constructed in 1985 during the military regime to symbolize the sovereignty of Brazil, the warriors stand 105 meters high (345 feet); the flag, which flies continuously, is particularly evocative when illuminated against the dark sky. The changing of the flag, accompanied by a military band, occurs at 9 a.m. the first Sunday of each month.

## Memorial JK

Erected by Niemeyer to honor Juscelino Kubitschek, the memorial looks like a submarine emerging out of water. A statue of Kubitschek sits atop a 28-meter (92-foot) pedestal on the roof; inside, his body is retained in a red-lit crypt that makes a dramatic, if avant garde final resting place.

The museum inside boasts a fascinating display of his personal and political life, told through photographs, ceremonial costumes, medals, and documents pertaining to the construction of the city. Born September 12, 1902, in Minas Gerais, Kubitschek studied to be a doctor, but found himself succeeding in politics. After he passed the next presidency to Jânio Quadros on Jan. 1, 1961, he became a senator, but in July 1964, his political rights were suspended for 10 years by the military dictatorship, during which time he took exile in Europe. When JK returned, he met his final demise in a suspicious car accident. Although he certainly went to his death with the accomplishment of building Brasília, many claim he was responsible for beginning the gargantuan foreign debt, which today still threatens to choke the country to death. The museum also has a library, art gallery, and small snack bar. The entrance fee is about a dollar.

## Palácio do Buriti

A short walk north from the JK Memorial is the seat of the local government, set in its own square dominated by a Buriti palm tree. It's also nicknamed Sweetheart's Square because of all the parked cars that congregate at night.

## Avenida das Nações

If you have time, take a drive down this street, where all the embassies have constructed residences following the architectural style of their own country.

## Spiritual Sights

### Santuário Dom João Bosco

*Avenida W-3 Sul, Q 702. Mass: Mon.-Sat. 1 p.m. and 6 p.m.,*
*Sun. 8 a.m., 11 a.m., 6 p.m., 7:30 p.m.*

This Gothic-style church dedicated to the Italian visionary who dreamed up Brasília is appropriately ethereal; the wash of color from the blue-stained glass (12 different shades) gives the effect of sitting in heaven. Designed by the architect Carlos Alberto Neves with gardens by Roberto Burle Marx, the church was founded in 1964 and the first mass was held Mar. 23, 1970. The sculpted bronze doors hold the story of Dom Bosco's dream; on top is the life of Jesus carved in stone. Above the altar is an eight-meter-high (26 feet) crucifix with the image of Christ carved from a single block of wood by Gotfredo Thaler. To the left of the altar is a statue of Dom Bosco. The most striking feature is the awesome chandelier, weighing over 1½ tons, with 74,000 pieces of glass.

Catedral Metropolitana Nossa Senhora Aparecida.

### Catedral Metropolitana Nossa Senhora Aparecida

*Esplanada dos Ministérios. Mass: Mon.-Fri. 6-12 p.m., Sat. 5:30 p.m.,*
*Sun. 8:30 and 10:30 a.m.*

Oscar Niemeyer once claimed to a journalist that he designed Brasília's cathedral in 30 minutes, trying to make something that did not remind people of their sins. In fact, his futuristic circular temple, with sculptures by Ceschiatti suspended from the roof, more resembles an inverted chalice and crown of thorns, though at night it looks to me just like a space center for ETs. In any case, the upward-thrusting movement seems to carry the eye and soul straight to heaven while the pill-like Baptistry to the right grounds one back to earth.

After the church was completed on May 3, 1957, the stained-glass windows were taken out to reduce the heat, and Niemeyer spent the next two years trying to make the structure look more like a church. As you enter the cathedral the dark corridor he called the Meditation Zone prepares you for the bright illumination of the sanctuary. The bells atop the candelabra were donated by Spain and are engraved with the names of Cabral's boats. The acoustics are excellent; experiment with the curved walls. The wooden cross on the left was used in the first mass of Brasília. Next to the church, a flower stand sells dried flowers typical of the *cerrado*. Note: Shorts are not permitted.

## Igreja de N.S. de Fátima

*107/108 South.*

Built by Oscar Niemeyer with gardens by Roberto Burle Marx, this small, modest chapel was the first church in Brasília, erected in 1958 at the request of JK's wife, Sara Kubitschek, in honor of the Virgin of Fatima. Some say the roof's flying triangle resembles a nun's habit. The street in front is the only one in the city that has a name, Rua da Igrejinha (Street of the Small Church).

## Templo do Boa Vontade

*SGAS 915, LT 75/76;* ☎ *245-1070.*

The heartchild of José Paiva, a well-known writer and broadcaster, this interfaith temple, opened Oct. 21, 1989, is the most inspiring chapel in Brazil. Built through local and international donations, the temple is dedicated to the idea that the "altar preferred by God for His Worship is the human heart." As such, every detail is geared towards instilling a meditative state of mind in order that the visitor may open up to greater energies. At the inauguration, the stunning jacaranda doors were knocked on 17 times, and since then have remained opened. (As the chapel is open to the public 24 hours a day, many people come to visit in the dead of night.) Every detail in the chapel involves the number seven (considered the number of perfection). In the Nave, the tradition is to walk slowly around the seven rings of black marble, meditating on releasing your negative energy, until you reach the center, over which presides the largest and purest crystal in the world. Then you slowly return on the white marble rings, absorbing positive energy, until you reach the front of the altar. (My guide claimed that Russian Kirlian photography has proven that those returning on the white lane have clearer auras than when they began.) There is also a *Sala do Silêncio* (Room of Silence), as well as an art gallery of Brazilian and international artists. (Look for the German artist Ula Haensell, who makes healing mandala plates corresponding to each chakra.) Also, walk past the natural font of water that flows from the earth below and is filtered in a spiral to receive energy from the crystal. Downstairs is a memorial room, considered the heart of the temple, where you are encouraged to pray according to your own path. A brilliant, multicolored tile panel represents yin and yang energies, the chakras, and the spirit's awakening to God. In the inner room, the violet-lit suspended coffin symbolizes the spirit's transcendance over death. Near the exit is a souvenir shop, where you may purchase literature by Paiva Netto in English as well as a variety of crystals.

## Vale do Amanhecer

*Just 45 minutes out of Brasília.*

This is a community of 3,000 "channelers" or psychic mediums, totally dedicated to the healing of others. (For more information, see *Brazilian Spirits*, under *Introducing Brazil*.) Visitors may attend healing sessions in the eclectically designed temple on Wed. and Sun. afternoons, when clients are received individually for psychic counseling and the "laying-on of hands." You may arrive without a reservation or you may arrange an English-speaking guide and transportation through the tourist agency **Prestheza**, ☎ 226-6224. There is a simple restaurant on the grounds.

# Ecological Sights

## Botanical Gardens

If the concrete and steel of Brasília becomes overwhelming, there are several well-designed parks and gardens in which to escape. Located on the South Lake, the gardens cover 1,500 acress, loaded with different environments representative of the region.

## Brasília National Park

From the north of the city is this reserve of 91,000 acres, where flora and fauna of the region are preserved. Open to the general public are mineral springs, two natural swimming pools, natural woodland, an orchidarium, and tourist facilities. For tourists, it's best visited during the week.

## City Park

Located at the heart of the city is this park, designed by Costa and Niemeyer, with landscaping by Roberto Burle Marx. Over the 40 acres is spread an artificial lake with a boat dock, ridges, waterfalls, and islands, where you can pedal-boat, fish, and kayak, as well as dine in an adequate restaurant. Other attractions include a swimming pool with waves, playground, and outdoor barbecue.

## South Lake Recreation Area

Along the banks of the Paranoá Lake and surrounded by a wooded section of eucalyptus trees is the recreation area, with a boat dock, restaurant, playground, and fishing pier. At the time of the construction of Brasília, Lago Sul had been a very small river that was damned and expanded to provide more humidity. On a nice night, it's a lovely place for drinks or dinner overlooking the lake. From a plane, you can see the chic homes of the area, each one boasting a swimming pool.

# Where To Stay

If you decide to stay overnight in Brasília, you won't find cheap accommodations easily. Most of the hotels, located in the **Hotel Sector** (*Setor Hoteleiro*), run from moderate to expensive. Because Brasília is a Mon.-Fri. business town, however, great discounts can be found at most hotels from Fri. night through Sun., although you may have to inquire pointedly if a discount is not directly offered. Also, traffic is less hectic on weekends, and if you plan to visit the spiritual community of Vale do Amanhecer, note that it is only open to the public on Sun. and Wed. Advance reservations are highly recommended at any time, particularly if you want a view (many people prefer to stay on the upper floors of high-rise hotels for the magnificent vistas). See page 26 for price chart.

## Hotel Nacional

*Setor Hoteleiro Sul, lote 1;* ☎ *321-7575, fax 223-9213.*

Inaugurated in 1960, the five-star Nacional was the first hotel built in Brasília and still attracts the big, traditional names, such as Queen Elizabeth, as well as Brazil's own top officials who do not live in the city. The streamlined lobby appears to be permanently time-warped in the 1960s, though it's usually filled with important-looking persons in expensive business suits. Hallways are carpeted in bright square patterns and wood-paneled walls, exuding a sense of decorum and propriety. The impossibly large Alvorada Suite has an impressive view of the Congress, Cathedral, and National Theater. Even standards have a touch of chic, though the furniture has not been updated for decades. The egg-shaped pool is the largest in the city and the sauna is especially clean. Guests particularly enjoy the connecting Galeria, owned by the hotel and housing numerous airline agencies, exchange house, car rental, bookstore, and boutiques. During high-priority news events, the hotel is jammed with journalists who hole up in the enormous convention center and transmit faxes all night, though the hotel is usually packed with politicians during the week. Thirty-percent discounts are available in July and Dec. Feb. brings special weekend rates. *346 apts. Expensive. All cards.*

## Naoum Plaza

*Setor Hoteleiro Sul QD 5, bloco H/I;* ☎ *226-6494, fax 225-7007.*
The chic lobby of this five-star high-rise is reminiscent of Rio's Caesar Park
– plush oriental rugs and highly polished marble floors. The elegant
restaurant looks onto a landscaped garden replete with waterfalls. The top
three floors, with private entrances, have VIP services. All rooms are
appointed with designer-styled spreads, walnut headboards, and
electronic controls; all have tubs. Prince Charles and Princess Diana graced
the Presidential Suite – a stunning expanse of five rooms, French
colonial-style furniture, outdoor jacuzzi, and wraparound verandas. The
small, rectangular-shaped pool has an outdoor sun deck, and a health club
and Turkish bath are also available. English-style afternoon tea is a tradition
here; a jazz bar offers fine music nightly. If you're in the mood, follow
Princess Di's habit and go jogging around Parque Cidade (City Park) across
the street. *200 apts. Expensive. All cards.*

## San Marco Hotel

*Setor Hoteleiro Sul QD 5, bloco C;* ☎ *321-8484, fax 224-3935.*
The rooftop pool of this five-star hotel offers a magnificent view of the TV
tower. Standards, with color TVs and mini-bars, are fashionably appointed
with gold carpets and peach spreads. Suites are gracefully decorated with
leather couches and a glass-top dining table in the adjoining room. All
rooms have verandas. There's also a gallery of small shops, including a car
rental and a travel agency. The rooftop restaurant is a bit spartan, but does
offer a 360° view of the city. A piano bar has live music nightly. *256 apts.*
*Expensive. All cards.*

## Eron Brasília

*Setor Hoteleiro Norte, QD 5, bloco A,* ☎ *321-1777, fax 226-2698.*
Pelé and Michael Forbes have stayed at this four-star high-rise, with a white
marble lobby dominated by a modernized painting of Jesus. Corridors are
well kept and exceedingly clean; apartment doors are painted in
blue-and-white colonial style. Rooms are adequately furnished, though on
the smallish side; the only difference between standard and deluxe is that
the latter has a better stocked mini-bar and electronic controls. On Wed.,
the restaurant serves a special buffet with delicacies traditional to the state
of Pernambuco. Clients may use the prestigious Golf Club, with whom the
hotel has an arrangement. Forty percent discount on weekends. *180 apts.*
*Moderate-expensive. All cards.*

## Bristol Hotel

Setor Hoteleiro Sul QD, 4, bloco F; ☎ *321-6162, fax 321-2690.*
The Bristol has the quality of a four-star hotel, but the management claims
it gets more business masquerading as a three-star. It's also the only
three-star hotel in Brasília that has a pool. Standard rooms, with gold satin
bedspreads, are quite acceptable, with large glass sliding windows. Deluxe
rooms have verandas. An indoor pool with a glass roof offers a fabulous

view of the city, particularly at night. The restaurant, which also doubles as a coffee shop, serves international food both à la carte and buffet. The hotel's one jarring detail is the salesmen allowed to stand at the entrance of the hotel hawking jewelry and crystals. Thirty percent discounts are available on weekends. *141 apts. Moderate. All cards.*

## Hotel das Nações

*Setor Hoteleiro Sul, QD 4, bloco I, ☎ 225-8050, fax 225-7722.*

The lobby of this three-star lacks even a pretense of luxury, but at least the brown-and-white marble floor matches the couches. The air-conditioned apartments are adequate, if a bit kitschy, with old-time phones, electronic controls, a small desk, and a mini-bar. The restaurant, called Panela o Brasil, offers a large buffet with cold and hot dishes good for vegetarians and an à la carte menu that specializes in *carne de rã* (frog meat!). A tiny bar has four tables. Weekend discounts up to 20% are available. *129 apts. Moderate. All cards.*

## Mirage Hotel

*SHN QO 02. bloco N; ☎ 225-7150.*

The lobby of this two-star has more oomph than others in the same inexpensive category. Apartments are clean and come with color TV, phone, but no mini-bar; the bathrooms are small but acceptable. Breakfast is served in a cheerful salon with plastic tablecloths and a snack grill for hamburgers and omelettes. The hotel is located in a complex with several other similar properties. Management does not accept credit cards, and a sign at the reception reads "Don't insist." *69 apts. Inexpensive. No cards.*

## Camping

Those wanting to feel the "vibes" in Brasília might do well camping. The most centrally located site is **Camping de Brasília** in Setor Áreas Isoladas Norte, behind the Kubitschek Monument and the Buriti Palace. The #100 bus gets you there from the *rodoviária* downtown. Fees are about $2-4 a night. About 46 km. (29 miles) out of town on Estrada da Ponte Alta/Estrada da Marila are the **Bela Vista Campgrounds**, ☎ 226-2663.

# Where To Eat

Though hardly the culinary capital of Brazil, Brasília does not lack for good meals. All hotels, even three-stars, have decent restaurants and fair prices. Execs tend to go out for drinks between 6:30 and 7:30 p.m., then return home and dress for dinner, which starts no earlier than 9 p.m. Most restaurants are hard put to serve decent fare at 7 p.m. On Sat. you can find *feijoada* everywhere except in *churrascarias*. See page 26 for price chart.

# Churrascaria

## Spettus

*Setor Hoteleiro Sul, QD 5, bloco E;* ☎ *223-9635. 11:30 a.m.-1 a.m.*

Near the TV Tower and across the street from the São Marco Hotel, this is one of the best all-you-can-eat steakhouses in Brasília. The extravagant options of 22 cold salads, 14 hot plates, and 18 types of Argentine meat will fill you for the day. The manager says, "If you don't have good service, you don't have to pay." Happy Hour takes place on a small veranda overlooking the highway, but that's Brasília. *Expensive. All cards.*

# Easy Lunch

## Coisas da Terra

*Avenida W-3, North, QD 703, bloco D, loja 41, subsolo;* ☎ *226-6748.*
*Daily 11:30 a.m.-4 p.m.*

Eat lunch on the covered patio or inside this airy restaurant trimmed with greenery, where the casual-chic buffet of salad, vegetables, fish, and chicken is filling. Sandwiches, such as the grilled chicken on French bread, are excellent. Women traveling alone will feel welcome. *Moderate. No cards.*

# Eclectic Funk

## Carpe Diem

*Coméreio Local Sul QD 104;* ☎ *225-8883. Mon.-Wed. noon-4 p.m., 7 p.m.-midnight; Thur.-Fri. noon-4 p.m., 7 p.m.-dawn; Sat. noon-dawn; Sun. noon-midnight. Beer garden open Mon.-Wed. noon-2 a.m.; Thur.- Fri. noon-dawn; Sun. 8 a.m.-midnight. Breakfast Sat. and Sun. 8-11 a.m.*

A waggish menu full of elaborate explanations, a bevy of tall, beautiful women (actually mannequins) and live music set the tone for this eclectic eatery owned by two journalists, two architects, and one engineer. The chef is Swiss, but the cuisine is funky Portuguese, with specialties like *feijoada com lirismo* (with lyricism), *peixe em alcaparras*, fish prepared in a vinegar base with capers and hot butter, and the *filé com 4 pimentas* (steak grilled with red, green, black, and white pepper). Friendly and breezy, the joint breaks open at midnight with the young and terminally hip, who gravitate between the outdoor beer garden, the restaurant, the piano bar, and a small import shop that sells Sidney Sheldon, Bulgarian jam, and Grey Poupon for outrageous prices. *Moderate. All cards.*

# French-Brazilian

## Gaf

*SHIS QI 05, bl. C, ljs. 16/24 in the Centro Comercial Gilberto Salomão;*
☎ *248-1754. Daily 6 p.m.-3 a.m., closed Sun.*

Dark, cushy, and chi-chi, Gaf attracts the haute couture of Brasília, namely politicos with their mistresses. An excellent jazz singer adorns the marvelous bar area, enhancing the romance. The menu is a French-Brazilian mix, specializing in seafood shipped from the Northeast and Santa Catarina. The house shrimp is flambéed in cognac; also intriguing is the *Filet à sauce d'escargots* with garlic. Since Gaf fills up fast after 11 p.m., make reservations for late-night dining, but also consider just coming for drinks and dessert after a night tour of the city. *Expensive. All cards.*

# French/International

## Florentino

*Comércio Local Sul, QD 402, bloco C, loja 15;* ☎ *223-7577. 11:30 a.m.-2 a.m.*

Top of the politicos' A-list, Florentino is, with the exception of Cachopa, the closest restaurant to the hotel sector. Outside is a lovely covered garden veranda; inside, a high-class, English-style pub with mahogany-paneled walls and tartan carpets. The French menu features *mini-lagosta* (small but tasty lobster) with fettucine, and grilled chicken with asparagus. Despite the menu, however, the chef will cook anything on demand – even cheeseburgers. At noon, the street in front of the restaurant is filled with chauffered limos. *Expensive. AE, MC.*

# Natural

## A Caminho do Natural

*Comércio Local Norte, QD 302, bloco B, loja 7;* ☎ *226-6733.*
*Noon-3 p.m. and 5-9 p.m., closed Sun.*

Just a small stool and tabletop, but the vegetarian self-service is hearty, including all kinds of beans, vegetables, and brown rice for under $5. Also the place to stock up on beans, wholewheat bread, granola, delicious oatmeal cookies, and sugarless sweets. A bulletin board details all the New Age activities of the city. *Inexpensive. No cards.*

## Vivalavanca

*HIGS 707, Boulevard L, Casa 48;* ☎ *244-2127. Noon-2:30 p.m., 6 p.m.-2 a.m.*

Located in a private home in the residential sector, this small but airy restaurant (and organization) promoting macrobiotics is my favorite lunch spot. Simple, but well-cooked plates of brown rice, salad, beans, and a little cake run under $5. You'll have to endure eating on wooden stools, but you're sure to find like-minded souls, especially if you're interested in healers. Honey, beans, wholewheat breads, etc., are also on sale; classes and courses are periodically given. The organization promotes the work of Tomiko Kikuchi, who brought macrobiotics to Brazil. *Inexpensive. No cards.*

## Portuguese

### Cachopa Restaurante

*South Sector QD 5, (Galeria Nova Ouvidor), subsolo 1, loja 127;* ☎ *224-9192. Noon-4 p.m., 7 p.m.-last client (about 2 a.m.), Sun., lunch only.*

The name of this Portuguese-style adega means *menina* or "girl," but there's nothing childish about the menu, except perhaps for the *Ovos Moles de Veiro*, a kicky-sweet concoction of egg yolk, sugar, and cinnamon that mothers traditionally serve their children. Gypsy shawls cover the rough-hewn walls of this traditional spot in Brasília for the last 25 years; specialties include *Bacalhau na Brasa* (codfish grilled in the Portuguese style). Even diet plates are available with vegetables grilled *sans* oil. Downstairs, a special lunch buffet charges per kilo. The music charge covers the solo singer from Sun.-Thur. and multi-stylistic house bands on the weekends; movement starts after 9:30 p.m. A special buy is the Portuguese clothes and wines on sale in the lobby. *Moderate-expensive. All cards.*

## With A View

### Pontão

*45 SHIS QL 10/12 (Ponte Costa e Silva). Noon-3 a.m.*

This outdoor/indoor restaurant overlooking the lake is a lovely place to contemplate the reflection of the city lights (though chilly in July). After 6 p.m. a fine local singer with guitar provides serenades. Pizza, pasta, and chicken are specialties, but it's best to come just for hors d'oeuvres and beer. *Music cover. Inexpensive. No cards.*

# Nightlife

Two excellent bars, usually with live music are **Bar Academia**, 308 Norte; ☎ *274-8828* and **Chorão**, 302 Norte; ☎ *226-0891*.

Many people head for the entertainment complex, **Gilberto Salomão**, where they can pick from a variety of bars, discos, and fine restaurants. The environment is dynamic and ever-changing to reflect trends. One of the most active clubs in the complex is **Hippus**, SHIS QI 5 Conj. Gilberto Salamão; ☎ *248-2890* (open nightly at 10 p.m.). Tues. and Thur. nights feature 60s music; Wed. is Afro-Caribbean; Fri. and Sat. bring pop; and Sun. from 4 to 8 p.m. is reserved for teens 12-16 years old. A cover is only charged on the weekends.

Another hot club is **New York New York**, SHIS QI 9, open nightly 10 p.m.-5 a.m. (closed Sun. and Mon). Music is changed according to the clientele; after 3 a.m. the DJ "lets the animal go," as he says. The small disco floor is tinged in blinking red lights, and the cushy banquettes are inviting. The young and hip patronize **Zum**, SHIS QI 5 Conj. Gilberto Salomão; ☎ 248-2890.

Older singles (especially women 30-40) frequent **Flash,** Setor Hoteleiro Norte; ☎ 225-3393.

# Gay Brasília

Since this is a political town, the gay scene is mostly underground, but I was informed by reliable sources that the town is full of transvestites (draw your own conclusions). **Aquarius** is one of the few "official" hangouts, but it's considered sleazy. Gays (and prostitutes) tend to gather at the **Edifício Eldorado**, a shopping complex, after 8 p.m. Consider the scene dangerous.

# Shopping

Brasília raises convenience shopping to an art, with a shopping complex every four superblocks. The major ones are **Conjunto Nacional** and **Park Shopping**. Located across from the National Theater, Conjunto Nacional can be recognized by its vertical ad panels as brightly lit as Times Square. A tourist guide (steep at $9) can be found at the Livraria Sodiler on the first floor. Near this bookstore, a bulletin board called Mural Comunitário lists different cultural events happening throughout the city. Park Shopping, with eight movie houses, is much more modern, featuring a large playground and lots of restaurants. The best place to buy precious and semi-precious gems is **Gemas do Brasil**, SQS 303 in the commercial district. An excellent esoteric bookstore, **Thot Livraria**, is located in the Edifício Eldorado shopping complex. A few books are in English, though most are in Portuguese. Among the many topics covered are works of French spiritualist Allan Kardec, who has influenced generations of Brazilian mystics, as well as fascinating tarot decks. The owner, who is also a publisher of esoterica, speaks some English and can direct you to any healer in the city. Also on sale is a video documentary of Brazilian esoterics. Nearby in the same complex is **Cheiro Verde**, a natural foods buffet luncheonette.

# Healers

Look for a copy of *Guia Ser Alternativo* (in Portuguese), a guide to the esoteric services in Brasília (available in health food stores, bookstores, etc.).

### Forças Ocultas

*SCLN 209, bloco D, loja 21;* ☎ *273-5680.*

An esoteric center sponsoring courses and individual sessions in tarot, astrology, practical magic, Bach Flower remedies, hypnosis, and numerology.

### Instituto Ser

*SHIS Q1 05, Chácara 81 (Lago Sul).*

An alternative spiritual center offering courses in astrology, Indian ayurvedic massage, Tibetan healing, rebirthing, and meditation.

# Hands-On Brasilia

## Climate

From Nov.-Feb., the countryside in Brasília is intensely green. In the winter months (June-Aug.), the land is very dry and often parched brown. Brush fires can easily occur. March receives the most rain. Temperatures in Jan. run 60-80°F, in July 50-67°F.

## Consulates

**USA**
SES Avenida das Nações, lote 1 . . . . . . . . . . . . . .   ☎ 223-5143
**Great Britain**
SES Avenida das Nações Q 801, cj. K, lote 8. . . . .   ☎ 225-2710
**Canada**
SES Avenida das Nações Q, 803, lote 16 . . . . . . . .   ☎ 223-7515
**Australia**
CP 11-1256, SHIS QI-09, Conj. 16, casa 1 . . . . . . . .   ☎ 248-5569

## Money Exchange

Money may be exchanged at the airport, as well as in hotels. Also, some tour guides will change money – generally a safe thing to do here. Good rates can be found at the following banks:

**Banco do Brasil**
SDS Q 1, bl. A; Ed. Sede 1 . . . . . . . . . . . . . . . . . . . .   ☎ 212-2230
**Banco Econômico**
SCS Q 1, bl. 1. Ed. Central Loja 15/16 . . . . . . . . . .   ☎ 225-8783

## Transportation

### Arrivals

The **international airport** is 13 km. (eight miles) from the city center. **Taxis** run about $10-$12. **Bus** #102 also runs to and from the airport, originating in the *rodoviária*. If you plan to fly into Brasília in the morning, sight-see, and fly out at night, you can leave luggage at the airport in secure lockers. (Also see *Points Beyond Brazília*, below).

### City Transportation

The bus system in Brasília is excellent, with the *rodoviária* located at the center of the city – walking distance from the cathedral.

### Points Beyond Brazilia

#### Air

**Varig** offers regular shuttle services daily to Rio and São Paulo and other major cities, and special regional services to the interior of Goiás, Pará, and more. **VASP** flies to Corumbá and Cuiabá daily. **Transbrasil** offers reduced-fare night flights to Manaus.

> **Varig/Cruzeiro**
> CLS 306 bl. B, loja 20 . . . . . . . . . . . . . . . . . . . . . . . . .  ☎ 242-4111
> **VASP**
> SCLS 304 Bl. E, loja 9 . . . . . . . . . . . . . . . . . . . . . . . .  ☎ 244-2020
> **Transbrasil**
> CLS 305, bl. C, loja 30 . . . . . . . . . . . . . . . . . . . . . . .  ☎ 248-6433
> **TAM** (Transportes Aéreos Regionais) . . . . . . . . . .  ☎ 248-6978
> **TAP-Air**
> Galeria Hotel Nacional . . . . . . . . . . . . . . . . . . . . . . .  ☎ 223-7138

#### Bus

Both regular buses and *leitos* (air-conditioned buses with food service) are available to Rio (20 hrs); São Paulo (16 hours); and Belo Horizonte (12 hours). Also, less comfortable buses go to Goiâna, Cuiabá, Campo Grande, Porto Alegre, Fortaleza, Natal, Salvador, and Recife. At the new bus terminal, you can leave luggage secured in lockers.

#### Train

The **O Bandeirante train**, opened in 1981, leaves Brasília only on Friday night for São Paulo (about 24 hours), with a connection made in Campinas. The station is located past the TV Tower, on the far side of the Eixo Monumental.

## Sports

There is free **Tai Chi** every day between superblock 104 and 105 at 6 a.m.

## Tourist Information

The local tourist board is **DETUR**, ☎ *321-3318*. Brochures may be picked up at the airport (international side) and at the bus station. For any kind of information, ☎ 156. For information about movies, ☎ 139.

## Travel Agencies & Tours

### Prestheza

*Hotel San Marco, Setor Hoteleiro Sul QD 5, bl. C, ☎ 226-6224.*

An excellent agency with a variety of touristic options, owned by a Japanese-descended Brazilian named Shiro. Guides are good English speakers and informative. Special excursions can be arranged to Vale do Amanhecer as well as forests and waterfalls in the surrounding area.

### Presmic Travel Agency

*Hotel Nacional, SHS, hotel, ☎ 225-5515.*

Group tours (half- and full-day) leave twice a day (9 a.m. and 2 p.m.) from the Nacional Hotel. All guides speak both Portuguese and English. Nighttime tours are another option.

## Private Tour Guides

An historically oriented guide who speaks excellent English is **James Roll,** SQS 404-F-306; ☎ *(61) 226-8855.*

## When To Go

Once a year at **Easter**, a great reenactment of the Passion of Christ takes place on the mountains of the Planaltina. As one local guide told me, "They really put him upon the cross and nail him." Hundreds of locals dress up in Biblical costumes and there are even Roman-like constructions erected along the way.

During the week, when the President is in town, he ascends up the ramp at the Palacio do Planalto, accompanied by a military guard and band, and descends on Fri. at 5:30 p.m.

## What To Wear

Brasília is a formal city, where most official political business is conducted in suits. Female visitors to government buildings should wear a dress or tailored pants; men, a sports jacket. Some churches do not allow Bermudas or shorts.

# BAHIA

The womb of black culture in Brazil – the state of Bahia, and especially, its capital city, Salvador – holds special meaning for Brazilians, no matter what their racial identity. The city of Salvador is also referred to as Bahia (Bah-EE-uh), a point of continual confusion among tourists. Those who have only heard reports of Bahia's exquisite beaches, fiery cuisine, magnificent colonial churches, and exotic voodoo sessions long to visit; those lucky enough to come here dream of returning. True, many of the treasures of Bahian culture can be sampled in the restaurants and nightclubs of Rio, but there is something in Bahia that must be experienced firsthand – and that is the heart of the Bahian people. Deeply rooted in a mysticism best expressed through joyous celebration, the Bahian passion for life arises directly from the profound devotion of the masses, descendants of African slaves who were dragged mercilessly to Brazil over 300 years ago by Portuguese merchants. Tortured, humiliated, and subjugated to the whims of the sugarcane plantation owners, these black immigrants clung to their African traditions, fiercely preserving their customs behind closed doors until today, when their celebratory festivals, music, and cuisine have fused with mainstream Brazilian culture.

Today, the word Bahia has become synonymous with "soul"; even in Rio's Carnaval, the *alas* (groups) of Bahian-dressed women, with their huge hoop skirts and dangling necklaces, bring tears to everyone's eyes – a reminder of the strong black maternal figures responsible for raising so many generations of Brazilian colonists. But the black culture of Bahia has done more than nurse Brazil; it has given birth to some of the country's greatest artists, including songwriter Dorival Caymmi, novelist Jorge Amado, poet Vinícius de Moraes, bossa nova great João Gilberto, and musical superstars Gilberto Gil, Caetano Veloso, Maria Bethânia, and Gal Costa. Without Bahia, one could argue, Brazil might never have been able to transcend the rather conservative, uptight attitudes of its Iberian mother.

## Islands of Pleasure

Most travelers are probably familiar already with Salvador as the major destination in Bahia – a magical, time-warped city where cows still walk down the highway beneath the shadow of towering skyscrapers. Yet the beachside capital city is far from being the only attraction in the state. Dotting the Bay of All Saints, on whose banks Salvador sits, are over 36 islands, easily reachable by public ferry or day cruises. Only 1½ hours away by bus is the well-preserved colonial town of **Cachoeira** – site of the most authentic *candomblé terreiro* (church of Afro-Brazilian trance worship) in Bahia. And secluded in the interior, not more than an hour from Salvador, are some of the greatest beach resorts in South America, namely **Comandatuba Island** (Transamérica Hotel) and **Praia do Forte**. Not only are these spectacular estates crime-free, they offer the finest combination of luxury service and natural beauty, including pristine beaches, fascinating excursions, and play-perfect weather.

# Salvaðor

*"About 11 o'clock we entered the Bay of All Saints, on the northern side of which it is situated. It would be difficult (to) imagine before seeing this view anything so magnificent... If faithfully represented in a picture, a feeling of distrust would be raised in the mind.* Charles Darwin (1832)

Two street boys selling *lembranças*.

One of the most beloved destinations in Brazil, Salvador is a city of mystics, magic and music – a sacred land where intoxication is often considered a prelude, or at least, the postlude, to religious salvation. Even the writer Jorge Amado, whose novels are virtual travelogues of Bahia, advises visitors to Salvador to make their first offering of *cachaça* (sugarcane liquer) to Exú, the wily, two-horned African god who guards the thoroughfares of the city. Such gestures are not even considered superstitious in Salvador, where animism is a form of daily life, and Christian saints and African gods are worshipped together in a sensual mess of devotion. Only in Salvador do you see the sacred images of Mary as the *Nossa Senhora do Leite* (Our Lady of the Milk) used to encourage women to breastfeed. Even businessmen and intellectuals tie fetishistic ribbons (*lembranças do Bonfim*) around their wrists and wait for their wishes to come true.

For the first-time visitor, Salvador can feel like a barrage of exotic sense perceptions, since everything, from business to love to extreme poverty, is lived out on the street. Even the smell of the city – a mixture of sea and sweat and spices – is enough to send you into a whirl. There are hundreds of magnificent baroque churches to visit, scores of beaches to scavenge, tiny colonial alleyways full of folkloric crafts and regional foods, but you could easily discover the heart of Bahia simply by soaking up the many faces of children on the Praça da Sé or in front of the Church of the Bonfim. Hunger has carved cunning desperation into many of these street children, but you haven't experienced Salvador until you've been suddenly corralled into a corner by a group of them desperate to sell you something – anything. Though these young children may irritate you or sometimes scare you, try to remember they are often working to support families of 10 or more, if they have not already been abandoned themselves. Simply, one cannot go to Bahia without acknowledging the extreme poverty experienced by a large percentage of the population. In fact, Salvador is the only Brazilian city where you'll see little boys selling coffee from a cart on the street or even trying to hawk a single cigarette.

Yet for all its despair, Salvador is also a city of rhythm and celebration. Next to Rio, it boasts the biggest Carnaval blowout in Brazil, not an organized parade in a sambadrome or coliseum, but an explosion in the city's streets jam-packed with percussion ensembles, *trio elétricos*, twirling, hoop-skirted women, and neighborhood *blocos*. Some say that until you come to Salvador, you haven't experienced the real Brazilian Carnaval.(For more information, see *Carnaval* chapter on page 60) During the rest of year, folkloric religious celebrations enliven the social calendar nearly every week, giving the people ample excuse to drink, eat, and dance until dawn.

## City Of Poetry

As one of the great architectonic centers in South America, Salvador is also a city of poetry. Even the street names are lyrical reminders of the colorful life that once teemed on its colonial-wrought cobblestones. Located in front of the Governor's Palace is **Rua do Tira Chapéus** (Street of the Hat-Tipping), where lines of royal subjects had to doff their hats obsequiously whenever the authorities passed by. **Beco da Maria Paz** (Alley of Maria Paz) was named after a prostitute well known for her charms during colonial times. Rebels fighting for independence from the Portuguese had their heads chopped off and displayed on **Rua da Cabeça** (Street of the Head), near Praça Piedade. In Ondina, **Rua Escravo Miguel** (Street of the Slave Michael) was inspired by the story of a farmer whose daughter ran off with his slave named Miguel; when the young girl died, Miguel threw himself, with traditional Latin passion, to his death in the sea.

## Goddess Of The Ocean

Today, the sea in Salvador retains such mystical power that the captains of the colorful *saveiros* criss-crossing the bay still sing that it's best to die in the foamy green waves thinking of Iemenjá. The Goddess of the Ocean, Iemanjá is not a figment of imagination in Bahia, but a living force that even today guides the conscious and subconscious habits of *Bahianos*. As Jorge Amado wrote, "Wherever there is a fisherman or sailor, there Iemenjá is with her love and seduction." Rumored to have a fondness for combs, mirrors, and bright red lipstick, she's said to live in diverse places – in the ruins of the Forte da Gamboa, in Rio Vermelho, in Barra, in Itapuã, Pituba, and Itaparica

– and makeshift shrines to her can be found everywhere, from dark alleys to coves along the beach. On Feb. 2, her feast day, the city is transformed by one of the most beautiful and impassioned celebrations of the year, with dancing, singing, and drinking, as canoes and sloops laden with presents are pushed far out to her home in the deep dark sea.

# History

Salvador's bay owes its name to Cabral's expeditionaries who first anchored in the harbor on Nov. 1, 1501, the Catholic feast day for All Saints. Among the first native people to greet the settlers were the warfaring **Tupinambá** (or Tupí), whose cannibalistic ways did not win them friends. Some less pious settlers – deserters, renegades, and shipwrecked sailors – did manage to commune with a few tribes by teaching them military tactics; in fact, Diogo Alvares, a shipwrecked Portuguese sailor, eventually married two Indian princesses and sired an entire dynasty of *mestizos* (mixed breeds). While the Jesuits tried to missionize the natives, the Portuguese authorities in Bahia preferred bartering labor for goods. The Indians, unaccustomed to European ways, soon succumbed to disease, exhaustion, and disinterest.

Securing the port of Salvador also did not prove easy. After numerous squabbles with Dutch and French pirates, Dom João III established direct royal control by sending a resident governor, **Tomé de Sousa**, to commence construction on Brazil's first capital. Impressed with the fertile lands in the coastal plains surrounding the bay, called the **Recôncavo**, the crown ordered the first sugar plantation built. The problem, however, was labor. When the native Indians quickly proved unreliable, the Portuguese turned to the one foreign labor pool they knew only too well.

In truth, it was precisely the nefarious **African slave trade** that populated colonial Bahia. By the beginning of the 18th century, more than 1.2 million black Africans had already been shipped to Bahia in shackles, many of them dying on the way; by the beginning of the 19th century, a third of the population was enslaved. Bahian society soon became based on the hierarchy of the plantation, where masters lived a seignorial life, protecting or abusing their retainers at will. The city of Salvador thus grew up as a complement to the state's agricultural industry – the place where merchants pushed papers and moved the plantations' goods on to other ports. Developing far away from the wharves on the upper city was the religious and governmental life: The first Jesuit college was established in 1549, followed by the monasteries of Franciscans, Benedictines, and Carmelites by the close of the 16th century. Later, when the cultivation of tobacco centralized in nearby Cachoeira, a less elite class of merchants began to emerge in Salvador. Still, the entire economy was dependent on slave labor and, although a slave revolt failed in 1835, the threat of losing its labor force sent shivers of fear through the white community. Ironically, even Abolition, in 1888, did little to change plantation politics, which simply moved into a neo-feudal model, indenturing the former slaves to their previous owners through debt.

The enormous inequalities rampant in Bahia (to this day) have not gone unheeded. In 1897, the longing for a better life led to one of the most extraordinary peasant revolts in Brazilian history. Starting in the *sertão* (backlands), the uprising consisted of followers of the mystic Antônio Conselheiro, who refused to submit their rustic settlement of Canudos to Portuguese authority. The simple *sertanejos* valiantly fought off not only the local police, but state troopers, until federal troops decimated the entire village shanty by shanty. A marvelous fictional account of this tragedy can be found in Euclides da Cunha's celebrated novel *Os Sertões* (published in English under the title *Rebellion in the Backlands*).

## Culture

### Candomblé

Though it is freely found throughout the country, the African-based trance-cult practice of *candomblé* finds its deepest roots in Bahia. For more detailed information, see *Traveler's Guide to Brazilian Spirits*, on page 54.) To seek out and attend authentic sessions of the religion, however, takes some private scoping. Do note that any *candomblé* performed in a theater or offered on a group tour by a travel agency is bound to be diluted – usually straw-dog performances that exploit the color, music, and dance of the religion without any genuine feeling. In Salvador proper, however, there are hundreds of *terreiros* (*candomblé* churches), though the sessions are usually held after midnight on Sat. in poor black neighborhoods verging on slums. If you tell the concierge of your hotel you would like to attend a "real" *candomblé*, he will most likely be able to arrange it for you – for a tip, that is; the session itself is free. If you do go, don't take much money and don't expect anyone to speak English. Plus, take a taxi, and pre-arrange for a pickup; the first time I went, my taxi driver was so surprised I was alone that he insisted on waiting for me – not a bad idea. The session can go on until dawn, though you will most likely be ready to leave in an hour or two – the tiny room gets hot and stuffy fast. Attend with a sense of decorum and utmost respect. (You are there only to witness quietly, not participate.) Do not wear shorts (anything white is best). And, under no circumstances should you ever record, videotape, or take photographs. (From experience, I can say that you will either be summarily dismissed from the room or stripped of your film.) If you're offered any food, it's most likely to be fried bean curd; accept it gracefully, though you needn't eat it. Donations are appreciated, but if an adult acting like a child demands money from you, it is most likely a practitioner incorporating the spirit of a childlike divinity; he or she only wants a few coins as a symbolic appeasement. Any donation you care to give for attending the session should be given directly to the *mãe* or *pai de santo*, the leaders of the *terreiro*. For more information, contact the tourist office **Bahiatursa;** ☎ *241-4333.*

## Capoeira

*Nowadays one does not need to feel the cold contact of the straight razor*
*on the skin, to regret the blood of another person on his or her hands ...*
*to feel goosebumps ... while walking through dark alleys to discover*
*the power of Capoeira ..."* Bira Almeida (1986)

*Capoeira*, the uniquely Brazilian martial art that you will see throughout
Bahia, has enjoyed a dark and steamy past. Even its historical origins are
controversial. Some claim that *capoeira*, born out of a fierce desire for
freedom, began as an acrobatic technique developed by slaves who were
forced to hide their self-defense practices from their masters. Others claim
the techniques derived from an African male puberty rite, or that the name
refers to the partridge, called *capoeira*, which fiercely engages in bloody cock
fights. Since the 18th century, the Brazilian police have considered
*capoeiristas*, the lowest of lowlife, once exiling a particularly scruffy bunch
of hooligans to the horrible penal colony on Fernando de Noronha. When
restrictions on popular culture were unexpectedly eased under the
repressive regime of Getúlio Vargas, *capoeiristas* finally began to enjoy some
freedom, facilitated by the teaching of the century's greatest master,
**Manoel dos Reis Machado** (known as Mestre Bimba). His school, opened
in 1932, is still located near the Pelourinho. As late as the 1950s and 1960s,
*capoeiristas*, always poor, still lived a knife-edged existence, populating
violent gangs and sharing the narrow *becos* (alleys) and honky-tonks of old
Bahia with prostitutes, drunken sailors, and other nefarious figures.

Today, the martial art has developed from being a fighting technique into
a spectacular visual show. The main moves are performed in pairs, in a
series of gravity-defying acrobatic attacks, including somersaults,
backbends, and head-high kicks. Training is not only physically but
artistically demanding, requiring the student to learn several instruments,
primarily the **berimbau**, a single-stringed gourd whose rhythms demand
a keen sense of timing. Some of the rhythms and chants refer to Catholic
saints and African deities; others originated from secret signs that warned
the *capoeiristas* of approaching police. Through the ever-changing music,
the *capoeirista* creates either a succession of harmonious forms, generates a
confrontation of strategies, or engages in slow-motion counterattacks, all
best performed by one whose spirit is equal to his or her technical skill.
Indeed, true *capoeristas* strive to attain *axé*, a special energy connected to the
universal flow. Those who have undertaken the sport as a martial art form
seek to transcend ordinary states of consciousness.

Unfortunately, most of the professional *capoeira* you will see in Brazil will
be tainted by egocentric showmanship (although the intense martial-art
movements still remain visually thrilling). The lithe, but well-developed
bodies of the practitioners, could themselves be considered art forms. Some
of the best performances can be seen at the restaurant **Solar do Unhão** or
in front of the market **Mercado Modelo** (although the latter performers may
turn aggressive if you don't donate some coins to their supposedly free
show). Many of the schools around the Pelourinho are considered rough to
visit, though there is an unusual school for small boys across the street from
a good youth hostel, **Solar**, Rua 223 Macapá, 461 in Ondina; classes there

are usually held in the late afternoon. The academy of **Mestre Bimba** is at Rua Francisco Muniz Barreto, 1 (1st floor) in the Terreiro de Jesus.

## Bird's Eye View

Salvador is perched on a privileged sight – a 200-foot bluff overlooking the glimmering All Saints Bay. For many *Bahianos*, the bay itself is nearly a personality; as Jorge Amado writes in his novel *Juiabá*, "the sea gives a peace the city cannot bring." In colonial times, the cliff acted as a perfect natural fortress for the port; today it divides the city into two parts: the **Cidade Baixa** (Low City), where the commercial district and wharfs are found, and the **Cidade Alta** (High City), heart of the historical center. Unless you embark on an island cruise, most of your tourist activity will be centered in the Cidade Alta. The fastest way to travel between the two levels is by the **Elevador Lacerda**, a lift connecting Praça Cairu and the Mercado Modelo with the Praça Municipal (Tomé de Sousa) in the Cidade Alta. Unfortunately, the lift is also the most dangerous way to go – probably the site of more assaults and thefts than any other place in Salvador. (See *Safety Alert*, below.) Steep hills, called *ladeiras*, also connect the two levels, but most tourists, especially those carrying anything valuable, should take a taxi.

With more than two million people, Salvador ranks as the third largest city in Brazil, behind São Paulo and Rio. A large percentage of the working poor are squeezed into the city's suburban areas; others – such as the more recent immigrants from Northeastern droughts – inhabit squatters' camps, *invasões*, along the outer circle of the city. Even in the historical district, near the Pelourinho, families of 10 or more are crammed into tiny apartments and you'll no doubt see homeless families camped out on the street. Most of the hotels and tourist activities focus along the shoreline in middle-to-upper class neighborhoods, such as Ondina, where singer Gilberto Gil has a penthouse. Enjoying a recent renaissance, the Barra district is one of the choicest places; the city's best hotels, bars, and restaurants are all located here within walking distance of each other, and the beach is superb (see below under *Barra*). Drive around the upper/middle-class neighborhood of Graça. The compelling geometric high-rises in shades of red, black, white, and orange are the works of Fernando Peixoto, whose avant-garde designs are now gracing other cities.

## Safety Alert

Salvador is so full of distractions that your attention may be diverted from your personal safety. However, the same kind of precautions suggested for Rio should be followed in Salvador – if not more so, since the level of extreme poverty and desperation is even more intense in this Northeastern city. Also, many of the poorer neighborhoods are situated within, or immediately adjacent to, the colonial area, where most of the tourist activity takes place. *Perspicacity*, rather than paranoia, should be your watchword. In general, don't walk around with much money, and separate your credit cards from your travelers checks. Lock up your passport, plane tickets and extra valuables in the hotel's safe. Avoid carrying expensive cameras. Don't ever exchange money on the street (there are too many tales of disappearing dollars). Most importantly, blend in with the vibe of the city.

Take taxis when you can or the special tourist bus that goes down the *orla* (strip), and take particualr caution in the following locations (all best avoided completely at night):

- ☐ **Lacerda Elevator**: Avoid day and night.
- ☐ **Praça da Sé**: The old, abandoned buildings on the street across from the Excelsior movie house are a center of crime, drugs, and prostitution.
- ☐ **Pelourinho**: Avoid after midnight.
- ☐ **Convento da Piedade**: Outside the Praça da Piedade.
- ☐ **Ladeira da Conceição**: An area of prostitution.
- ☐ **Any side streets** or **back alleyways** in the **colonial area** that are not well lit.

# Walking Tour

One of Dorival Caymmi's most famous songs extols the 365 churches in Bahia, one for each day of the year; in truth there are only about 165. Some of the best ones in the historical center are easily accessible on foot.

## Praça da Camara Municipal

The best place to start your walking tour of Salvador is the pigeon-strewn square, where the shimmering magnificence of the All Saint's Bay can embrace you. Dominating the square is the **Palácio do Rio Branco**, the former Governor's Palace, which was destroyed by war and restored several times; hence, the eclectic Greek columns, baroque windows, and neoclassical eagles. Unfortunately, the sumptuous interior, bedecked with a rococo ceiling and finely restored paintings, is only open to the public in the afternoon (Mon.-Sat., 2-5 p.m.). Also facing the square is the **Câmara Municipal**, the 17th-century city hall.

Walking towards the harbor, you'll glimpse the **Lacerda Municipal Elevador**, which can take you to the lower city, the departing dock for island cruises, and the **Mercado Modelo**.

## Forte de São Marcelo

From this privileged viewpoint above the harbor, contemplate the red-tiled roofs of the old city and this building in the middle of the bay, once a prison but now headed for a new life as a casino, if the law will permit.

Next, head down Rua 223 da Misericórdia to Praça da Sé, keeping to the middle of the street, whenever possible. (Be particularly careful when you pass Ladeira da Misericórdia because thieves tend to race down this alley after committing a crime.)

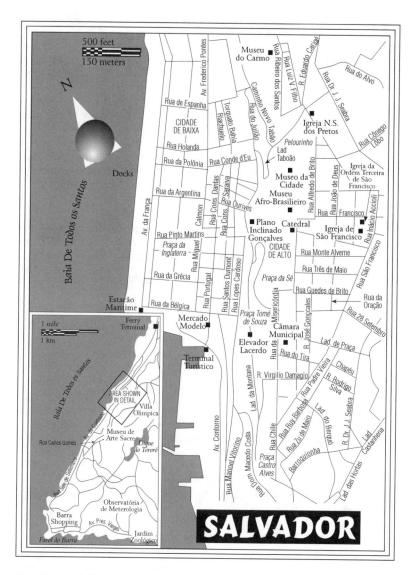

SALVADOR

## Igreja da Misericórdia

Before reaching the Praça da Sé, you'll pass by this church, opened only on Sun., featuring the largest ivory Christ in Brazil, about 3½ feet high. The plaza itself, one of the most colorful street scenes in Salvador, is a crossfire of *figuras* (characters) straight out of a Fellini movie – from the snake-oil salesman hawking a magic elixir for eternal youth to Sonia Braga lookalikes sauntering down the narrow alleyways with their (usually foreign) clients.

## Praça Terreiro de Jesus

Crossing the Praça da Sé and heading down Rua Guedes de Brito you'll enter the heart of colonial Salvador and the site of the city's original public water supply. Here, shaded by the large leafy branches of almond and poinciana trees, the many faces of Salvador come alive: from the homeless street boys who aggressively hawk souvenirs, to the old shoe-shine men sipping *cafezinho* on chairs made of rags, to the famous white-skirted *Bahiana* who ekes out a living selling *acarajé* – fried bean cake grilled on an open fire. Sun. morning is a lively time to visit, when the square is transformed into a weekly arts and crafts fair; you'll find homemade lace, leather goods, traditional musical instruments, such as the berimbau and the pandeiro, as well as fine primitive paintings.

## Pelourinho

It's from this plaza that you can directly enter the Pelourinho, the cobblestone square where colonial slaves were severely punished in front of their master. (The actual *pelourinho*, or whipping post, was removed as a humanitarian gesture by the government about 20 years ago.) Shaded by huge trees and lined with colonial mansions, the square has been designated a patrimony, or cultural treasure, by UNESCO since it is considered the site of the most important collection of 17th- and 18th-century colonial architecture in South America. Once a sad, deteriorated historical center, the Pelourinho has in the last several years experienced marvelous restoration ($43 million) funded by the state government; today it is a symphony of pastel-colored facades that glimmer in the bright sunlight, punctuated by antique street lamps, grilled balconies, and scores of chic tiny boutiques, delightful bars, and excellent regional restaurants. Even the buildings that have escaped restoration are fascinating to contemplate. Music abounds everywhere, from berimbaus to percussion bands, especially during summer (Dec.-Feb.), when everyone starts preparing for Carnaval. Best of all, the city has beefed up security so much that you can find policemen on every corner. (In the Praça da Sé, two policemen are stationed at every corner.) However, tourists must still be careful of prostitutes and avoid alleyways that have not been restored. In fact, anything that looks dark should be avoided.

(For numerous suggestions on where to eat and shop in the Pelourinho, see *Where to Stay* and *Shopping* at the end of the Salvador section.)

## Catedral Basílica

*Tues.-Sat. 9-10:30 a.m. and 2-5 p.m.; Sun. 9-10 a.m.*

Heading for the northwest corner of the Terreiro de Jesus, you'll find the green sculptured doors of the Catedral Basílica, originally a chapel built in 1557 for the Jesuit Seminary. After many restorations, it now boasts an eclectic facade that pits Greek classical columns against curvaceous baroque designs. Inside are the remains of Mem de Sá, the Portuguese nobleman/soldier who finally expelled the French from Rio de Janeiro in 1567.

## Museu Afro-Brasileiro

*Tues.-Sat. 9 a.m.-5 p.m.*

Next to the cathedral, this museum is housed in what was the first medical school in Brazil during the last century. On the ground floor is a marvelous exhibition heralding the richness of Brazilian black culture – from religion to music to martial arts and artisanry. Fascinating are the imaginative sculptures of *candomblé* divinities dressed in their uniquely personal styles (colors, jewelry, weapons, etc.) and surrounded by their favorite foods. (You can tell which divinity a devotee is dedicated to by checking out the colors of his jewelry and clothes.) While you're here, give a nod to Exú, the protector of the city, a devil-like figure with pitchfork, two horns, and erect penis, who is featured in many of Jorge Amado's writings. Most inspiring are the blown-up photos of *pais* and *mães de santo* – the formidable priests and priestesses of *candomblé*, whose enormous spiritual power was forged in the face of great poverty and despair. In the basement of this building you'll find the **Ethnological and Archeological Museum**, a showcase for Indian ceramics and fossils retrieved from native burial sites.

## Igreja e Convento de São Francisco

Crossing the Terreiro de Jesus on Ladeira do Cruzeiro, you'll come upon the finest 16th-century architectural treasure on the square. Built by slaves in the 16th century, the church is the essence of baroque, its cornucopia of winged angels, beatific saints, immaculate virgins, and pious-looking animals adorning every nook and cranny. What is shocking at first sight is that every hand-carved object appears to be covered in gold leaf – an ancient technique that can only be approximated today through using a mixture of yellow, green, orange, and brown paints to give the illusion of gold. Most amazing among the objets d'art are icons that the African slaves managed to slip in from their own cultures: notice the statue of the sea goddess Iemanjá riding the prow of the main pulpit, as well as the bare-breasted, pregnant women perched on the side of the jacaranda balustrades. The altar itself was inspired by Bernini's St. Peter's Altar at the Vatican, and the main statue of Saint Francis grasping Christ follows the painting of Murillo, which now hangs in Madrid's Prado Museum. From the front altar, turn around and look at the back choir loft, where the ceiling is made of wood boxes forming hexagons, stars, trapezoids, and crosses in representation of the Virgin's life. On the right side of the church (unfortunately, not illuminated) is one of the most sacred sculptures in Brazil – that of St. Peter of Alcântara, carved from one piece of wood. If you squint hard enough, you may be able to see his perfectly proportioned hands and the finely wrought muscles in his body. Next to him, with babe in arms, is St. Benedictine, the Ethiopian slave who saved a dying baby. In the side entrance hall, painted-tiled panels in sculpted wood frames retell the life of St. Francis de Assisi, whose philosophy of charity and service is still carried out by the church today. If you visit in the morning, you'll no doubt see a long line of Bahia's poor and crippled, who line up daily to receive free bread at 7 a.m. and free beans and meat at 11:30 a.m. The church is open 8-11:30 a.m. and 2-5:30 p.m. daily, though you must enter through the side door; when there is a service, you can enter through the front door. Mass is held daily at 7 a.m., 8 a.m., 6 p.m., 7 p.m., Tues. 7 a.m., 7:30 a.m., and 6 p.m., Sun. 7:30 a.m., 9:30 a.m., and 11:00 a.m. A blessing to St. Anthony is held every Tues. Pamphlets in Portuguese are sold for about $2 at the office on the right.

## Igreja de Ordem Terceira de São Francisco.

*Mon.-Fri. 8 a.m.-noon, 1-5 p.m. Services are held on the fourth Sun. of each month at 8:30 a.m., minimal fee.*

Next door on the left of the Igreja de São Francisco is this church, built in 1702-1703. The secular Third Order of São Francisco exerted a strong cultural and religious influence during the 18th and 19th century; today it boasts more than a thousand brothers and sisters, who support a hospital, an old folk's home, and ongoing social work with the prostitutes, thieves and addicts who live in the area. Ever since an unsuspecting painter chipped off a chunk of the original facade that had lain hidden for 150 years, the church has been slowly returning to its former glory; the interior, once entirely decimated, was restored to a neoclassical design in the last century. The saints' sculptures are original, but notice they are all wearing the robes of this order. Most stunning is the image of the Madonna on the altar; her facial expression is one of the purest in Brazilian art. (A better view can be had from upstairs.) The room to the right of the sanctuary is the eerie Room of the Saints, hosting the nearly life-sized statues that are carried through the streets during religious processions. In the cloister connected to the sacristy is a marvelous tiled mural that could be considered the wedding album of Dom José, the elder son of Dom João V, who married an Austrian princess. It even shows the carriage of the wedding party (not unlike Princess Di's), accompanied by a retinue of bowing and scraping courtiers. High society weddings are still held in this courtyard, and upstairs, the order holds its meetings around an immense antique jacaranda table, surrounded by sacred objects donated by the order's wealthiest families. The view from the shuttered windows upstairs will give you an intimate look on the neighborhood down below, a bevy of back streets and cobblestone alleyways full of tenement homes.

## Funerária Durán

It's an odd stop, I admit, but I find this store in front of the church endlessly fascinating. It sells marvelous wood-carved coffins, equal in artistry to those of the old masters.

## Olimpia – Múltiplos Artes & Turismo

Souvenirs of a more common variety can be found at this nearby shop, where you can purchase interesting local artwork, including miniature sets of *maracatú* bands.

Just in case you're tempted, the hotels around the Pelourinho here may look alluring – much of their colonial architecture is still intact – but it's my opinion that you're taking your life in your hands if you hang out here after dark. Even the beautiful Convento do Carmo Hotel, once located here, had to close its doors finally because of assaults on tourists. (For more information, see *Where to Stay*.) Cross to Rua Alfredo Brito, a narrow alleyway next to the Museu Afro-Brasileiro.

### Igreja Rosário dos Pretos

You will see the oriental spires of the church towering over the Pelourinho. Built by slaves for their own community, the church today still boasts a primarily black congregation. The last scene of the film *Dona Flor and Her Two Husbands* was shot here.

### Igreja do Senhor dos Passos

Turning right on Rua Ribeiro Santos, you'll come upon this church. The video for Paul Simon's 1990 album, *Rhythm of the Saints*, was filmed on the steps of the church.

### Dona Chika-ka

*Rua Luiz Viana (Ladiera do Carmo, no. 17.)*

Across from the street from Senhor dos Passos, stop for a typical tropical fruit drink – try the *abacaxi* (pineapple) – or an ice-cold *cerveja*. The delicious cakes and sweets are all home-made, typical of the region.

From here, gear yourself for a steep climb up Rua Luiz Viana.

### Igreja Nossa Senhora do Carmo

*Daily 9 a.m.-noon, 2-6 p.m. Mass only on Sun. morning.*

You'll pass the fantastic dilapidated arches of this church, founded 356 years ago. (A tourist police station is located here.) Inside is an inner courtyard of crafts, through which you'll have to pass to reach the main sanctuary. The church possesses one of the most vulnerable, beseeching images of the crucified Christ I have ever seen, entitled **Jesus Diante de Pilatos** (Jesus with the Crown of Thorns), positioned against a highly theatrical, red-curtained altar. In the sacristy is a stunning, though terrifying wood carving of the sleeping Christ, made by the same slave who carved the Christ image on the main altar; he accomplished the task in eight years using only two knives. Plant resin was used to get the exact color of skin, but the blood droplets were made from 2,000 rubies imported from India. The slave died immediately after finishing his masterpiece. On Good Friday, the image is placed on a silver platter and carried in procession through the Pelourinho.

### Souvenirs

If you have time and energy left, there are numerous stores for jewelry, handicrafts, and souvenirs around the Terreiro de Jesus, but be careful to stick to the main streets, avoiding any alleyways that seem particularly spooky. Fine lace stores can be found along **Rua Alfredo Brito**, and several jewelry stores are near the São Francisco Church. (Also see *Shopping*.)

> **UP CLOSE TIP:** *For a quick cheap lunch near the Pelourinho, head to* **Atabaque Ghandi**, *Rua Gregório de Matos, 53 (Pelourinho);* ☎ *321-7073, open noon-2 p.m., in the headquarters of the Filhos de Ghandi.*

In 1945 the Sons of Ghandi Organization was founded during a strike at the harbor; today they head up one of Carnaval's most famous *blocos* (groups) and help the homeless during the rest of the year. The mascot is a veritable Ghandi clone – Raimundo Quieroz, a 70-plus-year-old *Bahiano*, who needs only a little encouragement to put on his white loincloth and pose with his staff. From May to Carnaval, the group holds open rehearsals on Sun. from 3-10 p.m. Their simple luncheonette serves a hearty plate of beef, fried fish, or a typical dish at bargain prices.

# Other Sights

## Bonfim

The heart of Bahian religious culture – the fervor, the passion, and the poverty – can best be seen at the **Nossa Senhor do Bonfim**, Salvador's most popular Catholic church, located high up on a hill in the western suburbs. (Take a taxi or visit on a group tour.) No matter the time of year, the scene outside the church always looks frantic, but devoted *Bahianos* consider a trip to Bonfim a true pilgrimage. As soon as your bus or taxi arrives, a bevy of poor native boys will aggressively descend on you, hawking tiny ribbons (*lembranças*), a symbol of the church. (Warning: if you buy one ribbon from one boy, the whole crowd will attach itself to you.) Leaning against the front doors, with the saddest faces imaginable, are some of the city's most pathetic cripples. Inside the church, which is always at least half-full, is a shrine to the promise of a better life. *Bahianos* from all over the city come here to pray for the health of loved ones, for the healing of a marriage, for the manifestation of a boyfriend or girlfriend, for financial reversals – for anything that touches their everyday lives. And devotion often reaches fanatic heights; you just might see parishioners climbing up the steps on their knees or sunk into a prayer position for hours. Inside the Room of Miracles, plastic arms, heads, legs, and even hearts and lungs eerily hang from the ceiling; they are ex-votos, or offerings representing the parts of a devotee's body that have been or "will be" miraculously healed. The photos and signed letters adorning the wall tell manifold stories. One photograph even expresses thanks for the release from a kidnapping Jan. 23-Feb. 9, 1991 – an increasingly common occurrence among rich Brazilian families. Many of the notes pinned to the wall request healings and include lists of promises the petitioners will fulfill when they receive their healings. The huge and extremely heavy wood crosses stashed in the corner are used by suppliants who promise to carry them during a religious procession if their prayers are answered.

The *lembranças do Bonfim*, sold by the native boys outside the church, are actually more than souvenirs. Believers pin them to the walls of the church and loop them around candlesticks to remind God that they are asking for help. You'll also see *Bahianos* from all walks of life walk around with these gnarled ribbons on their wrists. Stemming from a *candomblé* practice, the tradition is to make a wish while the ribbon is tied on your wrist; when it falls off, you throw it away in water and your wish will appear. What tradition doesn't tell you is that after a week the ribbon starts to look ratty, but for some unknown mystical reason remains indestructible. (After one whole year, I'm still waiting for the stringy mess to fall off!) It's considered terrible luck to rip it off.

On the second Thurs. of Jan., one of the most important Bahian festivals – **Lavagem do Bonfim** – takes place at the church. Starting at the Igreja de Nossa Senhora Conceição, hundreds of *Bahianas* – native women dressed in traditional white hooped skirts, embroidered blouses, and turbans – progress along the seafront to the Igreja do Bonfim, where they scrub the steps and square clean and adorn the church with flowers and brightly colored lights. Joyous partying follows in the evening and every night until Sun., as the square fills up with drunken revelers.

## Barra

Squeezed between the Atlantic Ocean and the Bay of All Saints in the most southwestern nook of Salvador, the district of Barra might easily be considered the Ipanema of Bahia, except for the heavy current of bohemianism that runs through it. Once the home of industrialists and plantation owners, the neighborhood has been recently saved from decline by substantial restoration and the subsequent influx of young, beautiful people who stroll the beach day and night.

Many good, medium-range hotels are located here, as are some of the best restaurants – from casual outdoor eateries featuring Greek, Italian, and fast food cuisines to colonial-style mansions offering typical Bahian delicacies. The beach, while beautiful, is more for strolling than swimming, but that doesn't seem to deter sunworshippers who head for the fried fish and cold *cerveja* in the many *barracas* lining the shore.

One of the major sites in the area is the **Farol de Barra**, the city's lighthouse built in the 19th century and still in use every night. Most city tours stop here; inside are two museums containing various historical maps and centuries-old documents. From this hill, you'll have a good view of Itaparica Island and you may even catch a glimpse of pro-level surfers battling the high waves down below. In general, the beach is considered a family one, and at 5 p.m., hordes of teens converge at the lighthouse to enjoy the fabulous sunset. The **Forte de Antônio** was built in the 17th century as the first fortress to defend the bay.

For Barra's main street action, head for **Rua César Zame**. There you'll find **Tiffany's** restaurant (a new watering hole featuring moderately priced French dishes) and right next door, the **Cantina Roma**, a favorite Italian pitstop. At the corner with Rua 223 Barão de Sergipe, you'll see lots of bars, street fairs, and a constant crowd during high season. Nearby, **Bar Oceânia** is a traditional meeting place for singles.

Tourists and residents alike often head for Barra just for the shopping. Strewn with greenery, the **Barra Shopping Mall** makes an ultra-chic statement, with fine clothes stores, professional photo labs, cinemas, and a capuccino stand. One of the best places to buy high-quality Northeastern handicrafts is the **Instituto Mauá** (☎ *235-5440)*, Praça Azevedo Fernandes,

02; (Mon.-Fri. 8 a.m.-6 p.m., Sat. **8 a.m.-4 p.m.**) Nearby, **the Banco Econômico** gives a good exchange rate for the dollar.

# Museums

**UP CLOSE TIP:** *Most museums are closed on Mon.*

## Museu de Arte Sacra

*Rua do Sodré, 276;* ☎ *243-6310. Mon.-Fri.*

Not only does this museum have the largest collection of sacred art in the world, it's a marvelous oasis of peace, particularly on a rainy day when you can sit on a stone window seat and look out onto a tumultuous sea. Interestingly, the building's turbulent past belies its soothing ambiance. In 1665, a brotherhood of Barefoot Carmelites stopped here on their way to convert Indian tribes and asked permission from Portugal to build a church. One hundred and fifty years later, as the rest of Brazil was fighting for independence, the monks tried to persuade parishioners – during confession! – to remain Portuguese, but their subterfuge was soon discovered and they were immediately shipped back to Portugal. The original church, finished in 1697, retains elements of the baroque and manierista styles, while the museum, established in 1959, is elegantly arranged to offset the architecture. As you enter the monastery you'll pass through the tiled sitting room off the inner courtyard, where the monks' families came once a month to visit them. Marriages are often performed in the glorious baroque-rococo sanctuary, where there are tiled pictures of the original monks who arrived barefoot. The pure silver altar, crowned by a statue of St. Teresa of Avila, comes from the Cathedral da Sé, now defunct. Within the museum proper, a series of small galleries overflows with marvelous objects, including a wood sculpture of N.S. de Rosário by the 19th-century sculptor Pereira Baiõ (the robes appear to be blowing in the wind). Do note that the painted sculptures of the short-legged São Cosme and São Damião, with their black bowl-haircuts, look incredibly like the musician Paul Simon! (He must have some karmic connection with the city since he recorded with Bahian musicians in the late 1980s.) Also fascinating is the *Redoma com o Senhor Menino Deus* – a bell jar of the Baby Jesus surrounded by baby ducks and tiny teacups. On the first floor, the painting of N.S. Após a Flagelação from 1796 looks nearly black in closeup, but becomes hauntingly clearer as you step farther back. Before leaving, pick up a color booklet of the collection for about $2.

## Museu Abelardo Rodrigues

*Rua Gregório de Mattos, 45,* ☎ *321-6155. Mon.-Fri. 1-7 p.m.*

Collected by a Recife doctor (who was also a journalist and lawyer), this exhibition of sacred Northeastern art gives a fine perspective of the development of Brazilian styles from the 17th, 18th and 19th centuries. Unfortunately, the collector made no notes, so the researchers can only presume origins. Many of the magnificent pieces of carved wood have been stripped of gold so that you can see the virgin wood. In the 17th-century statues, you'll notice the carved vestments have less movement, rendering a greater sense of peace. During the 18th century, the baroque style transformed the saints into elaborate figures with flowing robes, wavy hair, and clear facial expressions. As the baroque was dying in the 19th century, the style regained an elegance of form and a simpler expression. The most treasured part of the collection is the 18th-century **São Miguel Arcanjo** (the Archangel Michael), a perfect representative of baroque movement and decoration. In the cabinet labeled "Popular," you can see how amateur artists tried to imitate the styles of the masters. In the lobby of this former colonial mansion, there's a map of the city with major tourist points labeled by pictures.

## Museu Carlos Costa Pinto

*Avenida 7 de Setembro, 2490. 3-7 p.m., except Tues.*

Settled in an old colonial house at an easily reachable address in Barra, this museum features jewelry, furniture, crystal, and perhaps the only examples of *balangandās* – silver chains of fetishes worn by slaves – in Salvador. Modern-day versions of the bracelets can be purchased in the Mercado Modelo.

## Museu de Arte da Bahia

*Avenida 7 de Setembro, 2340;* ☎ *235-9492. Tues.-Sat. 2-6 p.m.*

A rainy-day option, this collection in a colonial mansion includes diverse paintings, porcelain, and furniture from both Brazil and Europe.

# Rainy Days

It does rain in Salvador, especially in winter (June-Aug.), when it may get too cold and windy to enjoy the beach. Don't despair. Here are some cloudy day options.

- ☐ Take a leisurely stroll (rather than 20 minutes offered by tours) through the Mercado Modelo.
- ☐ Hang out in Barra Shopping Mall, complete with cinema and food complex.

# Beaches

As in most beach towns of Brazil, the *orla*, or shoreline along the Atlantic Ocean, galvanizes most of the touristic activity. Bahia has the longest coastline in Brazil, measuring over 15 miles. It's here, from Porta da Barra north to the beach of Itapoã, that the best hotels are found, as well as apart-hotels and small *pousadas*. Due to pollution and some natural characteristics, such as rocky shores and torturous waves, some of the beaches closest to the city are not suitable for swimming and are best

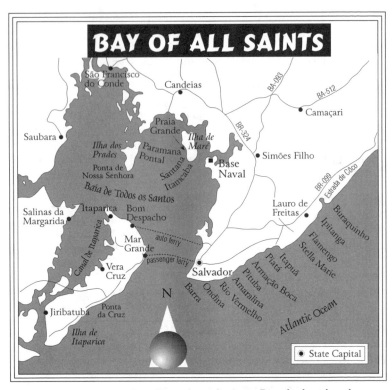

utilized as places to walk, talk, and gawk. As in Rio, the best beaches are farther out – sometimes a real trek – but special and regular buses go down the *orla* regularly. Along almost all the beaches are *barracas* selling food and drink, as well as vendors hawking beer and *acarajé*, fried bean cake.

The shoreline of Salvador actually begins at **Porto da Barra**, the site where Tomé de Souza, the first governor of Bahia and Brazil, arrived in 1549 and where the Dutch landed in 1624. It's now a small port, where the Western telegraph cables come ashore. The **Farol da Barra** is a fortress built in 1583; its lighthouse started to function in 1839. Barra, located where the Bay of All Saints meets the Atlantic Ocean, is one of the most active beach scenes, though swimming is not suggested (the only safe place to swim in Barra is near the lighthouse). **Praia do Farol**, near the Farol Flat Hotel, has become a family-oriented beach. As a swimming site, Ondina is not at all suitable, but it is picturesque, with artificial pools formed by the natural rocky coves. At Rio Vermelho, on the far side of Ondina, you'll find local native fishermen weaving their nets, which resemble enormous spider webs. Nearby an arts and crafts fair is held every Fri., sponsored by SESI. On the second of Feb., a celebration of *candomblé* offerings is held near the Casa de Iemenjá, a tiny house of worship built for such gatherings.

Originally a fishermen's village, **Pituba** has lots of restaurants and bars for flirting, but the sand is not clean and is often full of rubbish; still, lots of teens congregate here, as well as mothers and children. **Jardim de Alá** is a nice place to picnic, but the water is definitely polluted and often exudes an unappealing odor. At night, though, it's a beautiful place to sit at a grass-hut bar and contemplate the moonlight.

By all accounts, **Piatã** is Salvador's most beautiful beach. On its far side, Itapoã has been the subject of a beloved song by Vinícius de Moraes, which you are sure to hear at least once during your stay in Bahia. On New Year's Eve, **Itapoã** is the place to be, when *candomblé* devotees, dressed in white, place illuminated candles on the beach and offer food, money, and flowers to the sea goddess Iemenjá. As befits his poetic status, Vinícius de Moraes used to live in this neighborhood. Nearby are the dark waters and white sandy hills of the **Abaeté lagoon**, as well as an inlet formed by Ruas J and K, which makes for excellent sailing and diving. On the far side of Itapoã's lighthouse, **Stella Maris** attracts lots of surfers. Also known for surfers and lots of beautiful girls is **Jaguaribe Beach**. **Pitau** is where the chic people hang out, particularly by the Casquinha restaurant and the surrounding *barracas*. Corsário is the best beach for children, with calm, warm waters and clean sand.

Outside the city settlements, following the north coast along Coconut Road, small settlements between Arembepe and Praia do Forte still retain their rural simplicity; here, you'll find numerous fishing villages that haven't changed for centuries. The islands dotting the bay are also interesting to visit. (Also, see *Excursions* below.)

# Excursions

If you are staying in Salvador for a few days, hop on a **schooner** to one of the 36 adjacent islands – an excellent way to beat the heat and see the outer reaches of the All Saint's Bay. Numerous travel agencies offer daily schooner excursions that leave about 9 a.m., weather permitting. If you speak decent Portuguese, you might be able to bargain with the owners of the smaller *saveiros* (long, narrow fishing boats) moored near the Mercado Modelo.

## Ilha dos Frades

About 15 miles from Salvador rests Ilha dos Frades, one of the largest islands in the Bay of All Saints, with dense coconut groves and primitive settlements that still retain their colonial architecture. Many tourist agencies offer day excursions here, usually on tri-decker schooners serenaded by local *sambistas* singing at the top of their lungs.

My own adventure at Ilha dos Frades started a few feet from shore, when we were asked to wade the last few feet in ankle-high water (a few macho men dove in and swam to shore). Waiting for us on the strand was a lively band of natives vigorously hawking the crafts of the region – carved knives, handmade jewelry, wooden combs, and contraband snakeskins and turtle shells. As the sun reached its zenith we huddled under umbrella-shaded tables to enjoy cold beer and cracked lobster. An hour or two was spent inspecting the colonial church at the top of the hill and gingerly clmbing over the craggy reefs. Then we took another 45-minute cruise to Ponta d'Areia, a slightly more developed island, where we demolished a hearty lunch of *siri caranguejos* (soft crabs) under a grass hut. Afterwards, we strolled the dirt roads of the traditional village, then stretched out for a well-deserved afternoon nap. Around 5 p.m. the schooner made a bee-line back for Salvador as the sun dramatically set over the horizon.

Other schooner destinations offered by travel agencies include Ilha da Maré, which features the community of Santana, known for its handiwork of bobbin lace.

## Itaparica

The largest island of the bay is extraordinary for the fauna and flora that have been largely preserved in their original state. Only 12 miles from Salvador, it was first inhabited by the Portuguese in 1560; the name itself comes from the Indians and means "stone fence." You can reach Itaparica by the **São Joaquim Ferry**, which leaves several times daily from the dock adjacent to the São Joaquim Market. The crossing takes about 45 minutes (you can sit down below or lean over the railings for a better view), but you must book your trip two to three days in advance to avoid long lines, especially on weekends. On the other shore of Itaparica will be small buses waiting to take you to the various beaches (you can also rent a private car). Besides a famous mineral water spa (the only one set on a beach in Brazil), there are also good hotel accommodations, such as the Hotel Icaraí and the Grande Hotel, as well as numerous *pensões* (boarding houses). Among sites to check out are the **Fort of São Lourenço** and the 18th-century **Church of São Lourenço**. Eight miles from the township of Itaparica is the settlement of Mar Grande, where the best beaches are found: Barra do Gil, Barra Grande, Tairu, Aratuba, and others. Club Med is also there, as well as a few decent *pousadas*, such as Pousada Mar Grande (see under *Where To Stay*).

## Joanes River

This river makes an interesting ecological tour and should delight anyone in pursuit of birdwatching, jungle trekking, and swimming at deliciously deserted beaches. The tour follows trails through the Atlantic rainforest, where wild orchids, native fauna, and one of the largest mangrove areas in Bahia can be seen. For more information, contact: **Rio Joanes Viagens, Turismo e Eventos**; Terminal Turístico de Portão, loja 27; (Estrada do Coco, km. 9); ☎ *(71) 379-3615, fax 237-2580.*

# Where To Stay

Accommodations in Salvador and its environs run from the luxury resort to intimate *pousadas* with colonial charm. Unfortunately, with the exception of Quatro Rodas Sofitel, most hotels are not situated on beaches conducive to swimming; in most cases, you'll have to take a taxi or cab to a suitable strand. Because of the active nightlife and good shopping, many tourists like to roost in Barra. Although some travelers end up in dirt-cheap hotels near the Praça da Sé, I can't recommend them for safety or cleanliness; if you want to go the bottom-line budget route, you're better off in a youth hostel. See page 26 for price chart.

## Bahia Othon Palace

*Avenida Pres. Vargas, 2456 (Ondina);* ☎ *(71) 247-1044, fax 245-4877. Reserve in Rio,* ☎ *(21) 521-6262.*

With its impressive stucco facade and wraparound driveway, the five-star Bahia Othon affects the style of a tropical palace in the middle of suburbia. Its location is dramatic – in a grassy knoll jutting over a rocky coast pummelled by crashing waves. The enormous lobby, complete with tarot reader in a grass hut, is connected to a split-level mall full of boutiques and jewelry stores. Renovations in the past two years have created the best convention services in the city, attracting international congresses in banking, medicine, and industry. One huge meeting room can accommodate 600 people, while four others can serve 160 persons each. A new shopping corridor resembles the new face of the Pelourinho, with pastel shutters and grilled balconies. Antique-looking lamps and candelabras add historical dimension to the main restaurant overlooking the raging sea. A stunning pool complex offers extensive space for sunning. From June 15-Mar. 15, a leisure team organizes volleyball, aquatic games, walks, and bingo; programs for children above four, as well as babysitters, are available. The Othon loves to throw minishows and cultural events for conventions; non-participants can slip in unnoticed. Business execs who apply for VIP service receive a special breakfast on the 12th floor and free afternoon cocktails. Huge wall-to-floor glass windows in the main restaurant overlook the pool. Fabulous lunch and dinner buffets are offered. Best bets are deluxe rooms, appointed with wicker furniture and tartan spread, with a perfect vista of the sea from the windy verandas. Special cabana-type apartments are available for those who stay at least a month. The Hippopotamus nightclub is a popular hot spot. *277 apts. Expensive. All cards.*

## Meridien Bahia

*Rua Fonte do Boi, 216 (Rio Vermelho);* ☎ *(71) 248-8011, fax 248-8902.*

A massive high-rise on the dramatically craggy Rio Vermelho Beach, the Meridien attracts chic Europeans who appreciate the cool efficiency of the French-speaking staff. The lobby furniture is sleek rather than tropical, though the carved wood panels behind the reception are of native design. The outdoor/indoor restaurant poolside features a stunning view of the sea and provides a constant soundtrack of crashing waves. The pool boasts a voluptuous image of Iemenjá painted on its bottom. Equipped with small balconies, all rooms face the sea; the only difference between the standard and deluxe is the decoration. St. Honoré restaurant is an oasis of gourmet French cuisine and the nightclub Regine's is elite. The ear-shattering caws of caged *araras* (parrots) and toucans can be heard throughout the lower levels. Although you can't swim at this beach, Barra and Jaguaribe are 15 minutes away, as is Pituba. *426 apts. Expensive. All cards.*

## Enseada das Lajes

*Avenida Oceânica, 511 (Morro da Paciência, Rio Vermelho);*
☎ *(71) 336-1027; fax 336-0654.*

You'll feel at home the moment you enter this exquisite private residence transformed into a first-class *pousada*. Set high on a hill named Morro da Paciência, it's the perfect place to view the Festival of Iemanjá on Feb. 2, when a special boat laden with gifts is pushed out to sea. The fabulous living room and veranda, where breakfast is served, looks out onto a raging sea. An inner courtyard with an antique fountain is a lovely place to read books and meditate. Each apartment is individually furnished with antique furniture. If the daily rate is too stiff, at least come for lunch or dinner – a rustic, yet elegant, affair (reservations required). For special holidays, book months in advance. *9 apts. Very expensive. All cards.*

## Fiesta Bahia Hotel

*Av. Antônio Carlos Magalhães, 711 (Pituba);* ☎ *(71) 352-0000, fax 358-7810.*

This is the city's newest five-star hotel, sleek and marbled, with a brightly matched coffee shop overlooking an excellent pool, close to the Itaigara Shopping Center. The health room, though small, is equipped with free weights and bikes. The medium-sized apartments all have the same decoration; some rooms have a large veranda, but there is no view of the sea, only the cityscape. There are five handicapped apartments. Suites are lively, with carpet and jacuzzi. The city park nearby is good for jogging. The beach is 200 feet away. *Expensive. All cards.*

## Sofitel Quatro Rodas Salvador

*Rua Passáragada (Farol de Itapoã), 28 km.,* ☎ *(71) 249-9611, fax 249-6946.*

As is its style in other cities, the Sofitel Quatro Rodas is the closest thing to an island resort in Salvador proper. Located on Itapõa Beach, the hotel believes a guest should never be bored. As such, there is a constant stream of parties and leisure activities, as well as a luxurious pool, golf course, tennis courts, mini-spa, hair salon, and nightclub. Shows by Dionne Warwick, Tom Jobim, Júlio Iglesias, and others are presented in the gymnasium. Adorning the lobby is a gargantuan 18th-century sugar mill; the piano bar is filled with the statues and voodoo accoutrements of *candomblé* saints. The coffee shop is an intimate cove with native-dressed waitresses under a bamboo roof. New Year's Eve is famous for its big bash, as well as June 24, the São José Festival, when guests dress up in country-style clothes and dance *forró*.

Spacious and attractively appointed, the superior rooms face the sea, while deluxes face the sea and the pool (the latter are sometimes noisy). Unfortunately, the floors are carpeted which, in a seaside resort, often results in a slight musty odor. The closest beach is a five-minute walk away, but for better swimming, you'll have to walk twice as far. A hotel bus leaves four times a day to the Mercado Modelo, and twice a day to Farol da Barra

– about an hour away. Cars make the distance in half the time. *195 apts. Moderate-expensive. All cards.*

### Vitória Marina

*Av. Sete de Setembro, 2068 (Vitória); ☎ 336-7736, fax 336-0507.*

A semi-luxurious four-star hotel with a magnificent garden that leads down to its own pier (a cable car takes you down). An exquisite roof bar sits right above the ocean, and the medium-sized pool is good for sunning. Pay an extra $25 or so for a room with a sea view. The antique-style lobby looks better than the rooms themselves, which seem a tad worn. An overpriced souvenir store is in front of the entrance. *Expensive. All cards.*

### Tropical da Bahia

*Praça 2 de Julho (Campo Grande); ☎ (71) 321-3699, fax 336-0654.*

The only five-star hotel downtown, the Hotel da Bahia is a 10-minute drive to Barra, but the walk, down a tree-lined avenue, is extremely scenic. The breakfast room, decorated with lively wall murals, provides a huge breakfast buffet with traditional Bahian foods. Buffets are also offered for lunch and dinner, and the menu caters to American tastes as well, including triple-decker sandwiches and banana splits. A second, more elegant restaurant specializes in lobster, filet mignon, and pastas. Pleasantly arranged standards look out onto the avenue; the superiors look onto the pool area with a small veranda. When you buy your ticket at Varig, you can receive a 20% discount for the ticket and the room, including transfer from the airport. *292 apts. Moderate. All cards.*

### Apart Hotel Porto Farol

*Rua Eng. Milton Oliveira, 184 (Barra); ☎ (71) 247-5566, fax 247-6555.*

Lots of Germans and Italians stay in this apart-hotel, located on a leafy (and very safe) street two blocks from the beach in Barra. Apartments are identical, with living room, kitchen, marble table and chair, a pull-out couch; all have balconies, but there is no view. A coffee shop serves lunch and dinner, and there is small square pool. Service is exceptionally friendly. *Moderate. All cards.*

### Marazul

*Avenida Sete de Setembro, 3937 (Barra); ☎ (71) 336-2121, fax 235-2121.*

A lobby shaded with darkened glass provides a comfortable place to crash in this four-star hotel. The coffee shop, which serves breakfast and light meals, opens onto a small, circular pool. A restaurant featuring Brazilian specialties can serve large groups. Rooms are more serviceable than decorative, and run on the small size. *124 apts. Moderate. All cards.*

### Hotel do Farol

*Avenida Presidente Vargas, 68 (Barra); ☎ (71) 336-6611, fax 245-4436.*

The lobby has little space to mill, but Farol is right on the seashore, around the block from Barra's finest restaurants and bars, and across the street from a small shopping mall. Standards, with faux brick walls, are cozy and cheerful, with a veranda opening onto the beach and tiled baths with tubs. A fan-shaped pool gives you a full view of the surfers. The receptionist should speak English. *80 apts. Moderate. All cards.*

## Hotel Ondimar

*Avenida Presidente Vargas, 1843 (Ondina);* ☎ *(71) 245-0366, fax 245-4834.*

This three-star hotel in Ondina, near the Othon, provides service without frills. Standards are tight with no view; much larger deluxes, with seaside views, are worth the extra bucks. The breakfast room has American-style banquettes for fast foods, lunch, and dinner; there are no other restaurants nearby. A pool will be built. Shopping Barra is a 10-minute walk away. With advance notification, you can arrange a car to pick you up at the airport. Children up to age 10 stay free of charge. *24 apts. Moderate. All cards.*

## Farol Barra Flat

*Avenida Oceánica, 409 (Barra);* ☎ *(71) 237-6722.*

The best centrally located apart-hotel in Barra is spacious and colorful, and suited for families. Fully air-conditioned apartments, with a kitchen and bar, are built around a plant-filled inner courtyard. There's also a pool, sauna, and roof-top restaurant. Breakfast is included in the daily rate. Double and two-room flats available. *38 apts. Moderate-expensive. No cards.*

## Hotel Catharina Paraguaçu

*Rua João Gomes (Rio Vermelho);* ☎ *and fax (71) 247-1488.*

Named after the Indian love of a famous Portuguese adventurer, this absolutely charming *pousada* is Bahia's best bet, especially if you're shunning big hotels. A local female architect beautifully restored this old colonial house in 1994, keeping intact the high ceilings and adding traditional tiles, beautiful wood panels, flowering gardens, and antique lighting. The courtyard, full of white baroque garden chairs and plants, opens to the sun and is a lovely place to rest. The charming dining room is decorated with Bahian ceramics. Accommodations are available for the handicapped. The restaurant Zona Franca, across the street, is romantic and breezy. Standards start at $39; duplexes include a small kitchen.

## Villa Romana Hotel

*Rua Prof. Lemos de Brito, 14 (Barra);* ☎ *(71) 336-6522; fax 247-6748.*

One of the most charming options in Salvador, this is a country-style *pousada* full of antique tapestries and native pottery. Because they were built in phases over the last 20 years, rooms differ dramatically in size; some are tucked into cubbyholes, others are enormous. Make sure you ask for an *amplo*, with high-beamed ceilings. Even the corridors are romantic, rustically appointed with objets d'art collected by the owners on their international travels. Italians tend to stay here for a month, particularly for the Italian-oriented cuisine, a throwback to the owners' ancestry. The restaurant, with pretty waitresses in native costume, is particularly inviting.

A very unusually shaped pool with its own outdoor veranda overlooks the city. Low-season discounts range from 25-30%. *49 apts. Inexpensive. All cards.*

### Ondina Praia Hotel

*Avenida Presidente Vargas, 2275 (Ondina);* ☎ *(71) 336-1033.*

For a three-star hotel, the Ondina Praia has a decided upper-class feel, with a plant-dominated lobby filled with breezy, pastel furniture. The restaurant is tastefully appointed in shades of maroon; the breakfast room is full of hanging plants. Some rooms have front views to the sea, though they are obscured by large complexes, such as the Othon. All apartments are air conditioned and include TV and mini-bar, but bathrooms are tiny. The outdoor pool is not large. Discounts of 20-30% during low season. *46 apts. Inexpensive. All cards.*

### Barra Turismo Hotel

*Avenida 7 de Setembro, 3691 (Porto da Barra);* ☎ *(71) 245-7433.*

This is a good budget idea for those who want to take advantage of Barra's social scene. The lobby is dreary but the rooms have been restored and include a little balcony with a beautiful view of the sea. (Make sure you ask for the view.) City buses to downtown and the beaches stop at the front door. Nearby is a handicrafts market and many bars and luncheonettes. *60 apts. Inexpensive. All cards.*

### Golden Park Hotel

*Avenida Manoel Dias da Silva, 979 (Pituba);* ☎ *(71) 240-5622.*

This serviceable, friendly hotel is situated on the second avenue back from the shoreline. Although the beach here is not good for swimming, the bus stops in front of the hotel, and Itapoá is only 20 minutes away. Some rooms have a tiny view of the beach, but this is not a place to stay locked in your apartment all day. A small rooftop pool is served by a bar. The air-conditioned rooms are opened by electronic keys and include video, TV, and mini-bar. A pleasant restaurant serves lunch and dinner. *Inexpensive. All cards.*

### Hotel Villa da Barra Beach

*Av. Sete de Setembro, 3959 (Barra);* ☎ *(71) 247-7908, fax 247-9667.*

This small, tropical complex is geared to travelers with a high degree of tolerance. The rooms, simple and unadorned, verge on the grungy (the mattresses are nearly non-existent), but the outdoor plaza, where you can sip drinks under a huge mango tree, is friendly and breezy. The main hang-out room has the only TV. Good for kids wanting to crash during Carnaval, but reserve four months in advance. *Inexpensive. No cards.*

## Youth Hostels

### Solar

*Rua Macapá, 461 (Ondina); ☎ (71) 235-2235.*

Located a few blocks from the beach on a shady street, this youth hostel has a bright, clean aura. Across the street is a *capoeira* studio and next-door is a 24-hour luncheonette. Some rooms have eight bunk beds, with a cabinet that locks and a shared bathroom with hot and cold water. There's also a self-serve laundromat. All ages, all countries converge here – men and women are separated. About $10 per bed, including breakfast. *54 beds, three rooms for women, two rooms for men. Cheap. No cards.*

### Albergue da Juventude da Barra

*Rua Florianópolis, 134; ☎ 247-5678.*

Lots of American youths stay here, in this old colonial house, now a youth hostel that sleeps 44. Three bunk beds per room, one bathroom for the whole floor, a locked box for valuables (be careful). Attractive TV salon and restaurant next door. Fifteen-day maximum stay. Reserve two months before Carnaval. *Inexpensive.*

## In The Pelourinho

The historical center near the Pelourinho has a few hotels that are throwbacks to the rooming houses of centuries past. The architecture is dilapidated colonial, the atmosphere funky, and the prices unbelievably low but, unless you're looking for swashbuckling adventure, you won't feel safe here. Plenty of tourists get robbed in broad daylight; after dark it's even worse. Single women should forget it. If you're in the habit of braving these kinds of accommodations, I seriously suggest you travel with your own sheets and towels and wear your money strapped to your chest while you sleep.

### Hotel Colon

*Praça Anchieta, 20, beside the Igreja São Francisco; ☎ 321-1531.*

Old men and cats sleep in the hallways, and green fungus grows in the tub, but the original colonial architecture is appealing, particularly the wood-carved doors. An American professor of some obscure subject is reputed to be living here, though I never saw him. Rooms with bathroom and with shared bath are available. *30 apts. Cheap. No cards.*

## Carnaval Flats

Private flats for Carnaval can be rented through **Tatu Tours Ed**. Victória Center, room 1108; Av. Centenári 2883; ☎ (71) 247-9322, fax 237-7562.

## Resorts

### Club Mediterranée

*Highway to Nazaré, km. 13; ☎ (71) 833-7141; fax 833-7165.*

Located on the island of Itaparica, the Club Med Bahia offers that kind of insistently perky service known at Club Meds worldwide. The staff is young, sexy, and dedicated to making sure you don't stay cloistered in your air-conditioned, chalet-type apartment. The grounds are luxuriously landscaped with tropical vegetation, wood bridges, and a beach right out the backyard. Most of the social scene centers around the extensive pool area, though there are also horse rides down the beach, hikes to native villages, windsurfing, archery, aerobics, *lambada*, and more. Guest talent shows include stripteases performed by the guests. Even though 70% of the clientele are families (mostly Brazilians and Argentinians with a smattering of French, Americans, and Italians), I know singles who've gone home beaming. Children are kept wonderfully entertained all day long. Most remarkable is the quality and quantity of the cuisine – all-you-can-eat buffets of lobsters, prime rib, lamb, pastas, pâtés, French pastries, ice creams, and crêpes every day and night. The best time to go is Sept.-Mar. (Dec. is usually full). You must reserve in advance. *345 apts. Expensive. All cards.*

### Hotel Transamérica

*Highway to Canasvieiras (Ilha de Comandatuba); ☎ (126) 212-1122; telex, 2474. Reservations: Rua Colômbia, 587 in São Paulo; ☎ (11) 282-0999.*

Located on Comandatuba Island, Transamérica Hotel is the most luxurious resort in Brazil. Situated in a 25,000-acre grove of coconut trees, the hotel takes advantage of several islands, all pristinely maintained to ecological perfection. The ride to the hotel is a paradisiacal tour of Bahia's landscapes. An air-conditioned motor coach picks you up in Ilhéus (about 277 miles from Salvador), then follows the fabulous coastline south – past brilliant white beaches hugged by a dense tropical forest. After about 20 minutes, the sandy shore turns into an ocean wilderness as enormous palm leaves fan the highway and cattle graze over the high cliffs. Fifty minutes later, you cross the channel in a flat-bottom barge; on the opposite shore a cordial receptionist greets you with a tropical drink and leis. (All that's missing is a midget yelling, "Duh plane! Duh plane!") The main hotel, with three wings, plus a complex of private bungalows, is designed for total indulgence, its wood, rattan, and straw decor reflecting the island's natural but elegant lifestyle. The pool area is a voluptuous complex, enhanced by waterfalls and tropical bridges, yet steps away is a private beach so beautiful that you will never want to budge. All nautical sports from waterskiing to kayaks, sailboats, motorboats, and Hobie Cats, are concentrated along the Rio Doce channel; deep-sea fishermen come back with stories of dolphins, sea bass, red snapper, and more. Eco-minded adventurers will appreciate the mangrove-studded savannas perfect for exotic birdwatching. Four restaurants, including a special kid's club, an outdoor grill, an international buffet, and a special seafood restaurant, serve high-quality cuisine. Rooms in the main complex are luxuriously appointed, though the more rustic bungalows provide more privacy (especially great for honeymooners who are served candlelit dinners in bed). The most fun I had in my too-short stay was a motorboat jaunt to the island of Dona Vida, the resident mystic who even has a pyramid-shaped straw house. This feisty, 70-year-old European became so popular with the hotel's clients that the management gave her an island, where she receives guests for spiritual counseling and a great shrimp lunch. Rates for the resort depend on the accommodation, but generally start around $180 per person (breakfast and dinner included). To those looking for tropical luxury and security in Brazil, this must be heaven. For information, contact **F&H Travel Consulting** in the United States, ☎ *(800) 544-5503. 251 apts. Very expensive. All cards.*

## Agua Viva Praia Hotel

*Praia da Fazenda (Bom Jesus dos Pobres, 34 km.).*
*Reservations in Salvador, ☎ (71) 359-1132.*

Three hundred years ago the government gave this spectacular land with 16 miles of prime coast to the family whose descendants still own it. In 1989, they built 12 cabanas to share with the rest of the world, and they are planning more. Rustic and totally dedicated to beachlife, the "hotel" is a mere step away from the ocean, where you can indulge in all watersports and even horseback ride over the glorious dunes. The owner's wife is an international chef who prepares dishes that surpass even those at Bargaço's, one of Salvador's finest eateries. Tramping through the family's 1,000 acres of rainforest is great fun; a fabulous walk to a waterfall took us through knee-high rushes and rocky streams. Individual bungalows are smallish but air conditioned, and include mini-bar and tiled bathrooms; nights can be spent on the porch in a hammock. This is a great budget alternative to a high-class resort, with nary a reduction in beauty. Just coming for the day and eating lunch should be joyous. The hotel is about 50 miles from Salvador. If you whine, the hotel might pick you up in Salvador, but it's easy enough to take the bus from Salvador to Bom Jesus dos Pobres (four buses a day, about $3); it drops you 100 feet from the hotel. Alternatively, drive 2½ miles on the Santo Amara-Cachoeira Road, turn left, and go to Caubara Cabuçu and Bom Jesus dos Pobres. After Cabuçu, you will see the hotel sign; turn left toward the beach. *12 cabanas. Moderate. No cards.*

## Pousada Quinta Pitanga

*(Itaparica); ☎ (71) 831-1554, fax 831-1554.*

A very cozy *pousada* near Club Med, owned by a friendly American artist who painted the *pousada* himself. Six simple apartments, with excellent food, a front porch beach, and its own pier. *Inexpensive.*

# Where To Eat

Carybé, a famous Bahian painter, once said that "all Bahian food is holy." Indeed, many of the dishes served today in restaurants originated as offerings to the gods of *candomblé* and still have liturgical rituals attached to their preparation. Although both Portuguese and Indian influences can be tasted in the peppery cuisine, the kitchens of colonial plantations were dominated by African slaves – "usually two or three enormously large women," as historian Gilberto Freyre described them – who flavored their native dishes with a dendê palm oil, which turned everything reddish-yellow. Added to the pot were also generous doses of malagueta peppers, potent enough to draw tears from willing victims. Food was so important to the colonialists (little other entertainment did they have) that sometimes great chefs were given their freedom in gratitude for a memorable meal. At the very least, black cooks were often invited into the dining room to be toasted with song in front of the master's guests.

Among the most beloved Bahian dishes of African descent are *carurú* and *vatapá*. Eaten for centuries by slaves and masters alike, *carurú* is a stew made with okra, fish, shrimp, nuts, garlic, onion, and pimenta. An accompaniment to many dishes, *vatapá* is a type of porridge prepared from rice flour, ground cashews, peanuts, ginger, mint, and lots of palm oil. Even more exotic is **sarapatel** – a pork dish made with innards and other unmentionables, stewed in the pig's blood. Though the exact recipe varies from chef to chef, **xinxin** is a ragout of chicken prepared with salt, onion, garlic, oil, shrimps, and pumpkin. Bahian-style *feijoada*, enjoyed on Sat., is made with red beans, not black. In general, servings of all dishes in Bahia are generous, often accompanied by a series of side dishes, including *farofa de dendê* (manioc flour fried in palm oil).

Delicious desserts have long been the specialty of Bahian cooks, particularly during colonial times when a veritable war was waged between those made on the street and those made at home. Almost all Bahian sweets are made from coconut. *Cocada* – coconut candy boiled in sugar, water, lemon, and ginger – comes *branco* (white) or *preto* (black), depending on whether light or burnt brown sugar is used. Also delicious is **quindim**, a sticky little pudding cake made from egg yolks and coconut.

Many fine regional restaurants can be found throughout the state, especially in Salvador. One word of caution: be sparing when you first try the traditional dishes and see how they set with your stomach. The heavy palm oil and the profligate use of pepper could easily lay you up in bed for a few days. See page 26 for price chart.

## Bahian

### Casa da Gamboa

*Rua Newton Prado, 51 (Campo Grande);* ☎ *321-9776.*
*Noon-3 p.m., 6-11:30 p.m., closed Sun.*

Sixty-three-year-old Conceição Reis learned to cook on the farm where she was raised. Now her traditional/international cuisine is famous throughout the country, as is her motherly warmth, which she dispenses tableside. In her charming colonial-style house overlooking the bay, dine on Salvador's best examples of *moqueca* (fish or mussels simmered in oil and pepper) and *vatapá* (see above), as well as native desserts. Start off with *caranguejo na casca* – crab legs fried in a batter of egg, flour, and lemon. Lobsters are especially fresh, caught practically outside the front door, as are the many varieties of fish and shrimp. The octopus in vinaigrette, a cold salad, is unusual. What is special about Dona Conceição's kitchen is her creative use of condiments. "We spice with love here," she laughs, although she might be referring to the warmth of her folkloric-dressed waitresses, whose beautiful faces enhance the almost devotional service. Ask for a table beside the blue-shuttered windows; the view of the moored fishing boats is highly romantic. *Expensive. AE.*

## Tempero da Dadá

*Av. Texeira Mendes, 55; ☎ 235-4382 (Alto das Pombras). Mon.-Thurs. dinner only, Fri. and Sat. lunch only. Also in the Pelourinho: Rua 223 Frei Vincente. 1 a.m.-3 p.m., 7 p.m.-midnight, closed Sun.*

In Alto das Pombras, dogs sit at your feet and laundry hangs in the courtyard, but this dive serves the best Bahian food in the country. Dadá started cooking at the age of seven in a tiny interior town, cooked her way through the hotels of Bahia, and finally became a TV personality after she started this restaurant (and the one in the Pelourinho) three years ago. Music stars, such as Caetano Veloso and Gilberto Gil, come especially for the *bobó de camarão* (shrimp in *creme de leite*) and the singular dessert: *bolinho de estudante* (tapioca and coconut fried and rolled in sugar and cinnamon). What makes her cooking perfect is a light touch on the oil and a mastery of spices, not to mention her smiling face and busy hands as she supervises her turbaned assistants practically in your face. It's a real experience, particularly in the Alto das Pombras joint, since you venture into a slightly risky part of town, but the Mercedes Benzes are often lined up. Take a cab, and they'll call you one for the return. *Moderate. All cards.*

## Seafood

## Bargaço

*Rua P, QD 43, lotes 18/19 (Jd. Armação); ☎ 231-5141. Noon-midnight.*

This open-air restaurant with absolutely no ambiance has worked hard to garner acclaim as the best fish restaurant in Bahia. A great meal can be had from ordering a few of the enormous appetizers of shrimp, raw oysters, crab, and lobster. Or try traditional entrées, such as *mariscadas* and *ensopados*, fish stews simmered in a variety of sauces that arrive bubbling hot. *Expensive. All cards.*

## Casquinha de Siri

*Avenida Otávio Mangabeira (Pietá); ☎ 249-1234.*

Dance under the stars at Bahia's best beach (Piatá), where a live band swings to Brazil's golden oldies, and the regulars nosh on *tira gostos* (appetizers), such as the delicious *siri mole á Milanesa* (fried crabs) and *pitinga ao molho tartaro* (small fried fishbits). At night the atmosphere is unabashedly lively, but it's also a good lunch stop if you're sunbathing nearby. Music cover charge at night. *Moderate. No cards.*

### Frutos do Mar

*Rua Alm. Marquês de Leão, 415 (Barra);* ☎ *245-649. 11 a.m.-4:30 p.m.,*
*6 p.m.-12:30 a.m.*

Across from the Farol Flat Hotel, this fish eatery features waitresses in
folkloric dress and menus in English. Try the *siri mole* (soft shell crabs) or
the *sururu* (little mussels). *Moderate. All cards.*

## Churrascaria

### Churrascaria Rodeio

*Av. Otávio Mangabeira, 10;* ☎ *240-1762.*

An excellent steakhouse beyond Pituba Beach. *Moderate.*

### Baby Beef

*Avenida Antônio Carlos Magalhães (next to Hipermercado Paes Mendonça);*
☎ *358-0811. 11:30 a.m.-3 p.m., 6 p.m.-midnight.*

Excellent steaks à la carte, especially the huge *picanha.* Crispy French fries
and excellent *macaxeira frita,* fried macaxeira (a root plant). Check out the
mammoth supermarket Paes Mendonça next door. A second Baby Beef is
located in the Convention Center in Pituba. *Moderate. All cards.*

## Italian

### Il Forno

*Rua Al. Marques de Leão, 77;* ☎ *247-7287. Noon-3 p.m., 6 p.m.-1 a.m.*

An Italian bistro with American posters offers the best pizza (34 varieties)
in Salvador, not to mention a snazzy location in Barra. Steaks and chicken
are also available. Sit outside on the terrace and watch the world go by.
*Moderate. All cards.*

### Baguette e Cia

*Rua Marques de Leão (across the street from Il Forno).*

A cheerful counterette with long French bread sandwiches and excellent ice
cream sundaes. *Inexpensive. No cards.*

### La Gula

*Avenida Presidente Vargas, 2400 (Ondina);* ☎ *203-8314.*
*Noon-3 p.m., 7 p.m.-1 a.m., closed Mon.*

Among locals, this cantina is considered the best for Italian food – pasta,
lasagna, and pizzas. *Moderate. AE.*

# Arabian

## Aladin

*Rua Marques de Leão, 173. 11 a.m.-2 a.m.*

The "in" spot of Barra (at least this year) offers fine Arabic entrées, including stuffed cabbage and lamb. You can go just to nosh on hors d'oeuvres, such as *baba ganoush, kibe,* and *pastel de carne* and look over the young crowd (18-29) that hangs out here. Weekends are sardine-like. *Inexpensive. No cards.*

# Fast Food

## McDonald's

*Praça Tiradentes.*

Yes, the hamburger joint from up north gives new meaning to spic and span, conveniently located downtown across the street from the Varig Airline office on Praça Inglaterra. (The American Express office is also nearby, at the corner of Rua Miguel Calmon.) Another McDonald's is about a five-minute walk from the Mercado Modelo. *Inexpensive. No cards.*

## 1/2 Kilo

*Rua Florianópolis, 134 (Jardim Brazil). Mon.-Sat. 11:30 a.m.-5 p.m.*

Two blocks from the beach, this place is good for homemade fast foods. Pay by the kilo. They offer a decent lunch buffet, with eight hot plates and six cold. Next door is a youth hostel. *Inexpensive. No cards.*

# Natural

## Cozinha Natural

*Rua Belo Horizonte, 124 (Barra); ☎ 237-1012. 11:30 a.m.-8 p.m., Sat.-Sun. till 4 p.m.*

Health-oriented menu and natural foods. *Inexpensive. No cards.*

# Ice Cream

## Perini

Across the street from Barra Shopping Center, Perini offers the city's best ice cream, including a full array of tropical fruit flavors.

# In The Pelourinho

## Casa da Gamboa

*Rua João de Deus (Pelourinho). Noon-3 p.m., 7-11 p.m.*

One of the loveliest restaurants in Bahia, set in a restored colonial house open to the breezes. Voluptuous bare-breasted Bahian women adorn the paintings on the wall; if you can tear you eyes away, do try the *sopa de mariscos,* a delicious shellfish soup. Afterwards, walk out back to the *praça* to see the various stages of reformation in the area. *Moderate. No cards.*

## Tempero da Dadá

*Rua Frei Vicente, 05 (Pelourinho);* ☎ *321-5883. Tues.-Sun. noon-6 p.m. 7 -12 p.m..*

See review under *Where To Eat, Bahian* in Salvador, above.

## Pastel Mel

*Rua João de Deus. Noon-3 p.m., 6 p.m.-midnight.*

The bar downstairs is opened noon-midnight for desserts and light snacks; upstairs you can eat full meals. *Inexpensive.*

## Cafe Expresso LTDA

*Rua João de Deus, 03 (Pelourinho). 8 a.m.-11 p.m.;* ☎ *242-4459.*

Tiny shop for excellent espresso and pastries. *Inexpensive.*

## Cailler

*Rua Gregório de Matos, 16. 9:30 a.m.-10 p.m., bar service till 1 a.m.*

A perfect stop for excellent coffee and chocolates. *Inexpensive.*

## Cantina da Lua

*Terreiro de Jesus. 9:30 a.m.-10 p.m.*

Very popular, but can get a bit too boisterous. *Moderate.*

## El Méson

*Rua Alfredo Brito, 11 (Upstairs). Mon.-Sat. 11 a.m.-11:30 p.m., Sun. 6-11:30 p.m.*

Excellent seafood and meats. English spoken.

## Caso do Benin

*Praça José Alencar, 29;* ☎ *242-5529. Noon-6 p.m., 7-11:30 p.m., closed Mon.*

Afro-Bahian cuisine in fantastic folkloric surroundings. Specialty is the shrimp in cashew nut sauce. *Moderate.*

## Restaurant Vauá

*Rua Gregório de Matos, 36 (upstairs);* ☎ *321-3089.*
*11:30 a.m.-3 p.m., 7-11:30 p.m., closed Tues.*

Probably one of the best kitchens for Northeastern cuisine in the area. Don't miss tasting here the *carne de sol,* dried salty meat. *Moderate.*

## SENAC (Serviço Nacional do Comércio)

*Largo do Pelourinho, 13/19 (Pelourinho);* ☎ *321-5502. 12:30 a.m.-3:30 p.m.,*
*6:30-9:30 p.m.*

One of the most delightfully civilized dining experiences in Salvador, this state-run restaurant school, which trains young chefs in native Bahian cuisine, is a perfect place to escape the hubbub of the Pelourinho area. The waiters are young, attractive, and oh-so-serious. The massive buffet includes 40 native dishes. The 20 on the right are made with dendê (African palm oil) and the 20 on the left are without (take care: an excess of the oil can cause digestive problems). If the traditional food looks daunting, there is also excellent fried chicken and recognizable vegetables. The waiter might take your plate the moment you finish, but feel free to take a clean one and start over. Drinks are not included, but all diners receive a delicious *batida*, which tastes something like peach liqueur. Prices are kept low so tip the waiter well. A light tea is served from 5-7 p.m. If you don't want to eat, just stop to check out the view of Salvador's rooftops from the colonial-style, green-shuttered windows. Cookbooks of the house cuisine are for sale. *Moderate. All cards.*

### Filhos de Ghandi

*Rua Gregório de Matos, 53 (Pelourinho);* ☎ *321-7073. Noon-2 p.m.*
Good cheap meals. See under *Walking Tour*, above.

## On Sundays

A fishermen's colony during the week, Itapagipe Beach transforms into a weekend party when sunbathers pack the grass-roof *barracas* and chow down on fried fish and cold beer.

## Street Food

You may hear their nasal ê-ê-ê-ê-ê-ê cry before you see their huge white hoop skirts and colorful turbans, but the **Pretas do Acarajé** are an institution on Salvador's streets. These native women, who make and sell the delicacies called *acarajé* (fried bean cake), are beloved throughout the city; often their culinary secrets have been passed down through generations. The *Preta do Acarajé* makes her dish right on the street, grating fradinho beans on a stone and frying the mixture with dendê oil, dried shrimps, onions, and salt in a clay pan that sits on a little rustic stove. The taste differs slightly from cook to cook, so everyone has a different opinion over who makes the best *acarajé*, but the *Bahiana* who causes the biggest traffic jams is Dinah at the Largo de Santana in Rio Vermelho, in front of the old church of Sant'Ana. From 4-10 p.m., traffic stops and people cram the streets just to buy her soulfully cooked cakes.

> **UP CLOSE TIP:** *When the cook asks "Pimenta?" learn to say "Um pouquinho" (oom poh-KEEN-yoo) or your eyes will be streaming with tears from the pepper. The open-air market featuring Bahian delicacies and regional handicrafts takes place on Fri.*

## Fish Market

The new fish market at Largo da Mariquita in Rio Vermelho has become a popular place to eat traditional dishes and drink exotic-flavored *batidas*. Resident Americans tend to eat lunch here; at night the small tables and wood chairs served by various kitchen stalls are crowded with locals. The smell of fish saturates the air, but one *batida* at Diolino's (considered the best in Bahia) will cure anything. Insanely delicious is the **Gala Gay**, with coconut and guava mix (about 30 cents for a tiny cup); you'll probably want to stock up on bottles. Do take a browse through **Casa das Folhas #20,** a stand selling *candomblé* and medicinal paraphernalia.

# Nightlife

Salvador is a city to savor at night. Cool winds and fresh air make lingering at sidewalk cafés a tropical pleasure. Most tourists will want to spend one night watching a folkloric show; they are much more authentic in Bahia than in Rio. The best show is in the atmospheric colonial house of **Solar do Unhão** (see below under *Folklore Shows*), where you can also partake of a fine buffet of local foods.

## Bars

Bar-hopping in Barra is also a popular activity – easy to do since many of the liveliest pubs are located along **Avenida Setembro de 7.** Two of the best bars in Barra are: **Bacchus** (Avenida Presidente Vargas, 115, loja 3; ☎ *245-6749*), open Mon.-Sat. from 9 p.m. on.; and **Clube 45** (Rua Barão de Sergy, 196; ☎ *237-3778*), open 7 p.m.-5 a.m. with live music.

### In Rio Vermelho

The district of Rio Vermelho has nearly eclipsed Barra lately in the number of hot spots that offer good music. **Cheiro do Mar** (Rua dos Reis, 14; ☎ *247-1106*) is open noon-2 p.m., and 5 p.m. on. **Graffiti** (Rua Odorico Odilon Borges) opens Tues.-Sun. from 6 p.m. onward. **Bar 68** (Largo de Santana, 3rd floor) is open Mon.-Fri. from 6 p.m. and on Sat. from 7 p.m.

### In The Pelourinho

Nightlife in the Pelourinho has a special romantic quality, though it's often boisterous. These days it's much safer to walk around the Pelourinho area at night (four years ago I advised travelers to avoid the area altogether). Nevertheless, stay in lighted areas and don't lose consciousness!

The liveliest bars in the Pelourinho are in **Quadra 2M,** where you can find **Habeas Copos,** Rua Alfredo Brito, 31; ☎ 321-0340, and **Dom Crepe.** Live music often energizes the square, where passersby can sit on stone embankments and listen for free (daily, except Tues., starting at 8 p.m.). Just to sit on this *praça* and contemplate the symphony of pastel colors and angles created by the interplay of restored buildings and traditional rooftops is an historical delight.

#### Alambique Cachaçaria

*Rua 223 João de Deus.*

The place to hang during Carnaval, especially as many of the schools, including Olodum, start their parades down below on the corner. Climb the slightly tortuous stairs to the charming salonette (really a *cachaça* bar), where you can taste from one of the best selections in the city.

## Kibe & Cia

*Rua João Castro Rabello, 08 (Pelourinho); ☎ 226-3833. Mon.-Sat., 1 p.m. on.*

Live music on Fri., Sat. and Sun. One of several bars on the best *praça* to hang out on.

## Discos

There are also plenty of clubs for dancing. My favorite is **Casquinha de Siri,** Avenida Otávia Mangabeira s/no., Praia dos Coqueiro (Piatá); ☎ 249-1234, with a sprawling open-air dining room and a great dance band that plays Brazilian golden oldies (see *Where To Eat*, above). The disco **Hippopotamus** at the Bahia Othon Hotel is a popular spot for locals and tourists. One of the newest discos is **Zouk Santana** in Rio Vermelho, with an excellent sound system. The best *lambada* in the city is found at **Sabor da Terra**, near Boca do Rio (next door is another new disco, **Krypton**). Samba bands heat up at **Cartarerê** in Cardeal da Silva.

Reggae comes alive in the **Cidade Alta** on Tues. nights (the only relatively safe time to stroll through the historical center after dark); during the rest of the week, shops close up early. Most popular are the **Bar do Reggae,** Rua João de Jesus, 32 and **Bar Baro,** Rua Alfredo Brito.

> **UP CLOSE TIP:** *Don't miss the rehearsal of the drummers from Olodum, the Carnaval bateria (percussion group) featured on Paul Simon's 1990 album* Rhythm of the Saints, *but who are stars in their own right in Brazil. The event usually takes place from 7-11 p.m. behind the Teatro Antônio Miguel on Rua João de Jesus in an open field called the* **Quadra,** *as well as on Sun. in the* **Largo do Pelourinho** *from 6-11 p.m.*

## Folklore Shows

## Solar do Unhão

*Avenida do Contorno (Gamboa); ☎ 321-5551. Noon-midnight. Show starts at 11 p.m., closed Mon.*

Most consider the folkloric show in this renovated sugarcane mill to be the most artistic in the city. Native dancers in skimpy costumes, virile *capoeira* artists and a bevy of hot drummers keep the passions flowing; the colonial atmosphere adds even more romance. Enter the restaurant through the corridor of the former mansion, stepping over the railroad tracks that used to cart products to and from the harbor. Dinner is included – an all-you-can-eat buffet of native delicacies. Most travel agencies (check at your hotel) offer group rates (including transportation), which is the safest way to reach this isolated neighborhood. For the show, make sure your seat is around the stage, but not too close to the drummer! *Expensive. All cards.*

## Theater

### Teatro Maria Bethânia

Named after the sultry singer and sister of Caetano Veloso, this theater features plays, concerts, and a cinema that shows art films. Check the newspapers for listings.

# Gay Salvador

## Barra

The area in front of the lighthouse has become a popular hangout for gays. Downtown, two clubs are frequented: one mysteriously known as **Holmes 24th,** Rua Gamboa de Cima (opposite the Rua 223 Banco dos Ingleses near Campo Grande) is best reached by taxi; and the **Tropical Nightclub,** on Rua Pau da Bandeira. Also check out the courtyard near Tiffany's restaurant in Barra.

# Shopping

Native crafts are a true expression of Bahian culture. Artists display their wares in hotel lobbies, outdoors in the main *praças*, in fairs, and at state-operated institutes that assure quality and fixed prices. Principal materials employed by the artisans are wood, silver, gold, leather, lace, ceramics, clay, and sisal (entwined rope). Musical instruments, such as the berimbau, are good buys, and most airlines will let you board with the gourd in hand, though you may have to ship the bow (carefully wrapped in cloth or newspaper) with your luggage. If you're heading to the Amazon, it's cheaper to buy a hammock in Belém or Santarem.

## In The Pelourinho

Along the cobblestone streets of **Rua Alfredo Brito** are numerous artisan shops that are fun to peek in. Stores along the Pelourinho sell lacework, sculptures, and folkloric paintings.

### Instituto Mauá

*Rua Gregorio de Matos, 27 (Pelourinho);* ☎ *321-5638.*
*Tues.-Sat. 9 a.m.-6 p.m., Sun. 10 a.m.-4 p.m.*

Some of the best Northeastern handicrafts can be found at this tasteful store in the Pelourinho, supported by the state government. Quality is high and prices fixed, but numerous items can't be found elsewhere, such as straw ducks, *ocarinas* (flutes made out of pottery), and native paintings. Ceramic *orixás* – statues of *candomblé* divinities – are excellent buys.

## Artesanato Santo Barbara

*Rua Alfredo Brito, 7 (Pelourinho).*

Excellent handmade lace products.

## Artesanato Yemenjá

*Rua Alfredo Brito (Pelourinho).*

Typical Bahian clothes and handicrafts.

## Colibri

*Rua Alfredo Brito, 16; ☎ 233-8711 (Pelourinho). Mon.-Sat. 7 a.m.-6 p.m.*

Interesting native paintings with the new colors of Pelourinho in a naif style.

## Chá Chá Dum Dum

*Rua João de Deus, 32 (Pelourinho). Mon.-Sat. 10 a.m.-7 p.m.*

Exotic batik clothes from Indonesia, beautiful but pricey.

## Oficina de Papel

*Rua João de Deus, 26 (Pelourinho); ☎ 321-1453.*

A petite, but charming store with handmade paper products (boxes, stationary, etc.), all recycled.

## Atelier Portal da Cor

*Ladeira do Carmo, 31 (Pelourinho); ☎ 242-9466.*

An excellent local art gallery with good prices run by a cooperative of Bahian artists (Totonho, Calixto, Raimundo Santos, and Jô, among others.)

## Casa do Indio

*Ladeira do Carmo (across the street from Atelier Portal da Cor, above).*

Indian artifacts and art, including a restaurant and bar. Open till late in the evening.

## Loisa Nossa

*Rua Alfredo Brito, 45.*

Good naif art. Next door are wood carvings by a cooperative of sculptors, Palito and Negão Barão.

## Chez Lua

*Rua Alfredo Brito, 27.*

Handmade traditional percussion instruments. You can even receive lessons from local percussionist Dilson Lua.

## Oficina de Investigção Musical

*Rua Alfredo Brito, 24; ☎ 321-0339.*

Percussion lessons. Mon.-Fri. 8 a.m.-noon and 1:30-4 p.m.

## Brazilian Sound

*Rua Francisco Muniz Barreto, 18. Mon.-Fri. 9 a.m.-noon,*
*2-6 p.m., Sat. 9 a.m.-noon.*

A good record store. (The smallest record store in the world is Mini Som in Praça da Sé.) Go upstairs for a great selection of antique records that you can't find anywhere else. Japanese collectors crowd in here for good reason.

## Simon

*Praça Anchieta 1, Ed. Derike, lojas A & B, ☎ 242-5218. Mon.-Sat. 9 a.m.-6 p.m.; Sun. 9 a.m.-1 p.m.*

Simon features handmade jewelry and will deliver it to your hotel (an excellent idea). Prices, however, run about three times the amount I paid for similar quality in Ouro Preto (Minas Gerais) and may even be higher than prices in Rio. A special product is called "Mask" – the matrix rock of an emerald handworked by communities of Indians near Porto Seguro. Also sold are precious and semi-precious stones used for healing purposes (designed so that the stone of the ring can touch the skin). Also available are Bahian cigars made at Suerdieck, one of the biggest plantations in Bahia. Good English spoken. *All cards and cash.*

Nearer the church is **Las Bonfim Gems Jewelers**, the oldest jewelry store in Bahia. If you are buying for business, they will sell wholesale. Specialties are chess sets made of onyx and sodalite, as well as raw amethysts.

## Shopping Pelô

*Rua Francisco Muniz, 02; ☎ 321-4200. Daily until 6 p.m.*

Run by SEBRAE, the Brazilian small business authority, this market offers stalls filled with varied goods, clothes, and jewelry.

> **UP CLOSE TIP:** *The major Carnaval Afro blocos have boutiques selling T-shirts and fantasias (costumes). Try the* **Boutique Olodum,** *Praça José Alencar and* **Ilí Alyê,** *Rua Francisco Muniz Barreto, 16.*

## Beyond The Pelourinho

## Mercado Modelo

*Mon.-Sat. 8 a.m.-6 p.m., Sun. 8 a.m.-noon.*

The city's main market, located in from the Lacerda Elevator in the lower city, is usually the last stop on city tours. First installed in the old customs house in 1915, it has been ravaged by two fires and was rebuilt, the last time in 1984. With 190 stalls, this three-story market is like a Turkish bazaar, where the first price is a joke and bargaining is expected (though in Brazil, it should always be done with charm). Primitive Bahian art and sculptures are excellent buys, as are the chess sets with traditional figures (upstairs). You'll also find plenty of musical instruments and fine embroidered and lace tablecloths. Most interesting are the *carrancas* – sculptured miniatures of the monsters with winged ears, grizzly smiles and red tongues that hang on the front of ships to ward off spirits.

In the front of the market is a round stage where *capoeira* artists perform. They expect money if you take their picture or stand there more than three seconds, which offended me until I learned that *capoeira* artists are usually poor and receive no support from the government. Don't be intimidated. Of the two restaurants in the market, the best is the **Camafeu de Oxóssi**, which serves traditional dishes. It's open daily at 11 a.m. and overlooks the bay.

The intriguing sculptures near the Mercado Modelo that look like two big *bundas* (derrieres) are the work of Mario Cravo, who innocently claims he just liked the shape. *Bahianos* insist the shape represents one of two things: 1) the voluptuousness of Bahian woman or 2) things that both the mayor and the governor have.

## SESI

*Avenida Sete de Setembro, 261 (Mercês). Mon.-Fri. 8 a.m.-noon, and 1:30-6 p.m.; ☎ 245-3543. (Two other locations: Loja Rio, Vermelho Rua 223 Borges dos Reis, 9 and Loja Porto da Barra, Forte de Santa Maria, Barra.*

Walking distance from the Meridien Hotel this co-op crafts store in a colonial house was founded to support native craftspersons from the interior. Many of the patchwork items, sold here at fixed prices, can only be found in the countryside. Small postcard paintings from Itaparica are good buys, as are thumb pianos, Indian-made rain sticks (a musical instrument that sounds like rain), and wooden jewelry. Afterwards, walk over to Largo Santana and buy some *acarajé* from Dinah, the famous street vendor (see above under *Street Food*). Across the street is a popular bar **Cheiro de Mar**, and around the block is the **Teatro Maria Bethânia**. Nearby, at the corner of Rua João Gomes and Largo da Mariquita is the **Teresa Galerias de Arte**, a gallery featuring posters and painters from well-known Brazilians.

## Shopping Malls

### Shopping Barra

*Ave. Centenário. Mon.-Fri. 9 a.m.-10 p.m., Sat. 9 a.m.-7 p.m., Sun. 3-9 p.m.*

This three-floor, ultra-modern mall is a cool, dry place to get out of the heat or rain. A telephone company is on the first floor, as well as fast-food restaurants and cinema. Some of the best stores include **Timberland shoes**, **Cheda** for men, **Gas** for chic children, and **Dimpus** for hip women.

Next to Salvador Praia Hotel is a small shopping mall housing **Itaparica Turismo**, one of the city's best travel agencies. And next to that are two important art galleries: **Escritório de Arte da Bahia** (☎ 245-5033); and **Cavalete** (☎ 345-5033), both at Avenida Presidente Vargas, 2338 (Ondina). Another excellent gallery is **Limpia**, Praça Anchieta, 16; ☎ 321-8896.

On Rua João Gomes there are several fine antique shops.

# Hands-On Salvador

## Airport

**Aeroporto Internacional** (Dois de Julho Estrada do Coco, ☎ *204-1136*). This is a modern airport with various snack bars, restaurant with a fine buffet, souvenir shops, and even a hairdresser.

To reach your hotel, you can take special air-conditioned buses that run from the airport along the shoreline, but the easiest way is to reserve a special taxi by paying in advance at the white booth in the middle of the arrival lounge (where you exit from customs). The clerk will ask the name of your hotel, and you pay according to the neighborhood you are going to. Then you will be directed to hand your receipt to the first special taxi in line.

*Be careful:* There are also "regular" taxis waiting for customers, and unless you can firmly express yourself in Portuguese and know how to bargain, you will most likely be taken for a very long ride.

## Arrivals

Salvador may be reached directly from the States on **Varig Airlines**, which runs a direct flight from Miami to Salvador once a week on Mon., leaving at 5 p.m. and arriving the next day at 3:45 a.m.

Originating in Rio, daily flights to Salvador are handled by **Varig, Cruzeiro, VASP**, and **Transbrasil.** The trip takes about two hours and costs $376 round trip if you have not previously purchased a Varig Air Pass.

## Airlines Serving Salvador

**Varig/Cruzeiro**
Rua Carlos Gomes, 6 . . . . . . . . . . . . . . . . . . . . . . . . .   ☎ 243-1244
**VASP**
Rua do Chile, 27 (Cidade Alta) . . . . . . . . . . . . . . .   ☎ 243-7277
**Transbrasil**
Rua Carlos Gomes, 616 . . . . . . . . . . . . . . . . . . . . . .   ☎ 241-1044

The **bus station** (Rodoviária de Salvador) is on Avenida Antônio Carlos Magalhães (Iguatemí); ☎ *558-0124.*

## Car Rental

**Avis** . . . . . . . . . . . . . . . . . . . . . . . . . . . . . . . . . . . . .   ☎ 377-2550
**Hertz** . . . . . . . . . . . . . . . . . . . . . . . . . . . . . . . . . . . .   ☎ 373-2667

## City Transportation

Most of the historical sightseeing in Salvador is concentrated in the Cidade Alta and can be easily done on foot. To reach a good swimming beach you must either take a taxi or a bus. The Lacerda Lift connects the high and low cities, but it is best avoided due to the high number of assaults.

## Buses

Buses in Salvador tend to be hot, crowded, and unsafe for tourists not used to third-world travel. The best bets are the air-conditioned *frescãos*, air-conditioned express coaches, which you can catch on the sidewalk up from Praça da Sé for about 75 cents. The *frescão* has two routes: one to the Iguatemí Shopping Center (via Barra and Rio Vermelho beaches, stopping near the *rodoviária*), and one to the airport, which passes Pituba and Itapoã beaches.

## Taxis

Taxis are plentiful and relatively cheap in Salvador, but drivers here have been known to be as sneaky as they are in Rio. Frankly, their level of honesty and gentility seems to correspond with the fluctuations of the economy. However, since the city government implored the taxi drivers (*motoristas*) to clean up their act in the name of tourism (preceding some important conferences), and I have actually noticed a definite accentuation on the positive. To avoid getting taken for a ride, however, make sure you know where you're going, how to get there (ask your concierge), and about how much it will cost – in advance. I don't like to say it, but some hotel doormen have been found to be in cahoots with cab drivers, so stay alert.

**Alôtaxi** (radio).............................  ☎ 273-4411
**COMETAS** (special cabs) ...................  ☎ 244-4500
**COMTAS** (airport)..........................  ☎ 377-2498

## Ferry

The islands in All Saint's Bay may be reached by both ferry and tourist excursion boats, which leave from the Terminal Turístico, behind the Mercado Modelo. Ferries handling automobiles leave from the Terminal da Estação Marítima, past the docks to the right.

### Climate

Sunshine is Salvador's greatest free pleasure. Average temperatures range from the mid-70s to the high 80s, with a refreshing sea breeze cooling the peak heat of summer.

The best time to go, climate-wise, is Sept.-Mar. Rainy months are Apr., May and June, when you're most likely to run into a nasty ocean squall that will dampen beachdoings for days at a time. However, even in summer, a fast but brief downpour occurs about once a day, clearing the hot air for even brighter sunshine.

## Consulates

In case of lost passports, stolen merchandise, or extreme illness, contact your own consulate immediately.

**USA**
Ave. Antônio Carlos Magalhães . . . . . . . . . . . . . .    ☎ 358-9166
**Great Britain**
Avenida Estados Unidos, 4 . . . . . . . . . . . . . . . . . .    ☎ 243-9222

## Credit Cards

**American Express** (Kontik Franstur Praça Inglaterra 2, 1st floor; ☎ 71 242-0433) is open Mon.-Fri. 9 a.m.-noon, 2-4 p.m. The office is extremely friendly and will process emergency check cashing, card replacement, foreign currency exchange, and mail for all cardholders. A **Telephone Service Center** is available on a 24-hour basis: for lost and stolen cards, ☎ 800-5050; for lost travelers cheques, ☎ (11) 545-5018 or 545-6223 in Salvador.

## Money Exchange

As in Rio, it's best to avoid cashing travelers cheques or exchanging dollars at your hotel, where the rate will be somewhat lower than the official tourist rate. Better rates can be found at **Banco do Brazil,** Avenida 7 de Setembro, 733 and Avenida Estados Unidos, 561 (Cidade Baixa). Located across from the Ondina Apart Hotel, **Banco Econômico**, Avenida Oceânica, 2400, Mon.-Fri. 10 a.m.-4 p.m., is good for exchanging travelers cheques and American currency. Rates are substantially better here than at the nearby Bahia Othon Hotel. In Barra, the best places to exchange money are **Banco do Brazil**, Rua Miguel Bournier, and in **Shopping Barra**.

## Medical Emergencies

**Private Clinic**
Rua Barão de Loretto, 21 (English spoken).

## Photo Development

**FOTO Lab**
Shopping Barra, 1st floor . . . . . . . . . . . . . . . . . . . . .    ☎ 247-4004

## Police

For emergencies, ☎ 197. For any problems, contact the special tourist police at Rua Gregório de Matos, 16.

## Post Office

The only pink post office in Brazil is at Rua Alfred Brito 43. Hours are Mon.-Sat. 8 a.m.-5 p.m., Sun. 8 a.m.-noon.

## Public Telephones

For long-distance calls there are telephone stations at **Shopping Barra**, the **Mercado Modelo**, the **airport**, the **bus station**, and the **Centro de Convenções** (Convention Center).

## Tourist Information

The city of Salvador is now mining its own tourist charms madly, so help is more forthcoming these days. College students who speak other languages have been hired to run the tourist information booth at the airport (in the lobby, where you pick up taxis). They should have free copies of colorful brochures and maps. Inquire about the *Salvador Tourist Guide*, a 61-page book with some English translations published by Emtursa. Other information centers staffed by Bahiatursa, the state's official tourist board, are:

**Bahiatursa**
Rua Francisco Muniz Barreto, 12 . . . . . . . . . . . . .   ☎ 321-2463
Daily 8:30 a.m.-7:30 p.m.
**Porto da Barra**
Praça Azevedo Fernandes . . . . . . . . . . . . . . . . . . .   ☎ 245-5610
Daily 9 a.m.-6 p.m.
**Rodoviária (bus station)**
Avenida Antônio Carlos Magalhães (Pituba); . .   ☎ 231-2831
Daily 9 a.m.-9 p.m.
**Mercado Modelo**
Praça Visconde de Cairú . . . . . . . . . . . . . . . . . . . .   ☎ 241-0242
Mon.-Sat. 9 a.m.-6 p.m.

## Travel Agencies

Travel agencies in Salvador are best used for schooner excursions and general transportation, such as a panoramic tour of the city, or a trip to Solar do Unhão, a folkloric dinner show (it's a hefty taxi ride away from most hotels). Unfortunately, walking tours tend to treat clients as herds, and "English-speaking" guides don't always sound as if they are speaking your language. Large groups of Argentinians usually dominate these tours, so if you understand Spanish better than Portuguese, you'll be one step ahead.

### Tatu Tours

*Ed. Victória Center, Sala, 11008, Av. Centenário 2883 (Salvador);*
☎ *247-9322, fax 237-7562.*

This is probably the most efficient and creative travel agency in the city, specializing in cultural and spiritual tours, schooner expeditions, countryside excursions, and Bahia by night. Owned by Conner O'Sullivan, an Irishman who fell in love with Bahia, Tatu (which means armadillo) is sure to pick you up on time, regale you with interesting and accurate tidbits, and lead you to in-spots the more institutionalized agencies have never even heard of. A full-day tour can be taken to the historical village of Cachoeira (see description below), or the fashionable, though primitive, resort of Praia do Forte (see below). Special museum tours are also available, as is a tour of the Pelourinho by night (best on Tues. and weekends). If you want to visit an authentic *candomblé* session or receive a reading of the *jogo de búzios* (similar to a psychic reading), Tatu can arrange it. Tatu's close relations with community projects also offer the opportunity for visitors to interact with social welfare programs.

## Itaparica Turismo

*Avenida Presidente Vargas, 2338, loja 5; ☎ 245-1455, fax 245-8918.*

Itaparica offers historical tours, island excursions, and evening folkloric shows. Airport transfers are also available. Trips to Cachoeira and Praia do Forte can also be arranged; if you are staying at the Praia do Forte Resort, however, the hotel provides its own transfer.

## LR Turismo

*Avenida Sete de Setembro, 3959; ☎ 247-9211 (Barra).*

The leading agency in Salvador conducts up to nine different tours, including a walking tour of historical Bahia, Salvador by night, full-day trips to Cachoeira, island jaunts, and a handicraft and architectural tour. Tours are generally conducted in multilingual groups in comfortable air-conditioned buses. Make sure you request a guide who speaks English well.

### Private Guide

## Silvia Vannucci Chiappori

*Largo do Campo Grande, 124/1202; ☎ 245-3924 or 235-2047, fax 235-2047.*

Silvia is President of the Guide Association of Salvador and an excellent English-speaking guide herself. If she can't help you, she'll find someone who can. If you're planning to use her services, it's best to call in advance. She is well connected with many travel agencies.

### When To Go

*Bahianos* need little impetus to throw a celebration. Between Carnaval, Holy Week, feast days for saints, homages to *candomblé* divinities, and historical remembrances there seems to be at least one major festival here each month. All these colorful festivities are public affairs – usually involving street processions, native foods, music, dance, and, more often than not, drunken revelry by the end of the day. If you can make it to any of the following festivals, you'll get a rare glimpse into the real Bahia. Just watch your wallet and be prepared for voluminous crowds.

**UP CLOSE TIP:** *The rainiest months in Salvador are May and June.*

**JANUARY 6: Festa dos Reis Magos** (The Festival of the Three Kings) starts in the early hours in the Square of Lapinha as the Maji and shepherds pass through streets to the Praça da Sé, accompanied by brass bands, honor guards, gypsies, and folkloric characters.

**JANUARY** (second Thurs. for 8 days): **Lavagem do Igreja da Bonfim**, considered the major fetishist festival in Brazil, focuses on the washing of the steps at the Church of the Bonfim by local women. As participants chant African hymns, little donkeys garlanded with streamers parade single-file from the center of the city to the church, carrying barrels of water on their backs. During the week, bands of musicians play popular and classical music around the square while native-dressed girls sell traditional Bahian dishes. The final night is punctuated by a stunning display of fireworks.

First Monday after Bonfim: **Festa da Ribeira** is as wild as Bonfim is devoted, with young boys and girls, impervious to race, class, or position, dancing in the streets of Itapagipe, drinking traditional *batidas* and partaking of native foods.

**FEBRUARY: Carnaval** is characterized by enormous crowds following behind blaring *trios elétricos*, motorized open-air trucks carrying a small band. Music star Caetano Veloso traditionally composes a few *frevos*. Two weeks before the Carnaval on Sunday is **Festa do Rio Vermelho**. Fifteen days after Carnaval is the **Lavagem da Igreja de Itapoã**. (For more information, see the chapter on Carnaval, page 60.)

**February 2: Festa de Iemanjá** is a grand Bahian festival, honoring the protectoress and mother of the sea. It begins a week before with parades, dances, and special foods. On February 2 fishermen and devotees meet at the Largo de Sant'Ana in a simple church. A small stone house filled with presents is then launched out to sea.

**MARCH 29: Founding of the city.**

**MAY 19: Festa de São Francisco Xavier** celebrates the patron saint of the city.

**JUNE 13: Festa de Santo Antônio.** The patron saint of marriage (and Ogum's equivalent in *candomblé*) is celebrated with special dances. During the month of June there's also a 12-day *candomblé* festival honoring all the divinities.

**JUNE 29: Festa de São Pedro.** The feast, honoring Saint Peter, patron saint of widows, serves corn in every imaginable form, as well as grilled beef chunks washed down with *quentão* (hot spiced wine).

**JULY 2: The Independence of Bahia** is celebrated in the city's main square, Campo Grande.

**AUGUST: International Fair of Precious Stones.** Four days of exhibitions for buyers of precious stones, usually held at the Hotel da Bahia. Contact Bahiatursa for more information.

**SEPTEMBER 7: Independence of Brazil.** Parades and fanfares celebrating the release from Portuguese domination. Everyone dresses in white and carries green and yellow feathers.

**SEPTEMBER 27:** The whole month of September celebrates **São Cosme** and **São Damião**, the most important black Catholic saints. Special masses are held and traditional foods eaten, such as *vatapá, carurú,* and *efó.*

**DECEMBER 4: Festa de Santa Bárbara.** The festival of Santa Barbara (or Iansã, in *candomblé*) is celebrated with religious processions, lots of *cachaça,* and *capoeira* demonstrations. A local okra dish is served to all.

**NOVEMBER 29-DECEMBER: Festa da Conceição da Praia.** The protectoress of Bahia (the syncretic parallel to Iemenjá) is honored for a week, with festivities in front of the Cais Cairu. Beer, *batidas,* traditional foods, and samba.

**DECEMBER 31-JANUARY 1: Festa de Nosso Senhor dos Navegantes** is celebrated by the simple men of the sea, who give praise and thanks to the "God of Navigators" for helping them survive the previous year. Festooned with flowers, a vessel containing the image of Bom Jesus is sailed, in the company of hundreds of small boats, from the Igreja da Boa Viagem through All Saint's Bay to the Igreja da Conceição da Praia, where the statue of the Virgin Mary awaits. Later, the festival returns to the Largo da Boa Viagem with fireworks and native music.

# Cachoeira

For cultists in the know, the tiny, sleepy market town of Cachoeira, about 70 miles from Salvador, buzzes with spiritual fever – it's said to have one of the most authentic *candomblé* centers of worship in Brazil. Daring tourists have been known to make the two-hour trip to attend the Sat. night *terreiro* session in nearby São Felix, but getting there itself is a pilgrimage of endurance. About 12 hot, non-air-conditioned buses run daily from the main terminal in Salvador, but these sometimes rumble maniacally over the pockmarked highway (mine almost hit a dog), and their drivers tend to play scratchy boom boxes at peak volume. You may also have to share bus space with cats, squawking chickens and crowing roosters that often accompany their owners. Survivors of the trip will be rewarded, however, with a colonial village that still sports the fine buildings, churches, and cobblestone streets of its 18th-century heyday. Overnights can even be spent in a restored convent, complete with a bevy of bats that love to swoop down from the high-beamed ceilings.

Located in the Recôncavo, the fertile coastal plains surrounding the Bay of All Saints (Baía de Todos os Santos), Cachoeira was once the primary port and trading post for the sugarcane plantations that supplied the state with fruits and spices. In 1822, the inhabitants of the city gained a feisty reputation when they took on a Portuguese warship docked in the harbor, becoming the first community in the country to claim allegiance to Dom Pedro I. When Dom Pedro visited with his court, Cachoeira was even dubbed the capital of Brazil for a brief 48 hours. Today, the Recôncavo is one of the most important agricultural centers of the state (mostly harvesting tobacco, peppers, and cloves), although Cachoeira and its nearby twin town of São Félix have never quite advanced to the 20th century. The people still live a primitive life, embraced by religious devotion, farm life, and small-town intrigues. Folklorically, white, black and Indian cultures collide here to produce a rich tradition of song and dance, including *bumba-meu-boi, afoxé*, and *samba-de-roda*, all of which can be seen and heard during the various festivals held throughout the year. Among the liveliest is the **Festival of São João** on June 22-24.

If you're traveling along BA-026, you'll pass through the town of **Santo Amaro**, birthplace of Caetano Veloso and Maria Bethânia, two of the most lyrically inspired musicians of *música popular brasileira* (MPB). Indeed, talent still reigns in this region; the moment I stepped off the bus in Cachoeira, I discovered two young boys (the next Gilberto Gil and Caetano Veloso?) sitting on the dusty curb, working out tunes with their guitar. Offsetting the unpressured life, however, has been a series of disasters over the last few decades that have shaken Cachoeira's confidence. In 1969, a dam broke due to human error and kept the entire city under water for three weeks. Water marks left from the flood can still be seen along some of the old buildings.

# Walking Tour

Starting from the Pousada do Convento, turn right on Rua Inocêncio Boaventura to see the ruins of the **Convento do Carmo** from the 16th century. Like the São Francisco Church in Salvador, this stone-and-wood structure houses a shocking display of gold-leaf ornamentation. An old custodian with an ancient set of keys will open the church, which is only in use during Easter. Most interesting are the Oriental eyelids of many of the sculpted saints – these all hail from the Portuguese colony of Macau, China. Also startling are the shiny blood droplets on the Christ figures, made from a mixture of cow blood, rubies, and herbs. The life-like figure of Jesus with a red wig is carried through the streets on Good Friday.

Walk a few yards down to the **Casa da Câmara e Cadeia** (1698-1712) on Praça da Aclamação, the historical center of the city during the 18th and 19th centuries. During the fight for Independence in 1822, this yellow-and-white colonial building acted as the prison; now it is the mayor's office. On the Praça da Aclamação is the **Museu do Iphan**, an 18th-century landowner's house, where you can view typical furniture of the era. Notice the bars on the window, which kept the slaves out, and the antique chair in the lobby, used to transport the mayor. The theater in the backyard sponsors musical events and *capoeira* demonstrations.

Next door is the gallery of the 90-year-old artist Cincinho, whose primitive, naif style is typical of the region. The next shop houses **Casa Velha Arte**, open daily 8 a.m.-6 p.m., a handicraft store featuring the paintings of João Gonçalves, a sculptor and painter inspired by the rituals of the Nossa Senhora da Boa Morte.

Further up Rua 13 de Maio is **Igreja Matriz de Nossa Senhora do Rosário**, dedicated to the patroness of the city. During Pentecost Sunday, when I visited, the entire church was wrapped in white ribbons adorned with white plastic pigeons. An historian has claimed that the church displays the most blue Portuguese tiles in Brazil. The highly treasured sacraments are kept in a pure silver cabinet on the left behind the white-and-gold gates.

Turn uphill on Ladeira d'Ajuda to arrive at the first church in Cachoeira, built in 1595, the **Igreja de N.S. d'Ajuda**. You must ask the priest to open it, so bang loudly on the door. Next door is the **Museu Irmandade N.S. da Boa Morte**, documenting the history of a sisterhood of female slaves who banded together to buy the freedom of other slaves. Today the sisterhood still functions and holds a famous three-part feast in Aug. (usually the last Fri. before Aug. 15). On the first day, they commemorate the death of those who died seeking freedom; on the second day they hold a symbolic funeral; and the third day they celebrate the freedom of Nossa Senhora da Boa Morte as she ascends to heaven. The present members of the sisterhood must be black, over 45 years of age, and have had at least three years soliciting money for the projects of the organization, which includes social work and care for the homeless. During the festivities all the city's *candomblé* groups turn out in full white regalia, dancing and singing in African dialects.

Next door is the **City Hall** (Prefeitura Municipal). Follow the brick steps of the street to the right of the hall to the **Praça Doutor Milton**, where there is a bronze fountain (*chafariz*) from 1827; the city's inhabitants used to come here to fill their clay jugs. In front, the yellow church with the belfry is the 18th-century **Santa Casa da Misericórdia**. Turn right on Rua Ruy Barbosa, a main shopping street with a drugstore, bar, restaurant, and bookstore. Turning onto Rua Cons. Virgilio Damazio, you'll discover a great place to roam. Much of the town here is in evocative ruins, but you can also see the old train station from here and the iron box-girder bridge built by British engineers in 1885, which connects to the city of São Félix.

At Praça Manoel Vitorino, in front of the train station, you'll find the city's second best typical restaurant, **Gruta Azul**, filled with cages of tropical birds. After lunch, walk along the edge of the **Paraguaçu River** to Praça Teixeira de Freitas, where you can rent a canoe and guide to tour the river. A trip to the lighthouse and back (one hour) will run about $5. It costs about 30 cents to cross the river to São Félix. Nearby in the square on Rua 13 de Maio is the Atelier de Dory, the studio of one of the city's best sculptors. If you get desperate for entertainment, the movie house on the *praça* shows films on Fri., Sat. and Sun.

## Candomblé

*Candomblé* sessions are held at the **Terreiro de Vannuú** on Varre Estrada in São Félix on Sat. nights. To get there, cross the bridge connecting Cachoeira and São Felix, which starts after the cemetery. The walk takes about one hour and is relatively safe if you don't get lost, but it's best to go with a native of the city or with a guide from Salvador who has connections; remember, *candomblé* is a very insular, deeply serious religious practice of trance worship. (Contact Bahiatursa for information regarding attendance.

For more explanation about the actual practice, see *Traveler's Guide to Brazilian Spirits* on page 54.) The sessions are held in a small wood cottage, packed to overflowing with the congregants who arrive around 10 p.m. and stay until dawn. Guests are usually ushered to a seated position, but the room can get hot and claustrophobic.

# Where To Stay & Eat

See page 26 for price chart.

## Pousada do Convento

*Rua Inocêncio Boaventura;* ☎ *(71) 724-1716. Reservations in Salvador,* ☎ *(71) 235-3949.*

The timeless vibes of this old Franciscan monastery make for an atmospheric accommodation – the best in the city. The high-beamed corridors are so wide that at least 10 monks could walk side by side without touching. The rooms, built around an inner courtyard, are large, with the original stone window seats and carved jacaranda headboards. The antique keyholes don't always work, but even more unsettling are the black fuzzy balls that hang upside down from the high beams. Management nonchalantly assured me that these "house bats" weren't harmful and even offered to let me photograph them. Actually, the perpetual guests only add to the medieval allure. The restaurant, which serves all three meals, is considered the best in the city. All rooms have mini-bars, air conditioning, and modern plumbing. *25 apts. Inexpensive. No cards.*

## Restaurant e Pousada do Pai Thomaz

*Rua 25 de Junho, 12;* ☎ *(71) 724-1288.*

A two-in-one *pousada* with a reputable restaurant near the waterfront. Red-brown jaqueira wood lines the walls of the restaurant, which features *sarapatel*, the viscera of hogs boiled in their own blood (don't ask me, but rumor has it, the dish has a strange, "exotic" taste). You'll have to climb steep stairs to reach the simple rooms, which are several notches below the quality of the Convento. Cleanliness is not the best virtue here. *13 apts. Inexpensive. No cards.*

## Gruta Azul

*Praça Manoel Vitorino, 2;* ☎ *725-1295. 11 a.m.-6 p.m.*

This lively eatery, across from the ancient train station, is built around a courtyard. It has noisy parrots and excellent native dishes. The specialty is *maniçoba* – a stew of manioc leaves, okra, and a variety of dried, salty meats; it looks like gruel but tastes great. Ceramic handicrafts are for sale. *Inexpensive. All cards.*

# Nightlife

## Massapé

*Rua 25 de Junho;* ☎ *724-1319. 11 a.m.-midnight.*

The only restaurant where there's action at night. Specialties include *carne de sol com pirão* – dried salty meat with manioc flour boiled in water. *Inexpensive. All cards.*

# Hands-On Cachoeira

## Arrival

**Bus** tickets from Salvador to Cachoeira run about $5, one way. Buses are not air conditioned, and the ride can be riotous. About 12 buses run a day (the last leaves at 7 p.m.), and tickets are best purchased in advance. Bus lines include **Viazul** and **Princesa**. The *rodoviária* (bus station) office is open daily 5 a.m.-7 p.m.

**Schooners** may be hired to traverse the bay and the Rio Paraguaçu to arrive in Cachoeira.

## Tourist Information

A tourist post on Rua 13 de Maio will give you a brochure about the town and directions. Don't expect any English. Daily 8 a.m.-5 p.m., closed weekends.

# Praia do Forte

Praia do Forte is one of the last authentic fishing villages in Brazil – cocooned in a national park, yet featuring some of the best luxury resort options in Brazil. Fifty-odd miles north of Salvador, you can walk an hour over pristine beaches without discovering another footprint, but you can also enjoy comfortable lodging, excellent seafood, a turtle reserve, and intriguing wildlife. In recent years an elite mix of vacationers, from environmentalists and surfers to musicians and movie stars, have descended on this gorgeous stretch of sand, especially during high season, when the sea turns into a veritable fishbowl of windsurfers, sailboats, snorkelers, and divers. During off-season you'll have more opportunity to get to know the simple folk who populate the sleepy village, which, thanks to strict building regulations, has miraculously retained its unpretentious charm.

The recent revival of Praia do Forte can be taken as a model for eco-preservation. In 1972 W.H. Klaus Peters, the German-Brazilian mastermind behind the resort, bought a 25,000-acre coconut plantation that fronted 7½ miles of beach. The purchase gave him title to the fishing village of Praia do Forte, the castle ruins, and the surrounding rainforest. In the following years, he created a foundation to maintain the castle and turned the forest into a reserve administered by Brazil's federal environmental agency. In an unprecedented gesture in Brazilian history, he donated the land title of the village to its inhabitants, but only after the municipality in 1989 adopted a series of strict zoning regulations. Today, within the village of 3,000 inhabitants, no buildings may reach over two stories high, and all must be constructed of native traditional materials, such as piassava palm fronds and colonial tiles. Homeowners are required to plant four coconut palm trees for each one they cut down, and houses may only be passed on through families. All the streets, except the main highway, remain unpaved.

Also at Praia do Forte is the headquarters of TAMAR, the national conservation project for *tartarugas marinhas* (sea turtles) – now the symbol of the village since fishermen stopped killing them. Each Oct., hundreds of sea turtles lay their eggs along the seashore, with the help and protection of the conservationists; in 1992, they released the one millionth turtle hatchling into the sea. The TAMAR complex includes a small museum and water tanks, where you can observe the turtles close at hand.

# Ecology

The slogan of the eco-minded village says it all: "Enjoy, don't destroy." What is at stake is a marvelous ecosystem along the River Timeantube called *mangue* (pronounced man-gay), a swamp-like area full of mangroves whose roots have adapted to the twice daily rise and fall of the river (at least five feet). Acting as a breeding ground for microorganisms necessary for marine life, the marsh is full of shrimp and crabs that you can nearly catch with your hands. Visitors can take a windsurf board and paddles, and spoon 1¼ miles down to a lake, keeping watch on the profuse variety of tropical birds that perch near the banks. The best time to see the birds is at dawn, when you will also see *jacarés* (alligators), snakes, and turtles.

> **UP CLOSE TIP:** *Praia do Forte is one of the safest and most crime-free beaches in Brazil. Of course, no matter where you travel, personal safety precautions should always be followed (locking up valuables, etc.), but incidents here are practically non-existent.*

# Sights

Despite its small size, there are scores of things to do in Praia do Forte; in fact, you could spend your entire two-week vacation here and not get bored. Besides the watersports and horseback riding offered by the resort, some other suggestions are listed below.

## Papa Gente

A quarter-mile from the white-painted lighthouse are these natural pools, formed from the rocky reefs that dot the shore. During high tide, these sand-bottomed pools, a favorite among snorkelers, fill chest-high with crystal-clear water and become natural aquariums flush with tropical fish.

## Praia do Forte

A 20-minute walk down the paradisiacal shore takes you to this village full of *barracas* that serve fantastic grilled shrimp. Alongside a deserted boat wreck on the shore, you might find the village mystic, his dreadlocks flowing, banging out folkloric tunes on his berimbau. There's also a blue-and-white church, an excellent example of a colonial-style church still in use.

## TAMAR

From Praia do Forte, a five-minute walk takes you to this project, where you can view turtles in open tanks and stroll through the small museum. A small gift store features excellent T-shirts with "Save the Turtles" themes (all profits are funneled back to the project). A 20-minute video is available in Portuguese. (For an English version, ask at the Praia do Forte Hotel.)

## Imbassai

Take an energetic 10-mile hike along the isolated beaches to this spot – accessible only by foot, boat, or a jeep down a dirt track.

## Timeantuba Bird Reserve

Across the road from the entrance to the Praia do Forte Resort Hotel are the lagoon and wetlands. Exploring by canoe, the casual naturalist can easily spot alligators and some of the 173 bird species recorded here.

## Hilltop Ruins

A three-mile hike from the Praia do Forte Resort Hotel are the hilltop ruins of a fortified medieval manor house formerly owned by Garcia d'Avila, a mere bailiff to the governor of Salvador. In 1549, the Portuguese monarchy awarded him over 308,000 square miles of prime acreage, upon which he would build the largest secular edifice in colonial Brazil. Exactly how he built it remains a mystery – some claim he dismantled a castle in Portugal and reassembled it here. For over two centuries, the castle and its vast estate has stayed in the hands of the d'Avila family, constituting at the end of the 18th century the largest private property in the world. Today, the ruins, romantically overgrown with flowers and tall grasses, make a fascinating tour.

## Barraca Nativa

Schooners may be rented here for one to four hours.

# Excursions

**Odara Turismo,** ☎ *832-2333*, maintains its branch office at the Praia do Forte Resort Hotel. The company offers half- and full-day jeep trips. You can make a half-day excursion of the castle ruins, hike through the ecological preserve, visit a traditional manioc flour mill, or swim under the waterfalls of the Pojuca River. A full-day trip includes an outdoor barbecue and a visit to a remote duned beach.

# Where To Stay

Accommodations in Praia do Forte range from the elite and semi-elite to full-fledged primitive; if worse comes to worst, you could probably convince someone to let you hang your hammock on their porch. Even if you don't stay at the Praia do Forte Resort Hotel, you can still partake of their excursions, watersports, and restaurants – for a fee, of course. See page 26 for price chart.

## Praia do Forte Resort Hotel

*Estrada do Coco (Praia do Forte);* ☎ *(71) 876-1111, fax (71) 876-1112.*

This luxurious complex, the flagship property of the village, offers tropical accommodations in split-level wings that snake through a 35-acre seafront coconut plantation. The tiled apartments are big enough for a family with two children, with an area separated by a divider holding additional couches. The rooms are not air conditioned, but the cooling ocean winds provide comfort; guests can even sleep in hammocks on their own private veranda. With the accent on the natural, the resort offers windsurfing, sailing, scuba, two tennis courts, two restaurants, and four swimming pools. (Two-hour mini-courses in windsurfing are available.) In Nov. 1991, the Club Mistral was opened here by two Germans, featuring the newest equipment in the world. Horseback riding is available every day (warning: what they called "frisky" turned out to be nearly unmanageable), and a different tour is offered daily, such as a hike to the castle, a trek to a waterfall, passage down the river on a floatboat, and a tour of the Vila dos Pescadores on foot. Rates include breakfast, taxes, and all sports activities, except for windsurfing and catamaran, which are charged hourly. *132 apts. Expensive. All cards.*

## Pousada Praia do Forte

☎ *(71) 835-1410.*

Facing a reef and the open sea, about a 2½-hour walk from the Praia do Forte Resort Hotel, is this more rustic inn run by the same owner. The 17 igloo-shaped chalets have straw roofs and structural beams made from coconut palm trees. Hibiscus flowers invigorate the primitive landscape. Some rooms have fans, though you can sleep in a hammock on the private porches; all have mosquito nets. The expanse of sea seen from the lobby/dining room is awe-inspiring. The *pousada* is right next to TAMAR.

According to my Deep Throat, Bonnie Kassell: "Guests are no longer allowed privileges at the main resort. You can't even dine there and they are strict about it. I had to come back wearing white linen and beg!" Apparently, the guests at the hotel were paying a lot of money and complaining about the riffraff. *Expensive. All cards.*

### Pousada Tatuapara

*Praça dos Artistas;* ☎ *876-1015.*

One of the most charming *pousadas* in the village, and a cheaper alternative to the Praia do Forte properties listed above. Split-level suites feature a bedroom upstairs and downstairs dining room connected by a rustic wood stairs. Standards are one room. All apartments look out onto a flowered courtyard and come with fan and mini-bar. *23 apts. Moderate. No cards.*

### Pousada dos Artistas

*Praça dos Artistas;* ☎ *(071) 876-1147.*

Bonnie Kassell writes: "This *pousada's* got great charm – a homey quality as opposed to the more motel feel of the Tatuapara. Teresa, the owner, is an artist and her works are hung everywhere. She herself is lovely and low-key. But it can be a bit noisy, if you think Brazilian music and the choir practicing at the chapel across the street is noise." *4 apts. Inexpensive-moderate. V.*

### Sobrado da Vila

*Al. do Sol.;* ☎ *876-1088; fax 876-1033.*

Located on the village's main street. Bonnie Kassell considers these rooms (about $40) "the best value if you don't mind being not being at the beach, which is a lovely 10-minute walk away. At least it's right where the bus arrives and departs." Really new and clean, rooms come with small kitchen and fridge. Bar on premises. *Inexpensive. All cards.*

## Camping Grounds

Camping grounds are available near **Vila dos Pescadores.** For other options, call the **Praia do Forte Resort Hotel,** ☎ *(71) 876-1111,* fax *(71) 876-1112,* who will make reservations for you at any hotel or *pousada.*

# Where To Eat

The buffet and à la carte cuisine at the Praia do Forte Hotel are excellent, but eating every meal there can be costly. A short walk to the village will reveal a number of casual eateries for traditional dishes, excellent seafood, and snacks. See page 26 for price chart.

## Souza

*Rua Principal.*

Bonnie Kassell tells me I didn't rave enough about this bar, famous for its *bolinhos de peixe* (fish balls). She writes: "This is *the* in-place now and the *moquecas*, regional fish stews, served in black stone bowls, are the best we had anywhere – better than Casa da Gamboa in Salvador. Also the best *batidas* crammed with fresh fruit – some quite exotic. A very interesting crowd." *Inexpensive. No cards.*

## Starlight

*Praça dos Artistas. Noon-4 p.m., 8:30 p.m.-midnight, snacks 4-8 p.m.*

This is one of the village's most attractive restaurants, with brick floors, natural wood tables, and a spacious tropical feel. Stop by to check out the specialties of the day. Live music under the stars on Sat. makes a nice place to crash.

## Boca-Piu

*Al. do Sol, 10 a.m.-midnight.*

Heavy boat chains grace the doorway of this traditional white stucco house. The front room features *lambada*; the homey back patio surrounded by enormous trees is for dining. Try the *pitu à milanesa* – large shrimp native to the area – or just slow-sip some tropical drinks with a side plate of *bolinho de peixe* (pastry-stuffed fish appetizers). Work up a free sweat with *lambada* bands on Fri. and Sat. starting at 10 p.m. Somehow, the dear waitresses here manage to be tropical without even trying.

## Restaurante Casa da Dinda

*8 a.m.-midnight on the main street.*

For sandwiches and fast local dishes check out this straw-roofed spot.

## Casa Alemã

*Al. do Sol. Noon-10 p.m., closed Mon.*

Set on the main street, this is a good place for German cuisine. *Moderate. AE.*

## Pizzaria Gastón

Good pizza, on the main street, next to the pharmacy.

# Hands-On Praia do Forte

## Arrival

Every Mon. afternoon, **Varig** flies from Miami to Salvador. By special prior arrangement with the Praia do Forte Resort Hotel, a minivan shuttles visitors from the airport to Praia do Forte, 30 miles north (or about 45 minutes) on the newly paved Estrada do Coco, or Coconut Road. For one to three passengers, the van costs $47 on weekdays, $60 on weekends and at night. Group rates can be arranged.

**Taxi Cometas,** a 24-hour service at the Salvador airport, also offers car service; rates are slightly more expensive. For cheaper rates, contact Deborah Scott Leitsch, the English-speaking manager of **Odara Turismo,** ☎ *(71) 86-1080,* to arrange a pickup.

### When To Go

Temperatures rarely dip below 76°F or rise above 84°F. During the rainy season (Mar.-Aug.), the water loses its placid azure quality and turns choppy. Diving is best between Dec. and Feb., when the water is clearest, but remember that this is high season, so rates are at their peak and hotels are packed. From the middle of Aug. to Mar., the sun is stellar.

# Morro de Sao Paulo

In the opinion of Mike Salvo, my Deep Throat, Morro do São Paulo is "simply one of the best beaches in Brazil." Bonnie Kassel told me it was the "Ibiza of Brazil" and a "must for weekends."

On an island five hours south of Salvador, the overwhelming natural beauty and eclectic collection of people from Europe, South Africa, Scandanavia, Argentina, and Brazil all serve to "suspend any reality of the outside world." While the island retains the pristine beauty of a remote outpost, there is still an abundance of cafés, restaurants, and *pousadas* (inns) at all prices. There is also a fax/communications center, a photolab, electric service and telephone – Mike claims he even called New York City from a pay phone!

"Primal spontaneous combustion" is how Mike describes the action in Morro. The four beaches spreading out from the town – Primeira (First), Segunda (Second), Terceiro (Third), Quarto (Fourth), are so named for their proximity to the center of town. By day the beach scene, centralized on Primeira and Segundo *praias,* is vivacious with soccer and volleyball games, beautiful women, and friends sharing beers or *caipirinhas.* Out on Terceiro and Quatro *praias* the town influence gives way to vast fields of coconut palms and a pristine coast with an odd fisherman's hut here and there. Here, one can rest off a night's wildness in total peace.

Nightlife and impromptu jams also happen on Primeira and Segundo beaches, which alternate nights for the Big Fiesta – a huge dance party that takes place nightly around midnight at one of two bars featuring barefoot dancing on the beach. Mike writes: "The sound system is excellent and pumps out reggae, Bahian *axé,* and even Cypress Hill. The party lasts until 8 a.m., so there's plenty of time to nap after a beach day and a big meal. You only need to wander into town around midnight and meet with just-made friends, have a drink, then head for the fiesta and dance until sunrise."

Spreading out from the main event are bonfires on the beach, quieter bars with great music, elaborate carts with *pasteis* (baked snacks), and drinks, and all sorts of people.

Morro da Mangaba is the hill that runs through the center of the island. There are stone stairs at each end: one leads to town, the other to the beach.

There are fewer *pousadas* and more *nativos* living here and it makes a nice alternative to town.

Mike writes: "I stayed at a friend's house here. Trails cut across the island into a wild Bahian backcountry. If you cross all the way you'll eventually find Gamboa on the other side. In Morro, there's a great bakery that makes fresh *pão com coco* (coconut bread) every morning and some excellent restaurants, including *churasscaria*." Try something made from *cacau*, a natural fruit that tastes like chocolate. *Suco do cacau* (juice of cacau) is great anytime! There are many resident artists who sell their work nightly in town. In the town square there is an open jam hosted by a local guitarist and pastel guru who is accompanied by his wife on percussion. Other musicians pass by and play for awhile and anyone is welcome.

❖ **GETTING HERE:** *To reach these famous beaches, you must first pass through the lively town of Valença. Buses from all over Brazil eventually pull in here. From the rodoviária (bus station) in the center of town, you can walk or take a 10-minute cab ride to the dock where the ferry leaves for Morro and Gamboa on the island of Tinhare. The regular boat takes about five hours, but a speedboat will get you there in under two. The ferry sails through mangrove islands and other exotic terrain, first stopping at Gamboa on the far side of Tinhare.*

## Mike writes about Gamboa

"Gamboa is exclusively inhabited by natives – an idyllic, tranquil place with little or nothing to offer besides beer, fish, and beach. There are mud cliffs nearby where you can give yourself a natural mud bath – excellent for skin and hair. Once the ferry docks in Morro, you climb the old stone stairs and pass through the town's 300-year-old portal arch. Historical remnants from the Portuguese discovery in 1531, a Dutch occupation and numerous Indian rebellions can still be seen in the architecture. The ruins of an old fort look out over the sea; people gather here to watch dolphins frolic in the golden rays."

# Where To Stay & Eat

Bonnie Kassell tells me there are so many *pousadas* and restaurants here that you don't have to plan in advance. See page 26 for price chart. You might try:

## Pousada da Fazenda Caseiro

*Terceira Praia;* ☎ *783-1042; fax 741-1272.*

Small lodgings with restaurant, sports court and service on the beach. *15 apts. Inexpensive-moderate. V.*

**Belladonna**

*Rua da Prainha;* ☎ *783-1039. 6 p.m.-midnight, closed Thurs. (May and July).*
Italian cantina.

# PARTY BAHIA

## Porto Seguro

The resort town of Porto Seguro and its nearby beachfellows Arraial
d'Ajuda and Trancoso lie at the heart of the Brazilian party scene. Come
summer (Dec.-Feb.), sun-worshippers descend on this strip of Bahian coast
from all over Brazil; many stars, such as Gilberto Gil and singer Gal Costa,
own beachside villas here. Porto Seguro is also famous among Brazilian
history buffs, for it's here, at longitude 17 degrees south, that Pedro Alvares
Cabral first discovered Brazil on April 22, 1500. (See *Roots*, page 35) At the
very least, Cabral was lucky. The Indians who met him at shore were
reported to be friendly, unlike those a few years later who decimated the
first community of settlers, including the first church in Brazil and its two
priests. Built on a cliff, the colonial area of the city, called Cidade Alta, still
houses the reconstructed church, a small fort, and other 16th-century
buildings.

Down below, in Cidade Baixa, is where the party-time begins. While
Porto Seguro's beaches are not wide, they become as packed as Copacabana
in Dec., with the overflow of tourists clogging the narrow cobblestone
streets. Building regulations, which prohibit any structure over 25 feet, have
preserved the tropical simplicity of the skyline; in fact, any structure along
the beach line must also be made with small mud tiles or grass huts. During
Carnaval, which lasts for three days, the 56,000 population doubles, and
very drunken revelers can be seen traipsing after a *trio elétrico* (an amplified
band on the back of a truck). During low season, when the streets seem
nearly ghost-like, many writers and poets come here to revel in the silence.

The best beaches are in Arraial d'Ajuda and Trancoso, along with a most
rarefied social scene, one that mixes laid-back locals with gorgeous *carioca*
teens, aging hippies, bohemian movie stars, and international jetsetters. A
1½-hour ferry ride gets you there, though you can also take a schooner ride
from Porto Seguro. Accommodations in all three towns run toward the *au
natural pousada,* and excellent discounts can be found in off-season. Do note
that most people spend little time in their rooms.

## Sights

History buffs will not want to miss **Cidade Alta**, the Old City, perched on
a cliff high above the city. After the first community was burned by the
Indians, the next band of daring settlers moved to the top of this cliff, where

they could keep watch on the sea and the Buranhen River. The only image said to have survived the desecration was a statue of St. Francis of Assisi, now considered to be the oldest religious icon in Brazil; it can be seen high above the altar in the **Igreja de Nossa Senhora da Pena**, built in 1535. Unfortunately, the church, as brightly lit as a boardwalk and strewn with plastic roses, appears too kitschy to be real. An older church, **Igreja da Misericórdia**, dates back to 1526. Nearby is the **Museu da Cidade**, a two-room museum that includes images of saints from the 17th and 18th centuries and funeral masks from the Ticuna Indians. Most interesting is a display of the history of the Brazilian flag; the first flag of the republic, used only for four days between Nov. 15-19, looks amazingly like the Stars and Stripes. Also, in the area are a small fort, the remains of a Jesuit College, and the Marco do Descobrimento, the seven-foot column placed by the Portuguese in 1503 to proclaim their sovereignty over the land.

# Beach Eateries

Life along the beaches of Porto Seguro centers around lively *barracas*, open-air bars known for their excellent seaside cuisine and interesting clientele who hang out till all hours along the strand. The following are the most famous:

## Porto Fino Bar/Restaurant

*Porto Fino Beach, north to Cabrália.*

Owner Giuseppe is a friendly, blue-eyed Italian-Brazilian, whose love for pasta only equals his love for his clients. Indulge in the excellent Italian specialties under his sheltered restaurant or eat outside in your bathing suit under grass huts, where the water can tickle your toes. Giuseppe speaks English and will prove a fine navigator of the scene.

## Vira Sol

*Taperapuan Praia; ☎ 288-2350. 8 a.m.-5 p.m.*

This bar and restaurant on Taperapuan beach features a casual nautical theme and a young crowd that grooves on loud dance music. Children will love the tropical playground, and adults may rent jetskis. The bar, an upside-down canoe, serves typical foods, such as *peixe embriagado*, literally, "drunken fish," marinated in wine sauce.

## Neptunnos Bar and Restaurant

*Ponto Grande Beach.*

Boasting a magnificent view of the reefs, this restaurant sits where the beach converges at a point. From here, you can see why Cabral chose the area to land, because the bay, surrounded by reefs, makes for gentler waters. Typical foods, such as *peixe assado* (baked fish) and mussels, are considered tops. The best reason to stop by is to pet the house sloths, who look like E.T.s and hang upside down from their palm-leafed hut. If you appear kind enough, the owner may even let you hold them – it's an incredible feeling when this animal, the slowest in the world, puts his paws around your waist and falls asleep.

### Barraco do Mutá

Here, you can rent *voos de ultraleve*, a two-seater plane with a small engine and three wings that lands on water. One person goes at a time, accompanied by the pilot ($13 for 10 minutes). A culinary specialty here are the *bolinhos de bacalhau*, fried codfish balls, which are made hot on the spot.

# Where To Stay

See page 26 for price chart.

### Porto Seguro Praia Hotel

*Av. Beira-Mar km. 65;* ☎ *(73) 288-2321, fax 288-2069.*

Located across the street from the beach, this four-star is the city's best – a palm-lined, ranch-style complex replete with tropical ambiance and efficient service. The wood-planked large bedrooms are decorated with mahogany frame beds, and come with mini-bars, spacious bathrooms, color TV, and verandas. The huge, exotically shaped pool and bar make a relaxing alternative to the shore, as do the tennis courts surrounded by palm trees. There is also a gym, boutique, and 24-hour room service. During low season, there is a 30% discount if paying in cash; 20% with cards. *115 apts. Moderate-expensive. All cards.*

### Pousada do Descobrimento

*Avenida Getúlio Vargas, 330;* ☎ *(73) 288-2452/2004.*

A clean and perky *pousada* with a charming breakfast room just 650 feet from the beach. The chalet-like rooms, built around a tropical courtyard, come with verandas, air conditioning, phone, safes, and hammocks. *16 apts. Moderate. All cards.*

### Pousada Porto Príncipe

*Avenida dos Navegantes, 82;* ☎ *(73) 288-2003.*

Located on the main street, this slightly upscale *pousada* offers lovely colonial-style rooms with verandas, mini-bars, phone, modern bathrooms, color TV, and air conditioning. The beds have nice wood frames with matching cabinets. An attractive pool dominates the inner courtyard. Half-price rates in low season. *23 apts. Expensive. All cards.*

### Pousada Casa Azul

*Rua 15 de Novembro, 11;* ☎ *(73) 288-2180.*

Situated in the center of town, this 100-year-old home has now been named an historical patrimony. The blue-and-white exterior is so beautiful that the individual apartments hardly compare, but they are adequate. Housed in a building separate from the main house, the apartments have private patios, air conditioning, and mini-bar. The rooms do not have phones or

TV, but guests may use the phone in the reception and there is a small TV room. Nearby is the cultural center, where musical shows and events are often held. *Moderate. No cards.*

## Where To Eat

See page 26 for price chart.

### Casa Rústica Avenida

*Rua Getúlio Vargas, 348; ☎ 288-2399. 11 a.m.-11 p.m.*

Best place in the city for *parrilhada,* a regional dish, as well as steaks, chicken, and grilled pork. *Picanha* comes on a smoking grill at your table. *Inexpensive. MC, V.*

### Grelhados

*Avenida do Aeroporto, 666 (Cidade Alta); ☎ 288-1177.*

Fine grilled meats, chicken, and fish in attractive environs. *Moderate. No cards.*

### Três Vinténs

*Avenida Portugal, 246. Noon-2 p.m.*

Stone walls and a dramatic color scheme catch your eye at this bar/restaurant, which offers soulfully cooked Bahian specialties, such as *moqueca* (regional fish stew made with palm oil and coconut milk), *polvo* (octopus), and *bolo de camarão* (shrimp rolls). *Moderate. AE.*

### Populi

*Rua São Braz, 163 (Cidade Histórica).*

A boisterous pizzeria on a dirt street lined with coconut palms and flamboyant trees that bloom all summer. *Moderate. No cards.*

### Café La Pasarella

*Rua Portugal, 224.*

An all-purpose snacks hangout: pies, drinks, tea at 5 p.m., espresso day and night, and even breakfast. *Inexpensive. No cards.*

### Lótus Delicatessan

*Rua Pero Vaz de Caminha, 220; ☎ 288-2988.*

This teahouse makes a refreshing stop for a cold buffet and desserts.

### Sabor de Amor

*Av. do Descobrimento, 400, next to the Lambada Boca da Barra.*

Good for sandwiches and regional fruit juices.

# Nightlife

Even if you don't dance *lambada*, samba or reggae yourself, head for the **Boca da Barra** – a huge, brightly lit, open-air grass hut where the best dancers congregate. During the summer it's packed, while onlookers sit on bleachers. It's free, except for drinks.

### Lambada Boca da Barra

*Av. do Descobrimento, 400.*

The nickname of this dance club is "the sacred temple of *lambada*" – a success for the last 10 years.

### Porto Prega Bar

*Rua Pedro Alvares Cabral, 100.*

Porto Prega features live music lightly.

### Reggae Night

*Av. do Descobrimento (no number);* ☎ *288-1368.*

This is a new house close to Boca da Barra, capable of holding 2,000 people.

### Fliperama

*Avenida Portugal, 23.*

A popular video arcade.

# Shopping

The main drag beside the shore in Porto Seguro is named **Rua Portugal**, but everyone calls it "Passarela do Alcool" – a local joke that refers to the part-fact/part-fantasy that everyone here is reeling around drunk. At the very least, you'll find lots of tiny bars where you can sit outside and enjoy the cool breeze. If you want to pick up the local brew, head for **Colônia Brasil,** Avenida Portugal, 188; ☎ *289-2670*, which features the highly creative mixes of *cachaça* (sugarcane liquor) of owner Eduardo Caminha. Pure *cachaça* from Porto Seguro is called *aguardente verde*, and Eduardo has over 200 kinds, many with exotic fruits. For the macho at heart, he even sells a *cachaça* with a snake fermenting inside the bottle, a tradition among fishermen. This is, reportedly, good for the skin and blood as well as being a vaccine against the venom (of course, if the snake is inside the bottle, how can it bite you?). There's also a bottle fermenting with a crab, which is reputed to be a fine aphrodisiac/cold remedy. Another drink here is *Pau do Indio*, made of alcohol, guaraná, honey, and 32 herbs. The owner is generous about tasting; make sure you try the Gabriela liqueur, a silky-smooth concoction of clove and cinnamon.

At the **Coroa Vermelha plaza** you'll find an Indian crafts market run by a tribe of the Tupí-Guarani. About 1,000 Indians live on a 57-hectare reservation near the city, preserving their traditions and supplementing government subsidies through fishing and hunting. Life has hardly been idyllic for these natives, as they've become victims of a bureaucratic mess that has allowed industries and farmers to encroach on the borders of their land. In the past few years, an iron company took over the Vale do Rio Doce, which had been previously designated tribal land; fortunately, the company has now been indicted.

Among the crafts for sale are headdresses of brightly stained feathers (pink seems to be the favorite color), wood-carved combs, beaded jewelry, and bows and arrows. The chief of the tribe, Jocana Jiroa Baixu, is a charming, extremely handsome young man, often stationed at one of the main stalls. If you speak Portuguese, he will give you a rundown of tribal concerns. During the entire month of April, Indian celebrations are held featuring traditional foods, dance, music, and body-paintings.

**Praça da Bandeira** is the main courtyard of Porto Seguro, featuring a nightly hippie market of handicrafts. The surrounding streets are also full of shops.

# Hands-On Porto Seguro

## Arrivals

**Flights** to Porto Seguro leave from Salvador on **Nordeste Airlines**, ☎ *288-2108*, daily at 3:30 p.m. **Rio-Sul** (Hotel Seguro Praia, BR-367; ☎ *288-2321*) also flies to Porto Seguro, as do **VASP, Varig, Taba, Tam,** and **Pantanal.** Connecting cities include Rio, Salvador, São Paulo, Recife, Ilhéus, Natal, Porto Alegre, Belo Horizonte, Brasília, and others.

Just over 1½ miles from the center of the city, the *rodoviária* (**bus station**) is a stone-and-wood-beamed structure, with a snack bar that opens at 5:30 a.m. Two buses run daily from Salvador to Porto Seguro, on the Expresso São Jorge line, as well as direct buses to Rio. The bus trip between Ilhéus and Porto Seguro shows one of the most exotic tropical landscapes I have seen in Brazil – one that will make you truly believe in God's original plan for the planet. With a forest on one side and the gorgeous shoreline on the other, the bus snakes through a primitive landscape that reveals the depths of poverty, as well as the heart of interior Brazil: pastel-colored shanties, barefoot boys playing in the sand, and old women carrying heavy loads on their heads.

Buses also run to Belo Horizonte, Ilhéus, Rio, Salvador, and São Paulo.

## City Transportation

| | |
|---|---|
| **Taxi** . . . . . . . . . . . . . . . . . . . . . . . . . . . . . . . . . . . | ☎ 288-2400 |
| **Interlocadora** (car rental). . . . . . . . . . . . . . . . . . . . | ☎ 228-2335 |

## Money Exchange

See **Descobrimento Turismo**, below.

## Schooner Rentals

### Cia do Mar

*Praça dos Pataxós;* ☎ *288-2981.*

Owned by Arthur Priolli, Cia do Mar has two boats and chartered schooners.

## Tourist Information

The tourist office is at Praça Visconde de Porto Seguro (Casa da Lenha); ☎ *288-2126.* It's open Mon.-Fri. 8 a.m.-8 p.m.

## Travel Agency

### Mucugê Exotik Travel Agency

*Avenida dos Navegantes, 53,* ☎ *(73) 875-1238, fax 875-1238.*

This agency can arrange excursions anywhere throughout Brazil, as well as book rooms for the Mucugê Hotel Village in Arraial d'Ajuda. The owners of the agency are also presently selling prime real estate here that should prove fine investments in the future. English is spoken well.

### Descobrimento Turismo

*Avenida Getúlio Vargas, 330;* ☎ *(73) 288-2452/2004.*

Arranges city tours, schooners to Trancoso and the reefs of Coroa Alta, diving tours to Recife de Fora, a coral reef teeming with marine life, and treks through the national park of Monte Pascoal.

# Arraial d'Ajuda

Arraial d'Ajuda is not for the conventional tourist. Sometimes compared to Ibiza in Spain, this tiny fishing village across the river from Porto Seguro wallowed in obscurity for more than 500 years until it suddenly became the "Party City" of Brazil a few years back. Some even claim *lambada* was born here (see below). An odd mixture descends on the village in season – rich singles, movie stars, musicians, aging hippies, precocious teens, and anyone who is tall, tan, dark and handsome. Compared to Porto Seguro, which has only three bars, Arraial has more than 15 – some residents consider the whole city a bar. Certainly a kind of makeshift nightlife happens wherever it's ignited. The main action starts on **Broadway**, the central drag, sometime after 11 p.m. By 7 a.m., you don't know if the people you meet on the road are just waking up or on their way to bed.

A green courtyard separates Broadway from the city's one church, **Nossa Senhora d'Ajuda**. It might have been significant that an electric amp and guitar was lying beneath the altar when I checked it out. Built between 1549 and 1551, the church is the second oldest in Brazil.

By all accounts, Carnaval in Arraial is a wild and crazy time. Broadway gets so packed you can't walk through, and revelers generally push the outer limits of the Dionysian celebration. Rumor is, there are 10 girls to every two guys. There is no organized parade, but people generally follow after a *trio elétrico*, which fills the streets with high-volume samba. Given the various activities that go on in public, anyone adverse to drug consumption probably won't feel at home. Reservations for any *pousada* during Carnaval should be made at least two months in advance.

# Beaches

The beaches in Arraial are glorious, primitive, and models for Swept Away fantasies. Following **Mucugê** are: **Pitinga** (1¼ miles), **Lagoa Azul** (2 miles), **Taipe** (2½ miles), and **Rio da Barra** (4½ miles). Pitinga has long been known as a nude beach; these days it's one of the few completely nude beaches in Brazil.

# Where To Stay

See page 26 for price chart.

## Mucugê Hotel

*Village Estrada p/Mucugê, 6 km.;* ☎ *(73) 875-1238.*

Twenty years ago, Luiz Claudio Ferreira bought up a lot of land in Arraial when nobody could remember its name. Today, he's selling off prime lots (the last was to an Arab sheik), but is still keeping the best for himself – namely, the Mucugê Hotel. As a world traveler, he wanted to create his own fantasy *pousada*, and he has truly succeeded, with the prettiest, cleanest complex in the area, located on a spectacular landscape that includes a river, an ocean, and acres of coconut trees and tropical vegetation. The apartments are built into chalet-like structures, all with verandas; the duplex suites, which come with kitchens, are built on stilts with private patios. A common living room and bar is completely homey, and the staff is so hip you won't know who are guests and who are employees. Decor runs to the rustic, and you can wake up to the roar of the ocean; breakfast is on the other side of a wood bridge, just steps from the sea. Friends of the owner – only "interesting" people – drop in all the time; Robert de Niro stayed a week. During off-season, the *pousada* is nearly deserted so you're sure to enjoy peace and privacy. Any travel arrangements can be made by the family agency, which will arrange expeditions in the area and throughout Brazil, including the Amazon. Anyone interested in prime real estate (it's tripled in price in the last few years) should take a hike here – fast. Twenty percent discount in low season. Make reservation for high season two months in advance. *17 apts. Expensive. AE.*

## Pousada Fragata

*Estr. p/praia do Mucugê, 5 km.;* ☎ *(73) 875-2044.*
*Reservations in São Paulo,* ☎ *(21) 264-8569.*

This colonial-style *pousada*, located 1,000 feet from the beach, is one of the nicest in Arraial, its tropical ambiance preserved in the palm-lined courtyard. Apartments are rustically appointed with wood-frame beds; all come with air conditioning, color TV, mini-bar, and very clean bathrooms. Half-price in low season; eight-day package at Carnaval and Christmas/New Year's. Reserve a month ahead. *8 apts. Moderate. V, MC.*

### Pousada Brisas

*Saída p/Trancoso;* ☎ *(73) 288-2348.*

A driveway full of cashew trees that grow horizontally leads to the lobby of this *pousada,* looking out onto a fabulous panorama of grassy fields and raging ocean. A fantastic jungle is only steps away and the ocean about a five-minute walk.

The apartments – white stucco chalets with orange-tiled roofs – are simple, with a brick bed stand, mosquito nets, and mini-bar; no air conditioning or phone. If you want a fan, you must ask for one. Some rooms have extra space for children. During high season, three meals a day are served (breakfast included), along with 24-hour room service. The owner speaks English. Half-price in low season. *18 apts. Moderate. No cards.*

### Pousada da Estrela

*Rua do Campo de Aviação;* ☎ *(73) 875-1183.*

If you decide to stay in town here, head for this feel-good *pousada,* off a quiet street, across from the police station, and only a half-mile from the beach. The inner courtyard is so packed with plants you might have to slice your way through.

The five simple rooms come with double beds, mosquito nets, mini-bar, and an extra hammock: no TV, air conditioning, or phone. Duplos are split-levels, with two ceiling fans. *Inexpensive. No cards.*

### Hotel Porto d'Ajuda

☎ *(73) 288-2942.*

A rock concert producer named Sergio Pessoa opened this new complex for those who "want the feel of the sea"; in fact, it's the only hotel where the boats practically come up to your door. Located where you cross on the ferry (turn left to Coconut Grove), the hotel offers all watersports from skiing and sailing to windsurfing.

The restaurant serves Japanese food. All rooms are air conditioned and come with phone, TV with video, mini-bar, and an extra living room. Doubles run about $70-80. *10 apts. Expensive. All cards.*

## Where To Eat

See page 26 for price chart.

### Alto Astral

*Broadway.*

Located on the main drag, this hangout is so homey that some clients seemed to have grown into the woodwork. *Moderate. No cards.*

## Restaurante São João

*Praça Brig. Eduardo Gomes. 2 a.m.-11 a.m.*

Best homemade food in town, at the private home of Senhor Manoel. Don't be daunted by the screaming children in the living room or the laundry in the courtyard. Feast on six kinds of *moqueca*, shrimp stroganoff, or *frango ao molho pardo* (chicken in its own blood). Be prepared to bat away flies. *Inexpensive. No cards.*

## Varanda Grill

*Rua São Benedito. 4 p.m.-11 p.m., closed Mon.*

This is the best joint in town for grilled meats. Portions are for one person. The *torresminhos* (fried pork rinds) and French fries are excellent. *Inexpensive. No cards.*

## Mão na Massa

*Rua Bela Vista;* ☎ *875-1257. 1 p.m.-midnight (high season), 3-11 p.m. (low season).*

This "real-Italian" *adega* is one of the most romantic spots in town, with creamy lasagna, 10 kinds of pizza, and grilled meats. Start off with the great *pão de alho* (toasted garlic bread). Desserts are memorable. *Inexpensive. AE.*

# Nightlife

## Jatobar

*Praça Brigadeiro Eduardo Gomes, near the church.*

While others have claimed it was the creation of Madison Avenue, most residents here firmly believe that *lambada* was created at the Jato Bar. The official "papa" is Maroto, the owner of this wood-floor bar, a gorgeous, young man with flowing dreadlocks and a wild-Jesus look who could easily be Brazil's answer to Patrick Swayze. A natural dancer, Maroto claims to have mixed samba with Northeastern folkloric steps to create the first *lambada* – a fast-twirling dance where the couple literally looks joined at the hips.

Whether or not Maroto actually discovered *lambada*, he at least seems to have well trained the locals, who dance here with a grace and joy rarely seen in commercial demonstrations. During high season, Maroto gives classes that are not to be missed; during low season you'll have to negotiate privately with him. One warning: He is so shy that he actually turned down some Brazilian producers to headline an international *lambada* show. When he finally takes to the tiny dance floor with his wife, however, it's a major event. Other bars include **I Luminight Bar** and **Café da Mata**, both for dancing.

## Hands-On Arraial d'Ajuda

### Arrival

Arraial d'Ajuda and Trancoso may be reached from Porto Seguro by taking the **ferry**, which runs regularly (about every half-hour during high season). If you are coming from the tiny **airport** in Porto Seguro, you may take a **taxi** to the ferry (about $3) or all the way to your hotel in Arraial for about $12 (rates depend on the season). If you cross the ferry without a taxi, you'll have to find a cab on the other side. It's quite likely that you could hitch a ride anywhere along the route; people are extremely friendly and you'll be relatively safe.

### Climate

Hot during the day and refreshingly cool at night, with temperatures averaging 95°F. Rain at night is very common. Watch out for mosquitos – nets are *de rigueur* here.

### Rentals

**Wind Point Parracho**, a five-minute walk down the beach from Mucugê Hotel, rents kayaks, windsurfing equipment, and horses. Also contact the **Mucugê Travel Agency, ☎ *875-1238.***

### When To Go

Once a month there is a **full-moon festival**, with bonfire and live music – a big free party that starts after midnight. Mar.-Apr. is low season. May-June is the cheapest time to come, but the weather is not reliable and the social scene is nada. Sept.-Oct. the village comes back to life in preparation for the summer blitz.

# Trancoso

Walk about seven miles down the beach from Mucugê, or traverse a torturous dirt road through the forest (about half-hour by jeep) to reach Trancoso, a tiny fishing village seemingly in the middle of nowhere. The road there is full of potholes, but the scenery is pure folkloric Brazil – native fishing huts, crowds gathered before evangelicals screaming on scratchy mikes, chicken and horses blocking the road. The wind-swept beach is dramatic, flanked by high cliffs and washed by huge waves that send foaming crests to the strand. Inspired by such primitive natural resources, many bathers have been known to strip totally – an occurrence, if you can believe it, which is uncommon in Brazil. The most famous meeting point is the **Barraca Itaip**, a grass-hut bar where you can dine on catfish and crabs at tables made out of logs.

The village of Trancoso itself is the smallest I have seen in Brazil. High season turns the small football field in front of the church into a den of activity, but even during off-season, locals look for any excuse to have a celebration; once I ran across a group of school children giving a lively musical performance at their graduation. Mostly, you'll find old men playing dominoes in the shade or elderly ladies resting on their porches. Almost everyone seems to walk around barefoot, maybe because the beach is just down the hill behind the church.

> **UP CLOSE TIP from Theodore Folke:** *Visitors to Trancoso should bear in mind that during high season the place is jumping and it's hard to get a room on short notice.*

## Where To Stay

See page 26 for price chart.

### Hotel da Praça

*Reserve in São Paulo, ☎ (11) 813-6011.*

Located off the main square, this tiled-roof complex remains the most popular place to stay, featuring individual chalets on stilts, surrounded by a woody grove. All apartments come with fan and mini-bar. No pool, no TV, just a gorgeous tropical landscape with magnificent old trees. Theodore Folke swears that the hotel's bar is the best place to meet people. *11 apts. Inexpensive-moderate. No cards.*

### Capim Santo

*C.P.115, Praça São José s/n; ☎ and fax (73) 868-1122.*

My Deep Throat Theodore Folke tells me that this *pousada* has the "best food in Brazil" – after Agua Viva near Salvador (we both agree there!). The owners, he says, Sandra and Nano, are not only lovely, but they speak English! Rates are about $40 per night. *Inexpensive.*

### Pousada Sol da Manhã

*C.P. 86.*

Dutch owner Aart Tlan and his Brazilian wife, Dora, were the first in Trancoso to rent out rooms in their native-style house. He also now owns a pineapple farm, from which his guests eat the fruits. Five simple rooms come with a fan; you share bathrooms. The house has no phone, so leave a message for a reservation at Central Telephone, ☎ 867-1115. In off-season, Aart may be the only one in town who speaks English. *Inexpensive. No cards.*

### Pousada Hibiscus

*Reservations in São Paulo, ☎ (11) 826-4200.*

Wood-frame beds with mosquito nets and a ceiling fan in this simple eight-room *pousada*, with bathrooms cleaner than most. The beach is a 15-minute walk away. *Inexpensive. No cards.*

## Where To Eat

**Rama** is considered to be the best restaurant, built in front of a massive tree with elephantine gnarled trunks. Also try the pizzas at **Tucano** and the all-natural sandwiches at **Abacaxi.**

## Hands-On Trancoso

### Arrivals

A **bus** runs between Arraial and Trancoso about every hour. **Jeeps** can be rented through the **Mucugê Travel Agency** in Arraial, ☎ *875-1238.* A walk along the beach will take about an hour.

### Telephone

The only telephone is at the **Posto Telefônico,** near the bus depot, open 7 a.m.-10 p.m. The number of the central operator is ☎ *(73) 867-1115* or *867-1116.*

# THE NORTHEAST

The Northeast of Brazil is synonymous with the hard hot life. Cactus and dense shrub (called *caatinga*) dominate the region's interior, an unforgiving territory where the heat is fierce and the land is parched brown for most of the year. *Nordestinos*, as the residents are called, are legendary in South America for being survivors, forced by perpetual droughts, famines, and political upheavals to uproot their homes and migrate thousands of miles each year in search of water. Though the states of Bahia,* Sergipe, Pernambuco, Alagoas, Paraná, Rio Grande do Norte, Ceará, and Maranhão occupies 10% of the national territory, a fourth of the population of Brazil resides here, 30 million of them in substandard subsistence. Yet something in the Northeastern character is indefatigable; despite a life that teeters perpetually on the edge, *Nordestinos* always seem to find their way back home. They know in a moment of rainfall the vast, semi-arid backland (called the *sertão*) can suddenly transform, the cacti burst into bloom, and the parched brown earth returns overnight to life.

## The People

The racial mix in the Northeast makes a startling contrast to the predominantly white, European ancestry of the South. The largest concentration of blacks in Brazil are located here – descendants of African slaves imported to work the plantations. But a mixture of Portuguese and Indian influences also predominates, which can be seen in the hard, carved features and short stature of tan-colored *mestiços*. A deep-rooted spirituality also runs through the veins of Northeasterners. It's here, in the *sertão* of Bahia, that the first millenarian revolution took hold, when the mystic **Antônio Conselheiro** led his impoverished followers in a tragic rebellion against the federal government. And then there was the religious fanaticism inspired by the so-called miracles of **Padre Cicero Batista**, which profoundly affected the political developments of the state of Ceará. Today, almost a century later, Padre Cicero's image in the form of icons still exerts a powerful spiritual force on the people of the backlands.

## Pleasure Spots To Savor

Ironically, coastal cities of the Northeast are among the finest pleasure spots in all of Brazil, where the blue-green ocean water seems limitless and the sunshine a boon to pleasure rather than the bane of an impoverished existence. In fact, this northeast region has become such a sensation among Europeans and Argentines that it is expected to displace Rio as Brazil's

---

* Although the state of Bahia is technically a part of the Northeast, it has been given its own chapter, due to its rich resources for tourism.

destination of choice. As such, hundreds of millions of dollars are being spent to upgrade resorts, hotels, marinas, sewage systems, and roads, not to mention the historical preservation of artifacts and architecture located in towns with quaint historical areas. And for adventurers, the Northeast proffers some of the most exciting eco-treks to be found in Brazil.

The tourist sites covered in this chapter are principally the capital cities of each state, as well as the desert island of **Fernando de Noronha**) – all major destinations, complete with their own folklore and native cuisine. Although each city boasts fine beaches, they are individually known for their own specific virtues and adventures. For example, an exciting itinerary could begin with Salvador (see previous chapter on Bahia), then move up this Northeast coast, to include: **Maceîó** for its usual *jangada* (boat) ride out to the middle of an elevated ocean floor; **Recife** and **Olinda** for their historical architecture; **Natal** for exotic dunesurfing; **Fortaleza** for its rollicking music scene; and **São Luis** for its reggae clubs and historical renovation. In this edition I've added some extra excursions to even more exotic beaches and crafts villages about three to four hours from the main urban centers. By staying in the coastal communities, however, you will be blessed with cooling winds that temper the hot, nearly constant sunshine. As you go up the coast from Máceio to São Luis, approaching Amazônia, you will feel the temperature rise steadily higher until you think you can't stand it anymore; that's when it's time to head for the tree-shaded rainforest. However, the best places to escape the heat are the arts and crafts markets, where you will find jewelry and decorations made out of bone and leather, straw and lace, as well as fine ceramic and wood-carved sculptures, all traditional to Northeastern culture.

As for accommodations, hotel rates are generally cheaper in the Northeast than in the southern states and, accordingly, the rooms are rarely as nice. The *maresia*, or sea wind, is insidious, and even the best hotels retain a slight, musty odor. Primarily, English is spoken at four- and five-star hotels, and even if you speak Portuguese, you may find the hard and fast clip of *Nordestinos* difficult to grasp. (Even when asked to slow down, they seem totally incapable of doing so!) Besides the desert island of **Fernando de Noronha**, which is a scuba diver's paradise, one of the best resorts in Brazil is the **Pratagy Eco Resort** in Maceió, which hosts a veritable treasure trove of ecosystems that will leave any amateur or professional botanist thrilled.

# History

While the Northeast was the first part of Brazil to be settled by Europeans, it was, nevertheless, territory hard won by the Portuguese. As early as the 16th century, the **Portuguese** began to dominate the coastal regions with sugar plantations, giving rise in Olinda and Salvador to a prosperous merchant class often at odds with the noble elite.

Beginning in 1624, the **Dutch** kept the area in constant turmoil through their fierce invasion until they were finally expelled 20 years later, retiring to the West Indies, where they beat the Portuguese at their own sugarcane game. It was then that the colonization of the *agreste* and *sertão* accelerated – runaway Indians and escaped slaves mixing with a new breed of frontiersman, the *vaquiero*, or cattle driver. Today, cattle-raising continues to be a viable industry, though during periods of drought, the paltry ribs of the herds are acute reminders of the harsh Northeastern reality.

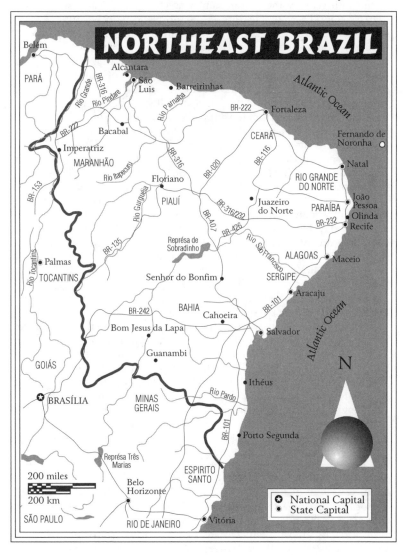

NORTHEAST BRAZIL

# Maceió

One of the Northeast's favorite beach resorts, Maceió is the capital of **Alagoas**, Brazil's second smallest state. When it was first discovered, the city was dedicated by settlers to São Gonçalves, a Portuguese saint; later, in the 18th century the patron saint was changed to *Nossa Senhora dos Prazeres* (Our Lady of Pleasures) – a prophetic nomenclature. Today, sunworshippers fill the wide promenade running along the shore where 75 *barracas* (or open-air bars) ply vacationers with food, drink, and live music all night long. Squeezed between the open sea and a lagoon, Lagoa do Mundaú, Maceió feels like a small city, although its population of 700,000 certainly cancels out any provincial status.

**Sugarcane** remains one of the principal industries both in Maceió and in the state; on the drive from the airport, you can spot a sugarcane factory, as well as large plantations along the road to **Marechal**, a nearby colonial town. Unfortunately, the chemical factory, Salgema, one of the state's most important enterprises, has become a notorious polluter of the city's lagoon and some surrounding beaches. As a result, tourists should avoid the beach in front of the Luxor Hotel.

The family of ex-President Fernando Collor de Melo has been a name of power and wealth in Maceió for the last 200 years. (The family name is de Melo.) Today his ex-sister-in-law (wife of his late brother Pedro, who caused his downfall) is now the glamorous Secretary of Tourism. And you might meet some of his other relatives on the beach, who are still complaining that he didn't tell his uncle or his cousins (or even his own mother!) before he froze the banks in 1990.

The people of Maceió feel a special connection with Americans. During World War II, after Brazil sided with the US following the Nazi decimation of several Brazilian ships, an airport was built here by Americans to control the sea. Behind the **Museum of Image and Sound** (*Museu de Imagem e Som*), you can still see the miniature **Statue of Liberty**, which was given to the city as a sign of friendship. The Kennedy family is also popular here. When JFK was President, he gave substantial monetary support to the city and years later the hospital boat *Hope* docked in the port for eight months. Residents deeply felt his death. Downtown, an avenue near the Gstaad restaurant on Ponta Verde Beach has been named Avenida Robert Kennedy.

## A Bird's Eye View

The best place to view the city is from the **Mirador de Santa Teresina**, where you can see the full expanse of the lagoon. Precious little is left of the historical city, mostly situated in the **Praça dos Martírios**, which is dominated by the neoclassical **Governor's Palace** on one end and the **Igreja Bom Jesus dos Martírios** on the other.

The one art museum worth seeing is the **Fundação Pierre Chalita**, owned by Maceió's greatest painter, who in 1980 created a foundation to house his own fabulous accumulation of 17th- and 18th-century sacred sculptures. One of the most extensive collections in Brazil, it also features French masterpieces, as well as Chalita's own fine works on the top floor. (His 1957 painting of Christ on the Cross created an immense scandal because he left the genitalia showing.) A **School of Beaux Arts** is also housed on the premises.

---

# Beaches

---

Maceió has made its beaches user-friendly with the mosaic promenade that runs the length of the major beaches; every few hundred yards, grass-hut cafés offer cool escapes from the sun, excellent seafood, and live music all night long. (The trend after dusk is to bar hop.)

The palm-lined **Pajuçara Beach** is the main city beach, excellent for bathing, as is **Jatuíca**. Nicknamed Little Riviera, **Ponta Verde Beach** attracts the "beautiful set," who like to pose on the many rocks jutting out to sea; the fact that you can't swim here makes the beach that much more elite. Although excellent for surfing, the violent waves at **Cruz das Almas** have caused many deaths and have inspired the appointment of lifeguards all week during high season (weekends in low). If you want to escape the crunch of the crowd on the northern beaches, head for **Praia do Francês**, 10 miles to the south, where you'll be greeted by an enormous stretch of pristine white sand, foresty borders, and an energetic surf. To get there, take the bus marked "Deodoro," which runs hourly from in front of the old train station. Then explore the well-preserved colonial town of **Marechal Deodoro**. (See *Excursions* below.)

The best *barracas* (grass-roofed bars) along the beach are listed here.

**Felline,** Praia Ponta Verde, offers candlelit jazz at night (piano, sax, and flute), as well as hors d'oeuvres, crêpes, and seafood. **Lampião,** Praia Jatuíca, features a hot dance floor propelled by live *lambada* and *forró* bands under a shady grove of coconut trees. **Ipaneminha,** Praia Pajuçara, serves excellent hors d'oeuvres, with music only at night. **Casa do Seresta,** Jatuíca Beach, attracts a young set who love to samba. Single women looking for dates are welcome.

---

## UP CLOSE ADVENTURE: A Jangada Party

They're called *jangadas* – flat-bottom canoes with droopy masts and enormous sails that create a floating village right in the middle of the ocean. They're easy enough to find. Even if you don't hear the hoarse yells of *"jangada,"* along **Pajuçara Beach** in front of the **Othon Hotel**, you can't miss their blue-and-white sails waving madly in the wind.

First, you mosey down to the shore and pick your boatman, bargaining him down to the going rate for a three-hour excursion (ask your concierge first). Then you wade out to the boat and settle into the wobbly hull as sails are arranged over your head.

Suddenly you're sailing off to an undisclosed destination, water raining down on you as the boatman wildly splashes his sails.

About 15 minutes later, you'll see 20 other masts bobbing up ahead. Your boatman pulls up and parks, then suddenly a handsome young man wearing nothing but a bowtie and swimtrunks jumps on board. Aghast, you think you're about to be robbed until he smiles and explains he's your waiter. Jumping back in the water, he swims over to a floating kitchen and brings you a cold beer and a plate of spicy lobsters. Soon an enthusiastic young local paddles over to your boat and invites you for a swim; to your surprise, you can actually stand up in this natural "pool" and the water doesn't even reach your waist. You wave back at the next *jangada*, full of sun-tanned Argentines, who catch you doing your best breaststroke on their camera. A floating samba band bangs out lively tunes as you sip tropical juice straight from a coconut shell.

A waiter delivers a plate of grilled lobsters at a *jangada* party.

Three hours later, you've been invited to two parties, a yacht cruise, and an evening at a beachside *barraca*. By the time you return to the beach, you're so exhausted you convince the boatman to carry you to shore in his arms.

**UP CLOSE TIP:** *If you only go to Maceió for one day, take this adventure. The sensation of being able to stand up and party in the middle of the ocean will make you feel like a sea god. But go light. Take a towel, enough change for food and drinks (tucked into a neck or waist pouch), and lots of suntan lotion. Leave your shoes on shore and wear shorts (or* *just swimsuit and a coverup). Note that camera equipment and notebooks (mine was a mess) can get wet easily. Boatmen prefer not to take singles and often wait for a full boat.*

---

## Excursions

---

### Marechal Deodoro

About 13½ miles from Maceió lies the quaint village of **Marechal Deodoro,** one of the best-kept colonial towns in Brazil. Once the capital of the capitânia in 1817, Marechal was for centuries reachable only by boat through the South Lagoon; 20 years ago a road was built, but the small-town tranquility hasn't been tinkered with. Barefoot children still play in the street (often swarming tourists for cash), women lay their colorful laundry out on the rocks to dry, and fishermen sit in the windowsills of their 19th-century houses repairing fishing nets. The beautifully landscaped **Praça João XXIII** leads to the city's major treasure, the 17th-century **Convento de São Francisco,** which has now been transformed into the **Museu de Arte Sagrada.** Inside, rich brown floors of pau-brasil (the tropical redwood from which the name "Brasil" is taken) lead to impressive displays of 17th-, 18th- and 19th-century sacred art – from life-sized, often terrifying wood carvings of Christ to charming miniatures of saints. Nearby is the unassuming birthplace of the **Marechal Deodoro,** the first president of the Republic in 1889; it's now a museum housing artifacts of his life. A controversial figure, Deodoro was a general of the Empire who mounted a military coup against the Emperor, ordering him to leave the country within 24 hours. Unfortunately, after assuming the first presidency, Deodoro made a mess when he dissolved Congress and had to resign during a state of siege in 1891. (The museum, on Rua Marechal Deodoro, 25, is open Tues.-Sun., 8 a.m.-5 p.m.) Next door to the museum is **Vera Artesanato,** Rua Marechal Deodoro, 2, an excellent shop for lace, linen, and embroideries made in the area.

---

#### UP CLOSE ADVENTURE from Mitchell Torton "The Changing Character of a Fabled Coastline"

Halfway between Maceio and Recife is the fishing village **Maragogi** (Mara-go-JHEE).

On the coastal side of the road, fishermen ply their trade in their simple, one-sail *jangadas* that somehow manage to survive day-long ocean excursions. On the inland side, waving fields of sugarcane plantations support a population of *fazendeiros* (farmers) and land-bound field workers.

Just for fun, ask a local pedestrian for directions to anywhere. Even if you speak Portuguese, you may not understand a word, since even those from Rio and São Paulo can't decipher the accent. But the rhythm of their speech is musical, especially as they roll out their favorite juices: *acerola, graviola, caju, laranja, umbu, acai...* I've noticed a full-blooded *Nordestino* will always think of one that hasn't been mentioned, and make a point of asking for it.

A bend in BR 101 reveals a sparkling contemporary facade, with a blue plaque bearing five white stars. This is **Club Hotel Salinas do Maragogi,** a luxurious Caribbean-style retreat along a pristine strip of South Atlantic Beach. Brazilian honeymooners look to this air-conditioned oasis owned by a rich Italian family; sun-starved Europeans spend two to three weeks going catatonic in the sun.

The night of my arrival, Salinas' director, Glenio Cedrim regales me with wild stories about "Jesus's massage" – a snorkeler's fantasy. So the next morning I join an early expedition to the warm, natural pools along the off-shore reefs. A strapping Argentine instructs us in basic snorkeling technique and rules of non-engagement with the reefs. Soon we are paddling through clear waters, immediately swarmed by gorgeous patterned species of aquatic life. Later we visit a family plantation house, set on a rise over an enormous sugarcane *fazenda* and a swath of untouched Atlantic forest. The Portuguese and Moorish elements of the 17th-century big house recalls the era when Portugal battled Holland for control of Brazil's destiny in the 1600s. A patron saint with a remarkably fussy haircut adorns the veranda.

Returning, we stop at a small fishing village, and Valeria, our guide, makes an intriguing comment – that the *jangadeiros* (*jangada* fisherman, who live and die on the sea) lack only gills to qualify as fully aquatic beings. And yet, just across BR 101, a short walk away, resides a population that wouldn't set a toe in the ocean. "They spend the whole day Saturday on the beach in the baking sun," she says, "but they are terrified of the real ocean." Two distinct cultures separated by a two-lane blacktop.

## Where To Stay

Tourism is on the upswing in Maceió and there aren't enough hotels. Do make reservations ahead of time.

See page 26 for price chart.

### Hotel Salinas do Maragoji

*AL-101 towards Maceió, km 124, 2 km;* ☎ *296-1122, fax 296-1158;*
*Res.(082) 221-5046.*

A full-service resort right on the beach, with diving equipment, kayaking, boats, tennis, horseback riding, bicycling, trekking, and windsurfing. Dinner included in rate. *132 apts. Expensive. All cards.*

## Village Enseada Pratagy

*Praia de Pratagy (dist. de Riacho Doce), 20 km; ☎ (82) 231-4598, fax 231-5134.*

Located about a half-hour's drive from Maceió, the Pratagy is one of Brazil's finest destinations – a fascinating ecological hotel and a romantic resort. The road there is a scenic adventure as the bumpy path takes you past tropical fields, traditional shack-like homes, and barefoot boys taking dips in the Riacho Doce River. The lobby is a surprise; marble floors vying with wood logs create the epitome of rustic elegance. The preserved ecosystem (approved by IBAMA) is endlessly intriguing: 150 miles of private pristine beach in combination with *mangue* (swamp), which harbors all sorts of critters, including snails and crabs.

Room are rustic, but fashionably appointed, with all the leisure comforts, except one – TVs. The hotel hopes the absence of TVs will inspire socializing. One night a month at full moon, magnificent *luaus* are held poolside with live music and bonfires. A huge breakfast buffet is served in a high-beamed, bamboo eatery that flows out to the innovative pool complex created with mineral water and waterfalls. Organized leisure activities, such as hydrogymnastics, volleyball, soccer, jogging, windsurfing, and kayaking keep guests active. There are even special *lambada* and *forró* classes. Behind the pool flows the Rio Caboclo, with its own wooden bridge, where guests may fish. A treat is the large number of *peixe-boi* (manatees), a species officially considered extinct in Brazil. Tennis, volleyball, squash courts, and a golf course should be completed by the time of your trip. *96 apts. Expensive. All cards.*

## Maceió Mar Hotel

*Avenida Alvaro Otacílio, 2991 (Ponta Verde); ☎ 231-8000, fax 327-5085.*

Marble floors and ceramic tile facades lend casual elegance to this new four-star across Ponta Verde Beach. The pleasant bar and snack shop downstairs is a meeting place for artistic types, who often make art expositions around the curvaceous bar. The 127 rooms, all with views, are stylishly decorated in bamboo and wood; deluxes have an extended area that holds a couch bed, desk, and chairs. The strangely shaped pool looks nearly unswimmable, but it runs provocatively through the open-air lobby. Upon advance request, airport transfers may be arranged. Cash payments receive a 20% discount. *121 apts. Expensive. All cards.*

## Matsubara Hotel

*Av. Brig. Eduardo Gomes, 1551 (Cruz das Almas). ☎ 235-3000, fax 235-1660.*

Owned by a prominent Japanese family, the Matsubara is one of Maceió's prime five-stars, with enough luxurious details to be considered a resort. The lobby is a sprawling atrium around which stand five stories of apartments overhanging with greenery. The exquisitely landscaped grounds inspire outdoor lounging and offer a viable alternative to beachcombing. The pool complex is massive, with wood bridges and islands of flowers shaded by coconut trees; even the tennis courts drip with flowers. Roaming the grounds are eight giant turtles, beloved by guests.

The suites are lusciously appointed with satin spreads. Standards are more sedate, but all rooms have verandas and most have ocean views. The hotel also has a hair salon, Turkish bath, boutique, jewelry store, and convention facility. The lushly appointed nightclub, usually opened on weekends, is a hot spot. Discount in low season is 30%. *110 apts. Expensive. All cards.*

### Jatiúca Resort

*Rua Lagoa da Anta, 220 (Lagoa da Anta);* ☎ *231-2555, fax 235-2808.*

Built around a lagoon and the ocean, and about 20 minutes from town, Jatiúca has the feel of a high-class resort village. The lobby is one of the most beautiful in Maceió, designed by sculptor Fernando Lopes with embroidery artists from Alagoas; the grounds are also artistically landscaped. The two parts of the hotel are connected by a grass-roofed walkway separating the apartments from the leisure activities and beach. Numerous fine restaurants and snack areas dot the grounds, including a romantic beachside bar. The beach, to which the hotel has immediate access, is not private, but tight security keeps non-guests from entering the grounds. Apartments are large and tastefully furnished, with verandas looking to the garden or pool. New Year's Eve, which draws elite Brazilians from all over, is an eight-day blowout with a huge bonfire on December 31. In high season (July and Nov.-Feb.), a full set of leisure activities is available, including tennis, volleyball, soccer, and walking. *95 apts. Expensive. All cards.*

### Hotel Enseada

*Avenida Dr. Antônio Gouveia, 171 (Pajuçara);* ☎ *231-4726, fax 231-5134.*

This black-and-white hotel resembles a cathedral with its angular geometric facade. Formerly an apart-hotel, the nine-story Enseada is built around an indoor pond and atrium of tropical vegetation. The air-conditioned rooms are all enormous, befitting its former status, fashionably styled in red, black, and white decor. Superior rooms are suite-like, with two rooms and a veranda. Guests may be picked up at the airport if requested in advance. Ten percent discount during low season. *101 apts. Moderate. All cards.*

### Ponta Verde Praia Hotel

*Avenida Alvaro Octacilio, 2933 (Ponta Verde);* ☎ *231-4040, fax 231-8080.*

Here's a good middle-range hotel well placed on Ponta Verde, a beach frequented by the young, rich, and chi-chi. The restaurant (all three meals) is cheerful with local avant-garde art. The small pool right off the street offers little privacy, but there are also a children's pool, pool bar and small playground. The seafront room, with a full beach view, is pleasant, with walnut headboards, full-length mirrors, and tiled bathrooms, but save a few dollars with the lateral sea view, which is sufficient. A panoramic glass elevator gives a magnificent view of the ocean. *68 apts. Moderate. All cards.*

## Jacarecica

*R.E, 141 (Conjunto Jacarecica);* ☎ *235-3598.*

A small house on Arredores Beach, close to a natural pool. Worth it for the locale and the budget price. *Inexpensive. No cards.*

## Pajuçara

*R. Quintino Bocaiúva, 63;* ☎ *231-0631.*

Located on Pajuçara Beach, this youth hostel offers rooms with three beds and individual closets with keys. The laundry and kitchen are at the disposal of the guests. The house is 200 feet from the beach, and has TV, video, and cassettes for rental. The reception is open 24 hours, and the telephone is public. *Inexpensive, No cards.*

# Where To Eat

Specialties in this seaside capital center are, of course, made from the freshest seafood. Lobsters are caught on the high seas, but there are times when it's forbidden to fish for them – specifically, in Apr. and June, when you'll be served frozen lobster. See page 26 for price chart.

## Gstaad

*Avenida Robert Kennedy, 2167;* ☎ *231-6275. Noon-4 p.m., 6 p.m.-1 a.m., Sat. 6 p.m.-1 a.m., closed Sun.*

The famous come to see and be seen at this elegant Swiss-style eatery, the most expensive in Maceió. Flowered upholstery lends a seaside tropicália; the marble floors and mahogany columns add élan. Dishes are named after the owners' friends; one wonders if the *filet à Senhorzinho Malta,* named after ex-First Lady Rosane Collor, is still on the menu. Fondues are specialties. After 10:30 p.m., a soft sax and piano kick in with moody jazz. Women in chic linen suits with short sleeves looked as if they were freezing in the strong air conditioning; ties are not necessary. *Expensive. All cards.*

## Fogão Gaúcho

*Via Expressa, km 4 (Serraria), 10 km;* ☎ *329-1681. 11 a.m.-10 p.m.*

One of the best steakhouses in the city. *Moderate. All cards.*

## Bar das Ostras

*Rua Prof. Teonilo Gama, 200 (Trapeche da Barra)* ☎ *223-4061. Noon-1 p.m.*

The simplest of ambiances but that special kind of place that's been in the same family for at least a century. Pig out on fresh oysters and tasty grilled lobsters. *Moderate. All cards.*

## Canto da Boca

*Av. Jatiúca, 654 (Jatiúca);* ☎ *231-8404. Noon-midnight.*

Featuring Northeastern dishes, such as *carne de sol, macaxeira, farofa, feijão tropeiro*, and *manteiga do sertão*. In high season and festivals you should make reservations. *Moderate. All cards.*

## Restaurante do Alipio

*Avenida Alipio Barbosa, 321 (Ponta da Barra, Lagoa Mundaú);*
☎ *221-5186. 11 a.m.-1 a.m., Sun. 11 a.m.-6 p.m.*

Prices have risen since this rock-simple eatery began to pack them in on the banks of the lagoon in Barra do Pontal. Still, fried fish is a good bet, as is *carne de sol*. Waiters have a strange sense of humor here. (One told us our wait would be 20 minutes, then brought the food in a matter of seconds.) Better to go after the sun sets, when live music is played nightly. *Moderate. AE.*

## Lagostão

*Avenida Dq. de Caxias, 1384 (Centro);* ☎ *221-6555.*
*6 p.m.-midnight, high season noon-midnight.*

Seafood *rodízio* (all you can eat) with 19 dishes of shrimp, lobster, *muqueca*, stuffed crabs, mollusks, etc. If you're a fish lover, how you can go wrong? *Moderate. No cards.*

## New Hakata

*Rua Dr. Antônio Conceição, 1198 (Ponta Verde). 11 a.m.-3 p.m., 7 p.m.-2 a.m.*

Casual to the point of unimaginative, this Japanese-inspired fisheria, with an outdoor patio and air-conditioned salon, is well known for its *carapeba* – the most famous typical fish found in Maceió. Specialty is cuisine cooked *na chapa*, served on a sizzling grill. If you look helpless, the waiter will skillfully deliver the head from the tail, but be careful of bones – I almost choked to death. Fish is priced according to size. Located near the Maceió Mar Hotel, the restaurant sits on an inner street a few blocks from shore. *Moderate. All cards.*

## Tia Julieta

*R. Gen. Hermes,* ☎ *223-6162.*

One of the best houses in the city for buffet, with a strong variety of dishes. The mother restaurant is on Ponta Verde. *Inexpensive. No cards.*

# Nightlife

## By Bar Brasil

*Rua C, 320 (Jatiúca). 6 p.m.-last client daily.*

A star bar in the city, where the garlic bread is as famous as the *chopp*. The *picanha* (prime beef) served with fried *macaxeira* comes in a close second.

## Fellini

*At the end of Avenida Robert Kennedy (Ponta Verde). 6 p.m.-last client.*

Nicknamed the *"pianos' mar"* (sea of pianos), this is the place to sink down into good local jazz.

> **UP CLOSE TIP:** *To dance samba, head for Casa do Povo on Jatiúca Beach. Female tourists looking for singles are a common sight.*

# Shopping

Take a hired car or bus out to **Pontal da Barra**, along the shores of the Lagoa do Mundaú, formerly a fishermen's village and now filled with stores of traditional lacemakers. Ask for the house of **Teka**, one of Maceió's most famous lacemakers, who in her youth was considered one of the most beautiful girls in the region. Today, her weather-drawn face tells the story of a hard existence, but the joy in her eyes when she shows you her designs brings back her former glory. To get to her house, you'll pass the quaint town square and walk through a dirt road past traditional cottages, where barefoot boys play in the mud and old women spend the day on their stoops. Teka learned her craft from her mother at the age of eight, and today can complete a wedding dress in about 10 days. Her designs have been featured in expositions throughout the country. Everyone knows where she lives, but her official address is: Travessa São Sebastião, 56, Pontal de Barra.

### Mercado de Artesanato (Crafts Market)

*Parque Rio Branco (downtown), 8 a.m.-6 p.m.*

This market offers a good choice of ceramics, wood-carvings, native paintings, and lace embroideries.

# Hands-On Maceió

## Arrival

**Flights** run daily to Brasília, Curitiba, João Pessoa, Natal, Recife, Rio, Salvador, and São Paulo. Connections can be made through numerous cities. **Buses** run to most large cities, such as Salvador, Brasília, and São Paulo.

The airport is 12½ miles from downtown. **Taxis** are about $25, or you can take a bus to the **train station** or near Hotel Beiriz on Rua João Pessoa, 290.

## Car Rental

| | |
|---|---|
| **Avis** ........................................ | ☎ 322-2125 |
| **Maceió** (dune buggies)...................... | ☎ 231-7375 |

## City Transportation

Both the city bus and a special *jardineira* bus make all stops along the *orla* (beach drag). The bus that goes from the center of town down the *orla*, is marked "Centro Barra Cruz das Almas."

## Money Exchange

**Aeroturismo**
Rua Barão de Penedo, 61 (Shopping Iguatemi).
**Caiçara**
Rua Jangadeiros Alagoanos, 617 (Pajuçara) . . . . . ☎ 231-0872

## Tourist Information

Try **Ematur**, Duque de Caxias, 2014 (downtown); ☎ *221-9393*, fax *221-8987*. Information booths are also located at the **airport** and the **bus station**, as well as Ponta Verde, Pajuçara and Jatiúca beaches.

## When To Go

High season (Dec.-Feb.) is hot and crowded; it's better to hit the beaches from Mar.-May. Avoid July and Aug. due to heavy rains. From Sept. to Dec., rain and sun alternate.

# Recife & Olinda

Home of one of the great Carnaval blowouts in the Northeast, **Recife** is the capital of the state of **Pernambuco** and one of the major industrial cities north of Salvador. What draws tourists, besides the pre-Lent festivities that usually last 10 days, is an excellent coastline of natural pools formed by the craggy reefs, or *recifes* (hence its name). Weather is uniformly beach-friendly, and there are also glorious stretches of primitive strands north and south of the city. In addition, four miles away, the colonial town of **Olinda** remains one of the country's greatest architectural treasures, a perfect city to experience cultural time-warp as you stroll leisurely over the 400-year-old cobblestone streets. It's not coincidence that *O Linda* means "oh, beautiful."

Recife beats to a different *ritmo* (rhythm) than the rest of Brazil. During Carnaval, which mostly descends on the tiny alleyways of Olinda, samba is all but obscured by the more frenzied, high-tempo beat of folkloric dances like the *frevo*, the *maracatú*, and the *caboclinho*. Towering *bonecos* – papier-mâché figures of folk heroes and caricatures of local politicians – dominate the *praças*, where it's said people spend more money on beer than on their costumes. *Trios elétricos* – small bands blaring away on the back of trucks – bring the decibel level over the edge. Certainly Olinda has gained the reputation for one of the wildest street Carnavals in Brazil; residents who can't stand the excitement often escape to the local Jesuit Seminary for four days of peace and quiet.

UP CLOSE TIP: *Start practicing now the high, nasal tongue of the locals. Recife is pronounced "he-SEE-fee." Throw away those Texas R's.*

# History

Although Olinda is today considered the bedroom community of Recife, it was founded before Recife and once overshadowed the harbor city in its colonial greatness. After Olinda was established in the 1530s, the **Portuguese** proceeded to plow most of the surrounding fields into sugar plantations. By 1630, forces from the **Dutch West India Company** expelled the settlers, burning down the glorious wrought churches and rebuilding the new capital, Recife, whose swampy lands opened onto a more favorable harbor. Conquering territory from the southern border of Alagoas all the way to Maranhão, the Dutch expanded their monopoly of the sugarcane industry by maintaining tight control on the slave trade, but they also introduced advances in tropical medicine, weather analysis, and zoology. They erred, however, on the side of politics, ignoring the tensions among the original settlers; by 1654, the Dutch were forced to surrender Recife to the Portuguese, and they never returned.

The mercantile Dutch transformed Recife into the first bourgeois commercial center of Brazil. By the time they left, the village of 100 houses had grown into a bustling port with over 2,000 houses. But they had also created a class struggle. The rural aristocracy based in Olinda began to feel threatened by this growing commercial class and labeled them *mascates* – a derogatory word employed by the aristocracy for those who had to work for a living. Tempers erupted, but by the end of 1711, a governor dispatched from Lisbon reconciled the **War of the Mascates** with a generous pardon for all. However, for two more centuries, the gap between the aristocracy and the bourgeoisie lingered. A conspiracy revolution in 1817, inspired by European enlightenment ideals, not to mention the War of 1812 in the States, abolished all titles of nobility, the brazilwood monopoly, class privileges, and even some taxes. This was considered the principal revolt of the colonial period, but it, too, was eventually quelled and Pernambuco returned to the fold of the new republic within three months.

# A Bird's Eye View

Perhaps it's more wish than reality, but Recife is often called the "**Venice of Brazil**," since the heart of the city sprawls over three islands – Santo Antônio, Boa Vista, and Recife proper – all connected by more than two dozen bridges over the Beribe and Capibaribe rivers. The business district is situated on Santo Antônio and surrounded by a few colonial churches. Most of the middle class crowds into the southern area along the Boa Viagem Beach, where the majority of the better hotels are located, as well as hundreds of beachside eateries and clubs. Stay away from the docks on Recife Island at night, a veritable sleaze center.

# Sights In Recife

## Pátio de São Pedro

To get a glimpse of colonial Recife, head for the large square in the district of Santo Antônio. Reminiscent of Rome with its dozens of flying pigeons, the plaza is lined with bars and artisan stores, but is dominated by a church.

## Igreja de São Pedro

*8 a.m.-11:30 a.m., 2-5 p.m.*

Constructed between 1728 and 1782, the church boasts an impressive facade that resembles an opera house, as do the gold-leafed boxes inside. The ceiling painting in the main sanctuary is a fabulous example of trompe l'oeil and provides an immense sensation of radiating energy. Go up three flights of rickety stairs (the kind seen in horror movies) for a fabulous panoramic view of the city from the rooftop.

## Livraria Cordel

On the corner of the Pátio you'll find the best sculpture shop in the city, which features the woodcuts of artists Amaro Francisco and Jota Borges. (Some of the sculptured saints seem so alive they look as if they could perform a miracle any second.) You'll also find excellent native paintings here, and scores of *cordels* – old poems, romances, and biographies in pamphlet form that take their name from the cords on which they are hung for sale. Since *cordels* were the primary form by which the natives in the interior passed on their news, their themes (wife abuse, murder, and politics) were always topical, if somewhat tabloidish. Even if you can't read Portuguese, the woodblock-cut designs on the front covers are usually sensational enough to rate as fine souvenirs.

At night, the bars around the Pátio teem with Recifenses, especially on the weekends when you can hear excellent live bands. With your purse tucked tightly under your arm or your wallet in an inside pocket, wander around the inner streets surrounding the Pátio.

## Mercado de São José

Packed with stalls hawking everything from herbs and dried fish to jeans and tablecloths, some of the alleyways in this market are barely big enough for two people to pass. But the scene is exciting – the epitome of a frenzied third-world marketplace. If your sandals need fixing, you'll even find shoemakers using sewing machines so ancient they have to be pedaled. Across the esplanade is a fruit and vegetable market open daily.

## Casa da Cultura

*Rua 223 Floriano Peixoto, ☎ 224-2084.*

Located on the shores of the Capibaribe River, you'll probably be feeling steamy when you arrive here, so buy a cold Coke and a bag of roasted cashews or boiled Indian corn, then stroll slowly around this former prison now transformed into the city's major arts and crafts market. Good buys are hammocks, lace handiwork, and straw pottery. My favorite purchases were the miniature *maracatú* and *frevo* bands bought at Kafua Artesanato (room 116). Just make sure you repack the fragile little sculptures yourself because the newspaper packing used by the store won't be sufficient. To get a better look at the impressive structure of the ex-prison, cross to the other side of the river.

## Museu do Homem do Nordeste

*Avenida 17 de Agosto, 2187 (Casa Forte); ☎ 441-5500. Tues., Wed. and Fri. 11 a.m.-5 p.m., Thur. 8 a.m.-5 p.m., Sat., Sun. and holidays 1-7 p.m., closed Mon.*

*Confirm in advance.*

It will take at least a half-hour by car to get here, but this is one of the best museums in Brazil for the study of Northeastern culture and history. Once inside, you'll find that the compulsory guided tour (in English) will give you a quick overview; afterwards, graciously inquire if you can wander around on your own. Several galleries are devoted to such topics as sugar, cattle, popular religion, pagan festivals, and ceramics. There are also impressive exhibits of native handicrafts. Make sure you check out the **Galeria de Arte Popular,** which features the sculptures of a peasant farmer named Mestre Vitalino, who became famous for his life-like clay portraits of the residents in his small village.

❖ **GETTING HERE:** *Hire a taxi for a ride through the leafy residential neighborhoods or take bus #552 Dois Irmãos Rui Barbosa.*

## Instituto Joaquim Nabuco

*Av. 17 de Agosto, 2187 (Casa Forte); ☎ 268-2000. Tues., Wed. & Fri. 11 a.m.-5 p.m. Thur. 8 a.m.-5 p.m., and Sat. and Sun. 1-5 p.m.*

The paintings of Mestre Vitalino can be found at this museum, which also features some of the best Northeastern folk art in Brazil.

# Walking Tour Of Olinda

Next to the cities of Parati, Ouro Preto, and São Luis, **Olinda** stands as one of the great architectural treasures still remaining from colonial Brazil. Spread across several small hills and fanning along the shore, Olinda is a mere four miles north of Recife – a wonderful maze of cobblestone streets, pastel-colored mansions, baroque churches, and market squares that invite leisurely strolling. Covering about 10 square km., colonial Olinda is but one-third of a modern metropolis of nearly 400,000 that stretches out behind it, but it's the center of excitement for the Northeast's most frenzied Carnaval. During the rest of the year, it acts as a magnet for the bi-cities' bohemians and intelligentsia, who congregate at night in the numerous bars along the shore and in the **Alto da Sé**. Since Olinda was designated a national historical patrimony in 1980 and a world monument by UNESCO in 1982, building regulations have forbidden construction of any modern architecture unless the lot is totally vacant.

Olinda has over 22 churches and 12 chapels, a few of which can be glimpsed on this energetic walking tour. Note that some of the slopes are steep and temperatures can rise sharply, so make sure you take a few rests in the shade.

❖ **GETTING HERE:** *To get to Olinda, take bus #902 or #981, both marked Rio Doce. From the center of Recife, buses marked Rio Doce or Olinda will also get you there.*

## Praça do Carmo

Begin here, site of the first Carmel church built in Brazil, the Igreja do Carmo (1588). The imposing church may still be closed for restoration, but knock loudly on the door and perhaps the *vigia* (watchman) will let you slip inside for a peek.

## Igreja de São Bento

*Wed.-Fri. 8-11:30 a.m., 4-5:30 p.m.*

Walk down Rua do Vasconcelos to this monastery founded by the Portuguese in 1736. The original site dates back to 1596, but the Dutch decimated this area when they invaded Pernambuco, and it wasn't until 1761 that the Portuguese could rebuild it. São Bento is considered the richest church in Olinda, with a cedar wood altar and two gold pulpits (the left one is used by the priests and the right by the richest family); slaves were not even allowed to enter the main sanctuary. The beautifully preserved ceiling was painted with colors made from tropical fruit condensed with banana oil.

## São Sebastian Church

To the left of São Bento, on Rua 13 de Novembro, stands this church. It was constructed in 1686 when the city was overrun with rats. (São Sebastian is the protector of rats.)

Walk uphill on Rua São Bento over the original stones forged by slaves who used particles from the reefs cemented with whale oil. The black stones are called *cabeça de negros* because the slaves carved portraits of heads into them.

## Mayor's Office

On the corner of 15 de Novembro and Rua São Bento stands this 16th-century yellow-and-white façade, rebuilt in neoclassical style.

## Alceu Valença

Number 182 on Rua São Bento is the home of the popular Northeastern singer who specializes in *frevo* and returns to Olinda every year for Carnaval.

## Pitombeira dos Quatros Cantos

Walk back to the *praça*, then left on Rua 27 de Janeiro. The yellow-and-black house is the meeting place of the principal *frevo* club that dances in Carnaval. At night it transforms into a popular bar. During Carnaval, the concrete walls around here are saturated with graffiti, a creative and often highly political outlet of expression that the entire city engages in; after Carnaval, the government keeps the best ones and washes off the rest – until the next Carnaval.

## Igreja de São Pedro

Walking down Rua 27 de Janeiro, you'll reach São Pedro, founded in the 17th century and rebuilt by the Portuguese in the 18th century in baroque style. During Carnaval, the steps of the church become an outdoor bed for anyone too drunk to go home. Walk around the church to Rua 7 de Setembro, turn right on Rua São Bento, and notice the #301 house with the Portuguese blue-tiled facade. About this time, you might be approached by a street artist like Jota Caxiado, who sells fine line drawings.

## Mercado da Ribeira

Walk straight on Rua São Bento till you reach the former site of slave auctions attended by sugar plantation owners, that is now a handicraft center; if you go behind the market on the right side, you can peep inside the backyard of some of Olinda's finest artists, restoring wood and plaster saints.

## The Principal Corner Of Carnaval

At this point Rua São Bento becomes Rua Bernardo Vieira de Melo, where the romantic **L'Atelier restaurant** is located. If you're not ready for a full meal, at least stop in for a drink on the back patio overlooking the city or dig into a *Coupe Atelier* – melon, vanilla ice cream, meringue, and cherry liqueur – just the thing for heatstroke. The restaurant is a block from the principal corner of Carnaval – Quatro Cantos – the meeting point of all the *frevo* clubs (specifically, the corner of Rua Bernardo Vieira de Melo and Ladeira da Misericórdia and Rua Prudente de Moraes).

## Misericordia

A short rest will be imperative if you continue up – this is the highest slope of Olinda and a killer on the calves. Turn left on Beco dos Quatros Cantos and go down the hill. There you'll find a mineral well with natural spring water that's perfectly safe to drink. During Carnaval, revelers come here to drink and shower at the same time.

## Rua do Amparo

Walk back up the hill to the oldest street in Olinda. Near here, at #91, is the home of **Antônio Cardoso**, who is famous for the *pau do indio* he sells – homemade *pinga*, with 32 ingredients, including herbs and other macrobiotic products that are supposedly good for the health. It's also a hefty shot of intoxication, about $5 for a liter bottle, and the major liquid consumed during Carnaval. (My Deep Throat, Bonnie Kassel, tells me that the new **Museu do Mamulengo** for old folk art puppets is a jewel, located at Rua do Amparo, 59.)

## Igreja da Misericórdia

Up the steep hill is this church, reconstructed in the 18th century. Between 4:30 and 5 p.m. you may be lucky enough to stumble upon the angelic all-female choir rehearsing with a nun who plays a tiny organ. The church is noted for having one of the most tasteful displays of gold in a Brazilian church; notice the Portuguese-tiled mural depicting scenes of Our Lady of Conception. The white inner door in the foyer was originally used to keep slaves from entering. Outside the church you can find some of the best lacework for sale in the Northeast, as well as a magnificent view of the shoreline.

## Museu de Arte Sacra

*Rua Bispo Coutinho, 726;* ☎ *429-0036. 9 a.m.-noon, closed Mon.*

Walking toward the seashore, you'll pass this museum that features some of the oldest examples of sacred art in the country.

## Praça da Sé

Nearby, on the Praça da Sé, you can find the lowest prices for native crafts. Sit down on the square and indulge in a *tapioca* (coconut shreds wrapped in manioc flour), a grilled wonder that needs to be washed down with a cold Coke. Ask for the vendor, Duda, who sits near the stone cross making probably hundreds of *tapiocas* a day. The *praça* is open around the clock, and it's a nice spot to come for a breakfast of *tapioca* and coffee. The church on this square, **Igreja da Sé**, is an original from 1537, though the interior has been subjected to numerous reforms throughout the centuries.

## Rua Coutinho

From the *praça*, walk down this street past the Jesuit Seminary, built in 1656; it is the highest point in Olinda. It was here that the first ideas of Brazilian independence sprang. During Carnaval, if you want to avoid the frenzied revelry, you can actually rent a room here for four days, though you must reserve a month or two in advance.

## Convento de Nossa Senhora das Neves (1585)

Turn right on Rua São Francisco to the first Franciscan church in Brazil. It remains a monastery for men, with the Sant'Ana Chapel still in use. Just don't walk around here at night because it's not safe due to the lack of traffic.

**UP CLOSE TIP:** *Shops in Olinda (at times other than Carnaval) tend to be less crowded than in Recife. For Brazilian arts and craft, try* **Mercado de Artesanato Eufrásio Barbosa,** *near the Contemporary Art Museum – a leisurely paced store with an excellent selection of Pernambucan figurines and less common local crafts. At all costs, avoid shopping at the airport, where the prices are extravagantly higher (though less than Rio's airport). Some of the best native paintings and Crafts can be found at* **Sobrado 7,** *below the Mourisco restaurant.*

## Beaches In Recife

Only a few minutes from the city's center lies Recife's principal beachhead, **Boa Viagem**, which, thankfully, remains relatively unpolluted. More than six km. (3½ miles) long, it's graced with fine white sand, leafy grass huts, and colorful *barracas*, not to mention the steady stream of activity day and night. Right offshore, hundreds of natural rock pools are formed by the craggy reefs, making them inviting coves to wade through when the tide is out. Special illumination after hours permits nighttime bathing.

Many of the best hotels are located along the beach drag, **Avenida Boa Viagem**, and you can also find quaint *pousadas* (small inns) tucked into the many side streets. Besides bathing and the occasional *jangada* ride, the main activity on the beach seems to be eating. Evidence is the perpetual parade of colorful native vendors down the strand hawking everything from fresh coconut milk to cut pineapples, boiled shrimps, beer, and *batidas*.

❖ **GETTING HERE:** *Transportation to the beach is exceedingly easy. From Avenida Dantas Barreto, you can pick up frescões (special air-conditioned buses for about 50 cents) to Boa Viagem.*

## Beaches Near Recife

Beaches north and south of Recife are considered by many to be far superior to Boa Viagem, and certainly the exotic flavor of small villages and fishing coves adds to the draw of strands that are near-deserted during the week and packed on the weekends.

The island of **Itamaracá** is the penal colony for greater Recife, a palm-covered patch of earth with a tiny village. These days it's often overrun by tourists, but if you venture forth, do check out the wonderfully weird **Porto Brasilis restaurant**, the opulent home of a funky artist named Luis Jasmin. There's a patio, a pool you can swim in, a magnificent ocean in the backyard, and a dog named Mike Tyson. After lunch, you can spend the afternoon with Luis doing nothing.

For a great view, head down the scenic coastal road PE-60 (called the *via litoral*) to **Gaibú**, about 12½ miles from Boa Viagem. Buses leave from Recife, or rent a car and driver. (Note: you may have to go to Cabu first.) But even the main highway, BR-101, will take you past silky stalks of sugarcane waving sensuously in the wind. (Frankly, either trip is a wonderful way to see rural Brazil, with its typical orange-tiled roofs and groves of coconut trees.) More like an obstacle course, the turnoff to Gaibú must be one of the worst roads in Brazil, but you'll be rewarded with a beach as deserted as you'll ever find.

## Gaibú

During the week, the craggy coastline is nearly deserted, but weekends teem with motorcycle couples who pat themselves on the back for having survived the 1½-hour trip from Recife. Because there are no reefs to cut the violent waves, be careful swimming. (Surfing, however, is great.)

## Cacheta

An even worse dirt road winds around the cliff to this spot, one of the most beautiful primitive beaches around. A rocky promontory juts out to a sea full of lobster boats and native children trying to surf on makeshift boards.

You can scamper over the rocks or get out of the shade at **Bar do Artur**. Do meet Artur, the bar's owner, a perpetually cheerful professional beach bum, who will take your photo for his "memories wall" and serve you the specialty – fried needlefish (*agulhas fritas*), though you'll need about five to fill you up. On the weekends, elite Recifenses groove on the excellent sound system, not to mention the snorkeling by moonlight.

## Porto de Galinhas

From Cabo, buses also head directly to this village, a community that's fast growing as a summer condo resort, although the sea is still full of traditional fishing and lobster boats. If you're looking for peace and quiet, go during the week; action turns steamy come weekends. At low tide, all the reefs appear and create natural pools.

At the end of the main street is **Bras Bar**, the principal hangout, where you can find excellent steel fish. A *jangada* trip out to the natural pool runs about $5 (though the boats looked dangerous to me, and if the sea is rough, you'd better be a very good swimmer). Snorkeling is also great here, though you should bring your own equipment. Most exciting is just the glorious color of the water, which changes from deep, deep blue in the winter to grayish green in the summer.

> ❖ **GETTING HERE:** *Take a bus in front of the airport to Gaibú, as well as to Porto das Galinhas about twice a day, for less than a dollar.*

Accommodations in Porto de Galinhas run from the elegant rustic charm of the Hotel Pontal de Ocaporá (see below) to seaside *pousadas*, such as Porto do Sol.

## Hotel Pontal de Ocaporá

*Access from Rod. PE-09, km. 6 (Praia do Cupe);* ☎ *678-1166, reservations in Recife:* ☎ *(81) 224-9193.*

Júlio Iglesias brought an entourage of Brazilian beauties to this picturesque villa of grass-hut chalets set on a stunning section of Porto das Galinhas. Cobblestone paths lead to tropical bungalows with verandas overlooking the sea; even the three-pool complex with its own waterfall looks out onto the ocean. All watersports equipment may be rented on premises. *Expensive. AE, DC, MC.*

## Solar Porto de Galinhas

*Reservations in Recife,* ☎ *(81) 325-0772.*

Rooms are simple but air conditioned in an attractive locale. Pool, horseback riding, and dune buggies are all available. *Inexpensive. All cards.*

## Pousada Marambi

*QD, M2, 56. (Praia de Serrambi). Reservations:* ☎ *(81) 228-4090.*

Simple inn with pool and air-conditioned rooms with fridge. Restaurant on premises. *Inexpensive. No cards.*

**UP CLOSE TIP from Mike Salvo:** *"Maracaípe is a cool surfing beach slightly south of Porto da Galinhas, with excellent waves and clear, clean water."* In fact, *Maracaípe holds Brazilian surfing competitions. In Pontal de Maracaípe, there appears at low tide a crown of rocks that stretches five km. (three miles) inside the sea. You'll find simple pousadas, bars, and locals who sell homemade sweets made of cashew. (It's best to stay in Porto de Galinas and visit.)*

## UP CLOSE ADVENTURE from Mike Salvo

"There is a great stretch of coastline to explore near the town of **Tammandare**, about 110 km. (68 miles) south of Recife, near the Alagoas border. This is dreamtime beach country, with a perfect tidal reef about a half-mile or so offshore. The fishermen do well here at low tide when the reef actually becomes exposed at some points. It's a long swim across a deep channel to the reef. If you're in the right place at the right time, you can also ride a *jangada*.

"The ocean is mostly calm here, protected by the reef at low tide. At high tide the reef becomes completely submerged and is inaccessible. It is important to get back before high tide starts really coming in because the reef becomes dangerous and the channel is more difficult to swim. The ocean and reef are crystal clear and full of wildlife. Lots of small colorful fish and black urchins. Make sure you have flippers and your feet are covered. I had to share a set of flippers with someone, one each, and it was difficult at times. In just a couple hours we saw a beautiful manta ray, some huge angel fish, a huge ray/shark-like creature and some octopi. The day before, I saw some guy skinning a huge eel he'd caught out at the reef near where we had been. My friend, who was a great fisherman, would bring home lobsters or great fish every trip. I was glad that we were swimming with my friend's speargun after I saw that eel.

"Time passes painlessly here, especially in summer, when you can live on lobster, mangoes, cashews, and coconuts. On weekends some of the towns get lively as people visit summer homes nearby, but during the week it stays pretty empty.

Another great place to snorkel is a small river that flows into the sea here; it leads back through some pretty rural country where people will be surprised to see you. If all you want to do is lie in a hammock after a swim and listen to the wind rustle through miles of coconut palms, Tammandare is ideal."

**Getting Here:** From Recife the "coastal" highway PE-060 parallells the coast (without going near it). Take the turn-off to Tamandaré on PE 076. The beach is reached by access roads, mostly dirt tracks that lead to numerous beaches and small towns. There is bus access and telephones in the town of Sirinhaem. You could probably negotiate to rent a hammock on a fisherman's porch, but there are also some simple *pousadas*.

## Excursion: Northeastern Crafts

Ninety miles west of Olinda lies one of the largest outdoor markets in northeast Brazil, in the dusty frontier town of **Caruaru**. A cheap bus ride will get you there in two rickety hours; though the market opens at 6 a.m., you won't have to fight off the crowds if you're there by 8 a.m. The best buys are Pernambucan figurines, especially the folkloric *bumba-meu-boi*, a mystical bull festooned in jewels that figures prominently in Northeastern mythology. Figurines of Brazilians at work – dentists, doctors, telephone repairmen, legendary bandits – can range from the clumsily crafted to wonders of miniature design. Look for those crafted by the artist Jandira.

For accommodations in Caruaru, the only luxury hotel in the vicinity (2½ miles from town) is the **Hotel do Sol**, corner of BR-104/Br-232; ☎ *(81) 721-3044*. Prices are low to moderate. If you prefer to stay in the city and walk to the market, the best option is the **Hotel Centenário**, Rua Sete de Setembro, 94; ☎*(81) 721-9011*.

## Where To Stay

See page 26 for price chart.

### In Recife

#### Mar Hotel

*Rua Br. de Souza Leão, 451 (Boa Viagem);* ☎ *341-5443, fax 341-7002.*

The steel-and-aluminum lobby of Recife's principal five-star ought to read "cold," but actually it's one of the most attractive foyers in Brazil. Plants and oriental rugs enliven the area that opens onto an exquisite pool complex with gushing waterfalls. The Mont Black Restaurant offers fine Swiss cuisine, and a Japanese sushi bar and coffee shop will satisfy other palates. The After Dark piano bar offers a fine view of the city, and dancing and dinner take place on the roof garden during the weekend. A teahouse serves colonial-style tea every afternoon. Deluxe rooms overlooking the pool are spacious and inviting, and the beds are probably the most comfortable in Brazil. Gal Costa graces the Presidential Suite when she's in town – a veritable wonder of stylish decor, complete with jacuzzi and sacred art sculptures. *207 apts. Expensive. All cards.*

## Recife Monte Hotel

*Rua Petrolina/ Rua dos Navegantes, 363 (Boa Viagem),*
☎ *326-7422, fax 326-2903.*

Only five minutes from the airport, this five-star doesn't match the ones in Rio, but it's an excellent choice for Recife. Antique chandeliers adorn the intimate lobby, while a fantastic aquarium perks up the restaurant serving international and Brazilian dishes. Laps can be easily negotiated in the huge pool, and a bevy of boutiques will serve all shopping needs. Standards do not differ radically from other rooms; all come with safes, color TV, mini-bar, and electronic keys. No rooms have a sea view, though some look out onto the pool. Excellent discounts are offered in low season. *173 apts. Expensive-moderate. All cards.*

## Recife Palace Lucsim

*Avenida Boa Viagem, 4070 (Boa Viagem),* ☎ *465-6688, fax 465-6767.*

The dark-speckled lobby of this five-star is ice-cold (a relief in Recife, where air conditioning is mandatory). Oriental rugs, tapestries, and a grand piano make you feel special. Standards are very large, with an extra sofa bed; only suites and super deluxes have full views. All rooms come with tubs, safes, color TVs, and electronic controls; the white marble bathrooms add a rich detail. The Savoir Faire, specializing in seafood crêpes, is one of the most sophisticated French eateries in the city, or you can choose to eat on the open-air terrace surrounding the small pool. The Happy Ending nightclub is a hot spot. Up to 30% discount in low season. *294 apts. Expensive. All cards.*

## Fator Palace Hotel

*Rua dos Navegantes, 157 (Boa Viagem),* ☎ *326-0040, fax 326-8953.*

Formerly an apart-hotel, the Fator is 800 feet from Boa Viagem Beach. Though it's rated as a four-star, the quality is more like that of a three-star. Antique wood tables and potted plants fill the lobby; live music is offered Mon.-Sat. in the pub. The small, oddly shaped pool is surrounded by high-rises, and elevators have been known to be temperamental. Standards and superiors differ only in the view; the latter comes with a balcony. Bedrooms are small, but white-and-beige decors lend lightness. Airport transfers can be arranged. *180 apts. Moderate-expensive. All cards.*

## Hotel Casa Grande & Senzala

*Avenida Conselheiro Aguiar, 5000 (Boa Viagem);* ☎ *and fax 465-2401.*

A stunning four-story colonial house with turrets and balconies, this *pousada*-like hotel offers service in the grand manner of the great sugar plantations. The wood-planked corridors gleam golden-bright under the antique illumination, and you must even use huge antique keys to enter your apartment. Old photos of Recife line the salmon-colored walls of the individual rooms decorated with colonial furniture, while greenery drips from the windows that look out onto an inner courtyard complete with an antique fountain. The suite, with an extra room, is totally charming. The elegant Mucama Restaurant is the most atmospheric in the city, with waitresses in folkloric costumes affecting obsequious airs. Fifty meters (800 feet) from the beach, the hotel can also arrange excursions, and clients have use-privilege at the Caxangá Golf Club. *50 apts. Expensive. All cards.*

## Hotel Praiamar

*Avenida Boa Viagem, 1660 (Boa Viagem);* ☎ *326-6905.*

Across the street from the beach, this tiny hotel has the charm of an *albergue* (inn). Antique ceiling lamps hang in the corridors of this former farmhouse; breakfast is eaten in a simple but friendly salon with antique grilled windows. The best room is #101, with an original wood-carved closet, sunken tub, and shower. Rooms are air conditioned; safes at the reception. The pool is the smallest I have ever seen. *14 apts. Inexpensive. All cards.*

## São Francisco Hotel de Campo

*Estrada da Aldeia;* ☎ *459-1306, fax 231-5487.*

More modern than the usual *pousada*, this is one of the best deals in the city, and only a 330-foot walk to the beach. Rooms are small but cheerfully decorated with native prints and woven bedspreads. Superior and deluxe rooms have verandas to the sea, and all rooms come with air conditioning, phone, and mini-bar; safes are at the reception. The two parts of the hotel are connected by a grass-roofed corridor. Across the street is one of the most beautiful colonial homes in Recife – now a psychiatric hospital. *32 apts. Inexpensive. All cards.*

## In Olinda

## Amoaras

*Rua Garoupa, 5525 (Praia do Pontal de Marinha Farina); 20 km.;*
☎ *436-1331, fax 435-1880.*

Very comfortable resort right on the beach. Full beachside facilities available, from jetskiing to diving. Bar, three restaurants, and pool round out the services. *77 apts. Expensive. All cards.*

## Pousada dos Quatro Cantos

*Rua Prudente de Moraes, 441;* ☎ *429-0220; fax 429-1845.*

Funky on the verge of seedy – but a favorite among adventurers – this budget *pousada* is located on one of the prettiest streets of colonial Olinda; during Carnaval, the best folkloric groups meet at the corner, an impressive sight you can enjoy from the grand colonial veranda. Once a fabulous mansion of interlocking balconies and balustrades, the *pousada* dates back to the beginning of the century; today it's only 10 minutes from Pau Amarelo Beach. Religious art peps up the wood-floor apartments;

bathrooms are as simple as they come. Some rooms have air conditioning; the lowest priced rooms have only a fan and share a bathroom; all rooms have color TV and phone. Safes at the reception. For Carnaval stays, you must reserve months in advance. *15 apts. Inexpensive. No cards.*

## Where To Eat

### In Recife

#### Marruá II

*Rua Ernesto de Paula Santos, 183 (Boa Viagem);* ☎ *325-1970. 11:30 a.m.-1 a.m.*

The closest translation I found for *marruá* is "cowpoke" – the guy who throws the lasso around the calf. An oddly suitable name for this pristine *churrascaria*, where the walls are so white you'll want to throw paint on them. Elegant service and superb steaks. Located in the convention center. *Moderate. All cards.*

#### Mucama

*Casa Grande Hotel, Avenida Conselheiro Aguiar, 5000;* ☎ *341-0366. Noon-3 p.m., 7 p.m.-midnight.*

The moment you sit down at this gorgeous colonial-style restaurant, a white-turbaned waitress arrives with a silver pitcher and bowl for washing your hands. Candlelight softly illuminates the Art Deco walls full of antique porcelain plates. When excellent live jazz isn't playing, a sophisticated hush prevails. The menu, developed by an Italian-trained chef, is highly imaginative, featuring native fish, such as *tainha* and *suburim*, as well as *filé colosso* (steak with caviar and salmon). The tasty *camarão na forca* is grilled shrimp skewered to a guillotine-like structure and flanked by pineapple chunks. Even more exquisite than the food is the graceful service, though the obsequious attention may make you feel like a plantation owner. *Expensive. All cards.*

#### Buongustaio

*Rua Sto. Elias, 350 (Espinheiro);* ☎ *241-1470. 7 p.m.-1 a.m., closed Sun.*

You may have to wait for a seat, but the cuisine is usually worth it. Homemade pastas filled with pâté and grilled steak with camembert sauce are winners. *Moderate. All cards.*

#### Porcão

*Rua Eng. Domingos Ferreira, 4215 (Boa Viagem),* ☎ *465-3999. 11:30-12:30 a.m.*

Marble floors and long tables for groups are available at this fine *churrascaria*, with a salad bar that will please any vegetarian. Children under five eat for nothing; ages 5-10 pay half. Live music. *Moderate. All cards.*

## Spettus

*Av. Agamemnon Magalhães, 2132 (Derby);* ☎ *221-3060. 11:30 a.m.-1:30 a.m.*

Excellent *rodízio* with 16 types of meat, plus 10 different vegetables and complements. The gigantic self-serve salad bar is included in the price, about $10. Live music at lunch and dinner. *Moderate. All cards.*

## Restaurante Danado de Bom

*Rua Dom José Lopes, 64 (Boa Viagem);* ☎ *326-5636.*

This tin-roofed, open-air eatery offers some of Recife's finest local cuisines. Waitresses are adorable in their khaki shorts and gun belts, dressed as *cangaceiras* – bandits who were troopers under the legendary highway robber Lampião. Order lots of different small portions here, like *mandioca* with *charque* (dried meat), *arrumadinho* (with shreds of beef with onions, tomatoes and parsley), *ovo de codornas* (tiny eggs of a tiny bird), *sarapatel* (interior pig organs boiled in its own blood), and *peixe frito* (fried fish). An excellent seafood plate is the *marinhada* (with shrimp, lobster, oysters, mussels, and rice). *Inexpensive-moderate. No cards.*

## Da Mira

*Av. Dr. Eurico Chaves, 918 (antigo Beco do Quiabo, Casa Amarela);*
☎ *268-6241. 11 a.m.-4 p.m., 7 p.m.-midnight, Sat.& Sun. 11 a.m.-6 p.m.*

Dona Mira and her sons serve regional delicacies in the rooms of their own simple home. Authentic and memorable. *Inexpensive.*

# In Olinda

## L'Atelier

*Rua Bernardo Vieira de Melo, 91 (Ribeira),* ☎ *429-3099. 7-11:30 p.m., closed Sun.*

Swiss owner Michel Barbault salvaged this abandoned Dutch-style mansion and transformed it into one of Olinda's most atmospheric eateries. Sit on the porch overlooking the city of Recife for an aperitif, then head for one of several small salons to indulge in a multinational menu featuring steak au poivre, duck pâté, lobster, and chicken in red wine sauce. The owner and his partner sell the avant-garde tapestries on the walls. Reservations should be made during high season. The restaurant is just one block from the principal corner of Carnaval. *Moderate-expensive. All cards.*

## Mourisco

*Praça Cons. João Alfredo, 7 (Carmo);* ☎ *429-1390. Noon-3 p.m., 7-11 p.m., closed Mon.*

Live music and fresh fish. *Moderate. MC, V.*

## Officina do Sabor

*Rua do Amparo, 335 (Amparo);* ☎ *429-33331. Noon-4 p.m., 7-11 p.m.;*
*Sun. noon-5 p.m.; closed Mon.*

Regional cuisine prepared with creativity and respect for fresh products. Try the *camarão ao coco* (shrimp in coconut). *Inexpensive-moderate. All cards.*

# Nightlife

## In Recife

Weekends start on Thurs. in Recife. Lots of activity happens around the numerous outdoor bars in the **Pátio de São Pedro**, especially on the weekends, when excellent live bands and folkloric dance troupes perform. One of the most romantic spots in the city, **Som das Aguas**, in the Graças district, features *lambada* and *forró* Wed.-Sat. Eat typical Northeastern food under straw roofs or smooch in near-total darkness under a palm tree while the neon-lit dance floor rocks. A small cover charge after 9 p.m.

## In Olinda

The **Alto da Sé** teems with activity 24 hours a day, especially on weekend nights. A mishmash of dance music, from *frevo* and *merengue* to samba and *forró*, breaks out every Fri. and Sat. night around 11 p.m. at the **Clube Atlântico**, on the Praça do Carmo. (Look for the sign showing a couple dancing on a crescent moon.)

# Shopping

### Casa da Cultura

*Rua Floriano Peixoto. Mon.-Sat. 9 a.m.-8 p.m., Sun. 3-8 p.m.*

Constructed in the 19th century, this former prison was transformed into an arts and crafts market in 1975, now replete with art galleries, artisanry stores, museums, theaters, bars, and snack counters.

### Shopping Center Recife

*10 a.m.-10 p.m.*

This modern two-floor mall is adorned with waterfalls, marble floors, and a select variety of stores. The all-purpose C&A department store predominates; there's also a food village on the second floor.

### Fundação de Cultura da Cidade de Recife

*Pátio de São Pedro, 10.*

The Cultural Foundation of Recife, where you may buy popular records and Portuguese books. Free folkloric dances are held here at 8 p.m. every Fri. Upstairs you can ask for a tourist map.

# Hands-On Recife & Olinda

## Arrival

Recife is reachable **by air** from many Brazilian cities, either direct or through connections. Recife can also be reached direct from Miami and Buenos Aires (Air France flies to Paris). **Varig Airlines** usually offers the best schedule for traveling. Otherwise, you may end up flying in the middle of the night.

The **international airport**, Aeroporto Internacional dos Guararapes, Praça Min. Salgado F; ☎ 341-6090, is located in Imbiribeira, 11 km. (6.8 miles) from downtown. Taxis to downtown cost about $15; tourist taxis are about twice as much as ordinary red taxis. There's also an airport bus that takes about an hour.

If you're arriving in Recife **by bus**, you'll find the *rodoviária* (bus station) seemingly in the middle of nowhere, but an underground rail (the **metro**) will whisk you to the **Estação Central** in the center of the city. The hotel district is a short cab ride away.

## Airlines Flying To Recife

**Varig/Cruziero**
Avenida Guararapes, 110 . . . . . . . . . . . . . . . . . . . . ☎ 341-4411
**VASP** now flies Miami-Recife direct.
Avenida Manoel Borba, 488 . . . . . . . . . . . . . . . . ☎ 326-1699
**Transbrasil**
Avenida Conde da Boa Vista, 1546 . . . . . . . . . . . ☎ 231-0522

## City Transportation

### Buses

**Santa Rita Bus Terminal,** Cais de Santa Rita (São José); ☎ 224-5499. Located just over a half-mile from downtown, the main bus terminal offers information centers and luggage storage on the ground floor. Other buses originate on Santo Antônio in Pracinha and along Avenida Guararapes. Buses tend to be crowded and hot. Air-conditioned buses *(frescões)* that run along the Boa Viagem Beach are a little more expensive it, but worth it.

### Taxis

Try **Coopertáxi (radio),** ☎ 224-8441, or **Coopseta (airport),** ☎ 325-5999.

## Car Rental

Cars may be rented at the airport.
  **Avis** . . . . . . . . . . . . . . . . . . . . . . . . . . . . . . . . . . . . . ☎ 341-2542
  **Hertz** . . . . . . . . . . . . . . . . . . . . . . . . . . . . . . . . . . . . ☎ 461-1222

## Climate

Summertime reigns mostly year-round in Recife, with temperatures averaging 72-85°F in Jan., 68-79°F in July.

## Consulates

USA . . . . . . . . . . . . . . . . . . . . . . . . . . . . . . . . . . . . . . . ☎ 421-2441
Great Britain . . . . . . . . . . . . . . . . . . . . . . . . . . . . . . . ☎ 326-3733

## Money Exchange

**Banco do Comércio**
Rua Matias de Albuquerque.
**Lloyds**
Rua do Fogo, 22.

## Tourist Information

Official state tourist posts for **EMPETUR** are located at the **airport** (24 hours), at the main **bus station** (7 a.m.-9 p.m.) and at the **Casa da Cultura** (Mon.-Sat. 9 a.m.-8 p.m., Sun. 3-8 p.m.). The **municipal tourist office** is at Store #10, in the Pátio de São Pedro. Ask for a copy of the *Historical Circuit of the City of Recife*, with an excellent map and tons of facts in English. Also, pick up the small brochure called *Viva Olinda*, which can give you some facts about the historical city.

## Travel Agencies

**Frevo**
Rua Ant. Gomes de Freitas, 131 (Ilha do Leite) . . ☎ 222-3127

## When To Visit

**Carnaval** explodes in typical Northeastern fashion in Feb. Don't miss **Easter**, when the Passion is reenacted at Nova Jerusalém, a city theater surrounded by wooden walls, where 500 actors in 12 plays reenact Christ's Passion on a mobile stage. *Forró* music is featured during **festivals in June**, along with typical foods such as corn. In July, **"Vaqueiro" worship**, promoting the Northeastern cowboy culture, is celebrated. Aug. has been dubbed **Folklore Month**, featuring native dances, expositions, ceramics, and poetry festivals. The **Festival of Iemenjá**, with a boat parade and typical foods, takes place the first week of Dec.

# Natal

For the last four years, Natal, the capital of **Rio Grande do Norte**, has replaced Salvador and Maceió as the hot-spot resort of the Northeast. Despite years of drought and poverty, the city of more than 500,000 inhabitants is now attracting even São Paulo businessmen, who are envisioning a future for the region, one full of exceedingly exotic sand dunes that some say were the inspiration for Antoine de Saint Exupéry's *The Little Prince*. Until 1983, the main beach drag, **Via Costeira**, was virtually empty; today it is the main tourist strip, with immense white sand dunes lining one side and modern hotels on the other. Despite its modernity, Natal still boasts beaches of pristine beauty, particularly those to the north and south of the city.

## History

Thousands of years ago, Natal was just water and sand. As the African wind, called *vento alisios*, swept through the region, dunes were created and vegetation blew in from the sea. Consequently, *falesias* were formed, those mountainous red-colored cliffs that provide the craggy vistas overlooking the shore. Presently Natal and its surrounding beaches offer over 4,000 acres of dunes, the inspiration for breathtaking, dune-buggy adventures that are more exciting than roller coasters. Botanists have also identified over 350 kinds of vegetation, mostly *catinga* – forests of knotted dwarf trees and stunted bushes that support the structure of the dunes. Once Natal's largest dune, **Morro da Careca** (or Bald Hill, so named because it didn't have any vegetation) has sadly been degraded by teenagers' dunesliding down the slopes; today the sport has been prohibited by law.

Located on the easternmost tip of the South American continent, Natal was founded on Christmas Day, 1599, by the Portuguese, who had to wrestle it first from the Potangi Indians and later from the Dutch who had arrived in search of brazilwood. During World War II, Natal became known as the "Trampolim da Vitória" because American soldiers used the area to depressurize before going home. (The city was the site of the largest US Air Force base outside its own territories.) Later, the Kennedys also came into vogue. Downtown, a bust of JFK is accompanied by one of his quotes that still speaks so poignantly to Brazil: "If a free society cannot help the many who are poor, it will not be able to save the few who are rich."

## A Bird's Eye View

The treasures in Natal are the sun and surf, and there is little of historical value left in the 400-year-old city. A good place to grasp the expanse of the city's beaches is atop the **Mãe Luiza Lighthouse**, where you can see **Praia do Forte**, **Praia dos Artistas**, and **Praia do Meio**, as well as the rocky vista of **Praia da Areia Preta**. Dominating the entrance of the Rio Potengi, on whose banks Natal is situated, is the **Forte dos Reis Magos** (Tues.-Sun. 8 a.m.-noon and 2-5 p.m.), founded in 1598 as a defense against marauding invaders. In the Cidade Alta, little remains of colonial times except for the small alleyways and squares, but of some interest is the 18th-century **Igreja de Santo Antônio**. (The bronze cock perched on the church's Moorish tower makes an ironic statement about the patron saint of marriage.) An obligatory stop for newcomers is the **Centro de Turismo,** housed in the old prison and now an enclave of artisan stores.

# Beaches in Natal

Natal's fine beaches begin in the city and extend north and south hundreds of kilometers. Even on rainy days, the windswept waves crashing against the reefs make for dramatic vistas. **Natural reefs**, which begin in front of the Othon Hotel, can be seen at low tide, but never swim beyond the second reef, as the open sea can often turn violent.

### Praia dos Artistas

One of the first beaches developed in the city was the site of bohemian activity during the 1960s. Today, the water is polluted, but surfers still enjoy the high waves, and a large crafts fair is held there from 4-10 p.m., daily.

### Praia do Forte

Six km. from downtown, this is the best beach for bathing, surrounded by voluptuous dunes and protected by reefs that form natural pools. The city's fortress is also here.

### Praia do Meio

Between Praia dos Artistas and Praia do Forte, this beach is also protected by natural reefs and boasts a vital infrastructure for leisure. Grass-hut kiosks line the strand, and on New Year's Eve a huge festival of *candomblé* is held around the sculpture of Iemenjá, created by Natal artist Jordão Arimatéia in 1985.

### Praia Areia Preta

On the far side of Praia do Meio, this beach is known for the black rocks that form provocative grottoes and caves. A more residential area, the beach houses numerous bars serving excellent *coquetel de fruta* (fruit cocktail) and *caipirinha.*

### Praia de Ponta Negra

The "in" beach lately is 8½ miles from downtown on the southernmost strand within the city limits. Considered one of the Northeast's most beautiful, this stretch features a small bay surrounded by tall dunes and palm trees. *Luaus* at full moon are great fun, illuminated by bonfires and serenaded by improvising guitarists. Down the strand, nightclubs, bars, and restaurants keep the action tight. On Sun., the streets are packed with young beautiful kids hanging out on their cars. Surfing is best near the Morro da Careca.

# Beaches Near Natal

## South

The best way to scope out the beaches south of the city is by boat. **Schooner trips** leave twice a day in high season near the dock at Cotovelo Beach. Sailing north, you will pass **Barreira do Inferno** (site of a rocket base), **Pirangi do Norte** (home to high-powered politicos), **Praia Pirangi do Sul** (a tiny fishing village), and the sophisticated condos of **Búzios**. Most schooner trips stop at a natural pool, where bathers can jump off and swim to a rocky outcropping in the middle of the ocean. Due to the high winds of Natal, these trips can be a little *lambada*-like, with the waves as big and curvaceous as the dunes. (For schooner information, contact **Marina Badauê**, ☎ 238-2066.)

### Cotovelo Restaurante

*Praia de Pirangi;* ☎ 237-2020. 10 a.m.-5 p.m.

Before or after your schooner trip, stop here for excellent *carne de sol* and grilled lobster. Wadeh Faraj, the hearty Lebanese owner, says he started this open-air restaurant – considered one of the most exotic in the Northeast – as a joke; he just wanted a place to drink with his friends. Today, the locale looks through a forest of palm trees onto a glorious ocean vista, where huge black boulders only add to the beauty. Senhor Wadeh is also building a series of chalets next to the restaurant (some with complete kitchens) that should prove paradisiacal accommodations – especially for families. You'll only need to scramble down a stone stairway or over the rocky cliff to the beach. A bus that stops at the restaurant transports guests to the marina, where you can catch an outgoing schooner.

### Further Exploration

Don't miss the **"Largest Cashew in the World!"** in the villa of **Pirango do Norte**. The grove is a delicious spot to come after the beach – a mysterious secret garden of trees growing in the sand. On the ground, the grove's gnarly roots spread out like scary tentacles; up above, the branches have become interlocked into a leafy arbor that whistles in the wind and makes leaf-like shadows on the sand below. The "world's largest cashew tree" is *definitely big*, and information concerning its history can be found in the adjacent artisanry shop, where you can also see women making traditional lace. The amusing double-entendre signs adorning the grove have all been posted by the Tahiti Motel (an hourly hideaway for lovers), imploring you not to violate the trees by touching or walking over the roots. Down the road a fantastic view shows you in contrasting colors where the Rio Pirongi and the Atlantic Ocean meet.

## North

### Genipabú

With access through RN 160, Genipabú is 22 miles from downtown, a pit stop for most dune buggy tours. Down the glorious (but these days, crowded) beach, you can either ride horseback, take a *jangada* trip on a flat-bottom boat, or rest in the shade of an open-air restaurant.

### Tabatinga

Three miles north lies Tabatinga, reportedly full of jumping porpoises (though I didn't see a one), where you can stop for a drink on a cliff overlooking a magnificent dune-swept beach. The best time to visit this *mirante* (lookout point) is at full moon, when the sea turns silvery and the grass-hut bars surrounded by coconut trees seem even more romantic. You'll find the **Mirante Turístico Bar** near the sign "Vista Panorâmica dos Golfinhos."

## A DUNE BUGGY ADVENTURE from the author

It's a cool windy day in Natal, and at the wheel of our four-wheel-drive jeep is dune buggy owner Zenilda Pinheiro, the kind of bronzed, muscular, long-legged gal who wouldn't flinch on a bucking bronco. Zenilda can read the dunes of Natal like the curves of her husband's back, both of them long-time pros who know that the slope and texture of the dunes can shift in an instant. If you want an adventure to remember (and one you'll survive), you need experts like the Pinheiros.

The trip starts sane enough, then slowly gains in momentum.

With the wind slicing our faces, we head out of Natal on the highway, crossing the Rio Potengi, bordered by a massive grove of *mangué*, a tropical ecosystem of tall trees rooted in water and chock full of crabs. The river from whose banks you can see the lights of Natal is itself a natural breeding ground for shrimp. (*Potengi* is Tupí-Guarani dialect for shrimp.) Though we're still within the city limits, we begin to pass traditional houses – pastel-colored shacks with orange-tiled roofs. After 10 minutes the famous dunes appear in the distance, voluptuous silver-gray mounds that seem almost ghost-like. Passing through the village of Santa Rita on Genipabú Beach, we watch fishermen cast their lines from rocky cliffs. Zenilda races the buggy near the edge of the shoreline, and as we lean out of the windows, we all get drenched.

At Genipabú Beach we pile out for a quick *água-de-coco* under the shade of the bar. From a native boy I rent a frisky horse and trot down the shoreline, barely staying upright when dune buggies full of drunken beachcombers zoom past me in the opposite direction. A braying burro plops in my path and I swerve to avoid hitting him. Passing up a ride on a *jangada*, we jump back in the jeep for the real rollercoaster ride. Zenilda gives us two choices: *emocional* or *calma* – referring to the level of thrill our stomachs can take. My friends, all locals, argue for calm. We agree on medium.

Zenilda heads for the dunes outside Genipabú, and suddenly we feel as though we're gliding on snow. In a minute, what had seemed like a straight plane quickly turns sideways as Zenilda tilts the buggy left, then right, jumping off cliffs, spiraling up and down the mounds. Screaming, we cling to the bars of the jeep as sand fills our hair, our eyes – and especially our mouths. Suddenly a lone native man appears like a mirage, holding a lassoed burro. For a buck, I ride the critter around for a few minutes. (Take care mounting – it's surprisingly easy to barrel over the ears of a burro.) After contemplating the crystal-blue lakes in the valley below, we climb back in the jeep as Zenilda steels her hands on the wheel for one last sensational dive – horizontally down a dune. Luckily, I'm seated in the front; my companions in the back look dazed.

Our final stop is Redinha Beach, from where we can see the port and the old fort from a bank of the Potengi River. Less sensational than Genipabú, Redinha has nevertheless retained the charm of its quaint village life – an atmospheric destination for the urban crowds that pile in on the weekends. Before we take shelter under the roof of O Pedro, an open-air eatery, we make a stop at the tiny local church to say a few thanks for surviving. Then we settle down to enormous plates of *camarões na casca* (garlicky shrimps encased in their shells) and tall, cold glasses of *chopp*. The only thing left to do after celebrating is wash the sand off from every part of our bodies. Luckily, the ocean is a mere step away.

**UP CLOSE TIP:** *The sun in Natal is fierce, and exposure in a dune buggy is maximal. Make sure you generously douse yourself with sunscreen, and you should consider taking a hat that ties under your chin. Cover-ups that you can easily tie around your waist would be helpful. On these cliff-hanging trips, be careful that your camera equipment or wallet doesn't fall out of the buggy.*

## Where To Stay

Most of Natal's best hotels are on the **Via Costeira**; if you don't have a car, you'll have to take a bus or cab to the main beaches. (The beaches along the hotel strip are too rocky to be safe for swimming.) Accommodations run from exceedingly comfortable resorts to less imaginative, but moderately priced hotels. The most atmospheric properties are outside the city – in *pousada*-like digs that give you the best feel of tropical living. See page 26 for price chart.

### Hotel Parque òa Costeira

*Via Costeira, km. 7 (Mãe Luísa Beach);* ☎ *222-6147, fax 222-1459.*

From the street, the Parque da Costeira looks like a module from Venus. Inside, the white curvaceous columns separating the rooms more resemble the resorts on the Greek island of Mykonos. The pool area is the most spectacular in the city – with two saltwater pools and a double slide kids will adore. Even the tanning area is split into three sprawling levels that wrap around the hotel. Wicker furniture enlivens the fully air-conditioned rooms, all of which have a fabulous view of the pool and the crashing sea. The owner, from São Paulo, attends constantly to creative details, especially at the indoor and outdoor restaurants, both of which offer fine cuisine. Keeping the feel of a beach resort, the hotel has no elevator for its three floors. If you pay in cash during low season, you might receive a 30% discount. *96 apts. Expensive. All cards.*

### Vila òo Mar

*Via Costeira, 4233;* ☎ *221-6000, fax 221-6017.*

Owned by the Secretary of Industry and Commerce, the Vila do Mar on Barreira d'Agua Beach is one of Natal's finest resort hotels, gracefully integrating the natural resources of stone, wood, and plant life with the dunes and sea that surround it. Just walking to your room is a tropical adventure, past artificial lakes brimming with flowers. The simple, but stylish apartments have sitting verandas with spectacular views. The Tuaçu restaurant is an elegant dining room in pastel oranges and pinks, and the breakfast buffet is one of the best spreads in Natal – the freshly fried tapioca pancake shouldn't be missed. The large pool and children's pool, surrounded by coconut trees, provide ample space for tanning. A hair salon, sauna, masseur, tennis courts, and travel agency are also on premises. *210 apts. Expensive. AE, V.*

### Marsol Natal

*Via Costeira, 1567 (Parque das Dunas);* ☎ *221-2619.*

High wood-beam ceilings and traditional tile roofs make this two-floor hotel a model of tropical comfort. A good-sized pool with a children's pool is surrounded by lush vegetation, with grass-hut umbrellas for shade. Standards with stone floors are extremely small, with bathrooms barely big enough for essentials. Considerably more spacious, the deluxes, with brown tile floors and wood carvings, are attractive; you can even sleep in a hammock on the veranda. Luxurious suites, with a couch bed in the living room, are tailored for families. An arched-roof structure that takes advantage of the city's strong breezes houses a multipurpose game room; there's also a playground. The restaurant is well known for its local foods, such as *carne de sol* and *galinha à cabidela* (stewed giblets). A veranda inside the grass-roofed bar offers an excellent view of the pool and the ocean. Children up to age five stay free. *90 apts. Moderate. AE.*

## Natal Mar

*Via Costeira, 8101 (Ponta Negra);* ☎ *219-2121, fax 219-3131.*

The first hotel to be built on the Via Costeira (1984), the Natal Mar exudes a friendly seaside ambiance; you'll feel totally surrounded by dunes and sea. Deluxes look out onto the ocean, but standards have verandas that give a spectacular view of the sand dunes, especially at sunset. All apartments are air conditioned, and come with color TV, two wicker chairs, and mini-bar. There is no elevator. A bar inside the circular pool, where you can sip tropical drinks, helps relieve the heat; you can also shade yourself under the grass-roofed umbrellas. The restaurant serves all three meals. Two boutiques, a playroom with pool, and a sauna complete the services. *176 apts. Moderate. All cards.*

## Barreira Roxa Praia Hotel

*Via Costeira, km. 5 (Mãe Luîsa); fax and* ☎ *222-1093.*

Once the governor's house, the Barreira Roxa Praia was later transformed into a school of tourism, but now functions solely as a private hotel. All 42 air-conditioned apartments are enormous, slightly resembling college dorm rooms, with little decoration. They feature color TV, mini-bar, and video; safes at the reception. All beds are singles and must be put together to make a double. The restaurant, integrated into the two-story lobby under high-beamed ceilings, looks inviting. The pool has a sunny disposition. *42 apts. Moderate. AE, MC.*

## Praia Center Hotel

*Rua Fabricio Pedrosa, 45 (Praia dos Artistas);* ☎ *211-6764, fax 211-4580.*

Two years old, this hotel is centrally located, near Praia dos Artistas. Breakfast is taken downstairs in a cove-shaped salon overlooking the pool. Air conditioning is cold, and rooms are on the smallish side. Suites are the best deal with two rooms and extra space. *35 apts. Moderate. AE, MC.*

## Serra do Mar

*Av. Hermes da Fonseca, 1329 (Tirol);* ☎ *222-4498.*

A large house adapted into a *pousada*, with nine apartments in good condition. It's located about three km. (1.8 miles) from the beach. *Inexpensive. No cards.*

## Pousada Ponta Negra

*Rua Dr. Raimundo Fonseca, 2277;* ☎ *236-3317.*

For budget travelers: large apartments, rustically appointed, with a pool on premises. About 800 feet from the beach. *Inexpensive. No cards.*

## Outside The City

### Pousada Villa do Sol

*Loteamento Tabu, QD 9 (Genipabú);* ☎ *225-2132; fax 225-2037.*

Owned by a young American named Ron whose hippie parents moved to Brazil in the 1950s, this moon-shaped *pousada* is on Rio Ceara Mim, where the river meets the sea. Entranced by the unusual ecological conditions, beachcombers love to walk here because there is no pollution and you can even catch crabs by hand in the nearby *mangue* (mangrove swamp).

The 15 basic apartments are fan-cooled, with tile floors and private baths; the daily rate includes breakfast. Restaurants are about a half-mile away at Genipabú Beach, or the *pousada* will transport you to Genipabú Hotel for a fine dinner. A lot of employees from the American Embassy in Brasília come here in July, but most guests are Brazilians. *Inexpensive. AE.*

### Genipabú

*Highway to Genipabú;* ☎ *225-2072, fax 231-4602.*

Two km. from the center of the village of Genipabú, this hotel is a fabulous option for families or anyone in search of tropical tranquility. Situated on a hill surrounded by dunes and groves of trees, the hotel is more like an upper-class *pousada*, dominated by an Olympic-sized pool shaded by grass umbrellas. Apartments, complete with verandas, are either spacious doubles or duplexes with three beds in the lower level. The chic native style is carried through the lounge and restaurant, with its wicker furniture, woven rugs, and folkloric paintings. Nearby, beaches may be reached with the help of the hotel's jeep, or you may roam the countryside on horseback. The Brazilian-Japanese owner, who speaks English, and her French husband lend their charming personalities to the homey ambiance and will fill any reasonable requests. Buses leave for downtown every hour, and free airport transfers are provided. *24 apts. Moderate-inexpensive. All cards.*

# Where To Eat

Natal is not particularly noted for outstanding cuisine. Due to electrical problems, food is often served lukewarm, and meat, if ordered rare, nearly always arrives "medium." Fish in this seaside town is your best bet, but excellent *carne de sol* (dried salted meat typical of the Northeast) can be found at the restaurant aptly named **Carne de Sol**. See page 26 for price chart.

### Camarões Restaurant

*Avenida Eng. Roberto Freire, 2610 (Ponta Negra);* ☎ *219-2424. 11:30 a.m.-4 p.m., 6 p.m.-midnight; Sun., 11:30 a.m.-5 p.m.*

Sit on the veranda overlooking Ponta Negra Beach or inside this fan-cooled restaurant with white brick walls and a few greens to offset the red tablecloths. The specialty is shrimp – 15 kinds – from *gratinado* (broiled under fire) to *empanado* (fried with flour). Try *camarões ao champagne,* flambéed with champagne, or the *camarão sertanejo,* sauteed with herbs and *nata do sertão,* a locally made butter. As with most restaurants in Natal, dessert concludes with Italian ice cream concoctions. *Moderate. AE, V.*

## Xique Xique

*Avenida Afonso Pena, 444 (Petrópolis); ☎ 222-4426.*
*11 a.m.-4 p.m. and 6 p.m.-1 a.m., closed Sun.*

Would-be plantation owners will love this white colonial house with its calm, sophisticated ambiance and top-class service. The folk paintings of Nilton Navarro make a fine setting for such seaside delicacies as *delícias do mar,* a delicate broth of lobster, fish, and shrimp. *Risoto de polvo* (with octopus) is excellent as is the lobster thermidor (even if the menu's pidgin English translates it as "with ketchup"). Entrées also include chicken and pasta. *Moderate. All cards.*

## Marenosso

*Rua Aderbal de Figueiredo (Centro de Turismo) (Petrópolis); ☎ 221-4022. Mon.-Sat.*
*11 a.m.-7 p.m., Fri. 11 a.m.-11 p.m.*

Located in the Centro de Turismo (the arts and crafts market), this restaurant opens its traditional green-shuttered windows to the sea, with golden corn fields waving in the foreground. Regional food, such as *carne de sol, paçoca* (a dish made of meat with manioc meal), and *galinha ao molho pardo* (chicken cooked in its own blood) are specialties. Every Thurs. night, a *forró* dance with big band kicks in from 10 p.m.-2:30 a.m. In high season, folkloric dances are held every afternoon at 3:30 p.m. and at night in the inner courtyard. Taxis are usually waiting outside the market. *Moderate. All cards.*

## Chaplin

*Avenida Pres. Café Filho, 27 (Praia dos Artistas); ☎ 211-4253. 5:30 p.m.-3 a.m.;*
*Sun. 11 a.m.-midnight.*

Dedicated to Chaplin memorabilia, this restaurant overlooking Artist's Beach is as elegant as Natal gets; in fact, anyone who's anyone comes for Happy Hour. The air-conditioned dining room upstairs serves an international menu, specializing in shrimp à Greta Garbo flambéed in a salmon bisque. You can also sit outside on the windy veranda for beer and hors d'oeuvres. *Moderate. All cards.*

## Calamari

*Rua Dr. José Augusto Medeiros, 2; ☎ 222-8148. 11 a.m.-2 a.m., Sun. 11 a.m.-5 p.m.*

There is room to dance at this informal open-air eatery with live music Sun. afternoon and Tues. and Sat. nights. The house shrimp is cooked empanada-style, with feta cheese purée and rice. The location on Artist's Beach is central, in the area of Rua Governador Silva Pedrosa. *Moderate. No cards.*

### Nemésio

*Rua Rodrigues Alves, 546 (Petrópolis);* ☎ *222-4658. Noon-4 p.m., 6 p.m.-midnight.*

The only place that serves codfish in Natal, this wood-beamed restaurant with rustic chandeliers offers Spanish-flavored cuisine at moderate prices. Sangria arrives in large jars, a mixture of chilled red wine and tropical fruits. Spanish paella for two is extremely good, as is the *pupurry marinho*, a potpourri of fish, lobster, and oysters. A grand piano provides music nightly. *Moderate. All cards.*

### Italia '90

*Praia dos Artistas.*

The waiters are young and flirty at this beachside, all-you-can-eat pizza and pastaria, with posters of a sobbing Sophia Loren on the walls. Simple chairs and wood tables; the only thing missing is a real view. Afterwards, walk catty-corner to **Gelare**, Ave. Gov. Silvio Pedroza, 134, an Italian ice cream parlor with 31 types of sundaes, including one with champagne. *Inexpensive. No cards.*

### Carne de Sol

*Rua Dionisio Filgueira, 799;* ☎ *222-9627. 6 p.m.-last client, weekends 10 a.m.-4 a.m.*

Walking distance from Praia dos Artistas, this stone-floor, open-air restaurant has a *piaçava* – a typical straw roof made from palm trees. The menu is nearly unilateral – *carne de sol* and *frango de sol* – but famous citywide. The meats are salted and left to dry for a week, then grilled with *manteiga da terra*, a cholesterol-laden butter that is addictive. One portion, big enough for two, comes with French fries. The house style here is to stuff the *carne de sol* with cheese, which makes it exceedingly tasty. *Inexpensive. All cards.*

### Tábua de Carne

*Av. Gov. Silvio Pedrosa, 54 (Praia da Areaia Preta);* ☎ *211-6920.*

Generous portions for reasonable prices right in front of the sea. Specialties include *carne de sol* and chicken. *Inexpensive. All cards.*

### A Macrobiótica

*Rua Princesa Isabel, 524 (Centro);* ☎ *222-6765. 11 a.m.-2 p.m.*

Self-service macrobiotic regime for lunch only. *Inexpensive. No cards.*

# Nightlife

### Natal Othon Hotel

*Avenida Presidente Café Filho, 822;* ☎ *222-2140. Thurs.-Sat. 11 p.m.-4 a.m.*

The best nightclub in town.

### Mandacaru

*Avenida do Jiqui, 201 (Neópolis);* ☎ *217-3008.*

The most popular dance hall for *lambada* can be found across from the Shopping Center Cidade Jardim. A one-hour folkloric show features young sexy dancers who actually look as if they're having a good time. Order wine, drinks, and hors d'oeuvres before you're pulled up to dance. Weekends are crowded, maybe because of the neon "Love Motel" sign that blinks in the background.

### Casa da Música Popular Brasileira

*Rua 25 de Dezembro (Praia do Meio);* ☎ *222-6277. Fri. and Sat. 9 p.m.-4 a.m.*

To dance *forró*, the native dance of the Northeast, head for this spot.

# Shopping

### Centro de Turismo do Natal

*Rua Aderbal de Figueiredo, 1976.*

Housed in the antiquated house of detention, the center now encloses the city's major arts and crafts enclave. Most of the small stores (housed in the original cellblocks) accept credit cards, though you're better off paying in cash. Traditional buys include wicker baskets and hats made out of *palha* (straw), as well as *feijoada* earthenware. *Nas coxinhas* – small phallic symbols made out of clay – are hot items here, as are tiny bottles of *cachaça* with pornographic labels. In the art gallery upstairs, antique sculptures of Catholic saints (which can be custom-made) make memorable purchases, as do cordéis, the Northeast's version of dime-store novels.

Few tourists head downtown for shopping, but there are some artisan stalls across the street from **Praça JFK**.

# Spiritualism

For several generations, the family of Dona Jânia has dedicated itself to a form of spiritualism in which troubled departed spirits are healed through group intervention. Only Portuguese is spoken, but if you contact the family directly, they may let you attend one of their sessions. The work, done with impressive commitment, is performed free of charge. For information contact **Jânia Góis de Muora,** Rua Dr. Luiz Antônio, 500 (Natal); ☎ 222-7425.

# Hands-On Natal

## Airlines Serving Natal

**Varig**
Avenida João Pessoa, 308 . . . . . . . . . . . . . . . . . . . . ☎ 272-2244
**VASP**
 Avenida João Pessoa, 220 . . . . . . . . . . . . . . . . . . . ☎ 272-2236
 . . . . . . . . . . . . . . . . . . . . . . . . . . . . . . . . . . . . . . . . ☎ 222-2290
**Transbrasil**
Avenida Deodoro, 363 . . . . . . . . . . . . . . . . . . . . . . ☎272-2235

## Arrival

**Aeroporto Augusto Severo**, Rua Eduardo Gomes; ☎272-2811. The local airport is about nine miles from the center of town. Taxis are plentiful.

The *rodoviária* (**bus station**) is at Rua Capitão-Mór Goubeia, 1237; ☎ 231-1170. The main bus station is some distance from town. Buses are available to Belém, Belo Horizonte, Brasília, Cuiabá, Fortaleza, Máceio, Recife, Rio, São Paulo, and others. Catch local buses into town on the far side of the street; those marked "Via Costeira" (the principal beach drag) run along the southern coast to Ponta Negro Beach.

## Car Rental

**Avis** . . . . . . . . . . . . . . . . . . . . . . . . . . . . . . . . . . . . ☎ 219-2882
**Localiza** . . . . . . . . . . . . . . . . . . . . . . . . . . . . . . . . . ☎ 272-2557

## Climate

The highest temperature in summer is about 84°F, with constant winds cooling the air. Winter is so-named, not because of a drop in temperature, but because it is more likely to rain. Its proximity to the Equator (three degrees), allows the city to enjoy up to 15 hours of sunlight daily.

## Taxis

**Cooptaxi** . . . . . . . . . . . . . . . . . . . . . . . . . . . . . . . . . ☎ 223-8366

## Travel Agency

**NatalTur**, Avenida Deodoro, 424; ☎ *(84) 222-5401*, fax *221-5956*. Offers city tours, as well as trips to the more exotic beaches, such as Genipabú, Litoral Sul, Praia de Pipa, and Praia Maria.

## Tourist Information

**Center of Tourism (Centro de Turismo)**, Rua Aderbal de Figueiredo, 980 (Petrópólis); ☎ *231-6729*. The tourist center is situated in the old prison on top of the hill overlooking the city. Brochures, maps, and assistance (sometimes in English) can be found Mon.-Sat., 2-8 p.m. There is also an enclave of artisan stores and a lively restaurant. Information booths are also located at the airport.

**EMPROTURN**, Avenida Deofore, 249; ☎*221-1452*. This is the state tourist board.

# Fortaleza

Like many of the states in the Northeast, the state of Ceará has long been subject to the hard facts of water – the deadly absence of it in the interior and the glorious abundance along the Atlantic Coast. Ever since its colonization in the late 18th century, the state has been the victim of severe droughts that parched the *sertão* and left millions of people starving and desperate for livelihood. And yet in one of those ironies of nature, Ceará also boasts some of the most beautiful beaches in all of the Northeast – almost 400 coastal miles of swaying palm trees, multi-colored sand dunes, dramatic cliffs, and rocky coves formed by the eternal rush of sea and air. No matter how stunning the natural resources are, however, it's in the gentle coastal fishing villages where the true spirit of Ceará can be felt. Village women, famous for their delicate artistry, still fashion lacework from century-old patterns while their fishermen husbands sail out to sea

A typical *jangada* prepares for a jaunt near Fortaleza.

on homemade *jangadas,* their fishing nets resembling enormous silvery spider webs against the azure-blue sea.

The capital of Ceará is Fortaleza, by far the largest metropolis in the Northeast, with over two million inhabitants. Offering perpetual sunshine and an exciting nightlife, the city rates as one of the best resort cities in the country. But wealth and poverty coexist closely here, and homeless beggars frequently ask for money. Since most of the beaches are polluted on the eastern shore, many tourists head out to those beyond the city limits for swimming and such exotic adventures as dune surfing. Within the city, however, even the polluted beachfronts are the site of continuous activity, with tourists crowding the arts and crafts fair along Avenida Presidente Kennedy or settling into one of the numerous *barracas* (straw-roofed bars) for a plate of fried crab legs and *chopp.* Not to be missed is the return of the local fishermen from the open sea (around 4 p.m.), when they dock their *jangadas,* roll up their nets, and clean their daily catch right on the beach.

## History

The first inhabitants of the Cearense region – the **Tabajara Indians** – did not easily give up their territory to the first **Portuguese** settlers, who arrived in 1603. In fact they killed and ate the first bishop (a fate the laity in Belém shared as well). The **Dutch** forced the remaining Portuguese out in 1637 and erected a fortress against the natives in 1639. Seventeen years later, the Portuguese returned in victory, founding their own fort (*fortaleza* means fortress), around which a settlement grew.

Independent political fortitude has continued to mark Cearense history. In 1824, Fortaleza was one of the few places where the continental Portuguese tried to quell the growing Brazilian independence movement, massacring the local patriots before being decimated themselves several months later. The state of Ceará was also the first to abolish slavery (although the absence of sugar plantations and the low number of blacks tended to make the noble act seem somewhat less than sacrificial). As Fortaleza became prosperous at the end of the 19th century, the backlands of Ceará also gained national prominence when Padre Cícero Romão Batista, a humble parish priest, effected a seeming miracle when the communion wafer he was administering to one of his flock turned to blood in her mouth. Overnight, the dusty village of Juazeiro became the site of religious pilgrimages while Padre Cícero himself came to be worshipped as a near saint, despite the Church's attempt to quell his religious influence. Until his death in 1934, Padre Cícero maintained intense political power, and at one point his followers even marched on Fortaleza and brought about the downfall of the state. Today, the city of Fortaleza remains a destination for thousands of migrants who arrive from the parched interior looking for a better life.

## Bird's Eye View

Located near the equatorial line on the northeast coast of Brazil, Fortaleza lies by the beach between the Ceará and Cocó rivers, in the middle of 578 km. (360 miles) of sandy beaches. The highest point in the city is only 30 meters (100 feet), and its beachfront is formed of sandy dunes (up to 10 meters/33 feet high) and coconut trees.

The main drag, called **Beira-mar Avenida** (officially known as Avenida Presidente Kennedy), is where the most important hotels are located, as well as the best opportunities for nightlife. From its beginning at Iracema Beach to its end at the yacht club, you will find restaurants, a handicraft fair (5-11 p.m.), tourist information centers, sports courts, and even free aerobic classes held every day (except Sun.) at Volta de Jurema court at dawn and dusk. At night, feel free to stroll down this street and partake of one of more than 30 different tropical ice cream flavors at the several parlors along the way.

**Barra do Ceará** (the mouth of Ceará River) is the place where Vicente Pinzon, one of Christopher Columbus' captains, arrived in the early 1500s. Here you can find small boats that make the crossing of the river to the far beaches, and a popular beach center where thousands congregate to swim, drink *caipirinhas*, and eat fried fish.

## Culture

The folklore from Ceará is among the richest in Brazil – do make every opportunity to experience it. Through dances and popular parties, the people from Ceará have found ways to express their deep religious and cultural roots. Among the most significant dances are *pastoril, caninha verde, coco de praia, banda cabaçal* and *maracatú*. The Cearanese folklore has also been spread by regional singers who improvise spontaneous songs according to their feelings. The songs are usually composed of numerous verses that retell political, social, or historical facts, most often accompanied by guitar.

Widely known through the Northeast, the *dança do coco* was created centuries ago in the old mills by the few black people living in Ceará. Born from work music, the genre boasts a rhythm set by the beat of the rocks used to break open coconuts. Eventually, the dance form developed into a rather complicated series of movements that utilized coconuts in its choreography. A variation, the *coco do sertão*, is a very sensual dance for couples.

The *pastoril* mixes dramatic scenes, narrative, song, and dance in front of the Nativity scene. As a performance of praise for the baby Jesus, it is presented at Christmas time by groups of actors dressed as shepherds and shepherdesses.

The *banda cabaçal* is the most typical style favored in the countryside, retaining some Indian influence in its choice of instruments. The name "cabaçal" came about because the sound produced musically by the ensemble is similar to that produced by the shock of hollow calabashes.

The *maracatú*, developed first in Africa, brings together totemic symbols from royal Congonese ceremonies with devotional practices toward the *Nossa Senhora do Rosário* (Our Lady of the Rosary). As one of the biggest attractions during Carnaval, it is presented as a processional, in slow and measured steps.

## Sights

### Conjunto Santa Teresinha

The best view of the city is from a cliff overlooking the twinkling lights of Conjunto Santa Teresinha. Below the rocky embankment lies a lower-class neighborhood from where the sounds of *candomblé* drums can be heard deep into the night. Atop the cliff is a complex of open-air restaurants frequented by the cognoscenti, who enjoy the terrific view, the fabulous sunsets, and the cool, windy nights. Here, at the **Mirante Restaurante** (open daily, 6 p.m.-midnight, closed Mon.) you can sit under a tiled roof or on the romantic terrace overlooking the hill. Specialties here come *na telha* (baked in a clay boat), but if you're brave, order the *arraia*, a special fish said to be descended from an underwater bat. Also in the area is the **Mirante Bar**, with a stunning view of the ocean and the city's port. The trip by car from Avenida Presidente Kennedy takes about 10 minutes. I don't suggest walking because you'll have to pass through lower-class *bairros* (neighborhoods), though the cityscape from this perspective can be quite enlightening. Taxis are usually waiting outside the restaurant for the return trip.

### Teatro José de Alencar

*Praça do Alencar; Mon.-Fri. 8 a.m.-11 a.m., 2-6 p.m.*

One of Fortaleza's finest showpieces, this metallic Art Nouveau theater was built in 1910, but looks like something out of the boardwalk in Atlantic City, with its military green grillwork, cut-glass dome, and antique street lamps. All types of shows, from folklore to popular singers, are presented here, but don't miss the opportunity to go for a tour. The view from the stage is awesome (try to jump up).

### Centro (Downtown)

In the city's center you can find the fortress where Fortaleza began its development and the headquarters of the army in this region. Also in the area is the city's main cathedral; the **Passeio Público**, a small park beside the fortress where rebels were once executed; **Praça do Ferreira**, the plaza still considered the heart of the city; **Emcetur**, the old prison and now a tourist center; and the old **train station**.

## Museu de Arte e Culturas Populares

*Avenida Sen. Pompeu, 360. 7 a.m.-6 p.m.*

This interesting historical museum is above the tourist complex. Recently expanded, it shows regional crafts and fine art, including a model *jangada* boat, a 40-year-old hammock-weaving machine and a raft made from logs.

# Beaches

## In Fortaleza

At least 19 beaches can be found along Fortaleza's eastern and southern shores, as well as points beyond the city limits. The bad news is that some of the inner-city beaches are now too polluted for swimmers. Today, the government of the state of Ceará monitors the water quality of the 70 km. (44 miles) of beaches in the metropolitan area through weekly lab tests. Look for signs posted by SEMACF, the Environmental Superintendency, which indicate that swimming is allowed. But this doesn't stop the continuous flow of tourists down the still-picturesque stretches; they come to contemplate the dramatic rocky vistas, embark on *jangada* trips, and cruise the arts and crafts fair that is held nightly along Av. Presidente Kennedy.

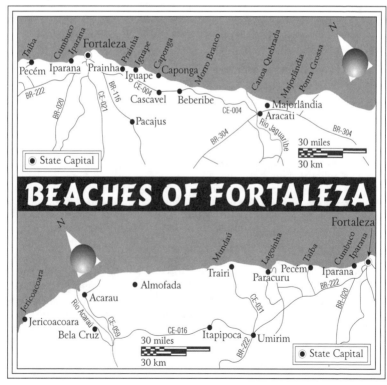

## Praia do Iracema

The city's most traditional beach is 10 minutes from downtown at the beginning of Avenida Presidente Kennedy. The rocky landscape acts as a natural breakwater. Bathing is allowed today, but take caution. Bars with all kinds of music are found here.

## Praia do Meireles

A few km. south of Praia do Iracema is where the majority of hotels are located. The artisan fair is held here along Avenida Presidente Kennedy.

## Praia do Mucuripe

Further east, *jangada* sails, lobster boats and the movement of local fishermen make for colorful activity on this beach. Photo ops abound around 4 p.m., when fishermen, mostly residents from the poor *bairro* (neighborhood) on top of the hill, return and sort through their day's catch. Not surprisingly, most of the best fish restaurants are located here, as is a statue of Iracema, considered the folkloric mother of Ceará, in front of the yacht club. This area was given the okay for bathing as of this writing.

## Praia do Futuro

On the eastern coast of the city,"Future Beach" runs three miles from Avenida Zezé Diogo to Clube Caça e Pesca. Crowded on the weekends, it's one of the few city beaches where you can swim. Every few yards you'll find open-air bars, restaurants, and hotels that serve excellent crabs, fried fish, and *batidas*.

## Praia da Barra do Ceará

Located where the Ceará River empties into the Atlantic Ocean, this lovely stretch of sand is an excellent place to take a boat ride. No bathing.

## Beyond Fortaleza

## Beach Park

An alternative to the city beaches is this more commercially developed "beach park," 12½ miles from Avenida Beira Mar. The brainchild of two Brazilian entrepreneurs who fell in love with Florida's Wet 'n Wild, this complex has its own exquisite beach and a massive water park with wave pools and slides. Equipment (including ultraleves, jetski buggies, kayaks and surfboards) can be rented. *Barracas* (straw-roofed bars) line the beach, employing enthusiastic young boys as waiters, and a good restaurant offers a cool refuge from the sun. An interesting boutique hawks over-priced bathing suits, T-shirts, and American candies. No regular buses come here; you'll have to hire a private car or take an excursion through a travel agency.

## Morro Branco

Fifty-four miles north of Fortaleza lies one of the most publicized beaches due to a TV soap opera in the early 1980s. The original settlement sprang up among petrified dunes, and today is known for its natural springs and spectacular *jangada* rides over red, yellow, white, black, and gray-tinted dunes. (The bottled sand paintings you see in crafts stores come from this region.) During high season, four daily buses leave from the Fortaleza terminal (note that the 2½-hour trip will be hot, crowded, and uncomfortable).

## Praia da Lagoinha (Litoral Norte)

About 62 miles from Fortaleza, this spot is excellent for camping. Full of coconut trees, the beach gets its name from the small, but very deep lake surrounded by dunes. The minimal infrastructure includes only two *pousadas* and very simple restaurants.

## Praia da Canoa Quebrada

Down the Litoral Sul, 100 miles from Fortaleza, is this beach in the municipality of Aracatí – a favorite resort among Europeans. During the 1960s, people from the interior moved to this paradisiacal retreat in search of tranquility. Buses that go to the village are always met by local dune buggies.

## Jericoacoara

About 175 miles from Fortaleza lies one of the most beautiful beaches in all of Brazil. Now the in-spot of the Northeast, Jericoacoara mixes the starkness of the *sertão* with the voluptuousness of wind-swept dunes that reflect a rainbow of colors at sunset. Here, the sea carves masterful designs into the rocky formations already sculptured by thousands of years of wind and surf. The fisherman's village still has its local charm, though there are many bars to waste away hours and a very famous hall to see real *forró* dancers.

As with most elite beaches in Brazil, Jericoacoara is not easy to reach. It's possible to take a local bus to Gijoca, but the trip will take at least eight hours and the driver stops at every village on the way. In Gijoca, you'll fnd locals from Jericoacoara waiting with dune buggies and pickups to take you on a wild, three-hour trek aross the dunes. Your best option is to sign up for a private excursion that includes direct transportation and two-night accommodations in simple *pousadas*.

The Hippopotamus Pousada provides transportation from Fortaleza every day except Mon. for an inclusive rate. In Fortaleza, contact **Hippopotamus Turismo**, Ave. Santos Dumont, 2459; ☎ *244-9191*. Also, the Pousada Matusa offers a transfer/accommodation package, including horseback riding, diving, and dune buggying. In Fortaleza, call **Matusa Turismo**, Avenida Dom Luís, 383, sala 2; ☎ *240-6500*.

It's also possible to stay at the simple dwellings of fishermen. Offer them some money and they'll probably show you to a hammock strung up on their porches. If you go this route, you'll have to rent your own dune buggy to get around; lots of Toyotas are usually waiting at the bus station.

## VP CLOSE ADVENTVRE from Mike Salvo

"Jericoacoara is a surreal place. Just before the town is a small cemetery with a 30-foot cross that stands isolated on a broad sweep of desert – so strange and yet so perfect. Near the center of the village is a 17th-century stone church around which a powerful hallucinogenic plant grows. On the main beach the immense sand dune is over five stories high – from the top you can see the Sahara-like oasis of the coastal desert, the town of Jeri, and the incredible pristine coast. When the sun finally broke through on the horizon and flooded us with light we were awestruck."

# Excursions

## Schoooner Trips

**MARTUR** (travel agency), Avenida Presidente Kennedy, 4301; ☎ 244-6203, offers schooner trips disembarking from Beira-Mar, near the Statue of Iracema. Two-hour boat trips also leave from Mucuripe and go to Praia Mansa, where you jump off the boat and spend about 20 minutes on the small, deserted beach. The best time to go is between 10 a.m. and noon, or for the sunset cruise at 4 p.m. Diving courses and fishing expeditions can also be arranged.

## Dune Surfing

Anyone with a yen for scaling the dunes should head for **Cumbuco Beach**, 45 minutes from Fortaleza. Despite its rapid development in recent years, the beach has retained its natural beauty, with coconut palms peppering the dunes and wild pigs strolling along the shoreline. Settle in under the shaded roof of the **Restaurante Sol e Sol** for a *bolinho de camarão* (shrimp roll) and a quick *caipirinha*, then hire a dune buggy (and driver) for a screaming-meemies adventure over the rolling sand dunes. The buggies stop along the Lagoa de Banana, where a mule team will be waiting; if you want to ride, tip the muleteer, but be careful getting on (I would have fallen right over that mule's ears if my cavalier muleteer hadn't pulled me back by my belt!). The *pièce de résistance* of this excursion is the body dune surfing over a substantial hill that requires the participant to stop himself just seconds before falling into a glorious azure lake – takers are thrown a rope to drag themselves back up the hill. Most people go tumbling into the lake, but I once saw a talented native boy stop on a dime at the foot of the hill. Even if you don't want to dune-surf yourself, the scenery alone is spectacular, and just watching the bikini-clad surfers is always a riot. After the excursion, head back to the Sol e Sol for a large plate of *mariscos*, fried crab claws, or a fine grilled lobster. *Pargo frito* is a huge fried fish suitable for two; it has few bones. If you decide to stay in Cumbuco, the **Hotel**

**Tendas do Cumbuco,** ☎ *231-5249* or *224-1670,* comes highly recommended. Nearby, the village women offer a variety of handmade crafts.

The easiest way to experience Cumbuco is to book a day-excursion through a local travel agency. Otherwise, you'll have to catch a bus to Caucaia at the Praça Estação in Fortaleza, then catch another bus to Cumbuco (which runs every three hours). Thirty minutes beyond Cumbuco is one of Fortaleza's most exotic beaches – **Taíba** – a fishermen's village where at ebb tide visitors can enter the numerous grottoes hollowed out in the rocks by the sea. The mile-high dunes here are separated from the sandy coastal plains by blue lagoons surrounded by greenery. At twilight, the landscape turns lunar as the mountainous dunes and craters form mysterious shadows under the illumination of the moon.

> **UP CLOSE TIP:** *Unless you're an expert, driving your own buggy over these dunes can be treacherous. Even Brazilians on weekend joy rides have tipped over. Note that only four-wheel-drive and special tires can safely navigate these beaches. And remember to cross rivers only at ebb tide because the mouths become too broad and deep to traverse at high tide. If your dune buggy does get bogged down, lower the pressure of the rear tires. Never speed on a beach and, when driving over dunes, don't go over 12 miles per hour; the sun creates optical illusions, flattening out slopes.*

# Where To Stay

Most of the best hotels in Fortaleza are set along **Avenida Presidente Kennedy;** unfortunately most of the beaches here have been polluted from overuse. You'll save a few dollars with smaller hotels and *pousadas* a few blocks away. If you prefer more rustic accommodations in fishing villages outside the city, head for beaches such as **Cumbuco** or **Jericoacoara.** See page 26 for price chart.

## Caesar Park

*Av. Beira Mar, 3980 (Praia do Mucuripe);* ☎ *283-1133, fax 263-1444.*

Built in 1992, this fine luxury hotel is a welcome addition to Fortaleza. With Japanese management, it offers consistently elegant service in five-star surroundings following the tradition already established in Rio and São Paulo. The elegant lobby was designed by Burle Marx. A complete fitness center features a Universal gym, massage, jacuzzi, pool, and sauna; convention facilities can serve up to 1,000. The Mariko Restaurant serves the best Japanese food in the city; the Le Caesar is famed for its French cuisine; and the Mucuripe serves regional dishes, including a fabulous *feijoada* feast on Sat. The lunch buffet is the best in the city, featuring different cuisines daily and an awesome dessert table. *Very expensive. All cards.*

## Esplanada Praia Hotel

*Av. Presidente J. Kennedy, 2000 (Meireles);* ☎ *244-8555, fax 224-8555.*

You'll find the Varig crew staying at this top five-star on Meireles Beach, the city's main drag, close to the hub of Fortaleza's nightlife. The sprawling lobby, full of abstract art and modern tapestries, is split-level, with various areas bordered by leather and chrome chairs and massive couches. The spacious apartments all have tubs and sport magnificent verandas that look onto the ocean; standards and superiors differ only in the size of the balcony. The reception and corridors are not air conditioned, though the rooms are well cooled. The coffee shop offers a fine breakfast (including hard-to-find cornflakes) and overlooks the sea. Pool, beauty salon, and boutiques are also on premises. Ask in advance for an airport transfer. *244 apts. Expensive. All cards.*

### Marina Park Hotel

*Av. Presidente Castelo Branco, 400;* ☎ *(85) 252-5253, fax 253-1803.*

More a tourism complex than a hotel, the Marina Park's huge grounds, include a modern, well-equipped marina. Six restaurants, coffee shop, nightclub, American bar, shopping mall with 24 stores, beauty salon, tennis courts, volleyball courts, health club, and water park suggest a tiny city. Tourists looking for an intimate Brazilian experience will be overwhelmed, with cold chrome and glass. Don't miss New Year's Eve, when more than 3,000 people crowd onto the grounds for a blow-out dusk-to-dawn marathon of food, song, and dance. *248 apts. Expensive. All cards.*

### Imperial Othon Hotel

*Avenida Presidente J. Kennedy, 2500 (Meireles);* ☎ *(85) 244-9177; fax 224-7777.*

This five-star Othon on Meireles Beach isn't as luxurious as similar Othons further south, but it does provide a full array of services and entertainment. During high season, a special "leisure director" whips up aerobic classes and parties, and a winding staircase from the tree-lined pool area leads to an underground mall of boutiques and crafts stores. There's also a beauty salon, sauna, and nightclub, and a doctor on 24-hour call. Standards are decorated simply with white walls, white spreads, and red rugs; the larger deluxes have wonderful sea views. Bathrooms are luxurious. Every floor has a small living room, though not air conditioned; neither is the lobby. The pleasant coffee shop, with a veranda overlooking the sea, also functions for dinner and a well-received folkloric show nightly. Weekend discounts. *264 apts. Expensive. All cards.*

### Hotel Praia Centro

*Avenida Mons Tabosa, 740 (Iracema);* ☎ *and fax (85) 211-1122.*

A few blocks from Iracema beach, the Praia Centro is a spiffy, well-serviced hotel. Sunsets from the rooftop pool area are so spectacular that even non-guests should drop by for a drink. Standards are not only attractive, but surprisingly ample; deluxes are not substantially bigger. The piano bar with live bands is a reasonable place to hang out at night; live music accompanies lunch and dinner. *Feijoada* is served on Mon. from 10 p.m.-3 a.m. *190 apts. Moderate-expensive. All cards.*

## Best Western Colonial Praia Hotel

*Rua Br. de Aracati, 145 (Meireles);* ☎ *211-9644, fax 252-3501.*

This four-star, with its white stucco walls, graceful arches and tiled roof, has the charm and repose of a country *pousada*. A tropical garden shades the attractive pool and children's pool, set far back from the bustle of city traffic. Standards and deluxes differ only in location; none has views. Colorful woven bedspreads coordinate tastefully with the brown carpet and exposed brick walls; bathrooms are small but clean, with hot and cold water. Tennis courts are available to guests. The restaurant serves all three meals. *99 apts. Moderate. All cards.*

## Hotel Praia Verde

*Av. Dioguinho, 3860 (Praia do Futuro), 16 km.;* ☎ *(85) 234-5233, fax 234-0808.*

Situated on Future Beach, this is one of Fortaleza's best bets, with medium-range rates, five-star service, and a two-level architecture that resembles a resort. The lobby is a breezy sprawl of white couches and marble, dominated by a wild carving of a nature spirit emerging from a piece of bark. The beautiful pool area is shaded by palm trees and graced by a voluptuous, but tortured statue of Iemanjá, goddess of the ocean. A small intimate bar offers live music in high season. The pleasant, air-conditioned apartments differ only in view; you can choose between dune or sea view. A small mall holds several boutiques, hair salon, tapestry store, and travel agency. There is no elevator. During low season, everybody receives a 30% discount. Across the street is the great musical bar **Chico e Caranguejo**. *150 apts. Moderate. All cards.*

## Samburá Praia

*Avenida Presidente Kennedy, 4530 (Meireles);* ☎ *(85) 263-1999; fax 263-2177.*

The small homey lobby has a tiled floor, framed by leather and woodframe couches and a protecting saint. Standards are small, with no view; deluxes look to the sea; superiors have a side view. The best rooms have two windows that look down on the fishing villages. Little decoration adorns the air-conditioned rooms except a color TV and mini-bar, but they are spunky clean. The tiny pool is set next to a covered area with a fantastic view of the fishing huts and sea. There's a very attractive, if slightly kitschy restaurant. Low season discounts can range up to 40%. *35 apts. Moderate. All cards.*

## St. Tropez des Tropiques

*Avenida dos Coqueiros, 4000;* ☎ *(85) 211-9644. (Write to Hotel Colonial Praia.)*

Now re-opening with its own freshwater lake, this rustic complex of grass-hut chalets on its own exquisite, deserted beach offers attractive accommodations that can sleep four. Unless you have wheels, you'll be dependent on the hotel's kitchen for meals, but spending the day in a hammock or sipping a drink in the open-air bar shouldn't prove all bad. The hotel is a favorite among the French, for whom Air France arranges direct flights. *Moderate. All cards.*

## Zen Praia Hotel

*Av. Antonio Justa, 1894 (Meireles);* ☎ *(85) 244-3213, fax 261-2196.*

Fortaleza's only officially sanctioned one-star hotel, with a charming tropical ambiance and *pousada*-like lobby. Clean, but simple, it is walking distance from the beach. *Inexpensive. All cards.*

## Hotel Nossa Pousada

*Avenida da Abolição, 2600;* ☎ *261-4699.*

This budget-styled property doesn't exactly retain the charm of a *pousada*, but its prices are low. Rooms (fan-cooled) are carpeted and include a mini-bar, but you must pay extra for TV and air conditioning. Showers have no curtain and practically rain down on the toilet. Breakfast is included, though the room is not spectacularly clean. Its prime advantage is that it's just one block from the beach. Twenty-five percent discounts are available in low season. *20 apts. Inexpensive. All cards.*

## Turismo Praia Hotel

*Avenida Presidente Kennedy, 894;* ☎ *231-6960.*

This hotel is only recommended for those on a minute budget or blessed with a backpacker's mentality. Rooms are small and the mini-bar rusty, but the bathrooms are tolerable. All rooms have air conditioning and phones. *Inexpensive. No cards.*

## Pousada Portal de Iracema

*Rua dos Ararius,2;* ☎ *(85) 231-0066 (Praia de Iracema).*

Located in front of the old Iracema Plaza Hotel on the side of the Igreja de São Pedro, this simple *pousada* has few amenities, except that some of the corner rooms have terrific views through shuttered windows. Do try to get a room with air conditioning; some only have fans.

# Where To Eat

As a cosmopolitan city in a folkloric area, Fortaleza offers everything, from regional dishes to haute cuisine. The typical foods show a heavy Northeastern influence, from *carne de sol* (dried salty meat) to *peixada*, (a fish stewed in vegetable sauce) and *pirão* (manioc flour and fish sauce cream). Fried fish in all forms is a particular delicacy seaside, washed down with a cold *chopp* (lager beer on draft) or locally made *cachaça*, a sugarcane drink, one of the region's principal products. Exotic tropical fruits are abundantly grown in this region, such as *sapoti* (sapodilla), *cajá* (hog plum), *meláo* (melon), *caju* (cashew), *maracuja* (passion fruit), and *coco* (coconut). See page 26 for price chart.

## O Alfredo

*Avenida Presidente Kennedy, 4616 (Mucuripe);* ☎ *263-1188. 11 a.m.-1 a.m.*

A popular open-air fisheria on the main beach drag – a great spot to watch fishermen arrive with their day's catch, as well as sailboats struggling to stay afloat. Try the *peixada*, fish, potato, and vegetable in a thin soup-like sauce, or the *ensopado*, more like a stew. *Moderate. All cards.*

## Peixada do Meio

*Avenida Presidente Kennedy (Mucuripe), 4632;* ☎ *224-2719.*
*11 a.m.-2 a.m., weekends till 4 a.m.*

Practically the same restaurant and menu as O Alfredo next door, but with added oomph: hanging fish nets and a tiny waterfall with lobster cages. Lobsters are a must, but steaks and chicken are also available. Take a leap and try the *Peixe Big Surpresa*: fish stuffed in a fried crust full of shrimp and cheese. *Moderate. No cards.*

## La Trattoria

*Rua dos Pacajus, 125; (Iracema);* ☎ *252-3666. 6 p.m.-midnight.*

A charming Italian place where the waiter's shirts match the red-and-white tablecloths. Italian-born owner Alfio claims he started the city's first Italian restaurant 13 years ago because the "Cearenses didn't have any food." At least you won't go hungry now: the garlic bread is delicious; 12 kinds of pizza are cooked in a brick oven over natural fire; and the antipasti diversi – a fantastic buffet of about 30 dishes – can be a complete meal. A good meal for two is to share an antipasto plate, split a lasagna, and go for the marvelous desserts, such as *cassata*, ice cream with crystallized fruit and liqueur, drizzled with chocolate. Reserve on weekends. Some American friends love the bar next door, **Casbar**. *Moderate. All cards.*

## Sandra's

*Avenida Eng. Luis Vieira, 555 (Future Beach);* ☎ *234-6555.*
*Weekdays 11:30 a.m.-midnight, weekends 11 a.m.-2 a.m.*

Surrounded by high-class beach homes 15 minutes from downtown, Sandra's is about as classy as an open-air restaurant gets. Under typical wood-beamed roofs and white stucco arches, diners enjoy a panoramic view of the city with the roaring ocean behind; waiters in white coats offer impeccable service. For starters, octopus salad is a true delicacy; good lobster is also served. A small inner salon with faux Indian calligraphy is cave-like; there's also an air-conditioned dining area with cushy banquettes. After dining, just sit outside under the gorgeous palm tree and meditate. *Moderate. All cards.*

## Tudo em Cima

*Rua do Mirante, 107;* ☎ *234-0777.*

An open-air café featuring honest *chopp*, crab claws and fish. *Moderate. All cards.*

## Ice Cream

### Tropical Sorveteria

*Avenida Presidente Kennedy, 4690.*

A necessary pit stop on Mucuripe Beach, featuring 50 different flavors, including such tropical fruits as *goiaba, melão, manga, tangerina, coco,* and *abacaxi.* Also ice-cold water!

# Nightlife

Fortaleza probably has the best line-up of music in the Northeast. A great show can be found on every night of the week; some of the hottest in-spots maintain a daily schedule. The preferred choice of those in the know are:

## Entertainment For Every Night

**MONDAY: Bar do Pirata Rua dos Tabajaras**, 325 (Praia de Iracema); ☎ *231-4030.* The place to go to have a *forró* party with lots of beautiful young people.

**TUESDAY: Iate Clube de Fortaleza**, Av. Mons Tabosa, 1381; ☎ 263-1744 (Mucuripe Beach). Folklore show; **Oasis Night Club**, Av. Santos Dumont 6061. Dance club hopping with tunes from the 60s and 70s.

**WEDNESDAY: Clube do Vaqueiro Anel do Contorno de Fortaleza,** entre BR116 and Ce O04; ☎ *276-3082.* An outdoor arena that offers regional *vaquejada,* a local sport where cowboys knock down a bull to the tune of *forró.* Also samba-reggae shows.

**THURSDAY: Chico do Caranguejo,** Av. Zezé Diogo, 4930 (Praia do Futuro); ☎ *276-2014.* A riotous outdoor bar on Future Beach. The scene is like a big party with everyone dancing between the tight tables and throwing their crab shells into green plastic tubs. All stages of flirting seem to be allowed. Live music starts at 9 p.m.

**TUESDAY, FRIDAY, SATURDAY, SUNDAY: Barraca Subindo ao Céu,** Av. Zezé Diogo, 5461 (Praia do Futuro); ☎ *234-3802.* Located along the beach, this seaside bar serves fine tropical dishes during the day and rocks out all night. Usually there is a comedy show with local performers on Thurs. night. Live music starts at 9 p.m.

**THURSDAY-SATURDAY: Eden Club**, Rua Carolina Sucuripa, 455. A fancy nightclub featuring an "American" bar, a restaurant and a disco.

**SATURDAY: Forró dos Três Amores**, Estrada Tapuio, s/n; ☎ *260-1603. Forró* shows, singers and national bands.

**WEEKENDS: Itaparika Bar,** Avenida Zezé, 6801 (Future Beach); ☎ *234-6061.* This huge straw-roofed bar is packed on weekends (day and night) with families and bikini-clad teens. You must like people here, because the wooden chairs and tiny tables are packed knee to knee. Little boys take your order; try the *caranguejos* (crabs). Live music on Thurs. nights, but dancing is strangely not permitted. **Praia de Iracema**, on the beach, is particularly the place to be on Fri. night. Stroll along the sidewalk and visit the various bars and restaurants. This is a great place to see the sun set.

**SUNDAY: Cajueiro Drinks,** R.G. Batista s/n BR116, km 20; ☎ 275-1482. *Forró* shows start at 4 p.m.

## Theater

### Pirata

*Rua dos Tabajaras, 3235 (Praia de Iracema);* ☎ 231-4030. *Shows at 9:30 p.m.*

Waiters are dressed like pirates in this restaurant/theater, where singers perform on a stage set that looks like the backyard of a house. Menu is basically brick-oven baked pizza and appetizers. Entrance fee about $10.

### Teatro José de Alencar

(See under *Sights*, above.)

### Oba Oba

*Avenida Washington Soares, 3199;* ☎ 234-4030. *Daily Thurs.-Sat.*

A venue for major musical shows, featuring singers from all over Brazil. Styles include lots of *forró* and *lambada*. Make sure to catch the singer **Beto Barbosa**, a part owner, who was born in Belém, but became famous in Fortaleza for singing *lambada*.

# Gay Fortaleza

I really had to dig for this information, but there is in Fortaleza a viable gay community, if slightly underground.

Among some of the bars and restaurants considered "gay hangouts" are **Galpão**, Rua Dragão do Mar (near Capitania dos Portos); **Barraca do Joca**, Av. Beira-Mar (in front of Hotel Beira Mar); **Bar do Joca**, Rua da Paz (near Av. Beira Mar); **Barraca Opcão Futuro**, Av. Zezé Diogo (Future Beach old); **Barraca Kabumba**, Av. Zezé Diogo (Future Beach new); and **Tabu Bat**, Av. Santos Dumont (in front of Centro de Fisioterapia).

# Shopping

Fortaleza is Brazil's second largest fashion center after Rio. Biggest buys are hand-embroidered cotton lace – tablecloths, bedspreads, placemats, and blouses. If you're going on to the Amazon, a smart buy would be a sturdy, brightly colored hammock, but wait until the end of an outing since they are heavy to carry.

The beginning of **Av. Monsenhor Tabosa** offers the largest concentration of clothes stores in Fortaleza, including locally designed clothes and crafts.

**Palácio da Microempresa,** a trade center for small businesses, features goods – furniture to regional foods – from all over the state. On Thurs. nights, it hosts a free popular show with a local band.

In an upscale neighborhood on Santos Dumont Ave., **Centro Artesanal Luiza Tavora** was designed for handicraft artists to sell their work directly to visitors. It also boasts a German and a Brazilian restaurant.

## Centro de Turismo

*Ave. Senador Pompeu, 350,* ☎ *231-3566; Mon.-Sat. 8 a.m.-6 p.m.; Sun. 8 a.m.-noon.*

The old public jail, constructed in 1850, was used for over 120 years before it was transformed into the Center of Tourism. It took three years to clean up the jail, whose former cells now house a complex of artisan and handicraft shops. Stop first in the Tourist Office for maps and brochures, then browse through the corridors. Wood carvings of Padre Cícero can be found here, as well as interesting sculptures and lacework, but in general the quality is kitschy. Bargaining is expected.

The best prices for lace are downtown at the Mercado Central. Do stop by the **Sorveteria Doce Sabor**, a stand across the street from the theater, and pick up a bottle of *Cajuina Nordeste* (a tangy fruit juice made from the cashew tree; when it's chilled, it tastes like alcohol but isn't). Also, roasted and raw cashew nuts from this tiny stand are delicious.

## Museu de Arte e Culturas Populares

*Avenida Sen. Pompeu, 360. 7 a.m.-6 p.m.*

Located upstairs from the tourist complex is this historical museum of popular culture that doesn't exactly overwhelm with interest, but it does show a good model of a *jangada* boat, a 40-year-old weaving machine for hammocks, and an authentic raft made out of logs. Some visitors slip money under Padre Cicero's statue for good luck.

## CEARTE

*Rua Costa Barros, 1650 (Aldeota); Mon.-Thurs. 9 a.m.-6:30 p.m.,*
*Fri. and Sat. 9. a.m.-8. p.m.*

Opened in May 1991, this complex of 14 stores was established by the government to promote native handicrafts in Fortaleza. The remarkable wood-beam and cut-glass structure also houses a restaurant serving local foods and a gallery. Good buys include leather moccasins, sand paintings made inside bottles, crochet rugs, woven baskets and large painted pottery from the city of Cascavel (the leaf design is its signature). A natural food store sells *cachaça* with fermenting fruits, roasted cashews, and *doce de cajú com castanha*, a sweet loaf of jelly-like substance made from the cashew fruit. Brightly colored hammocks go for about $55 (you can find them cheaper in Belém). Folkloric shows are presented at night only in high season.

## Mercado Central

*Rua Gen. Benzeril (downtown). Mon.-Sat. 8 a.m.-5 p.m.*

Hot, crowded, and exotic, these 600 stalls, featuring everything from clothes to live animals for dinner, is straight out of a Turkish bazaar. If you want to see how the general population shops, this is it. Bargaining is expected, and the best prices for lace are here. Watch your purse and backpacks.

### Feira de Artesanato

Beginning in front of the Praiano Palace Hotel along Avenida Presidente Kennedy, vendors start putting up tents at 5:30 p.m. All the crafts from Ceará are represented here. Bargaining is essential, and time is needed to scout out the blocks-long fair to find good buys. Make a stop at the stand called "Mágica" and you'll be treated to a series of Brazilian magic tricks. The area also has a snack bar and tables, and there is an information post in the center.

**Iguatemi Shopping Center** is the best shopping mall in Fortaleza.

# Hands-On Fortaleza

## Airlines

**Varig** offers nonstop flights (6½ hours) on Wed. from Miami to Fortaleza, which fly on to Recife. **VASP** also flies nonstop from Miami to Recife on Sun.

## Airlines Serving Fortaleza

**Varig**
Rua Miguel Calmon, 19 . . . . . . . . . . . . . . . . . . . . .    ☎ 243-1344
**VASP**
Rua Chile, 216 . . . . . . . . . . . . . . . . . . . . . . . . . . . .    ☎ 272-1353
**Transbrasil**
Rua Portugal, 3 . . . . . . . . . . . . . . . . . . . . . . . . . . .    ☎ 241-1044

## Arrival

**Taxis** from the Aeroporto Pinto Martins Praça Eduardo Gomes, ☎ *227-8066*, to downtown charge a fixed rate of $8; buses, about 30 cents, run every 20 minutes. As you leave the lobby boys will aggressively try to help you with luggage, but don't be intimidated. They are usually extremely poor and just trying to make a buck, but they are not official. If you accept their help, you should tip them. The main **bus terminal** is at Av. Borges de Melo; ☎ *186*.

## Car Rentals

**Locatur Hertz**
Avenida Br. Studart, 3330 . . . . . . . . . . . . . . . . . . .    ☎ 272-4322
**Buggy Tur** (only buggies)
Avenida Antônio Justo, 2236 . . . . . . . . . . . . . . . . .    ☎ 224-5000

## City Transportation

### Taxi

| | |
|---|---|
| Rádio Taxi . . . . . . . . . . . . . . . . . . . . . . . . . . . . . . . . . | ☎ 221-5744 |
| COOMETAS (special taxi) . . . . . . . . . . . . . . . . . . | ☎ 244-4500 |
| Air Taxi (TAF) . . . . . . . . . . . . . . . . . . . . . . . . . . . . | ☎ 272-7333 |

### Bus

Buses running along the beach strand are labeled according to the beach: Meireles, Mucuripe, Praia do Futuro, Caça e Pesca. After dark, take a cab; they're cheap and safer.

### Points Beyond Fortaleza

Air service and bus service are available to Recife, Rio, Bélem, and other major cities. Express bus service includes Recife (12 hours) and Rio (48 hours).

## Climate

Located three degrees below the equator, Fortaleza averages between 80°F and 89°F the year round, with high humidity. Nights are windier and cooler. July is considered summer since it tends to rain (a daily 15-minute spritz). High season months are July, Jan. and Feb., when the most tourists come. The *maresia* (sea wind) is strong and will rust equipment.

## Money Exchange

**Acctur Câmbio e Turismo**
Avenida Monsenhor Tabosa, 1600 (Meireles). . . .    ☎ 261-8900
**Banco do Brazil**
Rua do Rio Branco, 1515 (centro)   . . . . . . . . . . . .    ☎ 221-7555

## Security

Tourists need to be careful downtown, especially at night. However, Avenida Presidente Kennedy, where most visitors stroll, is safe due to the heavy police presence. Watch your backpacks and purses at Future Beach and the Mercado Central.

## Tourist Information

### Coditur

*Avenida Senador Pompeu, 350,* ☎ *231-3566.*

Located in the ex-municipal prison, Coditur offers information assistance, as well as a gallery of artisan shops. Ask to see the office's notebook with photos of Jericoacoara, Praia Lagoinha, Canoa Quebrada, and other beach destinations. Maps with some English are available.

### Posto Fortaleza Turistica

*Avenida Presidente Kennedy;* ☎ *261-4221. Daily 7 a.m.-midnight.*

This tourist information center, which looks like a caved-in grass hut, sits in front of the Nautical Club. Here, you can pick up brochures on beach excursions, as well as stock up on cigarettes, *cachaça*, maps, newspapers, and postcards. There's also a phone company where you can make long-distance and international calls.

## Travel Agency

### Ego Turismo

*Rua Barão de Aracati, 644 (Aldeota);* ☎ *221-6461; fax 231-3672.*

Offers city tours and excursions to Beach Park and other beaches.

## When To Visit

**Festas Juninas** takes place the first two weeks of June, with natives dressed in old-fashioned costumes performing *quadrilhas* (Northeastern square dances). Dedicated to Santo Antônio, the patron saint of marriages, the festival features the tradition of sticking a knife into a banana tree overnight to find out the name of one's future mate.

The **Regata de Jangada Dragão do Mar**, a well-known regatta, is held on July 29 in front of the Nautical Club. On Aug. 15, *umbanda* groups celebrate the **Festival of Iemenjá** on Praia do Futuro, filling the strand from dusk to dawn with rituals, drumming, and offerings that they throw into the sea.

# Fernando de Noronha

Three hundred and twenty-six miles north of Recife and 217 miles north of Natal is one of the last great, untouched paradises of the Southern Hemisphere. A miniature archipelago of 16 islands, Fernando de Noronha is also the name of the principal island first discovered by Amerigo Vespucci in 1503. Almost 500 years later, the island has retained its pristine ecosystem, despite having weathered a spooky history as a penal colony. Today, it harbors some of the rarest species of fish and fowl in the world; one bird species, *vireo gracilirostris*, a small brown brush bird, can only be found on this island. With a year-round underwater visibility of over 300 feet, the island is considered by divers as one of the greatest sites in the world for both scuba and snorkeling.

The fragility and preciousness of Fernando has fortunately been recognized by the Brazilian authorities. In 1988, the military returned control of the island to the civilian government, which was persuaded by conservatives to declare 70% of the archipelago a national marine park. Today, the island is under the jurisdiction of IBAMA, the national environmental protection agency, who tightly controls the waters and regulates the number of visitors. Since 1984, underwater fishing has been outlawed, which has inspired a profusion of tropical fish, from queen angels, butterflies, and honeycombs to yellow goats and parrot fish. Although the Bay of Dolphins has been closed to divers, they may swim outside the immediate boundaries of the bay, where many dolphins are seen.

Anyone wanting to meet human beings unpolluted by modern culture should come to Fernando de Noronha. Of the 1,600 residents (most of whom are descendants of the prisoners who inhabited the penal colony during the 18th and 19th centuries), about 800 are children; very few are educated and those who do not work for the hotel subsist off the land or from welfare. Almost none have ever left the island, and there is no TV in sight. The natives, however, are very friendly to visitors, and crime is virtually unheard of.

# History

In 1503, the great astronomer and mathematician **Amerigo Vespucci** miscalculated bearings on his fourth voyage to the New World and rammed into a rock at Fernando de Noronha. Immediately he sailed on to Cabo Frio, Brazil, where he paraded his hard-earned maps entitled "Land of the Americas" before the German government, thus altering the course of American history. In the early 1600s and 1700s, the **Dutch** and **French** repeatedly seized the island, using it as a springboard for invasions of the mainland. After expelling the last foreign occupants in 1736, the **Portuguese** colonial authorities completed the island's fort, whose cannon barrels still stand watch over the trans-Atlantic yachts anchored below in Santo Antônio Harbor.

In the early 1700s, Fernando de Noronha became a highly feared Devil's Island. Situated along a cliff overlooking a beautiful bay, a prison was built with stone beds, barred windows and ghastly holes for solitary confinement. The worst punishment was considered to be abandonment on Rat Island, far out to sea. In 1832, **Charles Darwin** sailed around the island and noted in his diaries that it was covered with vegetation. Twenty years later, another visitor remarked that the only trees to be found were in the prison governor's garden; all the others had been cut down to prevent the prisoners from building escape rafts. Until 1817 when inspectors complained repeatedly to the Portuguese crown of widespread homosexuality, women were banned from the community.

Incredibly, the American influence on this totally primitive island is still omnipresent, though hardly mainstream. During World War II, the **US Army** established a base to transport planes to Africa, and today their quonset huts have been appropriated by locals as igloo-type homes. The two-mile airstrip now used for tourist flights was built by American engineers. Most of the inhabitants receive power from a diesel station installed by Americans, and they drink water from an American-made cement rainwater catch basin. The summit of the island's landmark, the Pico, is reached by a series of cast-iron ladders riveted to the rock by American soldiers.

# Sights

## Pico Rock

Rising up like a fertility god, Pico stands as the major icon of the island – a 1,060-foot-tall finger-shaped rock formed by erosion over eons. Visitors first glimpse the extraordinary protrusion from the plane, as it rises high above the green foliage surrounded by a shoreline of white coral sand and large crescent bays. As is common in Brazil, many locals claim to have seen strange lights emanating from the center of the natural structure. For those who want to enjoy the spectacular 360° view from the top, the peak can be climbed with the help of cast-iron ladders attached to the rock. It is a good idea, however, to wear a climber's belt with clamps that hook to the ladder.

## Vila dos Remédios

This enclave is considered the most important historical point on the island. It includes **Forte de Nossa Senhora dos Remédios**, the principal fortification constructed in 1737 on the ruins of the Dutch invasion of 1629; **Igreja de N.S. dos Remédios**, the island's first church built in 1772 and restored in 1988; **Palácio de São Miguel**, administrative center of the district; and **Museu Histórico**, which records the history of the island.

## Baia dos Golfinos (Dolphin Bay)

This is the only place outside Kealakekua Bay, Hawaii, where white-belly spinner dolphins are known to live year round. Spotted here since 1700, biologists have actually recorded dolphins performing up to five somersaults, 14 leaps with body twists, and 10 consecutive straight leaps. Visible in the bay about a third of the year, they are best sighted between dawn and 3 p.m. The hotel can arrange a driver and car, which leaves at dawn and makes the 1½-hour trek (including climbing) up the bay's 350-foot cliff. Since the dolphins use the bay for mating, breeding, and nourishment, park authorities have banned swimming and boating here within demarcated buoys.

## Praia do Leão (Lion Beach)

Built up by sand dunes, this beach faces two small rocky islands known as the nesting place for the rare blue-faced booby. At the southern end of the beach, waves rushing the naturally formed reefs explode in 30-foot-high fountains. From Jan.-Mar. this beach is also the scene of a thousand-year-old ritual. Paddling feverishly from Ascension Island 900 miles to the west, green turtles return every year, dragging themselves, exhausted, onto the beach to lay their eggs. The TAMAR project, a national turtle preservation foundation, has been instituted here to protect the hatchlings. (During Feb.-May, authorities have banned visiting the beach from 6 a.m.-6 p.m.)

# Excursions

An ecological walk is organized by IBAMA for a minimum of five persons inside the Marine Park, Mon.-Fri. in the morning. Liliane Lodi, a biologist, accompanies the group and gives information where and how to spot the leaping dolphins. For more information, ☎ 619-1210.

**Aguas Claras,** ☎ 619-1225, is the dive operation owned by Randall Fonseca, who has three dive boats and equipment for rent. At the end of the dive, clients are awarded with popsicles and ice cream made of avocados, peanuts, and native *graviola* fruit.

**Bill Guarda** rents a battered military **jeep and driver** for about $35 a day. You can also rent fins, snorkel, and mask. He is not listed, but ask the locals and you're sure to find him.

For **fishing equipment,** contact: **Patrick Muller,** ☎ 619-1371.

**Boat excursions** around the island leave daily between 8:30 and 9:30 a.m. The price is about $25 with transfer and lunch ($15 without). It's best to reserve in advance. Among the agencies offering trips are **Alquimista,** ☎ 619-1114; **Atenas,** ☎ 619-1266; and **Neto,** ☎ 619-1242.

## Birdwatching

Birdwatchers will appreciate the gentle walk at low tide from Porcos Beach past American's Beach to Boldró Beach; sightings of boobies and frigate birds patrolling the crashing surf are common.

## Sunsets

The views on the wind-blown western side of the island facing Africa are fantastic. Also, check out Suest Beach, a calm bay about a two-mile walk from the hotel (see below), where the Dutch landed in the early 17th century.

## Surfing

Considered the Brazilian Hawaii, the beaches of Bolero, Conceicão, and Cachorro are the best in Brazil. Be careful with the sea, however. A local saying goes: After even calm waves, a strong one.

# Where To Stay & Eat

See page 26 for price chart.

### Hotel Esmeralda do Atlântico

*Al. do Boldró;* ☎ *(81) 619-1355, fax 619-1355.*

Most visitors stay here, which offers little more charm than it did when it was the American Army base. Guests are lodged in square-box rooms, furnished with at least two single beds, with no cross-ventilation, no window screens, and total dependence on air conditioning, which only runs between 10 p.m. and 7 a.m. Single guests should expect to share rooms with the same sex. Only cold-water showers are available, and cleanliness is such that you will want to wear sandals when you bathe. The only place to eat on the island is the hotel, which flies in fish from Recife or Fortaleza, served with tropical fruits from the island. The bar is well stocked with sodas, beer, and basic hard liquor. Minimum stay four days. Reservations in Natal, ☎ *(84) 221-3139*; in Rio, ☎ *(21) 262-8011.*

> **UP CLOSE TIP:** *Bring your own soap, towel and hard liquor. You will also be glad to have packed your own stock of chocolate, nuts, raisins, instant oatmeal, etc. Drink only bottled water.*

Some accommodations may be made with local residents, but reservations and confirmation must be made in advance. Don't expect anyone to speak English. Rates are about $60 per day with meals included.

### Verdes Mares

*Floresta Nova;* ☎ *619-1222.*
Lovely home with one apartment and one single. Try to get the hammock on the porch.

### Pituca

*Vila dos Remedios;* ☎ *619-1202.*
Don Pictuca has four very modest rooms in her 200-year-old house next to the church, owned previously by the governor. It rates as the first house on the island.

### Da Rita

*Av. Nice Cordeira (Florest Velha);* ☎ *619-1324.*
A spacious house with two singles and two doubles.

# Hands-On Fernando de Noronha

## Arrival

Nordeste Airlines flies from Recife to Fernando de Noronha, leaving daily at 12:30 p.m. and returning around 3:30 p.m. Two flights are made on Sun. Flights are also available from Natal. Since regulations keep visitors to a maximum of 100, park police will not allow you out of the air terminal without a confirmed reservation. No camping is allowed.

## Climate

The island is blessed with 200 days of sunshine annually. The rainy season peaks between Mar. and May, when the rain leaves most roads unpassable, but turns the island into a bright green paradise. Between Sept. and Feb.

(called the dry season), the island takes on a dusty brown shade. Daytime temperatures hover around 78°F, never dipping below 64°F. Since the island is only 3.5 degrees from the equator, the UV rays are among the most intense on the planet, so sun hats, coverups, extra-strength sunblock and extreme caution are mandatory.

## Packages

Because of the visitors' quota, it is easier to book a package deal rather than arranging your own accommodations, particularly if you are not fluent in Portuguese.

### Brazilian Scuba and Land Tours

*5254 Merrick Road, Suite 5, Massapequa, NY 11758.*
☎ *(800) 722-0205, (516) 797-2133; fax (516) 797-2132.*

This group offers an excellent 10-day package, including three nights in Recife, six nights in Fernando, five days of diving, accommodations at the Hotel Esmeralda, all meals, tour of the bay and islands, and roundtrip airfare for $1,999.

## Time

One hour ahead of Recife.

## When To Visit

The open Atlantic side of the islands can be dived only from Jan.-Mar. due to sea conditions. (Note: From Dec. through Mar., Brazilian tourists descend on the island and prices may be higher.)

# São Luis

São Luis is the capital of **Maranhão**, a state laden with *Nordestino* culture despite a climate and geography that nearly belongs in Amazônia. From the moment you step off the plane, the hot (very hot) humid air smacks you in the face, and if you visit from Jan.-June, you will understand the meaning of rain. West of São Luis, you'll find the beginnings of the rainforest, yet the southern coastline has often been called the "Pantanal of the Northeast," because between July and Dec. the land becomes so dry you can ride a truck over what was formerly water. Despite being one of the poorest states in Brazil, Maranhão has some of the most fertile plains in the Northeast, particularly along the banks of the Tocantins, a powerful tributary of the Amazon River.

As a tourist destination, São Luis is slowly crawling out of obscurity. The city has always boasted fine beaches, even if the weather can turn oppressively hot. Today, the interest is leaning towards history. The **Reviver Project**, funded by the state, has poured more than 25 million dollars over the last 15 years into restoring grand old mansions that once marked São Luis as a center of the aristocracy. Even cobblestone streets that were being decimated by heavy traffic have been closed to vehicles and transformed into pedestrian malls. Today, a very viable colonial area makes for picturesque strolling and at night the cobblestone streets, illuminated by authentic 19th-century gas lamps, resemble Bourbon Street, with local musicians and artists hanging out in the neighborhood bars.

## Bumba-meu-boi Festivities

In June, it's worth catching the *bumba-meu-boi* festivities, one of the most authentic folkloric events in the Northeast. The activities occur all month, but peak around June 24, when the interior towns send their troops of dancers and musicians into São Luis to perform outside the churches of São João Batista and Santo Antônio.

The festival's folklore revolves around the story of a bull that dies while under the care of a slave and then is magically resurrected. Center stage in the dancing is the *boi*, or bull – an enormous black velvet-and-sequined puppet that whirls around to the beat of the hypnotic *bumba* drums and the Mediterranean twangs of the mandolin. During the rest of the month, folkloric dances, foods, and crafts are exhibited at the Parque Folclórico.

### UP CLOSE ADVENTURE from Theodore Folke

"The origins of *bumba-meu-boi* are uncertain. Brazilian anthropologist Roberto Pinho speculates that it dates back to the bull in ancient Crete. Today, the festival tells the story of a young woman who wants her husband to kill a bull for her, and has all the trappings of a joyous fertility rite worthy of mythologist Joseph Campbell. The music and dance climax at the end of June, with nightly shows in three places – the old town of Projeto Reviver, the Ceprama Cultural Museum, and the Vila Palmiers outside of town. Each *bloco* has its own version of BMB. Some nights the festivities began with a *tambor de crioula* (regional dance) show, other nights with a *forró* band. Officially everything starts at 8 p.m., which means 1 a.m. Some of it was really wild – what I particularly liked was the spangled homemade costumes and the feathery headdresses, all of which reminded me of the Wild Magnolias and Big Chief Red of Mardi Gras fame. But I'm afraid the best show is in the Vila Palmiera, a few miles out of town, and alas, thanks to the personal soap opera I was embroiled in at the time, I didn't get to see it."

# History

São Luis is the only Brazilian capital founded by the **French**. The expedition, which arrived in 1612, was headed by Daniel de la Touche, Senhor de la Ravadiére, whose three ships maneuvered through the Bay of São Marcos to establish an island fort they dubbed Saint Louis in honor of the King of France. The land, however, already belonged to the **Portuguese**, who eventually expelled them, only to be taken over again by the **Dutch** in 1641. Three years later, the Portuguese regained control and initiated the expansion of a new city, whose streets were designed to take advantage of whatever refreshing wind blew in from the sea. During the 18th and 19th centuries, the majority of the great colonial mansions were built and decorated with imported blue tiles from Portugal called *azulejos*, thus giving the city its nickname: *cidade de azulejos* (City of Tiles).

# Sights

The old city of São Luis is a marvelous place to tour on foot. In fact, it's the only way to see the colonial area since the Reviver Project has prohibited traffic over a four-street complex that includes Rua Portugal, Rua Estrela, Rua Giz, and Rua Humberto de Campos. The following walking tour will give you a glimpse of some of the main attractions, including museums and marketplaces, but pace yourself because the heat may become oppressive. Along the way you'll pass numerous bars and restaurants where you can find a cool drink. Remember to wear good walking shoes for the cobblestone streets and slightly steep slopes.

## Walking Tour

### Praça João Lisboa

Begin the tour at the SEMATUR/MARATUR Information Office, in the Casa da Cidade de São Luis. This is the main square of the city which, during colonial days, featured the *Pelourinho*, a whipping post for renegade slaves. In the middle of the square is a statue of João Francisco Lisboa, a great journalist and historian who started the first newspaper of Maranhão called *Timon*. In this square is also the Igreja do Carmo and Convento do Carmo, as well as the offices of Transbrasil and VASP. Down the block from MARATUR is the post office, *Correios e Telegraphos*.

### Rua Osvaldo Cruz

Across the *praça* to the right, the houses in extreme disrepair look barely inhabitable, but they are actually lawyers' and engineers' offices, plus well-known boutiques with 200-year-old tiles. Turn left on Rua Osvaldo Cruz, the main commercial street, its cobblestones now closed off to all but pedestrians. On both sides of the street are wonderful, though ill-kept examples of art nouveau; notice the wooden shutters, the molded emblems, and the grilled balconies on the second story. At the Aky Disco record store, you'll find the latest regional cuts.

## Museu de Arte Sacra

To go directly to the restored part of the city, take a right on Rua Humberto de Campos, which arrives at Rua do Giz, Rua Estrela, and Rua Portugal. Or turn left from Rua 3 da Cruz at Unibanco (on the corner), then right to Rua 13 de Maio to reach the Museu de Arte Sacra at #500.

## Igreja de São João

In front of the museum is this church built by the governor Ruy Vaz de Siqueira in 1665 as penitence for a dalliance with a married noble lady that resulted in a child.

Continue until Praça do Santo Antônio, where there is a 19th-century monastery and church by the same name, notable for its pink-winged angels on the main altar. Next, turn left on Rua Santo Antônio to Rua Ribeirão.

## Fonte do Ribeirão (1796)

Sunk into a cobblestone square, this intricately carved fountain features a statue of Neptune flanked by two young imperial palms. (Many Maranhão natives believe that a legendary serpent sleeps with his head under the fountain and his tail under the cathedral; when he wakes up, he supposedly shakes the entire city.)

## Solar do Ribeirão

Across the street from the fountain is this excellent stop for lunch in an authentic 19th-century mansion.

## Teatro Artur Azevedo

From the fountain take a right on Rua do Sol and you'll pass this salmon-colored building that boasts a beautiful facade. São Luis' 1817 opera house has been transformed – after a two-year $8 million renovation – into an impressive arts center, directed by a dynamic Brazilian impresario who was ballsy enough to sign up the international operatic soprano Aprile Millo for inaugural night. Check out the performance schedules, which might include unknown operas by the Brazilian composer Carlos Gomes and dance and folklore spectaculars. Visiting hours are Mon.-Fri. from 2-5 p.m.

## Caixa Econômica Federal Bank

Cross the Rua do Egito and you will be face to face with one of the most beautiful glazed-tile facades in the colonial city. Take a rest on the benches next to the old men and the young boys chanting out their wares. Notice the antique lamps on this traffic-less cobblestone street, Rua de Nazareth e Odylo.

## Praça Benedito Leite

Cross to this plaza teeming with fruit stands, jewelry counters, and shoeshine men. This is a great place to pick up a bag of cashew nuts or Brazil nuts to munch on. There are also craft stores and an ice cream stand that features such tropical fruit flavors as *cupuaçu, bacuri,* and *graviola*.

## Praça Dom Pedro Segundo

The site of both touristic and political activity, the square is circled by the Hotel Central (the city's oldest), the Hotel Vila Rica (five-star), and the Lord Hotel (two-star). As it has for centuries, the café next to the Hotel Central remains a favorite place to meet. The Varig office is also located here, a pink-and-white restored building with splendid grilled-work windows. The cathedral is distressingly unattractive, but the government buildings that stretch out before it on Avenida Dom Pedro Segundo are impressive leftovers from the pre-baroque colonial era. Dating from 1688, the oldest building, next to the Panorama Café, still houses the mayor's office. It is called Palácio La Ravadière, after the French buccaneer who founded São Luis (his pirate-like bust can be found on the sidewalk).

## Palácio dos Leões

*Mon., Wed., and Fri. 3 p.m.-6 p.m.*

Next door to the mayor's office is the state governor's residence, built between 1761 and 1776. Originally a French fort, it now boasts sumptuous rooms fit for a king, with 200-year-old hardware floors, portraits of Dom Pedro I, and a fabulous courtyard overlooking the bay. The gardens, juxtaposing limpid pool and islands of trees, were landscaped by the famous Robert Burle Marx. Tours are usually given on Mon. and Wed. from 3 p.m.-6 p.m., but ask in advance at MARATUR.

From the Praça Dom Pedro II, you can reach the residence either through Rua da Estrela or through the Beco Catarina Mina. If you take the Rua da Estrela you will arrive at:

## Fundação da Memoria Republican Memorial José Sarney

*Rua da Palma (downtown);* ☎ *221-3317; Mon.-Fri. 2-5 p.m.*

Located at the Convento das Mercês, this 17th-century restored monastery and library of the ex-president José Sarney features the worldly goods and tomb-to-be of the still-living ex-President (who left office with few fans, but is still in politics as a senator from Amapá). Along this street there are also lots of artisan shops featuring straw and leather crafts, as well as an *umbanda*, Ogun Yara, which features the tricks of the voodoo trade.

## The Zona

If you take the Beco Catarina Mina from Dom Pedro Praça, you'll go through the heart of the Zona, block after block of historic buildings, some crumbling, others being revitalized. In general, however, what were once colonial mansions are now tenements, inhabited by very poor people whom you may see sitting on their porches or hammering on their houses.

## The Old City's Marketplace

*Feira da Praça Grande.*

Walking on Beco Catarina Mina from Dom Pedro Praça, you can reach the large grilled archway next to the building with the sign "Casa de Sucos Produtos Regionais." Here, in the old city's marketplace, ripe with fish smells and damp from constant washings, you'll find all sorts of regional products, from dried fish to exotic spices to Brazil nuts. The game the young boys are playing around the counters is a type of checkers called *jogo de damas.*

## Centro de Criatividade de Odylo

*Costa Filho Rampa do Comércio, 200;* ☎ 222-4844.

Walk from the old market down to this very old, restored building that used to be a warehouse and is now an art center, with a cinema, restaurant, artists' ateliers, and a theater that hosts *Segundo Arte,* a Mon. night musical show. Walk around to the painting and ceramic classes and watch the students at work; you'll be welcomed. There's also a bookstore, where you can buy books on folklore and *bumba-meu-boi* records.

## Museu de Arte Visuais

*Rua Portugal, 289. Mon.-Sat. 1 p.m.-6 p.m.*

Nearby the Centro de Creatividade de Odylo you'll find a full exhibit of Maranhão tiles from the 18th to 20th centuries. The building is a 19th-century house beautifully restored by the engineers from the Reviver Project. Upstairs are contemporary paintings from Maranhão artists, including lithographs and oil pastels. On the third floor is a fabulous view of the city's rooftops.

## Alcântara (restaurant)

Next door to the Museu de Arte Visuais is one of the city's most historically atmosphere restaurants, which is set in a restored house with a towering roof and ox-cart tables that hang from the ceiling by chains. On Fri. nights, troubadors sing *serestas* and there's even a bingo game played called *sorteios.*

## Secretaria da Cultura

On the same street as Alcântara, the Secretary of Culture's office is one of the most charming buildings in town, with blue Portuguese tiles and antique-grilled balconies.

## Cooperative Reggae (dance club)

At the end of Rua Portugal, this spot is open for reggae on Thurs. and Fri. nights. If you turn left onto Rua da Estrela, then another left on Rua João Gualberto, you'll discover a wonderful used bookstore at #52, with used Brazilian records and paperbacks on all topics. Pick up the small newspaper, *O Tambor,* written in São Luis, which covers the city's reggae scene. *Folha de Gaia,* a paper about tourism and ecology in Brazil, is another interesting publication.

# Museums

## Museu de Arte Sacra

*Rua 13 de Maio, 500. Mon.-Fri. 1-6 p.m.*

A project of Reviver, this colonial mansion boasts a fine collection of sculptured saints from the 17th-19th centuries. The extraordinary vista of the city from the top floor shouldn't be missed.

## Centro de Cultura Popular Domingos Vieira Filho

*Rua do Giz, 221; ☎ 22-4599. Mon.-Fri. 8 a.m.-5 p.m. Free.*

Near the Praia Grande market, this museum in a preserved colonial mansion features stunning folkloric costumes and other crafts of the region. Front and center are the elaborately sequined *bois* (or bulls), as well as a full cast of characters that parade through the streets of São Luis during the June *bumba-meu-boi* festivals.

## Museu do Negro

*Rua Jacinta Maia, 43. Mon.-Fri. 1:30-5 p.m.*

This former slave market, called *Cafuá das Mercês,* or Hovel of Mercies, has been transformed into a homage to black culture in Maranhão. Signs of the house's former function can be seen in the disturbing displays of manacles and chains that kept the newly arrived African slaves immobile until they were sold at auction. Upstairs, the indomitable spirit of the race can be seen in the black-and-white photos of the spiritual leaders of Tambor de Mina, Maranhão's version of *candomblé.* Notice the strength in the faces of these *mães* and *pais de santo* (mothers and fathers of the saints, as they are called), who by the sheer force of their personality and connection to the spirits were able to influence the moral outlook of their enslaved people. If you would like to attend a session of *tambor de mina,* inquire of the staff here.

# Beaches

São Luis has a fine chain of beaches, easily reachable by local bus. At high tide the water reaches all the way to the rock embankments, forming natural pools. Sometimes even small fish and shrimp appear. At low tide, bathers are treated to enormous expanses of sand.

## Ponta d'Areia

Now extremely crowded, this has become the beach of the masses, who have recently been provided transportation from the suburbs. The water is not good for swimming. The stone sculptured mermaid adorning the beach was made in 1983 by Cherubino, an eccentric ex-priest whose "castle" you may visit (see below).

### Avenida Litorânea

A new avenue called "Avenida Litorânea" extends from Praia do Calhau to Praia de São Marcos on the island's north side. Dozens of bars along the seven miles of sidewalk offer live music. Don't miss the great view close to the Hotel Sofitel at Avenida Avisência.

### Calhau

A direct walk from Ponta d'Areia is this highly inviting beach, where the Sofitel Quatro Rodas Hotel is located – a scenic 1¼-mile walk from Olho d'Agua when the tide is low. Full on the weekends, the beach is lined with *barracas* offering all kinds of snacks.

### Olho d'Agua

This is the best known beach in the entire state. The sand itself is extremely wide, and the activity colorful; donkey carts vie for space with speeding Volkswagens. An excellent *barraca* for seafood is Roseangelas.

### Aracagi

The elite of Maranhão head about nine miles out of town to Aracagí, which has the cleanest water and no crowds. Also here in the west is a large fishing and lacemaking community.

## Excursions

To **rent a catamaran** at the yacht club, either contact the English-speaking guide Simão Ramos at ☎ 236-4069 or come to the club at Praia da Ponta d'Areia and talk directly to the salesman. The cost for a full day (to Alcântara and nearby islands) runs about $60 and is a wonderful way to spend a hot day in Maranhão. Rumor is that guests rarely get sick because catamarans are propelled by motor.

(For more information on trips to Alcântara and Parque dos Lencois, see *Excursions Beyond São Luis*, below.)

## Where To Stay

See page 26 for price chart.

### Sofitel Quatro Rodas São Luis

*Avenida Aviscência;* ☎ *(98) 235-4545, fax 235-4921.*

Iguanas and peacocks roam this five-star resort on Calhau Beach, where the philosophy is Club Med without the frenzy. Folkloric programs throughout the week keep guests entertained with dance performances, local foods, and hot bands. The extensive pool complex invites all-day tanning, but the palm-tree-covered grounds lead directly to the lovely beach, where all manner of watersports can be enjoyed. Rooms are large and well furnished, though the *maresia* wind tends to leave a musty smell. The restaurants, though not inexpensive, offer excellent cuisine, attended by folklorically dressed waitresses. Usually, a 10% discount is given for cash payment. *195 rooms. Expensive. All cards.*

## Hotel Vila Rica

*Praça Dom Pedro II 299 (Centro);* ☎ *(98) 232-7245.*

This five-star is situated right next to the Archbishop of Maranhão, but that doesn't stop it from being a fine leisure hotel. The ice-cold lobby (a relief in São Luis) is constructed around a variety of intimate areas that resemble a private living room. The coffee shop, where breakfast is served, opens onto an exceedingly pleasant pool complex lined with coconut and palm trees and bouquets of tropical flowers. A fine international-style meal can be had at Restaurante dos Arcos, which strangely resembles the inside of a castle. Lushly decorated two-room executive suites sleep four; standards are more simply appointed with two sofa beds, color TV, and bamboo closet. Clients may patronize the beauty salon, sauna, massage, and small boutique. An attractive playroom looks out onto the bay, where guests may play pool and bridge. *213 apts. Expensive. All cards.*

## Pousada do Francês

*Rua da Cruz, 121;* ☎ *(98) 222-0334*

I saw this *pousada* in its last stages of construction, but it promises to become one of the most charming accommodations in the city. Located in the old city on a street replete with colonial grill work and wonderful arches, the original house dates back to 1712. Owner Airton Abreu has worked hard to follow the strict laws regulating historical renovation, including preservation of the original facade and tiled roof. Walls have been painted with oxidized whale oil to retain a warm burnish glow, and antique lamps hang from the walls. Rooms follow the eccentricities of the original design; hence, some of the 30 apartments are quite small, while others are spacious. All units are air conditioned, with color TV and a mini-bar; the bathrooms are small but modern. It's best to wander around and take your pick of what's available. Reservations recommended. *Moderate. All cards.*

## Aracagy Praia Hotel

*12 km.* ☎*(98) 226-1190, fax 226-2552.*

Built in 1989, this three-story property boasts some of the most pleasant apartments in the city, if not the cleanest. The hotel is equipped with verandas that provide a distant glimpse of the sea. All rooms are air conditioned and come with wood-frame bed, color TV, mini-bar, and tiled bathrooms. A good-sized pool and tanning patio provides an attractive alternative to the beach, which is only a five-minute bus ride away. Next door is a water park with numerous swimming pools, slides, and tennis courts, which hotel guests may use free of charge. The restaurant serves lunch and dinner (*feijoada* on Sat). *66 apts. Inexpensive. All cards.*

### Ilha Bella Hotéis

*Praça da Matriz (São Francisco);* ☎ *(98) 227-0921.*

A 10-minute walk to Ponta d'Areia Beach, this budget hotel opened in 1991 with five apartments; it has since expanded. The lobby is brief but clean; the rooms are all huge, with fine wood floors and nicely tiled (though small) bathrooms. There are no closets, but all rooms have air conditioning and phones; you pay an extra couple of bucks for TV and mini-bar. *Inexpensive. All cards.*

### Chale de Lagoa

*Praia do Araçagi;* ☎ *(98) 226-4916.*

A funky down-scale *pousada*, the Chale de Lagoa on the outside looks like a tiny charming village with traditional tile roofs and tropical vegetation. Inside, the apartments range from simple to questionable, but they are perfect for backpackers or those who don't mind bringing their own sheets. The owners, who are involved in *Tambor de Mina* (a form of *candomblé*, or voodoo worship) have named their apartments after the saints of the religion. Rooms have tiled floors, private baths, fan, and a sheet of burlap that passes for a closet. The *pousada* is next door to Castello, a castle-like private home built by an eccentric, but very friendly, ex-priest turned architect. *Inexpensive. No cards.*

### Tia Maria

*Quadra 1, lote12 (Ponta d'Areia);* ☎ *227-1534.*

A charming *pousada* close to the yacht club. Tranquil location with large apartments and a garden. Make reservations. *Inexpensive. No cards.*

# Where To Eat

See page 26 for price chart.

### Churrascaria Pavan

*Av. dos Holandeses (Calhau), 9 km.;* ☎ *248-1817.*
*11 a.m.-3 p.m., 6 p.m.-midnight, closed Mon.*

A no-fanfare *rodízio* with 12 kinds of meat, 12 salads, and 12 desserts (including watermelon) for a reasonable $8. Painted scenes of the old city adorn the walls; a large, traditional wood-beam and tile roof keeps the joint cool without air conditioning. Pavan is also one of the few places in the Northeast where you can find a Diet Coke.

### Tia Maria

*Avenida Nina Rodrigues, 1 (Ponta d'Areia), 4 km.;* ☎ *235-6979. 9 a.m.-1:30 a.m., Sun. 11 a.m.- 6 p.m.*

With one of the most beautiful vistas in the city, Tia Maria is a step away from the beach at Ponta d'Areia. At night, the twinkling lights of the city reflected on the water make a stunning panorama. Hanging lamps of woven rope and raw wood tables add to the rustic allure, but there's also room to dance to languorous Brazilian ballads played by live bands nightly. The menu includes 14 kinds of fish, 12 kinds of shrimp, 10 kinds of crabs, four types of oysters, as well as *hapossay*, a kind of paella with squid, shrimp, chicken, *sururu* (a mollusk), vegetables, and mushrooms in a Japanese sauce. Most famous is the *ensopado de caranguejo no leite de coco* (a kind of crab stew with coconut milk). The specialty of the house is *batidas* made with *pitanga* and vodka; the chocolate (*batida*) was so good I walked out with a bottle. After dinner, take a turn in the double-seated love swing or just kick up some sand on the beach. *Moderate. AE.*

### Solar do Ribeirão

*Rua do Ribeirão, 141;* ☎ *222-3068. 11:30 a.m.-3 p.m., 7-11 p.m., closed Sun.*

Overlooking the Fonte do Ribeirão, this restored colonial mansion dates back to 1884 and is a lovely place to dine à la 19th century. Specialties are regional delicacies, such as *cuxá com peixe frito* (fried fish) and *caldeirada* (fish stew). The lunch buffet is a good buy. *Moderate. All cards.*

### A Varanda

*Rua Genésio Regg, 185 (Monte Castelo);* ☎ *232-8428. Noon-midnight, closed Sun.*

Situated in the garden of the owner's house, this homey restaurant cooks to order. Fish dishes are unusual, but expect a wait. *Moderate. All cards.*

### Hibiscus

*Av. dos Franceses, 48 (Vila Palmeira);* ☎ *243-2236. Noon-3 p.m., 7-12 p.m.*

Next to the Folkloric Park where the *bumba-meu-boi* festivities are held, this tropical chic eatery serves politicos such as Sarney, who indulge in the *peixe frito com cuxá*. Fri. and Sat. you can dine to live *música romantica* from 9 p.m.-2 a.m. Try the *taioba*, a kind of mussel that comes in a tiny shell with a touch of cilantro. *Moderate-expensive. No cards.*

### Olho d'Agua

*Avenida Atlântica, 200 and Rua 223 dos Magistrados, 28;* ☎ *226-0435.*

Located on Olho d'Agua Beach at the *pousada* of the same name, this funky open-air eatery is one of the most popular in the area. Locals adore the "Jesus," an exceedingly sweet soft drink that nearly made me sick. Try the *torta de camarão*, a delicious shrimp pie for under $4. *Feijoada* is served on Sun. for a reasonable $4. *Inexpensive. AE.*

### Base do Germano

*Av. Venceslau Brás (Canto da Fabril);* ☎ *222-3276. 11 a.m.-4 p.m., 6 p.m.-1 a.m., Sun. 6 p.m.-1 a.m.*

Legendary for its *caldeirada de camarão*, a steamy shrimp soup. *Moderate. No cards.*

### Antigamente

*Rua da Estreia, 210 (Projecto Reviver);* ☎ *221-2020.*
Well-lighted restaurant featuring live MPB from Wed.-Sat. Pizzas and natural juices are good, as is the grilled shrimp. *Caldeirada marahense* – a fish stew Maranhão style – is a specialty. *Inexpensive. No cards.*

### Naturista

*Rua 3 do Sol. 11 a.m.-11 p.m.*
Macrobiotic menu. *Inexpensive. No cards.*

# Shopping

### CEPRAMA

*Mon.-Sat. 9 a.m.-8 p.m., Sun. 4-8 p.m.*
The handicraft center run by the state in a restored textile plant in the Madre de Deus district. Good buys are canned regional fruits made by Tia Noca, leather jewelry boxes, lacework, leather sandals, straw baskets, pottery, and Indian crafts from tribes in the interior. If you can stick it in your luggage, splurge on a "rain stick," a long bamboo-type stalk filled with seeds that emits the sound of rain; it's become a staple among Latin percussionists. I found a good one at Box da Tribo Guarajaras.

# Hands-On São Luis

## Arrival

Flights daily into São Luis are provided by **Varig, VASP,** and **Transbrasil.** The airport, **Tirirical,** ☎ *225-0049,* is 11 miles (18 km.) from the center of the city. **Taxis** are plentiful.

## Airlines Serving São Luis

| | |
|---|---|
| **Varig** . . . . . . . . . . . . . . . . . . . . . . . . . . . . . . . . . . . . | ☎ 225-1208 |
| **VASP** . . . . . . . . . . . . . . . . . . . . . . . . . . . . . . . . . . . . . | ☎ 245-1228 |
| . . . . . . . . . . . . . . . . . . . . . . . . . . . . . . . . . . . . . . . . . . . | ☎ 245-2822 |
| **Transbrasil** . . . . . . . . . . . . . . . . . . . . . . . . . . . . . . | ☎ 245-1604 |
| . . . . . . . . . . . . . . . . . . . . . . . . . . . . . . . . . . . . . . . . . . . | ☎ 225-1471 |

## City Transportation

### Bus

Adequate bus service is available to the various beachfronts.

## Taxi

| | |
|---|---|
| **Cobras Táxi Aéreo** (airport) ................. | ☎ 245-1268 |
| ........................................... | ☎ 222-3243. |

## Climate

Equatorial – which means hot and very humid. Rainy season peaks between Jan. and Apr., though it rains for short periods during the rest of the year. The coolest month is Sept. From Jan.-July it rains some every day.

## Money Exchange

**Baespa**
Rua do Sol, 404 (downtown) ................. ☎ 222-1281
**BASA**
Avenida Dom Pedro II, 140 (downtown).

## Travel Agencies

**Atlântica Turismo**, Rua 14 de Julho, 20 (downtown); ☎ 222-*8685*. Clients can use special VIP rooms at the airport.
   **Praia Tur**, Avenida São Marcos (Ponta d'Areia); ☎ 227-*4477*.

## When To Visit

June is the traditional month of festivities, with the most *bumba-meu-boi* celebrations in the Northeast. **Tambor de Mina** (homage to São Sebastião) is held Jan. 19-20.

# Excursions Beyond São Luis

## Alcântara

If you've made it as far as São Luis, a side excursion to the glorious ruins of Alcântara, 11 miles across the Bay of São Marcos, is a must. Formerly the center of the aristocracy in northern Brazil, the village today could be the setting of a ghost story about 17th-century spirits. Crawling ivy nearly obscures the once magnificent facades of colonial mansions; cobblestone streets are now fully overgrown with grass. A mysterious hush prevails over the entire 10-block historical area, and even the town's 2,000 inhabitants seem a bit other-worldly. If the dilapidated shutters and crumbling fountains could talk, they would surely tell quite a story.

   Officially founded in 1612, and named Alcântara in 1648, the area was originally wrested from the Tupinambá Indians by the Portuguese, who slaughtered them to make way for their own sugar, rice, cotton, and salt plantations. To facilitate production, thousands of African slaves were imported, many of whose descendants still live in the village today. When slavery was abolished, the thriving metropolis (and the first capital of

Maranhão) seemed to vanish into time. Although the state government these days is making stabs at restoration, the majority of the colonial houses, cathedrals, Portuguese-tile facades, and iron balconies remain in awesome, but strangely beautiful dilapidation. Ironically, this village, lost in the 17th century, has also been designated as a special site for spaceship launching. Though Alcântara has no real touristic infrastructure, you may be approached by young boys offering to be your guide (note that practically no one speaks English here). A visit can start at **Ladeira do Jacaré**, the main road, including a stop at the **Igreja de Nossa Senhora do Carmo** (the main cathedral), the **Igreja do Desterro**, the unfinished **São Francisco de Assis**, and the **Fonte das Pedras** (Fountain of Stones). Built in 1648, the main square, **Praça da Matriz**, was finally restored in 1948, having been buried underground for 50 years. Try to find Rua da Amargura, once a large promenade now completely covered with grass and weeds, though some of the most impressive ruins are located there, such as the **Passo** (Step of the Cross) at one end.

On the principal street, **Rua Grande**, you'll find the **Pousada do Mordomo**, as well as **Casa do Divino**, a center of artisanry, where you might see a native woman sewing lacework on a wooden loom. Most of all, just wander around and snatch glimpses of a village life that has remained as primitive as you'll ever find in Brazil.

**Museu Histórico de Alcântara Praça Gomes de Castro** features native pottery, primitive sculptures, and excellent black-and-white photos of religious festivals attended by native Indians in full regalia. It is open daily, 9 a.m.-2 p.m.

Local cuisine is simple but delicious: *arroz cuxá* (rice mixed with a special spicy sauce) and *torta de camarão* (shrimp pie). Try the mangoes, which are always superb. For a fabulous pit stop, settle in with an ice-cold coconut juice at the **Pousada Pelourinho** and order a sweet called *espécie*, a kind of coconut macaroon so utterly delicious that folks from Maranhão come just to take home a sack.

**Local handicrafts** (pottery, wood, straw) can be bought on the streets and squares. Excellent coconut sweets can be found on Rua das Marcas, 401.

❖ **GETTING HERE:** *The easiest way to reach Alcântara is by* **private plane** *(there are no regularly scheduled flights). For information regarding the eight-minute trip, contact the fine pilot* **Ilmo Antônio Klamt** *at* **CERTA**, *located at the airport in São Luis;* ☎ *245-2722.*

*The really exotic way to reach Alcântara is by* **boat**, *which departs from the Governador Luiz Rocha Terminal Hidroviário (Rampa Campos Mello) sometimes at 7 a.m., 9 a.m., and 10 a.m. and sometimes returns at 2 or 3 p.m. The "sometimes" depends on the tides and, incredibly enough, nobody seems to know exactly when they are. You'll have to return to the terminal several times to ask in advance, but be careful: It's a colorful, though rather seedy port, and brawls among drunken sailors tend to break out easily. The 90-minute "cruise" in the two-level wooden schooners tends to get rough, so arm yourself with whatever seasickness remedies you believe in. (A Brazilian once taught me to suck on a lemon and it worked.)* **Atlântica**

*Turismo, an excellent travel agency, now offers a modern schooner, Batevento, for excursions to Alcântara. (For more information, see Travel Agency, under Hands-On São Luis.)*

There are no telephones on the island. You might consider timing your visit to take in the **Festa do Divino Espírito Santo**, a marvelous festival held from May 8-19.

## Where to Stay

Simple *pousadas* are the only official offerings here, but local families also provide room and board for tourists. Contact **MARATUR** in São Luis. See page 26 for price chart. The following are recommended:

### Pousada Pelourinho

*Praça Gomes de Castro, 15;* ☎ *337-1150.*

This beautiful, sprawling *fazenda*-like house looks out on the principal square. Rooms are huge, but primitive, with traditional beam roofs. The top floor is the best bet, with private bathroom. There is no air conditioning. *1 apartment, 11 rooms. Inexpensive. No cards.*

### Pousada do Mordomo Régio

*Rua Grande, 134. Reservations in São Luis:* ☎ *(98) 222-3093.*

A simple house with simple rooms, TV and air conditioning. *4 apts, 7 rooms. Inexpensive. No cards.*

## Where to Eat

The best eateries – all simple and unpretentious – are the **Josefa**, Rua Direita (daily 11:30 a.m.-2 p.m., 6-11 p.m., closed Fri.) and the restaurant at the **Pousada Pelourinho**, Praça Gomes de Castro, 15 (2-9 p.m.).

## Parque Nacional dos Lençóis

Surely one of the most exotic landscapes in Brazil are the voluptuous white dunes and dark green oases of the Parque Nacional dos Lençóis. Called the "Brazilian Sahara," Lençóis is actually a desert without a desert: a veritable dance between dune and *mangue*, a kind of swamp vegetation teeming with marine life and small verdant shrubbery. Although about 70,000 inhabitants (mostly fishermen) live in this 383-acre national park, the only way to really see the landscape is from the air in a four-seater plane. The trip will be forever etched in your memory. About two hours from Barreirinhas, thousands of freshwater lakes nestling between the dunes begin to make a hypnotic design of sensuous proportion, and if you look hard you might even glimpse a stray cow or the tiny figure of a fisherman on his boat. Between Jan. and June, fishermen improvise boats made of straw; when dry season comes, they bundle up their belongings and head for the closest municipal for small-plot farming.

The very first inroads are now being made into this park by anyone other than the farmer-residents, who have existed precariously on its dunes for hundreds (if not thousands) of years in severe isolation. The nearest city to the park is Barreirinhas (about 30 minutes by air from São Luis), a municipality of 40,000 people which boasts a mere landing strip for air arrivals. The city itself has a few small hotels and restaurants. For simple lodging, try Gilmour at Av. Brasília, 285; ☎ (98) 22-2390. Rates are very cheap.

❖ **GETTING HERE:** *Bus trips from São Luis (four hours), arranged through a travel agency, run $50 per person (min. of nine people) and take four hours. From Barreirinhas, you may enter the park on a three-hour boat tour that includes stopping at the sand dunes and swimming in freshwater (aguá doce) lagoons. It should be a marvelous excursion, and since this park was just recently "discovered" by Fernando César Mesquita, former Secretary of Tourism of Maranhão, you will be among the very first tourists to visit. Go with respect and ecological care. For information, contact* **Atlântica Turismo,** *Rua 14 de Julho, 20 (in São Luis);* ☎ *(98) 232-1965/222-8585.*

The dunes at Parque Nacional dos Lençóis as seen from a plane.

## Tutóia

If you decide to fly over Parque Nacional dos Lençóis, carry on a few miles further (toward the border of the state of Piaiú) to Tutóia, a coastal city more than 400 years old, which has not yet even made it to the *Guia Quatro Rodas,* Brazil's travel Bible (neither has Barreirinhas). That means the native fishermen won't even know what to charge you for a day excursion around the untouched islands, and the only hotel may not even have clean sheets.

Women still wash their clothes in the river, children play nude in the streams, and a secret grotto bears excellent mineral water (when I was there, the Secretary of Tourism declared it drinkable after one courageous sip, but you couldn't pay me to taste it). Most charming are the little pigs that run around town with lamp-shade type collars to keep them from slipping under the log fences.

If you decide to visit Tutóia, you must first contact the Secretary of Culture, who will pick you up at the airport and fully arrange your stay. (American and Japanese scientists have visited the area to research the fishing industry, but few tourists are ever sighted, and nobody around here speaks English.) Negotiate with a resident to rent his mule for a tour around the town, although you'll be surprised to be passed by a few roaring motorcycles. The church, built in 1724, features a wonderful ceiling painting of a frolicking Jesus who looks like he's dancing through heaven. The beaches surrounding the city are nearly pristine, though you may have to share sand space with some wandering boars. The prettiest island to visit by boat is **Cajú**, which is nearly deserted, so you must bring your own food and water. The only restaurant on the beach of Tutóia is **Embarcação,** which serves hearty platters of fried fish and rice. Ask if you can see some folkloric dances, which will probably be the most authentic you'll ever see. The city is very proud that it has had phones for the last eight years, but there are only two lines: ☎ *(98) 471-1271* and *471-1027.*

❖ **GETTING HERE:** *Flights over Parque Nacional dos Lençóis and to Tutóia from São Luis are offered two times a week, on Mon. and Fri. Private planes may also be hired. For reservations call* **CERTA** *at the airport in São Luis;* ☎ *(98) 245-2722. The contact is Ilmo Antônio Klamt. Private flights can also be arranged.*

In Tutóia, authentic folk song and dance is performed from the heart.

## Where to Stay

**O Manelão,** Rua Senador Leite 178, is the simplest of accommodations and very cheap; you should probably bring your own sheets. All apartments have a bed and hammock. For reservations, call the Tutóio operator and leave a message or, better yet, contact the Secretary of Culture.

# AMAZÔNIA

*"The Amazon is the last unwritten page of Genesis."*
Euclides da Cunha, geographer and novelist

*"Imagine if the people in Amazônia decided in the next decade not to treat
the places they lived in as a commodity but as a sacred place."*
Ailton Krenak, Krenak Indian

To travel through the great Amazon River region is a nature experience
you will never forget. The innate wisdom of the forest – its voluptuous
beauty, the life-and-death dramas of millions of species – are realities that
will literally enter your bones as you tramp through the rainforest, cruise
down the tributaries, or raft over rapids. The Amazon is about challenge,
and ever since the first explorers set foot on the banks of the continent, the
dark, mysterious rainforest has inspired countless numbers to sacrifice life
and limb for a little excitement and the promise of treasure.

These days, of course, travel through the Amazon need not be
life-threatening, though it's still exciting, unpredictable and full of
challenge. Despite all the recent political controversy, there's still a lot of
poetry left in the rainforest: the liquid rustle of treetops, the elusive shadows
of animals, the cries of unseen birds. But for most travelers, the most
memorable part of a jungle adventure is the people – the locals who toil day
by day in the jungle; *caboclo* fishermen who live like Indians along the river
shores; old ladies who have fled to the jungle to escape city violence; little
girls who paddle to school every morning and brush their teeth in the river.
There are also Indians, those living on protected reservations, and others
trying to survive halfway between "civilization" and tribal security. Add
to that botanists, biologists, and scientific photographers who are trying to
capture the miracle of the ecosystem. And finally, there are the gold miners,
rubber tappers, ranchers, and industrialists – all, in their own way,
attempting to bend the will of nature to their own commercial desires. A
circus of cross-purposes, yes, but no matter what one's political allegiance
is, each "jungle" person you meet will only add to your understanding of
what the Amazon rainforest is – a fragile paradise.

Traveling through the Amazon is not for couch potatoes, and you may
have to do some solid soul-searching to see if you'll make a good candidate.
(The *"Should I Go to the Amazon?"* quiz will separate the gnats from the no's.)
The best way to indoctrinate yourself is rent a few videos (*The Emerald
Forest, Arachnophobia, At Play in the Fields, Medicine Man*) or dive into
travel-adventure narratives and novels that will let you feel the thrills
without the thorns. Some of the best books are *Tales from a Shaman's
Apprentice* by Mark Plotokin, *Running the Amazon* by Joe Kane, *The Cloud
Forest* by Peter Matthiesson, *Amazon Beaming* by Petru Popescu, *Amazônia*
by Loren McIntyre, and (for laughs) *Holidays in Hell* by P. J. O'Rourke.

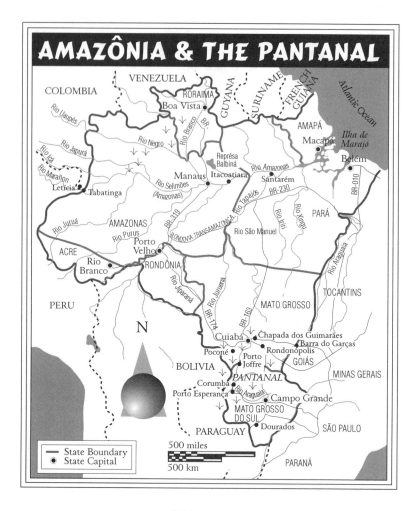

# History

It was myth that seduced the first European explorers to the Amazon. Four centuries ago, the most prevailing one was that of **El Dorado**, a tribal chieftain whose wealth was so vast that he supposedly tattooed his body daily with gold dust. In 1540, **Gonzalo Pizarro**, the brother of the conqueror of Peru, launched an expedition with Ecuadoran general **Francesco Orellana** to conquer the lands of El Dorado and the cinnamon forests. Confronted by disease and imminent starvation, Orellana broke off from the main troops and led a hunting party into the jungle, eventually discovering the mouth of the Amazon River. Although he never found gold, Orellana did tangle with fierce tribes, who told him about a community of women warriors who once a year invited male adults to participate in their mating rituals. Orellana may never have actually met these women, but the story soon became bloated with retelling and enflamed numerous *bandeirantes* and booty-seekers to follow in his footsteps. Later, Spanish scholars dubbed the region and its massive river the Amazon, in honor of the women warriors of Greek mythology who removed their right breast so that they could more easily shoot a bow and arrow.

## Botanists, Biologists, & Shutterbugs

Imagine the courage of those first Amazon explorers who didn't have the advantage of a travel guide, let alone good maps. Among the most intrepid were the 19th-century botanists and biologists whose journals recorded their profitable, but harrowing journeys. The Prussian naturalist **Alexander von Humboldt** was the first to prove that the Orinocco River and Rio Negro-Amazon rivers sprang from the same source in the Parima Range, but he soon lost his enthusiasm when the crocodile grease he daily smeared on his body failed to ward off mosquitoes. A half-century later, **Alfred Russel Wallace,** the English scientist, forged his way up the Rio Negro, experiencing first-hand the "survival of the fittest" and eventually co-authored the theory of evolution with Charles Darwin. **Henry Walter Bates**, the founder of protective mimicry, walked around like a human pin cushion, collecting over 14,712 species (8,000 which were new to science), but even he was unnerved by the screeching of howler monkeys and other mysterious sounds, such as the clanking of iron. Perhaps the best description of the frustration scientists felt came from Englishman **Richard Spruce**, who wrote: "Save willing Indians to run like cats or monkeys up the trees for me, the only way to obtain the wildflowers and fruits was to cut down the tree, but it was long before I could overcome a feeling of compunction at having to destroy a magnificent tree, perhaps centuries old, just for the sake of gathering flowers."

The tallest tales of the jungle came from **Percy H. Fawcett,** a retired British army colonel sent to the upper Amazon in 1906 to resolve the overlapping claims to Bolivia and Peru arising from the rubber boom. Fawcett reported rumors of anacondas, swallowing cattle whole and picking men right out of canoes at night, and he even claimed he once smelled a penetrating fetid odor emanating from one, "probably his breath," he wrote, "which is known to have a stupefying effect." Fawcett also complained about the anacondas' melancholy wails at night – a phenomenon never proven by scientists. Certainly a colorful figure, Fawcett carried no radio during his expeditions, which didn't seem to matter since several spiritualists, including his wife, claimed to be in psychic contact with him. Ever in search of the lost city supposedly discovered by the Portuguese explorer Francisco Raposo in 1754, Fawcett was eventually found dead near the mouth of the Xingú River, most probably murdered by Kalapalo Indians.

In this century one of the last great Amazon explorers is **Loren McIntyre**, a world-class photographer for *National Geographic*, who has done more to capture the ever-changing Amazon than any other chronicler. A must-read is Petru Popescu's *Amazon Beaming*, a riveting account of Mcintyre's capture by an isolated Amazonian tribe and his subsequent involuntary descent into their shamanistic reality. Mcintyre's own coffee-table book *Amazônia* is a thrilling visual testimony to the region and its people.

## Rubber Boom & Bust

It was **rubber**, not gold, that transformed the face of Amazônia. Contrary to popular belief, the rubber trade in Amazônia started long before Charles Goodyear accidentally discovered rubber in 1839. As early as 1750, **Dom José**, King of Portugal, was sending his boots to be waterproofed in Pará, and by 1800 Belém was exporting rubber shoes to New England. The famous Amazonian rubber boom, however, was fueled by the debt peonage of isolated *seringueiros* (rubber tappers) and *caboclos* (backwoodsmen), who sold their balls of latex to the trading post for a pittance. It's been estimated that in 1850 there were 5,200 rubber men. By 1912 when the boom peaked, no fewer than 190,000 Brazilians were tapping 88% of the world's rubber. During these giddy years, **Manaus** became a boom city, its wealth concentrated in the hands of about 100 men – so-called "rubber barons" – who drank Hennesey brandy, dined with Irish linen, and built palatial homes. Soon, electricity was installed and the first tramway in South America initiated. The crowning glory in Manaus was a massive customs building modeled on that of New Delhi, prefabricated in England and shipped to Brazil piece by piece.

In 1870 a young Englishman named **Henry Wickham**, in cahoots with the Royal Botanic Gardens at Kew, conspired a scam that would totally puncture the rubber future of Brazil. Working with the Tapiu Indians, a detribalized tribe, Wickham raced to gather hevea seeds at their prime, smuggled them past customs with a large dose of charm, then nursed them across the Atlantic to Le Havre, France, where a special chartered train delivered them to Kew. From there, the seedlings were rushed to Ceylon where, in the swampy fields of Sri Lanka, the few that survived came to form the basis of the great rubber plantations of Malaysia. In a mere 24 years, the trees matured, outstripping the Amazonian market, which burst totally in 1923. With frightening speed, tycoons, speculators, traders, and prostitutes departed from the tropics, leaving behind them decayed palaces, a boarded-up opera house and cobblestones full of weeds. The only beneficiaries were the native people, who would be left in peace for another half-century.

## The Last Great Gold Rush

In 1979, the owner of a two-bit cattle ranch, **Gensio Ferreira da Silva**, discovered that his scrubby grasses and skinny cows were astride the most important gold strike in Amazonian history. By 1985, over 500,000 prospectors were toiling up and down the vast pits dug into the mountainside – a frightening tableau of human mudmen right out of a Brueghel painting. The federal government, worrying about the potential danger of so many unruly men near Carajás, the largest iron development in the world, finally sent in troops. In May 1984, the military occupied the Serra Pelada, led by Major Curió who, descending from his helicopter, flashed his Magnum and cried, "The gun that shouts loudest is mine." Though the military occupation brought a much needed health center, bank, post office, telephone line and wholesale government store, the *garimpeiros* staged a rebellion down the Belém-Brasília highway, eventually forcing the government to retreat.

## The Indian Issue

The real history of the Amazon belongs to its native peoples – a subject that deserves not a few paragraphs but tomes (among the best of which are *Red Gold and Amazon Frontier: The Defeat of the Brazilian Indians* by J. Hemming). When the first explorers arrived in 1500, there were as many as nine million Indians in the Amazon basin; by 1900 they had been reduced to one million; today, there are fewer than 200,000. The Jesuit missionaries were only one form of unnatural control. What truly undermined the Indian was *cachaça*, happily provided by the *bandeirantes*, who soon discovered that

Amazonian Indians at the crossroads of civilization.

liquor was the only way to press-gang the natives into submission. The tribes that escaped such ignominy, including the rape of their women, the theft of their children, and a legacy of incurable alcoholism, retreated deeper and deeper inside the forest.

In the 20th century, the onslaught of "progress" has continued to devastate the native population. The construction of two highways – the Transamazônica and the Cuiabá-Santarém – has dislocated over 10,000 families (50,000 originally intended), and nearly wiped out through disease the tribes of the Araba, Parkana, Kreen Akarore, and Txukarramae. During the 1980s, Indians began to display political self-determination when a group of Txukarramae from the Xingú River basin held the director of the Xingú Park hostage to demand demarcation of their lands, severed from the rest of the park by Highway BR-080. For a short term, a Xavante Indian chief even enjoyed his own seat in Congress. In 1989, President Sarney brought national attention to the plight of the Yanomami Indians when their 9,000-square-km. reserve on the border between Brazil and Venezuela was overrun by gold miners. Military troops were sent in, but in the end the army simply refused to confront 45,000 burly *garimpeiros*, even though they were poisoning the Yanomami rivers with mercury and attracting new strains of malaria. Today, some 70% of the Yanomami reservation has already been confiscated by mining concerns, but even more tragic has been the physical devastation brought on by constant contact with the outside world; their first case of AIDS has already been reported. In the future, the Yanomamis will be facing the federal government's own Calha Norte plan to populate Brazil's remote borders with frontiersmen.

In Feb. 1989, in the town of Altamira, over 500 Indians from Amazon tribes gathered together with international environmentalists to protest the Brazilian Eletronorte's Xingú HEP Dam scheme. Few who were present (or saw the documentary film) will ever forget the sight of a Kayapó woman brandishing a machete at Eletronorte's CEO and fervently crying, "Do you think we are so stupid that we don't know your plans for us, for this forest?"

In the last few years, a Kayapó Indian chief – **Paulinho Paiakan** – has emerged as a worldwide icon of native power. Touted as Brazil's wealthiest Indians, the 5,000 Kayapó Indians earn millions of dollars a year in royalties from gold and mahogany reserves in central Brazil. Most recently, the chief has solicited the support of the rock star Sting, who founded the Brazilian Rainforest Foundation, and he even managed to sell brazil-nut oil to The Body Shop, an international cosmetic chain. But on the eve of a $40-million movie to be made of his life (not to mention numerous international awards), Chief Paiakan was abruptly arrested when the 19-year-old white Portuguese-language tutor of his children accused him of rape. In Brazil, a national furor erupted, turning environmentalists against feminists (the latter enraged that rapists rarely are punished in Brazil), and raising the ire of industrialists who were lying in wait to discredit the Indian rights movement. By press time, the crisis remained unresolved. (For more information, see my guide, *Amazon Up Close*, Hunter Publishing, 1997.)

## Amazon Heroes

The Amazon has given birth not only to exploiters, but also to heroes. One of the greatest champions of Indians was the **Cândido Mariano da Silva Rondôn**, the highest ranking officer in the Brazilian army and a great explorer who led Teddy Roosevelt on an historic expedition down the Amazon. (A river discovered on that mission, first called River of Doubt, was later renamed Rio Roosevelt.) In 1961, three brothers named **Orlando,**

**Claudio**, and **Leonardo Villas-Boas** persuaded the government to create a national park for the Xingú tribe, whose lands during World War II had been invaded by the construction of military airstrips connecting Rio to Manaus. Entranced by native life, the Villas-Boas brothers not only fought for their rights, but also managed to live with various tribes for many years. Until they succumbed to old age and malaria, the brothers fought valiantly to secure FUNAI's protection of the area from rubber tappers, hunters, industrialists, journalists, missionaries, and even anthropologists, but in 1971, builders overrode public sentiment and drove Highway BR-080 through the park.

The most prominent name in recent Amazonian activism is that of **Chico Mendes**, a poor rubber tapper born in Seringal, Cachoeira. Illiterate until the age of 18, he gained most of his worldly education from listening to Radio Moscow, Voice of America, and the BBC Portuguese Service; when he finally learned to read, he discovered the price of rubber was being outrageously exploited by the *seringalistas*. As ranchers and settlers came to clear the rainforest, the rubber tappers were forced to leave, but Chico refused, urging his fellow workers to unionize. With no knowledge of Gandhi or Martin Luther King, Mendes naturally hit upon the idea of non-violent resistance, and in 1976 organized a series of human stand-offs that prevented work crews from using their chainsaws. In 1989, Indians joined the lobby in favor of extractive reserves set aside for use by rubber tappers and gatherers of nuts, fruits and fibers; today over five million acres of forest have been preserved. In December 1988, after returning home from a labor-organizing trip, Mendes stepped into his backyard and was fatally blasted by a shotgun at close range. The 21-year-old son of a rancher who hated Mendes finally confessed to the murder, but general opinion conceded that his father, Darli Alves, was to blame. In 1993, father and son escaped from a loosely secured prison in Rio Branco, Acre, but were found in 1996. Following the murder of Mendes, Hollywood descended on his family and his wife, Ilzamar, who is reported to have received a million dollars for the rights to his life story.

# Legenòs Of The Amazon

Legends and superstitions seem to lurk behind every plant or animal in the Amazon jungle; don't hesitate to ask locals about their folk beliefs. Among the most "enchanted" of jungle beings are *botos*, or dolphins, who are thought to transform themselves at night into white-suited cads and seduce young virgins. It's even said that *botos* are particularly attracted to the scent of menstrual blood – a folk belief so powerful that girls often refuse to bathe in the river during their periods.

The **japiim**, an Amazonian bird, also enjoys a notorious reputation. Legend has it that in the early days of the jungle, the japiim had a very beautiful voice, which secured him a place in Heaven right next to God. One day he came to earth and tried imitating the songs of the other male birds. When he started attracting all the females, their enraged spouses told him to get lost or reap the punishment. Desperate, the japiim turned to the bees for help, who allowed him to make his nest right next to theirs. As such, you can always find a beehive near the nest of a japiim, whose song is often mistaken for that of other birds.

The mystical origin of the **lily pad** is particularly evocative. Once a beautiful but ambitious girl named Arari wanted to be just like the moon. She tried climbing a great mountain to reach it, but finally jumped to her death from despair, falling into a glimmering lake. The moon, who had a bigger heart than most imagined, took pity on the girl and decided to transform her into a part of the forest. Hence was born the lily pad, which is formed from a blossom that sinks to the bottom of the river, then resurfaces.

### Amazonian Facts

- Amazônia is the world's largest rainforest, covering 2.5 million square miles.
- The Amazon River system is the largest body of fresh water.
- The Amazon Basin, with six million square km. of river and jungle, is the world's largest in terms of volume and drainage. The basin holds two-thirds of all the flowing water in the world.
- Besides the Amazon River, there are 1,100 tributaries (17 of which are more than 1,000 miles long). All totaled, there are 48,000 miles of navigable rivers.
- The Amazon River is at times so wide (up to seven miles) that you can't see the other side of the shore.
- The flow of the Amazon River is 12 times that of the Mississippi.
- There are 15,000 known animal species, 1,800 species of butterflies, 1,200-2,000 species of fish, four types of big cats and 200 mosquitoes in the region. One-quarter of the world's 8,600 bird species live in the Amazon.

# A Bird's Eye View

Maybe it was all those Tarzan movies, but to most people the phrase "The Amazon" has come to suggest a vast, humid jungle. Technically, "The Amazon" refers only to the river itself, including more than 1,000 tributaries that stretch some 4,000 nautical miles from the Atlantic Ocean to its source, Lago Lauricocha, high in the Peruvian Andes.

Resembling a large funnel, the Amazon flows in a Y-shaped system into which its headwaters, the **Negro-Branco** from the northwest, and the **Madeira** from the southwest, converge. When the main trunk reaches the Brazilian border, it turns into the **Solimões**, a so-called "white river," dense with silt and microorganisms, until it meets the darker and clearer **Rio Negro**. Long a point of fascination among visitors, the "dark" and "light" rivers run parallel for several miles without mixing until they finally blend, forming the pale-brownish **Amazon**. The term *Amazonas* refers to Brazil's largest state (of which Manaus is the capital), which is part of Amazônia, a vast basin of forests and wetlands occupying about half of the South American continent (75% of Brazil, as well as parts of Venezuela, Ecuador, Peru, Suriname, Guyanas, and Colombia).

Within Brazil itself, Amazônia embodies the states of Amazonas, Acre, Rondônia, parts of Pará, Mato Grosso, and Maranhão, and the territories of Roraima and Amapá.

# A Quick Rainforest Tour

To the uninitiated, the jungle looks like so much green mess, but actually the terrain that runs through the Amazon river system is extremely diverse. Some soils are deeply fertile, others approach bleached sand; along the Negro River, the vegetation is stunted, whereas in southeastern Pará, the forest, with its purplish-red soil, abounds with wildlife. There are also huge areas of wetlands and large expanses of savannah.

The rainforest itself grows in distinct **layers**, a natural hierarchy formed by the access (or lack of access) to the sun. Most of the activity take place in the luxuriant **canopy**, 100-130 feet above the forest floor, where plants compete for sunshine and where the majority of animals and birds live. Above the canopy poke the trees that form the skyline of the forest. A poorly defined middle layer of understory merges with the canopy, hosting a variety of **epiphytes** – plants that derive moisture and nutrients from the air and rain, but live on the surface of other plants. About 50 to 80 feet above ground spreads a tangle of seedlings, saplings, bushes, and shrubs. On the forest floor, plant life is limited because the thick vegetation of the canopy blocks out all but 1-2% of available sunlight. Ants and termites live here among the scattering of leaves and decaying plant matter.

## Types Of Forest

There are three types of Amazon forest: *várzea*, or floodplain, regularly flooded by the rivers; the *igapós*, which are occasionally flooded; and the *terra firme*, generally unflooded land that forms the majority of the surface area. Much of the *terra firme* is high forest, where animal life exists as much in the canopy as on the ground. When the forest is destroyed, the land turns to scrub since its fertility is bleached out.

## Why Preserve The Forest?

Rainforests are intimately tied to global weather conditions, and their preservation helps prevent the global warming trend known as the **Greenhouse Effect**. Deforestation causes up to 30% of all human-produced carbon dioxide to the atmosphere, as well as unknown amounts of methane and nitrous oxide – gases that exacerbate global warming and threaten the quality of life worldwide. Rainforests also provide a natural defense against hurricanes, cyclones, and typhoons, absorbing the punch of howling winds and preventing storm tides from eroding beaches.

The products that come from the rainforest are part and parcel of our daily lives. As a fantastic natural pharmacy, the forest is home to thousands of medicinal plants that can be turned into antibiotics, painkillers, heart drugs, and hormones. The National Cancer Center in the US has identified 3,090 plants as having anti-cancer properties, 70% of which come from the rainforest. Other products that can be taken from the forest without destroying it are used to create everything from cosmetics to automobile tires.

Tropical forests also provide the planet with much of its **biological diversity**. Every species is a living repository of genetic information, i.e., the building blocks of life. If the food chain that binds them together in a complex web of relationships is disturbed, it is not clear that humankind itself could survive. At the very least, we'd be facing the future with a shrunken world, a hostile climate, and a genetic base vulnerable to mutations.

Last but not least, the forest is home to millions of **indigenous people**, who have known no other way of life for thousands of years. Within their memory banks is a trove of natural wisdom, including how to use plants medicinally, that can never be duplicated once they pass from the earth. The forced relocation of indigenous forest people in the face of the bulldozer has invariably spelled disease, despair, and death.

## Is Eco-Tourism Kosher?

Many eco-conscious travelers ponder whether joining the rank and file of tourists tramping through the rainforest will ultimately endanger it further. Truly in Brazil, the phrase eco-tourism has become the buzz word for the 1990s, though in many cases it's merely a marketing device referring to any outdoor adventure, be it beach, mountain, or forest.

There are a select number of travel agencies and operators, however, who are deeply dedicated to preserving not only the forest (as well as other ecosystems), but also the country's native peoples. Among these are **Lago Verde Turismo** in Santarém and **Ariaú Jungle Tower** outside Manaus. However, generally in Brazil these days the prevailing philosophy is that eco-tourism actually serves to preserve the forest by giving its residents another way of making a living besides cutting down trees. Of course, one need only imagine the trash and debris that could clog the mighty Amazon and its tributaries when gum-chewing, smoking, beer-drinking tourists hit its banks. The nightmare needn't happen, however, if each traveler takes responsibility for his or her actions.

---

### Eco-Alert

The best way to preserve a rainforest is to travel with a conscience. Here are some Do's and Don'ts for visiting natural reserves.

☐ Don't give food to the local animals. It disturbs their immune systems as well as the ecological balance of the environment. It might also be dangerous.

☐ Don't hunt.

☐ Don't destroy trees or break branches.

☐ Don't throw litter.

☐ Don't kill or mistreat fish, birds, or other animals except in self-defense.

☐ Don't make a fire.

☐ Always have a reliable guide who respects the environment.

☐ Do not cross into Indian reserves without special permission from FUNAI (nearly impossible to get). This law protects native peoples from diseases and cultural disturbance.

---

Federal law prohibits the killing of dolphins, turtles, alligators, *peixe boi* (cowfish), tortoises, birds, and capybaras. Any animal that lives in the forest belongs to the state. Anyone caught red-handed by IBAMA agents is sent to prison for three months to one year. You do not want to languish in a Brazilian jail for any amount of time.

# Options For Travel

In all honesty, it takes a certain kind of traveler to enjoy a jungle adventure. Sometimes, however, humans can vastly surprise themselves. I, who was nearly sent home in tears from Girl Scout camp, immensely enjoyed my Amazonian treks, but they were not always easy, nor was I left with an overriding desire to return for the *unbeaten* tracks. (The beaten tracks were plenty exciting.) On your first trip to the jungle, I would not suggest braving it alone or with unreliable guides; believe me, you will want to feel there is someone looking after your welfare. Good guides (usually those officially trained) know the trails where you are least likely to meet poisonous snakes, voracious ants, man-eating piranha, and malaria-infested pools, not to mention mudslides and other debacles of nature. As for travel options, there is such a variety of possibilities that anyone from senior citizens to responsible children (nine and older) can make the grade. My suggestion is to plan a number of different treks that will give you a multi-dimensional perspective of Amazonian life. Among the possibilities:

☐ **Packaged boat tours** (or special charters) through the *igarapés* (streams) shooting off from the Amazon near Belém, Manaus or Santarém.
*Advantage:* Good for those with limited schedule. Trips usu-

ally last between four and 28 hours. Can include fishing, jungle walks and overnight stays in the forest. The best trip is out of Belém, with **Amazon Star Turismo** (see *Hands-On Belém*). Travelers seeking air-conditioned cabins should investigate the 22-passenger *Tuna* or the eight-passenger *Hawk*, which conduct three-day and six-day cruises out of Manaus. For most information contact **Brazil Nuts**, ☎ *(941) 403-8837* in the US.

□ **Two- to three-day stays at lodges** built inside the jungle, mostly accessible by boat from Manaus.
*Advantage*: Secure accommodations with adequate-good food, bath, and organized excursions day and night.

□ **Two- to three-day trips down the Amazon on public river boats** (the region's buses), such as the *Cisne Branco*, which goes between Santarém and Manaus.
*Advantage:* Slow, relaxing, requires no effort and gives you a chance to hobnob with locals. Best for those who speak Portuguese and for those amenable to less than luxurious accommodations.

□ **Sidetrip excursions to river beach sites**, such as  Alter de Chão near Santarém, and Marajó Island, near Belém.

□ **Luxury resorts**, such as Floresta Amazônica in Alta Floresta, Mato Grosso, where you can sleep in comfort and take expeditions into the forest, down the river, to neighboring farms and even to gold mines.
*Advantage:* Offers the greatest options of adventures and the largest perspective of Amazonian lifestyles. Good for those who don't like sleeping on boats.

□ **Ocean-going cruisers,** which dock in Amazonian ports. (See *Specialty Tours* in the back of the book.)

# The Amazon Survival Kit

## In Preparation

Be in good physical shape; even though the terrain is more or less flat, hiking through a high-humidity jungle can be exhausting. (In contrast, river trips border on the soporific.) Time your vaccinations over the month before you leave; you can't take them all at the same time. To ward off mosquitoes, many people swear by taking daily dozes of Vitamin B two weeks to a month before the trip (and during). Some professionals even believe that foregoing sugar helps. If you are particularly allergic to bees, make sure you travel with your own remedies (emergency medical assistance will probably be miles away). And above all, break in your new boots before leaving.

# What To Wear

Light cotton clothing. Although native people walk through the rainforest barefoot and in shorts, I don't suggest it for foreigners, whose immune systems are unaccustomed to jungle life. Wearing jeans (tucked into boots) and light cotton long-sleeved shirts (with roll-up sleeves) will cut down on scratches and snake and bug bites. In both wet and dry season you'll need sturdy tennis shoes and/or waterproof hiking boots (I loved my lightweight, waterproof Merrell boots made with Gor-Tex). Heavy-treaded soles are needed to help you balance on tree logs. On any river trip you'll need a sunhat and good sunglasses with a strap to keep them from falling off. Kerchiefs are excellent for wiping sweaty brows. In rainy season, take a lightweight hooded rain poncho and an extra pair of clothes for when you get soaking wet. A swimsuit will come in handy, but pack a coverup. Some agencies supply rain gear (rubber boots and ponchos) when necessary.

# What To Pack

Swiss Army knife, canteen, or plastic water bottle, thermos (with cup big enough to eat from), compass, binoculars, journal, pens, small backpack, and collapsible fishing gear. Pack water purification pills (but use in emergencies only – it's better to drink bottled water). If you plan to take river trips on the public boats, a hammock is advisable, even if you secure a private cabin. Mosquito nets are not generally needed, unless you venture out into the jungle on your own. (See *Health Kit* in the back of the book). Take plenty of bug repellent and reapply, especially at dusk and before going to sleep. A fellow traveler in the Pantanal swore by Avon Skin-So-Soft bath oil as a natural repellent (available through Avon Products). Suntan lotion with a high SPF is an absolute must; the sun at the equator is the hottest in the world; and the river water will reflect even more intensely. You should wear sunblock even in the tree-shaded jungle. Pack extras of all personal medicines, contact lenses and eyeglasses, etc. If you're taking a two- to three-day cruise down the Amazon, a juicy paperback will be deeply appreciated after a few hours.

### Photographic Equipment

I went down the Amazon River with a professional German photographer who didn't give a hoot about humidity rot, bugs, or human carelessness – until I nearly knocked his equipment overboard. Truth is, bugs and infinitesimal-sized ticks are rampant on these boats and fungus abounds; the spray from the river alone is enough to render delicate mechanisms defunct. To avoid ruined film, keep rolls tightly secured in waterproof baggies and store all equipment with a small packet of silica gel. At least once a week, expose lenses and camera to direct sunlight (minus the film!). Also, remember to develop film promptly (Manaus has some good 24-hour processing shops), and if your camera allows for exposure adjustments, underexpose a ¼ F-stop.

## Mosquitoes & Bugs

Almost all lodges near Manaus were chosen for their mosquito-free locations. Even so, independent-party mosquitoes always managed to find me, especially on my boat cruise from Santarém to Manaus. Off-the-beaten trekkers must be careful; some areas of the Amazon are so ridden with mosquitoes that few human beings even venture there. In his book *The Amazon* (Time Life), Tom Sterling recalls how he had to wear a bathing cap to protect his bald head in the notorious Jari Region.

Yellow fever, transmitted by mosquitoes, is considered endemic in Brazil, except around the coastal shores. Health authorities advise that the most infected areas are Acre, Amazonas, Goiás, Maranhão, Mato Grosso, Mato Grosso do Sul, Pará, Rondônia, and the territories of Amapá and Roraima. Vaccinations are good for 10 years and are essential if you are traveling either to the Amazon or the Pantanal. You may be required to show proof of vaccination when entering the country from Venezuela, Colombia, Ecuador, or Bolivia. It's best always to travel with it. (For more information, see the *Health Kit* at the back of the book.)

## Malaria

To take malaria pills or not to take – that is the question that doctors north and south of the equator are still debating. On the con side: prophylactics tend to mask symptoms of malaria, and, once the illness is diagnosed, they make it more difficult to treat. Also, new species of mosquitoes (from which malaria is contracted) are always developing and the latest medicines are not usually up to date. On the pro-side: Pills give you some peace of mind. What's best is to wear strong repellent and avoid commonly known breeding grounds, such as stagnant water.

## Vaccinations

Frankly, I took every form of vaccination possible before heading to Brazil and the jungle, including yellow fever (required), tetanus, and gammaglobulin (for Hepatitis B), as well as a complete round of malaria pills before, during, and after my trip to the jungle. For the latest official advisories, contact the **Centers for Disease Control**, Atlanta, GA 30333 (Parasitic Division, Center for Infectious Diseases). Also see *Health Kit* in the back of the book.

## What You Should Worry About

**Snakes** are an Amazon reality, but poisonous snakes are rare in the forest where official tours go. The most feared, however, is the *surucu* (bushmaster), the largest snake in Brazil, which measures up to 10 feet. Also common is the *sucuri* (anaconda), the largest snake in the world, though not poisonous. Silverish-green in color, it's a member of the boa family, meaning it kills its prey by constriction and suffocation, feeding on fish, birds, mammals, and alligators. Don't worry.

Do beware, however, that some rainforest plants and animals mimic each other in order to hide from predators or sneak up on prey. Snakes, in particular, love to look like vines. For protection, wear ankle-high boots and tuck in your pants.

**Piranhas:** *Pira* means fish and *rana* means tooth – nasty, toothy little fish found throughout the rivers and lakes of the Amazon basin. Their viciousness, though exaggerated, is not exactly unfounded. Piranha only become dangerous when trapped in lagoons during dry season or when they smell blood. Waters in the Rio Negro around Manaus are harmless, but in general avoid swimming with open sores.

Squeamish tourists should enter the water only after their guide dives in first. More feared than piranha is the *candirú açu,* a minute catfish that forces its way into the urethra of the bather, making itself difficult to extract. Don't worry.

---

## Should I Go To The Amazon?

*Take the following quiz to determine if you are a good candidate for an Amazon adventure. Don't cheat or it will come back to haunt you. If you rate more than six "Trues," sign up immediately; you'll probably actually enjoy yourself.*

1. You are in good physical shape (heart and lungs), though you needn't be able to jog five miles.

2. You are able to withstand heat and high humidity while trekking through a rugged forest on relatively flat land.

3. You do not flinch in the face of flying bugs, ticks, gnats, ants, or spiders and will not falter in the face of a dead snake (screaming in the face of a live one is permitted, but not encouraged).

4. You can endure less than haute cuisine for a few days, and travel on a boat in severely cramped quarters.

5. Seasickness is not a problem for you, nor are you scared of small canoes with bad motors.

6. You are not overly allergic to bees or bug bites and are prepared to return with arms and legs eaten up by mosquitoes.

7. You like mud.

8. You can handle intense, frequent rain.

9. You know how to psyche yourself to withstand "green overload," fear of the unknown, and that kind of squishy, moldy feeling that comes from being rained on and not able to change your clothes immediately.

---

# Santarém

Located near the western border of the state of **Pará**, Santarém is the major city in the **Tapajós River Basin** – an enchanting, near magical region distinct from other Amazon terrains. Also called the Lower Amazon, this area is a verdant, almost continuous plain, rarely exceeding 1,000 feet high and overlaid with lakes, tributaries, island rivers and narrow streams, called *igarapés*. During low tide (July-Dec.), vast stretches of fine white sand and green water graced by pink porpoises turn the Tapajós into an Amazonian resort. Though there are roads in the region, they are dangerous during rainy season, so most people travel by way of the *estradas líquidas* (liquid highways). Travelers can pick from every kind of water transport imaginable – from flat-bottom barges to diesel-powered canoes to *barcos de linha* (water buses) where everyone, from teens to salesmen to old ladies with grandchildren, hang up their hammocks and settle in for the two- to three-day journeys. (For more information, see *Excursions* in the Belém chapter.)

Santarém is situated on the exact point where the Tapajós River pours its greenish waters into the brown waters of the Amazon. Ecologically, Santarém is fascinating because it represents an unusual microcosm of the Amazon, where all three types of jungle systems – *várzea* (flood plain), *terra firme* (flat forest ground), and *igapó* (stream) – can be fully experienced. Numerous cruise lines use Santarém as a stopover, not only because of the varied ecosystem, but because the city itself is a lovely Amazonian port to visit. Along the Avenida Tapajós, you'll see hundreds of boats loaded with goods that are sold to villagers within moments of arrival. There's also a colorful wharfside market, a few imposing colonial houses and several sleepy baroque plazas. Although you can browse through this Rip Van Winkle town easily on foot, the best way to see it is by hiring a cow-drawn cart and rambling down the dusty, cobblestone streets.

Cruiseliners also tend to stop at the nearby primitive community of Alter de Chão, known for its folklore and its "illusory" lakeside beach (some cruises leave their passengers off in Santarém and pick them up in Alter de Chão). Extra excursions can be made to Alenquer, a former Indian village, where an impressive assembly of hieroglyphics point to the remains of an ancient civilization. Also, a few hours away by boat is the community of Monte Alegre, a region ripe with rock paintings as well as amethyst mines and an unusual ecosystem: its meadows, part of the Great Lake, boast semi-submerged forests and an enormous variety of fish.

> **UP CLOSE TIP:** *Typical of the region are enormous water lilies that look like saucers right out of* Alice in Wonderland. *Called* Vitória Régia, *this lily has bright green leaves that measure almost 6½ feet in diameter and a one-foot flower, making it the largest in the Americas.*

# History

Prior to the European discovery, the Lower Amazon was inhabited by several indigenous groups, including the **Tupaius**, from which the Tapajós River got its name. In 1661, an Indian mission was founded, and in 1758 the name of the burgeoning settlement was changed to Santarém, after the town in Portugal. If you come across a few locals with last names like Vaughon, Jennings, Hennington, Wallace, and Riker, that's because two years after the American Civil War, one hundred Confederates immigrated to the region straight from the southern United States. (Unfortunately, hardly any of their descendants speak English today.)

Between 1821 and 1912, nearly half a million people from the Northeast migrated to the region in a desperate bid to flee a ravaging drought, helping the region become the world's prime producer of **natural rubber**. In 1927, the most curious jungle saga began when American mogul **Henry Ford**, after researching sites around the world, decided that the **Tapajós Valley** was the best region in which to cultivate rubber trees on an international scale. (Curiously, no Brazilian had ever given it much thought.) Capitalizing on a contract that awarded him 110,000 square km. of forest for 50 years, Ford actually transported an entire prefabricated city into the jungle, complete with all the modern facilities. The community, appropriately named Fordlilândia, was light years ahead of other cities in the Amazon basin: Workers reaped the benefit of free housing, electric lighting, running water, telephones, schools, theater, nurseries, orchards, and the best equipped hospital in the state of Pará. What Ford didn't anticipate was an explosion between the social classes, including an outbreak (known as the "saucepan-breaking incident") when the native workers demanded back their old food – beans, manioc flour, and *cachaça* – instead of the protein-enriched American rations. The real downfall of the enterprise, however, was attributed to a fungus known as **leaf blight** that devastated the plantation. In 1934, the same venture was attempted in another tract of land 60 square km. (23 square miles) south of Santarém (called Belterra), but it, too, was attacked by the fungus as well as by caterpillar blight. Today, ecologists understand that the root of the disasters was monoculture – the lack of any other species that could balance the delicate ecosystem of the jungle. After 17 years the Ford company finally gave up the enterprise and "presented" the government of Brazil with the remains of the two communities for $250,000 (a loss of more than $20 million). Fordilândia, though still inhabited, now resembles a ghost town, with its deserted sheds and picket-fence houses – a mere shadow of the imposing structures erected during the 20s and 30s.

In 1958, the Lower Amazon was shaken by another explosion when an enormous vein of gold was discovered in the Upper Tapajós River Valley, from Itaituba northwards. In 1969 the Santarém-Cuiabá Highway was opened, enabling makeshift towns and villages to multiply as thousands hurried to the river and its tributaries to *bamburrar*, or get-rich-quick.

Unfortunately, little money from the gold rush returned to Santarém, and many rivers were contaminated with mercury as a result of the rampant prospecting. In the last several years, however, Santarém has made a tremendous comeback. A new local government has stimulated substantial growth in tourism and agriculture, adding to the industrial economy based on extraction of gold, wood, Brazil nuts, rubber, and jute, as well as textile, cattle farming, and fishing industries. Qualification programs for hotel and restaurant employees, guides, and taxi and bus drivers have been developed, and school children are being educated about the historical and cultural aspects of the region. Impressed by the potential of the mineral-rich várzea, the World Bank is now investing time and research into extensive harvesting without insecticides or fertilizers. Even the Japanese government is investing in a recuperation program of the most devastated ecological regions.

## A Bird's Eye View

To get a pleasant picturesque view of Santarém, walk down Avenida Tapajós – past the river boats, chicken coops, and floating gas station – to where you can view the meeting of the Amazon and Tapajós rivers. From July to Jan., the beach in front of the avenue is full of sand and lined with mango trees. A night tour to scope out alligators can be taken to **Ilha de Ponta Negra**, an area known for its cattle and huge water lily lake. Early morning trips are best for birdwatchers. Beaches near Santarém are exquisite. Located about three hours away by boat, the **Arapiuns River** is reputed to have the most beautiful beach in the area, with 130 feet of white sand and dark rocks and excellent resources for fishing in unpolluted waters. Three or four km. (1.8-2.5 miles) into the forest, you'll discover a stunning waterfall. Four km. (2.5 miles) from Santarém is **Maracanã Beach**, which local people frequent. Among the chic beaches is **Pajussara**, about 30 minutes by boat from the city, full of lovely summer homes and palm-lined white sands. You must take your own food.

## Sights

Santarém is a cinch to see on foot; just be careful about the heat, or the rain (during the rainy season). If you want to tour the city in a cow-drawn cart, contact **Lago Verde Turismo**, ☎ 522-7577.

### Walking Tour

#### Marketplace

Start at the marketplace along the wharf near Praça do Relógio, where between 6-10 a.m. you'll find the picture-postcard version of an outdoor third-world marketplace. Nearby is the indoor market called Mercado Modelo; between the two you'll find everything from live chickens to tropical fruits to hammocks.

## Nossa Senhora da Conceição

Walk up Rua Siqueira Campos to the cathedral. The original structure was built in 1711 by French architects, but had to be rebuilt 20 years later when it collapsed. The fully clothed model of Jesus holding the Cross in the front right vestibule is paraded during the Círio Festival on the second Sun. in Oct. In front of the church is the Praça da Matriz, where, about 60 years ago, a band used to perform.

## Rua Siqueira Campos

Walking down the main shopping avenue you'll pass two record stores with good discount bins as well as recordings by regional musicians, such as Ray Brito and Tinho. Even if you're not heading out on a river trip, an interesting stop is the supermarket on this street called **Formigão** (Big Ant). You can stock up on beer, cookies, crackers, and especially Tang (the American orange drink mix, which is good for dehydration).

On the next block you'll find the **Varig** office, Rua Siqueiro Campos, 277, open 7-11:30 a.m. and 2-5:30 p.m. Closed Sun.

## Pastelândia

Across the street is this clean and airy snack bar specializing in *pasteis* (baked dough pastries filled with meat or cheese), cooked right before your eyes. Camera and film stores are next door. Along Rua Siqueira Campos are several drugstores that may exchange dollars; talk to the owner.

Turn left on Rua Senador Lameira Beiftencourt, also called Rua 15 de Novembro, past more shops, then right on Rua do Comércio, a pedestrian mall full of sportswear stores.

## Mascote Bar

On the right is this good lunch stop. Nearby, at Rua Sen. Lam Bittencourt, 31 (the street running into Rua Comércio) is one of the best artisan stores (for more information, see *Shopping*, below).

## Rua Francisco Correa

Turning left from Rua do Comércio onto Rua Francisco Correa, walk up the steep hill for a wonderful view of the Meeting of the Waters; you'll see the blue of the Tapajós River and the brown of the Amazon. Fortunately, there's also a cool breeze here, perhaps the only one in the city. The odd illusion is that you'll feel as if you are looking out onto the ocean; the water is so clear because the river is full of plankton (plants) and, therefore, does not allow for the penetration of light. Walk back toRua Siqueira Campos and turn left, passing the only banana stand in the city.

## Centro Cultural João Fona

*Rua do Imperador.*

Also called the Museu de Santarém, this fine museum was formerly the city hall, parliament, court and prison. Today it holds a famous collection of Tupaiu Indian crafts (there's also a good view of the Meeting of the Waters from here). Anthropologists and archaeologists have been studying the

Tupaius' pottery (*ceramica tapajônica*) and have concluded that these were the most culturally advanced Indians in the Amazon; some of their pieces date back 8-10,000 years. Ana Roosevelt, granddaughter of the American president, has led research teams in the area and may be producing a book soon about this tribe, considered to be the most ancient civilization in South America.

To end this walking tour, walk back along the wharf. The best place to watch the sun set is at Mascotinho, an open-air café where you can indulge in pizza and cold beer. You'll also find an ice cream parlor where you can stock up on sweets and pastries, a good idea if you're planning a boat trip. Along the wharf you'll see cows tied to carts, still used for transporting goods and people.

## By Car

### Aparecida Hammock Factory

*Av. Borges Leal, 2561;* ☎ *522-1187. 7:30-11:30 a.m., 1:30-6 p.m.*

Thousands of *redes* (or hammocks) are handmade daily at this factory, where you can watch artisans work (until 3 p.m.) on looms imported from southern England. Excellent quality is assured here, and you're sure to find all varieties and colors (if you're looking for cheap, better go to the Mercado Modelo). All profits here go to support social welfare programs. If you're making any jungle trips – by land or water – a hammock helps beat the heat. Do practice slowly getting in and out of your hammock; many a gringo has fallen flat on his or her face, to the enormous amusement of locals, who do it so gracefully. (One hint: The safest way is to lie slowly down diagonally.) Before you invest, note that a hammock takes up considerable bulk in a suitcase, but will fit nicely in a backpack.

### Herb Farm

For the past 15 years, Farmâcia Viva, a dirt-road community of 3,000, has supported this herb cooperative famous for its medicinal remedies. The village, about 10 minutes from the Tropical Hotel, is full of ethereal-looking children with curly, bright-golden hair that no one can explain; the old ladies who tend the garden seem like the salt of the earth. They'll love to show you their patches of patchouli, *capim santo* and other herbs whose aromas fill the air. And they'll be even more delighted if you buy some of their homemade tonics. The *banho capilar* is reported to grow hair on a bald head, and there's even a plant called "Vick" that is good for headaches. Since the route to the plantation often confuses even locals, you will need a guide to get there, but be careful about getting stuck in the mud (though the whole community will turn out to help you if you do).

❖ **GETTING HERE:** *Take the road to Cuiabám turn left on Av. Moaçara, right on Trav. Rouxinol and Rua Maravilha. Keep asking for directions.*

### National Forest

Thirty-nine miles (62 km.) by good road from Santarém is the Floresta Nacional de Tapajós, a virgin forest where you can see a variety of animals, including groups of wild pigs, monkeys, and tropical birds. Ornithologists often come to research South American landbirds, which appear in quantity early in the morning. To visit the park, call IBAMA ☎ 522-3032, and speak to Rionaldo Almeida, director of the National Forest. You must provide your own transportation (boat, plane, or jeep) and translator, but you are also required to be officially accompanied by one of their guides. Lago Verde Turismo, the local travel agency, also offers a five-hour walking tour of this forest.

# Excursions

## Alter de Chão

Eighteen miles (30 km.) from Santarém lies Alter de Chão, Santarém's weekend resort. It's an outgrowth of a village of the Borari Indians, a place of magical leisure because of the still-native community and unusual beaches that spread over the bay of the Tapajós River. Some cruises that anchor in Santarém often leave passengers at port, where they can take a bus to Alter de Chão (the ship, via regional boats, retrieves them later in the day). Some cruises drop anchor directly at Alter de Chão, requiring passengers to reach shore through tenders. The trip to Alter de Chão from Santarém by car was once rough and rugged, but the road is now paved. (Lago Verde Turismo can arrange passage to the island.)

### Muiraquitãs Lake

Alongside the village, this lake's clear water changes daily from deep blue to green. It provides the area's folklore, especially by the celebration of Festa da Sairé in the beginning of July. Slowly the village has been surrendering to modernism. Today, most of the locals, who used to fish and hunt, live mainly off tourism and their clay homes are now being squeezed in between more modern summer homes. During high season the city is so crowded you can barely walk through the dusty streets; at other times it looks deserted. One concession to modern life is that the beachside avenue is now paved. The city's "garbage collectors" can be seen flying over the city – huge black vultures or *urubus*. (They're also called turkey vultures because their heads look like those of turkeys.)

### Praça de Nossa Senhora da Saúde

The main square is fronted by a native church and shaded by big, leafy jambeiro trees, whose fruits are quite tasty. Here, you'll also find local women selling *tacacá*, a native dish usually served in coconut shells. On the far side of the plaza, down Travessa dos Mártires (a side street from the beach), is an area of rubber trees. At 4 p.m. every day, the seeds blow up and explode, sounding just like a revolution breaking out. Don't miss this pinch of excitement.

Between Jan. and June, an island in the bay appears out of nowhere with 132 feet of sand, becoming the makeshift summer residence for about 1,000 *caboclos*. For about a dollar each way, little boys will ferry you in rickety canoes across to the island; there you'll find *barracas* for drinks, snacks, and barbecue fish and chicken.

> **UP CLOSE TIP:** *Avoid swimming on the river side (south); instead head for the north side of the island, where trees are growing out of the lake and the water is cooler and cleaner. Windsurfing is excellent (though you must have your own equipment) and kayaking is superb (rentals available). A very healthy hike can be taken up Morro do Cruzeiro, the mountain with a cross on top (about 45 min. one way). At the peak, you'll get an impressive view of Piranha Lake, Tapajós River, and Green Lake.*

## Center for the Preservation of Indigenous Art & Culture

*Rua Dom Macedo Costa.*

This beautiful museum in Alter de Chão has one of the finest collections of Indian tribal art in the Amazon River, with over 75 tribes represented. Visitors say there is no other place like this in the Amazon. Fee is about $3 per person.

## Instituto de Pesquisa Amazônica

Buffalo fanatics can head for the *fazenda* of Will Ernestro Leal, Wil Ernesto Leal, whose 2,470-acre farm also houses the most famous research institute in the area. The land is primarily savanna, a vegetation uncommon to the Amazon, comprised of thin tall trees, around which scamper monkeys, capybaras and exotic birds. For more information contact **Lago Verde Tourism, ☎** *(91) 522-7577.*

## Hotels, Restaurants & Shopping

If you stay overnight in Alter de Chão during high season, you'll have to reserve a hotel in advance. Only primitive *pousadas* are available.

## Pousada Alter do Chão

*Av. Lauro Sodré; ☎ 522-3411.*

This is the best spot for location and food. Under Tia Deney's care you can find probably a room for less than $10 person, including breakfast served on the veranda facing Lago Verde. Bathroom, but no air conditioning. *12 apts. Inexpensive. All cards.*

## Lago Verde restaurant

*7 a.m.-6 p.m., weekends, open at 6 a.m.*

This is another good restaurant lakeside. Try the regional *tucunaré* (a family of black bass) or the *bolinho de pirarucú* (an extremely tender fish wrapped in a crispy fried crust).

## Arte Grupo Lago Verde

This handicraft store features an interesting snack called *beijo de moço* (kisses of a young girl), a kind of tapioca flour baked into crispy crackers. Also stock up on jars of *doce de cupuaçu* or *licor de cajú*, sweets and liquers made out of regional fruits. Native crafts include hand-painted logs and twigs found in the forest – a little kitschy for my taste since the local style is to paint over the natural bark with artificial colors.

# River Cruises

The oldest and still most common mode of travel in the region is boat, as witnessed by the 7,000 vessels operating in the municipality, from small wooden diesel-powered crafts to large catamaran passenger ships owned by the ENASA Company. Luxury liners from the States and Europe are becoming a more frequent sight.

Larger boats and ships dock at the deep-water pier (*Docas do Pará*) at the far northern end of the Santarém-Cuiabá Highway. Most other boats leave from the area between the Market Place and the Praça do Pescador (Fisherman's Square). Though they are not always safe, two-decker *gaiolas* are the most popular way to journey downriver. Some have been known to sink from being overloaded with chickens, pigs, and produce, but better precautions are taken these days to avoid the kind of tragedy that befell the *Cisne Branco* about eight years ago. (On a New Year's cruise the ship sank, drowning everyone aboard when all the passengers moved to the right side at the same time to see the approaching port of Manaus. I must add, however, in 1991 I risked everything (for the sake of a previous edition of this book!) and took a cruise on the newly resurrected *Cisne Branco*, obviously happily surviving. And I liked it! For reservations on any river cruises, contact Lago **Verde Turismo** or **ENASA** directly.

Most boats headed for Manaus or Belém offer a limited number of private cabins, and should be reserved as early as possible. The cabins in gaiolas are extremely small, but their virtue is privacy; if you rent one, you may also want to hang a hammock in the main galley to lounge during the hot days. Usually, there is an upper deck with a snack bar where you can sit and watch the banks pass by. More often than not, the price of the ticket includes meals, but do take a pile of bananas, oranges, and cashews because the food may not be up to your personal standards of cleanliness.

**ENASA Boats** have been one of the most popular tourist excursions between Belém and Manaus (with stops in Santarém). Made for touring, the boats boast air-conditioned cabins with private bathroom, restaurant, telephone, video lounge, bar, sun-deck, and swimming pool. The trip from Belém to Santarém runs three days; Santarém to Manaus two days. Schedules in the past have run once a month. In Santarém, contact **Representante ENASA**, Tr. Francisco Correa, 34; ☎ *(91) 522-1934*; in Belém, Av. Presidente Vargas, 41; ☎ *(91) 223-3011*; in Manaus, Rua Mal. Deodoro, 61; ☎ *(92) 232-4280*.

A favorite stop for cruises is about three hours by vessel from Santarém – the point where the Amazon River meets the Cruá-Una River. This tributary of the Amazon is singular in that its banks host the greatest amount of native wildlife to be found in the entire Amazon's *terra firme* (primary forest that never floods). Upriver is **Pacoval**, an original village settled by fleeing black slaves and native Indians.

## Romantic Cruises

### River Curuana

An excellent three-day/two-night package that could serve as an exotic honeymoon starts from Santarém's airport, where you transfer to a 10-person boat and head up the river. Here, a canoe with outboard motor will be awaiting you for navigation through the numerous *igarapés* (streams) full of water lilies, pink dolphins, alligators, and birds. The region is known for having more native trees than any other, and as the river meets the Amazon, *várzea* (flood plain) appears, which is good for piranha fishing

After lunch you return to the regional boat and go upriver to visit **Pacoval**, a village founded by runaway black slaves originally from Guyana. At dusk (5:30-6:30 p.m.), small canoes are taken out for alligator hunting. Afterwards, a special candlelit dinner is served in the middle of the forest. The next morning you visit the outdoor and indoor labs of SUDAM, a research center for reforesting projects. Then you cruise downriver to **Alter de Chão**, arriving at dawn and breakfasting on the island. After eating you are invited to climb the mountain; successful trekkers are rewarded with ice cream and champagne. The rest of the day is spent at Alter de Chão (on the beach or in canoes); then you may either head for the airport in the evening or spend the night in a hotel. Groups of 8 to 10 people pay $300 per person. A private package for two people runs about $1,900. **Lago Verde Turismo,** Rua Galdino Veloso, 384; ☎ *(91) 522-7577*; fax *522-2118*, one of the most reliable and creative agencies, offers this trip.

## Monte Alegre

Heading down the Amazonas River between Santarém and Belém is the town of Monte Alegre (10 hours from Santarém). Etched into the Ererê and Paituna mountain ranges are caves, rock formations, and primitive designs and paintings belonging to prehistoric Amazônia. Six hundred and sixty feet from the port is one of the largest egret rookeries in the region. At dawn and dusk, millions of birds can be seen flapping their wings in a magnificent display. Another attraction is the **thermal springs**, where pools of sulfurous water are used to treat skin diseases. For more information contact the **Secretaria da Cultura e Turismo**/Prefeitura Municipal de Monte Alegre, Av. Presidente Vargas; ☎ *(91) 533-1147*, Santarém, PA.

## Alenquer

Nicknamed the "City of the Gods," Alenquer can be found upstream on the Amazon River between Santarém and the border of Pará (six hours from Alenquer). About an hour from the town are lakes and streams with giant water lilies. A family of rock pedestals with smaller stones in identifiable shapes can be found in **Morada dos Deuses**. There is also a tall cliff in a valley that forms a canyon with a waterfall. The folklore event **Festa do Marambiré** is held every June.

Lago Verde Turismo also offers excursions to both Monte Alegre and Alenquer on a three-day package. (For contact information, see *Travel Agencies* under *Hands-On* section.)

# Lodge Expeditions

### Tapajós-Amazon Lodge Hotel Ecológico

*Av. Alvaro Adolfo, 1232;* ☎ *(91) 522-2330, fax 522-5866.*

Tucked on the left bank of the Tapajós River (two hours by boat from Santarém), this new and extraordinary lodge is the only one in the Amazon to offer a beach of white sand and crystal water for swimming. Built into 370 acres of natural wildlife (320 of which is untouched tropical forest), the palm-roofed lodge's 18 wooden bungalows (with bathrooms) actually sit on stilts in a lake, offering terrific views. A footbridge links the rooms to the restaurant, which is known for its fresh fish. Two-day/one-night packages run about $80 per person, including transfer, jungle walk, fishing, and cruise down the river. Contact directly or through **Lago Verde Turismo** in Santarém, ☎ *(91) 522-7577; fax 522-2118.*

# Where To Stay

In Santarém there is the Tropical Hotel and then there are the others – a gap of about three stars. If you're rugged enough to spend a few days in the jungle, you may be perfectly happy with low-star accommodations in the city, but there's nothing like coming back to clean sheets, civilized service, and reliable air conditioning. See page 26 for price chart.

### Tropical Hotel Santarém

*Av. Mendoça Furtado, 4120;* ☎ *522-1533, fax 522-2631.*

Not as elegant as the Tropical in Manaus, but it is the best hotel here. It's also owned by Varig, so you'll find an airline office in the lobby. Rooms are tiled to accommodate jungle trekkers, and every effort is made to maintain high standards of cleanliness. *122 apts. Expensive. All cards.*

### Santarém Palace Hotel

*Av. Rui Barbosa, 726;* ☎ *522-5688, 522-5993.*

The best of the budgets offers rooms that are spacious to a fault, with painted corridors and carpeted floors. All rooms are air conditioned and come with color TV, telephone, and mini-bar; even the lobby is air conditioned. Local tours are offered in the lobby. *Inexpensive. No cards.*

### Brasil Grande Hotel

*Trav.15 de Agosto, 213;* ☎ *522-5660.*

Nearly a dive, but at least it's clean and efficiently run. In fact, it was the cleanest hotel downtown, according to quality control in 1994. The fan-cooled restaurant with MTV is a favorite among locals. Across the street is Mascote Ice Cream Parlor, with exotic popsicles. Standards come with fan, color TV, and mini-bar; suites with air conditioning, color TV, and mini-bar. Rooms with only fan and collective bathroom are cheapest. *Inexpensive. No cards.*

### New City

*Trav. Francisco Corrés, 200/212;* ☎ *522-4719.*

Funky on the verge of sleazy, but at least this hotel is cheap. Splurge on a suite, since it's air conditioned, with a double and single bed, color TV, and mini-bar. Because rooms vary in size, however, check what's available when you arrive. The apartments on the second floor are the quietest and the best ventilated. The lobby is dominated by a color TV, dirty plastic plants and a grungy aquarium. Laundry service available. *Inexpensive. No cards.*

# Where To Eat

See page 26 for price chart.

### Mascote Restaurante

*Praça do Pescador, 10,* ☎ *522-5997. 11 a.m.-midnight.*

Santarém is not the culinary king of the Amazon, but a good value meal can be had here. Pizzas are tasty, as is the *peixe de tucunaré*, a fish similar to black bass that arrives in light soup. The service is not fast, but you can spend the wait gazing out the window at the *gaiolas* (boats) loading up.

### Canto do Sabiá

*Est. Santarém/Curuá-Una, 6 km. 10 a.m.-2 p.m., 5 p.m.-1 a.m.*

Set outdoors in the middle of a forest about 10 km. (six miles) from the city, this is a great place to see the Amazon's moon and stars. During the day you can swim in a natural pool made from *igarapé* or cool off at the big canopied tables. Local families crowd in on the weekend to feast on great barbecued chicken and beer. *Inexpensive. No cards.*

### Mascontinho

*Riverside.*

Perched on the bank, this "little" version of Mascote, is perfect for pizza, sandwiches and dock-watching. Sunsets are spectacular from here. *Inexpensive. No cards.*

### Lumi

*Av. Cuiabé, 1683.* ☎ *522-2174. 11 a.m.-2 p.m., 6-11 p.m.*

Authentic Japanese cuisine made by the descendants of immigrants who arrived during the rubber boom. *Moderate. No cards.*

### Peixaria Canta Galo

*Trav. Silva Jardim, 820;* ☎ *522-1174. Noon-5 p.m., 6 p.m.-1 a.m.*

Specialty is regional fish cooked Parense-style. Browse through the aquarium of local species.

### Tupaiu (Tropical Hotel)

*Av. Mendoça Furtado, 4412-;* ☎ *522-1533. Noon-3 p.m., 7-10 p.m.*

Air conditioning is high on the list of assets here, with a decent array of international cuisine. *Moderate. All cards.*

### Mutunui

*Tr. Turiano Meira, 1680;* ☎ *522-7909.*

Traditional *churrascaria* specializing in *galetinhos* – little chickens. *Inexpensive. No cards.*

> **UP CLOSE TIP: *Bolo de Macacheira*** *(macacheira cake) is a delicious sweet heavy cake made of shredded macacheira root (the non-poisonous variety of cassava root), sugar, eggs, coconut, and butter. You're not likely to find this on any menu, so stop by* **Dona Antonia's Lanchonete Quero Mais***, Av. Rui Barbosa, 23, for a taste treat.*

# Nightlife

A few years back, locals liked to confess that Santarém was no stranger to boredom at nights. But with the recent influx of capital, there are now several cafés offering regional and Brazilian music, as well as nightclubs for dancing. Ask someone in the know for details on who's playing where. Live music can be found at the **Mascote Restaurant** during dinner on Fri. and the **Mascotinho Café** on Fri. and Sat. (see *Where To Eat*).

### Denis Bar

*Av. Mendoça Furtado (corner with Irv. Barjonas de Miranda).*

Live music on Fri. and foods typical of the Northeast of Brazil.

### Babilônia

*Av. Menonça Furtado, 2940;* ☎ *522-7122. 5 p.m.-last customer.*

Snows are held in this 3,000-seat theater on Sat., Sun., and holidays. Top Brazilian musicians. Check the newspaper.

### Bom Paladar

*Av. São Sebastião, 309;* ☎ *522-3891.*

Live music Tues.-Sun., with a capacity of 600.

### Signus Club

*Av. Borges Leal, 2712.*

Live music on Sat. and Sun. only.

### Boite Tropical (Tropical Hotel)

*Av. Menonça Furtado, 4120;* ☎ *522-1533.*

The nightclub at the city's nicest hotel features live music only on Fri.

### Boite Ancora

*(at the yacht club) Av. 24 de Outobro.*

This nightclub for 500 features live music on Fri.

> **UP CLOSE TIP:** *Ask about Sebastião Tapajós, a fantastic local guitarist who's become well known in France and Switzerland for Amazon folk music.*

## Shopping

Santarém is just finding itself, touristically speaking, so the likelihood of finding serviceable souvenirs at the marketplace is negligible. Normal goods, such as sandals, can run at outlandishly high prices here. The following stores offer some unique crafts made by local artisans. Also, check record stores on Rua Siqueira Campos for regional music.

### Cerâmica Art Sousa

*Av. Gonçalves Dias, 747.*

Pottery specialists José Aniceto and his son Joel sell mainly to arts and crafts shops throughout the Amazon region, but they welcome visitors. Joel was an exchange student/professor at the University of Missouri-Rolla in 1981.

### Loja Regional Muiraquitã

*Rua Senador Lameira Bittencourt, 131;* ☎ *522-7164.*

João Mileo's store has the most complete assortment of regional handicrafts and souvenirs in town, including Indian arts. Take the time to browse. *All cards.*

## Artesanato Dica Frazão

*Rua Floriano Peixoto, 281.*

The most famous business in town, Dona Dica has been creating her own cottage industry since 1949, crafting natural bark, root, and vine fibers gathered by Indians on the Upper Tapajós River into dresses, tunics, purses, and fans. Some of her handmade arts are in the Vatican at the Pope's table and Queen Beatrice of Belgium bought one of her dresses.

## Galeria Dos Artistas Rock Lima

*Av. Alvaro Adolfo, 492.*

This father and his sons produce the most famous wood-carved furniture in town.

## Artesanato e Souvenirs

*Rua Senador Lameira Bittencourt, 69-B.*

You'll find a wide assortment of arts and crafts from the region here.

## Livraria e Papelaria Atica

*Trav. 15 de Novembro, 193; ☎ 522-2745.*

Stationery, fine gifts, and books by regional authors, such as Benedito Monteiro, João Santos, and Wilde da Fonseca.

## Prönatus

*Rua Galdino Veloso, 278. Mon.-Sat. 8 a.m.-noon, 2-6 p.m.*

Across the street from the Brasil Grande Hotel, this store sells natural products from the Amazon, such as herb soap, shampoo, and various herb capsules for impotency, urinary problems, etc.

## Cabana

*Travessa 15 de Agosto, 211. Mon.-Fri. 8 a.m.-noon, 2-6 p.m., Sat. 8 a.m.-noon.*

An endlessly fascinating store that sells *umbanda* and *candomblé* paraphernalia, including statues of Christian and African saints, incense, candles, and all types of potions. (I once spied a very serious middle-aged man buying a potion to attract love.)

## Manipulação

*Trav. Francisco Correa, 168, ☎ 522-1303.*

A homeopathic store selling brown rice, homeopathic medicines, and anti-diabetic teas.

# Hands-On Santarém

## Arrivals

### By Air

Flights are available from Belém, Campo Grande, Cuiabá, Alta Floresta, Manaus, Rio Branco, Rio, Recife, Fortaleza, Salvador, São Paulo and a few other cities. The airport is 13 km. (eight miles) from town. Taxis to downtown are readily available at the airport: the Tropical Hotel provides complimentary shuttle bus service for its guests.

## Airlines Serving Santarém

**Varig/Cruzeiro**

| | |
|---|---|
| Rua Siqueira Campos, 227.................... | ☎ 522-2084 |
| (at the airport)............................. | ☎ 522-1084 |

**VASP**

| | |
|---|---|
| Av. Rui Barbosa, 786......................... | ☎ 522-1680 |

### By Boat

See *River Cruises* below.

### By Bus

The *rodoviária* (bus station), ☎ *522-1342*, is on the Santarém-Cuiabá Highway. Conditions permitting, bus service is available to Belém (through connections) and other points.

## Car Rentals

**Localiza/National**

| | |
|---|---|
| Av. Mendonça Furtado, 1603 ................. | ☎ 522-1130 |

## City Transportation

**Aquila**

| | |
|---|---|
| (air and land taxis) .......................... | ☎ 522-1848 |
| (at the airport) ............................. | ☎ 522-2596 |

## Climate

Tropical temperatures range from 68-92°F in Jan. and 69-90°F in July. The dry season runs July-Dec.; the rainy season from July to Jan., when it precipitates copiously. Mar. receives the most rain and, therefore, is the coolest month. The annual alternation of low and high tide that occurs every six months makes for exuberant ecological contrasts. From July-Dec., the meadows become excellent pastures for cattle and buffalo; between Jan.

and July, wildlife must swim through swamps or be transported to *terra firme*.

## Medical Emergencies

**José Garcia**, M.D., ☎ *522-1044*, specializes in tropical diseases and speaks English and Spanish. **João Otaviano de Matos**, M.D., ☎ *522-5276*, specializes in internal medicine and cardiology.

## Money Exchange

No one officially changes money in Santarém (it's best to arrive with a sufficient pile of *cruzeiros*), but in emergencies, drugstores along Rua Siqueira Campos may comply; inquire of the owners.

## Post Office

**Correio**, Av. Rui Barbosa, 1169.

## Private Guide

A favored licensed guide these days is **Paulo Henrique Melchior**, who is fluent in both German and English, and particularly experienced in ecological tours. Contact him through Lago Verde Turismo, ☎ *522-7577* or privately at ☎ *522-6951*.

## Telephone

Local and international phone calls may be made at **TELEPAR**, Av. São Sebastião, 913.

## Time

Santarém is one hour earlier than Belém – a fact that sometimes confuses even airline officials.

## Tourist Information

Tourist brochures and information can be obtained at **Divisão Municipal de Turismo**, Centro Cultural João Fona, Rua da Imperador, no number; ☎ *523-2434*.

## Travel Agencies

### Lago Verde Turismo Ltda.

*Rua Galdino Veloso, 384;* ☎ *(91) 522-7577; fax 522-2118.*

One of the premier agencies in Santarém, Lago Verde offers personalized packages to large and small groups. Good English-speaking management and guides are available for fishing, trekking, scientific expeditions, photographic projects, and nature studies.

## Agências Tropicais de Turismo/Hotel Tropical

*Av. Mendonça Furtado, 4120,* ☎ *522-1533.*

This agency provides transfers from the airport to the hotel for its guests, as well as a variety of group tours, including half-day city tours and trips to Alter de Chão, Meeting of the Waters, Belterra, piranha fishing, and nighttime alligator hunts.

## Amazon Turismo Ltda.

*Trav. Turiano Meira, 1084;* ☎ *522-2620, fax 522-1098.*

This company offers overnight trips to Monte Alegre in a jeep, and Alenquer in a wooden riverboat, as well as day trips to Fordlândia and the national park.

## When To Go

From Aug.-Jan. the flowers become increasingly more profuse and there's more sand on the beach. Jan. is peak time, and **New Year's Day** is celebrated with big bashes. **Festa do Sairé** occurs the first week in July. On June 29, a procession of bumba-meu-boi, a regional dance with costumes and music, takes place during the **São Pedro Festival**. In Sept. there is the International **Tucunaré Fishing Championship**.

# Belém

Belém effectively entered the 20th century in 1961, when Juscelino Kubitschek's highway from Brasília reached its final destination. For centuries prior, however, the city, strategically placed on the Amazon estuary close to the mouth of the Rio Tocantins, had served nobly as a natural port for the steady stream of products extracted from the Amazon. Dating back to 1621, the city of Belém, which is also the capital of the state of **Pará**, was christened on the feast day of St. Mary of Bethlehem, and at times is still referred to by its long nomenclature: Nossa Senhora do Belém do Grão-Pará or, at least, Belém do Pará. The state, which is larger than most European countries, is the wealthiest in Brazil in regards to ore; even Indian tribes, such as the Kayapó, are sitting on some of the richest mahogany and gold reserves in the country.

It was the 19th-century **rubber boom** that transformed this natty little port into a graceful, Victorian city of *fin de siècle* arches and Italianate palazzos. What makes Belém truly beautiful are its avenues and plazas, shaded with magnificent *mangueiras* (mango trees) that cool the cobblestones when temperatures soar. Today, the historic quarter, which retains much of its art nouveau and neoclassical structures, is a pleasure to stroll through, butted on all sides by a thriving market. One need only step inside the famed **Teatro da Paz**, the city's all-purpose theater, to appreciate the ingenuity of the rubber barons who longed to recreate European culture in the middle of the **Ver-o-Peso market**, facing the waterfront, which outclasses any other outdoor marketplace in Brazil, and perhaps in South

America. Crammed, chaotic, and totally confusing to the uninitiated, the Ver-o-Peso market is a veritable lion's den of exotic sights and smells that could take days to exhaust.

Although most jungle-destined tourists have traditionally headed for Manaus, Belém shouldn't be missed. Not only is the city more navigable by foot, but the jungle expeditions I experienced here are some of the best in the region. Like Manaus, Belém is hot and humid, but the locals here have developed a sense of humor: They refer to themselves as fish because they feel they breathe more water than air.

A stalwart resident of the jungle near Belém roasts manioc on his plantation.

# Sights

## On Foot

Belém is a perfect city to stroll through. The following is a walking tour, which is completely safe to follow on your own during the day.

### Hilton Hotel

Start your walking tour in front of the Hilton. (If you're not staying there, you might take a peek at the lush breakfast buffet, open to the public but free for guests.)

### Praça da República

The park is directly across the street from the Hilton. Once dense with tropical forest, the site was cleared in the 17th century to make way for

Belém's first cemetery; later it became the city's principal park. There's even a *coreto*, an iron-grilled pagoda where brass bands used to perform.

## Teatro da Paz

*Mon.-Fri. 8 a.m.-noon, 2-6 p.m.*

Dominating the square is the city's pride and joy, the theater, an unabashedly neoclassical opera house surrounded by Greek columns and adorned at its entrance with the four busts of the Muses. Inaugurated in 1878, the plush theater, with its bronze staircases and fabulous tiled floors was fueled by the ostentatious passions of the rubber barons who continually looked to Europe for style. Consequently, the foyer's crystal mirrors are Italian, the massive chandelier in the lobby German, the pastel, fluted light fixtures Art Deco. The theater's ceiling is a finely orchestrated marriage of Italianate painting and grillwork from which is suspended an eight-tiered, 1½-ton crystal chandelier. The adjacent Salão Nobre is absolutely charming, once a salon for the elite balls and now the stage for chamber concerts and voice recitals. Note that the salon's ceiling painting is not from the original construction, but was designed in 1960 by São Paulo artist Armando Balloni to reflect the abundance of Amazonian animals. Walk out to the balcony and look up to see the four Muses: from right to left, Comedy, Poetry, Music, and Drama. In 1986 the building, after laboring under a blue facade for many years, was restored to its original pink color. Backstage, you'll see plaques honoring performances by the great ballerina Anna Pavlova in 1918 and the great Brazilian soprano Bidu Sayão. If you have the opportunity to catch a performance of theater or music, grab it; ask your concierge or check the daily newspapers for listings. Free tours are given continuously throughout the day, though only in Portuguese.

## Bar do Parque

This outdoor café, on the side of the theater near the Hilton, is where the city's artists, singers, and streetwalkers gather until the wee hours of morning. Nearby is a kiosk that sells bread and coffee in the morning and beer and *caipirinhas* in the afternoon.

## Teatro Experimental Walber Henrique

*Rua Pres. Vargas, 645;* ☎ *222-4762.*

Walking down Rua Presidente Vargas, you'll come upon this theater. Started in 1979, this experimental theater is a showcase for avant-garde music, plays, and dance, with preference given to non-professional artists. Due to their tight budget, shows are not given daily; they start around 9 p.m. when they do happen. Seats go for about $1.50.

## Rua Santo Antônio

Walk down Av. Presidente Vargas to the right of the theater, passing a travel agency, the Varig office at #363, and the Monópolio Turismo Câmbio (for exchanging money) at #325. Turn left on Rua Santo Antônio, a cobblestone street with no cars, down the middle of which are the remains of 19th-century trolley tracks. As the principal shopping avenue of the city (also called Comércio), the street overflows with shops and vendors hawking all kinds of third-world quality goods. As you wander, look up at the second-story houses, once 19th-century fashionable homes and still adorned with exquisite tile work and pastel-colored balconies and shutters.

## Restaurante Vegetariano e Mercadinho Natural

*Rua Santo Antônio, 264. Lunch Mon.-Fri. 11:30 a.m.-3 p.m.*

A vegetarian market where you can stock up on natural shampoos, whole foods and Amazon teas. Upstairs, the restaurant serves only lunch.

## Paris N'América

Down the street from the market, peek inside the Paris N'América, today a dry goods store but once a beautiful home constructed in 1906 for Francisco Castro by the Portuguese master Ricardo Salvador Fernandes Mesquita. From the sculptured ceilings to the dramatic grilled stairway, many of the original architectural details are still intact. The steel was imported from Scotland, the ceramic-tiled floor and mechanical clock from Germany, the bronze light fixtures from France, the crystal mirrors from Belgium, and the outside wall tiles from Portugal.

## Praça Mercês

A few steps further on, you'll reach Praça Mercês, home to many finely restored buildings. Dominating the plaza is the church known as Mercês, founded in 1640. Despite the graffiti, you can see that the facade is still intact. This may be just the time that you need an ice-cold *água de coco*, which can be bought in front of the church.

## Travessa Frutuoso Guimarães

Next, walk in front of the church on Rua Gaspar Viana and turn right on Travessa Frutuoso Guimarães. At #63, you can pick up decent mosquito nets and hammocks for good prices.

## Ver-O-Peso Market

Nearby, along Av. Castilhos, facing the pier, you'll enter into one of the great third-world marketplaces of all time. To a first-world eye, the open-air market may look like a den of iniquity, but it's actually the epitome of Amazonian life: hundreds of tiny stalls selling anything and everything that floats up the river – from fruits and vegetables and Brazil nuts to snake skins, turtle soap, and dolphin eyes (the last three items being all contraband materials). Begun as a checkpoint in 1688, the market received its name ("watch the weight") from the Portuguese habit of weighing all merchandise that passed through the port for taxation. Today, the market is also a food bazaar, with scores of native women cooking aromatic dishes for the workers who cram into the tiny pathways. The air in the market is hot and dense and barely conducive to dining, but if you're brave enough, browse around until you find something that looks edible. The dark-maroon, soup-like juice sitting in the large tin pans is *açaí*, a true Amazon delicacy made with sugar and manioc juice (it tastes a bit like avocado and goes well with fried fish). Take a moment to watch the workers squeeze the water out of the ground manioc with a long straw tool called a *tipiti*, which works something like an accordion.

As you walk through the market, each section will resound with its own sounds and smells. Not just business, but the very dramas of daily life are carried on here, with lots of flirting and cursing going on between stalls. A perusal of the tropical fruit stands will give you an idea of the enormous variety available here; note the Brazil nuts that come lodged in big brown shells, just as they're found in the forest. The large green spiny-looking fruit is a graviola. The herb section is particularly ripe with superstition and folklore. Good buys are small bottles of concentrated oils, such as *baunilha* (vanilla) and jasmine or more potent love potions such as the Corre Atrás, designed to make a man "Run After" you. *Tamaquaré* powder is a cooked lizard powder sprinkled on husbands to make them calm down sexually – a hot-selling item in the Amazon. (Some women actually buy the live lizards you see in the market and cook them into potions themselves. Another trick is to place the live lizard in the same water where the man regularly washes his clothes.) On the opposite extreme, stall #54 sells perfume that comes complete with a boa constrictor inside, well known as a "fatal attraction" potion.

> **UP CLOSE TIP:** *Due to the tight space and general mayhem, this market can be dangerous. Go with little money on you, do not wear gold chains or jewelry, keep your bag close to you at all times, and be cautious about taking photos. Since a number of vendors trade in contraband items (such as endangered species), they do not care to have their business recorded.*

## Meat Market

Don't miss the meat market nearby, a chrome-grilled structure brought from England in 1909; its cast-iron frame and Victorian turrets are souvenirs from the time when the British built most of the port a century ago. Inside, individual stands are manned by brawny workers who constantly yell at each other while slicing carcasses hanging from wires. The wet, smelly fish market in the same complex opens in the early morning and closes by 1 p.m.; here you can view full-sized samples of the region's most common fish. Buyers receive their merchandise wrapped in large leaves from the guarumã bush, then supply their own plastic bag – a traditional Amazonian way of economizing on paper.

In general, the entire area near the pier is endlessly fascinating and ripe with photo ops. Outside the market you may see baby monkeys for sale (illegal) or even baby sloths (also illegal).

## Boulevard Castilhos França

Make sure you walk down this boulevard next to the bay, where fishermen and merchants dock their schooners and canoes laden with goods. Unfortunately, a lot of trash litters the portside here, even though (or because) many people use their boats as floating lodges. You may even see rats scurrying about these barges to no one's apparent dismay. Do note the

Texaco floating gas station in the bay, an omnipresent reminder of Western influence.

## Praça do Relógio (Clock Square)

Across from the pier near the market, this square, with its large, monumental clock tower, is often used by guides as a meeting place.

> **UP CLOSE TIP:** *ENASA boats to Marajó Island leave from the port on the other side of the market.*

## Praça Frei Caetano Brandão

Walk from the market past the mango and bamboo tree-filled Dom Pedro II Park to the Praça Frei Caetano Brandão, dominated by the 19th-century Catedral de Nossa Senhora da Graça. Sadly run-down on the outside, the cathedral boasts some of Brazil's finest paintings inside, though the lights are rarely turned on. Hours for mass are Tues.-Thurs. 5:30 p.m., Sat. 6:30 a.m., and 7 p.m., and Sun. 7 a.m., 9 a.m., 5 p.m., and 8 p.m. It's from here that nearly one million strong begin their journey to the basílica each year during the Círio festival in Oct. Nearby is the Igreja Santo Alexandrian, an 18th-century church, whose small collection of religious art may be open.

## Forte do Castelo

*Open daily 8 a.m.-noon, 2-6 p.m.; restaurant 11:30 a.m.-3 p.m., 6:30-11:30 p.m.*

This is a good place to end the walking tour. This fort marks the city's founding, as it was the first building constructed in Belém, strategically located at the confluence of the Guajará Bay and Guamá River on a hill commanding a view of the bay. Once headquarters for the military operations that expelled the English, French, and Dutch, it also provided a refuge for the Caabanagem revolutionaries. Now the fort houses the Circulo Militar Club and Restaurant, open to the public. Actually, there's nothing to do here but sit and drink (better at night when the weather is cooler, though during the day the view of the port below is fantastic). From the perimeter of the fort you can also see the Feira d'Açai down below, where boats loaded with raw *açaí* start arriving as early as 4:30 a.m. You can also see large cargo boats transporting ceramics from the nearby islands and returning home laden with mineral water and sodas.

## Cidade Velha (Old City)

The area around the market and cathedral is full of quaint squares and colonial homes with grilled balconies and colorful shutters. Browse at will, but do try to avoid Rua da Ladeira – not a safe street to walk through due to the prostitutes and homeless who frequent its alleyways. (During the day, it's more or less okay, but avoid it completely at night.)

## More Sights

### Basílica de Nossa Senhora de Nazaré

*Praça Justo Chermont. 6:30-11:30 a.m., 3-9 p.m.*

One of the most stunning churches in Brazil, this basílica is the end point for the annual procession of Círio de Nazaré on the second Sun. in Oct. The church, which was initiated in 1909, took 40 years to build – a majestic blending of Italian granite and mosaics, French stained glass, and a ceiling of red cedar taken from the forest. The idolized statue of the Madonna, which is carried through the streets, rests above the altar in a circle of cherubs (a photo showing details can be found to the right of the altar). Devotion to the statue is so intense that you might see petitioners dragging themselves on their knees to the altar in payment of a promise. In front of the basílica is a modern, open-air complex consisting of high altar, amphitheater, pantheon, and war monument, where mass during the Círio festival is held.

### Museu Paraense Emílio Goeldi

*Parque Zoobotânico, Av. Magalhães Barata, 376; ☎ 249-1233. Closed Mon.*

Belém's premier museum was initiated in 1866 to record the richness of Amazônia's flora, fauna, rocks, indigenous culture, and folklore. The multi-media complex embraces a park, zoo, and indoor museum. The park, planned after an Amazonian jungle, has fewer trees per square foot than the forest, but offers more species, including rubber trees, guaraná (from which the herbal stimulant is taken), pau-brasil, cedro vermelho, castanha-do-pará (Brazil nut), and the huge sumaumeira (the biggest tree in the South American jungle). At the desk of the permanent exhibition, ask for a guidebook in English, then tour the fine displays of stuffed birds, basketry, Indian artifacts, and jewelry. Running freely outside in the zoo are *cutias* (a type of small anteater with the frisky personality of a raccoon). Also to be seen is a dazzling array of tropical birds, alligators, cats, tapirs, manatees, and electric eels. The souvenir shop is excellent.

### Parque dos Igarapés

*Conjunto Satélite WE 12, # 1000, Ananindeua, Pará. Office: Rua 223 Manoel Barata, 704, Edifício Paes de Carvalho, # 403, Belém, CEP 66020; ☎ 235-1910, 223-8324, 227-2588. Reserve only on Sun. or for groups.*

This tropical park owned by a private family is a welcome respite from the heat of the city and the ruggedness of the jungle. The $10 entrance fee goes toward food and beverages taken in the excellent open-air restaurant or beside the natural swimming pool (whose water was pronounced cleaner than the drinking water in Belém). Ecological walks can be taken through the forested grounds or you can hop in a canoe and navigate the narrow *igarapés* (streams) that seem to go everywhere and nowhere. Children will love the wood-log playground and there are so many animals here – including an *atú* (armadillo), *creatipurí* (squirrel), and *preguiçosa* (sloth) – that a staff vet is required by law. Belemites flock to this complex on weekends, when live bands turn the main arena into a outdoor nightclub.

## A JUNGLE ADVENTURE from the author

Jungle adventures start early in Belém – 4 a.m. at the Hilton, when my young handsome guide Tony Rocha picks me up, threading his way through late-night revelers on their way to bed. We drive to the docks at the Novotel Hotel, then board a skiff in the moonlight, the humidity dense around us. Illuminating our way with flashlights, we set off down the Guamá River, passing *caboclos* (local jungle-dwellers) already on their way to market. A mere 15 minutes later, Tony is pointing out a "brand-new" island, recently sculpted by the six-hour tides that continually change the face of Amazônia.

As the sky turns luminescent pink we settle in front of another island called **Ilha dos Papagaios** and watch as thousands of green parrots wake up, then fly off squawking in pairs. As the sun rises, we catch glimpses of river life – women carrying baskets, children paddling to school. Soon we bank and I take my first plunge into the jungle.

The feeling of being surrounded by literally millions of life forms – trees, shrubs, vines, birds, ants, bugs, and whatever is flying in my face – is absolutely thrilling, though not unscary. Cutting the path with a machete, Tony leads us deeper into the darkened jungle, pointing out the sumaumeira tree, an elephantine monster whose trunks are used by natives to beat out messages. We inspect the leaves of the guaramá tree, which are used to wrap fish at market, and another tree whose bark exudes a drinkable milky substance. My boots sink deep into fungus; my arms get scratched. Despite the incessant cawing of birds, it's difficult not to appreciate the eery green silence of the forest – what writer Peter Mathiesson once described as the "stillness of a cathedral."

Cruising down the river again, we make a pitstop at a riverside grocery – a mere counter crammed with *pinga*, the jungle's alcoholic cure – all made from sugarcane. The owners are an elderly couple whose eyes are incredibly similar – wet and suspiciously shiny. "Maybe we are brother and sister," Senhor Tomé laughs. "When we were young, my father was very active!" Their grandchildren, visiting from the city, scamper about in their marvelous backyard – the jungle! Dona Palmira talks about the time she saw a white-suited stranger dive into the river late at night ("obviously" an enchanted *boto*, or dolphin). As a full eclipse of the sun is about to occur, we rush to the pier of an abandoned pepper plantation to catch the magical display of fading color over the river.

At dusk, Branco, our boatman, invites us to sleep at his riverside house. The moment the sun sets, mosquitoes attack us in droves, but we bat them off long enough to devour an excellent dinner of fried catfish cooked by his wife. Before retiring, we pump Branco for tales of the *curupira*, the legendary master of the forest whose feet are turned backwards and who loves to befuddle humans. Branco tells of his troubles with a *matinta pereira*, a forest witch who wouldn't stop seducing him until he finally married his present wife. At midnight I wake up terrified since my hammock, which is strung over a boat anchored far up on the bank, is swinging wildly – and for no apparent reason. Soon Tony's hammock, hanging next to mine, also goes out of control, driving us both to hysterics. Then, all of a sudden, both hammocks stop swinging as fast as they started. Paralyzed with fear, neither of us can speak or go back to sleep. In the morning, over breakfast, Branco frowns darkly when he hears the story, mumbling into his coffee that the *matinta pereira* – without a doubt – had paid us a visit. Nobody is laughing now.

After breakfast, we head out to the tiny streams, or *igarapés*, overhung with luscious green vines just like in a Tarzan movie. Branco's nine-year-old nephew Fernando shows me how to climb a palm tree with a rope made from leaves – a true jungle monkey. After a hot, sweaty trek over *terra firma*, we reach a *casa de farinha*, a manioc plantation run by Dona Paula, a powerfully built woman with two grown daughters, and her much smaller husband.

Incredibly, the talk turns to the Gulf War. "I was so happy that President Bush decided to end it," she says in Portuguese to my utter amazement, though I soon learn she has watched the entire war on her battery-operated TV – accompanied, I am sure, by a hefty diet of Brazilian soap operas. Before we head back to our boat, she primes us with a delicious plate of hot manioc and beans, then warns us to look out for cobras – "It's the only thing I worry about with my daughter." The thought does not make me a happy camper. This time, however, the way back, through tangled vines and overgrown moss, with one eye out for fat snakes, seems a lot shorter. By the time we return to the dock only 24 hours after we began, it feels as though we've been gone a few lifetimes.

Something similar to the above tour can be arranged through **Amazon Star Tursimo**, Rua Carlos Gomes, 14; ☎ and fax 224-6244, who offers four kinds of tours:

- ☐ A half-day tour around Belém, in front of the Guamá River, including a forest walk (price includes hotel pickup and two guides).
- ☐ A full-day (eight-hour) tour down the Guamá and Acará rivers, including a walk in the forest and lunch.
- ☐ An overnight stay on the Guamá River and Parrot Island.
- ☐ An early morning jaunt to Parrot Island, leaving at 4:15 a.m. and returning 8:30 a.m.

# Excursions

## River Travel

The most utilized form of transportation in this region is the boat. Wooden multi-deck cruisers (*gaiolas*) regularly make trips down the Amazon River from Belém to Santarém and Manaus – a colorful way to make friends and enter into the heart of Amazonian life. Along with grandmothers, babies, and traveling salesmen, you might share quarters with dogs, chickens, and the family pig. Some boats rent only hammock space (you must provide your own hammock); others offer a few private cabins just big enough for a sink and two bunk beds, with a key to the private toilet. (Note well that the communal toilet is usually beyond description.) You might consider renting a cabin (for the privacy and the bathroom) and also hang your hammock in the main galley.

During sunlight hours, the boats usually cruise near the banks so you can spot wildlife and peek inside the native homes; people hang out on the top deck, where you can buy beer and snacks. Most exciting are the brief stops at port, where you can watch lovers parting, children hawking fruits and homemade foods, and dockworkers loading the ship's goods.

ENASA touring boats with air-conditioned cabins and private bathrooms are popular ways to cruise from Belém to Manuas through Santarém. In Belém, contact **ENASA** at Av. Presidente Vargas, 41; ☎ *(91) 222-3995/224-0528.*

The *Amazon Clipper* is a riverboat built along traditional lines for cruising the Amazon and its tributaries. Eight double cabins with bunks accommodate 16 passengers, with night-time air conditioning and private toilet facilities. Outboard-powered canoes are used for trips into lagoons, channels, and flooded forest. There's also an open salon, video library, and sundeck. Cruises run three, four, and six days. Four-day trips include meeting native *caboclo* families to see jungle life up close.

**Safari Ecológico**, Rua Monsenhor Coutinho, 119; ☎ *(92)* 233-3739; fax *233-3739*, also offers two double-decked vessels – the Tunã and Fagra II – regional vessels with air conditioning, fully equipped kitchen, video lounge, and library. These penetrate the tributaries of the Amazon. Cruises from two to 15 days include close contact with local people; crews include a multilingual guide and a trained biologist. Day and half-day excursions can be taken on the *Jacaré-Cu*.

## Mosquiero Island

Fifty-three miles (86 km.) from Belém is Mosqueiro Island, the main bathing beach of the capital that is well-connected by road and bridges. Back in the 19th century, the first tourists to the island were Portuguese, French, and English rubber barons enjoying the boom; today most of the village has retained its mud-hut look. The hour's drive from the city takes you over a decent highway (BR 360) lined with verdant forests full of *açaí* and dendê palm trees (the red flag in front of houses signify they sell *açaí*); after you pass over the nearly mile-long bridge, you'll be besieged by young boys hawking beer and bags of sun-dried shrimps. The bus from Belém stops at **Areão Beach**, where the city's main square and market are located. However, most of the popular beach action takes place at **Farol Beach**, where the sand is the widest and rock concerts last all night. The bay here is where all rivers meet and flow to the ocean, causing an intense wave reaction big enough for surfing. **Murubira Beach** is considered the chic beach, where most of the jetskiers, ultraleve daredevils, and windsurfers hang out. Swimming is considered relatively safe. During Carnaval, this beach is one of the hottest in the Amazon.

Since there are 16 *igarapés* in the middle of the island, the landscape is perfect for short jungle tours, which can be arranged through **Carlos Alberto Ribeiro**, owner of the Maresia Restaurant. For about $20 he'll take you on a 4½-hour tour of the *igarapés* by canoe, visiting a *caboclo's* house and wheat plantation, and fishing for fresh shrimp (you must provide your own transportation to the island). If you would like to spend the night, Senhor Carlos Alberto's colonial-style *pousada* offers an exotic hideaway on the beach for remarkably low prices. The restaurant itself, on Farol Beach, serves a fine *caldeirada* (soup stew with fish, octopus, egg, potatoes, onions, shrimps, and manioc flour) and a delicious *peixe tropical*, fish with Brazil nuts and the cream of Brazil nuts. Buffalo steak, another rare delicacy, must be ordered four to five hours in advance. For reservations for the tour and pousada contact the **Restaurante Maresia**, Av. Beira Mar, 29; ☎ *(91)* *771-1463*. Crafts can be found on the **Praça da Matriz** from 8 a.m. to 9 p.m., daily.

## When To Go

Mosqueiros Island seemed even hotter to me than Belém. After it rains at 1 or 2 p.m. (every day), the temperature cools a bit, making strolling more palatable. (In Belém the same shower is called the "three o'clock rain.") Oct. is the hottest month, when crabs appear in the saltier water. High season lasts from July to Nov., with the best months of sunshine being Aug. and Sept. The months notorious for rain are Jan. and Feb.

&#10087; **GETTING HERE:** *Buses leave hourly from the bus station in Belém (during vacations, every 15 min.). The trip takes about 1½ hours by bus, or one hour by car. Return buses can be found on the Praça da Matriz;* ☎ *(91) 771-1204.*

## Marajo Island

Just across the bay from Belém is Marajó, an island the size of Switzerland, and fast becoming the major tourist destination of the North. The major attractions are the water buffalo ranches, where enormous herds graze the open plains – a species that first came to the island by way of shipwreck. Also in profusion are hundreds of rare bird specimens, as well as numerous alligators, and monkeys, more easily seen here than in the jungle. Those who choose to stay along the coast are awarded with a rolling sea, whose crashing waves result from the confluence of the inland rivers and the ocean seas.

Those who want to truly feel the life of Marajó should go to **Bonjardim**, the most famous of the buffalo ranches. The owners, Eduardo and Eunice Ribeiro, are a charming couple who speak English, French, and Spanish and love to sit down for lunch and dinner with their guests (invariably a groaning table of fine delicacies). During the day you can ride the range with the staff, birdwatch, and fish for piranha; at night there are organized alligator hunts. Bookings can be made most easily through **Amazon Star Turismo** in Belém ☎ *(91) 224-6244*.

Beyond the ranch, the best *pousada* in the main town of Soure is **Pousada Marjoara**, Rua de Soure, 33; ☎ *(91) 741-1287*; in Belém, ☎ *(91) 223-8369*. It's walking distance from the waterfront and the center of town.

❖ **GETTING HERE:** *The fastest way to reach Marajó Island is by plane. Air taxis, which can be reserved for any time, run about $200. Much cheaper are the regularly scheduled flights on TABA (about $30), which leave Mon. and Wed. from Belém at 7 a.m. and return at 7:40 p.m. from Soure. On Fri. the flight leaves Belém at 4 p.m. and returns on Sun at 4 p.m.*

*You can also go by bus. Service leaves from Belém's bus terminal at 5 a.m. and includes a bus to Iguraci, a ferry boat to Câmara (across the Marajó Bay, about 3 hrs.), then a bus to Salvaterra and a small ferry to Soure. The return trip leaves from Soure at 2 p.m. Mon.-Sat.*

*ENASA boats leave Belém Wed. and Fri. at 8 p.m. and return on Thurs. and Sun. at 4 p.m., as well as Sat. at 2 p.m., returning at 5 or 6 p.m. (from Soure). The trip is colorful, usually accompanied by screaming babies, squawking chickens, and quacking ducks. Regional class is about $8, but tourist class (much preferred) runs about $18.*

*The easiest way to visit Marajó is to arrange a package deal through* **Amazon Star Turismo,** ☎ *224-6624, who will provide transfer to the pier in Belém, trip by ferry boat to the island (3 hrs., 2 buses) or boat (5 hrs.), city tour, lodge with breakfast, half-day tour to a fazenda to see buffalos and horses, stops at one or two beaches, and a folklore show on Sat. night.*

## Salinas

Situated 124 miles (200 kms) from Belém, Salinas has one of the most beautiful and longest  Brazilian beaches (at nine miles/15 km.). The water changes its color and taste according to the season, due to the influence of the Amazon River. The best hotel is **Brasil Palace**, Rua Ver. Corinto Pereira de Castro, 70 (Alvorado); ☎ *891-1064*. An exuberant folklore festival with capoeira (the Brazilian martial art) takes place in Aug.

# Where To Stay

Accommodations in Belém run from the ever-efficient, luxurious Hilton to the modest *pousada*. Air conditioning is a necessity. See page 26 for price chart.

## Belém Hilton

*Av. Pres. Vargas, 882 (Praça da Rep., Centro);* ☎ *(91) 242-6500; fax 225-2942.*

The Hilton is Belém's first and only five-star – a luxurious relief from the heat and humidity of the cityscape. Service is geared towards those who wake up at dawn for river tours or stay up till dawn to dance; breakfast opens at 4 a.m. An impressive underground mall includes a deli, famous for salamis, cheeses, and exquisite pastries. The pool is small and unusually shaped; it serves as a magnet on the weekends for chic cruisers. The gym is the best in the city, with free weights, aerobic classes, sauna, and massage. An elegant club serves exotic tropical drinks and offers live music on the weekends. Apartments are plush, with marble-topped bathrooms and comfortable beds. *361 apts. Expensive. All cards.*

## Equatorial Palace

*Av. Braz de Aguiar, 612 (Nazaré);* ☎ *(91) 241-2000, fax (091) 223-5222.*

This traditional four-star is located in a prime area of shady streets and chic stores, four blocks from downtown. Smaller and more intimate than the Hilton, the hotel boasts a fine, old-world restaurant, called 1900, famous for its Portuguese codfish. The circular, blue-tiled swimming pool is surrounded by a *churrascaria* and pool bar. The romantic piano bar is a favorite in the city. The older rooms, mostly used for long-term residences, have an old-world charm the newer apartments lack. Ignore the tacky lobby. *296 apts. Expensive. All cards.*

## Novotel Belém

*Av. Bernardo Sayão, 4804 (Guamá), 4 km.;* ☎ *(91) 229-8011, fax 229-8709.*

Near the University of Belém, the Novotel is a good, medium-priced hotel, particularly suitable for families who make a one-day stop in Belém; most three-hour river tours leave from the harbor located in the hotel's backyard. The pool area, lined with açaí trees, is extensive, with a children's pool, playground, and volleyball court. All rooms are air conditioned, and come with two double beds and an extra couch bed, color TV, and a large desk. Make sure you ask for a room with a view of the river. Laundry service available. *121 apts. Moderate. All cards.*

## Zoghbi Park Hotel

*Rua Pe. Prudêncio, 220 (Centro); fax and* ☎ *(91) 241-1800.*

This small but adequate three-star offers a good low-priced option for discerning travelers. Rooms, all air conditioned, are clean, with finely finished wood doors, closets, and headboards. A good buy is the *especial*, with a fascinating view of the city's back streets. The bar doubles as a TV lounge. All room keys are electronic and safes are available at reception. *36 apts. Moderate-inexpensive. V.*

### Regente Hotel

*Av. Gov. José Malcher, 485 (Centro);* ☎ *(91) 241-1222; fax 224-0343.*

Centrally located within walking distance of the Praça da República, the Regente is a reliable low-priced hotel; nearby is the fine restaurant Lá Em Casa. Apartments, with color TV and mini-bar, are cheerful and overlook the city's rooftops. A good budget idea is the standard central. Noise from the city traffic may filter up to the rooms. The restaurant offers standard fare without much style. Safes at reception. *149 apts. Inexpensive. All cards.*

### Manacá

*Rua Quintino Bocaiúva, 1645;* ☎ *223-3335.*

An old reformed house with large room, and an interior garden where breakfast is served. This hotel-residence is an oasis in busy downtown. You pay extra for breakfast and TV. *Inexpensive. No cards.*

### Vidonho's

*Rua O' de Almeida, 476 (Centro);* ☎ *(91) 225-1444.*

A simple, small hotel with rock-bottom rates that can't be beat (without being seedy). Apartments come with mini-bar and color TV, and furniture in good condition. The only drawback are the small windows. Safes at the reception. *48 apts. Inexpensive. DC, MC, V.*

## Where To Eat

Belém is one of the best places in the Amazon to sample native cuisine. Fish is excellent. Do try the native fruit juices, such as *cupuaçu* or *taperebá*, from the cashew family. You can't come to the Amazon, however, without tasting its most famous delicacy – ice cream made from tropical fruit flavors. Needless to say, it's the best way to beat the heat (and the parlors are usually air-cooled). See page 26 for price chart.

### Lá Em Casa/O Outro

*Av. Gov. José Malcheer, 247(Centro);* ☎ *223-1212. Noon-3 p.m., 7p.m-midnight.*

Some folks say the only native food in Brazil can be found in Belém, where it was taught to the first colonists by the Indians. Owner Ana Maria Martin, who learned to cook from her grandmother (she even went upstream to the family farm to learn from Indian women), has received international raves for her *maniçoba*, a concoction of meat or fish mushed with manioc leaves that must be cooked for four to five days to extract the poison. Warm and voluble, Dona Ana Maria has installed two restaurants in this colonial-style house: the air-conditioned salon, called O Outro (The Other), which serves hot and cold buffets; and the back patio, Lá em Casa (There at Home), with its gargantuan flamboyant tree in the middle. The Menu Paraense gives you a chance to try all the different regional tastes. A special lunch plate is a steal. *Pato no tucupi* (duck made with a manioc sauce available only in Belém) and *patinhas de carangueijo à Milanesa* (fried crab legs) are excellent. The fish *tucunaré* is best eaten in Santarém. *Moderate-expensive. All cards.*

### Restaurante Círculo Militar

*Praça Frei Caetano Brandão (Forte de Castelo);* ☎ *223-4374. Noon-4 p.m. and 6:30 p.m.-midnight.*

With its balcony-like salon overlooking the bay, this is the perfect place to lunch away from the hubbub of the marketplace. Located in the Castelo Fort, it's especially romantic at night, but also good for light lunches. *Lagostim* is a small freshwater shrimp breaded with egg and stuffed with cheese. *Moderate. All cards.*

### Augustus

*Av. Almirante Barroso, 493 (Marco);* ☎ *226-8317. Noon-2:30 p.m., 7:30-11:30 p.m., Sat. 7 p.m.-midnight, Sun. noon-3 p.m.*

Dark wood-beamed ceilings vie with tropical gardens in this chic restaurant. A specialty is *bochette misto à Piamonteza*, a mixed grill of steak, pork, and sausage. Don't miss the *coco branco*, an intensely sweet concoction of shredded coconut glazed in sugar and spiked with cloves. *Moderate. All cards.*

### Miralha Bar e Restaurante

*Av. Doca de Souza Franco, 194;* ☎ *241-4832. 8 a.m.-4 a.m.*

Hip Belémites come to this tropical beer garden near the docks in the Umarizal district for a drink after work (and a pickup). Families, however, will also feel at home. Music (usually MPB) is the best in the city, with live bands starting at 9:30 p.m.; a small cover is charged after 9:45 p.m. The special is Japanese food: *camarão na chapa miralha* comes with super-sized shrimp, vegetables, and fries on a simmering grill. *Moderate. No cards.*

### Na Brasa

*Av. Nazaré, 124;* ☎ *225-4541. Closed Mon.*

A reasonably priced *rodízio* for barbecued meat (all you can eat), with one salon for the young and noisy, and the other for the discreet. *Moderate. All cards.*

### Hilton Delicatessen

*Av. Pres. Vargas, 882 (Praça da República). 11 a.m.-9 p.m., Sun. 10 a.m.-2 p.m.*

Takeout deli in the Hilton Hotel. Excellent pastries, salamis, and cheese. Stock up if you're planning a river trip. *Moderate. All cards.*

### Panela de Barro

*Av. Dq. de Caxias, 602;* ☎ *246-2733. Dinner only, closed Sun.*

A fish house known for its good food, in particular regional cuisine. *Inexpensive. No cards.*

## Alternativa Natural

*Rua O. de Almeida, 306. Mon.-Fri. 11:30 a.m.-3 p.m.*

A nice, quick alternative for vegetarians – a natural foods buffet, including tropical fruit juices, noodles, soy meat, fried macaxeira, soup, salad, and dessert. The post office is nearby. *Inexpensive. No cards.*

## Nutribem Ltda.

*Rua Santo Antônio, 264;* ☎ *224-3429.*

Vegetarian restaurant and market for natural products.

## Tip Top

*Travessa Pariquis at the corner of Padre Eutiquip (Batista Campos).*

A tip-top ice cream parlor 4½ blocks from the Hilton, with more than 150 exotic flavors. *Bacuri*, made from the hard-shelled fruit, is particularly delicious.

> **UP CLOSE TIP: Street Food**
> *You're sure to see folks on the street slurping something from a shell. It's* tacacá, *made with dried shrimps and* tucupí *(a sauce made from manioc), served in a* cuia, *the dried shell of the fruit of the calabaça tree. Tacacá runs hot (both in temperature and in spices), and if you add pepper, you'll have even more sweat running down your brow – an effect strangely adored by locals.*

# Nightlife

## Sabor da Terra

*Av. Visconde de Souza Franco, 685 (Umarizal);* ☎ *223-8620.*
*Mon.-Sat. 8 p.m.-midnight.*

Come to dine on traditional Amazonian dishes or just enjoy the city's best folklore show, featuring backland dances such as *xote, forró, lundi, carimbó*, and *lambada*. The eight dancers are young, attractive, and lively. The show lasts about two hours; one fine number is a cowboy dance with lassos straight from Marajó Island.

## Boite Lapinha

*Trav. Padre Eutíquio, 3901;* ☎ *229-3290. Shows: Mon.-Sat. 8:30 p.m.*

The city's most famous nightclub hangs somewhere between funky and old-fashioned. A statue of Iemanjá surrounded by live ducks greets arrivals while inside, a 50s silver ball dominates the stage. The shows change every half-hour, from comedy to live bands to striptease after 11:30 p.m., all introduced by a transvestite MC.

The specialty is *língua de bumba-meu-boi* (bull's tongue), served with mashed potatoes. Dancing is fun, but beware of mosquitoes and be extra careful when you go to the bathroom: There are three of them (men, women, and "others"), considered a major accomplishment by gays in Belém. Bermudas are not allowed for men.

**UP CLOSE TIP:** *Check the newspaper for listings of local musicians such as Nilson Choves, a singer/guitarist; Jane du Boc, an ex-volleyball player who sings like Zizi Possi; Rosanna, a wonderful singer of versatile styles; Alibi de Orfeu, who sings Portuguese blues; Debson Tayonara, who sings MPB; and Officina de Samba, an eight-man group that performs popular sambas.*

# Shopping

## Markets

The main city market is the **Ver-o-Peso** (see under *Walking Tour*). There's also an **Artisan Fair** on Praça da República on Fri. and Sat. – not so big, but worth a look. Good buys here are drums, flutes, handmade leather-tooled jewelry, fiber crafts, and semi-precious stones. Aromatic oil essences, made from Amazonian plants, are popular. Many of these oils are related to *candomblé* practices (Afro-Brazilian voodoo worship), and often come packaged with promises of love, money, or good health. Roots and barks are also ground into pleasant-smelling powders and fashioned into dolls or simple sachets.

Pottery is particularly fine in Belém. One style, *tapajônica*, is characterized by fine line carvings and sculptured decorations, originally from Santarém but now made in Belém; they often resemble ceramics made by ancient civilizations. Of wider, heavier design – more colorful and slightly more modern – is the *marajoara* style. It can be recognized by its low relief sculptures, often brightly patterned in red, black, and white. Both can be seen at the PARATUR tourist office (see under *Hands-On Belém*).

The **Palha Market** takes place every day near the Novotel Hotel. It is small but exceedingly third-world, with the intense smell of fish and dried spices.

**UP CLOSE TIP:** *If you're in the market for an Amazonian icon, look for a* muiraquitã *– a piece of green jade (or ceramic) in the shape of a frog. Legend has it that once upon a time in the middle of the Amazon forest, a tribe of female warriors were desperately in search of men for reproduction. One full moon they waited for Yara, goddess of the water, who unearthed some green stones from the depths of the river. The women dove into the river to retrieve the stones, then shaped the jade (or malachite) into a frog, which they then wore as an amulet. (Since the jungle later became populated, we can assume the fetish worked.) Anyone who wears it today is said to enjoy protection and good luck. (Specimens in the museum were found on Marajó Island by the Aruã tribe who used them).*

### Cacique

*Av. Presidente Vargas, 892;* ☎ *222-1144.*

This is the best artisan shop in Belém.

# Herbs

## Casa das Ervas Medicinais

*Rua Gaspar Viana, 230.*

This "House of Medicinal Herbs" is veritably crammed with wooden bins of dried leaves, herbs, barks, and seeds for every illness imaginable – even cancer. The owner has been in business for years, and even makes mixtures that come refrigerated in tall glass bottles (the tonic I bought did wonders for me). You can also buy a two-volume book (Portuguese only), *A Flora Nacional na Medicina Doméstica*, which tells the story of each herb and the disease it cures.

## Perfumaria Chamma

*Rua Boaventura da Silva, 606; ☎ 224-7298 and Artesanato Juruá, across the street from the Equatorial Palace Hotel on Avenida Brás de Aguiar.*

Well known for natural soaps, shampoos, cosmetics, and perfumes made from Amazonian plants. Celebrities and actresses, in particular, swear by the products at Juruá.

# Pottery

## Stúdio Rosemiro Pinheiro

*# 100, Soledade (past Espírito Santo).*

On a dirt backroad about 11 miles (18 km.)from downtown Belém (a half-hour by car) is the village of **Icoracy**, an unusual community of craftsmen who maintain the age-old tradition of handmade pottery. One of about 20 master artisans in the area, 50-year-old Rosemiro Pinheiro works in a rundown shack that belies the extraordinary output of his "factory." (He personally makes 200 vases a day, while his 25-man team produces over 2,300 pieces a month.)

Young boys take their canoes down the *igarapé* in the backyard to find suitable clay, which is then brought back to be cleaned, fashioned on wheels, and baked in brick ovens fueled by wood scraps. Children play around Senhor Pinheiro's feet while he creates vases in the *marajoara* style, a technique he learned from his father, though he is constantly experimenting with new designs.

In the front room is a showcase, from which you may purchase 45-piece *feijoada* sets, vases of all sizes, commemorative plates, and even erotic beer mugs. Prices are extraordinarily low; shipping to the US doubles the price.

# Hands-On Belém

## Airlines Serving Belém

**Varig/Cruzeiro**

Av. Pres. Vargas (opposite Praça da República) . ☎ 768-3363

(airport). . . . . . . . . . . . . . . . . . . . . . . . . . . . . . . . . ☎ 233-3941

**TABA**

Av. Gov. José Malcher, 883 . . . . . . . . . . . . . . . . . . . ☎ 223-6300

(airport). . . . . . . . . . . . . . . . . . . . . . . . . . . . . . . . . ☎ 244-2866

**Transbrasil**

Av. Presidente Vargas, 780 . . . . . . . . . . . . . . . . . . . ☎ 224-6977

(airport). . . . . . . . . . . . . . . . . . . . . . . . . . . . . . . . . ☎ 233-3941

**VASP**

Av. Presidente Vargas, 620, loja B  ☎ 224-5588

(airport). . . . . . . . . . . . . . . . . . . . . . . . . . . . . . . . . ☎ 233-0941

**TAP**

Rua Senador Manoel Barata, 704, room 1401. . . . ☎ 222-5304

## Arrivals

**Cooperativos Taxis,** ☎ *233-4941*. Located at the airport, taxis run about $11-$12 into town and can be hired at the last counter near the Paratur office. Buses run every five min. from the airport for about 25 cents. The name of the bus to downtown is "Perpétuo Socorro" (Perpetual Help).

## Car Rental

**Avis**

Av. Brazil de Aguiar, 621. . . . . . . . . . . . . . . . . . . . ☎ 233-2066

at Hilton Hotel. . . . . . . . . . . . . . . . . . . . . . . . . . . . ☎ 223-1276

. . . . . . . . . . . . . . . . . . . . . . . . . . . . . . . . . . . . . . . .  (ext. 7573)

## City Transportation

Taxis . . . . . . . . . . . . . . . . . . . . . . . . . . . . . . . . . . . . ☎ 224-5444

. . . . . . . . . . . . . . . . . . . . . . . . . . . . . . . . . . . . . . . . ☎ 229-4799

### Points Beyond

The *rodoviária* (bus station) is at the end of Av. Gov. José Malcher, five km. (three miles) from downtown (☎ *228-0500*). Buses are available to Brasília, Santarém, Salvador, Recife, Fortaleza, and Belo Horizonte, among other places.

## Climate

Temperatures range from 82°F. in the Amazonian winter (June-Aug.) to 90-93°F. in summer (Dec.-Jan.). Rain occurs nearly every day around 3 p.m.; the months with heaviest rainfall are Jan. and Feb.

## Consulates

**U.S.A.**
Av. Oswaldo Cruz, 165...................... ☎ 223-0800
**Great Britain**
Rua Gaspar Viana, 490 ....................... ☎ 223-4353
**South Africa**
Av. Presidente Vargas, 351 ................... ☎ 224-8282

## Money Exchange

**Monopólio Turismo e Câmbio**
Av. Pres. Vargas, 325......................... ☎ 223-3177

## Police

**POLITUR,** ☎ *224-9469*, this is a special division of the local police force that provides security for tourists.

## Private Guide

Tony Rocha gets my vote for best English-speaking guide in Brazil. A tall order to live up to, but his charm, knowledge, and consideration made my first foray into the jungle a joy to remember. He can be reached through **Amazon Star Turismo,** ☎ *224-6244*.

## Time

Belém is one hour later than Santarém.

## Tourist Information

A visit to **PARATUR**, Praça Kennedy, ☎ *223-6118* (Mon.-Fri. 8 a.m.-6 p.m.), won't be your typical boring trip to the tourist office. An ancillary park is full of native animals, particularly little monkeys called *saguis*, who will come eat from your hand. (They love peanut candy.) The primary handicrafts of the area are sold in an adjacent gallery. Of particular value are the ceramics, whose designs are native to the area. You can also stock up on machetes and bows and arrows authentically crafted by native tribes in Amazonas. Brochures in English can be picked up at the information desk in the artisan store.

## Travel Agency/Tours

Most hotels do not have sufficient information regarding river and jungle tours. For the best service in Belém, contact **Amazon Star Turismo Ltda.**, Rua Carlos Gomes, 14; ☎ and fax *224-6244*. Owned by French immigrant Patrick Barbier, the agency offers four kinds of river/jungle tours as well as package deals to Marajó and Mosqueiros islands. Special chartered tours can be arranged for specific needs. (For more information, see under *Excursions*, below.)

## When To Go

The best time to visit Belém is June-Aug., when there is sun in the morning and a little rain in the afternoon. Dec.-Mar. you'll experience the very wet side of the rainforest and will need rubber boots and ponchos.

Don't miss the **Círio de Nazaré** procession on the second Sun. in Oct., which attracts over a million religious devotees. The last two weeks of Oct. are filled with celebrations. Make hotel reservations far in advance.

# Manaus

Cruising into Manaus along the Rio Negro is an awesome sight after spending even a few days in the jungle. I've often wondered what Indian or *caboclo* children feel when they first glimpse that skyline of 20 skyscrapers, the yellow construction cranes stretching to heaven, the improbable gold dome of the opera house, all towering over the pastel-colored shacks that cling precariously to the hillside. How could they possibly grasp the meaning of all that black smoke pouring from the refineries, the multicolored boats bobbing in the floating docks, the defile of cars and trucks on the steel-girded bridge? One look, I think, and some of them must go reeling straight back to the forest.

For others, however, Manaus is the technological oasis of the Amazon. Located on the left bank of the Rio Negro, just above its junction with the Amazon River, Manaus is not only the political capital of Amazonas, it's practically the only city with any gusto of civilization. During the rubber boom, it enjoyed a few decades of nouveau-riche expansion; after a long decline, it's been gaining a grittier, if just as economically voracious, reputation ever since being declared a free trade zone in 1966. Just a few hundred feet from the docks, the center of the city is a beehive of activity – noisy stalls and shops selling everything from knock-off electronic equipment to Persian rugs and Taiwanese toys. A few years back, the international airport resembled the remains of a wholesale festival as passengers boarded planes loaded with enormous packages, but with the opening of customs to imported goods, the activity of the free zone has mellowed.

The eccentricities of the Rio Negro's ebb and flow sculpt the ever-changing face of Manaus' port. Subject to biannual tides, the river rises and falls as much as 40 feet within a six-month period; hence, the necessity of floating docks, a marvelous feat of British engineering (installed during the rubber boom), which respond to the tiniest variation of volume. A fair number of huts along the shore are actually built on rafts, some merely strung together by chains.

For many, the so-called "Meeting of the Waters" is an awe-inspiring sight – the junction of the Rio Negro and the Amazon, where two rivers of different colors flow together without mixing for miles. Blessed with mosquito-free environs, the jungles around Manaus attract most of the Amazon's tourists, who usually head for the jungle lodges located three to six hours away by boat. Many visitors spend their first night in Manaus at the famed Tropical Hotel – a veritable palace with its own zoo. My suggestion is to stay there after your jungle expedition – to slowly reacquaint yourself with the luxuries of civilization.

Nineteenth-century biologists Wallace, Bates, and Spruce all set out from Manaus; today the city is home to several hundred international scientists who actively study the forest in the hope of preserving both its fauna and flora. Though severely underfunded, INPA, the **National Institute of Amazonian Research**, staunchly perseveres in its multi-environmental projects, including raising manatees, dolphins, and rare sea otters that have been confiscated from illegal fishing expeditions. Many are on display to the public, and a swim-with-the-dolphins project is presently being planned, though its future seems bleak: Brazilians are uncommonly suspicious of the breed.

Unfortunately, the prospects for seeing substantial numbers of animals in their natural habitat near Manaus are somewhat discouraging. Frightened by loud motors and the sound of crunching boots, the smaller, more timid animals have, for the most part, retreated from the banks of the river, while most of the birds are so high up in the canopy they are difficult to see. (If you are desperate for fauna, try the Pantanal.) Sadly, many animals in the Amazon have already become extinct; the endangered manatee, common in the time of Henry Bates, is now being illegally slaughtered by *caboclo* fishermen, who often torture the babies to attract the mother. More often seen on excursions (and definitely heard) are screeching howler monkeys and also capybaras, bear-sized rodents who can sometimes be glimpsed poking their snouts into vegetation. Jaguars are rarely encountered by tourists, but I was once lucky enough to be handed a live sloth to cuddle – an experience no one should ever pass up.

# History

In the early 19th century, what is today known as Manaus was a garrison village named **Barra** that grew from a small fort the **Portuguese** had built in 1669 to monitor Spanish invaders. When botanist d'Orbigny stopped there in 1830, he noted that its 3,000 ragtag inhabitants were impassioned traders in everything the region had to offer: dried fish, sarsaparilla, Brazil nuts, and turtle oil. As **rubber** became an exportable commodity, Barra evolved into the provincial capital of **Manaus**, shipping nearly 20,000 tons of rubber abroad by the turn of the century. As rubber barons swelled the city to a population of 50,000, well-attired citizens in European fashions transacted business in gold coins. In 1897 electric trolleys clanged down 10 miles of tree-shaded avenues, and there were even 300 telephone subscribers, used by international stock houses competing for the price of rubber. In 1900 a chicken in Manaus cost about $27, and a bunch of carrots went for $9.

Between 1908 and 1910, when Manaus was at its peak, over 1.2 million square miles of forest, housing 80 million rubber trees, were being developed. With 80,000 tons of rubber now being exported annually, the country heavily depended on the city's export duties, which covered 40% of the national debt. But the rubber bust in 1923 sent Manaus reeling, with many companies declaring bankruptcy. Ironically, that very year, the 200-mile **Madeira-Mamoré Railway** was inaugurated 1,200 miles away to create an easier transport between Bolivia and the Brazilian city of Porto Velho. Called *Mad Maria*, it was an awesome accomplishment since everything – charcoal from Wales, steel from Pittsburgh, and termite-resistant wood from Australia – had been shipped in by necessity. Sadly, the construction cost the lives of 6,000 laborers and the collapsed market deadened any interest in pursuing the connection.

---

# Sights

---

Manaus is a jumping-off point for excursions into the jungle (most visitors stay in lodges several hours by boat from the city), but the urban area is worth serious attention. Don't miss a stroll around the port area and the various markets. The Teatro Amazonas is fantastic. Do take care for your belongings.

---

## Teatro Amazonas

*Praça Sebastião;* ☎ *234-2776. 9 a.m.-6 p.m.*

Imagine the chutzpah, the ingenuity, and the sheer persistence it took to build a grand opera house in the middle of the jungle. Inaugurated after 12 years of construction on Dec. 31, 1896, the Teatro Amazonas (660 seats, including boxes) is still a wonder of artful design, built completely with materials imported from Europe, except for the wood, which came from the Amazon forest. The original curtains, still intact, were painted by the Brazilian artist Crispim do Amaral in 1896 and represent the meeting of the waters of the Rio Negro and the Rio Solimões (the goddess in the middle is Yara, the water princess). The bronze chandeliers, which descend for cleaning, are from France; the pillars are made of English cast iron; and the ceiling was painted in Paris by two Italians, showing the arts of opera, tragedy, dance, and music. Except for the chairs, everything in the house is original (the old wood and cane chairs were replaced when air conditioning was installed under the seats). The ballroom, now only used as a showpiece, consists of 12,000 pieces of Amazon mahogany. The wrought-iron staircases are covered with guaraná plants. The wall painting showing a group of Indians saving some desperate-looking Europeans is a scene from the Brazilian opera *I Guarani*, by Carlos Gomes. In olden times, musicians used to serenade guests from the balcony. In 1947 the Governor declared all public buildings should be colored gray; it wasn't until 40 years later that the front facade was restored to its original light mauve. The first opera given in the house was *La Gioconda*, performed by an Italian troupe imported for the occasion. Tours are given throughout the day at regular intervals (though rarely in English). The air conditioning is only turned on for performances, so bring a fan and prepare to swelter. The view from the balcony is wonderful, but be careful of flying pigeons, who may decide to use your shirt as a toilet.

## The Port

The docks in Manaus often look as if somebody threw all the people and goods up in the air and then let them fall back down willy-nilly, but actually there's a consumer's intelligence organizing the activity lining the waterfront. A stroll down the waterfront to the **Municipal Market** may well be one of your best moments in Manaus, as you elbow past brawny dockers, tired fishermen, and even steely-eyed sailors eyeing the crowd for a little companionship. If you're daring, ask around to see which boats may be going out for the day; you could probably hitch a ride or, at the very least, charter one. During the day, walking around here is reasonably safe, but at night do avoid loitering. Despite the enormous fluctuation in river traffic volume, these floating docks, a miracle of British invention, can accommodate anything from canoes to ocean liners all year round. Nearby is the Customs House, prefabricated in Britain, then shipped to Manaus piece by piece.

## Feira da Manaus Moderna

Around 10 p.m. nightly a fantastic commotion takes place behind the Municipal Market as the port fills up with fishermen unloading their day's catch from canoes. Often, they throw some of their fish away, and dolphins lurking nearby leap out of the water to catch them. You can even rent canoes here and row around to inspect the activity. Make sure, however, that your boat doesn't have a hole in it, and take precautions with your valuables. A block away is the new market where the fish are sold.

## Mercado Municipal

Located at the corner of Rua Rochas dos Santos and Rua dos Barés, the Mercado Municipal is a concrete-and-steel structure built in 1906 and painted the pastel gray of all government buildings. Small cubbyholes manned by swarthy-looking merchants sell fruits, beans, wheat, sweets, and popcorn in big burlap sacks; it's a good place to stock up on supplies if you're headed for the jungle. You can also buy camping gear here, including paddles and hammocks. Good prices for Indian and *caboclo* crafts can be found (bargaining is essential). Check out Store #67, teeming with fresh and dried herbs for medicinal purposes; #30 is an *umbanda* store selling candles, incense, and other paraphernalia for calling up the spirits. Be careful with your own worldly goods here; one merchant cautioned me to carry my backpack in front of me because several people were eyeing it longingly.

## Fish Market

The fish market next door to the Mercado Municipal is wet and slimy, full of merchants, women and children all juggling for a good price. Here you'll see *pirarucu* just off the boat, as well as many fresh counterparts to the stuffed fish on view at the Science Museum.

# Beaches

Manaus is hot and humid because it labors three degrees south of the equator, 100 feet above sea level, and 1,000 miles from the ocean. But you can find a beach, nearby **Ponta Negra**, to which locals flock during the dry season, June-Nov. About 10 miles from the airport is the city's elite bathing grounds, **Dourado Beach**. Ask locals about swimming conditions so you don't run into unexpected piranhas or electric eels.

# Museums

## Flora & Fauna

### Museu de Ciências Naturais (Museum of National Science)

*Colônia Cachoeira Grande (Aleixo);* ☎ *244-2799. Tues.-Sun. 9 a.m.-5 p.m., closed Mon. Small fee.*

Founded in 1988, this exceedingly creative and well-maintained museum was the brainchild of a Japanese businessman who came to Brazil 15 years ago and immediately fell in love with Amazônia's flora and fauna. Located 15 min. from downtown, the museum is situated in a Japanese community where children still speak Japanese and traditional customs are maintained. The museum's air conditioning makes it a most attractive location to plant an overheated nervous system. If you're heading off for some serious fishing, this is a great place to get oriented. All notations are in English, Japanese and Portuguese. Among the 20 stuffed and 15 live species of fish housed in a gorgeous outdoor aquarium you'll see the *pirarucu*, the largest scaled fish in the world (up to 440 lbs.); the vicious *canjirú*, a small leathery fish that is extremely carnivorous (the species of the genus *Vanellia* are feared by people living along the river because they can enter the genitals of unsuspecting swimmers); the *tucunaré*, a very delicious fish whose coloring confuses other fish as to which end is its head. The insect room is straight out of a horror movie, featuring locusts, scarabs, and elephantine beetles. The butterfly mounts are extraordinary, including some species whose coloring resembles leaves and owls. The souvenir shop is one of the finest artisan stores in Manaus; though the goods are pricey, the quality is superlative. Groups may make arrangements to come at night.

## INPA

*Al. Cosme Ferreira, 1756; ☎ 236-9400. Mon.-Fri. 8 a.m.-noon, 2-6 p.m. Tours 9-11 a.m. only. Free lectures (some in English) are given every Tues. at 3 p.m.*

The Instituto Nacional Pesquisada Amazônia (the National Institute of Amazonian Research) is a forested park utilized by research scientists studying the survival and maintenance of the Amazon region. Many foreign scientists are working here, and guests are welcome from 9-11 a.m., when free tours are given. You may see manatee pups in captivity that have been saved from fishermen who tried to use them as bait to capture their mothers, and there are usually several tanks of dolphins. A good show is always given by the *arainha*, a diva-like otter who has a special ability to amuse himself in front of adoring onlookers. In the past, tours of the sawmill belonging to the Center for the Study of Forest Products have been given upon request, and guests have sometimes been presented with free boxes containing many different types of Amazonian wood. Fine T-shirts with slogans like "Preserve the Manatee" can be purchased on the grounds. Permission to enter the INPA must be obtained from the security police at the front gate. Call about programs open to the public.

## Eco Park

*Praça Auxiliadora, 4, AP 203; ☎ 234-0939; fax 633-3170.*

You will probably see more animals at this privately owned 4,500-acre preserve operated by the nonprofit Living Rainforest Foundation than in the "real" jungle. Opened in 1991 for purposes of conservation and education, the aquarium and botanical garden are still under construction; the orchid garden is complete. There's also a visitor center, bird sanctuary, a restaurant designed as a gigantic Indian hut, and even bungalows to house overnight guests in the forest. The 150 monkeys in the monkey jungle, who might use your back as a rest stop, were rescued from areas that have been flooded or burned down as a result of development. They receive medical attention and are given time to acclimate in the region before being released into the wild. You can hike six miles of trails leading through the forest, accompanied by trained guides; a full-day "survival course" emphasizes the techniques of indigenous people in obtaining food, water, shelter, and medicine from the forest.

Half-day excursions run about $25, full day $50, boat transportation included. Two-day/one-night stays cost $155 per person, based on double occupancy, and include two-day tours and all meals. A five-day/four-night visit (which requires a minimum of eight persons) is $425 per person and includes two days in the park and a two-day river cruise. The Tropical Hotel also offers packages starting at about $180 a person (double occupancy). Each night includes a one-day tour of the park with lunch. Another package features a night tour with dinner and an Indian dance show.

For more information regarding Eco Park or the package tours listed, contact Max Blankenfeld at Eco Park's office in the US: 9434 Old Katy Road, Suite 230, Houston, TX 77055-6300; ☎ *800-255-4326, fax (713) 468-1213.*

❖ **GETTING HERE:** *To reach the park, you must take a half-hour boat ride from the Hotel Tropical.*

## Native Crafts

### Museu do Homem do Norte

*Av. 7 de Setembro, 1385 (Centro);* ☎ *232-5373. Mon. 8 a.m.-noon, 1-6 p.m., Fri. 1-5 p.m. Minimal fee.*

This hot and sweaty, two-room museum was founded in 1985 to show the culture and way of life in the north. If you can brave the heat, you'll find the Indian artifacts fascinating, especially those from the Xingú tribe, which Noel Nutel collected over a 30-year period. Most impressive are the ritual clothes, and masks, among them an exquisitely beaded mask used to celebrate a girl's passage to puberty, and an ant-filled glove called a *Luva de Tocandira*, into which young boys put their hands to prove their manhood. There is also a room full of *bumba-meu-boi* costumes and a typical manioc house. A guaraná display shows the development of the plant as well as its many uses. There is no guide, but we did locate a worker who spoke a little English.

### Museu do Indio

*Rua Dq. de Caxias/Av. 7 de Setembro;* ☎ *234-1422. Mon.-Fri. 8:30-11:30 a.m., 2-4:30 p.m., Sat. 8:30-11:30 p.m. Minimal fee.*

Another non-air-conditioned museum in Manaus – this one is owned by the Salesian nuns, who run an Indian mission along the Rio Negro. Each of the six rooms is dedicated to various facets of Indian life; there are fantastic ceramics, baskets, and weapons, and even a model of a Yanomami house, a circular, straw-roofed dwelling housing between 30-250 people. The museum's store sells crafts from tribes up the Rio Negro and from *cablocos*. Rumor has it you can buy here the best guaraná (an herbal stimulant) in Amazonas (called Marou de Maués). One interesting novelty is a *Pega Moça* ("catch the girl"), an Indian wedding ring that looks like a Chinese knot and is placed on the woman's finger to pull her along. Also fascinating is the display of a pajé's instruments – the magical tools of the tribal shaman, including various powders, rattles, and medicine pouches. Among the musical instruments are panpipes, maracas, turtle-shell rattles, rain sticks and instruments made out of the brain of a buck. The last room is full of neon-colored butterflies and humongous-sized creepy crawlers. To film or take pictures, you must pay an extra 30 cents.

**UP CLOSE TIP:** *Ponta Negra, the river beach next door to the Hotel Tropical, is the city's hot spot on weekends. Between Oct. and Mar., when the river is low, you'll even find sand for fresh-water swimming.*

# Jungle Excursions

What's the best way to "do" the jungle near Manaus? You have basically two choices: lodges or package cruises. Jungle lodges are pousada-type accommodations deep in the jungle (usually near the shore of a tributary), where trekkers stay for two to three days. Quality ranges from the semi-luxurious to the primitive; meals are generally served in an open-air communal dining room. If you like to cruise, you may be happier (and cooler) if you take a package boat tour, where you sleep in tight (usually cramped) quarters and take meals on board prepared by a crew member. (The schedule may include a night of sleeping in the forest.) Excursions from the lodge and boat tours are usually similar: canoe treks through tiny streams, piranha fishing in the afternoon, alligator hunts at night, and the proverbial walk through the forest. During rainy season, consider that the lounging space on a boat becomes even more cramped. Private boat cruises usually sleep up to eight, not including crew.

A third category of tourists fantasize about renting their own canoes, meeting up with crazy explorers and riding the rapids to the mouth of the Amazon. Before you do this, make sure you read Joe Kane's compelling account of his own hazardous trip in *Running the Amazon*. The Polish daredevils he traveled with now have their own agency, **CanoAndes**, 310 Madison Avenue, NY, NY 10017; ☎ *212-286-9415*. They arrange trekking, rafting and wildlife and cultural expeditions for all levels of fitness and expertise. Just be forewarned that their guides run on the wild side.

# Cruise Packages

There are over 150 travel agencies in Manaus offering river excursions. Some of the best are listed below.

For those in a hurry, there are excellent one-day cruises out of Manaus, which go to the **January Ecological Park**, leaving from the docks at 9 a.m. and returning at 3 or 4 p.m. (lunch included, about $20). You see the Meeting of the Waters, tour around water lilies and take a canoe ride to the *igapós*. For more information, call **Selvatur**, Av. Gétulio Vargas, 725 A; ☎ *(92) 233-8044*, fax *622-2177*. Also try **Amazon Explorers**, Rua Nhamunda, 21 (Centro); ☎ *(92) 233-4418*, fax *(92) 233-4418*.

Several different cruises are offered by **Fontur**, located at the Hotel Tropical, Estrada da Ponta Negra; ☎ *(92) 656-2167*, fax *(92) 656-2167*.

Some of the best tours outside Manaus these days are run by **Amazon Nut Safari**, Av. Beira Mar, 43 (São Raimundo); ☎ *(92) 671-3525*, fax *671-1415*. It's best to write or fax for their itineraries, but schedules vary from three days and two nights to five days and four nights. They also have private rentals. (The five-day jaunt tours the **Anavilhanas Arquipelago**, the biggest archipelago in fresh water, formed by 400 islands.) Among their boats is the *Cassiquiari*, a double-decker river schooner that sleeps 24, with private, air-conditioned cabins. Trips leave from the Tropical Hotel, and include a visit to **Novo Ayrão**, a tiny town where the company's owner maintains a farm inhabited by an Indian family. The *Iguana* is a 10-person boat, with remote engine controls, hydraulic steering, and a satellite navigation center. You can also hire *Catuque*, a small motor boat, for about $100 a day.

For information about Amazon Nut Safari's jungle lodge, see "Apurissara Floating Lodge" under *Jungle Lodges* in the Manaus section.

## Excursions: Ornamental Fish

Ever wonder where the neon fish in your aquarium come from? Thousands of collectors and vendors swarm the area near Barcelos, Amazonas (pop. 7,000), 300 miles northwest of Manaus, along the Rio Negro for its enormous stock of ornamental fish. In 1993 about 16 million cardinals were exported. The first annual ornamental fish festival was held in Jan. 1994. Studying these fish at the Dr. Herbert R. Axelrod Foundation in Barcelos is Dr. Ning Labbish Chao, who can be reached through his organization Bio-Amazonia Conservation International, Caixa Postal 2310, 69, 061, Manaus, Amazonas; ☎ and fax *(92) 644-1138*, or 3204 Beamont Drive, Tallahassee, Fl 32308-2806, USA; ☎ and fax *904-668-8225*. Arrangements can be made for groups (such as aquarium societies or classes) to visit Barcelos and work at Dr. Chao's lab. Charter boats to Barcelos are also available.

During Jan., the city of Barcelos hosts the annual **Festa de Peixes Ornamentais** (Festival of Ornamental Fish). Participants can buy aquarium fish collected by *piabeiros*, or collect their own (a license is required). Visit the fish and plant show, trade crafts, workshops, contests for children, sportfishing, and boat excursions, music, dancing, and a tour of the aquarium business in Manaus. Beautiful water and bog plants, and especially wild orchids and bromeliads, are everywhere. Turtles may be available for sale, but do note that their trade or transportation is illegal. For more information contact: **Il Festa de Peixes Ornamentais**, Prefeitura do Municipio de Barcelos, Av. Tenreiro Aranha, 204; Barcelos, Amazonas Brazil (CEP 69,700); ☎ (only Portuguese) *011-55-92-7221/1200*, fax *721-1191*.

Travel arrangements and boating accommodations can be made through Miguel Rocha da Silva, **Amazon Nut Safari**, Av. Beira Mar, 43 (São Raimundo) Manaus, Brazil; ☎ *(92) 671-3525/233-7282*; fax *671-1415*.

## Where To Stay

Manaus is one of the hottest places in the world (and I grew up in Houston!). So, there are several points to remember in selecting a hotel.

- ☐ The air conditioning must work.
- ☐ A good pool will be appreciated.
- ☐ Cleanliness is sacred (this close to the jungle, you should think twice about the type of bug in your bed).
- ☐ Laundry (no one has ever returned from the jungle without the devastating need to wash clothes).

Considering all that, good deals can be found in Manaus, but at least one night at the Tropical is a must. If you can't afford it, just drop by for a drink beside the fantastic wave-pool. See page 26 for price chart.

## Tropical Manaus

*Estrada da Ponta Negra (Ponta Negra), 18 km., ☎ (92) 658-5000; fax 658-5026.*

The palatial oasis of the Amazon jungle – if you have the money, spend it here. The hacienda-like hotel is a sprawling maze of 608 rooms; a newer building added six years ago doubled the capacity. Dominating the lobby is a three-story atrium housing a great white heron and tropical ducks that perform tricks between 6 and 7 a.m. A magnificent pool complex famous throughout Brazil sports waterfalls gushing over rock cliffs. A mini-zoo features jaguars and pumas.

Minimal differences exist between standard and deluxe rooms, both lavishly appointed, with a chic-rustic allure. (Rooms in the older section are slightly more expensive, but sometimes retain a musty smell.) The three restaurants are spectacular: a barbecue buffet poolside for about $16, a candlelit gourmet restaurant, and a charming coffee shop. Tennis courts are open from 9 a.m.-9 p.m. daily. A travel agency arranges river and jungle tours, and a Varig office is open during business hours. *605 apts. Very expensive. All cards.*

## Taj Mahal Continental

*Av. Getúlio Vargas, 741 (Centro); ☎ (92) 633-1010; fax 233-0068.*

Opened in 1991, the Taj Mahal is the premier property of a famous Indian family who also owns the Plaza and the Imperial. All apartments have a view of the city; standards and deluxes barely differ. Furniture is streamlined and functional. Special rooms are available for the handicapped. The roof pool is about three strokes long. A nightclub is being built here. The restaurant delivers a fantastic lookout over the opera house, and an upper level slowly rotates for a panoramic view. Standard doubles run $92, deluxe doubles $106. *190 apts. Expensive. All cards.*

## Imperial Hotel

*Av. Getúlio Vargas, 227 (Centro), ☎ (92) 622-3112; fax 622-1762.*

Brass sculptures of Buddha adorn the lobby of this Indian-owned hotel in downtown Manaus. Standard rooms sport brightly flowered spreads, but the rugs are not uniformly clean. The medium-sized pool looks up to the hanging laundry of the neighboring apartment. The best *tacacá* in Manaus – a native dish of tapioca, manioc juice, garlic shrimps, and pepper – can be purchased right outside the front door, between the Plaza and the Imperial. Doubles run $90-$102. *100 apts. Expensive. All cards.*

## Plaza Hotel

*Av. Getúlio Vargas, 215 (Centro), ☎ (92) 232-7766; fax 622-1761.*

Owned by the same family as the Taj Mahal, the Plaza carries over the Indian decor in its colorful tapestries and bedspreads. Service is friendly. Superior rooms are substantially larger than deluxes, with an extended area for an extra couch bed. Although the rooms are well cooled, the corridors are as hot as a sauna. A rectangular pool is covered by a glass ceiling, which keeps the pollution out. Laundry service, a travel agency, and an imported-foods store are also on premises. Deluxe doubles run about $71, superiors about $86. *80 apts. Moderate. All cards.*

## Hotel Amazonas

*Praça Adalberto Vale (Centro),* ☎ *(92) 622-2233; fax 622-2064.*

This four-star seems to be particularly accommodating to children, who were running their electric cars all over the lobby when I visited. Deluxes feature verandas offering a fantastic view of the port; standards are a bit depressing. Special discounts are available for those who eat lunch and dinner. A hair salon, barbershop, pool, luncheonette, and drugstore accommodate guests. Children up to age five stay free; those aged between five and 12 are charged half-price. *182 apts. Moderate-expensive. All cards.*

## Slaass Flat Hotel

*Av. Boulevard Alvaro Maia, 1442;* ☎ *(92) 233-3525/3519; fax 234-8971.*

This gorgeous three-star is such a steal that one is left wondering what's wrong with this picture. Built initially as an apart-hotel (with kitchenettes), the Slaass, about six minutes by car from downtown, suggests an elegance almost unknown in Manaus. Doubles are incredibly spacious, with attractive wooden floors and a breezy veranda overlooking the city's rooftops. Apartments for four include three bedrooms, two bathrooms, kitchen, and living room. Special long-term rates are available. The rooftop bar makes a great perch. A pool and shopping center are being planned. Restaurants within walking distance include Florentina (Italian), Canto do Peixada (fish), and Miako (Japanese). *Inexpensive. All cards.*

## Hotel Monaco

*Rua Silva Ramos, 20 (Centro);* ☎ *(92) 622-3446; fax 622-1415.*

The classic Hotel Monaco is something out of a Jim Jarmusch movie, where the receptionist resembles a hooker and the quirkiest people emerge from the rooms. Still, the rooftop restaurant is one of the great spots to witness the city's fabulous sunsets, and you're sure to meet some real characters. *112 apts. Moderate. No cards.*

## Pousada Montemurro

*Rua Emilio Moreira, 1442 (Praça 14 de Janeiro);* ☎ *(92) 233-4564.*

This *pousada,* in a middle-to-low-class residential neighborhood, is a viable budget option. A white stucco building holds six kitchenettes and three suites, all air conditioned, with sculptured stained-glass windows. Suites are the best bet, with an outer room that includes a couch, dining table, and crazy photos of the Swiss Alps. All apartments have color TV and tiled bathrooms; only the suite has a phone. Breakfast (included in the rate) is the only meal served, but a tiny luncheonette is across the street. A sunning patio with potted plants relieves any sense of claustrophobia. *Inexpensive. No cards.*

## Hotel Dona Joana

*Rua dos Andrades, 553; ☎ (92) 233-7553.*

If you're looking for a cheap night, this simple three-story pension might do, but check your room before you sign in; grunginess is in the mind of the beholder. There's no elevator, and the stairs are steep, but the deluxe room on the third floor has a good breeze and great view of the river. You pay extra for hot water, but the spacious rooms should all have air conditioning. Across the street is a famous fish restaurant. The lobby is more funky than tasteless, but do note: This is no place to leave valuables. *60 apts. Inexpensive. No cards.*

## Hotel Rio Branco

*Rua dos Andradas, 484; ☎ (92) 233-4019.*

Located across the street from the Dona Joana Hotel, this pension is the hangout for hard-core adventurers, with 90% of the clientele European. All rooms have private bathrooms, and if you're seriously backpacking, who cares if the rooms are a little musty, the showers cold, and the breakfast room small? PR man Christopher Charles Gomes organizes jungle tours with expert guides; among his best is Jerry Hardy (part Brit, Indian, and Brazilian) who has his own boat. Three-day/two-night tours run about $150. Reports from the bush have been raves. Doubles with air conditioning run $10, with fan $8; singles $5-$6. Bedrooms with three or four beds, called *coletivas*, are the cheapest; all rates include breakfast (coffee, bread and milk only). A pay telephone, which you can use for three minutes a shot, is in the lobby, as are safes. *Inexpensive. No cards.*

## Hospedaria de Turismo Dez de Julho

*Rua 10 de Julho, 679; ☎ (92) 232-6280.*

Located within walking distance from downtown, this youth hostel for all ages is perfect for trekkers. All rooms are air conditioned, and come with tile floor, two beds, and clean baths. Breakfast is included, and laundry service is available. Pay phone in the lobby. Janete Tôrres, the director, is a lovely, gray-haired lady who speaks some English. *13 apts. Inexpensive. No cards.*

## Jungle Lodges Outside Manaus

## Ariaú Jungle Tower

*2 km. from the archipelago of Anavilhanas; 60 km. (37 miles) from Manaus; 3 hrs. by boat.*

The Amazon jungle's premier accommodation, Ariaú is the brainchild of a Brazilian businessman who longed to be not only in the jungle but above it. The entire complex of 45 wood apartments are interlinked by wooden catwalks between the trees, affording a unique communication with the flora and fauna. Towering 130 feet above ground is an observation deck (the only one in Amazonas), which allows you to see the magnificent canopy of the forest from above – a thrilling experience. A special Tarzan

House on top of a 120-foot chestnut tree was especially erected for guests who want to live out tree house fantasies. All rooms, with air-ventilators only, have private bathrooms and verandas. The duplex Presidential Suite, where the owner stays when he visits, boasts a downstairs dining room, TV, VCR, and lush leather furniture. Upon arrival from the river, you'll no doubt be greeted by the resident monkeys, macaws, and coatis (charming anteaters with raccoon tails); just watch out for the monkeys, who love to rip off eyeglasses and throw them in the water. Two-day/one-night packages include all meals (except drinks), a visit to a *caboclo* village, an alligator hunt at night, forest walks, and fishing. (Longer packages are available.)

For reservations in the US, contact **F&H Consulting**, 2441 Janin Way, Solvang, CA 93464; ☎ (800) 544-5503, fax *(805) 688-1021*. The main office in Manaus: **Rio Amazonas Turismo**, Rua Silva Ramos, 41 (Centro) ☎ (92) 234-7308; fax *(92) 233-5615*.

## Amazon Lodge

*Lago do Juma, 100 km. (62 miles) from Manaus (4½ hrs. by boat).*

This is a two-story rustic *pousada* that actually floats on the water. The 17 apartments share two bathrooms (cold water only) and use candles for illumination. Various treks into the jungle are part of a package.

In Manaus, contact: **Transamazonas Turismo**, Rua Leonardo Malcher, 734 (Centro); ☎ *(92) 622-4144;* fax *622-1420*. In US contact **Brazil Nuts**, ☎ *(800) 533-9959*.

## Amazon Village

*Lago do Puraquequara, 60 km. (37 miles) from Manaus (2 hrs. by boat).*

These 64 wooden apartments in neat cabanas are favorites of Germans and Swiss. who appreciate the excellent service and reputedly good food. Perched on a small hill at the bend of an *igarapé*, it's two to four hours from Manaus, depending on the river's condition. There are no electric lights, no air conditioning, no doors, and no windows. The "main building" is a large, open-thatched shed with a dining area, living room, bar and mini-museum, all open to the wind. Guests sleep in cottages scattered around the main building, easy to find with flashlights. The house jaguar eats in the dining area and loves to be stroked like a kitten. A five-star banquet can be held in the middle of the jungle if you ask.

In Manaus, contact: **Transamazonas Turismo**, Rua Leonardo Malcher, 734 (Centro); ☎ *(92) 622-4144;* fax *622-1420*. In the States contact **Brazil Nuts**, ☎ *(800) 533-9959*, or **Expeditours** in Rio, ☎ *(21) 287-9697*, fax *521-4388* or direct, ☎ *(92) 622-4144;* fax *622-1420*.

## Acajatuba Jungle Lodge

*Lago Acajatuba, Rio Negro, 70 km. (44 miles) from Manaus (4 hrs. by boat).*

More primitive than the Ariaú, these recently built 16 apartments are contained in three grass-roofed huts with private bathrooms, all illuminated by gas lanterns. Two-day/one-night packages for $140 include all food and mineral water, as well as piranha fishing, alligator hunts, a river tour, and a jungle walk. No cards accepted, but traveler cheques, dollars and *cruzeiros* are welcome.

In Manaus, contact: **ECOTEIS**, Rua Dr. Alminio, 30 (Centro); ☎ *(92) 233-7642*, fax *233-7642*. Contact **Amazon Explorers** in Manaus, ☎ *(92) 232-3052*.

## Pousada dos Guanavenas

*Ilha de Silves, 320 km. (200 miles) from Manaus (4½ hrs. by car).*

The Hilton Hotel of jungle lodges, these 20 apartments overlooking the Urubu River sometimes embarrass tourists who  come to the forest to escape air conditioning, mini-bars, and excellent food. On the other hand, the two-story roundhouse with screened porches and hewn-log verandas has received architectural raves for its structure, made from regional materials.

> ❖ **GETTING HERE:** *From Manaus, it's a 3½-hour trip by jitney to Itaquatiara, where you must board a flat-bottomed boat for another 1½-hr. ride. You may also arrive by sea plane or take a bus to Itaqoatiara and continue by boat.*

Packages include all meals and guided jungle excursions, such as alligator hunts and piranha fishing. In Manaus contact the main office: Rua Ferreira Pena, 755; ☎ *233-5558* .

## Terra Verde Lodge

This is an attractive lodge with two towers and five exotic grass-topped cabins on stilts in The Forest of Life, a large ecological reserve of virgin jungle situated among the richly contrasting ecosystems of the Negro and Solimões rivers. Electric lights, complete bathroom facilities, floating pool for swimming, and facilities for fishing and horseback riding are available. The owner is the famous film director and ecologist Zygmunt Subitrowsky. Contact **Agencia de Viagens e Turismo Terra Verde**, Rua Dr. Moreira 270/207; ☎ *(92) 234-0148;* fax *(92) 238-1742*.

## Apurissara Floating Lodge

*Rio Cueiras.*

Owner Miguel Rocha was a world traveler who used to invite his friends to cruise the Amazon with him. Today he still leads tours, along with his sons and daughters, using a squad of four kinds of boats. Their flagship property is a floating lodge (about five hours by slow boat, one hour by fast boat) on the Rio Cueiras, a tributary of the Rio Negro. The style is primitive chic, with 14 beds, some private bathrooms, and a thatched-roof dining area with a 360° view of the river. A four-day program includes transfer from Manaus, a canoe trip through the woodlands, night-time alligator hunts, a visit to a native house, an orchid search, and an overnight stay in the jungle. The lunch I ate here, cooked by a local, was verging on haute cuisine. Swimming in the river is encouraged, and kayaks are available. On rainy afternoons you can curl up with one of the many ecological books on board.

For more information on their cruising boats, see above, under *Cruising*. For reservations, contact in Manaus: Miguel Rocha da Silva, c/o **Amazon Nut Safari**, Av. Beira Mar, 43 (São Raimundo); ☎ *(92) 671-3525/233-7282*; fax *671-1415*.

## Lago Salvador

*On the right bank of the Rio Negro.*

This floating restaurant on the banks of the river, with 12 cabanas, is more luxurious than the average. An excellent resting place with a superb view; locals go just to feel at home in the jungle. For reservations, contact: **Fontur** (Hotel Tropical), ☎ *(92) 658-5000*, fax *658-5026*.

# Where To Eat

No one really goes to Manaus for a memorable meal. However, if you're just coming out of the jungle, any food that's more sophisticated than a ham sandwich will probably taste great. Fish is the most famous Amazonian delicacy, in particular *pirarucu* (called the "codfish of the Amazon"), *tambaqui, tucunaré* (especially delicious), and the more common *jaraqui* and *pacu. Molho de tucupi*, a sauce extracted from the manioc plant, is also ubiquitous. Regional fruits, such as *cupuaçu, taperebá, pupunha, graviola* and *jaca*, are prepared as excellent ice creams, juices, and cream desserts. The finest cuisine can be found at the Tropical Hotel, which features an impressive (but pricey) outdoor barbecue, indoor Italian restaurant, coffee shop, and several bars, all open to the public. Throughout the Amazon region be careful to avoid raw vegetables, salads, sushi, and unpeeled fruits. See page 26 for price chart.

## La Barca

*Rua Recife, 684 (Parque 10);* ☎ *236-8544. 11:30 a.m.-3:30 p.m., 7 p.m.-midnight, Sun. 11:30 a.m.-4 p.m.*

This popular fishery is set in an open-air, white stucco building, with a glimpse of the encroaching forest seen through open arches. *Costela de tambaqui grelhado* (grilled fish) is native to the Amazon – big enough for three, and one of the best fish I had in Brazil. People with colds (everyone seems to get one in Manaus because of the heat and the air conditioning) will love the steaming bowl of *canja da galinha* (chicken soup). Beef, chicken, stroganoff, and omelettes are also available. Those who can't take the heat or the noise can escape into an air-conditioned salon. *Inexpensive-moderate. All cards.*

## Churrasco/Tropical Hotel

*Estrada da Ponta Negra (Ponta Negra);* ☎ *238-5757. 7 p.m.-midnight.*

This barbecue buffet held under a tent-like roof is a little steep at $16, but the quality of the meats, fish, chicken, and salad bar is superb. One meal could last you two days. *Expensive. All cards.*

### Búfalo

*Rua Joaquim Nabuco, 628A (Centro);* ☎ *232-3773. 11 a.m.-3 p.m., 6-11:30 p.m., Sun. 11 a.m.-3:45 p.m.*

An air-conditioned *rodízio* – all-you-can-eat meat for reasonable prices. *Moderate. All cards.*

### Tarumã

*Tropical Hotel, Estrada da Ponta Negra;* ☎ *238-5757. Daily 7 p.m.-midnight.*

Old-world romance, Spanish-style lanterns, and high-beamed ceilings make a welcome (read air-conditioned) oasis. The cuisine rates as some of the best in the city; roasted duck with a cashew-spiked sauce was memorable. Desserts are first-class. Music from a grand piano and strings wafts down from the upper staircase. *Moderate. All cards.*

### Fiorentina

*Praça da Polícia, 44 (centro);* ☎ *232-1295. 11:30 a.m.-11 p.m., closed Mon. and first Sun. of the month.*

In the heart of the duty-free zone, this is the closest you'll get to an Italian cantina in the Amazon – cheerful tablecloths, bustling waiters, wood-slat chairs, and the inevitable fan. An air-conditioned room is upstairs. The menu is in English and Portuguese. *Moderate. All cards.*

### Hakata

*Rua Jonathas Pedrosa, 1800;* ☎ *233-3608. 11:30 a.m.-2 p.m., 6:30-10:30 p.m., closed Mon.*

*Na chapa* (table-grilled) is the specialty at this air-conditioned Japanese restaurant. *Camarão na chapa* comes with six shrimp, fried cabbage, and fried rice – a bit greasy, but filling. *Moderate. No cards.*

### Restaurant Palhoça

*Estrada da Ponta Negra;* ☎ *238-3831.*

An open-air restaurant with excellent views overlooking the river and obsequious waiters who present your fish to you before cooking it. Specialties include the *caldeiradas* (fish stews) and *pato no tucupi* (spicy duck). *Moderate. All cards.*

### Panorama

*Rio Negro Boulevard, 199;* ☎ *624-4626.*

Half the price of La Barca (above) and Amazonian fare almost as impressive. Plus a wonderful view of the city.

### Canto da Peixada

*Rua Emilio Moreira, 1677 E;* ☎ *234-3021.*

Situated in an old house with a veranda, this very good fish house specializes in Amazonian delicacies, including *caldeirada*.

## Restaurante Suzuran

*Rua Senador Alvaro Maia, 1683 (Adrianópolis);* ☎ *234-1693. 11:30 a.m.-2 p.m.,*
*6:30-11 p.m., closed Tues.*

This is the best Japanese restaurant in the city. Personally, I wouldn't eat
raw fish here, but I'm in the minority.

## Churrascaria Búfalo

*Av. Joaquim Nabuco, 628;* ☎ *232-3773. 11 a.m.-3:45 p.m., 6 p.m.-midnight; Sun. 11*
*a.m.-3:45 p.m.*

A fine steakhouse *rodízio*-style. *Moderate. All cards.*

## Bar "Galo Carijó"

*Rua dos Andradas, 536. 10:30 a.m.-3 p.m., 5:30-9 p.m., closed Sun.*

Also known as O Rei Jaraqui Frito, this open-air dive across from the Hotel
Dona Joana is just a roof and tables, but it's famous citywide for fish. The
ones I saw were bigger than the plates, with the head and tail hanging over.
Tastiest is the *pirarucú*, one of the largest fresh-water species; one of the
cheapest is the small *jaraqui*. Fish is normally served lightly fried, with
tomatoes, onions, and a mixture of rice and beans. *Inexpensive. No cards.*

## Ice Cream

## Beijo Frio Ice Cream Parlor

*Av. Getúlio Vargas, 1289 (Centro). 8 a.m.-midnight.*

People go to Manaus just to indulge in the numerous tropical fruit-flavored
ice creams. This air-cooled parlor features 36 exotic tastes – *cupuaçu, goiaba,*
*tucumã, tapioca, graviola, castanha de cajú, açai,* and *maracujá* – as well as five
diet flavors. Sundaes and banana splits are delicious. Take your time tasting
flavors.

## Alema

*Rua José Paranaguá at the corner of Doutor Moreira.*

Located near the free zone, this is a good pit stop for cold tropical juices,
desserts, and ice cream.

> **UP CLOSE TIP:** *Do try tacacá – a street dish famous in the region made*
> *with tapioca, cupí (manioc juice and pepper), garlic, and shrimps. The*
> *most famous vendor sets up on the corner between the Plaza and the*
> *Imperial Hotels.*

# Nightlife

Nightlife is limited in Manaus, but it does exist. Clubs appear and disappear
in less than a year, so check out the latest hot spots with your concierge or
locals.

## Maloca

*Estrada da Torre, km. 6 (Marina Tauá). Mon.-Sat. 9 p.m.*

The major folkloric show of Manaus, set in a grass-topped open-air theater, telling the legend of *guaraná* (the Amazon herb used as a stimulant) through song, dance, and fantastically feathered costumes. Fixed prices include dinner, transportation, for around $42; tickets available for show only. Buses to the show leave from the Hotel Amazonas. With one exception, all songs are sung in Sateré-Maué, a native dialect. Free brochures with translations in various languages are distributed.

## Hotel Tropical

*Estrada da Ponta Negra (Ponta Negra);* ☎ *658-5000.*

You won't find many locals at the hotel's fine disco (due to the high price), but it's considered the best in the city. Just hanging out beside the wave pool and having a drink can be fun, even if you aren't a guest.

## Hagae 39

*Rua Djalma Batista.*

This was the top-rated bar in 1994.

## Kalamazon

*Highway to Itacoatiara. Thurs., Fri. and Sat., action starts after midnight.*

This is the best club to dance *lambada* and *forró*, situated on the road to Itacoatiara – a substantial taxi drive from downtown. All ages are welcome and sometimes folklore bands from Paratins perform *toadas*, songs from the *bumba-meu-boi* festivities.

## Jet Set

*Rua 10 de Julho, 439;* ☎ *234-9309.*

Manaus' version of tropical striptease; women welcome. Locals consider the show "cold," but tourists seem to get a kick out of it.

## Sabor Brazil

*Rua Leonardo Malcher, 1840. Fri. and Sat. from 10 p.m. on; Sun. at 7 p.m.*

Club to dance samba and *pagoda*.

> **UP CLOSE TIP:** *Live bands can be found at* **Praia da Saudade** *on the weekends.*

# Gay Manaus

**Turbo 7**, a well-known gay bar, has served at least three generations of gay clientele, near the docks.

# Shopping

## Downtown

The main street downtown is **Rua Eduardo Ribeiro**, full of large department stores like Mesbla (the Macy's of Brazil), and the even cheaper Lojas Americanas. The majority of **banks** are located along **Rua Djalma Batista**. Duty-free shopping (not of particular value to the foreign tourist) is concentrated in the **Calçadão area** around the streets of Doutor Moreira, Marcilio Dias, and Guilherme Moreira, crossed by Quintino Bocaiuva.

## Native Crafts

### Centro de Artesanato Banco e Silva

*Rua Recife (no number);* ☎ *236-1241. Mon.-Fri. 8 a.m.-7 p.m.; Sat. 8 a.m.-1 p.m.*

Located in Parque 10 de Novembro, these 20 stores carry various indigenous Indian and *caboclo* artisanry.

### Museu do Índio

*Av. 7 de Setembro at the corner of Duque de Caxias.*

Fine Indian artisanry, such as headdresses, bows, and arrows, and jewelry have been collected by the Salesians nuns who run the museum. Reasonable prices; considerably cheaper than the Science Museum store.

### Eco Shop

*Amazonas Shopping Mall.*

Unbelievably expensive, but you'll find lots of good quality handicrafts from Amazônia and Alta Floresta, including fine pieces of Indian art.

### Artindia

*Praça Aldaberto Vale, 2;* ☎ *232-4890. Mon. 8 a.m.-noon and 2-6 p.m.*

In front of the Amazon Hotel, this old white building houses the Funai store, with excellent prices and good variety. Amazon Indians from all over provide earrings, necklaces, pottery, straw baskets, bows and arrow, and tangas made from seed. The ambiance effects the boisterous spirit of an outdoor market.

## Herbs, Cosmetics & Whole Foods

### Chapaty

*Rua Saldanha Marinho, 702-A (Centro),* ☎ *233-7610.*

This natural health food store specializes in herbal medicines, teas, whole breads, wholewheat pastas, and natural sweets, as well as extraordinary shampoos made from Amazon products.

## Prönatus do Amazonas

*Rua Costa Azevedo, 11 (Centro), factory at Rua 223, Esconde de Porto Alegre, 440 (Centro);* ☎ *234-8754.*

Inspired by the richness of Amazônia, this company has an exclusive line of herbal pills and cosmetics culled from the jungle plants. All products are hypo-allergenic, and their processing is all timed in with the natural cycles of the forest. Soaps made from tropical herbs make great gifts, as do herbal formulas for anything from impotence and diabetes to weight control.

## Shopping Malls

### Amazonas Shopping Mall

*Rua Djalma Batista, on the corner of Rua Darcy Vargas (Chapada). Mon.-Sat. 10 a.m.-10 p.m. On Sun. movies open at noon, shops 3-9 p.m.*

Ten minutes from downtown by car (20 minutes from the Tropical Hotel), this new shopping mall is shockingly chic for Manaus. Six movie theaters, food fairs, fine clothes stores, a one-hour photo shop, pharmacies, and a store that sells American cosmetics. Go just to get out of the heat.

> **UP CLOSE TIP:** *Best place to buy hammocks is along Rua dos Bares. For international magazines and newspapers, try the **Livraria Nacional** on Rua de Maio and the kiosk near the Teatro Amazonas.*

# Hands-On Manaus

## Arrivals

**Aeroporto Internacional Eduardo Gomes** (Av. Santos Dumont; ☎ *212-1431*) receives flights from Rio, Belém, Brasília, Campo Grande, Cuiabá, Fortaleza, Natal, Recife, Porto Velho, and a few other towns. From the United States, Varig flies direct from Miami, and a new flight was recently installed from San Francisco and Los Angeles. Hotel Tropical provides shuttle bus service to and from the airport for guests.

## Airlines Serving Manaus

**Varig**
Rua Guilherme Moreira, 278/86 . . . . . . . . . . . . . . ☎ 621-1136
**VASP**
Rua Guilherme Moreira, 179 . . . . . . . . . . . . . . . . . ☎ 621-1355
**Transbrasil**
Rua Guilherme Moreira, 150 . . . . . . . . . . . . . . . . . ☎ 621-1356
**TABA**
Av. Ed. Ribeiro, 664 (Ed. Zulmira Bittencourt) . . ☎ 621-1480
**Air France**
Rua dos Andradas, 371, first floor . . . . . . . . . . . . ☎ 234-2798

## Business Hours

Banks are open Mon.-Fri. 9 a.m.-3 p.m. Stores are also open Mon.-Fri., 8 a.m.-noon and 2-6 p.m., and Sat. from 8 a.m.-1 p.m.

## City Transportation

### Car Rentals

| | |
|---|---|
| Hertz | ☎ 621-1376 |
| Nobre | ☎ 233-6056 |

### Taxis

| | |
|---|---|
| Amazonas | ☎ 232-3005 |
| Coopertaxi | ☎ 621-1544 |

### Buses

City buses run from 5 a.m.-midnight.

## Climate

Manaus is a sauna – hot and humid all year long with temperatures that start at 80°F and rise without mercy, sometimes up to 115°F. Nov.-Mar. is the rainy season, with precipitation a daily occurrence.

Temperatures are a bit cooler in May and June, with the water level reaching its peak in June. Dry season occurs July-Nov. During dry season, you may have to change routes. Canoe trips may be cancelled in downpours. In an open river with a real storm, strong winds can make canoeing dangerous.

## Luxury Cruise Liners

A number of luxury cruise liners dock in Manaus or travel up the Amazon River, among them: Odessa America Service Co., Sun Line Cruises, Regency, Royal Viking, Ocean Princess, Society Explorers, Sagafjiord, Stella Solaris, Berlim, and Fairwind.

## Money Exchange

**Casa Cortez**
Av. 7 de Setembro, 199 . . . . . . . . . . . . . . . . . . . . . . ☎ 232-2695
**Banco do Brasil**
Rua Marechal Deodoro and at the airport (24 hrs.)
Exchanges dollars at the tourist rate.

## Mosquitoes

The Amazon River has an acidity content that prevents the breeding of mosquitoes, but the white waters of the Solimões are seriously infested. There, mosquitoes attack mostly at dusk and after dark, when repellant is absolutely necessary. Most legitimate tours avoid this area at those times. (Also see the *Amazon Survival Kit*, under *Amazônia*.)

Yellow fever, transmitted by mosquitoes, is considered endemic in Brazil, except around the coastal shores. Health authorities advise that the most infected areas are Acre, Amazonas, Goiás, Maranhão, Mato Grosso, Mato Grosso do Sul, Pará, Rondônia, and the territories of Amapá and Roraima. Vaccinations are good for 10 years and are essential if you are traveling either to the Amazon or the Pantanal. You may be required to show proof of vaccination when entering the country from Venezuela, Colombia, Ecuador, and Bolivia; it's best to always travel with the document. (For more information on malaria, see the *Amazon Survival Kit*.)

## Photo Development

### Foto Nascimento

*Av. 7 de Setembro, 1194;* ☎ *234-4660, 234-4995.*

Film development in one hour. Major makes of cameras are for sale.

## Private Guides

**EMAMTUR**, the official tourist board, requires officially sanctioned guides to take three months of training, including courses in history, jungle survival, ecology, and Red Cross. If you hire a non-official guide, make sure he is reliable and knowledgeable or you will regret it dearly. Some recommended private guides are: **John Harwood** (☎ 236-5133), a British scientist formerly at INPA, who now works with cruise lines as well as individuals; Brazilian-born **Claudia Roedel** (☎ 244-2455) formerly an ecology student who now guides treks into the jungle with her husband; **Christopher Charles Gomes** conducts tours and individual expeditions that may be reserved through the Hotel Rio Branco, Rua dos Andradas, 484; ☎ 233-4019. (See more information under *Where To Stay*.)

Special interest groups may contact **Sherre P. Nelson** at Solução, Rua Monsenhor Coutinho, 1141; ☎ 234-5955/5400.

## Telephones

To make international calls, head for the telephone company **Telamazonas**, Rua Guilherme Moreira, 326 (downtown), open daily 6 a.m.-11:30 p.m. Another branch is on the corner of Av. Getúlio Vargas and Leonardo Malche. Both are downtown.

## Time

Manaus is one hour behind Brazilian standard time (two hours behind between Oct.-Mar., when the rest of Brazil is on summer time).

## Tourist Information

**EMAMTUR** (the state tourist board) is at Av. Tarumã, 379 (Praça 24 de Outubro); ☎ 234-2252, fax 233-9973. Information posts are also located at the airport and across from the opera house at the intersection of Eduardo Ribeiro Ave. and José Clemente. For information regarding native tribes and permission to visit reservations, contact **FUNAI**, Rua dos Andradas, 473; ☎ 234-7632.

## Travel Agencies

**Amazon Explorers**, Rua Quintino Bocaiúva, 189; ☎ *232-3511*, arranges boat excursions, overnight jungle treks, fishing trips, city tours and excursions specially tailored to the needs of clients. English-speaking staff available.

**The Hotel Tropical**, ☎ *238-5757*, maintains a fine agency for guests and non-guests alike.

Another full-service agency is **Selvatur**, Praça Adalberto Vale (Hotel Amazonas), ☎ *234-8984.*

## When To Go

**JUNE 12-30: Folklore Festival of Paratins**. Often as spectacular as Carnaval in Rio, these festivities divide the cities into rivaling groups with parades, typical foods, and music. The best time to go is the last three days.

**JULY 15-30: Folklore Festival of Amazonas.**

**AUGUST-DECEMBER:** The months with least rainfall. In July the river starts to recede and beaches sprout up.

**SEPTEMBER 21-28: Agricultural Fair.**

**SEPTEMBER 27-29: Itacoatiara Festival of Song.**

**JANUARY** (last weekend): **Ornamental (Aquarium) Fish Festival**, in Barcelos.

# Alta Floresta

In the southernmost part of the state of Mato Grosso, the grit-and-grizzle town of Alta Floresta is something right out of the Old West. The business at hand is gold. For the last 20 years, thousands have converged on the area to try their luck; some make it after two years; others are still following pipe dreams. Luck, not persistence, seems to be the deciding factor and, as one local explained, a kind of inbred culture prevails where rules are not made to be broken. "There are no thieves here," he told me matter-of-factly, "because if someone takes something, he dies." A pale orange dust storm seems to have perpetually enveloped the city; even the children playing outside are covered with it. The major activity during the day takes place at the **Aurim Gold Exchange**, where *garimpeiros*, from the slick to the mud-slung, come to exchange their gold nuggets for cash. Around 10:30 in the morning, you'll see *garimpeiro* wives, dressed in cut-offs, high heels, and lots of gold jewelry, forking over the husbands' hard-earned nuggets to be weighed and processed.

Alta Floresta is also fascinating because you can actually see rainforest burning. Perhaps that's not everyone's dream vacation, but there's nothing like ramming home the reality of the earth's plight than by seeing it up close and in your face. Just traveling the roads out of town will bring you past scorched earth and burnt trunks, and you'll no doubt see not only smoldering grass but groves of trees and shrubs in actual flames. I actually saw one farmer setting fire to a plot of land so he could plant cotton, but the most shocking scene I witnessed was that of a three-year-old playfully setting a tiny pile of twigs on fire with a match – obviously imitating the gestures of his dad.

There is, however, access to a wonderful jungle near Alta Floresta and the best way to see it is by staying at the Floresta Amazônica Hotel. This resort, unusually stylish for the area, is located on the junction of the TeleSpires and Cristalina rivers and is owned by a large landholder who is passionate about preserving the forest (she even hires young professional botanists as guides who do extensive

Gold miners near Alta Floresta in Mato Grosso do it the old way – by hand.

research over their six-month internships). The complex is unique for the multidimensional perspectives of Amazonian life it offers its guests, who can look forward to widely different adventures, depending on the season (routes navigated during the dry season by jeep are cruised by canoe during the rainy season). A day trip may be taken to a nearby *fazenda* (farm) that features an unusual zoo as well as an exciting display of *garças* roosting in the leafy trees at dusk. Other excursions include a coffee plantation and the muddy dregs of a gold mine, where you'll probably get a chance to speak with miners. Overnight excursions into the jungle are the most exciting: Guests are escorted down the Cristalina River in a canoe to a location in the jungle, where they bed down dormitory-style (beds or hammocks). Just waking up to the symphony of cawing birds is thrilling, not to mention the nightly orchestra of bullfrogs. Fishing expeditions and fresh-water swimming are also available. This resort is particularly fine for families.

# Culture

## The Forest People

The following interview was made with Luiz Pereira Andrade, a 57-year-old guide who lives with his wife, daughter, son-in-law, and grandchild in the forest connected to the Floresta Amazônica Hotel. He is a burly man with gray, bushy eyebrows and a paunch that pushes out of his shirt. He has lived in the forest for over 25 years.

### Spirits of the Forest

"Here, in Alta Floresta, we call the *matinta pereira* (forest witch) the *pai do mato* (father of the forest). The first clue to being in contact with him is when you suddenly feel lost in the forest. You go home and get something to give him – food, anything – and put it where you felt strange. If you don't do this, you'll be lost forever and won't find your way home. He's invisible but you can feel him. When I fish at night, sometimes I hear strange sounds, like tools falling, or somebody coughing. I never feel afraid – I just don't know what it means. Many times I've seen strange lights. When I'm fishing at night, a spot of light, yellowish with a blue tail, comes up behind me, goes to the river and disappears in the water. This light is strong and illuminates the whole river. Some people say it's the Gold Mother. I don't know.

"Do trees and animals have spirits? *Com certeza* (certainly)! If they are alive, they have spirits. Trees have a natural capacity to take energy, others to receive. When I embrace a tree, I feel it. I learned this by myself because one time I went to the shade of a tree when I was very nervous and suddenly calmed down. You saw that when you went to hug the embauba tree, it released your negative energy and when you hugged the castanha it gave you positive energy. How could trees do this if they don't have souls?

"When you go to the forest and watch birds, they are happy, so you feel happy. You start to join with their happiness. When you are unhappy and you go to the forest and look around, you know a human is not that big. You are just a small piece in this world. I will live in this forest till I am 90 because here the old people become young. We don't miss anything from the city. I just feel unhappy I didn't come sooner."

## A Gold Miner

The following interview was made with the owner of a gold mine in Alta Floresta, a well-dressed man in his late 50s who was waiting to exchange gold. His slicked-back gray hair, good linen clothes, diamond ring and gold watch made a sharp contrast to the rough, desperate-looking young men with muddy feet who were also waiting in line.

## Garimpo

"I came here nine years ago from Paraná just for gold – eight in the mine, one year making money. In the beginning you don't know much. You usually lose money. You get friends to work for you, but usually they steal from you. But I was lucky. I have a good life now – a good house, a car. I was rich also in Paraná – I had a shop of tools for cars. But I think life was better there. The city here doesn't have much society, but my wife likes it better here because it's hotter. I had malaria five times. Only last year did I have it badly – at Christmas, I was very ill. Is it worth the pain? For me it's been good. *Garimpo* is like a vice. When you start you can't stop. And sometimes you lose all your money just because you have to reinvest it to try again."

# Where To Stay

### Floresta Amazônica Hotel

*Av. Perimetral Oeste, 2001;* ☎ *(65) 521-3601; fax 521-3801.*

A clean, cheerful resort – the most comfortable you'll find for thousands of miles. An outdoor dining area looks onto a pleasant pool complex; meals can also be eaten inside a stylishly rustic restaurant. Excursions include jungle hikes, coffee farm, and gold mine. The landscape is an ebullient profusion of pink and blue flowers and the lobby sports a few caged spiders and snakes. Trained biologists serve as guides. Fishing and fresh-water swimming included. *Moderate. V.*

# Hands-On Alta Floresta

## Arrival

### By Air

Alta Floresta is serviced by the airline **TABA**, Av. Ariosto de Riva; ☎ *(65) 521-3360/521-3222* (airport), with flights from Altamira, Belém, Cuiabá, Itaituba, Jacareacanga, Juará, and Santarém.

### By Bus

The bus station is on Av. Ariosto da Riva; ☎ *521-3177/2710*. Connections can be made from Campo Grande, Cuiabá, Paranaiba, and other towns. Some parts of the road from Cuiabá are not paved. "Luxury" buses, *leitos*, are available from São Paulo to Cuiabá, where you must change buses. At Colida, you change to an even more primitive bus for another three hours (total trip from São Paulo runs 12-14 hrs., about $76).

## Air Taxis

| | |
|---|---|
| Jato. . . . . . . . . . . . . . . . . . . . . . . . . . . . . . . . . . . . . . . . | ☎ 521-3903 |
| Penna . . . . . . . . . . . . . . . . . . . . . . . . . . . . . . . . . . . . . | ☎ 521-2584 |

## When To Go

The rainy season runs Oct.-Mar.; mosquitoes are rampant after heavy rains. Best time to visit is May-Oct. The coolest months are Aug.-Oct.

> **UP CLOSE TIP:** *Mato Grosso is one of the most malaria-infected states in Brazil, and Alta Floresta has its fair share (mostly around the gold mines). Do come protected and wear plenty of mosquito repellent, reapplying it before dusk. Keep windows shut at night. (Personally, I never had a problem, but I did take precautions.) (See Health Kit in the back of the book.)*

# THE PANTANAL

**A**lthough nearly obscured by the eco-media's blitz on the Amazon rainforest, the Pantanal – an immense kidney-shaped swampland in western Brazil – is perhaps the country's greatest natural resource. Officially known as *O Grande Pantanal,* the region, which cuts across the states of Mato Grosso and Matto Grosso do Sul (as well as western Bolivia and northeastern Paraguay) is a multi-faceted ecosystem that changes its alluvial face every six months – not unlike the Everglades in Florida. During the rainy season (Oct. through Mar.) torrential rains inundate up to 85% of this region, causing rivers, lakes and ponds to merge into an inland sea. Five months later, the effect of the burning tropical sun and the north-south flow gives way to verdant grassy plains dotted by water holes teeming with fish, tall wading birds and alligators. As such, the Pantanal during the dry season becomes an acutely visible arena for the playing out of Mother Nature's food chain. Simply, what the Amazon is to flora, the Pantanal is to fauna. If you want to see Brazilian wildlife at its most exotic, come to the Pantanal.

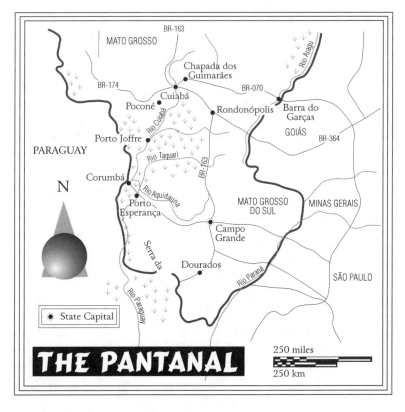

Although the word *"pantanal"* is usually translated as swampland, in actuality the Pantanal is a sedimentary basin into which drain numerous rivers, including the Rio Paraguay and its tributaries, as they make their way south to the Rio de la Plata and the Atlantic Ocean. More than 65 million years ago, the region was completely ocean; 7,500-year-old animal bones have been found here, as well as the remains of a 10,000-year-old human fetus. As recently as five hundred years ago, Kayapó, Iguato, and other tribes were known to migrate along the border with Amazonas. In the early 18th century, rumors of fist-sized emeralds and diamonds magnetized the first *bandeirantes* (pioneers) from São Paulo, though it was gold that was finally discovered along the banks of the Cuiabá River. After a 30-year rush, most miners moved on, but the few who stayed started sugarcane plantations and huge cattle ranches, piquing the interest of the King of Portugal, who established a captaincy in 1719 to collect taxes.

# A Wild West Fantasy

It would take another century until anyone intentionally returned to the Pantanal. As 17th- and 18th-century expeditions found the way nearly impassable, the region gained a certain wildcat reputation. In 1925, **Lt. Colonel Percy Fawcett**, one of the most indefatigable explorers, mysteriously disappeared while searching for the legendary city of El Dorado, but that didn't deter big-city slickers during the 1930s and 40s from zooming down in their German-made seaplanes to fish and bag game. With the construction of the highways between Cuiabá-Santarém and Cuiabá-Porto Velho, the Pantanal's fortunes, and especially those of Cuiabá (Mato Grosso's capital) improved dramatically. The booming frontier town, situated on the banks of the Cuiabá River, became a symbol of Manifest Destiny, a Wild West fantasy for those trapped in the drought-ravaged Northeast. Roads were planned for 150,000 new residents, but many more thousands were spellbound by the lure of gold, lumber, cattle, and diamonds. Nearly all had to pass through Cuiabá on their way to the yellow-brick plains.

Today, as the Pantanal loses its reputation as an intractable swamp, it is fast becoming the focus of enormous political and economic intrigue. Although two Brazilian areas are officially protected – a remote national park near Bolivia and a small ecological reserve in Mato Grosso – the rest remains the property of private cattle ranches, where frontier law prevails. Illegal hunters, miners, and commercial fishermen continue to blatantly exploit the region in the face of lax federal enforcement. The health of residents is threatened by mercury poisoning from gold mining, agrochemical pollution from crops, and malaria epidemics. Violent outbreaks take place daily between gold miners and native tribes, the latter which are being forced further and further into the interior. Sadly, with the exception of **Pantanal Alert**, an activist group made up of artists and musicians in São Paulo, there are very few private organizations dedicated to conserving the Pantanal with the same fervor as that of the Amazon rainforest.

Whether the land in the Pantanal is even economically viable is being hotly debated today behind closed doors. Although most of the land had been traditionally owned by a few families, it is now being divvied up into smaller plots, at great loss to the new owners. Rumor has it that, since such a large percentage of the land is flooded for most of the year, substantial agriculture is nearly impossible, and the exorbitant cost of constantly relocating grazing cattle makes for unprofitable business. Some factory owners are now using their newly claimed property merely as tax dodges. Beyond the great ranches, the only other residents of the region are poor fishermen, who eke out a subsistence level of existence. **Eco-tourism** is the Pantanal's brightest hope for the future.

# How To Visit

There are many ways to visit the Pantanal – all of them rugged, muddy affairs, but well worth the effort for a die-hard eco-tourist. The city of **Cuiabá** is only one of three gateways to the Pantanal; the other jumping-off points are **Campo Grande** and **Corumbá**. From any one of these cities you can journey into the interior and choose among several types of accommodations, from four-day cruises on fishing boats to lodges that allow you to comb the countryside on horseback, foot, and boat. Each of these accommodations have their own benefits and disadvantages, and each can be tailor-made to your level of physical fitness.

> **UP CLOSE TIP:** *Avoid Jan., when there are the most mosquitoes. Aug. and Sept. are the coolest months.*

# The Transpantaneira Highway

At least once in your stay, arrange to traverse the grand Transpantaneira Highway, a feat of civil engineering completed during the dictatorship (1964-85) that unwittingly created a stunning ex-post facto reserve. Accessed from the city of Cuiabá, the 150-km./93-mile road, elevated 8½ feet above the flooded plains, starts right after the quaint village of **Poconé**, where the asphalt road suddenly turns into what Pantanal vets sardonically call an "all-weather" highway. In the rainy season, the road becomes a linear refuge for wildlife; when the waters recede, millions of fish are trapped in the roadside trenches, offering a smorgasbord for predator and scavenger alike. During the dry season, riding over the bumpy highway with its bomb-sized craters is like journeying through a zoo on the moon – every few feet brings another "oh-oh-oh" experience. Large mounds become islands of refuge for snakes, capybaras, antbears, and jaguars, while caimans and great wading birds retreat to the artificial pools below to wait out the dry season. Seeds borne on the wind and in the guts of birds create the landscape of squat trees and scrub – a dried-out *cerrado* that nearly resembles parts of East Africa. The highway ends abruptly 150 km./93 miles south of Poconé at **Porto Jofre** on the banks of the Cuiabá River.

There are few people and no other towns in the Pantanal, so a look around Poconé is well warranted. Dating back to the 18th century, Poconé is a picturesque, well-kept colonial town, where most of the houses have traditional roofs and horse-drawn carts still meander down the cobblestone streets. A blue church dominates the main square, around which are general stores and the mayor's office. Just as it was 150 years ago, gold was "rediscovered" in Poconé about five years ago, turning the town upside down. Convinced there was gold hidden in the walls of the church, miners actually tore it down, finding only enough to rebuild a new church. Today, signs of *garimpeiros* (gold miners) are everywhere, from the picks and axes in the country stores to the smell of mercury in the air.

Travel can be as primitive as ox carts in the Pantanal.

**UP CLOSE TIP:** *Hitchhiking the Transpantaneira Highway (as opposed to going with a pre-arranged tour) seems to be the beloved pastime of male travel writers and gonzo photo-journalists who are mad for adventure and great photo-ops. Maybe I'm a sissy, but frankly I wouldn't suggest hitchhiking, at least not on your first trip to the region. Sure, you'll find a friendly ride eventually, and you're bound to meet lots of colorful cowboys, native fishermen, and even a few federal agents, but in the meantime you could be overcome by sunstroke, exhaustion, bee attacks, hungry capybaras, dazed crocodiles, and even swarms of malaria-ridden mosquitoes, not to mention sudden floodings. You might even stumble on illegal poachers who would like to scramble you for breakfast. You'd be better off with a reputable guide in a well-maintained vehicle (truck, boat, or plane) and a responsible driver who knows the terrain. The driving is rough; even Brazilian tourists have been known to topple over in their jeeps. Since there are no towns, restaurants, or phones on the highway, getting stuck will mean a very long wait.*

# Lodges

Besides trekking the Transpantaneira Highway there are several other travel options you can add to your Pantanal itinerary. First choice, in my opinion, is to book a stay at a rustic lodge. From here, you can initiate treks by foot, horseback, or canoe, always led by a guide – usually preferred by those who sleep more comfortably on dry land. A variety of lodges in all price ranges are available, from the most primitive ranches, where meals are cooked over an open fire, to the luxurious Pousada Caiman, the most famous lodge in the Pantanal. Package deals are usually the cheapest and the most sensible way to go; just make sure the lodge provides transfer from the airport.

## The Fazenda Experience

"I step off a 10-seater plane in Corumbá and find a rugged, four-word cowboy waiting for me in the lobby. He piles my gear in the back of his truck, and soon we're off on a rollicking ride to reach the Fazenda Xaraes. During rainy season, more than half of this trek would be navigated by canoe, when the annual rains floods the plains leading to the arm. On this Aug. day, the ride gives new meaning to 'wear your seatbelt.'"

After a dead-to-the-world sleep in my air-conditioned cabana, we fortify ourselves with a mule-teamer's breakfast, then hop in his truck to interface with the countryside. Julio, the driver of our jeep, seems to have preternatural sense where the wild animals are lurking, even before he sees them; along the highway we discover just-shed cobra skins, contemplate the jaws of alligators from bridges, and nearly get crushed by herds of cattle running Pamplona-style. Capybaras, bear-like rodents, sometimes plant themselves in our way; birds fly right in front of the windshield, barely surviving. If we were traveling at night, our guide informs us, we'd be running smack into alligators looking for dinner. Twice we catch toucans streaking past. In mid-sentence Julio jumps out of the running jeep to race after an armadillo, catching it by the tail so we can inspect its armored body. If you go to Bolivia by train, he says, they'll serve you *armadillo na casca* (in the shell). Soon we discover it's not just humans who scavenge the Pantanal. We drive past about 20 black *urubus* (vultures), feasting on the remains of a *jacaré* (crocodile).

In the afternoon, a canoe trip glides us through the leafy waterway of an *igarapé* – a miraculous vista at dusk where a crop of trees lining the banks become home to roosting garças that fly in for the night. The sight is something out of a tropical Christmas, the white birds hanging like snowy ornaments on the branches.

The next day we comb the enormous grounds of the Xaraes farm on both horseback and foot, exploring forests that seem nearly primeval – home to hundreds of monkey, capybaras, and rodents who scurry under the brush as we approach. From our guide, we learn that the only way to hear the voice of the Pantanal is to descend into silence – a kind of Zen in the wild. Crouching down behind bushes, we suddenly hear the terrifying screech of howler monkeys, a sound that even terrified the naturalist Henry Bates.

(For more information on Fazenda Xaraes, see below.)

## Fazenda Xaraes

*Rio Abobral, 130 km. from Corumbá. Reserve in Campo Grande.* ☎ *(67) 242-1102 or São Paulo,* ☎ *(11) 246-9934.*

This well-maintained, three-star lodge is rustic enough to be authentic and clean enough to be comfortable. Owned by the same group as the Nacional Hotel in Corumbá, it features wood-and-tiled rooms with shutters open to the river. The air conditioning is solid, and whatever dirt you trail in seems to mysteriously disappear in a matter of hours. The dining room is surrounded by screens so you can see and hear the chirping birds. Most impressive is the salt-of-the-earth staff, some of the nicest people I met in Brazil. Packages include all meals and a variety of daily excursions. Rates per person per night range from $58 (doubles $51); transfers from Corumbá $61 per person or $40 for doubles; three-hour horse treks run $8; a boat trip, $40. Two-day/one-night package, including one boat tour, runs $89; three-days/two-nights per person is $200 (doubles $162). (Rates may change.)

If you arrive in Corumbá, the staff will pick you up and transfer you by truck (or canoe during rainy season) to Fazenda Xaraes. You can also take the bus to Morro do Azeite, which leaves you out in the middle of the road, 31 km. (45 min.) from Xaraes, where the staff will pick you up. Flights to Corumbá are offered by VASP from Belo Horizonte, Brasília, Campo Grande, Cuiabá, Goiânia, and São Paulo.

## Pousada Caiman

*236 km. from Campo Grande, Mato Grosso do Sul.*

The five-star accommodation of the southern Pantanal, situated on a serious working ranch, is the eco-dream of Roberto Klabin, the energetic scion of a rich Brazilian family who wanted to create for his friends and tourists the height of luxury-in-the-wild. Of the ranch's 53,000 hectares, 7,000 (17,300 acres) has been set aside as an ecological reserve, but much of the land remains range for the 65 staff cowboys who live in a village adjacent to the lodge. The u-shaped hacienda (formerly the Klabin's family residence) houses 22 guests and offers every deluxe amenity, from swimming pool and Italian-tiled floors to comfy leather furniture, satellite-dish TV, and stylish apartments with excellent air conditioning. The cuisine is superb. The grounds have been called "an oasis for birds," since a large variety of species can easily be seen. Guests are led on morning and afternoon excursions on horseback, in canoe, and on foot. The lodge is about four hours by car from Campo Grande; transfers by air-conditioned micro-buses are offered every Sat. and Wed. from Campo Grande between 1:30-2 p.m., and after breakfast from the lodge. (Campo Grande may be reached by commercial flights from Belém, Brasília, Corumbá, Cuiabá, Rio Branco, Santarém, São Paulo, and others.) Three-day packages run from Wed.-Sat.; four nights from Sat. to Wed. In New York, contact **Brazil Nuts** (see *Specialty Tours*, at the end of this book, for address). In São Paulo, contact **Roberto Klabin Hoteis e Turismo**, Rua Pedrosa Alvarenga, 1208, first floor, CEP 045531; M *(11) 883-6566*. Contact **Pantanal Explorers**, ☎ *(065) 682-2800*, fax *682-1260*.

### Fazenda Boa Sorte Região de Abobral

☎ *231-1120 (in Corumbá); reservations can be made through Pantanal Explorers,* ☎ *(065) 682-2800, fax 682-1260.*

A rustic (read "primitive") farm without frills near the Fazenda Xaraes gives you a home-on-the-range ambiance. Sleep outdoors in hammocks, inside tents, or under grass-roofed huts with wood-slat floors. If you don't want to bathe in the river, there's a communal bath. Three daily meals are cooked over a wood fire; don't pass up a glass of freshly milked cow juice. The farm's parrots will sit happily on your shoulder and even the wild ducks and toucans are friendly. During the day you can make excursions on horseback, sleep in other *fazendas*, and take canoe trips. A three-day package for $70 includes all meals and treks.

### Fazenda Beira Rio

*Rod Transpantaneira, 150 km. from Poconé, 205 km. from Cuiabá. Reserve:* ☎ *(65) 322-0948; in São Paulo,* ☎ *(11) 35-4157, or (67) 725-5267 (in Campo Grande); or through Pantanal Explorers,* ☎ *(065) 682-2800, fax 682-1260.*

Located on 3,700 hectares of land right off the Transpantaneira Highway, this is considered the best *pousada* in the region for cleanliness and trek options. The hotel is seven years old, owned by the grizzly but *simpatico* Senhor Valdo de Luis. Running next to his property is the Pixaim River, which you can cross by motor boat, or canoe (monkeys upstream, herons downstream). You can also rent horses or explore the grounds by foot. Guides accompany guests without charge. Housed in a one-story white stucco building with traditional tile roofs, the simple rooms are all air conditioned and come with mini-bar, TV, and attractive tile floors. Suites sleep five. If you come through a travel agent, the package deal includes horse treks and boat excursions; otherwise, you pay extra. There are no phones, but there is radio communication with Cuiabá. Rates include all three meals; packages available. *13 apts. Moderate.*

### Araras Farm

*Reserve through Pantanal Explorers,* ☎ *(065) 682-2800, fax 682-1260.*

After nearly 20 years of working in the Pantanal, André von Thuranyi of Pantanal Explorers travel agency has now started his own lodge program in collaboration with native farmers in the Pantanal wetlands. A four-day, three-night package at this private reserve off the Transpantaneira Highway offers treks by foot, canoe, horseback, and jeep. An extra night in

Cuiabá and/or a tour of Chapada dos Guimarães (highly recommended) may be added.

### Hotel Santa Rosa do Pantanal

*Transpantaneira Highway, 150 km. from Poconé. Reserve in Cuiabá,* ☎ *(65) 322-0513/0077; in São Paulo,* ☎ *(11) 231-4511.*

Once a luxurious (for the region) hotel, this is still the best in Porto Jofre, located at the end of the Transpantaneira Highway on the banks of the Cuiabá River. One travel option is to trek or hitch your way here; then rent boats, horses, or guides at the hotel. The owner of the nearby campgrounds also rents boats. *54 apts. Moderate. No cards.*

# Botels & Boat Cruises

An alternative to bunking down at lodges is to take a package cruise. André Von Thurani, an energetic and devoted eco-tourism operator, offers numerous cruises through the Pantanal that combine water and road travel. One is the **Pantanal Ecological Triangle Tour**, a fine five-night/four-day package on the *Pantanal Explorer*, a modest, low-draft boat that sleeps 12, including crew (four air-conditioned bunks for  passengers, with two shared bathrooms, sun deck, and kitchen/bar). During the day, you can watch birds and other wildlife from the top deck of the boat; at night, special alligator expeditions are conducted in canoes. Tight quarters make sociable personalities a must, but humor is provided by outgoing guides who are able to identify most of the animals and birds sighted. Food is surprisingly good: a mixture of beef, fish, chicken, and pasta. The most exciting part of the trip is the roller-coaster ride over the Transpantaneira Highway – a must for Pantanal-goers. Among animals to be sighted are savanna hawks, Amazon kingfishers, snowy egrets, toucans, black-headed vultures, wood storks, herons, parrots, woodpeckers, cormorants, marsh deer, capybaras, caimans, iguanas, and lizards. The highway's 114 bridges are sometimes portraits of imminent disaster – weatherbeaten washboard planks crossed by moldy timbers, but the anything-can-happen ambiance is part of the fun. An hour and a half beyond Poconé you'll pass the Sao João ranch, owned by Sebastião Camargo Correia, one of the five richest men in the world. Ask if you can visit. A stop at the gold mines near Cangas, 10 minutes from Cuiabá, is also an eye-opener. (For more information about this tour and other land expeditions in the Pantanal, contact André Von Thuronyi, Av. Governador Ponce de Arruda, 670-Várzea Grande, Cep: 78038-500/MT, ☎ 065-6822800/fax 065-6821260, e-mail araraslg@nutecnet.com.br; on the Internet, www.Solunet.com.br\araraslodge.)

> **UP CLOSE TIP:** *If you're traversing the Transpantaneira Highway in a group tour, make sure the driver and guide know you want to savor every last scene. This will slow down the trip considerably, so if you have to catch a flight later in the day, leave a few hours earlier. You may never see anything like it again.*

# Independent Travel

The independent's way to see the Pantanal is to combine different options. First, hire a good guide who is ready to go anywhere, then improvise. You can go by car from Poconé to Barão de Melgão, then rent kayaks and paddle to Porto Cercado or, if you're crazy enough, all the way down to Porto Jofre (about four to five days). This way you can stop and take time to talk to the locals, who are usually friendly. Have a car waiting at Porto Jofre and go over the Transpantaneira Highway to Pixaim, camping or staying at a lodge. To do it right, you'll need eight to 10 days. To find a guide, call a travel agency and ask for the names of reliable guides without explaining exactly what you want; then make private arrangements with the guide.

# Pantanal Survival Kit

## Climate

During the dry season (Apr.-Oct.), temperatures range from 68-75°F, but can rise over 50° in a matter of hours. The hottest months in the Pantanal are Dec.-Feb., when 110-112°F is common. During dry season, it's important to drink lots of liquids to avoid dehydration. Starting in Nov., weather alternates between torrential rains and scalding sun. The most animals can be seen in Dec. and Jan.

## Medical Emergencies

It's best not to have them in the Pantanal. Decent hospitals will probably be boats, planes, and torturous jeep rides away. Take your own medicine kit (including gauze, antiseptic, allergy pills, and antihistamines, calamine lotions, aloe vera lotion for cuts and bruises, a snake bite kit, TANG for dehydration, and Pepto-Bismol for diarrhea, etc. Make sure you've had all the necessary inoculations (tetanus, yellow fever, typhoid, polio). And pray. (Hospitals are listed under *Hands-On Cuiabá*.)

## Bees

Anyone going to the Pantanal should read Vick Banks' riveting description of the "bees from hell" in his book *The Pantanal* (Sierra Club), 1991. According to Banks, 300-400 people a year die from bee stings in Brazil, more than from any other animal attack. In the Pantanal, Europa honeybees have interbred with African killer bees, making them capable of attacking aggressively en masse, even if just one drone is disturbed. Truly, Banks' encounter was most unfortunate, but frankly, I never met one bee in the Pantanal.

## What To Pack

Follow guidelines for Amazon treks (see *Amazônia*), but also dress in layers (for cool nights, a jean jacket and sweater is sufficient). Binoculars, telephoto lenses, and high-speed film are essential in the Pantanal. (Those magnificent close-up shots of birds seen in books and brochures are surely taken by professionals who spend days waiting silently under a bush for just the right moment.)

# Cuiabá

The capital of **Mato Grosso**, Cuiabá (pronounced Kwee-ah-bah) is the major gateway to the Pantanal, located about 102 km. (63 miles) from the northern entrance of the Transpantaneira Highway. Even so, it's not exactly a destination in itself, though a day or two stuck here won't feel like the end of the world. Most visitors use Cuiabá as a trampoline to visit other parts of the region, such as the magnificent rock sculptures in the national park and the caves and waterfalls of Chapada dos Guimarães, one of the most beautiful sites in all Brazil.

Once a frontier town, Cuiabá has boomed to over 330,000 people (some reports claim up to one million in the surrounding area); you will discover fine regional restaurants here, as well as some of the best crafts stores for Indian artifacts in the region.

The first *bandeirantes* in the early 18th century came in search of Indian slaves, but soon forgot their objective when they discovered **gold**. A *Paulista*, Pascoal Moreira Cabral, established the first settlement in 1719, having braved disease, mosquitoes, floods, and intense heat through his arduous five-month journey from São Paulo. Soon, thousands more were traveling the 3,000-km./1,865-mile route, boosting the population of Cuiabá far beyond that of São Paulo between 1719 and 1730. Because of the navigation systems, however, ties with Bolivians, Paraguayans, and Argentineans soon became tighter than with fellow Brazilians, resulting in a kind of trans-Latino culture. The flotillas of canoes and medium-sized ships that arrived laden with supplies and slaves invariably departed from Cuiabá groaning with gold.

In 1979, Mato Grosso was divided into two states, **Mato Grosso** in the north and **Mato Grosso do Sul** in the south. Since then, Cuiabá has enjoyed enormous development in education, tourism, and construction. In 1989-1990, three shows on TV claiming that gold had been found on the streets (!) of Cuiabá magnetized a stream of Northeasterners and *Mineiros*, who arrived with little more than dreams in their pockets. As a result, a rash of frontier towns rose up, most of them approximating slums. One such town is **Cangas**, 10 minutes from Cuiabá on the Cuiabá-Santarém Highway, the site of six or seven gold mines. Founded about seven years ago, Cangas today is a scene straight out of a Wild West movie, with two big bars, three small snack bars, one school, three churches, three gas stations, and a single public phone (for all 5,000 people). As one local told me, "There's only one phone because most people here have no one to call."

**UP CLOSE TIP:** *During the dry season, airplane descents into Cuiabá can be turbulent due to the smoky warm air from fires set by cattle ranchers every dry season to burn off undesirable vegetation and promote fresh grass for fodder. Aug. is the peak month for these fires, and sometimes flights are cancelled for several weeks, forcing travelers to take five-hour bus trips from the nearest open airport. During the rainy season, flights may be delayed due to inclement weather.*

# A Bird's Eye View

Cuiabá is nicknamed the **Garden City** because of its many trees, including 200-year-old palms. The main plaza, **Praça da República**, is dominated by an old church, the Hotel Excelsior, and a 12-story television tower on a nearby hill. Next to the tower is the alabaster minaret of a Muslim temple. The **Igreja de Bom Jesus dos Passos**, an 18th-century church with an exquisite Gothic facade, offers a great vista of the city. The tourist office, **TURIMAT**, is off the main plaza near the Igreja Matriz.

# Sights

## Praça Moreira Cabral (Geodesic Center)

Although the *mirante* in Chapada is considered a more scenic representation of the geodesic center of South America, the exact point is here, in Cuiabá. The site is marked by a monument and pyramid in a small concrete park facing the Legislative Assembly. It is considered to cover a 50-km./31-mile radius (of which Chapada forms one end). The *praça* can be entered from Rua Barão de Melgaço.

## Fish Market

Buying and selling the day's fresh catch takes place along the **Rio Cuiabá** daily from 4 a.m.-6 p.m.

## Horto Florestal Bairro Coxipó (City Park)

*At the confluence of the Rio Coxipó and Rio Cuiabá; access through Avenida Fernando Correa da Costa. Daily 7 a.m.-5:30 p.m. Guides available 2-5 p.m.*

The future park of the city is being planned on this tropical landscape where children can scamper around playgrounds made from logs. On the docket for the future is an orchid greenhouse, an exposition of seeds and plants natural to the forest, and a special display of medicinal plants.

### Comunidade São Gonçalo (Crafts Commune)

Located near the Fazenda de Mato Grosso, this primitive community sits on the banks of the Rio Cuiabá and supports itself totally through artisanry (especially pottery) and folkloric presentations. Visitors are always welcome; just seeing the rural lifestyle should prove fascinating. The community's major festival is held on Jan. 10, the **Feast of São Gonçalo**, when colorful boats proceed upriver to herald the arrival of the saint.

# Museums & The Zoo

### Museu de Artesanato

*Rua 13 de Junho, Praça Maj. João Bueno. Tues.-Sun. 10 a.m.-3 p.m., 6-11 p.m.*

Next door to the Casa do Artesão (a fine crafts store) is a museum of folkloric art situated in a frontier-styled, brick-and-wood house, complete with an antique kitchen. Featured are ornaments and weapons from the Xavantes and other Mato Grosso tribes, as well as leather goods from the home-on-the-range culture. Especially intriguing is the leather bornal, a contraption that was strapped around a horse's mouth so it could walk and eat millet at the same time.

### Museu do Indio Marechal Candido Rondon

*Located at the University Federal of Mato Grosso.*

This museum displays artisanry, weapons, and ornaments crafted by the state's indigenous peoples.

### Universidade Federal do Mato Grosso (Mini Zoo)

*Av. Fernando Correa da Costa. Best times to visit: 6-8 a.m. and 3:30-7 p.m. to avoid sunstroke (1 p.m. is deadly). Interior is open daily 7-11 a.m. and 1:30-7 p.m. Closed Mon.*

UFMT displays the fauna and flora of the region in an outdoor natural environment that features snakes, jaguars, monkeys, birds, and ostriches. On the far side of well-secured fences, animals such as capybaras, egrets, garças, alligators, and land turtles all seem to live in harmony, although some appear to be collapsed from the heat. A university restaurant near the parking lot goes on strike a lot, but is a nice place to meet young people. To reach the zoo, take the city bus labeled "Copamel Universidade" or "Santa Cruz."

# Where To Stay

If you don't want to find a veritable zoo in your hotel room (i.e., frogs in your toilet and cockroaches the size of capybaras in the closet), you'll have to pay for a bug-free environment in Cuiabá.

In the hot clime, air conditioning is essential, and if you are returning from an excursion, you'll appreciate a good laundry service.

See page 26 for price chart.

### Veneza Palace Hotel

*Av. Coronel Escolástico, 738 (Bandeirantes);* ☎ *(65) 321-4847; fax 322-5212.*

This perfectly respectable, impeccably clean three-star has an oriental lobby and a pleasant staff. The carpeted apartments are small, but the air conditioning is ice-cold, and the wood furniture attractive. All rooms come with color TV, mini-bar, and carpet. Safes are at the reception. Laundry is available.

The restaurant, which favors international cuisine, serves an excellent *canja de galinha* (chicken soup). There's also a pool, TV/playroom, and an American bar. Superior singles run $46, doubles $61. *78 apts. Moderate. All cards.*

### Hotel Fazenda de Mato Grosso

*Rua Antônio Dorileo, 1200 (Coxipó);* ☎ *361-2980.*

Only six km. from the city, this farm-like complex is surrounded by 19 hectares of forested land – a kind of "civilized wilderness." The rustic apartments are housed in one- and two-story buildings with traditional tiled roofs; all have air conditioning, color TV, mini-bar, and phone. Clean and attractive, the bathrooms are appointed in tile and marble.

On the grounds is a mini-zoo with snakes, garças and capybaras; there's also a large pool and playground surrounded by tropical vegetation. Horses, paddleboats and other sports are included in the daily rate, as is breakfast. Transportation to the city is provided for convention groups. *50 apts. Moderate. All cards.*

### Il Palace Hotel

*Rua Alziro Zarur, 312; (Boa Esperança);* ☎ *(65) 361-1858.*

For budget travelers only. A single in this three-story hotel is absolutely basic – little closet space, a slight mustiness, somewhat dirty walls, but a well-equipped mini-bar. Location is near a pharmacy and several restaurants. Singles have fans, but the doubles are worth splashing out on for the air conditioning. *Inexpensive. No cards.*

## Where To Eat

### Recanto do Bosque

*Rua Cândido Mariano, 1040;* ☎ *323-1468. 11:30 a.m.-3 p.m., 7 p.m.-midnight.*

Trees grow right through the middle of this open-air restaurant, the best *rodízio* in town, situated under a grass roof. Eighteen cold salads and all-you-can-eat meat; Sat. features *feijoada.*

After 5 p.m., beer is half price and barbecued fish is included. Discounts for groups of 15 or more. *Inexpensive. All cards.*

## Taberna Portuguesa

*Av. XV de Novembro, 40;* ☎ *321-3661. 11 a.m.-2:30 p.m., 6-11:30 p.m.*
*Mon. lunch only.*

About one km. from the center of town, this cozy, air-conditioned Portuguese tavern is piquant, with the smells of home cooking.

Codfish runs about $9, *caldeirada* (a thick fish soup made with white wine, potatoes, onions, pimentos, and tomato sauce) runs about $13, an award-winning paella about $20. Dishes usually serve two. *Moderate. No cards.*

## O Regionalissimo

*Rua 13 de Junho (Praça João Bueno);* ☎ *322-3908. 11:30 a.m.-2:30 p.m.,*
*7:30-11 p.m. Live music Thurs.-Sun., closed Mon.*

Next to the Casa do Artesão, this charming *adega* features some of the best regional cuisine in Cuiabá. Local folkloric musicians serenade the buffet, which changes daily; you might find fried fish, *peixe ensopado, farofa de banana, carne de sol,* and other delicacies.

Alas, no air conditioning, but a steady breeze whips through the open brick arches. *Moderate. No cards.*

## Mamma Aurora

*Rua Miranda Reis, 386;* ☎ *322-4339. 6 p.m.-midnight.*

Best pizzeria in town. Live music. *Inexpensive. No cards.*

# Nightlife

Nightlife in Cuiabá is as hot as you will find in the Pantanal, or even in Mato Grosso – north or south.

## Discoteca Logan

Best disco for the 18-40 set.

## Get Up Dance

*Avenida Fernando Corrêa da Costa, 1953;* ☎ *323-3335.*
Another dance spot.

## Mirante Bar

*Avenida Miguel Smith, in front of the Plaza Motel.*
For local bands and solo singers performing MPB.

# Shopping

## Casa do Guaraná

*Avenida Mário Corrêa, 310;* ☎ *321-7729.*

Situated in the *bairro* of Porto, the oldest district in Cuiabá, this "House of Guaraná" makes a fascinating showcase for Brazilian ingenuity, featuring products made from the plant most known for its stimulating kick to the nervous system. Here you can buy "sticks" of guaraná that you can grate into a powder in the traditional way, or you may buy the powder already formed. *Xarope de guaraná* is a syrup that is drunk as juice (just add water). The store also features *licor de Pequi* (a liqueur made from a typical fruit of the cerrado), as well as *serrinhas de unha* (nail files made from fish scales). You can also stock up on natural herb shampoos and cosmetics, as well as stunning Pantanal T-shirts.

## Casa do Artesão

*Rua 13 de Junho, 315;* ☎*322-3908, 321-0603.*

Founded on May 15, 1975, this store, situated in an 18th-century blue-and-white colonial house, features some of the best crafts for sale in the region. Good buys include *ganzas* (scraper-like percussion instruments made of wood) and handmade pottery. Absolutely exquisite are the embroidered hammocks that go for about $200 – steep, but so lovely you could hang them on the wall as decoration. Also for sale are indigenous Indian crafts such as bows, arrows, and basketry. A special room features homemade sweets and liqueurs; don't miss the antique sugarcane machine in the garden. Next door is the Regionalíssimo restaurant.

## Artindia

*Rua Comandante Costa, 942;* ☎ *321-1348, near the Praça Rachid Jaudy.*

The artisan store of FUNAI features crafts from the indigenous tribes of the Pantanal.

## Mercearia Banzal

*Av. Generoso Ponce (no number), Mercado Municipal Box 1/2/3 (downtown);* ☎ *321-7518.*

Macrobiotic and natural products, including brown rice, miso, and tofu are sold here.

# Healers

Cuiabá and Chapada dos Guimarães have attracted a steady stream of holistic health practitioners during the last 10 years. Among the best are those listed below.

## Centro de Vivências Para Integração do Ser

*Rua Balneário São João, 323 (Coxipó da Ponte);* ☎ *361-2215.*

The city's most active alternative health center, offering a fine acupuncturist, Décio Cesar da Silva, as well as other practitioners in the fields of rebirthing, oki-yoga, massage, and more.

## Ma Prem Dwari

*Rua Doze, 297 (Boa Esperança);* ☎ *361-5274.*

Excellent masseuse and practitioner of Bach Flower Remedies.

# Hands-On Cuiabá

## Airlines

Flights to Cuiabá can be arranged from Alta Floresta (TABA), Belém, Belo Horizonte, Brasília, Campo Grande (Varig), Natal, Porto Alegre, Rio Branco, Rio de Janeiro, Salvador, Santarém, and São Paulo, among others.

## Airlines Serving Cuiabá

**Varig/Cruzeiro**
Rua Antônio João, 258 . . . . . . . . . . . . . . . . . . . . . . ☎ 321-7333
**VASP**
Rua Pedro Celestino, 32 (Downtown) . . . . . . . . . ☎ 624-1313
. . . . . . . . . . . . . . . . . . . . . . . . . . . . . . . . . . . . . . . .   ramal 112
**Transbrasil**
Rua Barão de Melgaço 3508. . . . . . . . . . . . . . . . . ☎ 381-3347
**TABA**
Airport . . . . . . . . . . . . . . . . . . . . . . . . . . . . . . . . . . . ☎ 381-2233

## Arrivals

**Aeroporto Marechal Rondôn** is on Avenida Governador Ponce de Arruda (Várzea Grande); ☎ *381-2211.* The *rodoviária* (bus station) is on Avenida Mal. Rondôn (on the road to Chapada dos Guima rães); ☎ *624-2085.* For more information see *Points Beyond,* below.

## Car Rentals

**Nobre,** ☎ *381-1651,* can be found at the airport. There is also an office at Avenida Governador Ponce de Arruda, 980; ☎ *3811-2821.*
  **Localiza Nacional,** Avenida Dom Bosco, 965; ☎ *381-3773;* at the airport, open 24 hours.

## Climate

Weather can change very quickly within hours in Cuiabá. Basically, summers (Dec.-Feb.) are hot and humid (over 100°F), while winters (June-Aug.) are cool and dry (dropping to 60°F).

## Money Exchange

If you're flying into the state of Mato Grosso from a major Brazilian city, it's best to exchange money before you leave; rates will undoubtedly be better. Traveler's checks can be exchanged at **Banco do Brazil**, Rua Barão de Melgaço, 915. In addition, good exchange rates for dollars are offered at the **Abudi Palace Hotel**.

## Medical Emergencies

Hospitals are generally to be avoided in this region. For emergencies:

**Hospital Geral e Maternidade**
Rua 13 de Junho, 2101 . . . . . . . . . . . . . . . . . . . . . . .   ☎ 323-3322
**Pronto-Socorro Municipal**
Rua Gen. Valle . . . . . . . . . . . . . . . . . . . . . . . . . . . . .   ☎ 321-7404

## Pharmacy

**Drogaria Avenida**
Avenida Getúlio Vargas, 280 . . . . . . . . . . . . . . . . .   ☎ 624-1305

## Points Beyond Cuiabá

### By Bus

Buses run regularly between Cuiabá and Chapada dos Guimarães. (For times, see under *Hands-On Chapada*). Buses are also available to São Felix do Araguaia, São José dos Quatro Marcos, Guiratinga, Rio do Casca, Paranatingam, Paxaréo, and D. Aquino, among other places. You can also reach the Véu de Noiva (a waterfall and mountain) by local bus, which will leave you off after Buriti if you tell the driver in advance.

### By Air

Flights are available to Alta Floresta, Belém, Brasília, Belo Horizonte, Corumbá, Fortaleza, Manaus, Porto Alegre, Recife, Porto Velho, Rio Branco, Rio de Janeiro, Salvador, Santarém, São Paulo, and other towns.

## Private Guides

**Amilton Martins da Silva,** ☎ 322-3702, can provide names of city guides who speak English. He is the president of the local Guide Association, and is a very good guide himself. **Carlos Wolff,** ☎ 661-1469, is another English-speaking guide.

## Telephone

Local and international phone calls can be made from the telephone company **Telemat**, Rua Barão de Melgaço, 3195, during commercial hours. There is also an office at the bus station and the airport.

## Travel Agency

### Cidade Turismo

*Rua Duque de Caxias, 59 (Alvorada);* ☎ *(65) 322-3702.*

Director Amilton Martins da Silva specializes in cinematography, film crews, ecological tours, and VIP service. Arrangements for treks by boat, jeep, or plane can also be made. Four-hour city tours can be arranged, including lunch at a regional restaurant.

### Pantanal Explorers

*Av. Governador Ponce de Arruda, 670-Várzea Grande;* ☎ *(65) 682-2800, fax 682-1260; e-mail araraslg@nutecnet.com.br; www.Solunet.com.br\araraslodge.*

Perhaps the leading eco-tour agency in the region. One of the most serious eco-tour operators in Brazil, owner André von Thuranyi is not only deeply committed to preservation, but is also well tuned to the mystical aspects of the countryside. His efficient English-speaking staff can arrange accommodations at any of the *pousadas* listed below, as well as transportation and accommodations throughout the Pantanal.

## Tourist Information

The state tourist boar,d **Turimat**, is at Praça da República, 131 (downtown); ☎ *(65) 322-5363.* Information booths can also be found at the airport and the bus station, offering maps and some general assistance on car rentals and hotels. For major excursions, it's best to contact the travel agencies above.

## When To Go

**July** presents a **Winter Festival** in Chapada.

# Chapada Dos Guimarães

Chapada dos Guimarães is simply an extraordinary place. More than a half-mile above sea level, it boasts a variety of microclimates that allow for the coexistence of an enormous variety of plants and animals. Geological studies have shown that life existed here over 45,000 years ago, and mystics predict that future civilizations will be born here. Exactly what that means for the average visitor is obscure, but it can't be denied that most tourists immediately feel a strong sense of clarity and well-being here, and many are inclined to stay longer than they had initially planned. Frankly, it's my favorite place in Brazil, if not the world.

Chapada is at the 15th degree parallel, on line with such cities as Porto Seguro, Bahia (the birthplace of Brazil), Brasília (the futuristic capital), and Ilhéus. Such a location is rendered symbolic among Brazilians; many prophecies have suggested that Chapada dos Guimarães will be the birthplace of the Third Millenium. If you're a fan of Sedona, Arizona, you might recognize the same kinds of vibes here – a mixture of gorgeous landscape and mystical energy generated by numerous psychics, healers, and "Green People," who have moved to Chapada over the last 20 years. Not surprisingly, spiritual beliefs run rampant here. Some locals even believe there is a magnetic hole over Chapada that allows for communications with extraterrestrials. Indeed, something magnetically fishy is going on down here since car batteries and cameras are notorious for malfunctioning on cloudy days (mine did). Without much effort, you're sure to find residents who claim to have personally tape-recorded conversations with ETs; the topics generally seem to concern saving the environment.

## History

Chapada's recorded history began when the **Jesuits** built a little chapel in 1751. By 1779, Chapada had become a primitive baroque city, its newly built cathedral marked by two imposing towers that were later felled by heavy rains. *Bandeirantes* from São Paulo swarmed over the area, looking for gold to mine and Indians to subjugate; the first **sugarcane** plantation was established, later becoming famous for its *cachaça*. Supplies were so limited in this isolated region that locals were often forced to trade large hunks of gold for the simplest foods imported from São Paulo.

In the 1930s, a group of Americans left Bahia to found an evangelical mission at Buriti, Chapada's first farm. Today, the pastoral estate is an agricultural school, but the American-made church and colonial houses still look like something out of New England. In more recent times, Chapada has become famous for its waterfalls, rock formations, and UFO sightings. Every year a **Winter Festival** brings artists and craftspersons to the region in July.

## A Bird's Eye View

The town of Chapada is 73 km./45 miles north of Cuiabá, (with access on MT 251). No one quite knows how many people live there; some say about 6,000, but it's rumored another 15,000 live in the surrounding area. The main square is full of flowers and trees and makes a peaceful core to the town; the majority of restaurants are located here, as well as the oldest church in Mato Grosso, the **Igreja de Senhora Sant'Ana**, built in 1779 with the help of the local Indians. Today chickens scratch around in its courtyard, but inside is a magnificent dusty old chapel. Of particular note is the statue of Joseph wearing boots, a symbol of the gold miners who lived in the area. During my visit, an old couple was valiantly trying to clean the church from the soot that continually blows in from the burning fields – a sad reminder of the forest's destruction.

# Sights

The drive from Cuiabá to the national park of Chapada dos Guimarães offers some of the most thrilling vistas in Brazil. Taking MT-2551 (Cuiabá-Chapada Road), you'll first pass verdant rolling hills and glimmering lakes, behind which looms a massive mountain range washed in purples and blues. Suddenly, the rocky skyline is accentuated by vertical cliffs standing like sentinels – a dramatic contrast to the shrunken brown-and-green shrubbery lining the highway. This is the beginning of the Planalto Central (Central Plains) of Brazil, 10,000 years ago a magnificent inland sea that gradually dried to its present state.

## Salgadeira

The first stop you must make is at this weekend spot, originally built by the government for tourists, but now a private enterprise. Nicknamed the "Beach of Mato Grosso," the area boasts a stupendous man-made waterfall where bathers can take a dip, as well as a restaurant complex with four bars, ice cream stands, bathrooms, and playground. Walking along a path into the forest you'll come upon a turbulent double waterfall, and at every angle another mystical nature scene, including steamy falls, natural grottoes, and *macumba* offerings tucked inside coves. Campgrounds are available, but please don't litter; policemen keep close watch. A few years back, the "green" community made a fuss here when trees were cut down to build the complex, but the environs are still so beautiful that it's hard to complain.

## Portão do Inferno (Hells' Gate)

Nearby is this truly awesome canyon sculpted into dramatic shape more than a thousand years ago by natural erosion. The lookout point, a few feet beyond, is replete with gossip. Legend has it that the federal police threw "undesirables" off this cliff during the dictatorship, and at the beginning of Sarney's administration, a lot of Brazilians were rumored to have thrown themselves off when they lost all their money. Even today, a yellow car can be seen at the foot of the pit, reputed to have accidentally veered off the cliff, killing four or five people. These days, police maintain strong surveillance to avoid further incidents, but locals claim they can still hear the spirits of the departed crying at night. Three to four centuries ago, Indians roamed these areas, and the rock formations, which rise like phallic symbols along the highway, have helped create a number of legends. Local mystics like to think they are street signs for landing extraterrestrials. The big holes in the ground, however, are definitely made by local rodents. If you're intent on climbing these hills, be careful because the rock is soft.

## Cachoeira Véu de Noiva

Six km. after Salgadeira, take a right turn onto a red dirt road and go a few hundred feet from the rock formations. The road takes you down to an open canyon graced with a slender 200-foot waterfall that looks like the veil of a bride (hence its name). During rainy season, the fall is more voluminous, but can become yellow and dirty-looking; in Aug., when I saw it, it was simply stunning, rivaling Iguaçu Falls, perhaps not in volume, but at least in grace. Sturdy trekkers will love the half-hour climb down to the foot of the waterfall (one hour back), but be forewarned: the inclines are abrupt. Also, the route is deceiving and doesn't look the same on the way down – just stick to the wall on the right. The fall is actually a big lake, which you can only see from the base, and the water and surrounding air are always cold, no matter the season. The canyon itself is a natural wonder, embraced by a forest and accentuated by vertical backdrops of red rocks. A snack bar serves beer, light fare, and *galinha com arroz* (chicken with rice).

## Cachoerinha (Little Waterfall)

Eight km./five miles before you reach the city of Chapada (and an easy one-hour trek from Véu de Noiva) is this smaller waterfall. The *mata* (forest) here is being reforested by locals, since destruction of this environment could endanger the entire microsystem of the Pantanal. Walking down an idyllic woody path, you'll come upon a small waterfall jutting out of a rocky embankment; facing it is the perfect beachlet. A thatched-roof restaurant surrounded by a mixture of rainforest and cerrado is a perfect place to let the sound of crashing rivulets wash over you. It's also a great place to sun, but weekends are packed. The path to the left above the waterfall goes to Véu de Noiva.

## Mirante

Considered the "picturesque" geodesic center of South America, this magnificent rocky cliff and mountain range is felt by many to be a point of high magnetic energy and one of the best places to sight UFOs, particularly at night. At the very least on a clear day you can see Cuiabá, 50 km./31 miles to the southwest. Do take the exhilarating walk down the rocky path to the right, until you reach the half-mile drop-off plateau; the trip back up is tiring but worth it. Hopefully, the litter marring the landscape has been picked up; be careful with cigarettes since fires start fast. Near the rock formations is a large amount of burned land, probably caused by human carelessness.

## Parque Nacional

Founded about three years ago, the park covers about 33,000 hectares; it is a national park in name only as the government does little to no maintenance. **Eco Turismo** is the only agency that conducts tours to the park's wonderful **Cidades das Pedras**, seven "cities" of rock formations situated among the gnarled trees of the cerrado. During the rainy season, this route, which must be navigated by truck or four-wheel-drive, is considerably less dusty than in dry season, and more animals, such as pigs, foxes, jaguars, tapirs, wolves, and coatis can be seen scurrying over the landscape. But even dry season is exciting. In Aug., the stunted carrado lends an other-worldy air to the forbidding rock formations, which can look variously like sacrificial altars, alligators, or Indian faces. Animals do approach at times; we clocked an emu running chase in front of our truck at 50 mph. Many of the rocks are over three million years old; on their side you can often see stratification lines where the ocean left its indelible marks. It's even possible to find chips of hematite and crystals embedded in the ground, as well as fossils engravened with fish shapes.

At the **Nascente do Rio Claro**, you can walk to the edge of a 1,100-foot cliff and witness an awesome vista of rivers and plateaus that could keep you mesmerized for days. The most unforgettable thing I saw here was the **Casa de Pedra**, a natural house of stone situated over a running stream that was surely the home of native peoples thousands of years ago. I dream of making an overnight camp-out here; the nearby waterfalls boast such clean water you could probably safely drink it. Our final trek in Chapada took us down a slightly torturous descent to what must be the most perfect cove in Brazil – a gorgeous waterfall embraced by a thumb-sized strand of beach, behind which is a craggy outcropping of rock.

# Where To Stay

Chapada is a rustic town; so are the hotels. Fortunately, with such cool temperatures, air conditioning is not necessary. No *pousada* or hotel in Chapada has telephones inside the room. See page 26 for price chart.

## Pousada da Chapada   Lago Hotel

*Rodovia MT-251, km. 63, Estrada Chapada dos Guimarães/Cuiabá, 2 km.,*
☎ *791-1171. Reservations: São Paulo,* ☎ *(11) 231-4511; fax 791-1299.*

The nicest hotel in Chapada is, unfortunately, half a mile from the city, but the hotel provides free transportation. The red-tile, white stucco complex of four buildings retains a frontier colonial charm. Apartments, with raw wood furniture, are spacious, and tiled floors cut down on dirt. The deluxe suite, which sleeps four, is unusually elegant. On premises is a playground and outdoor pool, and a restaurant that serves all three meals. The owner also runs the Fazenda Porto Jofre in the Pantanal, as well as the Selva Turismo travel agency. Singles with fan run $27, doubles $32, double the price for air conditioning. *38 apts. Inexpensive. No cards.*

## Rios

*Rua Tiradentes, 333;* ☎ *791-1126.*

Among the lesser-priced hotels, Rios rates as the best. A block from the bus station and near the telephone company, it looks like a private residence. Families stay here, as do the kind of hippie clientele that sport feather earrings. Bathrooms are reasonably clean. Prices are rated according to the presence of air conditioning and TV. Singles and doubles come with air conditioning. *18 apts. Inexpensive. V.*

### Hotel Turismo   (Full)

*Rua Fernando Corrêa, 1065;* ☎ *791-1176.*

From the street, this small hotel looks like a residential house, complete with crowing roosters. The rooms are simple and clean, if overpriced. The dining room serves lunch, dinner, and a small breakfast of fruit, bread, and coffee). Sun. features all-you-can-eat *comida caseira* (home-cooked). Air-conditioned rooms with mini-bar and TV; some have fans $20. *14 apts. Inexpensive. No cards.*

### Pensão do Povo

*Rua Fernando Corrêa, 825.*

Located behind the church, Chapada's cheapest rooms are for those who don't care what bites them after they drop dead asleep. One communal bathroom for most rooms; two apartments have private baths. Some rooms have four beds, but there are no phones. *Cheap. No cards.*

## Where To Eat

See page 26 for price chart.

### Taberna Suiça

*Rua Fernando Corrêa.*

Open only on the weekends, but insiders consider this to be the best restaurant in town for international cuisine. Fri. serves only dinner. *Inexpensive. No cards.*

### Nivio's Tour Restaurante

*Praça Bispo Dom Wunibaldo, 631;* ☎ *791-1206.*

Don't let the word "tour" discourage you. This Portuguese-styled house with blue-tiled walls and white stucco arches offers a veritable feast. No one ever knows what will be served, but it's invariably good in this one-room house. If temperatures rise too high inside, you can sit outside on the veranda on a residential side street overlooking the public swimming pool. (The natural water is piped in from the Prainha River several hundred feet away.) Chicken and rice dishes are excellent, as is the *prato feito* (meal of the day). *Inexpensive. No cards.*

### Costelão

*Road to Cuiabá, 2 km. (Aldeia Velha);* ☎ *791-1102. 11 a.m.-3 p.m., 7-9 p.m.*

Good barbecue styled in a typical *gaúcho* house. *Inexpensive. No cards.*

### Chapadense

*Rua Ver. José de Souza, 535;* ☎ *791-1410.*

Open for lunch, dinner on Sun. only. Small salon with home-style regional cooking. *Inexpensive. No cards.*

### Gaia Bar

*Off the main plaza.*

This green-and-orange house is the denizen for the local "Green People," who are still reading Herman Hesse. Outsiders are sometimes scowled at, but yell out *"Preserva natureza!"* and you'll be fine.

### Borboleta Casa de Chá

*Rua Fernando Corrêa, 446-B;* ☎ *321-5307.*

A civilized teahouse in this dirty-boots wilderness is definitely refreshing. Indulge in *bolos* (cakes), *docinhos* (sweets), and *salgadinhos* (salty pastries), washed down with tea or cold beer.

# Shopping

### Achei Novidades

*Praça D. Wunibaldo. 8 a.m.-8 p.m.*

Next to the Gaia bar off the main *praça*, this is the city's premier crafts store, featuring jewelry made by the Xavantes Indians (who live about 750 miles from Chapada) and pottery from the Carajas tribe in the state of Pará. Other great buys are homemade liqueurs with *pequi cristalizado* (a tree typical of the cerrado). You can also buy modern art from regional artists. *No cards.*

# Healers

Chapada, like Cuiabá, has a strong Green movement, as well as a New Age/alternative health community. If you ask around, you can easily meet students of various gurus (such as Rajneesh, called Osho here), Zen meditators, yoga enthusiasts, massage therapists, acupuncturists, and even psychic healers. There may also be a few lingering souls who speak Esperanto. The small brochure-like magazine *Tempo de Crescer!* lists various professional holistic practitioners and organizations in the Cuiabá-Chapada region.

# Hands-On Chapada Dos Guimarães

## Arrival

The *rodoviária* (**bus station**) is at Rua Cipriano Curvo; ☎ *791-1280.* Buses run between Cuiabá and Chapada dos Guimaráes, at 7:30 a.m., 8 a.m., 10 a.m., noon, 2 p.m., 4 p.m., and 7 p.m., and returning at 6 a.m., 9 a.m., noon,

1 p.m., 1:30 p.m., 2 p.m., 4 p.m., and 6 p.m. Buses also run to Brasilan, Paranatinga, and other places.

## Climate

Between Apr.-Oct., – the dry season – temperatures run between 68 and 75°F, but temperatures can rise over 50° in just a matter of hours. The hottest months in the Pantanal are Dec.-Feb., when temperatures average between 110-112°F. During dry season, it's important to drink lots of liquids to avoid dehydration. Starting in Nov., weather alternates between torrential rains and scalding sun. The most animals can be seen in Dec. and Jan.

## Credit Cards

Chapada seems to have trouble processing American Express cards. A few businesses take VISA. (See below.)

## Money Exchange

Come with a full stash of *cruzeiros*; few people accept dollars or credit cards. Even the Banco Brazil will not exchange dollars, though it is rumored the **Hotel Turismo**, Rua Fernando C. da Costa, 1065, ☎ *791-1176*, will.

## Taxis

There's only one taxi in Chapada: contact **Eco Turismo**, ☎ *791-1393*, to find out who owns it that week.

## Telephone

**Posto Telefônico**, Rua 223 Tiradentes, 390.

## Travel Agency

### Eco Turismo Cultural

*Praça Dom Wunibaldo, 464;* ☎ *(85) 791-1393, 791-1305.*

One of Chapada's premier trek agencies is owned by Jorge Belfort Mattos Jr., a university professor who, despite his Santa Claus girth, scampers up and down steep hills like a master. All his trips last between four and six hours, including transportation, light lunch, and water. Three main tours include the **Parque Nacional** (with the Véu de Noiva), the **Caverna Aroe Jari** with the Lagoa Azul, and the **Cidades das Pedras** (City of Rocks). Exciting two- to five-day packages, from $100-$282, including breakfast and one meal a day, can also be arranged (accommodations at Hotel Pousada or Turismo). Five-day tours include city tour and geodesic site, caverns, National Park, Cidades das Pedras, and horseback riding. *V.*

## When To Go

**July: Winter Festival** mid-month.

# CONTACTS & MORE

## Specialty Tours

Specialty tours, especially in the Amazon, are often the easiest and safest way to travel. The following agencies, most of them US-based, are all reputable. Cancellations and price changes are a way of life, so you might take out insurance against cancellation. Also read the fine print; usually you are required to take responsibility for your own health and property.

### Brazil Nuts

*201 8th Street South, Naples, FL 34102; ☎ (941) 403-8837; fax (941) 403-8838; e-mail BrazilNuts@aol.com.*

Owner Adam Carter is a passionate Brazilophile offering packaged tours of Rio, the Pantanal, the Amazon, Carnaval in Rio, Salvador, and others. Travelers can also join the "Rio Like a Native" program on a day-by-day basis, which includes various trips to tourist sites and evening performances. The agency has sponsored exciting culinary tours and now has adventures through the Amazon, including Gabriel da Cachoeira. Clients rave about their services. The office in Rio is at *Blumar/Brazil Nuts,* Rua Visconde de Piraja 550, suite 108; ☎ *(21) 511-3636; e-mail Paula@ Blumar.com.br.*

### The Adventurous Appetite

*56 West 70th Street, New York, NY 10012; ☎ (212) 873-9067; fax (212) 496-1846.*

Owned by Bonnie Kassel, this company specializes in distinctive cooking pleasure trips throughout the world, including an extensive tour of Bahia. Groups of 10 explore local markets and cook in private homes and with chefs of outstanding restaurants. In Brazil, a 15-day tour, costing $3,395 per person, includes Salvador, Praia do Forte, a weekend at Morro de São Paulo, sailing around Parati, and Rio. Next trip: Mar. 15-30, 1997.

### Christine Chauvin, Ltd.
### Adventures on Horseback-Personalized Travel

*430 E. 56 Street, New York, NY 10022; ☎ (212) 421-0671, fax (212) 935-0559.*

Christine Chauvin both organizes and leads exciting horseback treks over the most exotic landscapes in the world, including South Africa, Uruguay, the Kalahari Desert, and Brazil. In Brazil she has designed two tours: Rio Grande of Sul and the Pantanal, which she leads yearly. She also creates and prepares itineraries for independent travelers on any budget, drawing from her vast international experience in out-of-the-way places. Get on the mailing list for her well-written newsletter, *Travel Log*.

## International Expeditions

*One Environs Park, Helena, Alabama 35080;* ☎ *(205) 428-1700.*

This company usually offers trekking journeys through the Amazon basin in Peru, but may have now extended trips into Brazil.

## ICS Scuba and Travel

*5254 Merrick Rd, # 5, Massapequa, NY 11758;* ☎ *(516) 797-2133, (800) 722-0205.*

This company specializes in scuba expeditions throughout the world, including an extensive program in Fernando de Noronha. (For more information, see the section on Fernando de Noronha.)

## Special Expeditions

*720 Fifth Avenue, New York, NY 10019;* ☎ *(212) 765-7740; (800) 762-0003.*

This company, aimed at the adventurous tourist, offers remarkable 16-day voyages aboard the 80-passenger *M.S. Polaris* from Manaus to Ciudad, Venezuela, traversing a thousand miles on the Amazon. Cost begins at $5,030 per person, double occupancy, including everything but airfare.

## Ecotour Expeditions

*P.O. Box 1066, Cambridge, MA 02238;* ☎ *(617) 876-5817.*

A three-year-old company, Ecotour offers a nine-day Amazon journey with three meals a day, including a tour of Manaus. The cost is about $1,895 (plus airfare to Brazil).

## Cosmos

☎ *(800) 851-0728.*

A pioneer of high-quality budget travel, Cosmos has developed seven escorted packages to Latin America. Tour prices, including airfare from Miami or Atlanta, range from $1,038 a person (double occupancy) for the seven-day "Mayan Mysteries of the Yucatan" tour, to $3,521 for the 22-day "South American Odyssey" package (Brazil, Argentina, Chile, and Peru). Airport transfers, accommodations, breakfast, and sights are included.

## Rainforest Alliance

*65 Bleeker Street, New York City, NY 10012-2420;* ☎ *(212) 677-1900; fax (212) 677-2187; E-mail: canopy@ ra.org.*

An international non-profit organization dedicated to the conservation of tropical forests for the benefit of the global community. Among the various programs they sponsor is a Conservation Media Center, the Amazon Rivers Program, Natural Resources and Rights Program, Small Wood Program and various grants for selected conservation projects. Recent publications include *Floods of Fortune* and *Tales From The Jungle,* two excellent books on the Amazon. Their website is: http://www.rainforest-alliance.org

## International Study Tours

*225 W. 34th St., # 913, New York, NY 10122;* ☎ *(212) 563-1327; (800) 833-2111.*

IST offers educational and cultural tours. Trips can be arranged for groups, including a rainforest expedition out of Manaus (or a combination including Manaus, the Pantanal, Iguaçu Falls, and Rio), "Carnaval of Cultures" 12-day tour of Rio, Salvador, and Recife to explore samba and Afro-Brazilian lore; and an "Art in Brazil" tour, including stops in Rio, Brasília, and Ouro Preto. Trips run from seven-13 nights. Lecturers are Brazilian university professors. Inquire about single arrangements.

## American Museum of Natural History Discovery Tours & Cruises

*Central Park West at 79th Street, New York, NY 10024;* ☎ *(212) 769-5700.*

The museum offers a cruise down the Amazon on the 98-passenger *Explorer* from April 11-21, 1997. Lectures will be given by a team from the museum. The price: $3,400-6,724 (no airfare).

## New York Botanical Garden

*Trav. pgrm/NY Botanical Gdn, Bronx, NY 10458-5126;* ☎ *(212) 220-8700, fax 6504.*

Special Amazonian tours for groups of eight-20 are planned for the early dry season of each year. Cruises are taken on a small river boat built especially for the program, accompanied by guides who lecture on the botanical aspects of jungle life. Fee, including roundtrip airfare from Miami to Manaus, all meals, transfers, expeditions, and reading material, is $2,495.

## Brazilian Views, Inc.

*201 East 66th Street, Suite 21G, New York, NY 10021,* ☎ *(212) 472-9539.*

This specialty consulting firm has previously offered several types of expeditions, including a 10-day Pantanal birdwatching tour, a (four-day minimum) fishing expedition to the Pantanal, a garden tour of Brazil and Argentina sponsored by four South American garden clubs, and a decorative fiber arts and folk crafts tour of Belém, Recife, Salvador, Belo Horizonte, Rio de Janeiro, and São Paulo. Write for current information.

## F & H Consulting

*2441 Janin Way, Solvang, CA 93463;* ☎ *(800) 544-5503, fax (805) 688-1021.*

This extremely reputable firm, co-owned by Claudio Heckmann, a native-born Brazilian, works only with five-star hotels and Brazilian-owned properties. Cludio is also the coordinator for the Brazilian Tourism Information Center. In the US, contact F & H for the most up-to-date information on resort facilities, spas, and private islands and the Ariau Jungle Tower outside Manaus.

## Brazilian Roots

*Rua do Riachuelo, 44, 4th floors (downtown). Rio de Janeiro, RJ Brasil 20.230-014;* ☎ *(21) 252-2759, fax 232-9643.*

Owned and run by two black Brazilians prominent in video, radio, and politics, this is a service promotion company specializing in international trade and tourism. The agency designs, plans, and executes international events and also offers special "Ethnic Cultural Tours" featuring the Afro-Brazilian culture of Brazil. They are skilled in bringing large groups of Afro-American tourists to Brazil.

## Travel Agencies & Tour Operators

### Abreu Tours

*317 E. 34th Street, New York, NY 10016;* ☎ *(212) 532-6550, fax (212) 532-7153.*

Handles group of 15 or more on custom basis. Also specializes in Portugal.

### Go To Rio Tours

*551 Fifth Ave., New York, NY 10176;* ☎ *(212) 682-5310, fax (212) 963-2398.*

Arranges FITs and groups throughout Brazil, with 24-hour guides and special requests. Also Amazon packages. Carnaval packages, minimum five night, average is nine nights.

### Equitable Travel

*654 Madison Ave., New York, NY 10176;* ☎ *(212) 682-5310, fax (212) 486-0783.*

Arranges trips for individuals, particularly businessmen.

### Panavian Travel

*25 W. 45th Street, New York, NY 10036;* ☎ *(212) 719-2270, fax (212) 719-2273.*

Discount airfares available throughout the year.

### Tourlite

*551 Fifth Ave., New York, NY 10176;* ☎ *(212) 599-2727, fax (212) 370-0913.*

Handles package tours. The *Carioca* package (New York-Rio) runs six nights, with airfare and three-star accommodations, for $1,339 in high season; $1,959 with five-star hotel. The "Ecological" packages include two days in Manaus, two days in a river lodge, and two days in Belém, including hotel, airfare, transfer, and half-day city tour (New York departure, $1,899).

### Transbrasil

*500 Fifth Ave;, New York, NY 10110;* ☎ *(212) 944-7374, fax (212) 944-7458.*

## Ocean Line Cruises

The following companies offer cruises that make port in various Brazilian cities, including Rio de Janeiro, Manaus, Recife, Salvador and Santarém.

**Holland America Line**
300 Elliott Avenue West, Seattle, WA 98119 . . . . . ☎ (206) 681-3535

**Odessa America Cruise Company**
250 Old Country Road, Mineola, NY 11501 . . . . .   ☎ (516) 747-8880
**Ocean Cruise Lines**
1510 S.E. 17th St., Fort Lauderdale, FL 33316 . . . .   ☎ (305) 764-3500
. . . . . . . . . . . . . . . . . . . . . . . . . . . . . . . . . . . . . . . .   or (800) 556-8850
**Regency Cruises**
260 Madison Avenue, New York, NY 10016. . . . .   ☎ (212) 972-4499
**Royal Viking Line**
95 Merrick Way, Coral Gables, FL 33134. . . . . . . .   ☎ (305) 447-9660
. . . . . . . . . . . . . . . . . . . . . . . . . . . . . . . . . . . . . . .   ☎ (800) 422-8000
**Sun Line Cruises**
1 Rockefeller Plz, # 315, New York, NY 10020 . . .   ☎ (212)  397-6400
outside New York City. . . . . . . . . . . . . . . . . . . . . . .   ☎ (800) 872-6400

Also see *Travel Agencies* under various *Hands-On* sections of each city.

# Online Information

*url*  http://www.deltanet.com/brazil/og.ag.atm
  Surf through this rainforest art exhibit offering native tribes, brightly colored birds and lots of green stuff.
*url*  http://www.ecobrazil.or.br
  In August 1994 a multidisciplinary group formed by government and non-government consultants established guidelines for Barzilian ecotourism. The group promotes the development of sustainable ecotourism, and also offers valuable information about projects, activities and tour operators.
*url*  http://www.embratur.gov.br/sBook/Poll/Lottery
  EMBRATUR, Brazil's official tourist board, presents information on each state and city, with hotel guides and a calander of upcoming events. Win free trips!
*url*  http://sensemedia.net/sprawl/21672
  A Brazilian goddess website featuring *lemnajá*, ruler of the oceans. E-mail direct to a Bahian guide Dona, Vani, and get information on beaches and restaurants.
*url*  http://darkwing.uoregon.edu/~sergiok/brazil.html
  Tour virtual street markets in Rio, behind the scenes of soccer teams, São Paulo and the Amazon jungle.
*url*  http://pasture.ecn.Purdue.edu/agentml/agenmc/brzil/rec ipes.html
  Choice recipes from superb Brazilian cooks.
*url*  http://www.solution.net/rec-travel/hostels/sa.br.htmlD
  Brazilian hostels, addresses, etc., with international affiliations.
**America Online** (keyword Travel Forum, Message Boards, World Traveler, Brazil). Chat with other Brazilophiles who will tell you how much they wish they were there – now!

# Rainforest Support Groups

## Arctic to Amazonia

*P.O. Box 73, Stafford, VT 05072.*

An educational organization devoted to constructive, non-violent change in the world by facilitating dialogue between indigenous and non-indigenous peoples, particularly regarding social justice and the environment. Publishes *Arctic to Amazonia Report*, available with a $25 annual membership.

## Rainforest Action Network (RAN)

*450 Sansome, Suite 700, San Francisco, CA 94111. ☎ (415) 398 4404.*

A grass-roots activist environmental organization working with indigenous land-based peoples in struggles to protect their rainforest homelands and cultures from rampant destruction. Available with a $25 annual membership is *World Rain Forest Report* quarterly, with monthly action alerts.

## Amanaka's Amazon Network

*339 Lafayette Street, #8, New York, NY 10012; ☎ (212) 674-4646, fax 274-1773.*

A nonprofit organization that sponsors an annual Amazon Week to promote public dialogues between Amazon leaders and their US supporters. Amanaka also publishes a quarterly newsletter on Amazon-related issues. Volunteer programs are available for those who want to commit themselves to political and social activism. Letter-writing campaigns and civil protests initiated by Amanaka have already had far-reaching consequences in the region. Other organizations involved in saving tropical rainforests include:

**Conservation International**
1015 18th Street NW, Suite 1002
Washington, DC 20036

**Friends of the Earth/U.S.**
218 DD, SE
Washington, DC 20003

**Greenpeace**
1436 U Street NW
Washington, DC 20009

**National Resources Defense Council**
40 W 20th Street
New York, NY 10011

**Rainforest Alliance**
270 Lafayette St, Suite 512
New York, NY 10012

**Sierra Club**
730 Polk Street
San Francisco, CA 94109

**World Wildlife Fund**
Panda House, Godalming
Surrey GGU 7 1 XRR
England

**COICA**
(Coordinating Body for the Indigenous Peoples'
Organizations of the Amazon Basin)
Jiron Almagro 614, Lima 11, Peru

# Health Kit For The Tropics

## Jet Lag

Overnight flights to Brazil (nine hours from New York to Rio) can easily cramp your style. The time change from the East Coast is only two hours, but it's the long hours spent cramped in a seat, the night of lost sleep, and the airline food and drinks that can get you down. Here are some tips to minimize discomfort:

- ☐ Drink as little alcohol as possible before and during the flight.
- ☐ Avoid large meals for several hours after landing to shrink your stomach to its normal size.
- ☐ Chew gum slowly only to relieve ear discomfort.
- ☐ Avoid gas-producing and greasy foods.
- ☐ Eat small portions starting two hours before takeoff. Eat high-fiber foods to avoid constipation.
- ☐ Drink one pint of liquid for every three flying hours to counteract the dryness of the cabin; water and fruit juices are best.
- ☐ Use eyedrops for dry eyes and take off your contact lenses.
- ☐ Eat simply and sparingly the first few days in Brazil.

## Sunburn

According to Dr. Howard Soble, Clinical Attending Physician, Dept. of Dermatology, Lenox Hill Hospital (NYC), Rio de Janeiro (and let's add all of Brazil) is one of the top 10 "sizzle-'n'-fry hot zones in the world (others include Death Valley, California; Nairobi, Kenya; and Phoenix, Arizona).

Primary factors that contribute to skin-cancer-producing conditions are hot temperatures, proximity to the equator, higher altitudes that are closer to the sun and have fewer atmospheric impurities to filter harmful rays (watch out for those Brazilian mountains), natural shade, and closeness to large bodies of water, which reflect and amplify light.

So, as the daughter of a dermatologist, I have to say that the best way to ensure a great time in Brazil is to first seriously protect your skin and hair from ultraviolet harm. My father would have told you that no tan is safe. Tanning is actually your skin's natural defense against ultraviolet rays. The pigment melanin helps to prevent radiation from altering the skin's cellular DNA. Over time, not all DNA damage is repaired, and the risk of skin cancer increases. Excessive UVA exposure also promotes premature aging of the skin.

To minimize hazardous exposure, Dr. Howard Soble suggests the following:

☐ Plan outdoor activities for early morning or late afternoon, because the midday sun causes the most damage to your skin.

☐ Administer sunblock at least 30 minutes before exposure, and always to dry skin since water dilutes it. UVA rays that burn are strongest at midday, but equally dangerous UVA radiation is present as long as the sun is up, even in a shadowed forest.

☐ Limit your first exposure to the sun to a few minutes, and gradually increase.

☐ Make sure you wear a strong enough sunblock to minimize the effects of the dwindling ozone layer. A sunblock with an SPF (sun protection factor) rating of 15 or higher should do the trick; reapply it after you perspire or swim. And don't neglect those easily forgotten places: neck, decolletage areas, hands, tops of feet, ears, lips, and bald spots.

☐ Choose clothing with a tight weave – fabrics with natural SPF are unbleached cotton, high-luster polyesters, and some silks. Wear a wide-brimmed hat and polarizing sunglasses.

☐ Treat sunburn pain with aspirin and a lubricating ointment like petroleum jelly or 0.5% hydrocortisone. By nightfall your skin will feel dry and tight.

☐ Do wear hair products that have sunscreen. (Fredric Fekkai, a famous New York hairstylist, suggests wearing botanical oil on your hair, then adding his Gel Coiffant and Texturing Balm to prevent it from drying out.)

# Diarrhea

Traveler's diarrhea is not preordained, though few escape it. It's usually caused by ingesting contaminated food and water or by placing your contaminated fingers in your mouth. The rule for all travelers: Boil it, cook it, peel it, or forget it. Also:

- ☐ Avoid street foods, shellfish, salads, and any uncooked or undercooked foods. Do not eat raw foods. Be careful which restaurants you choose. Deluxe international hotels are usually your best bet, since most use modern refrigeration, purify local water, protect foods from insects, wash vegetables in chemical solutions, and cook food properly.
- ☐ Eat only fruit with thick skins that you peel yourself. Don't drink milk in Brazil after noon (since it is rarely refrigerated and is delivered only in the morning).
- ☐ Always wash your hands before eating. Germs are picked up through handling money, souvenir shopping, door knobs, sand, and the ocean, etc. In remote areas, carry your own soap, toilet tissue, and handiwipes.
- ☐ Drink only bottled water. The carbonation in water (*água com gas*) acidifies it and kills microorganisms that may have gotten into the water prior to boiling. Be suspect of juices or fruit drinks not prepared in your presence.
- ☐ Minimize the water you swallow when swimming.
- ☐ Use bottled water when you brush your teeth (found in the mini-bar).

If you do get Montezuma's Revenge, minimize food intake for several meals and drinks lots of liquids. Medications that you should pack are Pepto Bismol and Immodium (both available over the counter), Bactrim (prescription), and Lomotil (prescription). If you have bloody stools or fever, feel unusually weak, or if your symptoms continue for three days, see a doctor immediately. Dehydration is a severe risk. Drink fruit juices, carbonated soft drinks, or mix eight ounces of carbonated or boiled water with a quarter-tablespoon of baking soda alternated with a mixture of orange juice, a half-teaspoon of honey or corn syrup and a pinch of salt. Drink alternately from each glass until thirst is quenched and supplement with carbonated beverages, water or boiled tea. *(Information courtesy of the Centers for Disease Control, Atlanta, GA.)*

### Tips For Drinking Water

- ☐ Always order mineral water (*sem gás*, without gas, or *com gás*, with gas). Insist it be opened in front of you.
- ☐ Avoid ice cubes in any drink; they are usually made from tap water. If you must have ice, put them in a small, clean, leak-proof bag inside your glass.
- ☐ Tie a colored ribbon around the bathroom faucet to remind yourself not to drink tap water.
- ☐ Carry an electric immersion coil for boiling water – to brush teeth or make tea or coffee. You will most likely need a current converter and a plug adapter (available in department stores and travel boutiques).
- ☐ Carry a small (unbreakable) bottle of chlorine bleach or tincture of iodine to disinfect water when boiling is not feasible. Add two drops of 5% chlorine bleach or five drops of 2%

tincture of iodine to a quart of clear water. Let stand for 30 minutes. Commercial tablets available in the US to disinfect water are Halazone, Globaline and Potable-Agua.

☐ Travelers using filters to purify river water may find them hopelessly clogged with sediment and thus be forced to drink river water straight – a perfect way to contract amebiasis. Best to take a safe water supply with you.

## Immunizations

**Yellow fever** is endemic in the northern half of Brazil, Vaccines are recommended for those going to jungle or rural areas. Suggested, but not required, are hepatitis and typhoid immunizations when traveling to areas of sub-standard sanitation outside the usual tourist routes. Persons working extensively in the countryside and on working assignments in remote areas should be vaccinated. **Tetanus** shots should always be updated.

## Malaria

Malaria is transmitted by the bite of the female Anopheles mosquito, which feeds from dawn to dusk. You can also get malaria from blood transfusions, or from using contaminated needles and syringes. Not every mosquito carries malaria, but one bite can give you the disease. In 1995 the Centers for Disease Control stated that all travelers to the Amazon Basin will be exposed to what is called chloroquine-resistant malaria. The recommended prophylactic is **mefloquine**, taken weekly and continued for four weeks after leaving the malarious area. You can also carry a treatment of Fansidar or doxycycline alone, taken daily. If you are pregnant or are planning to fly a plane or undertake any task requiring fine coordination, you should not take mefloquine since small doses have been known to cause dizziness and/or gastrointestinal upset.

## Other Bug-transmitted Diseases

Other mosquito-transmitted diseases found in jungle areas are listed here. **Dengue fever** has flu-like symptoms, with rash, over in about a week. Antibiotics do not help and no vaccine is available. Beware of hemorraghing. *Lleishmaniasis* is usually caused by sandfly bites; they attack most frequently at dusk and dawn. *Filariasis* is caused by larvae of worms injected into the body through the bite of a mosquito; usually only heavier exposure causes symptoms. Treat with Hetrazan. *Onchocerclasis* is a form of *filariasis,* or river blindness, borne by flies that breed in rivers. If parasites invade the eyes, total blindness can occur. Treat with Ivermextin early). **Chagas' disease** is spread by the reduid bug, usually found on roofs and walls of native huts. For more information, see the *International Travel Health Guide* by Stuart R. Rose, M.D.

---

# Prevention

Cut down on your chances of catching mosquito-transmitted diseases by protecting yourself. Search your sleeping quarters and bed for hidden insects. Use insecticides, preferably pyrethrum-based, in your living and sleeping quarters (RAID Formula II Crack and Crevice Spray is good). And protect your bed (if outdoors) with mosquito netting (spray the inside of the netting with RAID Flying Insect Spray).

Mosquito and tick bites can be reduced greatly by using the appropriate repellents. Insect repellents with a DEET percentage between 35 and 50 are recommended. Clothing may be sprayed with DEET-containing repellents and the insecticide permethrin, available in many states as Permanone, or PermaKill 4 Week Tick Killer. If you are using a mosquito net, spray it with the same product. A good, lightweight, compact mosquito net well suited for the vagabond traveler is "The Spider"; contact Thai Occidental, 5334 Yonge Street, Suite 907, Toronto M2N 6M2, Ontario, Canada; ☎ (416) 498-4277, price $69.95.

---

# Cholera

Cholera is an acute diarrheal disease caused by bacteria found in water contaminated by sewage. Although there have been serious outbreaks of cholera during the last few years in many Latin American countries, including Brazil, few Western travelers ever get seriously ill. Most illness occurs in native people who are undernourished and who regularly ingest large amounts of contaminated water. The main symptom is explosive, though painless diarrhea, which, if left untreated, may lead to fatal dehydration. Treating loss of fluids immediately is primary to recovery. A good idea is to carry Oral Rehydration Salts mixture distributed by the World Health Organization, which you should mix with safe drinking water and consume after every loose stool. If you can't drink enough to replace lost fluid because of vomiting or weakness, get to a hospital immediately. The best prevention is to pay attention to what you eat and drink.

---

# Other Diseases

### Schistosomiasis

Wading or swimming in fresh water can put you at risk for this disease, caused by parasitic blood flukes called schistosomes. The tiny larvae of these creatures bore into the skin and mature within the body. Some people disregard the initial symptom – a rash at the site of penetration – but four-12 weeks later, fever, malaise, and coughing, along with diarrhea, usually sets in abruptly. It's often curable, but if left untreated can progress to more severe stages.

### Hepatitis A

This disease can be transmitted by person-to-person contact or by contaminated food, water, or ice. The flu-like symptoms don't appear typically for two-six weeks and are soon followed by jaundice. The CDC recommends a **gamma globulin** vaccination for each three-month period. There's no specific treatment and normally healthy people recover on their own, but do see a doctor.

### Hepatitis B

Travelers to the Amazon basin are at high risk for hepatitis B. Vaccinations are not required, but the CDC recommends one for health-care workers, long-term travelers, or anyone expecting to have intimate relations with locals in rural areas. The virus is transmitted through the exchange of blood products, daily physical contact, and sexual intercourse. The vaccine involves a series of three intramuscular doses, which should be begun six months before travel; the series should be started.

### Typhoid Fever

Travelers in Brazil are at risk for typhoid fever when in small cities, villages, and rural areas. Although not required, the CDC recommends a vaccination for those straying from the regular tourist itinerary or staying more than six weeks. The disease is transmitted through contaminated food and water. Currently, the vaccine only protects 70-90% of cases, so continue to drink only boiled or bottled water and eat well-cooked food, even if you've taken the vaccination.

## AIDS

As of press time, Brazil does not require foreign travelers to take AIDS tests. For a free four-page leaflet on how to travel abroad and not bring home acquired immunodeficiency syndrome, write Global Programs on AIDS, World Health Organization, Avenue Appia, 1121; Geneva 27, Switzerland. (Also see *Safe Sex*, in the introductory section of this book.)

## Information Sources

For the most current information on traveling to tropical countries, contact the **Centers for Disease Control**, ☎ *(404) 332-4559*, using a touch-tone phone 24 hours a day. A recorded voice will direct you through a menu of information.

For an extremely useful bimonthly newsletter on travel precautions, write *Traveling Healthy*, 108-48 70th Road; Forest Hills, NY 11375.

An excellent 51-page booklet published by the American Society of Tropical Medicine and Hygiene discusses such topics as pre-trip preparations, immunizations, malaria prevention, traveler's diarrhea, etc. Write: Karl A. Western, MD c/o **ASTMH**, 6436-31st Street, N.W., Washington, D.C. 20015-2342. Price $4.00. Everything you need to know about the latest travel-health requirements worldwide (updated annually) can be found in *International Travel Health Guide*, by Stuart R. Rose, M.D. Published by Travel Medicine, Inc., 351 Pleasant Street, Suite 312, Northampton, MA 01060.

## Post-trip Checkups

Many specialists feel there is no reason to have a post-tropics checkup if you are feeling well. In some cases, however, symptoms don't appear for weeks, months, or a year after the trip; you may even suffer intermittent attacks followed by periods of subsidence. The incubation period for malaria varies from five days to a month, and longer in some cases. In its initial stages, it causes flu-like symptoms, and if treatment is delayed, it can become potentially fatal. If you have any of the following symptoms, don't delay seeking immediate medical attention:

- □ **Gastrointestinal distress** (if diarrhea, loose stools, abdominal pain, or excessive flatulence continues for a week or more, you could be harboring parasites).
- □ **Fever** (never ignore fever coming out of the tropics – it could be malaria, schistosomiasis, roundworms, hepatitis A, or a sign of tuberculosis).
- □ **Rashes**, change in skin pigmentation, or swelling.
- □ **Persistent coughs**, possibly due to parasitic worms in the lungs or tuberculosis.
- □ Unexplained **weight loss.**

In all cases, it is best to go to a tropical disease specialist straight away. To find one in your area, call the local health department or the tropical disease unit of a nearby hospital. The new **International Society of Travel Medicine**, Box 150060, Atlanta, GA 30333; ☎ *(404) 486-4046*, should have a list of specialists. To request a nationwide directory of tropical disease specialists, send a stamped, self-addressed business-size envelope to Dr. Leonard C. Marcus, 148 Highland Avenue, Newton, MA 02165.

# Books & Films

## Books

**Luso-Brazilian Books,** Box 170286, Brooklyn, NY 11217; ☎ *(718) 624-4000, (800) 727-LUSO*, fax *(718) 858-0690*. This is one of the leading distributors of Brazilian and Portuguese-oriented material. Write for a free catalog.

## Photography

Manor, Graciela, text, and Mann, Haus, photos. *The Twelve Prophets of Aleijadinho*. Austin and London: University of Texas Press, 1976. Black and white photos, a short text, and a poetic essay by Carlos Drummond de Andrade on the character of Minas Gerais as seen through the eyes of the baroque sculptor Aleijadinho.

Verger, Pierre. *Historical Center of Salvador (Centro Histórico de Salvador 1945-1950)*. Rio de Janeiro: Câmara Brasleiro do Livro, 1989. Black and white photos by a French documentary photographer in the 1940s whose reminiscences are still fresh.

Bruce Weber. *O Rio de Janeiro*. New York: Knopf, 1986. A sensual photographic journal by one of the world's leading photographers.

## History

Alden, Dauril., ed. *Colonial Roots of Modern Brazil*. Berkley: University of Press, 1973.

Burns, E. Bradford. *A History of Brazil*. New York: Columbia University Press, 1980. Perhaps the most readable history of Brazil readily available in bookstores.

Conrad, Robert Edgar. *World of Sorrow: The African Slave Trade in Brazil*. Baton Rouge & London: Louisiana State University Press, 1986. A rich resource of details and culture, particularly helpful for anyone writing an historical novel.

Diffie, Bailey W. *A History of Colonial Brazil 1500-1792*. Malabar, Florida: Robert E. Krieger Publishing Co., 1987.

Freyre, Gilberto. *Order & Progress: Brazil from Monarch to Republic*. Berkeley and Los Angeles: University of California Press, 1986. A three-volume masterpiece by the premier Brazilian sociologist.

Freyre, Gilberto. *The Mansions and the Shanty: The Making of Modern Brazil*. Berkeley and Los Angeles: University of California Press, 1986.

Freyre, Gilberto. *The Masters and the Slaves: A Study in the Development of Brazilian Civilization*. Berkeley and Los Angeles: University of California Press, 1986.

Maxwell, Kenneth. *Conflicts and Conspiracies: Brazil and Portugal 1750-1808*. Cambridge University Press, 1973. Interesting analysis explaining why Brazil adopted monarchical system of government instead of fragmenting into separate states.

## Street Life

De Jesue, Maria. *Child of the Dark: The Diary of Carolina Maria de Jesus*. New York: Penguin, 1963. An extraordinary diary of a poor woman living in a São Paulo ghetto, originally written on scraps of paper. After her writings were discovered by a journalist, they were first serialized in the newspaper, then made into an instant best-seller. Nothing more honest and direct exists to describe the day-to-day struggle of living in a *favela*.

Dimenstein, Gilberto, introduction by Rocha, Jan. *Brazil: War on Children*. London: Latin America Bureau, 1991. One of Brazil's most outstanding journalists investigates the tragic world of underaged pimps, muggers, prostitutes, and petty criminals – all homeless children who live in fear of sudden death at the hands of vigilantes.

Trevisan, João, translated by Martin Forman. *Perverts in Paradise.* London: GMP Publishers, 1986. Written by one of the founders of the Brazilian gay movement, this is a fascinating, if severely biased, history of homosexuality in Brazil, from the Papal Inquisition to today's pop music idols. A provocative analysis of how homosexuality dovetails with the Brazilian traits of extravagance and social repression is followed by a startling interview with a *candomblé* priest. Write: GMP Publishers, Ltd., P.O. Box 247, London N15 6RW, England.

## Native Peoples

Davis, Shelton H. *Victims of the Miracle: Development and the Indians of Brazil.* Boston: Cambridge University Press, 1977, reprint 1988. An anthropologist examines contemporary Indian policy in Brazil and discusses the devastation wrought on tribal life by highway construction and mining.

Hemming, John. *Amazon Frontier: The Defeat of the Brazilian Indians.* London: Macmillan London, Ltd., 1987. Covering the period from the mid-18th century to the early 20th century, this compelling analysis explains how and why the native cultures fell into demise. The author is Director and Secretary of the Royal Geographic Society.

## The Amazon

Head, Suzanne and Heizman, Robert, editors. *Lessons of the Forest.* San Francisco: Sierra Club Books, 1990. Essays from 24 leading authorities (biologists, ecologists, economists, and political activists) all committed to finding alternatives to rainforest decimation.

Hecht, Susanna and Cockburn, Alexander. *The Fate of the Forest: Developers, Destroyers and Defenders of the Amazon.* New York: Harper Perennials, 1990. A deeply researched and searing work exploring the history of the rainforest from the *conquistadors* to the gold miners to the military dictatorship. It also sheds new light on the role of Chico Mendes and other activists.

Lamb, F. Bruce. *Wizard of the Upper Amazon: The Story of Manuel Córdova-Rio.* Boston: Houghton-Mifflin, 1975. Written by a Peruvian healer held captive by Amazonian Indians, this is a mesmerizing document of life in a South American tribe, including descriptions of *ayahuasca* rituals – a hallucinogenic tonic made from Amazonian plants.

Lewis, Scott, preface by Robert Redford. *The Rainforest Book: How You Can Save the World's Rainforests.* Los Angeles: Living Planet Press, 1990. An extremely easy-to-read book that explains how rainforests are being destroyed, why we should preserve them, and what we can do to save them from destruction.

Kane, Joe. *Running the Amazon.* New York: Knopf, 1989. A must-read for the armchair adventurer, this eyewitness account of traversing the

Amazon River was written by a formerly office-bound journalist whose pre-trip naiveté was matched only by his unexpected fearlessness.

Matthiessen, Peter. *The Cloud Forest*. New York: Penguin, 1961, 1989. Zen master Matthiessen criss-crossed 20,000 miles of South American wilderness, from the Amazonian rainforests to Machu Picchu and Mato Grosso. Stylish, ironic, and insightful.

Plotkin, Mark. *Tales From A Shaman's Apprentice*, Viking, 1993. One of the world's leading ethnobotanists recalls his harrowing adventure with some remote medicine men in the Amazon. Great to read before, during, and after your trip.

Popescu, Petru. *Amazon Beaming*. New York: Viking, 1991. When world-class photographer Loren McIntyre was kidnapped by an Amazonian tribe, he found himself descending, unwillingly, into another level of perceptual reality that ultimately changed his life. This amazing *Twilight Zone* story is told by Romanian filmmaker Petru Popescu.

Shoumatoff, Alex. *The Rivers Amazon*. San Francisco: Sierra Club Books, 1978 and 1986. A staff writer for the New Yorker and a premier commentator of Brazilian affairs resolved to spend his 30th birthday in the Amazon. His reminiscences of negotiating headwaters, mosquitoes, exotic vegetation, and wildlife, as well as all manners of bureaucratic red tape lie somewhere between poetry and science.

## Pantanal

Banks, Vic. *The Pantanal: Brazil's Forgotten Wilderness*. San Francisco: Sierra Club Books, 1991. Photojournalist and cinematographer Vic Banks chronicles his lively adventures in the Pantanal, accompanied by photos. Also included is a good overview of the political dilemmas of the region.

## Art & Architecture

Epstein, David. *Brasília: Plan and Reality. A Study of Planned and Spontaneous Urban Development*. Berkeley: University of California Press, 1973.

Holston, James. *Brasília: The Modernist City. An Anthropological Critique*. Chicago & London: University of Chicago Press, 1989.

## Music

McGowan, Chris and Ricardo Pessanha. *The Brazilian Sound*. New York: Billboard Books, 1991.

Perrone, Charles. *Master of Contemporary Brazilian Song: MPB 1965-1985*. Austin: University of Texas Press, 1989.

## Roots & Culture

Amado, Jorge. *Bahia de Todos Os Santos (Guia de ruas e mistérios)*. A mystical guide to Salvador's streets and icons by Brazil's foremost novelist (Portugtuese).

## Religion

Brumana, Fernando Giobellina and Elda Gonzales Martinez. *Spirits from the Margin: Umbanda in São Paulo.* Stockholm: Wicksell International, 1989.

Bastide, Roger, translated by Helen Sebba. *The African Religions of Brazil: Toward a Sociology of the Interpretation of Civilizations.* Baltimore and London: Johns Hopkins Uniiversity, 1960. The leading analysis of Brazilian religious cults by a noted French social scientist.

Galembo, Phyllis. *Divine Inspiration: Benin to Bahia.* New Mexico: University of Albuquerque Press, 1993. An exquisite photo album with a foreword by David Byrne and various essays celebrating the ritualistic "theater" of African and Afro-Brazilian trance cult religions. The folkloric-rich photos help explain how African traditions, as living elements transmitted orally, were adapted in Brazil without losing their sacred fire.

McGregor, Pedro. *Jesus of the Spirits.* New York: Stein & Day, 1966. An interesting analysis of African myths and rituals and their influence on the religious beliefs of Brazilians.

O'Gorman, Frances. *Aluanda: A Look at the Afro-Brazilian Cults.* Rio de Janeiro: Livraria Francisco Alves Editora S.A., 1979.

St. Clair, David. *Drum & Candle.* New York: Doubleday, 1971. An American journalist made a personal investigation into the psychic/spiritual side of Brazil and came out a believer.

Wofer, Jim. *The Taste of Blood: Spirit Possession in Brazilian Candomblé.* Philadelphia: University of Pennsylvania Press, 1991.

## Samba/Carnaval

Guillermoprieto, Alma. *Samba.* New York: Random House, 1990. A marvelous account of one year in the life of Rio's Mangueira samba school, written by a former journalist with the soul of a poet.

Gardel, Luis. *Escolas de Samba.* Rio de Janeiro: 1967. Subtitled "A Descriptive Account of the Carnival Guilds of Rio," this book is a bit out of date, but the historical details of Carnaval are interesting. (The English edition is available in Rio's best book stores; try the one next door to the Copacabana Palace Hotel.)

## Dance

Bira, Almeida. *Capoeira: A Brazilian Art Form: History, Philosophy, and Practice.* Berkeley: North Atlantic Books, 1986. The student of one of the great *capoeira* masters of the 20th century and now a master teacher himself in California, the Brazilian-born author writes poignantly about the history, philosophy, and form of the country's premier martial art. The book is filled with legends, songs, and tricks of the trade – valuable for anyone interested in ethnocultural studies.

## Cuisine

Rojas-Lombardi, Felipe. *The Art of South American Cooking.* Harper Collins, 1991. Innovative Latin cooking by the late Peruvian owner of The Ballroom restaurant in New York City. Superb Brazilian delicacies.

## Health

Rose, Stuart R., MD. *International Travel Health Guide.* Northampton: Travel Medicine, Inc., 1991. Written by a physician who is a member of the AMA and the American Society of Tropical Medicine and Hygiene, this book gives excellent advice about traveling in third-world countries and tropical jungles. Specific guidelines for individual countries, including Brazil, are denoted in detail.

## Guides

*The Best Of São Paulo.* Hard-cover pocket-size guide written by a native *Paulistano.* Price, including shipping and handling, is $10. Write to: Editora Marca D'Agua, Avenida Cidade Jardim, 427 #124, São Paulo, Brazil 01453; ☎ *(11) 881-0753,* fax *(11) 883-5965.*

## Humor

O'Rourke, P. J. *Holidays in Hell.* New York: Vintage, 1989. An irreverent and world-weary foreign correspondent for *Rolling Stone* reports from hellholes around the world. His chapter about driving on third-world roads is required reading for anyone heading to the Amazon or Pantanal.

# Films

*Black Orpheus.* Directed by Marcel Camus, with music by Antônio Carlos Jobim and Luis Bonfá, this stunning movie retells the Orpheus tale through the eyes of a *carioca* streetcar conductor who figuratively descends into hell to save the woman he loves. A lush, if fantastical, view of Carnaval during the 1960s. Portuguese with English subtitles. (Available from Luso-Brazilian Books, see address above.)

*At Play in the Fields of the Lord.* Directed by Hector Babenco, this 1991 film preserves the moral intelligence of Peter Matthiessen's 1965 novel, but loses some of the adventure. Aidan Quinn plays a nerdy evangelist sent to convert an Amazonian tribe, which is also being invaded by a half-Cheyenne mercenary with his own savior complex. The footage of the jungle near Belém is colossal.

*Medicine Man. New York magazine* called this film "the most enjoyable bad movie in some time" – a big, messy emotional drama starring Sean Connery as a research scientist obsessed with finding a cure for cancer in the Amazon jungle. The shots of Connery and his sidekick, Lorraine Bracco, swinging over the forest on cables are exciting, but her jungle attire is all wrong.

***Blame It on Rio.*** Michael Caine plays a businessman in São Paulo seduced by the nubile virgin daughter of his best friend. The film gives a beautiful view of Grumari Beach, but the token toplessness is not authentic to the region. Anyone going to Rio for the first time might tolerate the horrible script for the cultural glimpses of *candomblé, capoeira,* and samba.

***Flying Down to Rio.*** This 1933 music and dance extravaganza featuring Fred Astaire and Ginger Rogers is unabashedly fun, especially the chorus line dancing samba on the wings of the airplane. Unfortunately, the music is more mariachi than Brazilian.

***The Emerald Forest.*** A marvelous, near-mythical tale of an Amazonian Indian who tries – literally – to save civilization. The score alone is superb, and the clash between the white and native cultures is thought-provoking.

# Selected Discography

The following is an extremely subjective list of some of the best recordings ever. Stars (★) represent the music I cannot live without. Large stores in major US cities carry good selections; ask for a catalog. Do set aside time in Brazil to visit record stores, where you can listen before you buy.

## Singer/Songwriters

★ Ben, Jorge. *Benjor*. Tropical Storml/WEA, 1989.
Ben Jorge and Gilberto Gil. *Gil Jorge*. Polygram/Verve, 1975.
Ben, Jorge. *Live in Rio*. Warner Bros., 1992.00
★ Bethânia, Maria. *Alibi*. BR/Philips, 1988 (rpt.)
Bethânia, Maria. *Memória de Pele*. BR/Philips, 1989.
Bethânia, Maria. *Personalidade*. Polygram/Brazilian Wave.
Biglione, Victor. *Baleia Brazil*. Tropical Storm/WEA, 1989.
★ Bonfá, Luis. *Non Stop to Brazil*. Chesky Records, 1989.
Bosco, Joäo. *Dá licença meu senhor*. Song Discos, 1996.
Buarque, Chico. *Construção*. BR Philips, 1980.
Buarque, Chico. *Malandro*. Barclay, 1985.
Buarque, Chico. *Personalidade*. Polygram/Brazilian Wave, 1987.
Buarque, Chico. *Vida*. BR/Philips, 1980.
Carlos, Roberto. *Roberto Carlos*. BR/CBS, 1986.
Djavan. *Lilás*. CBS, 1984.
★ Djavan. *Luz*. BR/CBS, 1982.
Djavan. *Não é Azul, Mas é Mar*. CBS, 1987
Djavan. *Seduzir*. World Pacific, 1990 (rpt).
★ Gil, Gilberto. *Dia Dorim Noite Neon*. Tropical Storm/WEA, 1985
Gil, Gilberto. *Parabolic*. Tropical Storm, 1992.
Gil, Gilberto. *Raça Humana*. Tropical Storm/WEA, 1984.
★ Gil, Gilberto. *Realce*. Tropical Storm, 1979.
Gil, Gilberto. *Um Banda Um*. Tropical Storm, 1982.
Gilberto, João. *Chega de Saudade*. BR/EMI, 1959.
Gilberto, João. *Interpreta Tom Jobim*. BR/EMI, 1985.

★ Gilberto, João. *The Legendary João Gilberto*. World Pacific, 1990.
  Gilberto, João. *Live in Montreaux*. Elektra/Asylum, 1987.
★ Gonzaga, Luiz. *0 Melhor de Luiz Gonzaga*. BR/RCA, 1989.
  Gonzaguinha, É. World Pacific, 1990 (rpt.)
★ Horta, Toninho. *Diamond Land*. Polygram/Verve, 1988.
  Horta, Toninho. *Moonstone*. Polygram/Verve, 1989.
  Joyce. *Language and Love*. Verve, 1991.
  Joyce. *Music Inside*. Verve, 1991.
  Lins, Ivan. *Awa Yiô*. Reprise, 1991.
  Lins, Ivan. *Harlequin*. GRP, 1986.
  Lins, Ivan. *Love Dance*. Reprise, 1989.
★ Lins, Ivan. *0 Talento de Ivan Lins*. EMI. Maria, Tânia. Bela Vista. Capitol, 1990.
  Maria, Tânia. *Love Explosion*. Concord, 1984.
  Nascimento, Milton. *Amigo*. Warner Bros., 1995.
★ Nascimento, Milton. *Anirna*. 1982.
★ Nascimento, Milton. *Ao Vivo*. *Polygram*. 1983.
★ Nascimento, Milton. *Clube da Esquina 2*. BR/EMI, 1978.
★ Nascimento, Milton. *Geraes*. BR/EMI, 1976.
★ Nascimento, Milton. *Milagre dos Peixes*. Intuition Records, 1992 (reissued).
  Nascimento, Milton. *Missa dos Quilonibos*. Polygram/Verve, 1982.
  Nascimento, Milton. *Txai*. CBS, 1992.
  Toquinho. *Canta Brasil*. CGD, 1989.
  Toquinho. *Made in Coração*. Elektra, 1990.
  Toquinho e Vinícius. *Personalidade*. Polygram/Brazilian Wave.
  Valença, Alceu. *7 Desejos*. EMI, 1992.
★ Veloso, Caetano. *Cinema Transcendental*. BR/Philips, 1979.
★ Veloso, Caetano. *Circuladô*. *Elektra*. 1992.
  Veloso, Caetano. *Estrangeiro*. Elektra/Musician, 1989.
★ Veloso, Caetano. *Personalidade*. Polygram.
★ Veloso, Caetano. *Totalmente Demaiis*. Verve, 1987.
  Vila, Martinho da. *Martinha da Vida*. CBS, 1990.
  Viola, Paulinho da. *0 Talento de Paulinho da Viola*. EMI Odeon.

### Singers

  Alcione. *Emoções Reais*. RCA, 1990.
  Alcione. *Fogo da Vida*. RCA, 1985.
  Andrade, Leny. *Embraceable You*. Timeless Records, 1991.
  Barbosa, Beto. *Beto Barbosa*. BR/Continental, 1988.
  Belém, Fafá de. *Atrevida*. BR/Som Livre, 1986.
★ Calcanhoto, Adrians. CBS Discos, 1992.
  Caram, Ana. *Rio After Dark*. Chesky Records.
  Carvalho, Beth. *Das Bêncãos que virão com os novos amanhã*. RCA, 1985.
  Carvalho, Beth. *0 Carnaval de Beth Carvalho and Martinho da Vila*. BMG, 1990.
  Caymmi, *Nana*. *Atrás da Porta*. BR/CID, 1977.
  Costa, Gal. *Bem Bom*. RCA, 1985.

★ Costa, Gal. *Gal Canta Caymmi.* Verve, 1976.
Costa, Gal. *Personalidade.* Polygram/Brazilian Wave.
Gilberto, Astrud. *Astrud Gilherto Plus the James Last Orchestra.* Polydor, 1987.
Kenia. *Initial Thrill.* MCA, 1987.
Leão, Nara. *Personalidade.* Polygram/The Best of Brazil.
Lee, Rita. *Rita Lee.* BR/Som Livre, 1986 (rpt.).
Matogrosso, Ney. *Matogrosso & Mathias, vol. 14.* Chantecler.
Menezes, Margareth. *Kindala.* Mango, 1991.
Menezes, Margareth. *Elegibo.* Mango, 1989.
Mercury, Daniela. *Samba.* Sony, 1994.
Miranda, Carmen. *Carmen Miranda.* BR/RCA, 1989.
★ Monte, Marisa. *Marisa Monte.* BR/EMI, 1988.
Purim, Flora. *Midnight Sun.* Virgin Records, 1988.
Purim, Flora. *Queen of the Night.* Sound Wave Records, 1992.
Ramalho, Elba. *Personalidade.* Polygram/The Best of Brazil series.
Regina, Elis. *Elis.* BR/Philips, 1988 (rpt.).
★ Regina, Elis. *Elis & Tom.* Verve, 1974.
★ Regina, Elis. *Essa Mulher.* WEA Latina, 1988
★ Regina, Elis. *Fascinação.* BR Philips, 1988.
Regina, Elis. *Falso Brillhante.* BR/Philips, 1988 (rpt.).
Regina, Elis. *Nada Será Como Antes.* Fontana, 1984.
Regina, Elis. *Personalidade.* Polygram/Brazilian Wave, 1987.
★ Regina, Elis. *Samba Eu Canto Assim.* 1983.
★ Sá, Sandra. *Sandra!* BMG Ariola Discos, 1990.
Simone. *The Best of Sinione.* Capitol Records, 1991.

## Rock

Baby Consuelo. *Sem Pecado E Sem Juizo.* BR/CBS, 1985.
★ Cazuza. *Burguesia.* BR/Philips, 1989.
Kledir. *Kledir Ao Vivo.* Som Livre, 1991.
Lobão. *Sob 0 Sol de Parador.* BMG/RCA, 1989.
Paralamas do Successo. *Bora Bora.* Capitol/Intuition, 1989.
Paralamos do Successo. *Selvagem?* EMI, 1989.
RPM. Rádio *Pirita Ao Vivo.* BR/CBS, 1986.

## Gaucho

Borghetti, Renato. *Renato Borghetti.* BR/RCA, 1987.
Gaucho da Fronteira. *Gaitero, China e Cordena.* Chantecler.
Gildo de Freitas. *Successos Imortais de Gildo Freitas.*

## Minas School

Azul, Paulinho Pedra. *Sonho de Meniio.* 1988.
Azul, Paulinho Pedra. *Uma Janela Dentro dos Meus Olhos,* 1984.
Franco, Tadeu. *Captivante.* Barclay, 1983.
★ Franco, Tadeu. *Animal.* Barclay, 1989.

Guedes, Beto. *Viagem das Mãos*. EMI, 1987.
Guedes, Beto. *Alma de Borracha*. EMI, 1986.

## Instrumentalists

Airto, Moreira. *Saniba de Flora*. Montuno Records, 1988.
★ Moreira, Airto. *Identity*. Arista, 1975.
★ Moreira, Airto & Flora Purim. *The Colors of Life*. W. Germany/In + Out, 1988.
★ Assad, Sérgio and Odair. *Alma Brasileira*. Elektra/Nonesuch, 1988.
Alameida, Laurindo & Carlos Barbosa-Lima, Charlie Byrd. *Music of the Brazilian Masters*. Concord Picante, 1989.
Alemão (Olmir Stocker). *Longe dos Olhos, Porto do Coração*. Happy Hours Music.
Banda Savana. *Brazilian Movements*. Libra Music (Denmark).
Barbosa-Lima, Carlos & Sharon Isbin. *Brazil, with Love*. Concord, 1987.
Biglione, Victor. *Victor Biglione*. Tropical Storm, 1987.
★ Castro-Neves, Oscar. *Maracujá*. JVC, 1989.
★ Castro-Neves, Oscar. *Oscar!* Living Music. 1987.
Cayymi, Dori. *Brasilian Serenata*. Qwest/Warner, 1991.
★ Elias, Eliane. *Eliane Plays Jobim*. Blue Note, 1990.
Elias, Eliane. *So Far So Close*. Blue Note, 1989.
★ Favero, Alberto. *Classical Tropico*. Tropical Storm/WEA Latina, 1989.
★ Gandelman, Leo. *Leo Gandelman*. Secret Records, 1989.
★ Geraissati, André. *Dadgad*. Tropical Storm/WEA, 1989.
Gismonti, Egberto. *Amazônia*. EMI, 1991.
★ Gismonti, Egberto. *Dança das Cabeças*. ECM, 1977.
Gismonti, Egberto. *Dança das Escravos*. ECM, 1989.
★ Gismonti, Egberto. *Sol do Meio Dia*. ECM, 1978.
Gismonti, Egberto and Nana Vasconcelos. *Duo Gismonti-Vasconcelos*. Jazz Bühne Berlin/Repertoire Records, 1990.
★ Jobim, Antônio Carlos. *Passarim*. Polygram/Verve, 1987.
Jobim, Antônio Carlos. *Personalidade*. Polygram/Brazilian Wave.
Jobim, Antônio Carlos. *Urubu*. BR/WEA, 1985 (rpt.).
★ Jobim, Antônio Carlos & Gal Costa. *Rio Revisited*. Verve, 1989.
Lyra, Carlos. *Carlos Lyra: 25 Anos de Bossa Nova*. 3M, 1987.
Tiso, Wagner. *Baobab*. Antilles/Island, 1990.
Silveira, Ricardo. *Sky Light*. Polygram/Verve, 1989.
Uakti. *I Ching*. Point, 1993.
Vasconcelos, Naná. *Storytelling*. EMI, 1995.

## Compilations

*Alô Brasil*. Tropical Storm/WEA Latina, 1989.
*Afro Brasil*. Verve, 1990.
*Bahia Black Ritual Beating System*. Island Records, 1992.
*Black Orpheus* (soundtrack). Verve, 1990 (rpt.).
*Brazil Classics 1: Beleza Tropical*, compiled by David Byrne. Luaka Bop/Sire, 1989.

*Brazil Classics 2*: *O Samba*, compiled by David Byrne. Luaka Bop/Warner, 1989.

*Brazil Classics 3*: *Forró*, etc., compiled by David Byrne. Luaka Bop/Warner, 1989.

*Brazil Classics 4*: *The Best of Tom Zé*, compiled by David Byrne. Luaka Bop/Warner, 1989.

*Luaka Bop*. Sire, 1990.

*Brazil is Back*. Braziloid Records, 1987.

*Brazilian Groove: Melting Pot*. Lux Music Corp., 1994.

*Djavan, João Gilberto, Toninho Horta*. Capitol Records, 1990.

*Lambada Brazil*, featuring Caetano Veloso and Margareth Menezes. Polygram, 1990.

*Nordeste Brazil*. Verve, 1991.

*Samba Brazil*. Verve, 1991.

*Sampler '89*. Tropical Storm/WEA, 1989.

*Sounds of Bahia* Volume 2. Sound Wave records, 1991.

★ *Violões*. Banera. (São Paulo), 1991.

## Best Samba Recordings

*Escolas de Samba Enredo*. Sony Music. Collection with 10 CDs, each dedicated to one of the great samba schools in Rio – from Portela to Beijo Flor, with famous interpreters like Beth Carvalho, João Bosco, and others.

*Olodum, O Movimento*. Continental/Warner. The famous percussion band from Bahia, which made international headlines with Paul Simon.

*A História da Musica de Carnaval*. Collector's. Eight cassettes with rare recordings of sambas and marches extracted from 78s, compiled by the famous musicologist José Maria Manzo. For more information, call in Rio, ☎ *(21) 239-6367*.

For Brazilian-influenced recordings by non-Brazilians, check out the releases of Stan Getz, Pat Metheny, Basia, Chick Corea, Ella Fitzgerald, Manhattan Transfer, Dave Grusin, Lee Ritenour, Sara Vaughan, Weather Report, and Paul Winter, among others.

The best cities to buy and hear music in Brazil are Rio and São Paulo (all genres), Belo Horizonte (especially the Mineiro School), Fortaleza (*forró* and *lambada*), Salvador (*afoxé*), Recife/Olinda (*forró*).

# Language

It's often been said that Portuguese is one of the sexiest languages in the world. If you are planning to spend any time in Brazil, it's well worth studying it seriously, even for a few months. Those who do are usually deeply moved by the sensuosity of the cadences and the vibrant vowel sounds – surely the secret behind the beauty of Brazilian music. Accents notwithstanding, continental Portuguese (that which is spoken in Portugal), varies only slightly in word usage, although natives from Portugal are constantly lamenting the damage Brazilians have wrought on the mother tongue over their 500-year history. (Brazilians, for their part, consider their contributions enlivening.) Among other things, Brazilians have usurped a lot of Tupi, Arabian, and French words, not to mention English phrases, particularly in the field of advertising. Don't be surprised if, in the middle of a whirl of Portuguese, you suddenly hear more familiar words like "know-how," "marketing," "design," "outdoor," and "brainstorm" – all somewhat mangled by the Brazilian accent.

The easiest way to reap a smile from a Brazilian is to learn one choice phrase of slang and use it at just the right time.

## Slang

| | |
|---|---|
| Cool, neat (literally, legal) | *Legal! (leh-gow)* |
| How great! | *Que legal!* |
| Really, really great! | *Tri-legal!* |
| How neat! | *Bacana!* |
| What a joy! Neat! Cool! Fantastic! | *Jóia!* |
| Wow! No kidding. | *Puxa! (or Puxa vida!)* |
| Oh, my gosh (literally, Our Lady) | *Nossa Senhora (Nossa)* |
| Keep cool. | *Fica frio.* |
| Keep it going. Chill out. | *Fica numa nice.* |
| expert (adjective) | *craque* |
| You said it! | *Falô!* |

Super (and even hiper, which is bigger and better) can be added to any word in Portuguese, i.e., *supermercado* (supermarket), *hipermercado* (even bigger supermarket), *super legal* (better than great), and *super bonita* (really beautiful).

## Time

These three proverbs should cover almost any situation you will encounter in Brazil.

Don't create a tempest in a teacup
*Não fazer tempestade em copo d'água.*

One who doesn't have a dog hunts with a cat (in other words, make do with what you have).
*Quem não tem cão caça com gato!*

A man is a devil that no woman can deny, but every woman wishes to be taken away by him.
*O homem é um diabo não há mulher que o negue, mas toda mulher deseja que um diabo a carregue.*

## Airplane/Customs

| | |
|---|---|
| Have you anything to declare? | *Tem alguma coisa a declarar?* |
| One suitcase of mine is missing. | *Faltame uma mala.* |
| Smoking is not allowed. | *É proibido fumar.* |
| I feel air-sick. | *Sinto-me enjoado(a).* |

## Common Questions & Phrases

| | |
|---|---|
| Where is the bathroom? | *Onde fica o toilete (banheiro)?* |
| Flirting Hello | *Alô* |
| Hi, hey | *Oi* |
| Oops | *Opa* |
| Bye | *Tchau (as in ciao)* |
| Good-bye (until later) | *Até logo* |
| Good morning | *Bom dia* |
| Good afternoon | *Boa tarde* |
| Good night (good evening) | *Boa noite* |
| What's your name? | *Qual é seu nome?* |
| My name is . . . | *Meu nome é . . .* |
| How are you? | *Como vai?* |
| I'm fine, thank you. | *Bem, obrigado(a).* |
| Thank you (very much). | *Obrigado (muito).* |
| You're welcome. | *De nada.* |
| Excuse me (apology). | *Desculpe.* |
| Excuse me (to pass by someone). | *Com licença.* |
| Where are you from? | *De onde você é?* |
| I'm from . . . | *Sou de . . .* |
| Do you speak Portuguese/ English/Spanish? | *Você fala português/inglês/ espanhol?* |
| I don't speak Portuguese. | *Não falo português.* |
| Do you understand? | *Você entende?* |
| I don't understand. | *Não entendo.* |
| Please speak more slowly. | *Por favor, fale mais devagar.* |
| How do you say . . . ? | *Como se diz . . . ?* |
| What do you call this in Portuguese | *Como se chama isto em   português?* |
| What does "—" mean in Portuguese? | *Que quer dizer "—"?* |
| Want to go out with me? | *Quer sair comigo?* |
| Want to have a drink? | *Quer tomar alguma coisa?* |
| You're very beautiful. | *Vocé é muito bonito (a).* |

**UP CLOSE TIP:** Gosto de você *is perhaps the most misunderstood phrase in Brazilian Portuguese. Depending on the tone, the body gesture, and the look in the eye, it can variously mean I like you (you're a nice*

person), I like you a lot (I hope we see each other again), I really like you
a lot (let's be friends for life), or I really, really like you a lot (do you want
to go to bed with me?).

# Directions

| | |
|---|---|
| left | *esquerda* |
| right | *direita* |
| there (where you are) | *aí* |
| over there or yonder | *lá* |
| pull | *puxe* |
| push | *empurre* |
| here | *aquí* |

# Brush-offs For Street Punks

| | |
|---|---|
| Leave me alone | *Deixe-me em paz.* |
| Go away. | *Vá embora.* |
| Don't touch me. | *Não me toque.* |
| Don't bother me. | *Não me chateie.* |
| Don't bother me (stronger). | *Não enche.* |
| Help! | *Socorro* |

# Dates

| | |
|---|---|
| Monday | *segunda-feira* (written as 2a) |
| Tuesday | *terça-feira* (3a) |
| Wednesday | *quarta-feira* (4a) |
| Thursday | *quinta-feira* (5a) |
| Friday | *sexta-feira* (6a) |
| Saturday | *sabado* |
| Sunday | *domingo* |
| weekend | *fim de semana* |
| yesterday | *ontem* |
| today | *hoje* |
| tomorrow | *amanhã* |
| the day | *o dia* |
| the month | *o mês* |
| the year | *o ano* |

# Numbers

Numbers in Portuguese use periods instead of commas, and commas instead of periods. For example, cr $3.500,75.

| | | | |
|---|---|---|---|
| 1 | um/uma | 17 | dezessete |
| 2 | dois/duas | 18 | dezoito |
| 3 | três | 19 | dezenove |
| 4 | quatro | 20 | vinte |
| 5 | cinco | 21 | vinte e um |
| 6 | seis | 30 | trinta |
| 7 | sete | 40 | quarenta |
| 8 | oito | 50 | cinquenta |
| 9 | nove | 60 | sessenta |
| 10 | dez | 70 | setenta |
| 11 | onze | 80 | oitenta |
| 12 | doze | 90 | noventa |
| 13 | treze | 100 | cem |
| 14 | quatorze | 101 | cento e um |
| 15 | quinze | 500 | quinhentos |
| 16 | dezesseis | 1000 | mil |

# Time

| | |
|---|---|
| What time is it? | *Que horas são?* |
| At what time? | *A que horas?* |
| How long does it take? | *Leva quanto tempo?* |
| When? | *Quando?* |
| Which day? | *Que dia?* |

Official time in Brazil (buses, airplanes, etc.) is reported on a 24-hour system. Midnight is *meia noite*; one, two, three o'clock in the morning is *uma hora, duas horas, três horas*, etc., until noon, which is *meio dia*. One o'clock in the afternoon is reported as *treze horas*, two o'clock as *quatorze horas*, etc. In general conversation, use the 12-hour system (i.e., you'll meet for dinner at *oito horas* (eight o'clock).

| | |
|---|---|
| at 1 a.m. | *a uma hora* |
| at 3 p.m. (official) | *às quinze horas (15:00 hours)* |
| an hour from now | *daqui a uma hora* |
| yesterday | *ontem* |
| today | *hoje* |
| tomorrow | *amanhã* |

| | |
|---|---|
| this week | *esta semana* |
| last week | *semana passada* |

## Dining

| | |
|---|---|
| Waiter | *Garçon* |
| Maitre d' | *Maitre* |
| The menu, please. | *O cardápio, por favor.* |
| What's the specialty? | *Qual é a especialidade da casa?* |
| I don't eat meat/fish. | *Não como carne/peixe.* |
| A little more. | *Um pouco mais.* |
| The bill, please. | *A conta, por favor.* |
| Is service included? | *O serviço está incluido?* |
| I want a receipt. | *Quero recibo, por favor.* |
| I want my change. | *Quero meu troco, por favor.* |
| The meal was superb. | *A refeição estava ótima!* |
| I'm full. | *Estou satisfeito (a).* |
| breakfast | *café da manhã* |
| lunch | *almoço* |
| dinner | *jantar* |
| a napkin | *um guardanápio* |
| a plate | *um prato* |
| a glass | *um copo* |
| a cup | *uma xícara* |

## Beverages

| | |
|---|---|
| mineral water | *água mineral* |
| carbonated | *com gás* |
| noncarbonated | *sem gás* |
| coffee | *café* |
| tea | *chá* |
| milk | *leite* |
| black coffee in demitasse | *cafezinho* |
| soda pop | *refrigerante* |
| beer/draft beer | *cerveja/chopp* |
| wine | *vinho* |
| red wine | *vinho tinto* |
| white wine | *vinho branco* |
| with ice | *com gelo* |
| without ice | *sem gelo* |

## Cover/Condiments/Hors d'oeuvres

| | | | |
|---|---|---|---|
| cover | *couvert* | bread | *pão* |
| butter | *manteiga* | salt | *sal* |
| pepper | *pimenta* | sugar | *açúcar* |
| oil | *azeite* | vinegar | *vinagre* |
| without sugar | *sem açúcar* | sauce | *molho* |

## Fruits

| | | | |
|---|---|---|---|
| fruits | *frutas* | apple | *maçã* |
| banana | *banana* | grapes | *uvas* |
| lemon | *limão* | melon | *melão* |
| orange | *laranja* | pear | *pêra* |
| orange juice | *suco de laranja* | strawberries | *morangos* |

A smoothie with fruit, juice, and often milk and sugar is a *vitaminas*

## Seafood

| | | | |
|---|---|---|---|
| seafood | *frutos do mar* | codfish | *bacalhau* |
| crab | *siri* | lobster | *lagosta* |
| octopus | *polvo* | oysters | *ostras* |
| shrimp | *camarão* | sole | *linguado* |
| squid | *lula* | | |

## Beef

| | | | |
|---|---|---|---|
| beef | *bife* | all-you-can-eat | *rodízio* |
| chops | *costeletas* | goat | *bode* |
| ham | *presunto* | lamb | *carneiro* |
| pork | *porco* | rabbit | *coelho* |
| sausage | *linguiça* | turkey | *peru* |
| veal | *vitela* | barbecue | *churrasco* |
| chicken | *frango/galinha* | | |

## Vegetables, Beans & Pasta

| | | | |
|---|---|---|---|
| salad | *salada* | carrot | *cenoura* |
| cucumber | *pepino* | green beans | *vagens* |
| lettuce | *alfaçe* | tomato | *tomate* |

| bean | *feijão* | pasta | *massa* |
|------|----------|-------|--------|

Cooked vegetables are referred to as *legumes cozidos*.

---

# Money

| cash | *dinheiro* |
|------|-----------|
| credit card | *cartão de crédito* |
| traveler's check | *as is, or cheque de viagem* |
| exchange house | *câmbio* |
| I want to exchange money. | *Quero trocar dinheiro.* |
| Do you exchange money? | *Você troca dinheiro? (dólares)* |
| What is the exchange rate? | *Qual é o câmbio?* |
| Can you cash a traveler's check? | *Pode trocar um traveler's check (cheque de viagem)?* |

---

# Getting Around/Directions

| Where is the . . . ? | *Onde é o (a) . . . ?* |
|----------------------|------------------------|
| I want to go to . . . | *Quero ir para . . .* |
| How can I get to . . . ? | *Como posso ir para . . . ?* |
| Does this bus go to . . . ? | *Este ônibus vai para . . . ?* |
| Please, take me to . . . | *Por favor leve-me para . . . ?* |
| airport | *aeroporto* |
| bathroom | *toilete* |
| beach | *praia* |
| bus station | *rodoviária* |
| bus stop | *ponto de ônibus* |
| embassy/consulate | *embaixada/consulado* |
| gas station | *posto de gasolina* |
| supermarket | *supermercado* |
| market/street market | *mercado/ feira* |
| street arts fair | *feira hippie* |
| movies | *cinema* |
| police station | *delegacia de polícia* |
| post office | *correio* |
| subway station | *estação de metrô* |
| theater | *teatro* |
| train station | *estação de trem* |
| Please stop here. | *Por favor pare aqui.* |
| Please wait. | *Por favor espere.* |
| I want to rent a car. | *Quero alugar um carro.* |

# Driving

| | |
|---|---|
| Danger | *Perigo* |
| Dangerous bend | *Curva perigosa* |
| Service station | *Posto* |

# At the Doctor's Office

| | |
|---|---|
| Call for the doctor. | *Chame o médico.* |
| I have a . . . | *Estou com dor . . .* |
| headache | *de cabeça* |
| sore throat | *de garganta* |
| stomach ache | *de estômago* |
| toothache | *de dente* |
| backache | *nas costas* |
| I have a bad sunburn. | *Estou queimado(a) do sol.* |
| sunstroke | *insolação* |
| food poisoning | *intoxicação alimentar* |
| I have a fever. | *Estou com febre.* |
| I sprained my arm/ankle. | *Torci o braço/o tornozelo.* |
| injections | *injeções* |
| cough medicine | *xarope* |
| aspirin | *aspirina* |
| tablets | *comprimidos* |
| ointment | *pomada* |
| tonic | *tônico* |
| vitamins | *vitaminas* |
| I need to go to the hospital. | *Preciso ir ao hospital.* |

# At The Hotel

| | |
|---|---|
| I have a reservation. | *Tenho uma reserva.* |
| I need a reservation. | *Quero fazer uma reserva.* |
| I want to see the room. | *Quero ver o quarto.* |
| I want to see the manager. | *Quero falar com o gerente.* |
| a single room | *um quarto de solteiro* |
| a double | *um quarto de casal* |
| double room with bath | *quarto de casal com banheiro* |
| triple | *triplo* |
| with air conditioning | *com ar condicionado* |
| mini-bar | *frigobar* |
| safe | *cofre* |

| | |
|---|---|
| key | *chave* |
| What time is breakfast served? | *A que horas é o café da manhã?* |
| Can you wake me up at seven? | *Pode me acordar às sete horas?* |
| I need another pillow/blanket. | *Preciso de outro travesseiro/ cobertor.* |
| Where can one hire a car? | *Onde se pode alugar um auto móvel?* |
| The air conditioning/heat doesn't work | *O ar condicionado/aquecimento central não está funcionando.* |
| Does that include all service & taxes? | *Estão incluídos o serviço e o imposto?* |
| Where is the manager? | *Onde está o gerente?* |
| I enjoyed my stay. | *Gostei da estadia.* |
| Thank you for your help. | *Obrigado/a pela sua ajuda.* |

## Shopping

Brazilian salespeople, especially those barely out of their teens, are sometimes overly eager to help. To have some breathing space, it's absolutely necessary to learn the password *Só olhando,* or "just looking." Other helpful phrases are:

| | |
|---|---|
| How much? | *Quanto?* |
| How much does it cost? | *Quanto custa?* |
| That's too expensive. | *É muito caro.* |
| I want something cheaper. | *Quero alguma coisa mais barata.* |
| Can I try this on? | *Posso provar?* |
| I want to buy (this). | *Quero comprar (isto).* |
| Do you sell film? | *Vende filme?* |
| batteries | *pilhas* |
| cassette | *fita cassete (K-7)* |
| Where can I buy . . . ? | *Onde posso comprar . . . ?* |
| postcards | *cartões postais* |
| soap/shampoo | *sabonete/xampu or champoo* |
| toothpaste/sunscreen | *pasta de dente/filtro solar* |
| stamps | *selos* |
| condom | *camisinha* |
| newspaper | *jornal* |
| shoe store | *sapataria* |
| These shoes do not fit me. | *Estes sapatos não me servem.* |
| What size do you take in shoes/clothes? | *Qual é o tamanho/número que calça/que veste?* |
| This color does not suit me. | *Esta cor não me fica bem.* |
| This coat is tight on me. | *Este paletó está apertado.* |

| | |
|---|---|
| silk | *seda* |
| cotton | *algodão* |

## Clothes

| | |
|---|---|
| suit | *terno* |
| skirt | *saia* |
| jacket | *casaco* |
| dress | *vestido* |
| trousers | *calça* |
| swimsuit/bikini | *maiô/ fio dental/tanga* |
| blouse | *blusa* |
| raincoat/umbrella | *capa de chuva/guarda-chuva* |
| girdle/stockings/panties/bras | *cinta/meias/calcinha/soutien* |
| socks/nightgown | *meias/camisola* |
| tie/shirt | *gravata/camisa* |

# INDEX